WORLD ERAS

VOLUME 8

ANCIENT MESOPOTAMIA
3300 - 331 B.C.E.

WORLD ERAS

VOLUME 8

ANCIENT MESOPOTAMIA
3300 - 331 B.C.E.

RONALD WALLENFELS

A MANLY, INC. BOOK

THOMSON

GALE

Detroit • New York • San Francisco • San Diego • New Haven, Conn. • Waterville, Maine • London • Munich

World Eras
Volume 8: Ancient Mesopotamia, 3300–331 B.C.E.
Ronald Wallenfels

Editorial Directors
Matthew J. Bruccoli and Richard Layman

Series Editor
Anthony J. Scotti Jr.

LIBRARY OF CONGRESS CATALOGING-IN-PUBLICATION DATA

Ancient Mesopotamia, 3300–331 B.C.E. / [edited by] Ronald Wallenfels.
    p. cm.—(World eras ; v. 8)
"A Manly Inc. book."
        Includes bibliographical references and index.
        ISBN 0-7876-4502-8 (hardcover : alk. paper)
        1. Iraq—Civilization—To 634.
        I. Title: Ancient Mesopotamia, 3300–331 BCE.
        II. Wallenfels, Ronald. III. Series.

DS69.5.W35 2004
935—dc22   2004010242

Printed in the United States of America
10 9 8 7 6 5 4 3 2 1

ADVISORY BOARD

In Memory of my Beloved Sister
Jennifer Ruth Swift
née Wallenfels
1948–2004

CONTENTS

CHAPTER 4: COMMUNICATION, TRANSPORTATION, AND EXPLORATION

CHAPTER 5: SOCIAL CLASS SYSTEM AND THE ECONOMY

CHAPTER 6: POLITICS, LAW, AND THE MILITARY

CHAPTER 7: LEISURE, RECREATION, AND DAILY LIFE

ABOUT THE SERIES

PROJECT DESCRIPTION

Patterned after the well-received *American Decades* and *American Eras* series, *World Eras* is a cross-disciplinary reference series. It comprises volumes examining major civilizations that have flourished from antiquity to modern times, with a global perspective and a strong emphasis on daily life and social history. Each volume provides in-depth coverage of one era, focusing on a specific cultural group and its interaction with other peoples of the world. The *World Eras* series is geared toward the needs of high-school students studying subjects in the humanities. Its purpose is to provide students—and general reference users as well—a reliable, engaging reference resource that stimulates their interest, encourages research, and prompts comparison of the lives people led in different parts of the world, in different cultures, and at different times.

The goal of *World Eras* volumes is to enrich the traditional historical study of "kings and battles" with a resource that promotes understanding of daily life and the cultural institutions that affect people's beliefs and behavior.

What kind of work did people in a certain culture perform?

What did they eat?

How did they fight their battles?

What laws did they have and how did they punish criminals?

What were their religious practices?

What did they know of science and medicine?

What kind of art, music, and literature did they enjoy?

These are the types of questions *World Eras* volumes seek to answer.

VOLUME DESIGN

World Eras is designed to facilitate comparative study. Thus, volumes employ a consistent ten-chapter structure so that teachers and students can readily access standard top-

ics in various volumes. The chapters in each *World Eras* volume are:

1. World Events
2. Geography
3. The Arts
4. Communication, Transportation, and Exploration
5. Social Class System and the Economy
6. Politics, Law, and the Military
7. Leisure, Recreation, and Daily Life
8. The Family and Social Trends
9. Religion and Philosophy
10. Science, Technology, and Health

World Eras volumes begin with two chapters designed to provide a broad view of the world against which a specific culture can be measured. Chapter 1 provides students today with a means to understand where a certain people stood within our concept of world history. Chapter 2 describes the world from the perspective of the people being studied—what did they know of geography and how did geography and climate affect their lives? The following eight chapters address major aspects of people's lives to provide a sense of what defined their culture. The ten chapters in *World Eras* will remain constant in each volume. Teachers and students seeking to compare religious beliefs in Roman and Greek cultures, for example, can easily locate the information they require by consulting chapter 9 in the appropriate volumes, tapping a rich source for class assignments and research topics. Volume-specific glossaries and a checklist of general references provide students assistance in studying unfamiliar cultures.

CHAPTER CONTENTS

Each chapter in *World Eras* volumes also follows a uniform structure designed to provide users quick access to the information they need. Chapters are arranged into five types of material:

- **Chronology** provides an historical outline of significant events in the subject of the chapter in timeline form.

- **Overview** provides a narrative overview of the chapter topic during the period and discusses the material of the chapter in a global context.

- **Topical Entries** provide focused information in easy-to-read articles about people, places, events, institutions, and matters of general concern to the people of the time. A references rubric includes sources for further study.

- **Biographical Entries** profiles people of enduring significance regarding the subject of the chapter.

- **Documentary Sources** is an annotated checklist of documentary sources from the historical period that are the basis for the information presented in the chapter.

Chapters are supplemented throughout with primary-text sidebars that include interesting short documentary excerpts or anecdotes chosen to illuminate the subject of the chapter: recipes, letters, daily-life accounts, and excerpts from important documents. Each *World Eras* volume includes about 150 illustrations, maps, diagrams, and line drawings linked directly to material discussed in the text. Illustrations are chosen with particular emphasis on daily life.

INDEXING

A general two-level subject index for each volume includes significant terms, subjects, theories, practices, people, organizations, publications, and so forth mentioned in the text. Index citations with many page references are broken down by subtopic. Illustrations are indicated both in the general index, by use of italicized page numbers, and in a separate illustrations index, which provides a description of each item.

EDITORS AND CONTRIBUTORS

An advisory board of history teachers and librarians has provided valuable advice about the rationale for this series. They have reviewed both series plans and individual volume plans. Each *World Eras* volume is edited by a distinguished specialist in the subject of his or her volume. The editor is responsible for enlisting other scholar-specialists to write each of the chapters in the volume and for assuring the quality of their work. The editorial staff at Manly, Inc., rigorously checks factual information, line edits the manuscript, works with the editor to select illustrations, and produces the books in the series, in cooperation with Gale Group editors.

The *World Eras* series is for students of all ages who seek to enrich their study of world history by examining the many aspects of people's lives in different places during different eras. This series continues Gale's tradition of publishing comprehensive, accurate, and stimulating historical reference works that promote the study of history and culture.

The following timeline, included in every volume of *World Eras,* is provided as a convenience to users seeking a ready chronological context.

TIMELINE

This timeline, compiled by editors at Manly, Inc., is provided as a convenience for students seeking a broad global and historical context for the materials in this volume of World Eras. *It is not intended as a self-contained resource. Students who require a comprehensive chronology of world history should consult a source such as Peter N. Stearns, ed.,* The Encyclopedia of World History, *sixth revised edition (Boston & New York: Houghton Mifflin, 2001).*

CIRCA 4 MILLION–1 MILLION B.C.E.
Era of *Australopithecus*, the first hominid

CIRCA 1.5 MILLION–200,000 B.C.E.
Era of *Homo erectus*, "upright-walking human"

CIRCA 1,000,000–10,000 B.C.E.
Paleolithic Age: hunters and gatherers make use of stone tools in Eurasia

CIRCA 250,000 B.C.E.
Early evolution of *Homo sapiens*, "consciously thinking humans"

CIRCA 20,000 B.C.E.
Migrations from Siberia to Alaska lead to the first human inhabitation of North and South America

CIRCA 8000 B.C.E.
Neolithic Age: settled agrarian culture begins to develop in Eurasia

5000 B.C.E.
The world population is between 5 million and 20 million

CIRCA 4000–3500 B.C.E.
Earliest cities in southern Mesopotamia: artificial irrigation leads to increased food supplies and populations

CIRCA 3200 B.C.E.
Writing comes into use in Mesopotamia and Egypt

CIRCA 3000 B.C.E.
Bronze Age begins in western Asia and Egypt where copper alloys, including bronze, are used for tools, weapons, and sculptures

CIRCA 2900–2300 B.C.E.
Proto-Elamite-like literate urban centers dominated by large ceremonial compounds spread from Elam eastward across Iran

CIRCA 2700–2200 B.C.E.
Egypt: Old Kingdom and the building of the pyramids

CIRCA 2600–1900 B.C.E.
Harappan culture develops along the Indus River valley (present-day Pakistan and northwest India): large, well-planned cities, writing, specialized stone-working techniques, copper and bronze metallurgy

CIRCA 2334–2194 B.C.E.
Akkadians establish world's first empire uniting all of Mesopotamia and north Syria under a central royal authority

CIRCA 2100–1800 B.C.E.
Central Asia: monumental urban sites established at oases across Bactria and Margiana

CIRCA 2080–1640 B.C.E.
Egypt: Middle Kingdom plagued by internal strife and invasion by the Hyksos

CIRCA 2000–1380 B.C.E.
Minoan society on Crete: lavish palaces and commercial activity

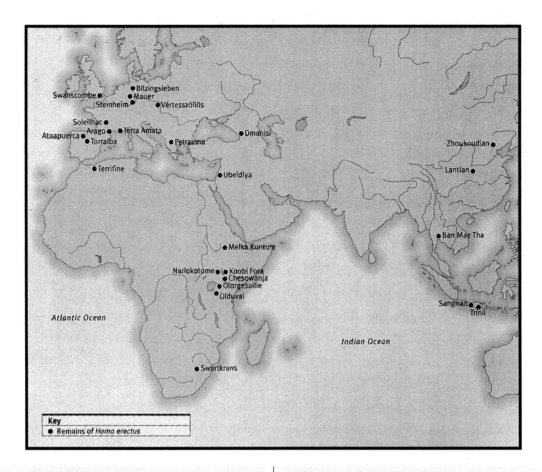

Key
● Remains of *Homo erectus*

CIRCA 1792–1750 B.C.E.
Old Babylonian Kingdom; one of the oldest extant legal codes is compiled

CIRCA 1766–1122 B.C.E.
Shang Dynasty in China: military expansion, large cities, written language, and introduction of bronze metallurgy

CIRCA 1700–1200 B.C.E.
Hittites build a powerful empire based in Anatolia (present-day Turkey) by using horse-drawn war chariots

CIRCA 1570–1075 B.C.E.
Egypt: New Kingdom and territorial expansion into the Levant and Syria

CIRCA 1500 B.C.E.
The Aryans, an Indo-European people from the steppes of present-day Ukraine and southern Russia, expand into northern India

CIRCA 1500 B.C.E.
Canaanites in the Levant develop the first alphabetic script

CIRCA 1400–1200 B.C.E.
Hittites develop the technology of iron smelting, improving weaponry and agricultural implements as well as stimulating trade

CIRCA 1200–800 B.C.E.
Phoenicians establish colonies throughout the Mediterranean

CIRCA 1200–800 B.C.E.
"Dark Age" in eastern Mediterranean and coastal western Asia: foreign invasions, civil disturbances, decrease in agricultural production, and population decline

CIRCA 1122–221 B.C.E.
Zhou Dynasty in China: military conquests, nomadic invasions, and introduction of iron metallurgy

1020–586 B.C.E.
Israelite monarchies consolidate their power in the southern Levant

CIRCA 1000–400 B.C.E.
Mexican Gulf coast: Olmec civilization flourishes

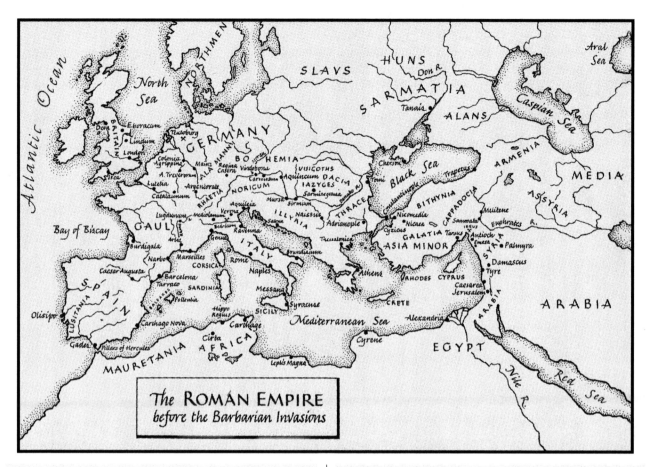

The ROMAN EMPIRE
before the Barbarian Invasions

1000 B.C.E.
The world population is approximately 50 million

CIRCA 934–609 B.C.E.
Assyrians create an empire encompassing Mesopotamia, Syria, the Levant, and most of Anatolia and Egypt; they deport populations to various regions of the realm

CIRCA 860 B.C.E.
Nubia: kingdom of Kush rises at Napata, to the south of Egypt

CIRCA 814–146 B.C.E.
The city-state of Carthage is a powerful commercial and military power in the western Mediterranean

753 B.C.E.
Traditional date of the founding of Rome

CIRCA 750–700 B.C.E.
Rise of the polis, or city-state, in Greece

558–331 B.C.E.
Achaemenid Dynasty establishes the Persian Empire (Iran, Mesopotamia, Syria, the Levant, Egypt, Thrace, Turkey, Afghanistan, and central Asia); satraps rule the various provinces

509 B.C.E.
Roman Republic is established

500 B.C.E.
The world population is approximately 100 million

CIRCA 400 B.C.E.
Spread of Buddhism in India

338–323 B.C.E.
Macedon, a kingdom in the central Balkan Peninsula, conquers the Persian Empire

323–301 B.C.E.
Ptolemaic Kingdom (Egypt), Seleucid Kingdom (Syria, Mesopotamia, Iran, and central Asia), and Antigonid Dynasty (Macedon) are founded

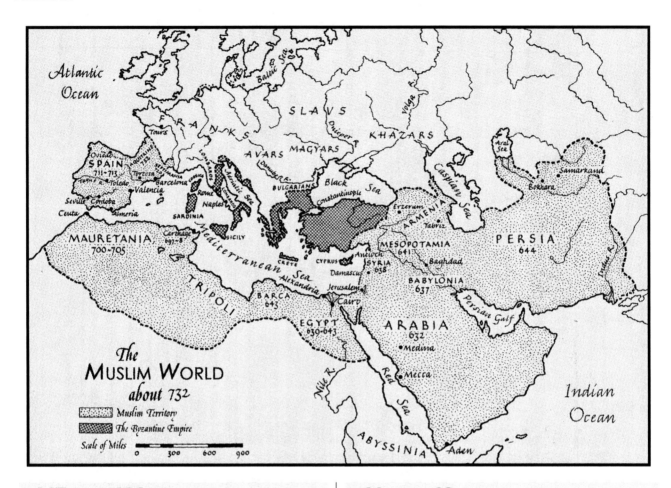

The Muslim World about 732

Muslim Territory
The Byzantine Empire
Scale of Miles
0   300   600   900

247 B.C.E.-224 C.E.
Parthian Empire (Iran, Mesopotamia, and north Syria): clan leaders build independent power bases in their satrapies, or provinces

221-207 B.C.E.
Qin Dynasty in China: previously warring states forged into unified empire with centralized administration

215-146 B.C.E.
Rome establishes hegemony over the Mediterranean world

206 B.C.E.-220 C.E.
Han Dynasty in China: imperial expansion into central Asia, centralized government, economic prosperity, and population growth

CIRCA 100 B.C.E.
Tribesmen on the Asian steppes develop the stirrup, which eventually revolutionizes warfare

CIRCA 100 B.C.E.
Founding of the monumental ceremonial site of Teotihuacan in central Mexico

44 B.C.E.-68 C.E.
Rome is transformed from a republic into an empire under a dynasty of hereditary rulers

1 C.E.
The world population is approximately 200 million

CIRCA 100 C.E.
Invention of paper in China

224-651 C.E.
Sassanid Empire (Iran, Mesopotamia, north Syria, Caucasus, Afghanistan, and central Asia): improved government system, founding of new cities, increased trade, and the introduction of rice and cotton cultivation

CIRCA 320-550 C.E.
Gupta dynasty in India: Golden Age of Hindu civilization marked by stability and prosperity throughout the subcontinent

340 C.E.
Constantinople becomes the capital of the Eastern Roman, or Byzantine, Empire

380 C.E.
Christianity becomes the official religion of the Roman Empire

CIRCA 400 C.E.

The first unified Japanese state arises and is centered at Yamato on the island of Honshu; Buddhism arrives in Japan by way of Korea

CIRCA 400 C.E.

The nomadic Huns begin a westward migration from central Asia, causing disruption in the Roman Empire

CIRCA 400 C.E.

The Mayan Empire in Mesoamerica evolves into city-states

476 C.E.

Rome falls to barbarian hordes, and the Western Roman Empire collapses

CIRCA 500-1500 C.E.

Middle Ages, or medieval period, in Europe: gradual recovery from political disruption and increase in agricultural productivity and population

618-907 C.E.

Tang Dynasty in China: territorial expansion, government bureaucracy, agricultural improvements, and transportation and communication networks

632-733 C.E.

Muslim expansion and conquests in Arabia, Syria, Palestine, Mesopotamia, Egypt, North Africa, Persia, northwestern India, and Iberia

CIRCA 700 C.E.

Origins of feudalism, a political and social organization that dominates Europe until the fifteenth century; based on the relationship between lords and vassals

CIRCA 900 C.E.

Introduction of the horseshoe in Europe and gunpowder in China

960-1279 C.E.

Song Dynasty in China: civil administration, industry, education, and the arts

962-1806 C.E.

Holy Roman Empire of western and central Europe, created in an attempt to revive the old Roman Empire

CIRCA 1000 C.E.

Norse (Viking) settlements established in Newfoundland, Canada

LATIN AMERICAN STATES after the REVOLUTIONS

0   500   1000   1500
Scale of Miles

1000 C.E.

The world population is approximately 300 million

1096-1291 C.E.

Western Christians undertake the Crusades, a series of religiously inspired military campaigns, to recapture the Holy Land from the Muslims

1200-1400 C.E.

The Mali Empire in Africa dominates the trans-Saharan trade network of camel caravans

1220-1335 C.E.

The Mongols, nomadic horsemen from the high steppes of eastern central Asia, build an empire that includes China, Persia, and Russia

CIRCA 1250 C.E.

Inca Empire develops in Peru: civil administration, road networks, and sun worshiping

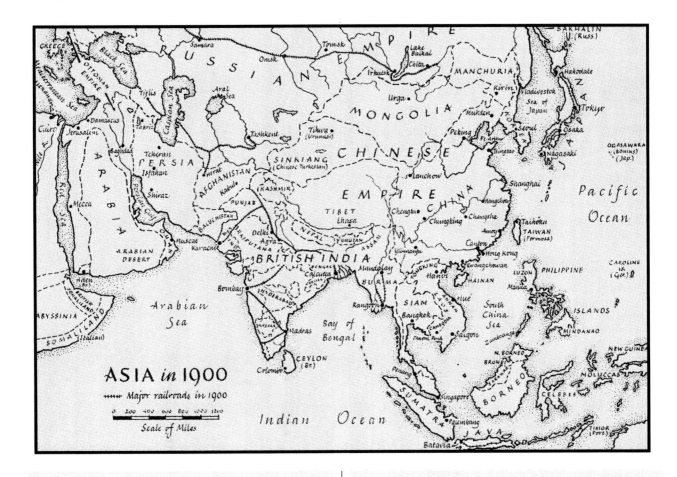

1299–1919 C.E.
Ottoman Empire, created by nomadic Turks and
Christian converts to Islam, encompasses Asia
Minor, the Balkans, Greece, Egypt, North Africa,
and the Middle East

1300 C.E.
The world population is approximately 396 million

1337–1453 C.E.
Hundred Years' War, a series of intermittent military
campaigns between England and France over control
of Continental lands claimed by both countries

1347–1350 C.E.
Black Death, or the bubonic plague, kills one-quarter of the European population

1368–1644 C.E.
Ming Dynasty in China: political, economic, and
cultural revival; the Great Wall is built

1375–1527 C.E.
The Renaissance in western Europe, a revival in the
arts and learning

1428–1519 C.E.
The Aztecs expand in central Mexico, developing
trade routes and a system of tribute payments

1450 C.E.
Invention of the printing press

1453 C.E.
Constantinople falls to the Ottoman Turks, ending
the Byzantine Empire

1464–1591 C.E.
Songhai Empire in Africa: military expansion,
prosperous cities, and control of the trans-Saharan
trade

1492 C.E.
Discovery of America; European exploration and
colonization of the Western Hemisphere begins

CIRCA 1500–1867 C.E.
Transatlantic slave trade results in the forced migration of between 12 million and 16 million Africans to
the Western Hemisphere

1500 C.E.
The world population is approximately 480 million

1517 C.E.
Beginning of the Protestant Reformation, a religious movement that ends the spiritual unity of Western Christendom

1523-1763 C.E.
Mughal Empire in India: military conquests, productive agricultural economy, and population growth

1600-1867 C.E.
Tokugawa Shogunate in Japan: shoguns (military governors) turn Edo, or Tokyo, into the political, economic, and cultural center of the nation

1618-1648 C.E.
Thirty Years' War in Europe between Catholic and Protestant states

1644-1911 C.E.
Qing Dynasty in China: military expansion and scholar-bureaucrats

1700 C.E.
The world population is approximately 640 million

CIRCA 1750 C.E.
Beginning of the Enlightenment, a philosophical movement marked by an emphasis on rationalism and scientific inquiry

1756-1763 C.E.
Seven Years' War: England and Prussia versus Austria, France, Russia, Saxony, Spain, and Sweden

CIRCA 1760-1850 C.E.
Industrial Revolution in Britain is marked by mass production through the division of labor, mechanization, a great increase in the supply of iron, and the use of the steam engine

1775-1783 C.E.
American War of Independence; the United States becomes an independent republic

1789 C.E.
French Revolution topples the monarchy and leads to a period of political unrest followed by a dictatorship

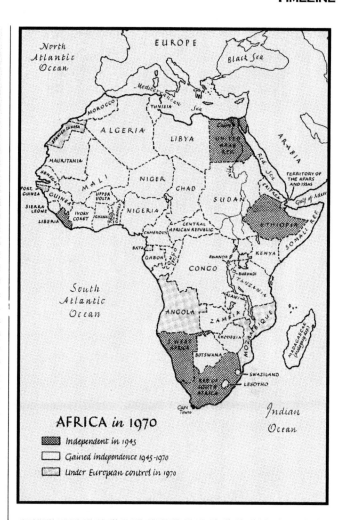

AFRICA in 1970

▓ Independent in 1945
□ Gained independence 1945-1970
▒ Under European control in 1970

1793-1815 C.E.
Napoleonic Wars: Austria, England, Prussia, and Russia versus France and its satellite states

1794-1824 C.E.
Latin American states conduct wars of independence against Spain

1900 C.E.
The world population is approximately 1.65 billion

1914-1918 C.E.
World War I, or the Great War: the Allies (England, France, Russia, and the United States) versus the Central Powers (Austria-Hungary, Germany, and the Ottoman Empire)

1917-1921 C.E.
Russian Revolution: a group of Communists known as the Bolsheviks seize control of the country following a civil war

1939-1945 C.E.
World War II: the Allies (China, England, France, the Soviet Union, and the United States) versus the Axis (Germany, Italy, and Japan)

1945 C.E.
Successful test of the first atomic weapon; beginning of the Cold War, a period of rivalry, mistrust, and, occasionally, open hostility between the capitalist West and Communist East

1947-1975 C.E.
Decolonization occurs in Africa and Asia as European powers relinquish control of colonies in those regions

1948 C.E.
Israel becomes the first independent Jewish state in nearly two thousand years

1949 C.E.
Communists seize control of China

1950-1951 C.E.
Korean War: the United States attempts to stop Communist expansion in the Korean Peninsula

1957 C.E.
The Soviet Union launches *Sputnik* (fellow traveler of earth), the first man-made satellite; the Space Age begins

1965-1973 C.E.
Vietnam War: the United States attempts to thwart the spread of Communism in Vietnam

1969 C.E.
U.S. astronauts land on the moon

1989 C.E.
East European Communist regimes begin to falter, and multiparty elections are held

1991 C.E.
Soviet Union is dissolved and replaced by the Commonwealth of Independent States

2000 C.E.
The world population is approximately 6 billion

INTRODUCTION

Mesopotamia. To Classical writers, the term *Mesopotamia* designated the land between the Tigris and Euphrates Rivers north of the point where they nearly converge near Baghdad. The land to the south was called *Babylonia*. In common modern usage, however, *Mesopotamia* refers to all the land between, and immediately on either side of, the two rivers for their full length and often along both sides of their major tributaries. Today, these lands fall within the territories of the modern nation-states of Iraq, Syria, Turkey, and Iran.

The Time Span. The time period covered in this volume, circa 3300–331 B.C.E., is enormous and remote—the Proto-literate period inhabitants of Uruk, circa 3300 B.C.E., are half again further removed in time from Alexander the Great in 331 B.C.E. than he is from people today. During this vast period a wide variety of peoples of diverse origins, speaking a multiplicity of tongues, contemporaneously or successively inhabited Mesopotamia. Yet, despite its heterogeneous population, there are two aspects of Mesopotamian history that maintain a continuous, unifying thread across three millennia: the domination of the great urban centers by temple and palace hierarchies and their recording of their activities and thoughts in cuneiform on tablets made of clay.

Western Interest in the East. Before the eighteenth century of the Common Era (C.E.), the Bible was accepted as a trustworthy history of antiquity. Young European men of privilege might spend several years after their university training on the "Grand Tour," traveling by boat and carriage, on horseback, on camelback, and on foot through often-hostile regions to see for themselves some of the still-standing wonders of the ancient Near East, such as the pyramids and Sphinx in Egypt, the Jerusalem Temple Mount, the ruins of Babylon, and the Persian royal tombs. However, by the nineteenth century, with its emphasis on philosophies of evolution and scientific naturalism, all records of antiquity, the Bible especially, came to be questioned closely. The Bible clearly describes the land of ancient Israel and the great ancient empires of Egypt, Assyria, Babylon, and Persia. Their great cities and monuments, especially those thought to be lost, were systematically sought out, and many were eventually uncovered and scrutinized by a new class of scientifically oriented world travelers, the archaeologists. Nineteenth-century newspapers regularly devoted their front pages to new discoveries, especially if they involved monumental works of art or, even better, treasures of gold, silver, and precious stones.

The First Decipherments. Not quite as dramatic, but ultimately of much greater significance, was the discovery of vast quantities of ancient writings. Egyptian hieroglyphics, or at least the basics, were deciphered in 1822 by the Frenchman Jean-François Champollion, after studying the Greek-Egyptian bilingual Rosetta Stone. Mesopotamian cuneiform proved much more difficult, but by 1850 its secrets had been uncovered by the little-known Irish Protestant clergyman Edward Hincks and his better-known but less competent rival, the flamboyant Englishman Captain Henry Rawlinson. Other scholars, following in their footsteps, eventually recovered from Egypt and Mesopotamia detailed royal annals, chronicles, and "king lists." These included various sorts of information, including the names of dozens upon dozens of kings, their supposed chronological order, the lengths of their reigns, and descriptions—sometimes quite detailed—of significant events during their reigns. For those interested in the historicity of the Bible, it was quite gratifying to find in these inscriptions some names known from the Bible: among them, the ancient kings of Israel Omri and Ahab, as well as kings of Israel's neighbors, such as Sargon II and Sennacherib of Assyria, Merodoch-baladan II and Nebuchadnezzar II of Babylon, Taharqa and Necho of Egypt, and Cyrus and Xerxes of Persia. Several significant biblical events were eventually confirmed, including the Assyrian capture of Samaria, the capital of Israel, and Nebuchadnezzar's conquest of Jerusalem and the exile of its last kings to Babylon.

Further Discoveries. More tantalizing were descriptions of events involving biblical figures that were not mentioned in the Bible. In one of his inscriptions, the ninth century B.C.E. Assyrian king Shalmaneser III described his attempt to invade neighboring Syria, where he was—reading between the lines—apparently stopped by a coalition of a dozen local princes including king Ahab of Israel. Ahab showed up with a force of considerable size—2,000 chariots and 10,000 foot soldiers. Probably because Ahab and his wife, Jezebel, a Phoenician princess, were worshipers of Baal, the writer of the biblical account of Ahab's reign omitted his heroic defense of Israel. Also omitted from the Bible was the fact that, following his bloody purge of Ahab's dynasty, king Jehu did not have sufficient forces to withstand the renewed threats of Shalmaneser and had to submit to him and pay tribute, an event the Assyrian king prominently depicted on an obelisk recovered from Nimrud by British archaeologists.

New Fields of Study. As significant as Mesopotamian archaeology has been to the examination of the Hebrew Bible, its importance certainly does not end there. The study of the cultures of ancient Mesopotamia is a major field of intellectual interest, revealing the very origins of what William W. Hallo has termed the essential ingredients of civilization, including the growth of cities, the formation of capital, and the invention of writing—followed almost immediately by such secondary elements as the beginnings of copper-alloy metallurgy, the rise of kingship, specialization of crafts and professions, and the application of writing, originally a bookkeeping tool, to record history and literature. Then followed other more-specialized developments, raising existence—at least for the elite classes—to a new level of refinement and luxury. The examination of these ingredients—the roots of modern civilization—provides the rationale for this volume.

Terminology. In general, geographical, rather than modern political, terminology is used wherever possible throughout this book; for example, Mesopotamia rather than Iraq, Anatolia rather than Turkey. In some cases—such as Syria, Iran, and Egypt—geographical and political terms coincide. The term *Levant* is used in its broadest sense to designate those lands in western Asia at or near the eastern shore of the Mediterranean Sea: modern Israel, Jordan, Lebanon, and the West Bank and the Palestinian Authority.

Transcription Conventions. The languages and writing systems of the ancient Near East and their evolution and development over a period of more than three thousand years are at best only imperfectly understood. During the past century and a half, the study of these ancient dialects and scripts has been the chosen field of a comparatively small number of scholars scattered around the world. As a result, a variety of frequently inharmonious methods has developed for transcribing the phonemic inventories of the relevant ancient languages into modern scripts and translating the ancient texts into modern languages. Further complicating matters is the fact that there are also inconsistencies in transcribing the modern languages of this region.

Therefore, beyond striving for internal consistency within this volume, transcriptions of personal and place-names are, for better or worse, rendered on a rather *ad hoc* basis. Thus, for example, the reader may encounter the name of an ancient king written in a manner consistent with the way that king's ancient dialect might be taught in a modern American university (for example, Naram-Sin), although here without the special diacritical marks used by scholars to indicate certain subtleties of the native phonology. Another name might be rendered in a common but less precise form as it was first read in the earliest days of modern scholarship (Hammurabi rather than Hammurapi). In other cases, names are transcribed as they were recorded in classical Greek (Darius rather than Darayavaush) or in biblical Hebrew (Sennacherib rather than Sin-ahhe-eriba). The transcription of Sumerian names follows a recent scholarly move away from orthographic spellings (Inana rather than Inanna). Cuneiform signs are often polyphonic; that is, they may be read in any of several different ways. Thus, in some cases there remains uncertainty in the reading, and the names of the signs are represented in small capitals (for example, Ninni-ZA.ZA). Where ancient texts are quoted, square brackets are used to indicate breaks in the text; any words enclosed within square brackets are modern restorations. Words within parentheses are interpolations—additions to the translation to produce a smoother rendering in modern English.

Problems of Chronology. There is currently no single universally accepted chronology for the absolute dating of events in Mesopotamia prior to the first millennium B.C.E. The same can be said for the ancient world at large; in fact, systems of dating are often inconsistent with each other. In Babylonia, regnal dates can be determined with certainty on the basis of the *Royal Canon* of Ptolemy, a second century C.E. Alexandrian astronomer, only as far back as the first regnal year of Nabonassar in 747 B.C.E. In general in Mesopotamia, a king's "accession year" was the time between when he first came to the throne and the last day of that calendar year, and this year was not counted toward the length of his reign; his first "regnal year" began on the first day of the first month of the new year, typically in the spring. The system of accession-year dating was abandoned with the coming of the Macedonians in 331 B.C.E. The chronology of Assyria can be confidently extended back—through the judicious use of excavated royal annals, chronicles, and lists of annually appointed *limmu*-officials (eponym lists)—to the first regnal year of Adad-nirari II in 911 B.C.E., and perhaps as far back to the first regnal year of Ashurnasirpal I in 1049 B.C.E. The Assyrian sack of the Egyptian capital at Thebes in 664 B.C.E. establishes the earliest certain link with Egypt, whose own chronology prior to this date is replete with difficulties and the source of much contention among both Egyptologists and historians of the ancient Near East at large. Among the royal inscriptions of the Assyrian king Shalmaneser III, two dated references to Israelite kings Ahab and Jehu suggest the last year in the reign of Ahab as the earliest certain date in the Hebrew Bible, 853 B.C.E. For earlier periods, it is often possible to locate events in Mesopotamian (and Egyptian) history quite precisely relative to each other, but neither archaeology nor such scientific dating methods as carbon 14, dendrochronology, thermoluminescence, and archaeoastronomy are sufficiently accurate and/or well-enough developed to provide absolute dates. When historians attempt to relate widely scattered ancient cultures beyond Mesopotamia, establishing even a relative chronology becomes, to say the least, difficult. This volume employs the conventional practice common among Assyriologists of using, without prejudice, the so-called Middle Chronology, by which events are dated in relation to the reign of Hammurabi of Babylon, which is defined as circa 1792 – circa 1750 B.C.E. Specific regnal dates follow those of A. J. Brinkman's "Appendix: Mesopotamian Chronology of the Historical Period" in A. Leo Oppenheim, *Ancient Mesopotamia: Portrait of a Dead Civilization*, revised edition, completed by Erica Reiner (Chicago: University of Chicago Press, 1964), pp. 335–348. For events in the fourth and third millennia B.C.E., this volume follows, again without prejudice, the dating schemes presented in Robert W. Erich, ed., *Chronologies in Old World Archaeology*, third edition (Chicago & London: University of Chicago Press, 1992). The dates of events prior to the first millennium B.C.E. offered by other competing dating schemes may be higher or lower than those of the Middle Chronology by just a few years, by a few decades, or by as many as several centuries.

Problems of Periodization and Nomenclature. It is often more convenient—as well as more evocative—to refer to some specific periods of history by distinctive names rather than by their (purported) dates. The terms used might reflect some dominant aspect of the material culture (such as Bronze Age or Iron Age), the political situation (Early Dynastic period) some underlying historical uncertainty ("Dark Ages"), the name of the capital city (Akkadian period), geographic region (Persian period), the ethnic identity of the predominant power (Kassite period), or the name of the eponymous founder of the ruling dynasty (Achaemenid period or Seleucid period). When speaking of these periods from a political perspective, applying absolute dates to them is subject to the constraints mentioned above. Still more caution is required when using these terms to designate cultural and artistic periods. From this perspective the material culture of the period immediately following the foundation of a new dynasty is often indistinguishable from that of the previous period. Thus, for example, the founder of the Akkadian Empire, Sargon (circa 2334 – circa 2279 B.C.E.), is depicted on his victory stele in a manner not unlike that in which his Early Dynastic period Sumerian predecessors are portrayed. Although artistic innovations are readily identifiable in the few surviving works of Sargon and his immediate successors, "classic" Akkadian art is not in full evidence until the reign of his grandson, Naram-Sin (circa 2254 – circa 2218 B.C.E.). Similarly, the stereotyped imperial "Persian" style of art does not really make itself evident until well into the reign of Darius I (512–486 B.C.E.), the fourth Persian ruler of Mesopotamia, and there is clear evidence of its continuation well into the early decades following the advent of Alexander in 331 B.C.E. Also, Greek artistic influences were already readily discernible in the Near East, especially in seal forms and designs, during the Persian period, decades before the onset of the Hellenistic period.

Identifying Sites. For many of the same reasons outlined above, there are no clear conventions for referring to specific sites. The ruins of many ancient cities, even for such once-great capital cities as Akkad and Washukanni, have yet to be identified. For many—perhaps even most—archaeological sites, the ancient name is not known, and such sites are most often referred to as the *tell* (Arabic for "mound") at whatever modern village is nearest. Even for those towns and cities where the ancient name is known with certainty, modern scholarly usage is still inconsistent. For some, the preference is for the ancient name, thus Mari rather than Tell Hariri, Ur rather than Tell el-Muqayyar. For others, the modern name is more commonly used: Tell Leilan rather than Shubat-Enlil, Balawat rather than Imgur-Enlil. Some sites are called, alternately and seemingly indiscriminately, by both their ancient and modern names (such as Uruk/Warka or Ebla/Tell Mardikh), while others had two or more different names in antiquity (such as Yorgan Tepe, called Gasur in the third millennium B.C.E. and Nuzi in the second millennium B.C.E.). There are also sites best known by their biblical or Greek renderings, such as Nineveh rather than Ninuwa (modern Kuyunjik), or Babylon rather than Babili(m).

Illustrations. Whenever possible, the objects chosen to illustrate this volume came to light in the course of controlled scientific archaeological excavations. Nonetheless, as a practical matter, several unprovenanced pieces—objects acquired from uncontrolled excavations or looted from archaeological sites—have also been included. It must be stressed that, even if they are unquestionably genuine, such objects—because they lack the historical context of objects found and documented on controlled digs—can offer only mute testimony on their own behalf. Furthermore, the market is awash in forgeries. Many are readily detectable by experts, but others are extremely sophisticated. It is regrettable to note that many of the objects indicated in the illustration captions as being in the collections of the Iraq Museum, Baghdad, have been missing since the looting of the museum in April 2003.

INTRODUCTION

Topics. All the volumes in the World Eras series share a common arrangement. The rationale for this organization is obvious and commendable, allowing the interested reader to compare and contrast different cultural attitudes to such specific topics as marriage, divorce, war, death, and taxes around the world and across the ages. There is no doubt that this approach provides the reader with a well-founded introduction to the cultures examined in this way. At the same time the reader should always be aware that in any general and introductory work, including the World Eras series, only a most select few highlights can be addressed in any detail. Much of what is also of great significance to specialists within the field can be mentioned only in the most general way, and much more is never mentioned at all, not because it is not important but because it is at best only tangential to the topics at hand.

Sources. A wide range of modern sources is cited within the pages of this volume—including entries in dictionaries and encyclopedias devoted to Mesopotamia specifically or to the ancient Near East at large, volumes of collected essays (some broad in scope, others limited to quite specific topics), and highly specialized scholarly monographs. Wherever possible, English-language sources are listed, but in some cases—given the small number of scholars in the field and their nearly global distribution—it was necessary to include sources in other languages. Readers are encouraged to pursue their interests in the additional, generally more specific, works listed in this book.

Acknowledgments. This volume is the product of a truly collaborative effort on the part of a diverse array of professional linguists and art historians, each a recognized scholar, working together toward a common purpose: to produce an accessible work that might bring alive to the interested reader some aspects of that now-remote world that was ancient Mesopotamia. Each of the scholars who has participated in this undertaking has been most gracious in sharing their expertise and learning, as well as their passion for teaching, and I am personally most grateful to each for their fine contributions. An equally large debt of gratitude is owed to the staff of BCL/Manly, Inc., especially to Karen Rood, who tirelessly and always in good cheer transformed the contributors' diverse styles, including my own, into a unified form and level that nonetheless accurately reflects each of our intentions. Finally, I wish to thank from the bottom of my heart my wife, Catherine Herriges, and our sons, Joshua and Jesse, without whose daily love and support I could not pursue my life's passion.

Ronald Wallenfels

Fair Haven, N.J.

ACKNOWLEDGMENTS

This book was produced by Manly, Inc. Karen L. Rood, senior editor, was the in-house editor. Anthony J. Scotti Jr. is series editor.

Production manager is Philip B. Dematteis.

Administrative support was provided by Ann M. Cheschi and Carol A. Cheschi.

Accountant is Ann-Marie Holland.

Pipeline manager is James F. Tidd Jr.

Copyediting supervisor is Sally R. Evans. The copyediting staff includes Phyllis A. Avant, Caryl Brown, Melissa D. Hinton, Philip I. Jones, Rebecca Mayo, Nadirah Rahimah Shebazz, and Nancy E. Smith. Freelance copyeditor is Brenda Cabra.

Editorial associate is Joshua M. Robinson.

Permissions editor is Amber L. Coker.

Layout and graphics supervisor is Janet E. Hill. The graphics staff includes Zoe R. Cook and Sydney E. Hammock.

Office manager is Kathy Lawler Merlette.

Photography editors are Mark J. McEwan and Walter W. Ross.

Digital photographic copy work was performed by Joseph M. Bruccoli.

Systems manager is Donald Kevin Starling.

Typesetting supervisor is Kathleen M. Flanagan. The typesetting staff includes Patricia Marie Flanagan and Pamela D. Norton.

Walter W. Ross supervised library research. He was assisted by Jo Cottingham and the following librarians at the Thomas Cooper Library of the University of South Carolina: circulation department head Tucker Taylor; reference department head Virginia W. Weathers; reference department staff Laurel Baker, Marilee Birchfield, Kate Boyd, Paul Cammarata, Joshua Garris, Gary Geer, Tom Marcil, Rose Marshall, and Sharon Verba; interlibrary loan department head John Brunswick; and interlibrary loan staff Robert Arndt, Hayden Battle, Alex Byrne, Jo Cottingham, Bill Fetty, Marna Hostetler, and Nelson Rivera.

WORLD
ERAS

VOLUME 8

ANCIENT MESOPOTAMIA
3300 - 331 B.C.E.

WORLD EVENTS:

SELECTED OCCURRENCES OUTSIDE MESOPOTAMIA

by RONALD WALLENFELS

3300*-3000* **B.C.E.**	• Syria, Anatolia (modern Turkey), and western Iran become the sites of urban colonies established by Uruk, a city-state on the lower Euphrates River. The well-constructed monumental buildings, regular networks of roads, and enormous settlement walls of these colonies are the results of tremendous efforts in organization and labor.
3150*-3000* **B.C.E.**	• Competing southern Egyptian regional leaders ("Dynasty Zero") vie for territorial, social, and ideological control. The emerging national state adapts aspects of Late Uruk styles and material culture—most notably niched brickwork, a hallmark of Mesopotamian temple and civic architecture—to Egyptian royal and funerary contexts.
3000* B.C.E.	• Upper and Lower Egypt are unified under a king (known in a Hellenistic tradition as Menes), who establishes the First Dynasty. • The city of Troy (modern Hissarlik) is founded in northwestern Anatolia.
2630*-2611* **B.C.E.**	• The architect Imhotep builds the Step Pyramid at Saqqara for king Djoser of the Egyptian Third Dynasty.
2600* B.C.E.	• Cities emerge on the alluvial plain of the Indus River and its tributaries. At sites such as Harappa and Mohenjo-daro (both in the modern nation of Pakistan), well-planned cities are erected on massive mud-brick platforms. Among the characteristic artifacts of this culture are square stamp seals, carnelian beads with bleached ("etched") geometric designs, an ideographic writing system (as yet undeciphered), and standardized cubical weights.
2551*-2528* **B.C.E.** *DENOTES CIRCA DATE	• The Great Pyramid and the Great Sphinx are built at Giza for king Cheops (Khufu) of the Fourth Dynasty of Egypt.

WORLD EVENTS 3300-331 B.C.E.

2500* B.C.E.

- In the Honan and Kansu Provinces of central China the peoples of the Yang-shao culture begin to establish many large and populous villages. The Yang-shao survive by farming, raising stock, and hunting. Among them are skilled carpenters, weavers, and potters.

2500*-2100* B.C.E.

- Seafaring contacts between Anatolia and Greece via the islands of the northeast Aegean and the Cyclades yield exchanges of cultural and artistic influences. In Greece, village farming settlements develop into more-centralized social structures.

2500*-1800* B.C.E.

- Permanent settlements, some with as many as several thousand occupants, are established along the Pacific Chinchaysuyu coast of South America. Impressive public architecture is evidence of the growth of local elites able to mobilize and coordinate a substantial workforce.

2250* B.C.E.

- As a result of an attack by Akkadian king Naram-Sin, a fire destroys the palace in Ebla, Syria, and also damages the lid to an alabaster jar for perfumed ointment, which has been imported from Egypt. The lid bears the name of the Egyptian Sixth Dynasty king Pepi I (circa 2289 – circa 2255 B.C.E.).

2205*-1766* B.C.E.

- According to tradition, the Hsia, the first Chinese dynasty, is established. (It is mentioned in legends but is of undetermined historicity.) Its founder is said to be Yu, who is credited with draining the waters of a great flood; later he is deified as lord of the harvest.

2200*-2000* B.C.E.

- Royal tombs are built at Alaca Höyük in central Anatolia. Each of these Anatolian Early Bronze Age shallow rectangular earthen tombs, perhaps originally roofed over with logs, contains a single elite burial accompanied by vessels made of gold and silver, copper-alloy standards, and jewelry of lapis lazuli and other stones.

2150*-2040* B.C.E.

- With the collapse of central power at the end of the Sixth Dynasty, Egypt enters the dark age of the First Intermediate Period.

2100*-1800* B.C.E.

- More than a dozen extremely large, heavily walled sites enclosing monumental buildings are established at oases scattered across western Central Asia. The material culture of this Bactria-Margiana Archaeological Complex includes evidence of interactions with western China, the Indus Valley, and the Iranian plateau.

2046*-1995* B.C.E.

- King Mentuhoptep II (Eleventh Dynasty) re-unifies Egypt and establishes his capital at Thebes.

*DENOTES CIRCA DATE

WORLD EVENTS 3300–331 B.C.E.

2000* B.C.E.	• Cultural contacts between western Asia and the Yang-shao and Lung-shan cultures of China result in similarities in the shapes, decorations, and techniques of their respective pottery.
2000*–1700* B.C.E.	• On Crete, in the eastern Mediterranean, an elaborate civilization (termed "Minoan" by modern excavators) is centered at Knossos, Phaistos, and Mallia, where palaces are built around open rectangular courts and without defensive walls. The Minoans develop a fast potter's wheel and a hieroglyphic writing system (which modern scholars have not yet deciphered).
1910*–1740* B.C.E.	• At emporia (trading centers) in Anatolia, merchants from the city of Ashur on the Tigris exchange finished textiles and tin, which they import via donkey caravans, for gold and silver.
1900* B.C.E.	• Indus civilization fragments into smaller regional cultures, a result, in part, of disruptions to the agricultural and economic systems following major natural diversions within the Indus River system.
1800*–900* B.C.E.	• During the Initial Period of cultural development in Peru, village agriculture is established in the inland valleys leading from the coast. Villagers practice weaving, pottery making, and stone carving.
1766*–1122* B.C.E.	• According to Chinese tradition, the Shang Dynasty begins with T'ang's overthrow of the emperor Chieh, the last king of the Hsia Dynasty. An urban culture of competing city-states is located in northern China around the eastern parts of the Huang (Yellow) River; it is best known for its bronze working and its large numbers of written records on "oracle bones," used to divine the future.
1700*–1550* B.C.E.	• On Crete, the palaces are rebuilt on a grander scale following a disastrous earthquake. Cretan influences begin to spread to the islands of the Aegean. A cursive linear-writing system, which modern scholars call "Linear A," is developed. (It remains undeciphered by modern scholars.) The script is adapted for writing Greek ("Linear B").
1650*–1620* B.C.E.	• Hattusili I, the founder of the Hittite Old Kingdom, establishes his capital at Hattusa (modern Boghazköy) and fights to gain control of territory in north Syria.
1595* B.C.E.	• After successfully overthrowing the powerful kingdom of Aleppo in north Syria, the Hittite king Mursili I attacks Babylonia, bringing the Old Babylonian period to an end. On his return to Hattusa, the king is murdered by his brother-in-law.

* DENOTES CIRCA DATE

WORLD EVENTS 3300-331 B.C.E.

**1575*-1475*
B.C.E.**

- Two circles of "Shaft Graves" at Mycenae on the Greek mainland show strong Cretan influences. These royal burials for local rulers, their families, and their retainers contain gold and silver vessels.

**1550*-1525*
B.C.E.**

- Amose, the founder of the Eighteenth Dynasty of Egypt, completes the expulsion of the Hyksos, western Asiatics who conquered Egypt and have ruled it for about a century. Amose pursues the Hyksos deep into the Levant and, later, extends Egyptian control south into Nubia. His emphasis on militarism establishes a pattern for his successors that brings Egypt up to the level of an international power.

1525* B.C.E.

- Hittite king Telipinu promulgates a strict law of succession. He inaugurates a policy of peaceful co-existence with his neighbors, concluding a treaty with the kingdom of Kizzuwadna in Cilicia.

**1504*-1491*
B.C.E.**

- Tuthmosis I, king of Egypt, moves his capital from Thebes north to Memphis, from where he launches his wars into the Levant, eventually reaching the Euphrates. Rather than building a pyramid, Tuthmosis is the first Egyptian king to be buried in a rock-cut tomb in what later becomes known as the "Valley of the Kings."

1500* B.C.E.

- The volcanic island of Thera (Santorini) in the Aegean Sea explodes catastrophically. The local civilization, a hybrid of Cycladic and Cretan origins, is destroyed. Earthquakes cause severe damage at Knossos on Crete.

- In Meso-America, more-or-less-permanent village farming is supported by a domesticated mutant corn (maize) with husks and supplemented by beans, squashes, chili peppers, and cotton.

- Aryan-speaking peoples migrate into India.

- Peoples of the Wessex culture complete the final stage of construction at Stonehenge on the Salisbury Plain in England.

**1479*-1458*
B.C.E.**

- Hatshepsut, widow of the Egyptian king Tuthmosis II, assumes the titles and regalia of kingship while acting as regent for her stepson, the young Tuthmosis III. She does not seem to be particularly active militarily, and—judging by the impressive buildings and monuments constructed—her reign is one of great prosperity.

**1479*-1425*
B.C.E.**

- Egyptian king Tuthmosis III re-establishes Egyptian militarism, mounting seventeen campaigns into the Levant and Syria. He erects a stele next to that of his grandfather, Tuthmosis I, on the bank of the Euphrates River.

*DENOTES CIRCA DATE

WORLD EVENTS 3300-331 B.C.E.

1401* B.C.E.

- In China, a Shang ruler named Pan-keng moves his capital to Yin by the Huan River, where he and his successors remain for the next two and a half centuries.

1379*-1362* B.C.E.

- Egyptian king Amenophis IV (Akhenaten) establishes his new capital, Akhetaten, at Amarna, where he and his wife, Nefertiti, devote themselves to the exclusive worship of the god of the sun disk, the Aten. At Akhetaten, there accumulates a voluminous cuneiform archive containing the correspondence of several late Eighteenth Dynasty kings with the rulers of city-states in the Levant, Syria, and Cyprus, and the Great Kings of Hatti, Mitanni, Assyria, and Babylonia.

1370*-1330* B.C.E.

- Suppiluliuma I establishes lasting Hittite control over much of Anatolia. During his expeditions into Syria, he sacks the Mitannian capital of Washukanni. He installs two of his sons as governors, one at Aleppo, the other at Charchemish. A third son, sent to Egypt at the request of the widow of a king, perhaps Tutankhamun, is murdered on his journey.

1305* B.C.E.

- While making regular calls at ports throughout the eastern Mediterranean, a Levantine cargo ship sinks off the coast of Anatolia, near Uluburun. The ship is laden with raw materials and manufactured goods originating in Cyprus, the southern Levant, Syria, Anatolia, Egypt, Greece, and the Aegean.

1279*-1213* B.C.E.

- In the fifth year of his reign, Egyptian king Ramesses II fights to a draw with the Hittite king Muwatalli at the Battle of Qadesh on the Orontes River in Syria. Ramesses concludes a formal peace treaty with Muwatalli's eventual successor, Hattusili III; copies are written in both Egyptian hieroglyphics and Hittite in cuneiform.

1275*-1240* B.C.E.

- The Elamite king Untash-napirisha erects his new capital city, Al-Untash-napirisha, at the site of Choga Zanbil in southwestern Iran. The city is dominated by a walled religious compound with a ziggurat at its center.

1200*-1175* B.C.E.

- The eastern Mediterranean Bronze Age draws to a close as dozens of royal cities and palaces in southern Greece, Cyprus, western and central Anatolia, western Syria, and the southern Levant are burned; many smaller communities in these regions are abandoned. (The cause or causes of these disasters are much debated by modern scholars.)

1185*-1155* B.C.E.

- The Elamite king Shutruk-Nahhunte invades Babylonia. Included among the booty he brings back to his capital at Susa are such ancient Mesopotamian monuments as the victory stele of Naram-Sin and the polished diorite statue of Manishtushu from Akkad, as well as Hammurabi's law stele from Sippar.

*DENOTES CIRCA DATE

WORLD EVENTS 3300-331 B.C.E.

1184* B.C.E.

- According to later calculations by Eratosthenes of Cyrene (circa 275–194 B.C.E.), this year is the traditional date for the fall of Troy to the Achaean Greeks, as related in Homer's *Iliad*. (Modern archaeologists tend to equate the event with the burning of level VIIa at Troy, datable to the latter half of the thirteenth century B.C.E.)

1184*-1152* B.C.E.

- In the eighth year of his reign, Egyptian king Ramesses III repulses an attempted land and sea invasion of his country by an alliance of so-called Sea Peoples.

1150* B.C.E.

- In Meso-America, the oldest known Olmec center flourishes at San Lorenzo on the Gulf coast of Mexico. This religious ceremonial center has the earliest ball court, stone drains, and colossal sculptured stone heads, some nearly three meters in height.

1150*-1120* B.C.E.

- The Elamite king Shilhak-Inshushinak expands Elamite control over the regions east of the Tigris River, north into the Zagros Mountains and Assyria, and eastward onto the Iranian plateau.

1122*-771 B.C.E.

- The Zhou (Chou), a people living to the west in the region of modern Sian in the Wei Valley of China, overthrow the Shang Dynasty and establish the early or Western Zhou period. The power of the provincial lords, in concert with incursions by the Shanrong nomads, eventually weakens the state to the point of collapse.

945*-715* B.C.E.

- Libyan warrior nobility, long resident in the Egyptian delta, establishes the Twenty-second Dynasty.

930* B.C.E.

- According to biblical tradition, the nations of Judah and Israel are established following the death of king Solomon and the division of his kingdom.

900*-300* B.C.E.

- The Middle Formative period in Meso-America is one of increased cultural regionalism. The La Venta urban complex rises and flourishes.

900*-200* B.C.E

- The Chavín culture, unified by a common ideology or religion, flourishes in the northeastern highlands of Peru. At the site of Chavín de Huántar, a massive temple complex is constructed of dressed rectangular stone blocks and decorated with elaborately carved stone-relief sculptures. At Chongoyape perhaps the earliest gold products in America are created.

860* B.C.E.

- The kingdom of Kush rises in the region of Napata, to the south of Egypt.

*DENOTES CIRCA DATE

WORLD EVENTS 3300-331 B.C.E.

842*-800*
B.C.E.

- Hazael seizes the throne in Damascus. His ability to resist the Assyrians and his attacks to the south—where he reduces Israel and Philistia to perhaps vassal states—make the state of Aram-Damascus the leading political power in Syria.

841 B.C.E.

- At the instigation of the prophet Elisha, Jehu stages a bloody coup d'état, overthrowing the Omride dynasty in Israel as well as the ruling dynasty in neighboring Judah.

840*-825*
B.C.E.

- The Urartian capital city of Tushpa (Van) is established by Sarduri I on the eastern shore of Lake Van.

840*-643*
B.C.E.

- The kingdom of Urartu is the dominant power in mountainous eastern Anatolia, from Lake Urmia in the south to Lake Sevan in the north and Lake Van in the west. The kingdom is the regular focus of Assyrian aggression.

814 B.C.E.

- According to later tradition, colonists from Tyre found the city of Carthage (Phoenician, Kart-hadasht) on the Tunisian coast. Later legends ascribe the founding of the city to Dido, the daughter of a Tyrian king.

785-714
B.C.E.

- Under a succession of militaristic kings, the kingdom of Urartu expands to become the most powerful state in western Asia. Its armies are active from central Anatolia in the west, across north Syria, to Trans-Caucasia in the northeast. In 714 B.C.E. the Assyrian king Sargon II marches north into Urartu, defeats its king, Rusa I, and proceeds to plunder the country.

776 B.C.E.

- According to Greek tradition, the Olympian Games are founded in this year and subsequently held every four years. A list of winners is drawn up and continued to 217 C.E., providing a basis for the dating of historical events in Greece.

775 B.C.E.

- Greek colonists establish Pithekoussa on the island of Ischia in the Tyrrhenian Sea off the coast of Italy. This event marks the beginning of the entry of Greek colonists on the Italian Peninsula and the island of Sicily.

770*-760*
B.C.E.

- Phoenician colonists settle at Cadiz on the Atlantic coast of Spain.

*DENOTES CIRCA DATE

WORLD EVENTS 3300-331 B.C.E.

770-256 B.C.E.

- Following the fall of the Zhou capital and the death of the king at the hands of invading nomads from the steppes, the Zhou Dynasty of China moves its capital eastward to Luoyang (modern Honan Province), initiating the period of the Eastern Zhou Dynasty. Construction of the Great Wall begins in the seventh century B.C.E. as the vassal states in the northern parts of the country build individual walls for defensive purposes. Luoyang remains the capital of the Eastern Zhou kings until the state is annexed in 256 B.C.E. by Qin Shihuangdi, the First Emperor of Qin (Ch'in).

753 B.C.E.

- According to later tradition, the mythical twins Romulus and Remus found the city of Rome. Virgil's *Aeneid,* written in the first century B.C.E., says that the two boys have been raised by a she-wolf following their abandonment by their mother, a Vestal Virgin and descendent of Aeneas, a member of the Trojan royal family who took to wandering the Mediterranean after the Greeks sacked Troy at the end of the Trojan War.

750*-720* B.C.E.

- Phoenician colonies, consisting of well-planned towns with imposing buildings and wide roads, are erected at several sites along the Mediterranean coast of Spain.

750*-580* B.C.E.

- At Tartessus, in the Guadalquivir Valley in southern Spain, the indigenous culture is influenced by its contacts with Phoenician settlers in Cadiz.

750*-500* B.C.E.

- The Upanishads, the chief mystical and philosophical scriptures of Hinduism, are written.

734-732 B.C.E.

- Phoenician king Hiram II of Tyre is defeated by Assyrian king Tiglath-pileser III, who captures the city of Tyre and forces it to pay tribute.

728*-675* B.C.E.

- According to later legend, Deioces founds the Median kingdom in western Iran, establishing his capital at Ecbatana (modern Hamadan).

723 B.C.E.

- Samaria, the capital of the kingdom of Israel, is captured following a three-year-long siege by the Assyrian king Shalmaneser V; the population of the city is deported and replaced with deportees from elsewhere within the Assyrian Empire.

722*-600* B.C.E.

- The Cimmerians, a nomadic people, flee south across the Caucasus Mountains to avoid the pursuing nomadic Scythians. Assyrian spies near Urartu in northeast Anatolia are the first to recognize the Cimmerians, horse-borne warriors who inflict defeats on the Urartians, Assyrians, Phrygians, and Lydians. According to Herodotus, Lydian king Alyattes finally drives the Cimmerians out of Anatolia.

* DENOTES CIRCA DATE

WORLD EVENTS 3300-331 B.C.E.

715-673 B.C.E.
- According to later traditions, Numa Pompilius, the second king of Rome, organizes priestly colleges and reforms the calendar by fixing the dates of festivals and adding two months to an earlier ten-month calendar.

715*-664 B.C.E.
- Nubian king Shabako marches north from his capital at Napata and, following his re-unification of Egypt, declares himself its king.

685* B.C.E.
- Gyges establishes the Mermnad dynasty in Lydia in western Anatolia, following his murder of his predecessor, Kandaules, whose wife Gyges takes in marriage.

685-643 B.C.E.
- Huan Kung, ruler of the state of Ch'i on the Shantung Peninsula, achieves leadership over many other Chinese states and successfully resists pressure from non-Chinese states to the north and south.

683 B.C.E.
- The Athenians begin the practice of listing the name of the annually appointed *archon eponymos*. This chief magistrate gives his name to the year in which he holds office. Lists of eponyms provide the means by which intervals between given years are calculated.

664 B.C.E.
- The Egyptian capital at Thebes is sacked by the Assyrians, bringing to an end Kushite rule in Egypt. The Egyptian Twenty-sixth (Saite) Dynasty is installed with Assyrian support.

650* B.C.E.
- The first coined metal is minted in Lydia as a means of providing standardized payments to mercenary soldiers.

646 B.C.E.
- The Elamite capital of Susa is devastated by Assyrians under the command of Ashurbanipal.

640-609 B.C.E.
- Under Josiah, the kingdom of Judah regains its independence from Assyria. Josiah institutes sweeping religious reforms, abolishing all foreign and local cult practices and replacing them with a newly centralized cult at the Temple in Jerusalem.

636-628 B.C.E.
- Leadership in China passes to Wen Kung of Chin.

*DENOTES CIRCA DATE

WORLD EVENTS 3300-331 B.C.E.

625-585 B.C.E

- During his reign (according to later traditions), Cyaxares drives the Scythian nomads out of Media and reestablishes Median royal power.

621 B.C.E.

- According to later Athenian tradition, Draco promulgates the first written laws in Athens. The penalties are severe, with death being specified for most offenses.

610-595 B.C.E.

- Egyptian king Necho II of the Twenty-sixth Dynasty marches his army north toward Syria in support of Ashur-uballit II and the last remnants of the Assyrian army under his command at Harran. In an unsuccessful effort to forestall Necho's advance, Josiah, the king of Judah, engages the Egyptians in battle at Megiddo, where he is slain. Necho begins a canal linking the Nile to the Red Sea, which is apparently not completed until the reign of the Persian king Darius I. Herodotus reports that a Phoenician fleet commissioned by Necho has circumnavigated Africa.

604*-531* B.C.E.

- According to later Chinese tradition, the founder of Daoism is one Lao-Zi ("The Old Master"). His exact identity is disputed by modern scholars. He may be a contemporary of Confucius, possibly his teacher. Lao-Zi is best known for his Daoist work, the *Daodejing* ("The Way and its Power").

599*-527* B.C.E.

- According to the Jain tradition of the Ganges basin in eastern India, Vardhamana, or Mahavira ("Great Hero"), is the twenty-fourth and last Tirthankara (one who leads the way across the stream of rebirths to salvation), a teacher of "right" knowledge, faith, and practice. Two of his disciples, Indrabhuti Gautama and Sudharman, found the historical Jain monastic community.

594 B.C.E.

- As chief archon, Solon, an Athenian statesman and poet, institutes social and political reforms in an effort to alleviate the increasing discontent of the underprivileged classes. He later promulgates a new law code abolishing all the earlier ordinances of Draco, except those concerning homicide.

587 B.C.E.

- Following a long siege, the Phoenician city of Tyre is captured by the Babylonian king Nebuchadnezzar II.

586 B.C.E.

- Jerusalem, the capital of Judah, falls to the Babylonian king Nebuchadnezzar II; the Temple is destroyed, and a significant portion of the population of the city is deported to Babylon.

585 B.C.E.

*DENOTES CIRCA DATE

- A solar eclipse on 28 May is taken as a bad omen and brings to an end six years of war between Alyattes of Lydia and Astyages the Mede, who have been in conflict over control of Cappadocia in south central Anatolia.

WORLD EVENTS 3300-331 B.C.E.

563-483 B.C.E.

- Siddhartha Gautama, called the Buddha, "The Enlightened One," is born to a ruler of the small republic of Sakka in southern Nepal. In an effort to open a path to enlightenment, he joins the spiritual teachers of his time, masters their disciplines, and relentlessly practices asceticism. Only after renouncing his family life and ascetic practices and gaining insight through meditation does he believe that he has discovered why people suffer and has found a way of escaping it.

551*-479* B.C.E.

- Confucius, born in the feudal state of Lu (the modern province of Shan-dong, China), is the founder of Confucianism, a complex system of moral, social, political, and religious teaching built on ancient Chinese traditions and perpetuated as the state religion.

550 B.C.E.

- Persian king Cyrus II overthrows his overlord Astyages, king of the Medes, seizing the capital at Ecbatana and taking over the vast Median kingdom.

547-546 B.C.E.

- In the absence of a Median presence in central Anatolia, Croesus, king of Lydia, crosses the Halys River in an attempt to expand his kingdom eastward. The Lydians are confronted by Cyrus II of Persia, who drives them back to the capital at Sardis. Abandoned by his allies, Croesus surrenders.

543*-459* B.C.E.

- Under Bimbisara and his successors, Maghada emerges pre-eminent from among the monarchical Vedic kingdoms of the Gangetic plains in India.

539 B.C.E.

- Cyrus II captures Babylon. The deportees from Jerusalem are released and are given permission to return home and rebuild their Temple.

535 B.C.E.

- In alliance with Etruscan forces, naval forces from the city of Carthage in north Africa defeat the Greek Phocaeans in a naval battle off the coast of Corsica.

525-522 B.C.E.

- The Persian king Cambyses II defeats the Egyptian army and their Carian and Greek auxiliaries, placing himself on the throne of Egypt and initiating the Twenty-seventh Dynasty. In Egypt, Cambyses plans expeditions against the Carthaginians in the west and against the kingdom of Meroë to the south.

522 B.C.E.

- Cambyses is recalled to Persia to quell a rebellion led by his brother Bardiya and dies en route in Syria. Darius, a Persian noble with designs on the throne, accuses the usurper of being a Magus with an uncanny resemblance to Bardiya, whom Cambyses has already secretly killed.

*DENOTES CIRCA DATE

WORLD EVENTS 3300-331 B.C.E.

521-486 B.C.E.

- On taking the Persian throne, Darius I moves to quell revolts in virtually every quarter of the empire. He records his victory in a monumental trilingual cuneiform inscription on a cliff face at Behistun overlooking the highway from Babylon to Ecbatana. In an effort to determine whether the extremities of the empire can be linked together with the center, Darius launches a thirty-month-long expedition from the Indus to the Nile. In the west, Darius moves into Thrace in Europe to prevent Scythian nomads from crossing the Danube. A revolt of the Ionian city-states in western Anatolia, instigated by the Athenians, is met with Darius's full-scale invasion of Greece, which is finally halted at Marathon.

509 B.C.E.

- According to later tradition, the Roman Republic is founded by Lucius Iunius Brutus, following the expulsion of Tarquinius Superbus, the last king of Rome.

500* B.C.E.

- The Zapotec people found Monte Albán on a commanding hilltop site in the Oaxaca Valley of Mexico. They produce the first local hieroglyphic writing and written calendar, probably borrowed from the Olmecs.

480 B.C.E.

- Greece is invaded by Persian king Xerxes, who defeats the Spartans at Thermopylae and pillages Athens before suffering a major naval defeat at Salamis.

475-221 B.C.E.

- The Warring States period in China is a time of almost constant strife as powerful feudal states struggle for supremacy, leading to the rise of Qin Shihuangdi, the first emperor of China.

471 B.C.E.

- In Rome, the Plebeians win official recognition of their assembly, the *concilium plebis*.

467 B.C.E.

- Cimon of Athens achieves a major naval victory at the Battle of the Eurymedon River, effectively ending the Persian threat in Greece.

461-451 B.C.E.

- During the First Peloponnesian War, Athens is victorious over the Peloponnesian League, led by Sparta in alliance with Corinth.

431-404 B.C.E.

- During the Second Peloponnesian War, Athens is defeated by Sparta, which has Persian monetary support.

429*-347 B.C.E.

- Plato founds the Academy, a philosophical school, at Athens.

*DENOTES CIRCA DATE

WORLD EVENTS 3300-331 B.C.E.

401-342 B.C.E.

- After several unsuccessful attempts by the Egyptians, with the aid of Greek mercenaries, to free themselves from Persian rule, the Libyan king Amyratos achieves success and establishes the Twenty-eighth Dynasty. His reign is followed by the native Egyptian Twenty-ninth and Thirtieth Dynasties that rule until the Persians retake the Delta in 342 B.C.E.

399 B.C.E.

- Athenian philosopher Socrates, charged with introducing strange gods and corrupting the youth, is brought to trial, found guilty, and sentenced to death.

395-386 B.C.E.

- In the Corinthian War, Sparta battles a coalition of Greeks and at the same time engages in conflict with Persia in Asia Minor. The war ends with the "King's Peace," which acknowledges the Persian claim to Asia Minor and recognizes the autonomy of the Greek city-states.

390 B.C.E.

- The Gauls sack Rome.

359-336 B.C.E.

- Through war and diplomacy, king Philip II of Macedon unifies Macedonia and then brings to an end Greek independence by forcing a federal constitution on the Greek city-states.

348 B.C.E.

- In a treaty with Rome, Carthage re-asserts its trade interests in Sardinia and the northeast coast of Africa (Libya).

343 B.C.E.

- King Philip II of Macedon invites the philosopher Aristotle to Pella, the capital of Macedon, to act as tutor to the king's son, Alexander.

336 B.C.E.

- Philip II is murdered as he is about to lead the combined forces of Macedon and Greece against the Persians; he is succeeded by his son, Alexander III.

334-323 B.C.E.

- Alexander III of Macedon crosses the Hellespont with 40,000 men and launches his assault against the Persian Empire. By 331 B.C.E. he is in control of all of western Anatolia, the Phoenician city-states, Egypt, and Babylonia, whereupon he assumes the title of "Great King." From 330 through 325 B.C.E., Alexander expands his empire eastward through Central Asia to the Hyphasis and lower Indus Rivers in northwestern India. He spends the remainder of his years in Babylon, where he attempts to integrate the Persian and Graeco-Macedonian noble classes.

*DENOTES CIRCA DATE

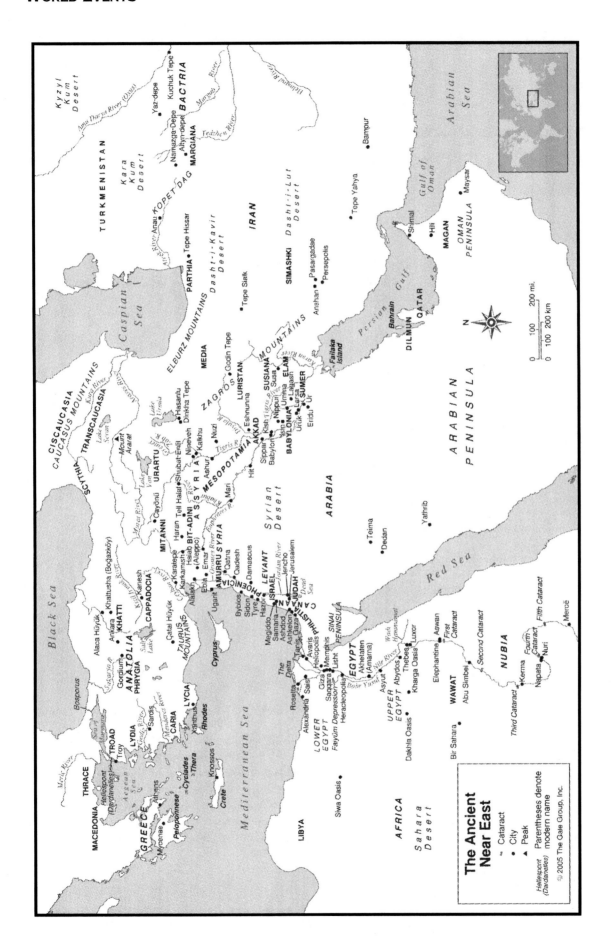

Map of Mesopotamia and the surrounding regions of the ancient Near East and the eastern Mediterranean

CHAPTER TWO

GEOGRAPHY

by RONALD WALLENFELS

CONTENTS

Sidebars and tables are listed in italics.

IMPORTANT EVENTS OF 3300-331 B.C.E.

2334*-2279*
B.C.E.

- The Akkadian king Sargon assembles the first empire in the world through military conquest. His realm includes the formerly independent Sumerian city-states in southern Mesopotamia, areas of western Iran, and the powerful city-states of Mari and Ebla in Syria. He claims to have reached the Cedar Forest and the Silver Mountain (Lebanon) and to have washed his weapons in the Lower Sea (Persian Gulf) and Upper Sea (the Mediterranean). During his reign, ships from Dilmun (Bahrain), Magan (Oman), and Meluhha (the Indus Valley) are said to tie up at the docks in the capital city of Agade.

2334*-2193*
B.C.E.

- The oldest known map on a cuneiform tablet is drawn during the Akkadian period at Yorgan Tepe (ancient Gasur, later renamed Nuzi). Depicted are two ranges of hills bisected by a watercourse, and nearby cities.

2254*-2218*
B.C.E.

- The Akkadian Empire reaches its greatest extent under Sargon's grandson, Naram-Sin. Carved rock reliefs in southeast Turkey and in the Zagros Mountains in southeast Kurdistan commemorate some of his more distant exploits.

2193*-2112*
B.C.E.

- At the time of the collapse of the Akkadian Empire, the Guti people from the Zagros Mountains in Iran descend upon lower Mesopotamia. Of this period, the *Sumerian King List* observes, "Then who was king? Who was not king?" The Guti are expelled by Utu-hengal of Uruk, who achieves brief control over the region.

2112*-2004*
B.C.E.

- The kings of the Third Dynasty of Ur establish direct control over Sumer and Akkad— southern Mesopotamia. Aggressive military campaigns east of the Tigris River bring northern Mesopotamia and western Iran into a frontier zone controlled by local leaders loyal to the kings of Ur. The middle Euphrates region beyond the "Amorite Wall" is ceded to the Amorites in Syria. In the end the state of Ur is overrun by the Amorites, and the city of Ur itself is sacked by the Elamites from southwest Iran.

2100* B.C.E.

- In a dream Gudea of Lagash is commissioned by the god Ningirsu to build a temple. A statue of Gudea depicts the seated city ruler holding on his lap a tablet bearing an engraved architectural plan of the E-ninnu temple.

2025*-1763*
B.C.E.

- Local Amorite rulers throughout Syria and Mesopotamia establish competing dynasties. Among the most significant are those at Ashur on the Tigris in the north, Mari on the middle Euphrates in the west, Eshnunna in the Diayala valley to the east, and Larsa and Isin in the south.

1822*-1763*
B.C.E.
* DENOTES CIRCA DATE

- A text records the day-by-day itinerary of a journey apparently taken by king Rim-Sin of Larsa, from the city of Larsa in southern Babylonia to Emar in Syria and back again. The round trip—perhaps a diplomatic mission or a military campaign—takes 194 days.

IMPORTANT EVENTS OF 3300-331 B.C.E.

1792*-1750*
B.C.E.

- Hammurabi of Babylon is able to extend political control in all directions from an initially small area in central Mesopotamia by successively defeating his most significant rivals at Larsa, Eshnunna, Ashur, and Mari. The First Dynasty of Babylon is now in direct control of the trade routes along which pass silver and gold, copper and tin, lapis lazuli and carnelian, exotic woods, and horses.

1749*-1712*
B.C.E.

- Under Hammurabi's successor, Samsu-iluna, the rival First Dynasty of the Sealand establishes itself in southernmost Mesopotamia, seizing control of the Persian Gulf trade. Terqa becomes the capital of an independent kingdom on the middle Euphrates.

1595*-1155*
B.C.E.

- The Hittite king Mursili I invades Mesopotamia from his base in central Anatolia and sacks Babylon. On his withdrawal, the Kassites, who may have originated in the Zagros Mountains, gain control of southern Mesopotamia.

1504*-1491*
B.C.E.

- At Tumbos, in the vicinity of the Third Cataract on the Nile River in Nubia, Egyptian king Tuthmosis I erects a commemorative stele on which he claims to have reached the Euphrates River in north Syria.

1500*-1350*
B.C.E.

- The Hurrian kingdom of Mitanni, centered within the Habur triangle in northern Syria, emerges; from its capital at Washukanni, the kingdom rules a vast area from the Mediterranean in the west to Assyria in the east.

1479*-1425*
B.C.E.

- The Egyptian king Tuthmosis III mounts seventeen campaigns into the Levant and Syria. In his thirty-third regnal year he crosses the Euphrates River and invades Mitanni. He records in his annals at Karnak that he erected a commemorative stele on the banks of the Euphrates next to the one of his grandfather Tuthmosis I.

1390*-1295*
B.C.E.

- During the so-called International Period, the later kings of Egypt's Eighteenth Dynasty correspond in cuneiform and exchange lavish gifts with the great kings of Babylon, Assyria, Mitanni, and the Hittites, as well as with Cypriote and Levantine princes.

1363*-1328*
B.C.E.

- Following the invasion of Mitanni by the Hittite king Suppiluliuma I and the subsequent assassination of the Mitannian king Tushratta, the Assyrian king Ashur-uballit I is able to establish his independence from Babylon and begins to expand Assyrian control westward. Tensions between Assyria and Babylon increase.

* DENOTES CIRCA DATE

IMPORTANT EVENTS OF 3300-331 B.C.E.

1350* B.C.E.
- A map of the Kassite-period city of Nippur is drawn on a clay tablet. The features include the walls and their lengths, the course of the Euphrates River west of the city, the area called the "Gardens in the City," and the general course of the "Canal in the heart of the City."

1305*-1274* B.C.E.
- Assyrian king Adad-nirari I enlarges his kingdom southward, pushing the Babylonians south to the Diayala Valley. In the west, he seizes the kingdom of Mitanni from the Hittites, but he stops short of the city of Charchemish on the Euphrates. The Hittite king Muwatalli denies Adad-nirari's request to visit the Amanus Mountains near the Mediterranean coast.

1243*-1207* B.C.E.
- The Assyrian king Tukulti-Ninurta I reinforces his position along the upper Euphrates River and campaigns extensively in the mountains to the north and east of Assyria. In the south the Assyrians defeat the Babylonian king Kashtiliash IV, capture Babylon, and come face-to-face with the Elamites of southwestern Iran, who are seeking to control the region east of the Tigris.

1200* B.C.E.
- The Babylonian national epic, *Enuma elish,* is written. Part of it recounts the creation of the universe.

1185*-1150* B.C.E.
- Led by king Shutruk-Nahhunte I, Elamites from southwest Iran invade Babylonia and heavily loot the country.

1158* B.C.E.
- Kassite rule of Babylonia is effectively ended as a result of the military activities of Elamite king Shutruk-Nahhunte I.

1125*-1104* B.C.E.
- Babylonian king Nebuchadnezzar I successfully repels the Elamites and returns to Babylon the cult statue of Marduk that was removed following Shutruk-Nahhunte's invasion.

1114*-1076* B.C.E.
- A period of Assyrian weakness in the aftermath of the murder of Tukulti-Ninurta I, circa 1207 B.C.E., is ended when Tiglath-pileser I is able to re-establish an Assyrian presence across northern Syria, from the Mediterranean Sea to the Zagros Mountains. During a campaign north of Lake Van, the king commissions a rock inscription there. To the south, the Babylonians remain a threat, but the Aramaeans from Syria are the greatest threat to both the Assyrians and Babylonians.

934-859 B.C.E.
- A succession of Assyrian kings re-assert their control over the mountainous regions to the east and north, westward into Syria, and southward toward Babylonia, laying the foundation for the Assyrian Empire.

* DENOTES CIRCA DATE

IMPORTANT EVENTS OF 3300-331 B.C.E.

858-824 B.C.E.

- The Assyrian king Shalmaneser III claims to defeat a coalition of Syrian and Levantine princes, including king Ahab of Israel, that is seeking to resist Assyrian expansion to the west. The king commissions a monument ("The Black Obelisk") to commemorate the tribute he has received from the furthest reaches of his realm. The text accompanying the reliefs on the obelisk identifies the Israelite king Jehu kneeling at Shalmaneser's feet; it also depicts Bactrian two-humped camels, an elephant, a rhinoceros, and monkeys.

826-820 B.C.E.

- A general insurrection breaks out in Assyria, precipitating yet another prolonged period of weakness, when Shalmaneser's son Ashur-da'in-aplu rebels, seizing control of twenty-seven cities, including the religious center at Ashur.

744-722 B.C.E.

- During the reigns of the Assyrian kings Tiglath-pileser III and Shalmaneser V, Assyria's military and political influences undergo their greatest expansion to date, reaching the border of Egypt in the west. The rise of the state of Urartu in eastern Anatolia to the north leads to conflict over control of the trade routes to the north and east through the Zagros Mountains into western Iran. In the west, Samaria, the capital of Israel, is captured and its population deported. To the south, Assyrian domination of Babylonia is undermined by local Chaldaean groups who, enjoying Elamite support, attempt repeatedly to seize the Babylonian throne.

721-705 B.C.E.

- Following his usurpation of the Assyrian throne in a violent coup, Sargon II suppresses a revolt in Syria and expands his territorial control into northeast Iran and central Anatolia. He suffers significant defeats at the hands of the Elamites and Babylonians before finally reestablishing control over the south. In the west his expansionist policies against Judah and Philistia provoke interference from the Egyptians, who are ruled by their Nubian conquerors. Sargon attempts to find common cause with the central Anatolian Phrygian king Mita (Midas) against the Urartians. Late in his reign Sargon receives embassies from local rulers in the Lower Sea—Dilmun (Bahrain), and the Upper Sea—Cyprus. Sargon is killed in Anatolia while battling Cimmerian nomads who have crossed the Caucasus Mountains from central Asia.

704-681 B.C.E.

- The Assyrian king Sennacherib finally suppresses the Babylonian revolts, still abetted by their Elamite allies, by destroying the city. He campaigns against Arab tribes advancing from the western desert, and in the Levant he confronts Egyptian support of revolts among local city rulers in Phoenicia, Philistia, and Judah.

700*-600* B.C.E.

- A map of the world is drawn on a clay tablet. An ocean encircles a single circular continent, with Babylon at its center.

* DENOTES CIRCA DATE

IMPORTANT EVENTS OF 3300-331 B.C.E.

680-669 B.C.E.

- Following the murder of his father, Sennacherib, Esarhaddon succeeds to the Assyrian throne and invades Egypt, capturing the northern capital at Memphis. He is unable to establish effective control over the country.

668-627* B.C.E.

- Esarhaddon's son and successor, Ashurbanipal, invades Egypt and captures and sacks the southern capital at Thebes. The Assyrians drive out the Nubian rulers of Egypt, and a vassal king is installed in Memphis. In response to a request by Gyges, king of Lydia in western Anatolia, Ashurbanipal dispatches troops in support of Lydian resistance to the continued Cimmerian threat there. In the east, Ashurbanipal successfully defeats the Elamites and sacks their capital at Susa.

627*-609 B.C.E.

- At the height of its power and greatest territorial expansion, the Assyrian Empire descends rapidly into chaos following the death of Ashurbanipal. The Assyrian capital cities are systematically destroyed by a coalition of Babylonians and Medes (from Iran), perhaps abetted by Scythian nomads. The last Assyrian king, Ashur-uballit II, despite the efforts of his Egyptian allies, disappears after the fall of the remaining provincial capital at Harran in Syria.

625-539 B.C.E.

- In the aftermath of the collapse of the Assyrian Empire, the Neo-Babylonian Empire succeeds in asserting control over all of Mesopotamia, Syria, and the Levant to the border of Egypt. Nebuchadnezzar II captures Jerusalem and deports much of its population. The Medes exercise control to varying degrees over lands from the Halys River in central Anatolia east to the Iranian plateau.

559-522 B.C.E.

- Cyrus II, the ruler of Persia, overthrows his Median overlord and secures his power throughout Iran. In the absence of a Median presence in Anatolia, Croesus, king of Lydia in western Anatolia, attempts to move east but is defeated by Cyrus, who gains control of the entire region. The Babylonians, former allies of the Lydians, are defeated in battle. Cyrus triumphantly enters Babylon and gains control over all its former territories. Cyrus turns to the east and campaigns deep into central Asia, where he is killed in battle. Egypt is added to the Persian Empire by Cyrus's son, Cambyses II, who dies attempting to return to Persia to quell a revolt by his brother Bardiya or by a magus posing as his dead brother.

521-486 B.C.E.

- The Persian Darius I claims to have killed the usurper and to have been selected as king by lot by his peers. He moves quickly to quell successfully uprisings that break out virtually across the entire breadth of the empire. Darius expands the empire eastward into northwest India, and westward into Europe, being halted in September 490 B.C.E. at Marathon by the Greeks.

335-331 B.C.E.

- The last Persian king of the empire, Darius III, is confronted with the invasion of western Asia and Egypt by Alexander III of Macedon, who goes on to amass an empire stretching from Greece and Egypt in the west to India in the east; Alexander establishes Babylon as his capital.

* DENOTES CIRCA DATE

OVERVIEW

The Origins of Agriculture. The great ice sheets that covered much of the northern hemisphere for more than one hundred thousand years during the last Ice Age reached their greatest extent about twenty thousand years ago, whereupon they slowly began to recede. Some fourteen thousand years ago, the pace of the melting quickened, causing widespread and rapid changes in local climatic conditions as large-scale climatic zones shifted and reformed. Scattered bands of humans who subsisted by hunting and gathering found it necessary either to adapt themselves to new local environmental conditions or to move in search of an environment with a flora and fauna on which they could more readily subsist. Some thirteen thousand years ago a new culture, termed *Natufian*, emerged in the Mediterranean Levant—an area stretching from modern-day southern Israel northward across western Syria into the foothills of the Taurus Mountains in southern Anatolia (modern Turkey)—throughout which edible cereal grasses grew. These people are defined on the basis of their characteristic stone and bone tools and their burial practices, which included decorating the body of the deceased with headgear, necklaces, earrings, pendants, belts, and bracelets made of seashells from both the Mediterranean and Red Seas, as well as with teeth and bone and colored stone beads, including obsidian from Anatolia. These people lived in semipermanent villages and were the first to develop and use the sickle—consisting of small stone blades (microliths) set in a wooden or bone handle—rather than beaters and baskets to harvest more efficiently wild stands of cereal, which they exploited intensively and extensively. The cereals—together with the pulses (the edible seeds of peas, beans, and lentils), nuts, and fruits that they gathered—were processed with stone mortars, bowls, and pestles for consumption. Hunting and fishing provided animal protein in the form of gazelle and other game, birds, and fish. The climate in this period was unstable, and a thousand-year-long return to colder, drier conditions beginning about eleven thousand years ago appears to have brought Natufian culture to an end.

The Neolithic Revolution. V. Gordon Childe, a twentieth-century British philosopher and archaeologist, coined the term *Neolithic Revolution* to describe the origin and consequences of farming and the widespread development of settled village life. Archaeological excavations reveal that, following a return to wetter climatic conditions about 10,300 years ago (circa 8300 B.C.E.), Neolithic ("new stone age") village-farming communities began to appear in an arc extending up the Mediterranean Levantine coast eastward across the river valleys and well-watered steppe between southern Anatolia and northern Syria and Iraq (northern Mesopotamia), then southward along the foothills of the Zagros Mountains in western Iran—the "Fertile Crescent." Here, over approximately the next two millennia, cultivation and domestication of native plants (such as wheat, barley, bitter vetch, pea, and lentil) and domestication of native animals (sheep, goats, cattle, and pigs) began to occur and supplied an ever-greater proportion of the villagers' diet. The earliest villages may have held many hundreds of individuals, necessitating the development of new means to maintain social cohesion, perhaps through public ceremonies and rituals in shrines and newly designated public spaces. The largest known Neolithic site in western Asia, Çatal Hüyük in Anatolia, may have supported a population of five thousand people.

The Neolithic Period in Mesopotamia. Northern Mesopotamia is characterized by higher elevations than in the south, rocky steppe lands, and gorges cut by the Tigris and Euphrates Rivers and their tributaries. The region is bordered to the north and west by the foothills and mountains of the Taurus range, with the Syrian Desert to the southwest. The northern- and eastern-most portions of northern Mesopotamia lie within a zone where reliable annual average rainfall is sufficient for "dry farming"; that is, seasonal rainfall and groundwater alone are able to sustain a crop. Southern Mesopotamia, on the other hand, consists of a broad, flat, low-lying alluvial plain created by the rivers, with levees formed along their banks, and lush marshlands toward the Persian Gulf. This region does not receive sufficient rainfall to permit dry farming, although hunter-gatherer and fishing communities might thrive. Beginning about 6500 B.C.E. a sequence of cultures began to establish new agricultural settlements within the dry-farming belt across the northern Mesopotamian plain and southward along the flanks of the Zagros Mountains. These communities, increasingly surrounded by defensive walls, produced clay pottery—some quite fine and beautifully decorated and painted—for storing and serving food and beverages. Native copper, as well as copper smelted from ore, began to be used for tools and jewelry. Eventually, molded rectangular mud bricks began to replace packed mud for building construction, with buttresses supporting the walls of some larger buildings. At several sites within the dry-farming zone, irrigation canals were built and maintained in an effort to increase the efficiency and production of the farming.

Occupation of the Southern Plain. The earliest evidence for a permanent farming settlement on the southern alluvial plain is dated to approximately the early sixth millennium B.C.E. The culture that evolved there is termed *Ubaid*, after the name of the site where its distinctive material culture was first identified by archaeologists. During the fifth millennium B.C.E. Ubaid-style painted pottery is found across an ever-broader area, spreading northward into northern Mesopotamia, where it replaced the earlier local Halaf painted-pottery tradition. Ubaid pottery has also been found across north Syria toward the Mediterranean, in south central Anatolia, and along the Arabian coastline of the Persian Gulf as far south as modern-day Qatar. In this period, at the site of what in the historical period was the southernmost Sumerian city of Eridu (modern Abu Shahrain), the rise to prominence of the priesthood can perhaps also be traced. At this site, archaeologists uncovered a sequence of temples, one built upon the leveled remains of another. The smallest and simplest is dated to circa 5400 B.C.E.; the latest, largest, and most complex dates to the proto-historic period, circa 3300 B.C.E.

Early Urbanization. During the millennium beginning circa 4000 B.C.E., the stages of urban development from village to city and from prehistory to the historical period are most clearly seen at the site of Uruk (Warka), whose name designates this period. During the period there was a change in population pattern. From a remarkably even distribution of towns along the watercourses of central Mesopotamia there was a southward shift toward Sumer, where clusters of small communities surrounded ever-larger urban centers, the foremost of which was Uruk. During this period there was also a marked increase in the size and complexity of the irrigation system, and the fields it watered produced vast quantities of grain for human consumption and of plant fodder to support herds of small and large cattle, which produced milk for dairy products; in addition, sheep provided wool for textile manufacturing. Religious architecture developed new monumental propor-

tions. Mass-produced wheel-made pottery, wheeled vehicles, the ox-drawn plow, and carved stone bowls and cylinder seals were introduced. There was also a dramatic increase in the use of copper for tools. Toward the end of the fourth millennium B.C.E., proto-cuneiform writing appeared at Uruk as a tool for maintaining administrative control over raw materials and finished goods and their producers and consumers.

The Proto-Literate Period. The ubiquitous mud of the southern alluvial plain was used to build dikes as part of the irrigation system, to make bricks for building, and to create clay tablets as a writing surface. The region is almost completely bereft of other natural resources; there are only small outcrops of comparatively soft stone, which is not particularly suitable as building material; there are no metals or metal ores in the region; nor are there hardwoods suitable for construction. The Uruk ruling elite began to obtain these materials through trade, exchanging the significant surpluses of agricultural products and textiles that the Uruk economic system was generating. During the Late Uruk period (circa 3500 – circa 3000 B.C.E.), Uruk's influence was felt beyond Sumer, throughout the rest of Mesopotamia, deep into Syria and into southern Anatolia, as well as at Susa in southwestern Iran. Late Uruk cylinder seals, artistic motifs, and building techniques have even been observed in Egypt. The available evidence suggests that, during the last century of the Proto-Literate period, also known as the Jamdat Nasr period (circa 3000 – circa 2900 B.C.E.), Sumer's foreign links were severed. However, central Mesopotamian pottery has been found at sites in Oman at the southern end of the Persian Gulf. At Susa, the Proto-Elamite urban culture arose, and evidence of its spread has been found across the breadth of the Iranian plateau. By circa 2900 B.C.E., southern Mesopotamia had entered a period of prolonged decline; its cause—whether social, political, economic, or environmental—remains much debated.

Climatic Changes in the Historical Period. Modern studies of the ancient climate have suggested that prior to the first millennium B.C.E. overall levels of precipitation in the ancient Near East were low, with several protracted periods of significantly below average rainfall. The first of these periods, circa 3200 – circa 2900 B.C.E, appears to be contemporary with the Late Uruk and Jamdat Nasr periods, a time of intense expansion of the system of irrigation canals in southern Mesopotamia. Recent paleoclimate studies of the ancient Near East point to a second, extremely severe period of drought that began suddenly circa 2075±125 B.C.E., and lasted for some three hundred years—contemporary with the period of the Akkadian Empire, the Guti invasion, and the Third Dynasty of Ur. It has been suggested that this dramatic climatic shift caused catastrophic crop losses in the dry-farming regions of north Syria, depriving the Akkadian Empire of its "bread basket," and thereby precipitating the sudden collapse of the empire. The protracted drought may then be seen as a significant factor in the subsequent migration of foreigners into the heavily irrigated areas of Mesopotamia: the Guti from the Zagros Mountains to the east at the time of the Akkadian collapse and—in much greater numbers—the Amorites from the west during the Ur III period. A brief dry spell at circa 1300 B.C.E., perhaps coincident with the end of the "International Period," was followed by fluctuating, but overall above average rainfall throughout the first millennium B.C.E., during the time of the Assyrian, Babylonian, Persian, Macedonian, and Seleucid empires. Although these coincidences between climatic variations and political events are suggestive, not all ancient historians are convinced of their connection.

TOPICS IN GEOGRAPHY

ANCIENT MESOPOTAMIAN WORLDVIEWS

The Creation of the Universe. There exists no single Mesopotamian text solely devoted to the topic of creation. Rather, there are many, often conflicting, accounts embedded within larger works. None is similar to the account in Genesis in the Hebrew Bible, with its ordered creation culminating in the formation of mankind. Perhaps the most-detailed Mesopotamian creation account is to be found in the so-called Babylonian Genesis, *Enuma elish.* The poem opens with the creation of the first gods, male and female, from the mixing of the waters of the primeval ocean, Tiamat, with the primeval fresh waters, Apsu, her consort. As a result of this union, a second generation of gods is born. Their clamor is disturbing to Tiamat and Apsu. When Apsu and his vizier Mummu attempt to destroy the young gods, one of them, Ea, magically defeats Apsu and Mummu. On Apsu's corpse, Ea builds his home, where he and his wife, Damkina, give birth to Marduk. Tiamat, who has taken a new spouse, Kingu, and given him the Tablets of Destinies, now undertakes to avenge the death of Apsu. In exchange for supreme and undisputed authority over the gods, Marduk faces Tiamat and her hordes in battle and defeats them. From her corpse, Marduk erects the heavens and the earth; her eyes become the sources of the Tigris and Euphrates Rivers. Marduk also arranges the stars, moon, and sun in the visible heavens and sets them on their courses. He completes his task by fashioning the cosmic bonds that hold the universe together and its parts in place.

The Structure of the Universe. Despite diverse traditions that treat of the creation of the heavens and the earth, the ancient Mesopotamians, throughout most of their history, maintained a remarkably consistent picture of the universe itself. They envisioned it as consisting of a series of superposed levels separated from each other by open spaces. The uppermost levels were where the gods of heaven lived. Beneath them were the starry sky, then the earth's surface, then the underground fresh waters of the Apsu, and, at the bottom, the underworld of the dead. Presumably the floor of each level served as the roof for the level beneath it. A first millennium B.C.E. Neo-Assyrian text identifies the floors of each level as being made of specific stones. The floor of the starry sky was said to be made of jasper, which can vary in color from sky blue to sunny yellow to the reds of sunrise and sunset to cloudy gray—all the colors of the sky as seen from the earth's surface. A similar tradition is found in the Hebrew Bible, where the heavenly floor is described as made of (blue) sapphire bricks. The fixed stars were inscribed onto the undersurface of the sky, which rotated once a day. The sun, moon, and five visible planets moved about beneath this floor, although no preserved Mesopotamian text says precisely how. The Assyrians described the "disk" of the sun as being sixty *beru* in diameter while that of the moon was forty *beru*. (One *beru* is over ten kilometers or somewhat more than six miles.)

The Earth. First millennium B.C.E. cuneiform sources provide a fairly consistent picture of the Mesopotamian conception of the earth's surface as a single circular continent amid a surrounding ocean. These texts include an incised map of the world with explanatory captions; a description of the realm of Sargon of Akkad, the third millennium B.C.E. "king of the world"; and descriptions of foreign lands listed in itineraries, especially of military campaigns undertaken by several Middle and Neo-Assyrian kings from the fifteenth to seventh centuries B.C.E. At the center of the world are the lands of Assyria and Babylonia, which are traversed by the great Euphrates and Tigris Rivers. To the north are the mountains of Anatolia, where the Tigris and Euphrates rise, and beyond, the Black and Caspian Seas. To the northeast are the lands of Urartu encircling Lake Van, and beyond, the Caucasus Mountains. To the east lie the Zagros Mountains, and beyond, the vast Iranian plateau. To the southeast, the Lower Sea (the Persian Gulf) leads to Dilmun, the island of Bahrain in the Gulf, and across the sea, to Magan and Meluhha. To the west lies the Upper Sea (the Mediterranean) with its coastline reaching south to Egypt; in this sea lie the islands, foremost Cyprus and Crete.

Sources:

Alexander Heidel, *The Babylonian Genesis: The Story of Creation,* second edition (Chicago & London: University of Chicago Press, 1951).

Wayne Horowitz, *Mesopotamian Cosmic Geography,* Mesopotamian Civilizations 8 (Winona Lake, Ind.: Eisenbrauns, 1998).

CARTOGRAPHY

The Oldest Map? A wall painting in a shrine at the site of Çatal Hüyük in central Anatolia, while not a map in the strict sense, may be the oldest cartographic artifact. Dated to circa 6200 B.C.E., this painting was interpreted by the excavator as representing a bird's-eye view of the ancient site, the largest known Neolithic town in the Near East, with its congested rectangular houses packed tightly against each other without intervening streets. Behind the town, there is a view of an erupting volcano.

District Maps. The oldest map on a cuneiform tablet was found at Yorgan Tepe (ancient Gasur, later renamed Nuzi), dated to the Akkadian period (circa 2334 – circa 2193 B.C.E.). On it are indicated two ranges of hills bisected by a watercourse, nearby cities, and even the cardinal directions. From later periods come district maps in the region of Nippur, one showing an agricultural area near the city, another perhaps used as a reference tool for tax collectors.

City Maps. Clay tablets bearing ancient maps of the cities Ashur, Babylon, and Nippur—or sections of these cities—are known. When the modern excavators of Nippur superimposed a transparency of the map of the fourteenth-century-B.C.E. Kassite-period city over aerial photographs and their site plan, they noted that the ancient map fit reasonably well. The observed features of the site on the old map include the walls and their correct lengths, the ancient course of the Euphrates west of the city, the area called the "Gardens in the City," and the general trend of the "Canal in the heart of the City."

A Map of the World. On the obverse of a Neo-Babylonian period (early to mid first millennium B.C.E.) tablet is a map of the world. A single circular continent is shown as a disc surrounded by an ocean, which is indicated by a double ring. The Euphrates, originating in the mountains to the north, flows through the middle of the earth. Babylon, indicated by a rectangle placed just above the middle of the map, sits astride the river. Cities and districts are indicated by circles with cuneiform captions, but not all are in their correct relative geographical order. Five triangular areas, perhaps distant islands in the sea, radiate from the outer circle. (The accompanying text suggests that there were originally eight triangles.) The northernmost region is labeled "where the sun is not seen," suggesting that the Babylonians, during the first millennium B.C.E., may have known of the polar night. Internal evidence suggests that the map was originally composed in the late eighth or seventh century B.C.E. and the present copy made one or two centuries later.

Field Plans. Field or estate plans are the most common kinds of maps known from ancient Mesopotamia. The drawings are often rough sketches with simple notations in the plan or along the borders. In the late third millennium B.C.E., measurements were given to calculate little more than the area of the field in order to assign the proper quantity of seed grain or to collect the appropriate amount of harvest. With the increase in private ownership of land in the early second millennium B.C.E., notations included compass directions and the names of the adjacent property holders, in addition to the basic field measurements. Field plans of the first millennium B.C.E.—both of cultivated land and lots with, or intended for, buildings—appear to have served as surveys to be used in conjunction with title deeds.

Building Plans. Among the many statues of the late third millennium B.C.E. city ruler Gudea of Lagash, perhaps the best known is the one called "Architect with Plan." In this nearly life-size statue, Gudea sits with his hands clasped reverently at his chest. On his lap rests a tablet bearing an engraved architectural plan of the E-ninnu temple, together with a stylus and a graduated ruler. Outlined in this orthogonal projection are the thick walls of the temple enclosure; details include the reinforced external buttresses and six fortified doors flanked by towers.

Itineraries. Ancient maps would not have been practical for a traveler to use when he wanted to find his way over any distance. A merchant, for example, would have needed to know how far he had to travel on any given day before he could find food and shelter. Several tablets are known, however, that either give actual distances between major resting places or list resting places that are spaced at approximately one-day travel intervals. Such lists have been of great value to modern historians attempting to locate on the ground cities whose names are mentioned in ancient texts. One such text, known from three later copies, gives the day-by-day listing of cities, towns, and caravansaries stopped at during a journey that was apparently taken by king Rim-Sin (circa 1822 – circa 1763 B.C.E.) from his capital city, Larsa, in southern Mesopotamia, to

Map from the Akkadian period (circa 2250 B.C.E.), drawn on a clay tablet (approximately three inches wide) excavated at Yorgan Tepe (ancient Gasur, later renamed Nuzi). At center, below a river flowing from north to south (left to right) between two ranges of hills (indicated by overlapping semicircles) is a circle indicating a thirty-acre field "belonging to Azala." Other circles on the map indicate cities; Mashkan-dur-ibla is at the lower left (Iraq Museum, Baghdad).

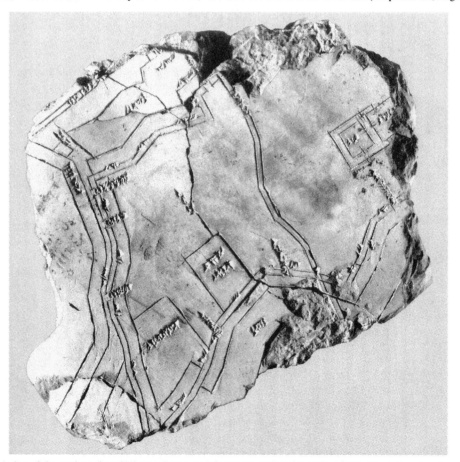

Ground plan of the ancient city of Nippur drawn on a fragmentary Kassite-period (circa fifteenth – circa fourteenth centuries B.C.E.) clay tablet from Nippur. At left the Euphrates runs south, parallel with the city wall; a canal runs through the heart of the city; the E-kur temple is at the right (Hilprecht Sammlung, Jena, Germany).

Late Babylonian (circa mid-first millennium B.C.E.) cuneiform tablet with a map of the world sketched on the lower half of the obverse (front side). The city of Babylon (indicated by a rectangle) straddles the Euphrates River, running north to south across a circular continent surrounded by a circular sea; the circles on the continent are other Mesopotamian cities. The accompanying cuneiform text may describe the triangular regions beyond the ocean (British Museum, London).

Diorite dedicatory statue (top) of Gudea, city ruler of Lagash circa 2100 B.C.E., height 36 5/8 inches. A tablet on his knees (bottom) bears an engraved architectural ground plan of the E-ninnu temple, showing its buttressed walls and six gates set between pairs of flanking towers; a stylus is at left, and a graduated rule is at the bottom (Louvre, Paris).

the city of Emar on the upper Euphrates in Syria. The route did not lead directly along the Euphrates, a course that would have taken the travelers through Mari, which at the time was in the hands of the ambitious native king Zimri-Lim. Instead, the travelers took a more circuitous route that led from Larsa north through such major cities as Babylon and Sippar on the Euphrates, to Ashur on the Tigris, then westward across north Syria via Shubat-Enlil and Harran, and finally southward again through Tuttul to Emar. Traveling at a rate of approximately twenty-five to thirty kilometers (fifteen to nineteen miles) per day, the round-trip journey took 194 days, including various layovers along the way. The reason for the journey, whether military or diplomatic, is nowhere stated and remains unclear.

Lists of Geographical Names. Part of the cuneiform curriculum, probably from its inception, was the copying of word lists. These lists were often organized around some common theme, such as the names of cities and towns. These lists provide another view of the ancient Mesopotamian world. However, they are not organized around any readily discernible cartographic principles.

The Sargon Geography. The Akkadian king Sargon (circa 2334 – circa 2279 B.C.E.) is credited by modern scholars with establishing the world's first empire. In his inscriptions he claimed that his realm stretched from Anatolia to Iran and from the Mediterranean Sea to the Persian Gulf and that his influence extended across the Lower Sea (the Persian Gulf) to what are believed to be the coastal lands of the Arabian Sea, perhaps as far as the Indus Valley (ancient Meluhha). Two first millennium B.C.E. cuneiform tablets, one from Assyria and the other from Babylonia, preserve portions of a text purporting to detail Sargon's empire, but the sources from which the text draws its details are unknown. The text equates the entire earth's surface with Sargon's empire, thus providing a detailed geography of the entire known world. In it are listed the names of all the lands he is said to have ruled; in some case their dimensions and the names of their inhabitants are also given. His domain is said to stretch to the lands of Anaku and Kaptara beyond the Upper Sea (the Mediterranean) and to Dilmun and Magan beyond the Lower Sea (the Persian Gulf). One possible interpretation of the data in the text suggests that in the Mesopotamians' conception of world geography, the earth's surface, centered on Mesopotamia, was a single circular continent with a diameter of approximately 4,500 kilometers (2,800 miles).

The Distant Reaches. Throughout the duration of ancient Mesopotamian history, a fairly stock repertoire of place-names was used to designate those most distant realms at the edges of the known world. These sites are usually associated with the sources of the rarest of woods, ivory, precious stones, and metals, but it is not always

clear to the modern scholar whether in every case they were real locations. Nor is it clear that in different periods a given name represented the same location, whether real or imagined. Overland to the east were said to be Marhashi, Shimashki, and Tukrish in Iran, and Aratta, possibly as far east as Afghanistan. In the Persian Gulf lay Dilmun, assumed to be the island of Bahrain and the mainland opposite it, and further yet, Magan and Meluhha. Magan is usually taken to be the Arabian coast in the vicinity of the Oman Peninsula, and perhaps the facing Iranian coastline. Meluhha, during the third millennium B.C.E., appears to refer to the region of the Indus Valley civilization, but in Assyrian texts of the first millennium B.C.E. Meluhha refers to Nubia, the land south of Egypt. To the west, across the Mediterranean lay Alashiya, the island of Cyrus; Kaptara, perhaps Crete; and Anaku, the "tin" land.

Sources:

Béatrice André-Salvini, "Seated Statue of Gudea: Architect with Plan," in *Art of the First Cities: The Third Millennium B.C. from the Mediterranean to the Indus*, edited by Joan Aruz with Ronald Wallenfels (New York: Metropolitan Museum of Art, 2003), pp. 427–428.

William W. Hallo, "The Road to Emar," *Journal of Cuneiform Studies*, 18 (1964): 57–87.

Wayne Horowitz, *Mesopotamian Cosmic Geography*, Mesopotamian Civilizations 8 (Winona Lake, Ind.: Eisenbrauns, 1998).

James Mellaart, *Earliest Civilizations in the Near East* (New York: McGraw-Hill, 1965).

A. R. Millard, "Cartography in the Ancient Near East," in *The History of Cartography*, volume 1: *Cartography in Prehistoric, Ancient and Medieval Europe and the Mediterranean*, edited by J. B. Harley and David Woodward (Chicago: University of Chicago Press, 1987), pp. 107–116.

Karen Rhea Nemet-Nejat, *Late Babylonian Field Plans in the British Museum*, Studia Pohl: Series Maior 11 (Rome: Biblical Institute Press, 1982).

Richard L. Zettler, *Nippur III: Kassite Buildings in Area WC-1*, Oriental Institute Publications, volume 111 (Chicago: Oriental Institute of the University of Chicago, 1993).

CLIMATE AND TOPOGRAPHY

The Land. *Mesopotamia* in Greek means the "land between the rivers," in this case the rivers Tigris and Euphrates. In its broadest sense, however, Mesopotamia encompassed not only the land between these two rivers, but the lands (occasionally for hundreds of kilometers) on both sides of their banks and of their major tributaries. Throughout prehistory and history, this vast area was occupied by a wide range of ethnic and linguistic groups. Thus, it becomes both convenient and necessary to distinguish specific areas in specific periods of time. In the third millennium B.C.E., on the alluvial plain—a broad flat land covered by thick layers of sediment deposited by the flooding rivers—between the marshlands at the head of the Persian Gulf north to the area of modern Baghdad were the lands of Sumer, to the south, and Akkad, to the north. During the latter half of the second and early first millennia B.C.E., the region bore the Kassite name Kar-

Set among date palms and built of bundles of reeds, this modern Marsh Arab's *mudhif* (guest house) closely resembles
buildings depicted on Uruk period (circa late fourth millennium B.C.E.) cylinder seals and stone reliefs
(photograph by V. Southwell; from Michael Roaf, *Cultural Atlas of Mesopotamia and the Ancient
Near East*, 1966).

duniash. However, as a result of the rise to prominence
of the city of Babylon, Sumer and Akkad are more con-
veniently referred to by the later Greek designation
Babylonia; the southernmost marshy region was termed
the Sealand. To the north, the region along the Tigris
above its confluence with the Lower Zab is the land of
Ashur, or Assyria, while to the northwest, the middle
Euphrates runs through Syria. The name *Syria* is a shortened form of *Assyria;* the Assyrian Empire dominated the
region for centuries, and the two names became synony-
mous in the classical period. To the east of southernmost
Mesopotamia, Elam, dominated by the city of Susa,
occupied Khuzestan, the lowland regions of southwestern Iran.

The Rivers. The Tigris and Euphrates rise near each
other in the mountains of eastern Anatolia, modern-day
Turkey. The more easterly Tigris heads almost directly
southeast, while the more westerly Euphrates initially
heads to the southwest. As the two rivers cross the modern border between Turkey and Syria, they are some 400
kilometers (250 miles) apart. At this point the Euphrates
turns to the southeast, converging on the Tigris as both
rivers near the region of the modern city of Baghdad.

From here the rivers continue to traverse the length of
modern Iraq, their braided streams meandering broadly
through their common delta toward the head of the Persian Gulf, which in antiquity may at times have been as
much as two hundred fifty kilometers (150 miles) further
inland than today. Over the millennia, the rivers' channels have wandered east and west to such a degree that it
is not always possible to say with certainty today whether
an abandoned channel was once a branch of the Tigris or
the Euphrates. Today the rivers enter the Gulf via a common channel, the Shatt al-Arab. The Euphrates flows a
total distance of some 2,720 kilometers (1,690 miles),
while the Tigris, with its more direct route, covers 2,033
kilometers (1,263 miles). Several important tributaries
join the rivers along their routes. The Balikh and the
Habur enter on the left bank of the Euphrates north of
the modern Syria-Iraq border. The Tigris is joined on its
left bank, from north to south, by three major rivers
flowing out of the Zagros Mountains to the east, the
Greater and Lesser Zab and the Diayala, and, in antiquity, by two rivers from Khuzestan in southwest Iran, the
Karkheh (which now ceases before it reaches the Tigris)
and the Karun.

The Climate. The climatic conditions of Mesopotamia are generally believed not to have changed substantially, on average, during the past five thousand years. Nonetheless, modern climatic studies suggest that the overall level of precipitation was low during circa 3800 – circa 1000 B.C.E., with two protracted periods of significantly below average rainfall circa 3200 – circa 2900 B.C.E. and circa 2350 – circa 2000 B.C.E. Rainfall throughout the first millennium B.C.E. fluctuated at overall higher than average levels. Along the foothills of the Taurus Mountains to the north and the Zagros Mountains to the east, summers are generally warm and dry, winters mild and moist. Vegetation includes oak, pine, and terebinth trees, and such grasses as barley and wheat. A wide grass-covered steppe zone south of the Taurus range has mild dry winters and hot dry summers.

ANCIENT FLOODS

During the most recent Ice Age, enormous quantities of water were tied up as ice in vast continental glaciers that covered much of continental Europe, Asia, and North America. In places these glaciers became as much as four kilometers (two and a half miles) thick. As a direct consequence, sea levels fell dramatically. It has been estimated that at the peak of the last Ice Age, some 20,000 years ago, mean sea levels were more than one hundred meters (some 350 feet) lower than at present, exposing up to one hundred miles of additional shoreline that is today underwater. Recently, some geologists have produced dramatic hypotheses based on observations made while drilling into the floors of the Persian Gulf, into which the Tigris and Euphrates Rivers empty, and the Black Sea, which forms the northern coastline of Anatolia to the north and west of Mesopotamia.

In the Gulf, the evidence indicates that 16,000 years ago the river delta was located at the Straits of Hormuz, 900 kilometers (560 miles) southeast of its present location. By circa 5000 B.C.E., the sea had entirely refilled the Gulf, having driven into southern Mesopotamia or southwestern Iran Neolithic hunter-gatherers, pastoralists, or agricultural villagers who may have been living along the ancient river valley. The Gulf waters had advanced to the point where the new shoreline lay as much as 250 kilometers (150 miles) further inland than today; the site of ancient Eridu may have been established on that ancient seashore. Between circa 5000 B.C.E. and circa 2000 B.C.E., the Gulf receded to more or less its present position.

It has been suggested that the Black Sea began to evaporate when worldwide sea levels fell below the level of the floor of the Bosporus Strait, which ordinarily connects the Black Sea to the Aegean Sea, an arm of the Mediterranean. Evaporation gradually lowered the level of the Black Sea, eventually by more than five hundred feet, leaving a brackish plain at the bottom of the empty seafloor. When the ice cap began to melt some 20,000 years ago, meltwater initially pooled into great lakes at the foot of the glaciers. From there, via several great rivers, the meltwater flowed southward. Water accumulated in the empty Black Sea basin, forming there a vast freshwater lake. However, by circa 9400 B.C.E., meltwaters no longer entered the Black Sea valley, and evaporation began to lower the lake even as worldwide sea levels beyond it were rising. Apparently, a natural dam had formed at the mouth of the Bosporus that prevented Mediterranean-Aegean seawater from gradually re-entering the Black Sea basin. By circa 5600 B.C.E., the shoreline of the ever-receding lake lay 350 feet below the top of the Bosporus dam, which is believed to have then catastrophically ruptured. Torrents of seawater descended in a vast waterfall to the valley floor below. Initially, the water is estimated to have accumulated at the rate of a half-foot a day. At that rate it would have spread rapidly across the relatively flat valley floor, and displaced, if not overwhelmed, any bands of Neolithic hunter-gatherers, pastoralists, or agricultural villagers who might have been living along the edge of the former freshwater lake. Any presumed refugees would most likely have fled up the major river valleys entering along the northern and western rims of the Black Sea basin into the Ukraine and eastern and central Europe or along the southern rim into Anatolia, and thence on to the Levant, Syria, and Mesopotamia. In addition to speculating on the identity of those presumed refugees among the known populations of sixth millennium B.C.E. Europe and Mesopotamia, the geologists further imagined that the event itself, as remembered by its survivors, may have become the basis of the Near Eastern Flood myth. This interpretation has not been widely embraced by historians of ancient Mesopotamia.

Sources: William Ryan and Walter Pitman, *Noah's Flood: The New Scientific Discoveries about the Event that Changed History* (New York: Simon & Schuster, 1998).
Juris Zarins, "The Early Settlement of Southern Mesopotamia: A Review of Recent Historical, Geographical, and Archaeological Research," *Journal of the American Oriental Society*, 112 (1992): 55–77.

Much of Mesopotamia proper, within the borders of the modern state of Iraq, lies in a semi-arid or arid region where little grows naturally, except along the banks of the rivers and at spring-fed oases; there tamarisk and similarly hardy bushes and trees thrive. At the head of the Persian Gulf date palms grow in the reed-filled marshes.

Taming the Land. Farming without irrigation (dry farming) is possible only with a minimum reliable annual rainfall of at least twenty centimeters (approximately eight inches); above thirty centimeters (twelve inches) per year farming becomes secure and profitable. Such rainfall levels occur only on the hilly flanks of the Zagros and Taurus Mountains and on the grassy steppe immediately to the south of the Taurus. Indeed, this area is the heart of the "Fertile Crescent," where the so-called Neolithic Revolution began some ten thousand years ago. The autumn rains softened the ground for planting cereals and vegetables, which were sustained by the winter rains; the harvest came in late spring.

Agricultural Settlers in the South. When agricultural settlers first began to exploit southern Mesopotamia early in the sixth millennium B.C.E., they were confronted with several factors restricting the ability of the rich but dry soil of the southern alluvial plain to support a considerable population. Foremost was the lack of adequate reliable annual rainfall throughout the region. Then there were the sudden and catastrophic floods that strike the region each April and May as the Tigris and Euphrates successively overflow their banks—the result of spring storms and the melting of the snow cover in eastern Anatolia. In addition, the slope of the southern alluvium is so gentle that when the riverbanks are breached, the waters flood a vast area. Unlike the Nile in Egypt, which floods in mid to late summer and recedes quickly enough for autumn sowing to begin immediately, the flooding in Mesopotamia occurs in the spring, thus potentially washing away or drowning a standing crop ready for harvesting. In the autumn planting season, the rivers run low within their banks, necessitating some means of irrigating the fields.

Thriving Population. The region possesses only the most limited natural resources with which to work: no hardwoods, little stone, and no metals; it has only reeds, softwoods, and mud. Nonetheless, by the late fourth millennium B.C.E., southern Mesopotamia had a thriving population, supported by an intricate system of dikes to protect fields and homes from flooding and canals to carry water onto the land when and where it was needed. The canals also provided a means of communication and transportation by boat and yielded fish, and the birds they attracted, for food. The coordinating and control of the enormous manpower required to build and maintain such a complex system, and the overseeing of the redistribution of the great wealth generated in the form of huge agricultural surpluses, was precipitated by, and in turn further precipitated, a highly organized and centralized administration. The religious and political hierarchies that arose in Sumer at this time established the basic patterns of governance in Mesopotamia that lasted for more than three thousand years.

Sources:

Robert McCormick Adams, *Heartland of Cities: Surveys of Ancient Settlement and Land Use on the Central Floodplain of the Euphrates* (Chicago: University of Chicago Press, 1981).

Karl W. Butzer, "Environmental Change in the Near East and Human Impact on the Land," in *Civilizations of the Ancient Near East*, 4 volumes, edited by Jack M. Sasson (New York: Scribners, 1995), I: 123–151.

Christopher J. Eyre, "The Agricultural Cycle, Farming, and Water Management in the Ancient Near East," in *Civilizations of the Ancient Near East*, 4 volumes, edited by Sasson (New York: Scribners, 1995), I: 175–189.

Richard N. Frye, "Assyria and Syria: Synonyms," *Journal of Near Eastern Studies*, 51 (1992): 281–285.

Michael Roaf, *Cultural Atlas of Mesopotamia and the Ancient Near East* (New York: Facts on File, 1966).

H. W. F. Saggs, *Babylonians*, Peoples of the Past 1 (Norman: University of Oklahoma Press, 1995).

Piotr Steinkeller, "New Light on the Hydrology and Topography of Southern Babylonia in the Third Millennium," *Zietschrift für Assyriologie und Archaeologie*, 91 (2001): 22–84.

Eva von Dassow, "On Writing the History of Southern Mesopotamia," *Zietschrift für Assyriologie und Archaeologie*, 89 (1999): 227–246.

ETHNOGRAPHY

Of Peoples and Pots. Ethnic identity depends on the recognition of significant similarities within a group and significant differences to distinguish members of one group from another. Any combination of differences in language, social customs, material culture, religion, mode of subsistence, political organization, and territorial contiguity might, under various conditions, come into play in the process of defining one ethnic group in contradistinction to others. Modern knowledge of the peoples of ancient Mesopotamia depends largely on those ancient texts that have by happenstance survived since antiquity to be recovered and interpreted by modern scholars. On the basis of these texts ancient culturally distinct groups who share a common ancestry—ethnic groups—may be distinguished on the basis of the languages and dialects they chose by which to name themselves, to speak, or at least in which they chose to write, and by the terms they applied to people they defined as "themselves" and "others." Further indications of ethnicity may be judged from the facial features, hairstyles, and dress of peoples represented artistically in various media, including wall paintings, carved relief, and sculpture in the round—subject, of course, to the skill of the artisan and to any artistic conventions that he might have employed. In the absence of any of these indicators of ethnicity, ceramic types and styles, in combination with other characteristic features of material culture, including the materials and forms of tools and weapons, the style and

FOUNDING MARI

The city of Mari (modern Tell Hariri) was founded in the middle Euphrates River valley by unknown builders early in the third millennium B.C.E. This part of Syria is a semi-arid region with insufficient rainfall to support dry-farming agriculture. Nonetheless, the founders of Mari established their city on a canal-laced terrace a few kilometers west of the river. They surrounded the city with a circular dike to protect it from floods and connected it to the river through a diversion canal. Behind the dike stood a 6.7-meter-thick (22 feet) defensive rampart. The area is at an important juncture between the main irrigation-based Sumerian city-states along the lower Euphrates River to the south and the dry-farming plains of north Syria along the upper Euphrates and Khabur Rivers, but Mari itself is of no agricultural significance. The position of Mari seems rather to have been determined by the location of trade routes through the area, which its leaders must have sought to control. The city was equipped with metalworking furnaces, as well as workshops for dyeing and pottery making, suggesting that supplying refined metals to the metal-poor south may have been one of its principal sources of wealth. For reasons that remain unknown, the city was abandoned for about a century, beginning about 2550 B.C.E. The ruins of the first city were leveled, and an even greater city was erected in its place, one that remained a major urban center until its destruction at the hands of an Akkadian king, circa 2300 – circa 2250 B.C.E. The city was rebuilt a third time by a dynasty of local governors serving the Akkadian Empire. During the early second millennium B.C.E., the city became the focus of attention of the rulers of several competing Amorite kingdoms, among them Hammurabi of Babylon, who, circa 1760 B.C.E., captured the city and destroyed it forever.

Sources: Jean-Claude Margueron, "Mari," in *The Oxford Encyclopedia of Archaeology in the Near East*, 5 volumes, edited by Eric M. Meyers (New York: Oxford University Press, 1997), III: 413–417.
Margueron, "Mari and the Syro-Mesopotamian World," in *Art of the First Cities: The Third Millennium B.C. from the Mediterranean to the Indus*, edited by Joan Aruz with Ronald Wallenfels (New York: Metropolitan Museum of Art, 2003), pp. 135–138.

iconography of seals, building design, and burial practices, are often taken as indicators of particular cultural groups. The limitation here, of course, is that readily portable objects, especially distinctively decorated pottery containing some desirable commodity such as oil or wine, might travel through trade far greater distances than the peoples who created them.

Ethnicity and Language. It is pointless to attempt to discuss the population of ancient Mesopotamia in terms of modern concepts of "culture" and "race." The earliest identifiable inhabitants of Mesopotamia, the Sumerians, who referred to themselves as the "black-headed" people, were speakers of a *language isolate*, that is, a language unrelated to any other known language, living or dead. The Sumerians appear as the masters of the southern Mesopotamian city-states in the earliest decipherable texts of the first half of the third millennium B.C.E. Whether the Sumerians had been present in the region for just a few centuries or for one, two, or three millennia prior to the mid-third millennium B.C.E. remains a topic of much discussion. Surviving texts from the latter half of the third millennium B.C.E. include evidence that during that period, as the political fortunes of the Sumerian rulers waned and as cuneiform writing spread up the Tigris and Euphrates River valleys to urban centers in Akkad and Syria, there were in the region a variety of speakers of Semitic languages, principally Akkadian, as well as speakers of other language groups, including Hurrian. In addition, even in the earliest texts, the names of cities and other place-names, as well as personal names, include evidence of other, often unknown, languages and presumably their associated ethnic groups. Further, some groups, such as the Semitic Amorites and the Kassites (another language-isolate group) became so thoroughly assimilated following their entry into Mesopotamian urban culture that, but for their foreign names, they are indistinguishable from "native" Mesopotamians.

Ethnicity and Appearance. The first evidence of Mesopotamians' interest in representing the human form in some detail in both two and three dimensions dates from toward the end of the fourth millennium B.C.E., with depictions of the so-called "priest-king" and those who supported him, typically in hunting and ritual activities. The essential conventions for representing the human form remained more-or-less fixed until the Hellenistic period. The highly stylized art depicts Mesopotamians typically with faces that are round or oval, with prominent cheekbones, thin lips, large high-bridged noses, and almond-shaped eyes—occasionally inlayed with blue or black stone—set beneath a single double-arching eyebrow. Their hair—colored black, where preserved—is curly, and the men, when not clean shaven, have curly beards. There is little in the art, except in renderings of hair style or costume, to distinguish sharply any one Mesopotamian ethnolinguistic group, even enemies, from any other.

City Dwellers and Nomads. Perhaps the most fundamental characteristic by which the ancient Mesopotamians defined themselves was their urban lifestyle. Among the suggested translations for *Ki-en-gir*, the Sumerian name for their land, are "civilized land" and "noble land." Early urban Mesopotamians apparently accepted without question the city as the sole communal organization, with no

Captive and tributary foreign peoples depicted in Neo-Assyrian palace wall reliefs (late eighth through seventh centuries B.C.E.): (top) marsh dwellers, perhaps Chaldaeans, (middle, left) Judaeans, (middle, right) Medes, (bottom, left) Arabs, and (bottom, right) Elamites (middle right: Louvre, Paris; all others: British Museum, London)

evident vestiges or memories of earlier tribal organizations. By and large they were not antagonistic toward those who dwelled in the open countryside. In fact, they were intimately and irrevocably connected, exchanging raw materials and finished goods. But hostile nomads and uncouth mountain folk were to be pitied—in a text assigned the modern name *The Sargon Geography*, they are as those

> who do not know construction . . . whose ha[ir-style] is chosen with a razor, devoured(?) by fire, who do not know burial. Meat-eaters, milk (and) roasted-grain eaters, whos[e insi]des do not know oven-baked bread, bellies (do not know) beer. (Horowitz)

Sources:

Geoff Emberling and Norman Yoffee, "Thinking about Ethnicity in Mesopotamian Archaeology and History," in *Fluchtpunkt Uruk: Archäologische Einheit aus methodischer Vielfalt. Schriften für Hans Jörg Nissen*, edited by Hartmut Küne, Reinhard Bernbeck, and Karin Bartl, Internationale Archäologie Studia honoraria 6 (Rahden: Marie Leidorf, 1999), pp. 272–281.

Henri Frankfort, *The Art and Architecture of the Ancient Orient*, fifth edition, with supplementary notes and bibliography by Michael Roaf and Donald Matthews (New Haven: Yale University Press, 1996).

Wayne Horowitz, *Mesopotamian Cosmic Geography*, Mesopotamian Civilizations 8 (Winona Lake, Ind.: Eisenbrauns, 1998).

A. Leo Oppenheim, *Ancient Mesopotamia: Portrait of a Dead Civilization*, revised edition, completed by Erica Reiner (Chicago: University of Chicago Press, 1964).

SIGNIFICANT PERSON

SARGON II

721-705 B.C.E.
ASSYRIAN KING

Usurper. In 722 B.C.E. Sargon, whose Akkadian name (*Sharru-kin*) means "the king is legitimate," overthrew the Assyrian king Shalmaneser V (726–722 B.C.E.), who may have been his brother, at the moment the king's troops were besieging Samaria, the capital of ancient Israel. Although in his later years, Sargon claimed that on taking the throne, he completed the conquest of Samaria and the deportation of its population; the Hebrew Bible, which is probably correct, mentions only Shalmaneser in this regard. In reality, after staging his coup, Sargon faced rebellion and belligerent adversaries on virtually all the borders of Assyria. Sargon spent practically his entire reign in military campaigns suppressing rebellions and attempting to complete the strategy of expansion and consolidation initiated during the reign of Shalmaneser's father, Tiglath-pileser III (744–727 B.C.E.). Yet, Sargon also managed to have built a magnificent new capital city named after himself, Dur-Sharrukin (modern Khorsabad). Sargon's artisans adorned the walls of his palace with large carved blocks of stone, many of them vividly depicting his military victories.

Rebellions in the South. Immediately after Sargon's coup, Marduk-apla-iddina II (the biblical Merodoch-baladan), the leader of Bit-Yakin, a local Chaldaean tribe, seized the throne in Babylon, which had previously been occupied by the Assyrian kings Tiglath-pileser III and Shalmaneser V. The defeat of the Assyrian army by the Elamites of Iran, allies of the Babylonians, during an otherwise unsuccessful Elamite attack on the city of Der, forced Sargon to concentrate his efforts in areas other than Babylonia for a full ten years. He returned to Babylonia in 710 B.C.E. and managed to isolate the Babylonians from their erstwhile Elamite allies, driving Merodoch-baladan to flee for his life.

Rebellions in the West. Following the initial stalemate in the south, Sargon immediately turned his attention to the west. Among the rebellious former vassal states was Hamath on the Orontes in Syria. The king of Hamath, Yau-bidi, led a coalition of neighboring states in revolt. In an inscription, Sargon called Yau-bidi "a *hupshu* (a Hurrian loanword that originally designated a member of one of the lower classes and later became a term of abuse) without claim to the throne, a cursed Hittite." Sargon fitted out an army and besieged Yau-bidi in the city of Qarqar. The city was captured and burned; Yaubidi was captured and flayed alive. Sargon then continued south, retaking Gaza and defeating an Egyptian force at Raphia on the Egyptian border. Later, an Assyrian garrison was posted at the border, and the Egyptian king sent diplomatic gifts to Sargon. In 712 B.C.E., Sargon successfully pacified the Philistine city-states. Sargon's power was felt as far west as the island of Cyprus, some 100 kilometers (60 miles) off the north

Syrian coast. An Assyrian royal inscription excavated on Cyprus records the gifts of seven local kings sent to Sargon.

Enemies to the North. Two major powers on Assyria's northern and northwestern frontiers presented Sargon with further difficulties: Phrygia and Urartu, in central and eastern Anatolia respectively, attempted together and individually to pressure border states into allying themselves with either of them. In the annals of his Eighth Campaign (714 B.C.E.), Sargon vividly described the difficult march into the highlands, where he defeated the Urartians and their allies. With the movement of the nomadic Cimmerians across the Caucasus Mountains into Anatolia, and the general threat they posed to all, the Phrygian king Mita (Midas) sought to bring hostilities with Assyria to a close; eventually the two states exchanged ambassadors. In 705

B.C.E. troubles in the border state of Tabal took Sargon into the northwest on one last campaign, in which he was killed in battle.

Sources:
Pauline Albenda, *The Palace of Sargon of Assyria: Monumental Wall Reliefs at Dur-Sharrukin, from Original Drawings Made at the Time of Their Discovery in 1843–1844 by Botta and Flandin*, Synthèse, no. 22 (Paris: Éditions Recherche sur les Civilizations, 1986).

J. A. Brinkman, *Prelude to Empire: Babylonian Society and Politics, 747–626 B.C.*, Occasional Publications of the Babylonian Fund, 7 (Philadelphia: Babylonian Fund, University Museum, 1984).

A. Kirk Grayson, "Assyria: Tiglath-pileser III to Sargon II (744–705 B.C.)," in *The Assyrian and Babylonian Empires and Other States to the Near East, from the Eighth to the Sixth Centuries B.C.*, edited by John Boardman, I. E. S. Edwards, N. G. L. Hammond, and E. Sollberger, volume 3, part 2 of *The Cambridge Ancient History*, second edition (Cambridge: Cambridge University Press, 1991), pp. 71–102.

DOCUMENTARY SOURCES

Enuma elish (late second millennium B.C.E.)—The best-known and best-preserved Mesopotamian creation myth is found in this Babylonian national epic, named from its *incipit* (opening words), which may be translated as "When on high." The myth celebrates the elevation of the god Marduk to the head of the Babylonian pantheon. To achieve this position, Marduk has to slay the monster Tiamat, the embodiment of the primeval ocean, and from her corpse Marduk erects the heavens and the earth.

Etana and the Eagle (Old Babylonian period, circa 1750 B.C.E.) —In this myth, incompletely known from fragmentary Old Babylonian and Middle and Neo-Assyrian copies, Etana, a king of Kish mentioned in the *Sumerian King List,* rescues an eagle from a pit into which it had been cast by a snake. The eagle agrees to help Etana—who is unable to produce an heir—find the "plant of birth." During their search, the eagle carries Etana up to the Heaven of Anu. From high in the air, Etana looks back to see that "The sea has turned into a gardener's ditch."

KAR 307 (Neo-Assyrian period, mid seventh century B.C.E.) —This tablet was recopied by Kisir-Ashur, a prolific scribe and an exorcist from the temple of

Ashur in the city of the same name. The tablet is identified as containing secret lore of the gods, forbidden to all but the initiated, and includes a description of the levels of the universe and their composition. The heavens are subdivided into an upper, middle, and lower level, each with its own resident deities. Similarly, the earth is subdivided into an upper earth, where mankind lives, and middle and lower earths, also the residences of deities.

Map of the World (circa eighth – fourth century B.C.E.)—A bird's-eye view of the world as conceived by the Babylonians is sketched on the lower half of the obverse of a Late Babylonian tablet in the British Museum. The purpose of this map and the accompanying text may have been to locate and describe faraway regions in relation to the more immediate world of Babylon and the Euphrates River.

The Sargon Geography (first millennium B.C.E.)—Two tablet fragments preserve portions of a text describing the "World Empire" of the third millennium B.C.E. Akkadian king Sargon. Lists of names of peoples and places are interspersed with material relating to the king's reign.

Crew members unloading timber onto the shore from Phoenician transport ships, with horse-head bows and fish-tail sterns;
in the sea are a merman, fish, aquatic lizards, turtles, crabs, murex shells, and serpents; alabaster wall relief
(height 9 feet 3 5/8 inches), Palace of Sargon II (721–705 B.C.E.), Khorsabad (Louvre, Paris)

by PAUL COLLINS

CONTENTS

Sidebars and tables are listed in italics.

IMPORTANT EVENTS OF 3300-331 B.C.E.

3300*-2900* B.C.E.

- Many of the themes of Mesopotamian art are established, including the image of a ruler defeating the forces of chaos, which are represented by a lion and human enemies.

- Monumental buildings decorated with mosaics, some raised high on mud-brick platforms, are constructed in a style that expands on much older traditions of architecture.

- Administrative systems are developed, and cuneiform writing emerges to record accounts and administrative actions.

- Cylinder seals are invented, representing some of the earliest examples of narrative art.

- Lost-wax casting is developed, allowing artists to create more-complex imagery in metal.

2900*-2600* B.C.E.

- Art focuses on two main themes: ceremonial banquets and combat among heroic men, wild animals, and supernatural creatures.

- Artworks include composite animal-human forms.

- Votive sculptures depict men and women in an attitude of prayer.

2600*-2450* B.C.E.

- Temple hymns and texts giving wise counsel are written, becoming the earliest surviving literary works.

- The Royal Graves of Ur reveal the metalworking skills of Sumer and the connections of the region with other civilizations.

- Cuneiform spreads beyond southern Mesopotamia to Iran and Syria.

2400* B.C.E.

- The earliest surviving record of an historical event—the conflict between the city-states of Umma and Lagash—is narrated and depicted on two sides of a stele, an engraved, upright stone slab.

2300* B.C.E.

- Much of Mesopotamia is united under the rulers of Akkad. The earliest art of this period continues the traditions of the Early Dynastic period (circa 2900–2340 B.C.E.).

2250* B.C.E.

- During the reign of Naram-Sin, an imperial art arises depicting an empire and a deified king. Royal art is naturalistic with an emphasis on the conquering ruler.

2100* B.C.E.

- Under Gudea of Lagash the longest and most-complex surviving Sumerian literary works are created.

- The art of this period emphasizes temple building rather than warfare.

* DENOTES CIRCA DATE

IMPORTANT EVENTS OF 3300-331 B.C.E.

2100* B.C.E. (CONT.)

- Ziggurats, monumental mud-brick, stepped, pyramid-like structures with steps leading to a temple at the top, are constructed in major cities.

2100*-2000* B.C.E.

- During the Third Dynasty of Ur, the scribal curriculum is reformed to reflect the concerns of king Shulgi of Ur (circa 2094 – circa 2047 B.C.E.).
- New literary works focus on the legendary rulers of Uruk.
- Shulgi is glorified in a series of hymns.

2000*-1800* B.C.E.

- The literary and artistic production of southern Mesopotamia is rooted in that of the Third Dynasty of Ur.

1800*-1500* B.C.E.

- Akkadian literary traditions become apparent in enlarged accounts of ancient themes, such as the Flood and the tales of Gilgamesh, a legendary ruler of the city of Uruk.
- Monumental inscriptions, such as Hammurabi's stele, emphasize the responsibilities of kings to their subjects as well as to the gods.
- The manufacture of glass is developed in northern Mesopotamia.

1400*-1200* B.C.E.

- Diplomacy across the Near East results in a fusion of regional styles to produce an International Style, evident most clearly in metalwork.
- National epics such as *Enuma elish* are written in Babylonia; they are later adopted and adapted in Assyria.

1100* B.C.E.

- Annals of royal achievements are written in Assyria.
- Many features of Assyrian royal relief imagery are established, such as depicting the king in profile with his hand raised in prayer.

883-859 B.C.E.

- Assyrian king Ashurnasirpal II founds Kalhu (modern Nimrud) as his Assyrian capital city.
- Ashurnasirpal II decorates his palace with wall reliefs showing his conquest of wild animals and human enemies while he is supported by the gods.

721-610 B.C.E.

- Assyrian king Sargon II (721–705 B.C.E.) establishes Dur-Sharrukin (modern Khorsabad) as his residence.

* DENOTES CIRCA DATE

IMPORTANT EVENTS OF 3300-331 B.C.E.

**721-610
B.C.E.
(CONT.)**

- A new use of space creates a sense of depth in the scenes on decorative wall reliefs, as opposed to the flat backgrounds of earlier reliefs.

- At Nineveh, Assyrian king Sennacherib (704–681 B.C.E.) builds his "Palace without Rival."

- Narrative art on wall reliefs shows an increasing interest in the details of characters and landscapes.

- The royal library of the Assyrian kings Sennacherib and Ashurbanipal (680–669 B.C.E.) preserves copies of older texts from throughout Mesopotamia.

**604-562
B.C.E.**

- Babylonian king Nebuchadnezzar II rebuilds Babylon and Borsippa, constructing palaces and cult buildings.

- Royal inscriptions are modeled on ancient texts.

**538-331
B.C.E.**

- During the Persian Empire, a court style develops in portable objects.

- Mesopotamian artistic traditions are blended with Egyptian, Greek, and Lydian influences in art and architecture.

- Cylinder seals are gradually replaced by stamp seals and engraved metal finger rings.

**331 B.C.E.-
75 C.E.**

- The largest ziggurat and two of the largest Mesopotamian temples ever built are erected at Uruk.

- Hellenistic art evolves from a fusion of classical Greek motifs and styles with older Mesopotamian and other Near Eastern types.

* DENOTES CIRCA DATE

OVERVIEW

Visual Arts and Architecture. The surviving artworks of Mesopotamia relate largely to royalty, especially the male ruler, or to wealthier members of the community. These elements of Mesopotamian culture include not only sculpture and painting but also religious and secular monuments and buildings, temples, and palaces. There are no Mesopotamian written accounts about art, but there are references in texts to the effort involved in artistic production and the experience of viewing the finished work. Mesopotamia was a crossroads for many different peoples during the three millennia from 3300 to 331 B.C.E. and, as a result, home to many forms of expression. Yet, what is perhaps most remarkable about Mesopotamian art is the great uniformity in its themes, symbols, and motifs—and perhaps also in some of the beliefs that inspired them. A major problem, however, is the identification and interpretation of many symbols or themes.

The First Cities. What appears to be clear, however, is that the basic grammar of Mesopotamian art and architecture was established around 3300 B.C.E. in southern Mesopotamia with the emergence of the world's first cities. In images, and later in texts, the settled community is contrasted with the chaotic and dangerous world beyond the city. The urban area is embodied in the image of its ruler, who defeats chaos in the shape of human enemies and wild animals. The ordered world of the city is also emphasized in the development of recording systems, including the use of cylinder seals, which produced miniature reliefs when they were rolled across clay. In later periods both texts and imagery depicted the Mesopotamian rulers' relationships with the gods. Much art emphasizes the royal duty to build houses for the gods (temples) and to feed and clothe them. As city-states developed into kingdoms and empires, the imagery associated with kingship remained largely consistent with earlier portrayals. Occasionally the association between gods and mortal ruler became so close that the king was deified. This changing approach to kingship is apparent in the visual messages. The relationship between royal inscriptions and sculptural images was a close one from its first appearance in the late fourth millennium B.C.E. until the end of the Achaemenid Persian Empire in the late fourth century B.C.E. Writing was not in a separate category from the sculpted images but was an integral part of the monument; that is, text and image in ancient Near Eastern art were viewed as a whole, one re-inforcing the other. Writing on monuments also expressed royal control of state administration (the scribes).

Literature. Although some texts written around 3200 B.C.E. may be considered literary, they are chiefly archival (that is, lists of commodities). Poetry and consciously literary prose were not committed to writing until the mid-third millennium B.C.E. and continued to be created throughout Mesopotamian history. Many literary forms were developed. Surviving religious works include hymns, prayers, and rituals; many poems describe the creation of the world and the relationship of gods to their human servants. Depicting a natural order that can be upset by both men and gods, these texts emphasize the importance of obedience to the gods and, by association, their representative the king. The role of the king is extolled in relation to his religious-building projects. By the end of the third millennium B.C.E., living and legendary rulers were described in heroic terms, and this theme was developed in epic poems, such as the *Epic of Gilgamesh,* during the second millennium B.C.E. Some literature was created to justify a king's claim to rule. Such texts often provide semi-historical connections with earlier rulers. In Babylonia these texts were developed into so-called chronicles, which describe events in chronological order but do not necessarily cover every year within a given time span, while in Assyria the king's ancestry and achievements are presented in annals, which present information for each and every year. A recurring theme in tales such as the *Poem of Erra and Ishum* and the various Flood myths is the possible or actual collapse of order. In the first millennium B.C.E. poetic accounts of dreams, allegedly provided by the gods, and royal letters addressed to deities, continued to emphasize the association between the ruler and the divine world. Like other Mesopotamian rulers before them, Achaemenid monarchs emphasized in texts that their right to rule is dependent on their maintaining a divinely ordained social order.

Music and Dance. Musicians played percussion, wind, and stringed instruments in ensembles and in solo performances. Singers also performed. Although the surviving lyrics are religious in nature, sculpted and inlaid scenes depict musicians and singers at banquets, some of which are in secular environments. Repetitions in poetic texts suggest that a musical form with a chorus might have existed. Surviving musical notation has allowed scholars to reconstruct some of the sounds of ancient Mesopotamian music. Dance forms are more difficult to identify, but some images appear to show people dancing in groups or singly. There is little information about the occasions for dance.

Theater. There is no evidence for the existence of drama in ancient Mesopotamia before Alexander III of Macedon (ruled 336–323 B.C.E., known to the Greeks as Alexander the Great) conquered the region in the late fourth century B.C.E. Some evidence suggests that mythological stories were recited at public festivals, such as the New Year festival, and these recitations may have included some form of enactment.

The Legacy of Mesopotamian Arts. Some of the artistic and literary traditions of Mesopotamia survived the cultural changes brought about by the conquest of Alexander in the late fourth century B.C.E., the domination of the Iranian Empires of the Parthians (247 B.C.E. – 224 C.E.) and Sasanians (224–651 C.E.)—both punctuated by periodic Roman incursions—and, in the seventh century C.E., the spread of Islam. Mesopotamian literary forms and ideas were preserved to some extent in the Hebrew Bible and Greek sources. A few Mesopotamian artistic themes were also retained and ultimately carried to Europe as contact between East and West was gradually re-established during the Middle Ages.

Hellenistic Art. With the conquest of the Achaemenid Persian Empire by the Macedonians in 331 B.C.E., classical Greek traditions of art and architecture were gradually fused with various Near Eastern traditions, including elements of Mesopotamian imagery, resulting in Hellenistic art. Under the Seleucid dynasty (311–129 B.C.E.), founded by one of Alexander's generals, Seleucus I Nicator, Greek traditions in architecture, especially for monumental buildings, were introduced in Mesopotamia, but they were seamlessly combined with local styles that preserved ancient forms of layout. During the same period occurred the final stages of the compilation of the Hebrew Bible, incorporating such Mesopotamian motifs and themes as the Flood and the Tower of Babel.

Rome and Parthia. During the first to third centuries C.E., as cities along trade routes linking the empires of Rome and Parthia were enriched, enormous temples were constructed in the Levant (the region bordering the eastern Mediterranean), Syria, and north Mesopotamia. They followed a traditional Near Eastern approach to temple design, with the sanctuary surrounded by an enormous walled *temenos,* or compound. Although the exterior looked like a Roman temple, the interior layout of the sanctuary was typically Near Eastern, designed as a throne room for a deity, usually with a raised platform approached by stairs. Among these gigantic constructions were the Temple at Jerusalem, begun by Herod in 20 B.C.E., the Temple of the Sun at Hatra in Iraq, and the Temple of Jupiter at Baalbek in Lebanon.

Rock Reliefs. The Parthians revived the tradition of carving rock reliefs at the same sites used by the Achaemenid Persians but introduced a frontal representation of humans that marked a break with earlier Near Eastern traditions. The Achaemenid Persians also influenced the art of the Sasanians, who defeated the Parthians in 224 C.E. Rock reliefs depict the Sasanian kings as successful warriors and hunters in the tradition of Mesopotamian royalty. The Sasanians particularly favored the image of the royal hunt for decorating bowls made of precious metals.

Ongoing Themes. In the Roman Empire a continued interest in Greek authors ensured that earlier writings on Mesopotamian art were preserved. At the same time, Roman, and later Byzantine, interest in acquiring the wealth of Mesopotamia from the Parthian, Sasanian, and Islamic Empires guaranteed a sustained contact with and recording of Near Eastern traditions. For example, Mesopotamian themes such as heraldic pairs of animals, the master of animals, griffins, interlaced animals, and eagles grasping pairs of animals appear in the architectural ornamentation of many Romanesque churches. The image of the eagle grasping serpents, which appeared on Mesopotamian seals as early as the third millennium B.C.E. and then spread widely across western Asia, was adopted in the Byzantine Empire and appeared in European sculpture and manuscript illuminations from the tenth century C.E. Eastern traditions are evident in Celtic art, especially in manuscripts, as in the interlacing animals decorating the *Book of Kells* (eighth century C.E.). The route of transmission for these motifs was largely through the East-West trade of Islamic textiles employing Mesopotamian motifs preserved in Sasanian art.

Royal and Divine Creatures. Other symbols may have been adopted directly from the Near East. The image of the royal lion—known through three thousand years of Mesopotamian art from the Late Uruk period, through the lion hunts of Ashurbanipal, and the Persian kings—found its way onto the royal coat of arms of England, probably as a result of European contact with the Near East during the Crusades. The Mesopotamian tradition of composite divine creatures was also preserved. Examples include the cherubim on the cover of the Ark of the Covenant, the animals of Ezekiel's vision, and the goat and fish combination, first found in the third millennium B.C.E., that stands for Capricorn among the signs of the zodiac (one more Mesopotamian legacy). Another combination creature is the *senmurv* (a dog or lion with a peacock's tail) that appears on Sasanian silks.

Modern Times. Mesopotamian imagery has also influenced artists and writers in recent centuries. Before the nineteenth century, artists drew inspiration from Hebrew and Greek sources for depictions of such originally Mesopotamian images as the Flood, the Garden of Eden, and the Tower of Babel. During the eighteenth century, however, contact between Europe and the East resulted in increased interest in Mesopotamia. The first European translation of the *Thousand and One Nights* was published in 1704. These tales, which had been collected since about the year 1000 in Persian-speaking Iran, or in an Arabic-speaking country, include stories about Sinbad the Sailor that have character types and narratives paralleling episodes of the *Epic of Gilgamesh*. Great epics such as Homer's *Odyssey*—which modern scholars have demonstrated to be dependent on the Gilgamesh stories and other Mesopotamian traditions—have been a popular subject for paintings since the eighteenth century. During that same period

"Oriental tales" such as Voltaire's *Sémiramis* (1748), *Candide* (1759), and *La Princesse de Babylone* (1768) became popular. The biblical and Greek view of Mesopotamia, which is generally negative, is also presented in such works as George Gordon, Lord Byron's *Hebrew Melodies* (1815) and his play *Sardanapalus* (1821). Nineteenth-century excavations of Mesopotamian sites and the translation of cuneiform did little to change attitudes about Mesopotamia except that unrealistic, negative, and sexually suggestive depictions began to include references to actual Mesopotamian art and literature. Beginning around 1850 the discoveries of Assyrian reliefs resulted in a brief flourishing of "Assyrian Revival" art in England and France, during which jewelry, sculpture, and architecture incorporated Mesopotamian motifs and themes. However, European and American artists and writers have continued to be largely influenced by the Bible and, as a result, their portrayals of Mesopotamia have been largely negative. A rare departure is D. W. Griffith's representation of Babylon in his motion picture *Intolerance* (1916), in which Prince Belshazzar is portrayed anachronistically as a supporter of religious freedom.

TOPICS IN THE ARTS

ARCHITECTURE

Mesopotamian Architecture. Knowledge of architecture in Mesopotamia is generally restricted to monumental public buildings such as palaces and temples. Occasionally, however, archaeological excavations have uncovered ordinary houses and other sorts of buildings.

Late Uruk Period, circa 3300 – circa 2900 B.C.E. During this period urbanism took spectacular form in southern Mesopotamia. The site of Uruk provides the most extensive evidence. In an area later dedicated to the heaven god Anu, a temple was built on top of a high terrace that had been rebuilt at least seven times. The best-preserved shrine is the so-called White Temple, which has a tripartite plan, identical to the layout of ordinary buildings known elsewhere in Mesopotamia a millennium earlier. The terrace, built of thousands of small rectangular mud bricks known as *Riemchen*, rose with sloping and recessed walls. The tops

of the terrace and stair walls were strengthened and decorated with inset rows of clay beakers, their open mouths at the surface. Some fifty meters to the east of the Anu terrace was the E-ana Precinct, probably dedicated then, as later, to the Sumerian goddess Inana. This area had a variety of buildings with plans that are often complex tripartite arrangements. (In a tripartite building, a rectangular floor plan is divided in thirds lengthwise; the central third is usually left as a long narrow room while the flanking rooms are often subdivided. More-complex buildings were made by assembling tripartite subunits parallel to and/or at right angles to each other.) These buildings in the E-ana complex are usually described as temples, but they lack altars or other features often found in such buildings. One of the earliest structures is the stone-built Limestone Temple (70 x 30 meters). Close by, the walls of the Cone Mosaic Court were decorated with zigzag and lozenge patterns formed by the black, red, and white painted heads of thousands of

Reconstruction of the columns decorating the court and staircase in the E-ana Precinct at Uruk,
Late Uruk period, circa 3300 – circa 3000 B.C.E. (Vorderasiatisches Museum, Berlin)

baked clay cones inserted into the plaster. Alongside was a raised area consisting of a double row of massive cylindrical columns, more than two meters in diameter, which—together with four half columns at either end—probably supported the roof of a hall. The columns too were decorated with painted clay cones. The Cone Mosaic Court was later filled in and replaced with even more massive buildings. In the Late Uruk period, southern style Mesopotamian settlements were established on the upper Euphrates. The best-known sites are at Jebel Aruda and Habuba Kabira, the earliest example of a planned city with the kind of mud-brick wall that became common in the later part of the Early Dynastic Period.

Early Dynastic Period, circa 2900 – circa 2340 B.C.E. Some temples built in this period resemble private houses in plan, with shrines and other rooms grouped around an open courtyard. Others—such as those at Khafajeh, Lagash, and Tell al-Ubaid—are raised on platforms within large oval enclosing walls. Surviving shrines are narrow with an altar at one end. The entrance was normally through a door in the long wall, giving a "bent axis" approach to the altar. Temples such as the one to Inana at Nippur could have accommodated only a few people, presumably priests.

The First Palaces. The first evidence of palaces dates from the Early Dynastic Period. (Some of the earlier monumental buildings at sites such as Uruk may have

had both ceremonial and administrative uses.) At Kish, the so-called "A" palace is one of the best examples of royal architecture. It is divided into several separate units that seem to include domestic, administrative, and storage areas. The building has an exceptional ceremonial suite with a pillared portico that is decorated with stone and shell inlay representing soldiers and naked prisoners. Parts of the building date to Early Dynastic II (circa 2750 – circa 2600 B.C.E.), though much of the surviving evidence is from the Early Dynastic III (circa 2600 – circa 2340 B.C.E.) period. Further north, in Syria, the Royal Palace at Ebla also consisted of a large complex of units. One of these, the so-called Administrative Quarter, stretched east of an open square with porches from which a monumental gateway, with a long staircase, led to the central area of the Royal Palace. The Administrative Quarter included several rooms, some of which served as an archive for cuneiform tablets. At Mari, on the middle Euphrates, parts of a third-millennium B.C.E. royal palace have been excavated. As at Ebla, the Mari complex consists of various units including a temple and a throne room with columns. In addition, six separate temples have been unearthed: the Shamash and Ishtarat temples, one on a raised platform; the so-called Massif Rouge; and buildings dedicated to the goddesses Ishtar, Ninni-ZA.ZA, and Ninhursanga. Each temple has a large covered hall, where offerings were made and which provided access to the cult room. The hall of the

Ninni-ZA.ZA temple was equipped with a *baetyl*, an oblong stone standing upright in the center. In the Nin-hursanga and Ishtar temples the cult room was compact, while in the Ninni-ZA.ZA temple, it was longer. At Tell Asmar in the Diyala region, a palace has an audience hall attached to the administrative block.

Akkadian Period, circa 2340 – circa 2200 B.C.E. There is evidence that during this period, at the so-called Northern Palace at Tell Asmar, some industrial activity may have taken place within the complex, which was well supplied with drains. The succeeding phase of construction was apparently not a palace but a building devoted to manufacturing.

Ur III and Early Isin-Larsa Periods, circa 2100 – circa 1900 B.C.E. In the two centuries following the collapse of the Akkadian Empire, there were changes in the architectural layouts of palaces and temples. In shrines the approach to the image of the god changed from "bent axis" to a direct path from a door opposite the altar. This new orientation may have resulted either from a change in religious thought or perhaps in the way people now approached kings, who, beginning in the reign of Shulgi (circa 2094 – circa 2047 B.C.E.), were deified. The most spectacular religious monuments of this period are the great ziggurats, or staged towers, of which the best surviving example is that of Ur-Namma at Ur. The exterior is decorated with buttresses and recesses to break the monotony of the flat surfaces and allow the play of light and shade. Ziggurats may have been thought of as ladders to heaven, or perhaps they symbolized the mountains in which the gods were believed to live (like Mount Olympus in later Greek mythology). Also at Ur was the subterranean vaulted tomb or "mausoleum" of the Ur III kings. It may originally have had a structure at ground level where offerings were made to the dead rulers. Some of the best evidence for private houses of the Ur III period and the succeeding Isin-Larsa period comes from Ur. They were built around courtyards with blank walls on the narrow streets. The wealthier houses, which may have had an upper story, sometimes had a private chapel and a paved bathroom with a lavatory. Late in the Ur III period the city ruler of Eshnunna, a city on the Diyala River, had a temple built to his overlord, the deified king of Ur, Shu-Sin (circa 2037 – circa 2029 B.C.E.). The temple was square in plan with exceptionally thick walls. With the collapse of the Ur III Empire (circa 2004 B.C.E.), a palace of the local rulers of Eshnunna was built abutting the Shu-Sin temple, which was incorporated into the palace.

Old Assyrian (circa 2000 – circa 1780 B.C.E.) and Old Babylonian (circa 1894 – circa 1595 B.C.E.) Periods. Impressive architecture at Ashur on the Tigris dates back to the time of Shamshi-Adad I (circa 1813 – circa 1781 B.C.E.). There were three ziggurats, one of which consisted of two temple towers dedicated to the gods Anu and Adad. Of the thirty-eight temples mentioned in inscriptions, only four have been excavated. The Ishtar Temple went through seven rebuildings. Like the palace further south at Eshnunna, on the Diyala, the so-called Old Palace next to the main ziggurat at Ashur has many chambers and storerooms ranged around courtyards. During the early first millennium B.C.E. the Old Palace was converted into a royal mausoleum. One of the best-known palace buildings of the second millennium B.C.E. is at Mari, on the middle Euphrates. It had nearly three hundred rooms at ground level covering an area of some six acres. The rooms are ranged around two open courtyards. There was probably a second story over most of the building. During this period monumental mud-brick buildings were often decorated with half columns. Tell el-Rimah in northern Mesopotamia had some of the most elaborate examples of columns, hundreds of which adorned the external and courtyard facades of a temple. To make these columns, carved bricks were laid in complicated sequences to represent spirals or two kinds of palm trunk. A sharing of style across Mesopotamia is suggested by palm-trunk columns at Ur, far to the south, which show an identical construction technique. Unlike ziggurats built in the south, which stood apart from other structures, the ziggurat at Tell el-Rimah was attached to a temple and was approached from the temple roof.

Middle Babylonian and Middle Assyrian Periods, circa 1500 – circa 1200 B.C.E. From around 1500 B.C.E. Mesopotamia was divided between the Kassite-dominated south (Babylonia) and the northern power of Mitanni. At Uruk an elaborate Kassite baked-brick facade, with images of deities set in niches, decorated the Inana Temple. To the west of modern Baghdad was founded a grandiose new city, Dur-Kurigalzu, consisting of several palaces, temples with rectangular platforms faced with baked bricks, and a ziggurat. Nothing is known of Mitanni architecture—its capital city, Washu-kanni, remains undiscovered—with the exception of a "palace" at Tell Brak in the Khabur plains. This large building combined administrative, manufacturing, and residential functions. The best evidence about architecture of this period comes from the site of Ugarit on the coast of Syria, where a royal palace was constructed in several phases. It covers three acres, and the quality of its construction from cut stones, wood, and rubble is superb. A dozen stone staircases and several walls to the floor of the upper level have been preserved. As at Mari and elsewhere, the floor plan includes complexes of rooms devoted to administrative, public, official, and private uses.

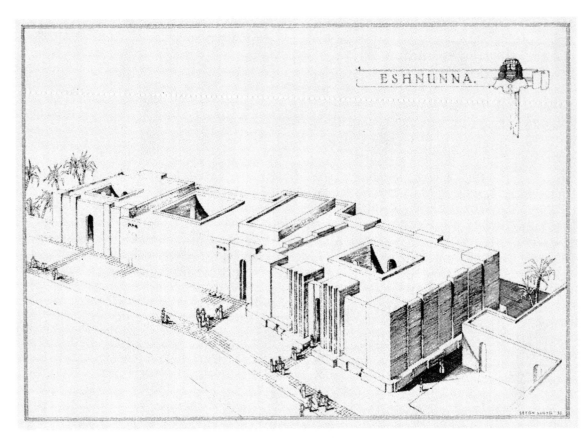

Artist's reconstruction of the temple dedicated to king Shu-Sin of the Third Dynasty of Ur (circa 2037 – circa 2029 B.C.E.), deified within his own lifetime; behind it is the adjoining palace of the governors of the city of Eshnunna (Tell Asmar) on the Diyala River (drawing by Seton Lloyd; from Joan Oates, *Babylon,* 1979).

Artist's reconstruction of the city of Ashur, situated on a rocky plateau overlooking the Tigris River, as it would have appeared from the northwest during the Middle Assyrian period, circa 1300 – circa 1100 B.C.E. (drawing by Walter Andrae; from Seton Lloyd, *The Archaeology of Mesopotamia,* 1978)

Neo-Assyrian Period, 934–610 B.C.E. The imperial power of the Assyrian Empire period is represented by the palaces and temples built at Ashur, Nimrud, Khorsabad, and Nineveh. These huge buildings were constructed almost entirely of mud brick and usually built on solid mud-brick foundation platforms. Floors open to the elements were paved with baked bricks or stone slabs. Temples and palaces were constructed around courtyards. Exterior doorways, which were often arched, led through gate chambers into a courtyard, and interior rooms opened either from courtyards or other rooms. Many such palaces have been excavated. The best understood are the so-called Northwest Palace at Nimrud (dating from the reign of Ashurnasirpal II, 883–859 B.C.E.), the palace at Khorsabad (dating from the reign of Sargon II, 721–705 B.C.E.), and the Southwest Palace at Nineveh (dating from the reign of Sennacherib, 704–681 B.C.E.). As part of their building programs the Assyrian kings also had extensive aqueducts constructed to bring water from the highlands to their cities.

Late Babylonian Period, 610–539 B.C.E. With the collapse of the Assyrian Empire in 610 B.C.E., major building projects shifted to the new capital of Babylon. The first evidence for a ziggurat at Babylon appears in the inscriptions of Sennacherib, though it may have been a more ancient structure. Greatly refurbished under Nebuchadnezzar II (604–562 B.C.E.), this ziggurat may have been the archetype for the Tower of Babel referred to in the Hebrew Bible. The royal palaces at Babylon are known as the Southern palace, the Northern palace, and the Summer palace. Their design was similar to that of Neo-Assyrian palaces. Decoration using glazed bricks, an ancient tradition in Babylonia, replaced the stone wall reliefs found in Assyria.

Achaemenid Period, 538–331 B.C.E. The early rulers of the Achaemenid Empire established administrative and ceremonial centers in the Persian homeland of southwest Iran. After his conquest of Lydia, circa 547 B.C.E., Cyrus II (ruled Persia 559–530 B.C.E. and Babylon 538–530 B.C.E.) founded his royal city at Pasargadae. Its buildings incorporate Western techniques and forms such as characteristic Lydian and Ionian stone-working methods and styles. However, Near Eastern forms of decoration—such as colossal Assyrian-style guardian bulls at the main doors—are also evident. This mixture of styles resulted from the use of craftsmen brought to Iran from throughout the empire and the incorporation of ideas from the conquered regions. This assimilation of different forms continued under Darius I (521–486 B.C.E., also known as Darius the Great) when he founded the city of Persepolis around 520 B.C.E., not far from the earlier capital at Pasargadae. Here the architecture draws on Egyptian, Mesopotamian, and East Greek traditions. The message presented by the architecture and decoration is of a harmonious world order in which the king defeats the forces of chaos. Persepolis was set on fire and destroyed by Alexander in 330 B.C.E.

Seleucid Period, 311–129 B.C.E. The survival and reworking of traditional Mesopotamian temple forms appears to have been a deliberate policy on the part of the Seleucid rulers to foster traditional religious forms in the old cities. At Babylon, archaeological and textual evidence suggest restoration work was carried out on the great ziggurat E-temenanki and on the E-sangil temple. At Uruk the largest ziggurat in Mesopotamia was erected and dedicated to the sky god Anu. Nearby the massive Resh temple was constructed for the god and his consort, Antu. A second great sanctuary, the Irigal, was built nearby, dedicated to the goddess Ishtar.

Sources:

John Boardman, *Persia and the West: An Archaeological Investigation of the Genesis of Achaemenid Art* (London: Thames & Hudson, 2000).

Susan B. Downey, *Mesopotamian Religious Architecture: Alexander through the Parthians* (Princeton: Princeton University Press, 1988).

Henri Frankfort, *The Art and Architecture of the Ancient Orient*, fifth edition, with supplementary notes and bibliography by Michael Roaf and Donald Matthews (New Haven: Yale University Press, 1996).

Ernst Heinrich, *Die Paläste im alten Mesopotamien*, Deutsches Archäologisches Institut, Denkmäler antiker Architektur, 15 (Berlin: De Gruyter, 1982).

Heinrich, *Die Tempel und Heiligtümer im alten Mesopotamien*, Deutsches Archäologisches Institut, Denkmäler antiker Architektur, 14 (Berlin: De Gruyter, 1982).

John Malcolm Russell, *Sennacherib's Palace without Rival at Nineveh* (Chicago: University of Chicago Press, 1991).

C. Leonard Woolley and others, *Ur Excavations*, Publications of the Joint Expedition of the British Museum and the Museum of the University of Pennsylvania to Mesopotamia, 10 volumes (London & Pennsylvania: Published for the Trustees of the British Museum and the Museum of the University of Pennsylvania, 1927–1976).

GLASS, FAIENCE, AND GLAZED TILES

Glass, Second Millennium B.C.E. Glass was one of the earliest artificial materials. Glass beads have been found at sites in Mesopotamia dating from the second half of the third millennium B.C.E. Major developments in glassmaking took place in north Mesopotamia during the mid-sixteenth century B.C.E., possibly among the Hurrians. Glass vessels were manufactured by making a clay core and covering it with hot glass. The core was removed after the glass cooled. While still hot and on the core, the vessel was often decorated by winding threads around it or placing blobs of differently colored glass on its surface. During the same period, objects such as pendants were also cast in molds, and marbled and mosaic glass were invented. A few surviving contemporary cuneiform texts give instructions on glassmaking.

Glass, First Millennium B.C.E. Following the general upheavals in the Near East during the twelfth century B.C.E., glassmaking re-emerged in the Neo-Assyrian

The "Sargon Vase," an eighth century B.C.E. light green core-formed glass vessel with angular shoulders and two vertical lug handles (height 3½ inches), possibly of Phoenician origin and excavated from the North-West Palace at Nimrud. In a band between the handles are an engraved striding lion and a cuneiform inscription that reads "Palace of Sargon King of Assyria" (British Museum, London).

period (934–610 B.C.E.). Carved ivories from Phoenicia were sometimes inlaid with glass. More widely, glass bowls were cast in molds, probably using the lost-wax technique, and finished by grinding, cutting, drilling, and polishing. The finest examples of cast and cut glass date to the Achaemenid period (559–331 B.C.E.). Many of these bowls were made to resemble metal vessels. Glassmakers also produced cylinder seals and scaraboid and conoid stamp seals, usually in translucent-blue or light-green glass. (Scaraboid stamp seals are in the general shape of Egyptian scarab seals but without any indication of the beetle's body parts; conoid stamp seals are made in various cone-like shapes.)

Faience. Before the development of glass, a widely used substance known as *frit* was made by melting quartz dust or sand, and the frit was then modeled or molded to form objects. When frit is covered with a glaze it is called *faience*. Faience may have been invented as a cheap substitute for stones such as lapis lazuli and turquoise. Faience first appeared in Egypt and Mesopotamia in the fifth millennium B.C.E., and it later spread throughout the Near East. In Mesopotamia, the earliest use of faience was for jewelry. It remained popular until the second millennium B.C.E., when glass beads appeared.

Glazed Clay. Some objects in Mesopotamia were made of glazed clay, which cannot always be distinguished from faience. Some of the earliest examples are large figures of guardian animals made of terra-cotta onto which a glaze was poured. They date from the fifteenth century B.C.E. and come from north Mesopotamia. During the fourteenth century B.C.E. clay vessels were glazed, first on Cyprus and in Syria. The technique spread to Mesopotamia, where it survived into the Islamic period.

Glazed Tiles. Wall decoration in glazed, colored, sometimes molded, bricks was developed during the first millennium B.C.E. Some of the finest examples come from Babylon and date from the sixth century B.C.E. The Ishtar Gate, Processional Way, and part of the royal palace were decorated with panels of colored bricks depicting palm trees and symbolic animals, such as lions, dragons, and bulls, alternating with abstract symbols. During the Achaemenid period the use of faience bricks was perfected at the site of Susa. A procession of Persian archers and spear carriers are finely molded with delicate use of color and glazing. This tradition survived for a long time and was employed during the Seleucid period at Uruk (311–145 B.C.E.) as well as in the Islamic period.

Polychrome glazed-relief brick panels (79 inches tall) depicting guards, each armed with a long spear, bow, and quiver, from the eastern door of the late sixth century B.C.E. Apadana, a large palace at Susa (Louvre, Paris)

Sources:
Dan Barag and Veronica Tatton-Brown, *Catalogue of Western Asiatic Glass in the British Museum* (London: Published for the Trustees of the British Museum, 1985).

A. Leo Oppenheim and others, *Glass and Glassmaking in Ancient Mesopotamia: An Edition of the Cuneiform Texts Which Contain Instructions for Glassmakers, with a Catalogue of Surviving Objects* (Corning, N.Y.: Corning Museum of Glass, 1970).

IMAGES OF KINGS

Late Fourth Millennium B.C.E. Coinciding with the emergence of the first cities in southern Mesopotamia during the Late Uruk period (circa 3300 – circa 2900 B.C.E.) are some of the earliest images of kings. The so-called priest-king is distinguished in sculpture and relief by his fillet (a narrow headband worn high on the forehead and above the ears) and by wearing his hair in a bun and a beard without a mustache. Writing, which was invented in the same period, is often combined with imagery, either indirectly when cylinder seals were impressed on clay tablets or directly such as on the "Blau Monuments" that show the image of the priest-king alongside proto-cuneiform signs describing the transfer of goods.

Early Dynastic Period, circa 2900 – circa 2340 B.C.E. As royal inscriptions developed they combined traditional and new stylistic techniques to extol the ruler in contemporary terms and convey various images of kingship. The majority of early royal inscriptions, from the mid-third millennium B.C.E., are short and are found on objects dedicated to the gods or on bricks and foundation deposits. There are, however, longer, elaborate texts in which past events are used to justify the present and confirm that the king acted according to right and justice as determined by the gods. One of the best known (circa 2400 B.C.E.) is the account of the war between the rulers of Umma and Lagash, which is preserved on fragments of a large stele found at the site of Tello. The god Ningirsu, acting through the ruler of Lagash, is depicted and described as restoring the natural order and re-establishing justice. The cuneiform inscription surrounds a relief image of king Eanatum, who wears a distinctive fleece-like robe over his left shoulder and is shown leading his army, first on foot and then in his chariot.

Alabaster statue (height 7 inches) of a Late Uruk–period (circa 3300 – circa 3000 B.C.E.) "priest-king" from Uruk; and Akkadian king Naram-Sin (circa 2254 – circa 2218 B.C.E.) wearing a horned crown, holding a bow and arrow, and facing a mountain at the top of a relief carved on a limestone stele (79 inches tall), originally erected at Sippar and taken as booty to Susa circa twelfth century B.C.E. (left: Iraq Museum, Baghdad; right: Louvre, Paris)

King Ur-Namma (circa 2112 – circa 2095 B.C.E.), wearing a round wide-brimmed cap and carrying building tools and a basket for making bricks, in the middle of the bottom register of a fragment (40 inches tall) of a monumental limestone stele from Ur. He is led by a god and followed by a servant. In the middle register, the king (only lower half preserved) pours a libation before a seated god (University of Pennsylvania Museum of Archaeology and Anthropology).

Akkadian Period, circa 2340 – circa 2200 B.C.E. With the Akkadian dynasty, sculpture and texts portray the king as an heroic individual. On the stele of Naram-Sin (circa 2254 – circa 2218 B.C.E.), the king dominates the scene and wears a helmet with horns, a sign of his deification. Akkadian rulers presented themselves as not only restoring order but actually, with the will of the gods, changing things for the better. This depiction is appropriate to a dynasty that created an empire equaled by no previous king, and the heroic image formed the basis for future models of kingship.

Ur III Period, circa 2112 – circa 2004 B.C.E. Beginning in the late third millennium B.C.E., hymns were used to narrate royal achievements, some more fictitious and literary than others. The intended audience was the gods and the temple and palace personnel appointed by the ruler—not ordinary people. Under the Ur III kings, texts and art emphasized cultic and civic activities rather than warfare. For example, a large stele of king Ur-Namma (circa 2112 – circa 2095 B.C.E.), discovered at his capital city of Ur, depicts his participation in the construction of a temple. Royal administrative skills (king Shulgi, circa 2094 – circa 2047 B.C.E., claimed he could read and write) and public works, including great monuments such as ziggurats, are presented as ensuring the country's welfare. However, although they stressed different aspects of kingship, the images of superhuman or deified kings were the same under both the Akkadian and Ur III rulers.

Second Millennium B.C.E. In northern Mesopotamia during the early second millennium B.C.E., the focus was on military achievements. Lengthy accounts of "historical" conquests by kings such as Shamshi-Adad I (circa 1813 – circa 1781 B.C.E.) of Assyria were composed. Stone reliefs also emphasize military activities with scenes of warfare

Assyrian king Ashurnasirpal II (883–859 B.C.E.) carved in relief on a stele (more than 9½ feet tall), which stood outside the Temple of Ninurta at Nimrud (ancient Kalhu). He is raising his right hand in a gesture of respect before the symbols of five of his gods (British Museum, London).

and royal triumphs. The rulers of the Old Hittite kingdom in Central Anatolia, and those of northern Syria, also followed this approach. In the south, however, there was less emphasis on war in royal literature and more of a focus on the king as judge. Royal praise is an essential element of the Stele of Hammurabi. It combines the image of Hammurabi (circa 1792 – circa 1750 B.C.E.) standing before the enthroned sun god with a long text that creates an idealized view of the king as the dutiful dispenser of justice. During the later Kassite period (circa 1595 – circa 1155 B.C.E.) in Babylonia, the legal tone of elaborate poetic royal inscriptions demonstrates the internationalism of the period with Egyptians, Hurrians, Hittites, Kassites, Assyrians, and Elamites all justifying their reasons for going to war while portraying the enemy as wrong or even evil.

Middle Assyrian (circa 1400 – 1050 B.C.E.) and Neo-Assyrian (934–610 B.C.E.) Periods. By the later second millennium B.C.E., under the Middle Assyrian kings, royal inscriptions become longer and more complex. Appearing during the reign of Tiglath-pileser I (circa 1114 – circa 1076 B.C.E.) an annalistic arrangement of military-campaign descriptions, with stock sentences and stylistic features, introduced a literary form that lasted for almost a millennium. These texts are often associated with monuments such as wall reliefs or large-scale sculpture, particularly during the Neo-Assyrian Empire. The reliefs present a version of history that is selected and arranged to convey the chief roles of the king, perhaps organized similarly to accompanying cuneiform annals. Both the pictorial and written narratives have simple structures, and their subject is always the victorious king. The Assyrian king is shown in two main roles: as commander in chief of the army and as chief priest of Ashur, the supreme Assyrian god. These political addresses were designed for an audience who could, with sufficient learning, "read" the images. In addition, epic poems were composed to celebrate the kings. A prayer addressed to Ashur during the reign of Sargon II (721–705 B.C.E.) is a real historical narrative. Elaborate propagandistic works include such texts as the so-called *Vision of the Netherworld*, while fictional biographies of ancient kings, especially Sargon of Akkad (circa 2334 – circa 2279 B.C.E.), are similar in style to inscriptions carved on stone monuments. Fictional, literary letters were also created and read as if dictated by famous kings or leaders.

Achaemenid Period, 559–331 B.C.E. The king maintained his central position in the art of the Achaemenid Persian Empire. Reliefs from the royal cities of Pasargadae and Persepolis in southwest Iran represent him as defeating the forces of chaos, which are depicted as wild animals. Unlike the Assyrian reliefs, however, Achaemenid reliefs include no scenes of military conquest; instead, the king is shown supported by loyal subjects of a united empire. Texts

also emphasize this aspect of Persian kingship. It is clear that there were many stories circulating about the Achaemenid kings of Mesopotamia, Cyrus II (538–530 B.C.E.) and Darius I (521–486 B.C.E.), especially their fictional (usually heroic) early years. Many of these, recorded by Herodotus of Halicarnassus (fifth century B.C.E.) and other classical writers, were based on traditional Mesopotamian ideas of kingship provided by both texts and images. From the time of Darius I the inscriptions of the kings emphasized their relationship with the great god Ahura-Mazda. By association all owed the king reverence, obedience, and tribute. The use of trilingual inscriptions (Elamite, Persian, and Akkadian) was part of a deliberate attempt to show the diversity, yet unity, of the empire. The texts describe how only those who are false and trust in the so-called lie are to be dealt with harshly while obedience to the god and his servant the king brings peace and security.

Sources:

Amélie Kuhrt, *The Ancient Near East, c. 3000–330 BC*, 2 volumes (London & New York: Routledge, 1995).

John Van Seters, *In Search of History: Historiography in the Ancient World and the Origins of Biblical History* (New Haven: Yale University Press, 1987).

IMAGES OF THE DIVINE

Religious Symbols. Much of the art of the ancient Near East was of a religious character and can, as a result, be difficult to interpret. Gods were depicted more often in some periods than in others, and there is a relative dearth of representations of deities from particular periods. Depictions of supernatural beings were generally of minor deities, monsters, demons, or symbols of the gods. The symbols remain the most consistent aspect of religious imagery. From prehistoric times until the fall of Babylon to the Persians in 539 B.C.E. there was little change in their form or meaning. Some of the best evidence for understanding these symbols comes from the second half of the second millennium B.C.E., when symbols of gods were used on the so-called Babylonian *kudurru* (entitlement monuments). These legal records of land transfers were decorated with divine images as a protection from transgressions against landowners' property rights, and these stones are often the only surviving artifacts on which gods and their symbols are labeled.

Standards and Animals, Late Uruk Period, circa 3300 – circa 2900 B.C.E. Little evidence of how the Mesopotamians perceived their gods has survived from before the middle of the third millennium B.C.E. It is possible that deities were not represented in human form. Images carved on cylinder seals, reliefs, and sculpture in the round from the late fourth millennium B.C.E. portray what are interpreted to be standards or symbols

Black limestone entitlement monument (so-called *kudurru*, height 24 inches), depicting king Marduk-nadin-ahhe of Babylon
(circa 1099 – circa 1082 B.C.E.). The image of the king, the divine symbols above him, and the divine curses inscribed
in cuneiform are intended to protect the monument and the contract it records (British Museum, London).

Fragment (height 71 inches) of the relief-carved limestone Stele of the Vultures from Tello (ancient Girsu), circa 2450 B.C.E.,
depicting the god Ningirsu holding a mace and a battle net filled with the defeated warriors of Umma (Louvre, Paris)

of gods. They take the form of poles with attached rings or streamers and are often associated with domesticated animals such as sheep and cattle. It is possible that some of the animals were also thought to represent the gods or to embody specific divine attributes. One of the best understood, most widely represented symbols is a pole with a ring and streamer, which is known to stand for Inana, goddess of Uruk. Some scholars have interpreted the sign as representing a doorpost and door hanging, perhaps at the entrance to her temple. The symbol is used to write her name on some of the earliest tablets from Uruk and also appears on cylinder seals and as clay wall inlay. It is often depicted alongside images of sheep

and the so-called priest-king. The Inana symbol continued to be used to write her name even after she became associated with the Akkadian goddess Ishtar during the Akkadian period (circa 2340 – circa 2200 B.C.E.). Since the association between deity and sign often did drop out of use, other symbols are more difficult to equate with gods known from later texts. One of the most common forms in early art is the ring-post, a pole with four or six rings at the top, which scholars have suggested might be connected with either the storm god Adad (Sumerian Ishkur), the sun god Shamash (Sumerian Utu), or the heaven god Anu (Sumerian An). Like the ring-post, the Inana symbol is often associated with

Bird-headed winged apkallu (sage) in the posture of an exorcist on a carved limestone relief (height 94 inches) from a doorway in
the North-West Palace of Ashurnasirpal II (883–859 B.C.E.) at Nimrud (The Metropolitan Museum of Art, New York,
Gift of John D. Rockefeller, Jr., 1932)

Akkadian period (circa 2254 – circa 2193 B.C.E.) cylinder seal (left, height 1½ inches), belonging to the scribe Adda; in the modern impression (right), the sun god Shamash (center) rises between two groups of mountains; he is attended on the left by the winged goddess Ishtar and a god holding a bow and on the right by the water god Ea and his two-faced vizier, Usmu (British Museum, London)

scenes of animal husbandry and continues to be represented until the second millennium B.C.E.

Anthropomorphic Deities: Early Dynastic Period, circa 2900 – circa 2340 B.C.E. By the middle of the third millennium B.C.E., after several centuries of economic and political recession, the emergence of rival city-states across Mesopotamia was accompanied by a flourishing of the arts. During this period, gods began to be portrayed in anthropomorphic form and were identified as divine by their distinctive horned headdresses. The emergence of the god in human form may be related to the politically fragmented nature of southern Mesopotamia, where rival city-states and their rulers associated themselves with specific deities in a pantheon of gods. Inscriptions and the representations of a god's symbol or sacred animal allow a few images of deities to be identified. One of the best examples appears on the fragmentary remains of a large stele from the city of Girsu (modern Tello) in the state of Lagash. A bearded male, depicted on a much larger scale than the humans portrayed on the other side of the stele, brandishes a mace. In his left hand he holds a giant net that contains the captured human enemies of Lagash. The net is sealed at the top by a lion-headed eagle (called Imdugud or Anzud in Sumerian and Anzu in Akkadian). The scale of the man suggests that he is in fact a god. (He probably wore a horned helmet as well, but that part of the stele is missing.) The appearance of the Anzu symbol and the accompanying cuneiform inscription enable scholars to identify the figure as Ningirsu, the patron god of the state of Lagash. Other gods may never have been depicted. For example, later texts suggest that a god such as Enlil was so powerful even the other gods could not look at him.

Anthropomorphic Deities: Akkadian Period, circa 2340 – circa 2200 B.C.E. The number of representations of gods increased after circa 2340 B.C.E., when the ruling dynasty of the city of Akkad came to control much of Mesopotamia by military force. This line of kings belonged to the Semitic element of the southern Mesopotamian population. The Akkadian dynasty appears to have standardized the pantheon, perhaps as a form of control, and in so doing they formalized a process of fusion, assimilation, and syncretism between Sumerian deities and Semitic Akkadian gods, which already probably had a long history. During this period, gods were portrayed wearing crowns with multiple rows of horns and flounced or tufted robes. Contemporary cylinder seals are the best source of information regarding the characteristic imagery of these gods. Among the most widely represented deities is the sun god Shamash (Sumerian Utu), symbolized by the sun disc. Shown with rays rising from his shoulders, he often carries a serrated saw and rests a foot on a mountain or a human-headed bison, symbolizing the eastern mountains through which he cuts his way each morning. Another popular deity was Ishtar, a goddess of sexuality and warfare who absorbed many of the attributes of the Sumerian fertility goddess Inana. Ishtar is often shown in her warrior aspect with weapons rising from her shoulders. She is the first Mesopotamian god to be depicted with wings, and, in the tradition of earlier female deities, she is usually shown full face. Her symbol is an eight-pointed star (the planet Venus). Ea

(Sumerian Enki) is surrounded by water, or has streams in which fish swim flowing from his shoulders. His symbols, which appear in later depictions, are a ram-headed staff, a turtle, and a creature with the foreparts of a goat and the body of a fish, the prototype of the zodiac sign Capricorn. (Ea himself was the prototype for Aquarius.) The storm god, Adad (Sumerian Ishkur), is represented by a lightning bolt or fork. He is generally shown standing on the back of a bull or a lion-dragon.

Minor Deities. During the Akkadian period, figures with horned crowns, but often without distinctive symbols or associated animals, appear alongside the major deities. They represent minor gods. From the late third into the second millennium B.C.E., one of the most commonly depicted is the protective spirit *lamassu* (Sumerian *lama*), shown with a horned crown and a long, tiered dress. She is often depicted on cylinder seals accompanying a person, either grasping his wrist or standing with both her hands raised before her face in a form of greeting. She introduces the human to a seated god or king, the latter identified by his distinctive round brimmed cap. This role may reflect the fact that people were no longer able to approach their kings without the aid of royal intermediaries, because rulers were starting to claim divine status during the period 2300–1800 B.C.E. Small amulets of precious stones and metals representing *lamassu* were possibly worn on necklaces and date from the second millennium B.C.E. onward.

Cult Statues. In the Old Babylonian period (circa 1894 – circa 1595 B.C.E.) terra-cotta figures depicted gods. These small-scale images may have been intended for private devotion or small chapels. There are no surviving examples of cult statues, but images on Assyrian reliefs of the eighth century B.C.E. show near-life-size statues of gods being carried off by the Assyrian army. From descriptions in texts of refurbishing divine statues, scholars have learned that they were sometimes made from precious materials that were melted down or re-used over time. In the fifth century B.C.E., Herodotus of Halicarnassus wrote about a golden statue of a god, some fifteen feet tall, that, he was told, had been carried off from a temple in Babylon by the Persian king Xerxes (485–465 B.C.E.).

Heroes. Heroic figures appeared in the late fourth millennium on cylinder seals. A nude bearded man with belts tied at his waist and holding snakes or lions continued to be depicted through the third millennium B.C.E., where he combated lions, bulls, or leopards, often alongside the human-headed bison, which is associated with the sun god and the mountains to the east of Mesopotamia, where the wild bison lived. He probably figured in mythology that is now lost.

Demons. Some of the *apkallu* (sages) have wings and faces of birds or humans; they carry a bucket and a purifier that looks like a fir cone. Other *apkallu* are fish-like creatures with a human face, arms, and legs. They are represented during the Neo-Assyrian period (934–610 B.C.E.) as small figurines and on the wall reliefs at Nimrud and Nineveh. Besides the gods and semi-divine heroes, the Mesopotamian cosmos was filled with monsters and demons, which are rarely depicted. One known representation of a demon is the female Lamashtu, who is shown as a wingless lion-headed bird-taloned humanoid who suckles a dog and a pig. She could be frightened away by representations of another lion- or dog-headed demon, Pazuzu.

Monsters. A popular representation in the third millennium B.C.E. was the lion-headed eagle, the Anzu (Sumerian Imdugud or Anzud), who was possibly a personification of storms. This creature is sometimes shown attacking the human-headed bison (perhaps symbolizing storm clouds covering the mountains to the east of Mesopotamia). A later version of the Anzu bird was possibly the "roaring weather-beast."

Sources:
Jeremy A. Black and Anthony Green, *Gods, Demons and Symbols of Ancient Mesopotamia: An Illustrated Dictionary* (Austin: University of Texas Press, 1992).

Anthony Green, "Ancient Mesopotamian Religious Iconography," in *Civilizations of the Ancient Near East*, 4 volumes, edited by Jack M. Sasson (New York: Scribners, 1995), III: 1837–1855.

Ursula Seidl, *Die babylonischen Kudurru-Reliefs: Symbole mesopotamischer Gottheiten* (Freiburg: Freiburg University Press / Göttingen: Vandenhoeck & Ruprecht, 1989).

E. Douglas Van Buren, *Symbols of the Gods in Mesopotamian Art* (Rome: Pontificum Institutum Biblicum, 1945).

JEWELRY

Stone Jewelry. In prehistory humans used stones and animal bones to make beads and pendants, but it was not until the fourth millennium B.C.E.—when unusual sorts of stone were imported into Mesopotamia and the technological ability to work metal had developed—that more-elaborate forms of jewelry were possible. The little surviving Mesopotamian jewelry of the Late Uruk period (circa 3300 – circa 2900 B.C.E.) largely consists of beads, sometimes made of exotic stones such as lapis lazuli imported from northern Afghanistan. This tradition continued into the third millennium B.C.E., when, as trade routes expanded, carnelian was imported from the Indus Valley. The Royal Graves at Ur (circa 2600 – circa 2500 B.C.E.) contained beads and pendants in which colored stones are often combined with gold. Sometimes the forms of the gold beads, such as a popular biconical shape, copy those of stone.

Gold Jewelry. Gold jewelry was largely made from metal hammered into thin sheets and then cut to shape. Sometimes the sheet was decorated with scored lines or

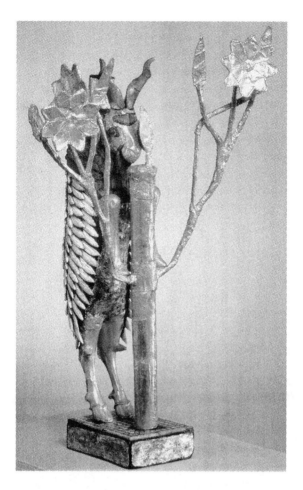

Two objects from the Royal Graves of Ur: (top) from the Great Death Pit, the "Ram in the Thicket," height 16¾ inches; (bottom) from a royal grave, possibly that of king Ur-Pabilsag, the "Standard of Ur," height 20 inches (top: University of Pennsylvania Museum of Archaeology and Anthropology; bottom: British Museum, London)

punched dots. Soldering was occasionally used to join elements. Spiral-cone beads or pendants were created from gold wire, which was also soldered onto sheet gold as decoration or used to make chains or loops. Sheet gold was also used to make boat-shaped earrings found in the Royal Graves at Ur. Simpler wire hoops or elaborate multilobed earrings with granulation are also known. Popular from around 2000 B.C.E., granulated designs were created by forming patterns of tiny gold spheres on a metal sheet. Fine examples of granulated gold work date to the seventeenth and sixteenth centuries B.C.E. and come from royal tombs at Ebla in Syria.

First Millennium B.C.E. Some of the beads in the jewelry of the first millennium B.C.E. are made of colored glass. Much evidence, particularly for the kind of jewelry worn by men, can be gleaned from Neo-Assyrian reliefs of the ninth to seventh centuries B.C.E. The reliefs depict the king, courtiers, and supernatural genii wearing bracelets, armlets, earrings, and necklaces with elaborate pendants. The armlets and bracelets often end in animal heads. These forms became popular throughout much of the ancient world. A gold bracelet with lion heads (seventh century B.C.E.) was discovered in the palace at Karmir Blur in Urartu, the northern rival of Assyria, and is one of the earliest datable examples of this type. Gold jewelry discovered in the tombs of Assyrian queens at Nimrud (ancient Kalhu) demonstrates the extraordinary quality of gold work produced in Mesopotamia in the eighth century B.C.E. Elaborate crowns, necklaces, headbands, and bracelets were deposited in the tombs and include examples with enamel and inlay work.

Oxus Treasure. Some of the finest jewelry of the Achaemenid period (559–331 B.C.E.) comes from the so-called Oxus Treasure, named for the river in Central Asia (the modern Amu Dariya) near where the hoard was said to have been found. The objects in this collection range in date (fifth to fourth centuries B.C.E.) and

THE ROYAL GRAVES OF UR

The most important evidence for art of the Early Dynastic period comes from the vast Royal Cemetery at Ur (circa 2600 – circa 2500 B.C.E.). Among the hundreds of graves excavated there by Sir Leonard Woolley in the 1920s, sixteen were extremely rich graves and contained multiple sacrificial victims, an extremely rare practice in Mesopotamia. The owners of the majority of the graves are unknown, but the wealth buried with them, together with the presence of human victims—seventy-three in one grave—suggest that they were "priest-kings" and queens. Evidence of virtually every type of metallurgical technique known in antiquity, except the working of iron, was found in the graves. Among the grave goods were weapons and vessels in copper, gold, and silver, and a large amount of elaborate jewelry. Sumerian jewelers exploited organic forms, such as flower-head rosettes, fluted beads, and leaves, or simple geometric shapes, such as cones, spirals, and circles. Some of the earliest known gold chains of the loop-in-loop style, decorative rings, and cloisonné inlay were found in the graves.

Other skillfully fashioned pieces include a sheet-gold helmet from a grave without sacrificial victims, and two examples of the "Ram in the Thicket," sculptures made of gold, shell, copper, and lapis lazuli and depicting a goat standing on its hind legs while resting its front hooves on the branches of a flowering plant. Each of these sculptures was originally the lower part of some sort of stand that probably supported a small table or tray. The materials used in such grave goods testify to long-distance trade. Metal deposits are unknown in Mesopotamia, so gold, silver, and copper would have been imported from Iran, Anatolia (modern Turkey), and possibly even Egypt. Similarly, exotic stones would have been brought into the region; lapis lazuli was imported from Afghanistan and carnelian from the Indus Valley. Inlay was a common feature on many objects including scepters, musical instruments, and the "Standard of Ur." This box-like object, of unknown function, is inlaid with lapis lazuli as a background for pieces of cut shell. On one side, chariots pulled by donkeys are trampling enemies; infantrymen carry spears, and enemy soldiers are killed with axes; other enemies are paraded naked and presented to a taller male figure, perhaps the king, who holds a spear. On the other side of the box, animals, fish, and other goods are brought in procession to a ceremonial banquet with religious overtones. Seated figures, wearing fleece or fringed skirts, drink and are entertained by a singer and a musician playing a lyre. These two scenes portray the chief aspects of Sumerian kingship: the divine world supports the ruler as both military leader and bountiful provider.

Sources: J. E. Reade, "Assyrian King-Lists, the Royal Tombs of Ur, and Indus Origins," *Journal of Near Eastern Studies*, 60 (2001): 1–29.
Richard L. Zettler and Lee Horne, eds., *Treasures from the Royal Tombs of Ur* (Philadelphia: University of Pennsylvania, Museum of Archaeology and Anthropology, 1998).

One of a pair of gold armlets (height 4¾ inches) from the Oxus Treasure, fifth–fourth centuries B.C.E. (British Museum, London)

may not belong to a single hoard. The treasure includes magnificent jewelry, such as two inlaid gold bracelets ending in winged griffins, several torques, and bracelets ending in the heads of animals. The animal imagery links the pieces stylistically with nomadic art of Central Asia as well as with Greek gold work.

Sources:

O. M. Dalton, *The Treasure of the Oxus, with Other Examples of Early Oriental Metal-Work,* third edition (London: Trustees of the British Museum, 1964).

K. R. Maxwell-Hyslop, *Western Asiatic Jewellery, c. 3000–612 B.C.* (London: Methuen, 1971).

Jack Ogden, *Jewellery of the Ancient World* (London: Trefoil, 1982).

LITERATURE

The Scribal Tradition. The oldest surviving literature in the world is written in the Sumerian language. Although these works may preserve parts of an ancient oral tradition, it is also possible that what was written was as fundamentally new as writing itself. Literacy was highly restricted in the ancient Near East. Only an elite could read and write. Most of the Sumerian literature that survives was written after about 2000 B.C.E., at a time when that language was no longer spoken by the general population but was maintained in schools and temples. Most people at that time spoke various Semitic languages, primarily Akkadian, which has its own literature. The creative process took place in a temple or palace, and it is possible that few ordinary people understood the meaning or imagery of the literature. Little is known about the poets. Few authors are named, and few works are attributed. A rare exception is the earliest known poet, the daughter of the Akkadian king Sargon, Enheduana, who wrote in about 2300 B.C.E.

The Earliest Sumerian and Akkadian Literature.

The earliest writing, from the late fourth millennium B.C.E., is mostly economic and administrative in nature. There are also lexical lists—words arranged by theme such as kinds of animals, plants, or professions. Presumably learning exercises for the administrators, these lists continued to be copied for more than three thousand years as part of the scribal literary tradition. Some of these texts have been interpreted as early forms of literature, but the first real Sumerian narrative and poetic texts date from around 2500 B.C.E. and have been found in excavations at two main cities, Fara (ancient Shuruppak) and Tell Abu Salabikh (possibly ancient Eresh). These texts are extremely difficult to understand because the scribes supplied only some of the meaning, expecting the reader to understand and fill in the missing elements. In other words, the writing was a guide to meaning, not a representation of the actual spoken language. Some tablets include magical charms against diseases. One text describes the adventures of a legendary king of Uruk named Lugalbanda. Another text, known as the *Instructions of Shuruppak*, is proverbial advice given by a king to his son. Most texts, however, deal with mythological subjects. Some of these describe how the cosmos was created and ordered by the gods. These early texts were written in Sumerian, with one exception: a hymn to the sun god, written in a dialect of Akkadian and found in two versions, one at Fara and the other at Ebla in Syria. Its existence suggests that more early texts in Akkadian are yet to be discovered.

The Sumerian Revival.

There is little evidence of a new literature during the Akkadian Empire (circa 2340 – circa 2200 B.C.E.), a dynamic imperial period whose vitality is clear in its art. Any literature (possibly written in Akkadian) of this period may have been expunged by the next dynasty. With the fall of the Akkadian Empire and the rise of the Third Dynasty of Ur (circa 2112 – circa 2004 B.C.E.), kings were celebrated in Sumerian poetry. The songs and poems of this dynasty were copied and adapted by later generations of scribes, and it is generally these later versions that survive. Among the most elaborate literary creations of this period are the Gudea Cylinders, A and B. These large clay drums, nearly two feet high, represent the longest and most-complex surviving Sumerian texts. They describe how

the god Ningursu, patron deity of the state of Lagash, appeared to Gudea in a dream and instructed the ruler to build his temple E-ninnu in the capital city of Girsu (modern Tello). Although they are literary masterpieces, these works never entered the Mesopotamian scribal curriculum and would have been lost had they not been recovered by modern archaeologists.

Sumerian Literature in the Old Babylonian Period.

The largest numbers of Sumerian compositions survive from the Old Babylonian period (circa 1894 – circa 1595 B.C.E.). By this time Sumerian was no longer spoken, but it was preserved as a written language for the scribal elite and used for monumental and religious texts. These texts include compositions that described a trainee scribe's schooldays, but they may be idealized representations of school life. Many texts were selections from older works, and a large number concern earlier rulers of Mesopotamia, who date back to the Ur III period (circa 2112 – circa 2004 B.C.E.), particularly king Shulgi (circa 2094 – circa 2047 B.C.E.), who seems to have restructured much of the school curriculum to reflect the concerns of his dynasty. He was one of the few Mesopotamian kings who claimed to be able to read and write. It is likely that the heroic tales of legendary kings of Uruk, such as Enmerkar and Gilgamesh, were composed at this time because the Ur III kings traced their ancestry to the city of Uruk. Other texts were copied and expanded or adapted by Old Babylonian scribes. Tales of kings were shaped to convey specific ideas about kingship and human destiny. Hymns, such as the *Lamentation over the Destruction of Sumer and Ur*, were popular, and more than 120 hymns honoring most of the major deities are known. Some of the more interesting texts focus on the goddess Inana and the betrayal and death of her lover Dumuzi. Royal letters, which may or may not be authentic writings of the Ur III period and the succeeding Isin period (circa 2017 – circa 1794 B.C.E.), were also included in the curriculum. Also popular were debate poems in which opposites or complementary characters such as Summer and Winter, Silver and Copper, or Cattle and Grain, attempt to demonstrate verbally which is more important. From cities north of Nippur, such as Sippar and Kish, come specific cultic compositions written in Sumerian, but the use of a literary dialect known as Emesal is characteristic of that region. Differing in pronunciation from the main Sumerian literary tongue, the word *Emesal* may mean "thin tongue" and seems to have been reserved for a special group of priests and for the direct speech among women or goddesses in literary texts.

Akkadian Literature in the Second Millennium

B.C.E. Although the Akkadian language had been written using cuneiform since the middle of the third mil-

FLOOD STORIES

Before the advent of modern dams and water management on the flat plains of southern Mesopotamia, a rise of as little as a foot in the rivers or the sea covered miles of land with water. Cataclysmic floods were frequent and violent enough to become subjects for ancient Mesopotamian poets. Near Eastern archaeology does not confirm the historical occurrence of one major flood, and it is clear that for ancient Mesopotamians the stories about floods or storms represent no one actual event; rather the Flood is a metaphor for inescapable destruction.

The Epic of Atra-hasis

This story from the first half of the second millennium B.C.E. is concerned with the early history of mankind, in which the Flood is only one element. The tale begins with the minor gods complaining about their hard work. Enki, god of wisdom, provides the answer, advising that humans be created as servants for the gods. Seven men and seven women are formed by mixing clay with the blood of a god slain for the purpose. From the initial seven pairs, humanity quickly multiplies across the earth. Their noise, representing the breakdown of order, disturbs the sleep of the supreme god, Enlil, who tries to silence humanity by sending plagues, droughts, and famine against them. However, he is always frustrated by Enki, who instructs his servant, the mortal Atra-hasis (which means "Exceedingly Wise"), how to survive. Eventually Enlil sends a flood. Having sworn not to communicate directly with humans again, Enki gives advice to a reed wall, through which Atra-hasis listens. Atra-hasis builds a boat and fills it with his family and animals. For seven days and seven nights the flood destroys the world. Eventually the flood subsides, and Atra-hasis makes a burnt offering to the gods, who swarm "like flies" around the offering and realize that they need human servants. They decide, however, to limit the human population by making some women sterile, creating stillbirths, and introducing chastity. The story thus explains why life has been so harsh "since the flood."

The Sumerian Deluge Myth

Written in the Sumerian language during the mid-second millennium B.C.E., this text describes the creation of humanity but also includes the foundation of kingship and cities and their re-establishment after the Flood. The tablet on which the text was inscribed is damaged, and the beginning and end are missing. The hero of the flood is Ziusudra ("Life of Long Days"), a king of the city of Shuruppak (modern Fara). The surviving text starts with Enki suggesting that humans, who have already been created, should come together to build cities. The new cities are inspected by Enki, and kingship is established in five of them—Eridu, Badtibira, Larak, Sippar, and Shuruppak—each dedicated to a particular deity. There is a break in the tablet, and then the story continues with the decision of the gods to bring about a great flood. One of the gods (probably Enki) warns Ziusudra, who finds a boat. After seven days and nights of flood, Ziusudra steps onto dry land and makes an offering to Utu (or Shamash), god of the sun and justice. Enlil relents, deciding not to destroy humanity. Ziusudra is rewarded with immortality and taken to the land of Dilmun, the place where the sun rises (a mythical paradise equated with the real island of Bahrain).

The Epic of Gilgamesh

In the late second millennium B.C.E. *Epic of Gilgamesh*, the account of the Flood represents only one element of the hero's attempt to understand his mortality. Gilgamesh finds Uta-napishti ("He/I found life"), whom the gods made immortal after he survived the great Flood. Uta-napishti explains how Ea (Sumerian Enki) warned him of the coming catastrophe by speaking through a reed hut and brick wall. Uta-napishti then built a boat, telling his neighbors that he had to leave the city because Ellil (Sumerian Enlil) had rejected him. The boat was loaded with precious metals and all forms of life, including his family and artisans. The flood lasted six days and seven nights until all humanity—except the people on the boat—was destroyed, or returned to clay. Afterward Uta-napishti sent out a dove and then a swallow, both of which came back because they could find no place to perch. A raven, however, did not return, indicating that it had found land. Uta-napishti then made sacrifices to the gods, and they swarmed around like flies. However, Ellil was furious. Ea chastised Ellil, suggesting that if humans need control in the future, Ellil could send out the plague god Erra. In response Ellil makes Uta-napishti and his wife "like the gods" (that is, immortal). Uta-napishti brings his account to an end by advising Gilgamesh that mortality is the fate of humans.

Sources: Stephanie Dalley, trans., *Myths from Mesopotamia: Creation, The Flood, Gilgamesh, and Others* (Oxford & New York: Oxford University Press, 1989).

Andrew George, trans., *The Epic of Gilgamesh: The Babylonian Epic Poem and Other Texts in Akkadian and Sumerian* (London: Allen Lane, 1999).

Brian B. Schmidt, "Flood Narratives of Ancient Western Asia," in *Civilizations of the Ancient Near East*, 4 volumes, edited by Jack M. Sasson (New York: Scribners, 1995), IV: 2337–2351.

lennium B.C.E., the real beginning of Akkadian literature was in the Old Babylonian period (circa 1894 – circa 1595 B.C.E.). Some of these texts were based on Sumerian myths and legends such as the *Descent of Ishtar into the Netherworld*, adapted from the Sumerian *Inana's Descent to the Netherworld*. Other Sumerian forms and themes, such as the Temple Hymns and the idea of divine kings, do not appear in Akkadian literature. As southern Mesopotamia was united under Semitic Amorite dynasties, new literary models began to appear in written Akkadian; many—such as the *Epic of Gilgamesh*, the story of *Atra-hasis*, and the creation epic *Enuma elish*—were much broader in scope than the Sumerian works. Akkadian writings of this period also include theological speculations, such as the *Dialogue of a Man with his God*. Archaeologists have found hardly any Mesopotamian literary texts dating from some two hundred or three hundred years after the end of the Old Babylonian period (circa 1595 B.C.E.). However, by the fourteenth century B.C.E. the cuneiform script and Akkadian language were in use throughout the Near East, and some literary texts from this period have survived from the Hittite city of Hattusa in central Anatolia, Ugarit on the Syrian coast, and even Egypt.

Enuma elish: **A National Epic.** The poem known as *Enuma elish* ("When above") explains the rise of Marduk to the position of supreme god in the Mesopotamian pantheon. It is often described as "The Babylonian Epic of Creation," but creation is a small element in the poem. It was under Nebuchadnezzar I (circa 1125 – circa 1104 B.C.E.) that Marduk was first called "king of the gods," suggesting that *Enuma elish* was probably composed at about this time. Surviving copies are all later in date. During the Late Babylonian period (610–539 B.C.E.) the text was recited, perhaps even enacted, as part of the New Year festival at Babylon. As in later Greek mythology the poem tells of an older generation of gods who attempt to destroy their offspring but who are defeated in battle.

Creation of Gods. The poem begins with the creation of generations of gods by mixing saltwater (Tiamat) and freshwater (Apsu):

> When skies above were not yet named
> Nor earth below pronounced by name,
> Apsu, the first one, their begetter
> And maker Tiamat, who bore them all,
> Had mixed their waters together,
> But had not formed pastures, nor discovered reed-beds;
> When yet no gods were manifest,
> Nor names pronounced, nor destinies decreed,
> Then gods were born within them. (Dalley)

Noise and disorder among the new gods frustrates Apsu, who decides to destroy his offspring:

> Apsu made his voice heard
> And spoke to Tiamat in a loud voice,
> "Their ways have become very grievous to me,
> "By day I cannot rest, by night I cannot sleep.
> "I shall abolish their ways and disperse them!" (Dalley)

Ea, the god of wisdom, knows of Apsu's plans:

> He (Ea) poured sleep upon him (Apsu) so that he was sleeping soundly,
> Put Apsu to sleep, drenched with sleep.
> Vizier Mummu the counselor (was in) a sleepless daze.
> He (Ea) unfastened his belt, took off his crown,
> Took away his mantle of radiance and put it on himself.
> He held Apsu down and slew him. (Dalley)

Making his home inside the waters of Apsu, Ea and his wife, Damkina, conceive Marduk, cleverest of the clever, sage of the gods. Marduk is so powerful that he causes flood waves that disturb Tiamat and the elder gods:

> They (the elder gods) were fierce, scheming restlessly night and day.
> They were working up to war, growling and raging.
> They convened a council and created conflict.
> Mother Hubur, who fashions all things,
> Contributed an unfaceable weapon: she bore giant snakes,
> Sharp of tooth and unsparing of fang(?).
> She filled their bodies with venom instead of blood.
> She cloaked ferocious dragons with fearsome rays
> And made them bear mantles of radiance, made them godlike. (Dalley)

The goddess Tiamat's army of gods and monsters marches against the younger gods, who are all afraid to join the battle, except Marduk. On condition that he is appointed king of the gods, Marduk offers to fight Tiamat. The young gods agree to his terms, and Marduk fashions his weapons: a bow and arrow, a mace, lightning, a battle net, and seven winds. He mounts his storm chariot, which is drawn by a team of four horses: Slayer, Pitiless, Racer, and Flyer:

> Face to face they came, Tiamat and Marduk, sage of the gods.
> They engaged in combat, they closed for battle.
> The Lord spread his net and made it encircle her,
> To her face he dispatched the *imhullu*-wind, which had been behind:
> Tiamat opened her mouth to swallow it,
> And he forced in the *imhullu*-wind so that she could not close her lips.
> Fierce winds distended her belly;
> Her insides were constipated and she stretched her mouth wide.
> He shot an arrow which pieced her belly,
> Split her down the middle and split her heart,
> Vanquished her and extinguished her life.
> He threw down her corpse and stood on top of her. (Dalley)

Tiamat's army flees before Marduk, who catches them in his net. Next Marduk slices Tiamat in two and forms the roof of the sky from one half and the earth from the other. From Tiamat's spittle he makes wind and rain and from her eyes pour the rivers Tigris and Euphrates. The gods crown Marduk as their king, and to relieve them of hard work Marduk creates humans as their servants, using blood from a slain monster. In gratitude the gods offer to build a home for Marduk. After two years his temple of E-sangila in Babylon has been created. The epic ends with a list of fifty honorific names of Marduk.

Gilgamesh. One of the greatest, perhaps the greatest, literary masterpiece from Mesopotamia is the *Epic of Gilgamesh.* According to Sumerian tradition, Gilgamesh (or as he is known in the earliest texts, Bilgames) was a ruler of the city of Uruk. His name is included on the *Sumerian King List,* composed around 2000 B.C.E., and, if the text is accurate, his position on that list places him around 2750 B.C.E. Nothing is known of this man, but later tradition describes him as a great warrior and builder of the walls of Uruk, which may have some basis in truth. Not long after 2700 B.C.E., Gilgamesh appeared in a list of gods. At the end of the third millennium B.C.E. memories of Gilgamesh were committed to writing in a series of short poems about his heroic achievements. Five of these Sumerian tales have survived and, as often with stories and epics, were known in antiquity by their *incipit,* that is, the first few words of their opening line: *The Envoys of Akka; The Lord to the Living One's Mountain; Hero in battle; In those days, in those far-off days;* and *The great wild bull is lying down.*

The Envoys of Akka. Akka, the king of the city of Kish, demands that Uruk submit to him. Bilgames gathers an assembly of elders and argues that Uruk should go to war with Kish. After the elders reject his advice, Bilgames turns to the assembly of young men, who agree with their king. Akka and the forces of Kish lay siege to Uruk, whose army defeats the attackers. Bilgames recalls how Akka had once given him refuge and returns the favor by letting Akka go free.

The Lord to the Living One's Mountain. Bilgames, in search of deeds of glory, journeys with his servant Enkidu and the young men of Uruk to the fabled Cedar Mountain in the east. On arrival Bilgames fells a cedar, waking Huwawa, the semi-divine guardian of the forest. After Bilgames tricks Huwawa into giving up his divine protection by promising him luxuries of the city, Enkidu cuts off the creature's head.

Hero in battle. As Bilgames is sitting in judgment in Uruk, he is approached by Inana, the goddess of sexual love. The king rejects her, and Inana seeks vengeance by asking her father, the heaven god An, to send the Bull of Heaven (the constellation Taurus) to destroy Bilgames. An hesitates but eventually leads the Bull of Heaven to Uruk, where it eats all the vegetation and drinks the river dry. Inana watches as Bilgames and Enkidu kill the monster. The horns of the giant beast are dedicated to Inana in her temple.

In those days, in those far-off days. In her garden the goddess Inana has planted a willow tree from which she hopes one day to make furniture. Unfortunately, the tree becomes infested with evil creatures. Bilgames fells the tree and presents the wood to Inana. With some of the wood he makes two toys, which fall through a hole into the Netherworld, and Enkidu volunteers to fetch them. He is warned about the ruler of the Netherworld, the goddess Ereshkigal, who should be treated with respect, but he ignores the warning and is taken captive. The sun god Utu lifts the spirit of Enkidu from the Netherworld, and the spirit describes to Bilgames the gloomy conditions there, particularly for the dead who have no sons to provide offerings of water.

The great wild bull is lying down. Bilgames lies dying. Reviewing his heroic achievements, the gods question whether he should be made immortal. They decide Bilgames should die but on entering the Netherworld sit in judgment on the dead. He will, therefore, be commemorated among the living. Bilgames builds himself a tomb in the bed of the Euphrates River, and his household joins him there.

The Old Babylonian Version: *Surpassing all other kings.* Sometime early in the second millennium B.C.E. some of the various Gilgamesh traditions, Sumerian and perhaps Akkadian, oral or written, were probably transformed into a single composition. This *Epic of Gilgamesh* is known today as the Old Babylonian Version, but in ancient Mesopotamia it was called *Surpassing all other kings.* Written in the Babylonian dialect of Akkadian, it is not a translation of the Sumerian compositions but, instead, a unified poem focusing on the hero's quest for immortality. The poem begins with a hymn of praise of Gilgamesh, who is presented as a superhuman, powerful oppressor of his people. In answer to the people's prayers for help, the gods create Enkidu as a match for Gilgamesh in strength. This Enkidu is different from the earlier character in the Sumerian tales, where he is Bilgames's servant. Initially, he is a wild man, hairy and animal-like. However, after seven days of making love with a temple prostitute, being bathed and clothed and consuming human food—bread and beer—he is transformed into a man worthy of meeting Gilgamesh. The two become friends and set out together to achieve fame by journeying to the Cedar Forest to do battle with Huwawa, whom they kill after initial hesitation. Enkidu dies, perhaps because he has helped in the killing of Huwawa or because he has completed the task of divert-

Old Babylonian period (circa 1750 B.C.E.) terra-cotta plaques depicting what appear to be episodes from the Gilgamesh cycle of stories: (top) the death of Huwawa; (bottom) the slaying of the Bull of Heaven (Vorderasiatisches Museum, Berlin)

ing Gilgamesh to heroic activities befitting a king. Another innovation in the story line is that Gilgamesh is consumed with grief for his friend. Faced with the reality of death, he seeks not the sort of immortality achieved through fame but everlasting life itself. After a long journey Gilgamesh finds Uta-napishti, who has received immortality from the gods after he and his family survived the Flood. At this point in the story the tablets containing the Old Babylonian Version are fragmentary.

He who saw the deep. In the centuries following the Old Babylonian period, knowledge of the *Epic of Gilgamesh* spread into Anatolia, Syria, and the Levant. Fragments of the epic in Akkadian, Hittite, and Hurrian adaptations have been found. Dating to the fourteenth and thirteenth centuries B.C.E., they incorporate material not included in the Old Babylonian Version and are part of the later, so-called Standard Version. Late in the second millennium B.C.E. the text of the *Epic of Gilgamesh* seems to have become stabilized in form. Tradition credits this edition to a scribe called Sin-leqe-unnini, who lived around 1200 B.C.E. The text of this version is known mainly from seventh century B.C.E. copies in the library of the Assyrian king Ashurbanipal (668 – circa 627 B.C.E.) at Nineveh, but parts have been found at other sites, such as Nimrud, Assur, Babylon, and Uruk. In total the epic runs to eleven tablets with an appendix on a twelfth.

The Standard Version. This version starts with a summary of Gilgamesh's achievements. He has both strength and wisdom—the essential attributes of a king. The prologue addresses the reader (not a listener) and says to inspect Gilgamesh's building works, especially the great wall around Uruk, and then to find the chest containing a tablet of lapis lazuli inscribed with the tale of Gilgamesh and read it. The poet emphasizes at every opportunity the hardships that Gilgamesh had to face to complete his journey.

Journey to the Cedar Forest. The story proper starts as in the Old Babylonian Version. Gilgamesh is oppressing his people, and they pray to the gods, who answer with the creation of Enkidu as a rival to Gilgamesh. The story of the adventure to the Cedar Forest appears to locate it in the mountains of Lebanon, while in the Sumerian story it seems to be in the closer Zagros range, to the east of Mesopotamia. The purpose of the journey is expanded; the battle with the giant, now called Humbaba, is described as an attempt to destroy evil. It also appears that Enkidu knows killing Humbaba will bring down upon his slayer the wrath of the gods, but, nonetheless, he urges on the hesitant Gilgamesh. As an attempt to appease the gods, Gilgamesh and Enkidu cut some of the great cedars to make a door for the temple in Nippur and then head back to Uruk.

Defeating the Bull of Heaven. Back in Uruk, Gilgamesh washes and dresses in his finery, attracting the attention of the goddess Ishtar, who offers him marriage. Gilgamesh, however, rejects her and lists her various lovers, all of whom died. The furious Ishtar rushes to her father, the heaven god Anu and demands that he send the Bull of Heaven against Gilgamesh. Anu hesitates because the Bull would bring famine and destroy the world, but after Ishtar offers to feed the people from the stores in her temple, Anu allows the Bull of Heaven to attack Uruk, and the creature's snorting opens up chasms into which the people of Uruk fall. Gilgamesh and Enkidu kill the Bull. As a final insult to the goddess, Enkidu tears off the Bull's haunch and hurls it at Ishtar, who is standing on the city wall.

The Death of Enkidu. After a great celebratory banquet, Enkidu (according to the Hittite version) learns in a dream that the gods have decided he must die. After a twelve-day sickness, he dies. Gilgamesh buries his friend and erects a statue in his honor. Devastated by his friend's death and his own inevitable end, he begins a journey to find the secret of immortality. He meets a scorpion man and his wife, who try to dissuade him, but he journeys deeper into the darkness at the edge of the world before emerging into a garden with trees covered in jewels. Here, Gilgamesh meets a divine tavern keeper called Siduri who also tries to persuade him not to go on. Eventually, however, she tells him how to reach the immortal Uta-napishti. By using a boatman, the hero crosses the Waters of Death and is greeted by Uta-napishti who explains why men have to die by recounting the story of the Flood.

The Flood. It is recognized that the Flood story was not part of the original epic and is drawn from an independent story, the myth of *Atra-hasis*. Having explained that the gods made men mortal to prevent them from becoming noisy and disturbing the natural order, which caused the gods to send the flood originally, Uta-napishti tests Gilgamesh: if Gilgamesh can stay awake for seven nights, he will prove he is worthy of immortality. But Gilgamesh falls asleep, and Uta-napishti's wife bakes a loaf of bread each night and places it under the sleeping hero's cheek. When he wakes, Gilgamesh sees seven loaves bearing his cheek impression and realizes that his goal of immortality is unreachable. However, Uta-napishti feels sorry for him and tells Gilgamesh about a plant that causes rejuvenation. The hero picks the plant from the bottom of the sea, but, while bathing in a pool, he loses it to a snake that immediately sloughs its skin as it is renewed. By recognizing that he cannot cheat death, Gilgamesh has achieved wisdom. He journeys back to Uruk, and the poet brings the story full circle with the same description of Uruk that began the epic— a description of the ordered world of a city and its king.

The twelfth tablet, which is a later addition to the Standard Version, is a translation of part of the Sumerian composition *In those days, in those far-off days*, in which Gilgamesh meets the spirit of Enkidu.

The First Millennium B.C.E. The literary creations of the first millennium B.C.E. are generally revisions of those created in the second millennium, or they deal with the role and image of the king. One exception, however, is the *Poem of Erra*, esteemed in antiquity, a masterpiece of Akkadian epic literature. Although the last known dated cuneiform tablet is an astronomical text from Babylon in 75 C.E., a small number of Sumerian texts of the sort used in scribal training continued to be copied until the early centuries C.E.

Sources:

Jean Bottéro, "Akkadian Literature: An Overview," in *Civilizations of the Ancient Near East*, 4 volumes, edited by Jack M. Sasson (New York: Scribners, 1995), IV: 2293–2303.

Stephanie Dalley, trans., *Myths from Mesopotamia: Creation, The Flood, Gilgamesh, and Others* (Oxford & New York: Oxford University Press, 1989).

Andrew George, trans., *The Epic of Gilgamesh: The Babylonian Epic Poem and Other Texts in Akkadian and Sumerian* (London: Allen Lane, 1999).

Piotr Michalowski, "The Earliest Scholastic Tradition," in *Art of the First Cities: The Third Millennium B.C. from the Mediterranean to the Indus*, edited by Joan Aruz with Ronald Wallenfels (New York: Metropolitan Museum of Art, 2003), pp. 451–456.

Michalowski, "Sumerian Literature: An Overview," in *Civilizations of the Ancient Near East*, IV: 2279–2291.

Jeffrey H. Tigay, *The Evolution of the Gilgamesh Epic* (Philadelphia: University of Pennsylvania Press, 1982).

METALWORK

Early Sumerian Metalwork. Evidence of metalwork in certain periods of Mesopotamian history is lacking. Because there are no natural deposits in the region, metal was always a precious commodity. As a result, metal objects were frequently melted down so that the metal in them could be re-used. In the Late Uruk period (circa 3300 – circa 2900 B.C.E.) metal casting using the lost-wax process appeared, probably stimulated by technological developments near metal sources in Anatolia and the Levant. During the Early Dynastic period (circa 2900 – circa 2340 B.C.E.), this technique was used to produce metal objects of extraordinary artistic quality. A copper model of a chariot pulled by four onagers (wild asses) comes from Tell Agrab, and a copper figure of a double jar supported by a pair of wrestlers was found in nearby Khafajeh. Also from Khafajeh are three copper statuettes designed as vessel stands and depicting male hero figures, each one nude apart from a belt. During the Early Dynastic III period (circa 2600 – circa 2340 B.C.E.) at Tell al-Ubaid, metal fittings of a temple were either taken down and stacked at the base of the temple platform for later re-use, or they fell from the decayed facade of the temple. They include a hammered copper

LOST-WAX CASTING

One of the most impressive technological developments in the ancient Near East during the fourth and third millennia B.C.E. was the invention of lost-wax casting for making objects of metal or, later, glass. The artisan begins by sculpting a wax model, which is then covered with clay and fired, causing the wax to melt out through channels pierced through the clay. Molten metal (or glass) is then poured into the mold through these channels, which also allow hot gases to escape. A sizable mold requires a large amount of metal, which was expensive in ancient Mesopotamia because it had to be imported. To reduce the amount of metal used, the wax can be sculpted over a core of clay. This core is held in place after the wax is removed from the mold and during the casting by metal supports inserted through the outer clay. Once the metal has cooled and solidified, the outer clay is broken away, and, if core supports have been used, they are ground down to the surrounding surface.

Source: J.-F. de Lapérouse, "Lost-Wax Casting," in *Art of the First Cities: The Third Millennium B.C. from the Mediterranean to the Indus*, edited by Joan Aruz with Ronald Wallenfels (New York: Metropolitan Museum of Art, 2003), p. 210.

panel depicting a lion-headed eagle grasping a pair of stags. There are also free-standing bulls and lions, each formed from copper alloy sheets nailed over a wooden core and coated with a thin layer of bitumen. The most important metalwork evidence from this period comes from the Royal Graves at Ur (circa 2600 – circa 2500 B.C.E.). Other important examples of the skill of ancient metalworkers comes from Girsu. These objects include a silver vase of king Enmetena, finely engraved with a representation of a lion-headed eagle grasping two lions, and a giant engraved copper spearhead dedicated by a king of Kish.

Akkadian Metalwork. From the time of the Akkadian Empire (circa 2340 – circa 2200 B.C.E.) are two copper-alloy objects of high quality. The first is an almost life-size male head from Nineveh, possibly depicting Naram-Sin (circa 2254 – circa 2218 B.C.E.), with long beard and elaborate hairstyle held in place by a headband that is part of a long tradition of similar royal headdresses. Although intentionally disfigured in antiquity, this head still retains its original vitality and majesty. The second masterpiece, found near Bessetki in northeast Iraq, is the lower part of a male figure, nude except for a belt, seated, with legs splayed, on a large circular drum bearing a cuneiform inscription of Naram-Sin. These large castings were probably done in multiple-piece molds.

Copper alloy relief (height 42 inches) depicting a lion-headed eagle grasping a pair of stags, probably a decorative element from above the temple door at Tell al-Ubaid, circa 2500 – circa 2340 B.C.E. (British Museum, London)

Late Third Millennium B.C.E. At the end of the third millennium B.C.E., under Gudea of Lagash, and the kings of the Ur III period (circa 2112 – circa 2004 B.C.E.), copper-alloy figures in the shape of pegs were placed in the foundations of temple buildings as a record of the royal builder. At Lagash they represent either Gudea's personal god grasping a peg or a sacred animal atop a peg. Under the Ur III rulers, the foundation figures took the form of a standing, robed king, or the peg was transformed halfway up into the king's nude upper torso, and above his head the king holds a basket of earth from which he will symbolically make temple bricks.

The First Bronze. Although bronze (an alloy of copper and tin) was employed during the third millennium B.C.E., it was only in the second millennium B.C.E. that its use became widespread. A finely modeled bronze figure from Larsa depicts a man kneeling on his right knee. His face and hands are overlaid with gold leaf. A cuneiform inscription on the base informs the reader that it was dedicated for the life of king Hammurabi (circa 1792 – circa 1750 B.C.E.).

The "International Style." In the second half of the second millennium B.C.E., diplomatic contact between Egypt and states in the eastern Mediterranean and Mesopotamia created an "International Style" for elite metal objects. Finely made bowls decorated by repoussé (a process of creating a pattern in relief in thin metal by hammering or pressing from behind), particularly those from the trading center of Ugarit on the Syrian coast, display a fusion of a dynamic Aegean animal style with Egyptian and Syrian imagery and compositions. Elements of this Mediterranean "International Style" in metalwork, as well as in ivory carving, survived into the early first millennium B.C.E., especially in the Canaanite (Phoenician) cities along the coast. Evidence for the use of other metals at this time comes from Ashur, where lead was extensively used to produce plaques and figurines as well as lead blocks. In northwest Iran local imagery on finely crafted gold vessels from sites such as Marlik and Hasanlu shows the wealth of settled communities with links to the art of nomadic groups in Central Asia.

Neo-Assyrian Metalwork. In the ninth century B.C.E. a transition took place from bronze tools and weapons to versions made from iron. Copper and bronze continued to be used to produce other kinds of objects. Indeed, Assyrian texts record that vast quantities of bronze came to Assyria as booty and tribute. Assyrian royal inscriptions describe monumental works. For example, at Nineveh under king Sennacherib (704–681 B.C.E.) massive castings produced lion colossi said to weigh 11,400 talents (about 42 tons). Among the surviving Assyrian metalworks are bronze bands decorated in repoussé with scenes similar to the palace wall reliefs. These bands adorned doors at the site of Balawat (ancient Imgur-Enlil). Elaborate furniture was also produced with component parts in bronze similar to those

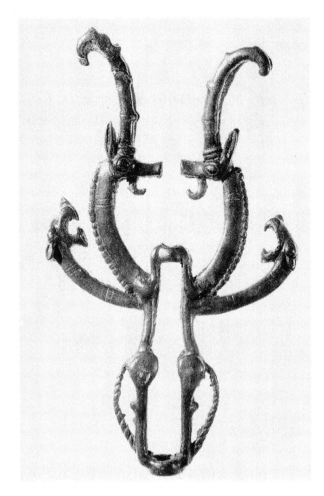

Copper alloy head of an Akkadian ruler, perhaps Naram-Sin (circa 2254 – circa 2218 B.C.E.), height 12 inches, excavated at Nineveh; the inlaid eyes, likely of precious stone, were forceably removed in antiquity; and a bronze finial for a standard, height 7 1/8 inches, two stylized upright ibexes with lion heads emerging from their shoulders, said to be from Luristan, circa tenth–ninth centuries B.C.E. (left: Iraq Museum, Baghdad; right: British Museum, London)

known from the kingdom of Urartu to the north. Evidence for the beauty and skill of eighth-century B.C.E. gold work is revealed by jewelry discovered at Nimrud. Under the floor in the North-West Palace were the remains of three tombs, inside of which were sarcophagi containing the bodies of royal ladies along with elaborate crowns, necklaces, and bracelets, all made of gold and decorated with inlays of precious stones.

Urartian Metalwork. In the early first millennium B.C.E. the powerful kingdom of Urartu in eastern Anatolia rivaled the Assyrian Empire. Urartu is renowned for its remarkable lost-wax-cast decorated bronzes, which originally adorned furniture. Some of the best examples come from the temple at the site of Toprakkale on the shore of Lake Van. As with the evidence from Assyria, some surviving Urartian metalwork is military in nature and includes objects such as helmets, shields, belts, and quivers decorated in repoussé. Assyrian influence is strong in the style and form of

Urartian metalwork, but north Syrian influence appears on objects such as cauldrons with *protomes,* decorations shaped like the foreparts of animals. In the mid-seventh century B.C.E., mythical creatures such as centaurs, winged horses, scorpion-tailed lions, and human-headed birds appeared in Urartian metalwork.

Luristan Bronzes. During the period of Assyrian domination in the first half of the first millennium B.C.E., extraordinary bronze objects were manufactured in the region of Luristan in western Iran. Elaborate standards with complex animal imagery are part of a repertoire of objects found in cemeteries. Unfortunately, scientific analysis has been hampered by the fact that many examples were plundered from illegally excavated sites; modern forgeries further complicate matters.

The Late Babylonian Period. The evidence for metalwork during the Late Babylonian Empire (610–539 B.C.E.) is minimal. There are references by Nebuchadnezzar II (604–562 B.C.E.) to his setting up monumental

Bronze bowl (5 7/8 inches in diameter) from a grave at Ashur, circa ninth–eighth centuries B.C.E.
(Vorderasiatisches Museum, Berlin)

bronze figures made in the form of bulls and dragons at the main gate of Babylon. In the fifth century B.C.E., Herodotus of Halicarnassus recorded that he was told of a fifteen-foot-high solid-gold statue of a man, presumably a deity, encountered by Persian king Cyrus II (538–530 B.C.E.) in a temple in Babylon. Evidence for metalwork from the Achaemenid Persian period in Mesopotamia is more plentiful, and a distinct Persian court style is clear. Gold and silver rhytons (drinking vessels decorated with animal bodies and heads and having a hole in the front for pouring) are found across the empire. Precious metals were widely used to produce vessels that were also copied in glass. Delegations portrayed on the reliefs at Persepolis carry similar vessels, as well as jewelry and ceremonial weapons. Actual examples of the metal jewelry are also known. Some of the best examples are part of the so-called Oxus Treasure, which includes massive gold bracelets with elaborate cloisonné decoration in multicolored inlay. Metal equestrian and other statues are referred to in Greek sources, but none survives. Herodotus mentioned a gold statue of the favorite wife of Persian king Darius I (521–486 B.C.E.). Herodotus also claimed to have seen in Babylon a statue of the god Bel seated on a throne supported on a base, with a table standing beside it, all of gold, totaling more than twenty-two tons.

Sources:

John Curtis, ed., *Bronzeworking Centres of Western Asia, c. 1000–539 B.C.* (London & New York: Kegan Paul / British Museum, 1988).

P. R. S. Moorey, *Materials and Manufacture in Ancient Mesopotamia: The Evidence of Archaeology and Art: Metals and Metalwork, Glazed Materials and Glass*, British Archaeological Reports (Oxford: Oxford University Press, 1985).

Oscar White Muscarella, *Bronze and Iron: Ancient Near Eastern Artifacts in the Metropolitan Museum of Art* (New York: Metropolitan Museum of Art, 1988).

MUSIC AND DANCE

Textual Evidence. Sumerian musical technical terms have been identified in cuneiform texts, but they are difficult to interpret. Several cuneiform tablets from the mid-second to mid-first millennium B.C.E. provide Akkadian technical terms relating to a set of seven musical scales and nine musical strings. A tablet from the Syrian city of Ugarit (circa 1400 B.C.E.) preserves a cult song, written in Hurrian, alongside terms for musical notation that are also used in a Babylonian description of how to tune a lyre. It has, therefore, been possible to reconstruct the sound of this song. Unfortunately, there is no knowledge of rhythm or tempo. Depictions of musical instruments occur on seals, terra-cotta and stone plaques, ivory carvings, and sculpture. The Mesopotamians used percussion, wind, and stringed instruments.

Stringed Instruments. Some of the earliest musical instruments recovered in Mesopotamia come from the Royal Cemetery of Ur (circa 2600 – circa 2500 B.C.E.), where the remains of lyres and harps were found. The lyres were generally portable, although one with approximately eleven strings was large enough to be played by two standing musicians, and the sound boxes were decorated with the head of a bull. The lyre was perhaps intended for the accompaniment of liturgical chants, and in ancient texts its sounds are associated with those of the divine bull. A boat-shaped lyre was decorated with the figure of a stag. After 2000 B.C.E. some sound boxes were shaped like animals. Harps were usually smaller than lyres and could be played in either a horizontal or vertical position. Marching and playing harpists and lyrists appear on Neo-Assyrian palace reliefs (883–610 B.C.E.). The long-necked lute appeared before 2000 B.C.E. King Shulgi (circa 2094 – circa 2047 B.C.E.) of the Third Dynasty of Ur claimed that he learned to play the instrument immediately. Two-stringed lutes are most common and often depicted while being played by nude, perhaps dancing, figures. Many Sumerian and Akkadian words for instruments are known, but relating terms to specific instruments is difficult.

Wind Instruments. Wind instruments were made of reed, wood, bone, and metal. The fragmentary remains of a pair of silver flutes were found in the Royal Graves of Ur. The earliest representation of a vertically played flute appears on a cylinder seal from the Akkadian period (circa 2340 – circa 2200 B.C.E.). Double pipes appeared around the second millennium B.C.E. and remained popular, supplemented by pan pipes, which were introduced from the West in the late first millennium B.C.E. Trumpets are shown on a stone plaque from the Early Dynastic period (circa 2900 – circa 2340 B.C.E.) and were used by soldiers depicted on Assyrian reliefs two thousand years later to direct prisoners of war dragging a stone sculpture. Miniature versions of trumpets are found in graves in western Central Asia. Sumerian hymns refer to the blowing of bull and ibex horns to produce a sound.

Percussion. Copper clappers were found in the Royal Graves at Ur, and similar clappers—two thin strips of metal mounted on wood—were also found at Kish. Drums of various shapes and sizes with skin drumheads are frequently depicted. Small, hand-held drums are the earliest and are usually shown being played by nude women. Frame drums appeared later, and in Neo-Assyrian reliefs soldiers play large versions. Kettledrums were in cultic use. From the second half of the third millennium B.C.E. large drums—lying on their sides and beaten by hand or with drumsticks by two men—are associated with ritual activities such as temple building and wrestling.

Song. Instrumental music and singing were probably features of every aspect of life. Although there is little information about everyday living, surviving texts of poems about Inana and her husband Dumuzi may have served as marriage songs. In temples there were professional cult lamentation priests and musicians (*kalu* and *naru* in Akkadian). Hymns devoted to specific deities or their temples were produced from the mid-third millennium B.C.E. Enheduana, the daughter of king Sargon (circa 2334 – circa 2279 B.C.E.), is credited with composing several temple hymns. Texts refer to songs for different occasions, such as work, battle, love, and funerals. One Middle Assyrian text of circa 1100 B.C.E. lists more than 360 titles belonging to thirty-one different song types. Men and women singers and instrumentalists performed in a variety of situations. A singer possibly appears on the Standard of Ur and is accompanied by a lyre player. Depictions of ceremonial banquets on stone plaques and cylinder seals often include musicians and singers. Such scenes are sometimes cartooned to show animals replacing the humans. The scenes look similar to modern comic strips, with humans replaced by a variety of animals chosen to add symbolic meaning to the activities they perform. It is possible that epics, myths, and celebratory texts such as *Enuma elish* were sung.

Dance. There are no texts describing dance, but depictions of people performing in groups or solo have been identified. The majority of examples date to the second millennium B.C.E.

Sources:
Anne Draffkorn Kilmer, "Music and Dance in Ancient Western Asia," *Civilizations of the Ancient Near East*, 4 volumes, edited by Jack M. Sasson (New York: Scribners, 1995), IV: 2601–2613.

Subhi Anwar Rashid, *Musikgeschichte in Bildern Band 2: Musik des Altertums Lieferung 2* (Leipzig: UEB Deutscher Verlag für Musik, 1984).

PAINTING

Late Uruk Period, circa 3300 – circa 2900 B.C.E. Because buildings in Mesopotamia were made from mud brick covered with plaster, they were regularly repaired, rebuilt, or left to decay. As a result, few examples of wall paintings have been found, but surviving evidence suggests that it was a widely used form of decoration. Wall paintings discovered in a temple of the Late Uruk period at Tell Uqair depict leopards and other animals and a procession of humans, all with their feet on the same ground line. The main altar was painted to represent a temple facade with vertical panels of imitation-cone mosaic. These paintings were done on a white background in a great variety of colors.

The Second Millennium B.C.E. The best-preserved wall paintings of the second millennium B.C.E. come from the palaces at Mari and Nuzi. At Mari on the middle Euphrates, ritual scenes show the king and goddess

Male figure wearing a fringed shawl and felt cap, from a group leading a sacrificial bull; detail (height 23 inches)
from a fragment of a wall painting in a courtyard of the Palace of Zimri-Lim at Mari,
circa eighteenth century B.C.E. (Louvre, Paris)

Ishtar and processions of people and animals. At Nuzi in northeastern Iraq, friezes depict heads like that of the Egyptian cow-faced universal mother goddess Hathor, cattle heads, and trees—all painted in black and ochre on white or gray. Later, at Kar-Tukulti-Ninurta (circa late thirteenth century B.C.E.), typical Assyrian designs of palmettes, bird-headed genii, goats, and geometric designs were painted in black, red, and blue on a white background. From about the same period, processions of

male figures were painted at doorways of the Kassite palace at Dur-Kurigalzu.

The First Millennium B.C.E. In Neo-Assyrian palaces and temples of the eighth and seventh centuries B.C.E., wall reliefs were often complemented or replaced by wall paintings. Painted bricks and wall paintings found at Nimrud were mainly in geometric patterns but also included animal and plant designs. Fine examples of Neo-Assyrian wall paintings come from the palace at the provincial center of Til Barsip in northern Syria. The subjects include protective genii, military campaigns, royal audiences, and lion hunts.

Sources:

Henri Frankfort, *The Art and Architecture of the Ancient Orient*, fifth edition, with supplementary notes and bibliography by Michael Roaf and Donald Matthews (New Haven: Yale University Press, 1996).

Eva Strommenger, *5000 Years of the Art of Mesopotamia*, translated by Christina Haglund (New York: Abrams, 1964).

POTTERY

The Earliest Pottery. The term *pottery* may refer to any variety of vessel or plate made of clay that has been fired, or hardened by heating, typically in an oven, or kiln. Because styles of pottery change over time and between regions, it is one of the most important diagnostic tools available to archaeologists for dating sites and distinguishing cultures. For example, undecorated pottery shapes, made for everyday use, are useful for understanding what people cooked, stored, or carried between sites. The earliest known pottery was found in northwest Syria and dates to around 8000 B.C.E. These clay containers may have been accidentally fired. It was not until the seventh millennium B.C.E. that the use of pottery became widespread in the farming villages of the Near East. Over time, distinctive styles of pottery emerged in different regions. In Mesopotamia, northern forms are called Hassuna and Halaf, and styles that developed further south are Samarran and Ubaid. During the Jamdat Nasr period (circa 3000 – circa 2900 B.C.E.) some vessels were painted with geometric designs in a distinctive, plum-colored paint. Sometimes, figures, animals, and vegetation were also included within panels. A later form of this pottery, known as "Scarlet Ware," is found in the Diyala region of eastern Mesopotamia and dates to the Early Dynastic I period (circa 2900 – circa 2750 B.C.E.).

Southern Pottery Traditions. Unlike the often elaborately decorated and finely made vessels of the earliest periods, Uruk period pottery of the late fourth millennium B.C.E. is notable for its lack of decoration and its mass production in molds or on the newly developed fast wheel. From the Akkadian period (circa 2334 – circa 2154 B.C.E.) through the Achaemenid

Scarlet Ware vessel decorated with red and black paint (height 11¾ inches) from a house in Khafajeh in the Diyala region, circa 2800 B.C.E. (Iraq Museum, Baghdad)

empire (559–331 B.C.E.), southern Mesopotamian pottery was largely undecorated and utilitarian. Vessels were made on potters' wheels and generally buff in color. In the Isin-Larsa period (circa 2004 – circa 1763 B.C.E.) white inlay was sometimes used to decorate jars.

Northern Decorative Traditions. Until the end of the second millennium B.C.E., styles of northern Mesopotamian pottery were distinct from those of the south. In the north, a style of pottery painted with geometric designs in dark paint, known as Ninevite 5, was first identified in level 5 at Nineveh, which dates from circa 3000 – circa 2500 B.C.E.; later forms included incised and excised patterns in the surface. A distinctive pottery form that is often associated with Hurrian peoples of the mid-second millennium B.C.E. is found widely over much of north Mesopotamia, from Alalakh in the west to Nuzi in the east. The finest examples of this pottery, known under a variety of names, are beakers with black paint overpainted with delicate white designs.

First Millennium B.C.E. In the first millennium B.C.E., pottery across Mesopotamia was largely utilitarian. One exception was what is now called "palace ware," eggshell-thin vessels produced by the Assyrians. In the Achaemenid and succeeding empires (from 539 B.C.E.) surface designs made by impressions of stamp seals became common. The use of glaze on pottery, known from the second millennium B.C.E., became much more popular following the Hellenistic period.

Sources:

Ian Freestone and David R. M. Gaimster, *Pottery in the Making: World Ceramic Traditions* (London: British Museum Press, 1997).

P. R. S. Moorey, *Materials and Manufacture in Ancient Mesopotamia: The Evidence of Archaeology and Art: Metals and Metalwork, Glazed Materials and Glass,* British Archaeological Reports (Oxford: Oxford University Press, 1985).

Max Wykes-Joyce, *7000 Years of Pottery and Porcelain* (London: Owen, 1958).

SCULPTURE

Late Uruk Period, circa 3300 – circa 2900 B.C.E. Large-scale sculpture in the round and relief carving appeared for the first time in the Late Uruk period. A new realism is apparent in the treatment of the human form. A frequent subject is the figure of the "priest-king." He has a fillet (a narrow headband worn high on the forehead and above the ears), has his hair in a bun and a beard without a mustache; he is attired in a skirt (often crosshatched like a net) to the knee or ankle. From the city of Uruk (modern Warka) comes the Lion Hunt Stele, on which two priest-kings (or one man shown

Late Uruk period sculpture (circa 3300 – circa 3000 B.C.E.): the Lion Hunt Stele (basalt), height 31½ inches, and the Warka (Uruk) Vase (alabaster), height 41¼ inches (both: Iraq Museum, Baghdad)

Standing male worshiper wearing a long skirt with a fringed hem (height 11 5/8 inches); gypsum, with shell and black-limestone inlaid eyes, hair and beard colored with bitumen, from Tell Asmar, circa 2750 – circa 2600 B.C.E (The Metropolitan Museum of Art, New York, Fletcher Fund, 1940)

twice) attack a lion, one with a bow and arrow and the second with a spear. This stele is the earliest example of the "royal lion hunt," a frequent theme in Mesopotamian art. Several known statues in the round also portray the priest-king. Excavated examples come from Uruk, where some fragments belong to a more than life-size figure. Other images in the round represent nude and bound prisoners. Many of these statues are geometric in style, with heavy legs, but others are naturalistic, with an emphasis on the musculature of the chest and arms that continues as a tradition in Mesopotamian portrayals of kings. A beautiful alabaster mask of a woman is another important find from this period at Uruk. It was part of a composite statue (a work made of more than one material). Constructing statues from different materials was popular in Mesopotamia during the late fourth and third millennia B.C.E. and later as far east as Central Asia. This method was probably used regularly in making divine images that, according to later texts, were formed from precious stones and metals. Many carved stone bowls date to the Late Uruk period and the Jamdat Nasr period (circa 3300 – circa 2900 B.C.E.). Carved in relief on these vessels are processions of animals, usually cattle, with the heads often turned to face the viewer. The best-known vessel of the period is the so-called Warka Vase, which is more than one meter high. Like designs on cylinder seals of the period, it portrays an ordered world. The vase is divided into horizontal bands, or registers, showing (from the bottom up) waters, grain, a line of small cattle, a procession of naked men holding a variety of vessels and apparently moving toward the uppermost frieze, where a priest-king (whose image is largely broken away) presents offerings to a priestess of the Inana temple. These two figures may also represent the goddess Inana and her consort Dumuzi, whose union, acted out by the king and priestess, ensured the continued fertility of Sumer. Behind the female are the symbols of Inana and the interior furnishings of her temple. A similar use of registers is found later on such masterpieces as the Standard of Ur.

Early Dynastic I Period. Sculpture, like other art forms of much of the third millennium B.C.E., has usually been divided into three phases based on perceived changes. While such a tripartite art-historical division is questioned today, the system remains a useful way of dividing some six hundred years. Some finely carved stone sculpture probably belongs to the long Early Dynastic I phase (circa 2900 – circa 2750 B.C.E.). These works include two well-modeled representations of men with bison's body and horns (bull-men) and statues from the Diyala River region (to the east of the Tigris) of naked bearded "heroes" wearing belts and grappling with lions and bulls. They demonstrate continuity with the naturalistic forms of the Late Uruk period and also

Two fragments of the relief-carved limestone Stele of the Vultures from Tello (ancient Girsu), circa 2450 B.C.E. In the lower
fragment (height 71 inches), king Eanatum of Lagash rides in a battle cart at the head of his troops (lower register)
and marches on foot ahead of his troops, who tread on the dead soldiers of the city of Umma (upper register).
In the upper fragment vultures peck at the decapitated heads of enemies (Louvre, Paris).

Diorite statute of Gudea, city-ruler of Lagash, circa 2100 B.C.E. (height 17 3/8 inches, probably from Girsu), with his hands clasped in a gesture of piety; and diorite head of an unknown ruler (height 9 3/4 inches), circa twentieth-eighteenth centuries B.C.E. (left: The Metropolitan Museum of Art, New York, Harris Brisbane Dick Fund, 1959; right: Louvre, Paris)

link with southeastern Iran, where similar images, particularly of composite human and animal creatures or animals acting as humans, were made.

Early Dynastic II–III Periods, circa 2750 – circa 2340 B.C.E. During Early Dynastic II (circa 2750 – circa 2600 B.C.E.) and III (circa 2600 – circa 2340 B.C.E.), statues of men and women, many identified by short cuneiform inscriptions, were set up in temples. They were dedicated to specific gods and may have been intended to represent either a donor who would receive the god's blessing or a deceased person. One of the largest collections of such figures comes from a deposit in a temple at Tell Asmar in the Diyala region. They have angular bodies, enormous eyes inlaid with lapis lazuli and white stone, large noses, and small mouths. Other more naturalistically carved votive statues suggest that both abstract and modeled forms of sculpture existed contemporaneously and may have been the styles of different temple workshops rather than a chronological development. Similar figures are also represented on stone plaques carved in relief, sometimes divided into registers, and pierced in the center so they

can be fixed to a wall. The upper register often shows a seated couple drinking from cups with other humans playing music and serving drink. The humans wear skirts or cloaks, with tufts covering the entire garment or fringes hanging at the hem. Below these figures, various domesticated animals are sometimes shown, and in the bottom register may be wrestling men, or processions, or a chariot or boating image.

Eanatum's Victory Stele. During the Early Dynastic III period, as the city-states apparently became stronger economically and politically, connections were established with other civilizations from the Aegean Sea in the West to Central Asia and the Indus Valley in the East. Exotic metals and stones not native to Mesopotamia were increasingly used in art. Temple and palace workshops, such as the one in the town of Girsu in the city-state of Lagash, produced astonishing works. The first known depiction of an historical event, king Eanatum of Lagash's victory over the warriors of Umma, is shown on the so-called Stele of the Vultures. Eanatum is shown twice, once leading his army on foot and then in his chariot from which he brandishes a spear. A simple register system is used, with each register standing for a whole and not to be "read" as representing a sequence in time. On the other side of the stele the god Ningirsu holds a net full of the defeated enemy soldiers. In this way the divine world parallels the mortal world, and the actions and will of the gods are reflected on earth.

Third Millennium B.C.E. Syria. Exquisite sculpture in the round was also made in north Mesopotamia and Syria during the Early Dynastic III period. At Ebla in Syria composite statues were created from different colored stones (a tradition that can be traced back to the Late Uruk period). At Mari on the middle Euphrates such a master-piece as the votive statue of the administrator Ebih-il was made. He is depicted as a bald man with a beard drilled to form rows of curls in the typical fashion of Mari, inlaid bitumen eyebrows, and eyes of shell and lapis lazuli. He sits on a wicker stool, with hands clasped. His skirt is realisti-cally rendered with tufts of hair that contrast with his bare torso. The naturalistic modeling found in much of this northern sculpture is comparable with that in works of the later Akkadian period, in which modern scholars often locate the development of the style.

Akkadian Period, circa 2340 – circa 2200 B.C.E. The dynasty of Akkad, which came to control much of Meso-potamia through military force, displayed strong continuity with the Early Dynastic period, and the idea of a complete break with earlier artistic tradition is no longer accepted. On reliefs, the theme of royal victory was still developed in registers. However, under Naram-Sin (circa 2254 – circa 2218 B.C.E.), the formal registers were discarded. The royal victory was treated in a single composition of grand sim-plicity on a stele originally erected in Sippar, but discovered at Susa in southwestern Iran, where it was carried as booty in the twelfth century B.C.E. On Naram-Sin's Victory Stele, columns of Akkadian warriors arrayed in ascending diagonals climb a hill toward the monumental image of the king, who is trampling his enemies underfoot. The figure of Naram-Sin is transformed, not only by the delicate and naturalistic modeling of his muscular body, but by his

Cult stand (alabaster, height 23 5/8 inches) from Ashur, depicting Assyrian king Tukulti-Ninurta I (circa 1243 – circa 1207 B.C.E.) twice, in two moments of prayer before a cult stand like the one on which he is depicted (Vorderasiatisches Museum, Berlin)

NIMRUD IVORIES

The great wealth of the Assyrian Empire in the first millennium B.C.E. is apparent in extraordinary art that often originated outside Assyria proper. The booty that Assyrian kings had brought back to their capital from military campaigns included ivories, such as furniture decoration and beds, as well as daggers, cups, and dishes. Huge quantities of ivories were found in the palaces, temples, and private houses at Nimrud (ancient Kalhu). Sometimes the Assyrians described the ivory as being overlaid with gold or silver, or inlaid and bejeweled. Occasional remnants have survived.

Three main styles of ivory carving can be identified: a local "Assyrian" style similar in design to the royal stone reliefs; a "North Syrian" style, with designs related to stone carvings of north Syrian cities; and a "Phoenician" style, with designs that reveal Egyptian influence. Within each of these major styles were several distinct schools of carving. Flame-like muscle markings on the animals and frond-like foliage give one North Syrian school the name "Flame and Frond." Most of the ivories were probably produced when the eastern Mediterranean kingdoms of the Levant were independent. They were incorporated into the Assyrian Empire during the reigns of Tiglath-pileser III (744–727 B.C.E.) and Sargon II (721–705 B.C.E.). It is not known when production started, but undeniable links with the "International Style" eastern Mediterranean art during the late second millennium B.C.E. suggest an early date.

Source: M. E. L. Mallowan, *The Nimrud Ivories* (London: British Museum Publications, 1978).

horned headdress, which was formerly the exclusive prerogative of the gods. Other stone sculptures from this period were made with the same concerns of naturalism and sensitivity.

Gudea of Lagash. With the collapse of the Akkadian Empire, circa 2100 B.C.E., some city-states, such as Lagash under the rule of Gudea, regained their independence. The many statues of Gudea from the site of Girsu (modern Tello) show the ruler with muscular arms symbolizing the strength of kingship. His hands are elegantly folded, and he stands or sits in the tradition of earlier votive figurines. He is either bareheaded and bald or wearing a straight-sided fur hat, his beardless face radiating a calm, otherworldly expression. Cuneiform inscriptions in Sumerian on the statues indicate that they were set up in temples that the ruler had refurbished. The diorite from which the statues were carved was imported from the region of modern Oman on the Persian Gulf.

Third Dynasty of Ur, circa 2112 – circa 2004 B.C.E. Possibly contemporary with Gudea was Ur-Namma, who founded the Third Dynasty of Ur. Ur III imagery preserves many motifs developed in the Akkadian period, including, under Ur-Namma's successors, the royal assumption of divine status. In contrast to Akkadian sculpture, however, there are no clear representations of warfare. Ur-Namma had a large stele carved. He is depicted in the upper register honoring the moon god Nanna and his consort. In the scenes below he—like earlier Mesopotamian rulers—officiates at the ceremonies for the building of a temple.

Isin-Larsa and Old Babylonian Periods, circa 2000 – circa 1595 B.C.E. With the fall of the Third Dynasty of Ur and the rise of rival dynasties at Isin and Larsa, the Amorite names of the rulers indicate the growing power of West Semitic Amorite tribes. Traditions in sculpture remained alive, with an emphasis on styles of the Ur III period. One of the best surviving examples of this period is a finely modeled black-granite head of a king that was excavated at Susa, where it had been brought as booty in the twelfth century B.C.E. Although damaged, the rugged yet world-weary face makes a contrast with the placid appearance of Gudea, and this black-granite image has been compared with roughly contemporary sculpture of Sesostris III from Egypt. During the eighteenth century B.C.E. the city-state of Babylon came to dominate much of Mesopotamia under king Hammurabi (circa 1792 – circa 1750 B.C.E.). Perhaps the best-known artwork of this time is a large diorite stele known as the Stele of Hammurabi, which originally stood in the temple of the sun god Shamash at Sippar. This stele was also part of the booty removed to Susa in the twelfth century B.C.E. The relief decorating the top of the stele shows the king wearing a royal hat—like that of Gudea—before the seated sun god. Both the king and Shamash are depicted for the first time with eyes in profile; thus a real gaze is established between god and ruler. From the north Mesopotamian city of Mari comes a beautiful life-size stone figure of a goddess holding a vase from which water must have poured; a channel drilled through the statue from the base to the vase no doubt had plumbing connected to an external water source.

Kassite and Middle Assyrian Periods. With the collapse of Babylonian power around 1595 B.C.E., southern Mesopotamia (Babylonia) was united under the rule of Kassite kings. The characteristic Kassite sculptures are the entitlement monuments (so-called *kudurru*) bearing the texts of royal donations placed under the protection of carved symbols of the gods. Further north in Assyria, an alabaster altar from the capital Ashur shows in relief two images of king Tukulti-Ninurta I (circa 1243 – circa 1207 B.C.E.) in two moments of worship, standing and

One of a pair of nearly identical Phoenician-style ivory plaques, originally inlaid with lapis lazuli and carnelian (height 4 inches), from Nimrud, mid-eighth-seventh centuries B.C.E. Amid a field of lotus and papyrus blossoms, a lioness embraces a Nubian boy wearing a gold-leaf-covered short skirt, and turns her head to tear at his throat (British Museum, London).

kneeling before the emblem of a god set on an altar identical in shape to the altar on which the relief is carved. It is one of the earliest depictions of an Assyrian ruler in characteristic poses of the Neo-Assyrian Empire (934–610 B.C.E.).

The Early Neo-Assyrian Period. The art of the Neo-Assyrian period, when Assyria emerged as a world power, consists mainly of architectural decoration in the form of reliefs. Almost without exception, they were made for the king, and most are wall reliefs in the form of stone slabs that lined the walls of important rooms in palaces and temples. The slabs, which bear images and texts recording the activities of the ruler, are carved in low relief, generally in soft alabaster. Figures are shown in the pose commonly used in Mesopotamian sculpture, with the head, arms, and legs in profile and the torso generally shown frontally. Obelisks and stelae, free-standing monuments depicting the king, were some-

times set up in public locations. In addition, rock reliefs were carved on natural rock surfaces to mark areas reached during royal campaigns or the location of royal construction projects.

The Palace at Nimrud. It is possible that the earliest known reliefs from the so-called North-West Palace of Ashurnasirpal II (883–859 B.C.E.) at Nimrud (ancient Kalhu) were inspired by local Syrian palace and temple decorations, which derived from earlier Hittite monuments. The dating of these Syrian decorations, however, is disputed, and the inspiration may have been the other way. Indeed, an earlier sequence of Assyrian wall decoration may have been copied and depicted in miniature on the so-called White Obelisk from Nineveh, possibly dating to the eleventh century B.C.E. The throne-room facade and several other major entrances were decorated with human-headed, winged bull and lion colossi. The largest were nearly six meters in length and height.

Black Obelisk of king Shalmaneser III (858–824 B.C.E.), from Nimrud (alabaster, height 79½ inches); five panels engraved in relief on each of the four sides depict the presentation of tribute and booty described in the cuneiform text on the monument (British Museum, London)

THE BLACK OBELISK

On one of twenty relief panels on the Black Obelisk of Shalmaneser III (858–824 B.C.E.), the caption to an image of a foreign dignitary kneeling before the Assyrian king has occasioned much interest ever since its discovery at Nimrud in 1846. The caption reads: "Tribute of Jehu 'son' of Omri: I received from him silver, gold, a golden *saplu*-bowl, a golden vase with pointed bottom, golden tumblers, golden buckets, tin, a staff for a king, (and) wooden *purihtu*." Jehu, according to the Hebrew Bible, was not literally the son of king Omri; rather he was the trusted, but soon-to-be insubordinate, commander of the army of king Joram, who was Omri's son. At the instigation of the prophet Elisha, Jehu overthrew the Omride dynasty in Israel, as well as the ruling dynasty in neighboring Judah, in a bloody coup d'état (II Kings 9:1 – 10:36). Nineteenth-century Londoners flocked to the British Museum to see the first indisputable evidence for the existence of two kings of ancient Israel. Later, in 1870, was published a fragment of an annalistic text in which Shalmaneser claimed that in his eighteenth regnal year he extracted tribute from Jehu; that year would have been 841 B.C.E., Jehu's first year on the throne of Israel.

Sources: Mordechai Cogan and Hayim Tadmor, *II Kings. A New Translation with Introduction and Commentary*, Anchor Bible, volume 11 (Garden City, N.Y.: Doubleday, 1988).
A. Leo Oppenheim, "Babylonian and Assyrian Historical Texts," in *Ancient Near Eastern Texts Relating to the Old Testament*, edited by James Bennett Pritchard, third edition with supplement (Princeton: Princeton University Press, 1969), pp. 265–317.

When approached from the front the creatures appear unmoving and unmovable. From the side, however, they stride forward with four legs, metaphorically preventing any evil forces from entering the palace. The spaces between the legs and behind the tails were carved with a text that identifies the king and summarizes his achievements. Relief slabs depict figures standing against a blank background that sharply defines them. Themes include foreigners bringing tribute to the king, images of the monarch beside protective stylized palm trees ("sacred trees"), and winged genii that are intended to protect the ruler and, by association, the land of Assyria from malevolent supernatural forces. Carved across the middle of each slab is a cuneiform inscription, known as the "Standard Inscription," recording the king's name and a summary of his military and building accomplishments. Slabs running along the long walls are divided into three unequal registers. The wider upper and lower registers display a series of images that are often termed "narratives," though they are more like snapshots of important moments. They depict royal hunts and military conquests. The narrower, central register is carved with the Standard Inscription. Sculpture in the round is rare, although one example (found in the Ishtar temple at Nimrud) shows Ashurnasirpal II standing in a formal attitude. Despite its small size (about 42 inches tall) the image is monumental in its presence. The king is also shown on a stele, where he is depicted facing left in a standard pose, pointing with his raised right hand and holding a mace in his left, with symbols of deities in front of his face. Inscriptions cover the back and sides. From the reign of Ashurnasirpal's son, Shalmaneser III (858–824 B.C.E.) comes the Black Obelisk. Found at Nimrud, it has twenty relief panels arranged around four sides in five registers, each labeled and showing the delivery of tribute to the king from a different part of the empire.

Khorsabad and Nineveh. The relief decoration of the palace of Sargon II (721–705 B.C.E.) in the later capital of Dur-Sharrukin (modern Khorsabad) was modeled on that of Ashurnasirpal II. The most spectacular reliefs come from the throne-room court, which is decorated with a scene depicting the transport of timber by water. It is shown as if viewed from above, with small figures dotted across the surface of the slabs, giving the impression of depth, which distinguishes it from earlier reliefs, where figures exist against a flat background. Sargon's son Sennacherib (704–681 B.C.E.), who moved the capital to Nineveh, exploited this artistic innovation. At Nineveh the entrance colossi have four rather than five legs. Military campaigns were the theme of the reliefs in the majority of rooms. Other scenes show the collection of building materials, including the quarrying and transportation overland of human-headed bull colossi. Instead of a band of inscription dividing the slabs into registers, relief images are often carved over the entire surface, allowing the artist to play with space and time. A sense of depth is achieved when subjects are presented against a patterned background, such as mountains or water, or the slab is divided into registers by ground lines. Some of the finest reliefs come from the

Divine human-headed winged lion guardian (alabaster, height 10 feet 3 ½ inches) from a gateway of the palace of Ashurnasirpal II (883–859 B.C.E.) at Nimrud (The Metropolitan Museum of Art, New York, Gift of John D. Rockefeller Jr., 1932)

Limestone relief (height 34 inches), from a palace at Persepolis, 358–338 B.C.E. A Persian servant holding a wineskin mounts a stairway, following a Mede with a covered vessel (The Metropolitan Museum of Art, New York, Harris Brisbane Dick Fund, 1934).

palace of Ashurbanipal (668 – circa 627 B.C.E.) at Nineveh. Scenes of the king hunting lions, gazelle, and wild horses are beautifully carved in great detail, particularly the richly decorated dress of the king and the sensitively depicted animals. One relief, which portrays Ashurbanipal and his queen banqueting in a garden, is an extremely rare depiction of an Assyrian woman. The carving appears to have been undertaken by crews of artisans. On some of the reliefs depicting large-scale lions, some of the animals were originally carved with longer tails, which were shortened, perhaps on the orders of the master sculptor.

The Late Babylonian Empire. Few sculptural works of the Late Babylonian Empire survive. Two poorly preserved images of Nebuchadnezzar II (604–562 B.C.E.) carved on a rock wall at Wadi Brisa in Lebanon depict the king slaying a lion and felling a cedar tree. The last king, Nabonidus (555–539 B.C.E.), had himself portrayed in an attitude of prayer on stelae where he is depicted in the standard royal pose with thickly styled body.

Persian Imperial Art. The Persians, from southwest Iran, consciously adopted and adapted images of power and royalty from their predecessors. The sculptured imagery of the Persian Empire, like that of the earlier Neo-Assyrian Empire—aspects of whose art the Persians particularly emulated—addressed the king and an audience of courtiers, thereby reinforcing a sense of belonging. Among the few surviving sculptures at Pasargadae in Iran, the royal center created under Cyrus II, who came to power in Persia in 559 B.C.E. and became king of Babylon in 538 B.C.E., is a winged genius carved in relief on a doorjamb; the figure has four Assyrian-style wings and wears an Elamite fringed garment and an elaborate Egyptian-style divine crown. Column capitals take the form of the heads and necks of two animals, the lion or bull, back to back. A lion-like monster was also used as column capitals at the later Iranian centers of Susa and Persepolis. Supernatural creatures, royal figures, and attendants carved in relief, similar to those found in reliefs at Neo-Assyrian palaces, guard some of the doorways in Persian palaces. Some of the garments and shoes depicted were originally decorated with attachments of metal.

Darius the Great. At Behistun (Bisutun), a mountain in northwestern Iran, Darius I (521–486 B.C.E.) had a relief and inscription carved on the side of a cliff some five hundred feet above the adjacent plain. Rather than depicting a series of events, it is a symbolic representation of the king's triumph over his enemies. This relief is the only Achaemenid royal image that depicts a specific historical episode rather than a standardized and repetitive ceremony or symbol. The relief is close in style to Neo-Assyrian imagery, particularly that of Ashurbanipal. Darius is also represented in a colossal statue (missing its head and shoulders) found at Susa but possibly originally from Egypt. He wears the Persian court robe rendered in a late Archaic Greek fashion, but he stands in the traditional Egyptian fashion with his left foot forward. The base is inscribed in Egyptian hieroglyphs with the names of the countries and regions under Achaemenid control. It also includes images of the various peoples of the empire. Similarly, the diverse population of the empire is represented with distinct costumes on reliefs decorating the royal tombs set in the cliffs above Persepolis.

Persepolis. The best-known sculptural works of the Achaemenid Empire come from the royal city of Persepolis, where many of the artistic traditions found at Pasargadae were continued. Massive, carved, six-foot-tall animal capitals were placed atop sixty-foot columns. Carved reliefs frequently depict a royal hero mastering or slaying powerful animals or monsters. Doorways are decorated with this image, so that the hero protects the interior rooms from the invading creature. Other reliefs show the king and attendants moving through doorways, having battled with monsters at the entrances to inner rooms. The king is also shown being held aloft on a dais supported by the people of his empire. As at Pasargadae, there are slots in the reliefs to insert metal ornaments, particularly on the king's crown.

Some of the most spectacular sculptural reliefs decorated staircases leading to the audience hall, or Apadana—the north and east stairways show the enthroned king with an official bowing before him. Behind the king are Persian nobles in alternating military and court clothing. In front of the king is a row of representatives bringing gifts to their emperor from twenty-three lands that make up the Persian Empire. A Persian courtier holds by hand the leader of each group—adopting a pose found in earlier Mesopotamian works where a figure is brought into the presence of a god.

Sources:
Joan Aruz with Ronald Wallenfels, eds., *Art of the First Cities: The Third Millennium B.C. from the Mediterranean to the Indus* (New York: Metropolitan Museum of Art, 2003).

T. A. Madhloom, *The Chronology of Neo-Assyrian Art* (London: Athlone Press, 1970).

Julian Reade, *Assyrian Sculpture* (Cambridge, Mass.: Harvard University Press, 1983).

Margaret Cool Root, "Art and Archaeology of the Achaemenid Empire," in *Civilizations of the Ancient Near East*, 4 volumes, edited by Jack M. Sasson (New York: Scribners, 1995), IV: 2615–2637.

John Malcolm Russell, *Sennacherib's Palace without Rival at Nineveh* (Chicago: University of Chicago Press, 1991).

Agnès Spycket, *La Statuaire du Proche-Orient ancien*, Handbuch der Orientalistik (Leiden: Brill, 1981).

SEALS AND SEALINGS

The Earliest Seals. The impressing of carved stones into clay to seal containers had a long tradition in Mesopotamia, with the earliest evidence found in Syria and dating to the seventh millennium B.C.E. In the fourth millennium B.C.E. various styles of stamp seals were made. In northern Mesopotamia, seals, which probably also served as amulets, were shaped like animals and may have represented votive offerings of the animals depicted since they are found in temples such as at Tell Brak. Northern Mesopotamian stamp seals of other shapes had animal motifs carved on them. In southern Mesopotamia stamp seals also had animal motifs, while in neighboring regions of Iran, geometric, animal, human, and demonic imagery—as well as heroes with animals—appeared on stamp seals.

Cylinder Seals. During the second half of the fourth millennium B.C.E., stamp seals were largely, though not completely, superseded by cylinder seals in Mesopotamia and southern Iran. A small cylinder of stone was carved with a design. (It is possible that some cylinder seals were made of wood, but none has survived.) Rolling a cylinder seal on a sufficient quantity of damp clay produced a frieze-like image. The invention of the cylinder seal was probably connected with new developments in recording and administration that accompanied the rise of the first cities and major institutions such as the temple. The shape of the seal allowed the user to cover a large, curved surface area and to employ a wider range of motifs, which produced

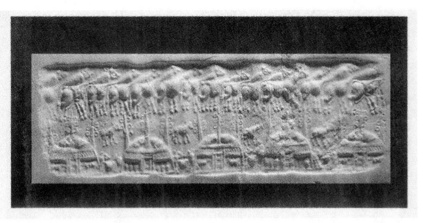

Cylinder seals and modern impressions: (top) file of overlapping cows above reed sheds (magnetite with copper handle, height 3 1/8 inch), Late Uruk; (bottom) banquet scenes, seal of queen Pu-abi of Ur (lapis lazuli, height 1 inch), Early Dynastic IIIA (top: Ashmolean Museum, Oxford; bottom: University of Pennsylvania Museum of Archaeology and Anthropology)

some of the earliest narrative art. Seals of the Late Uruk period (circa 3300 – circa 2900 B.C.E.) may be divided into two main groups. The first comprises large cylinders with modeled, naturalistic, and rounded forms that depict real and imaginary animals either in heraldic groups or being hunted and herded, often by the priest-king. The second group includes much smaller cylinders that are drilled or incised with characteristic pigtailed figures engaged in domestic or agricultural work. Also in this group are seals with rows of fish, scorpions, or gazelles. At the end of the fourth millennium B.C.E. similar schematic designs on cylinder seals were used over a wide area, a result of trade relations from southwestern Iran through Syria to Egypt. By the early third millennium B.C.E. the designs had become even more schematized; they are called Piedmont because they are found at sites along the foothills of the Zagros and southern Turkey. Patterns were based on lozenges, circles, and chevrons. Some seals in southern Mesopotamia used cuneiform signs, apparently to represent groups of city names on so-called City Seals.

Early Themes. In the Early Dynastic period (circa 2900 – circa 2340 B.C.E.) the variety of scenes on cylinder seals became larger. One of the two main themes on these seals, many of which are made of lapis lazuli imported from Afghanistan, is a banquet scene. Such scenes, which also appear on contemporary stone plaques, are representations of ceremonies in which music appears to have been an integral part. The banquet seals from the Royal Cemetery of Ur (circa 2600 – circa 2500 B.C.E.) may have been associated exclusively with women. The other common theme is contests of strength among animals, heroes, and, later, bull-men. By the time of the Akkadian Empire (circa 2340 – circa 2200 B.C.E.) the contest had split into two antithetical groups of well-matched opponents and perhaps represents a cosmic battle between order and chaos. Occasionally, brief cuneiform inscriptions appear in the field.

Akkadian Seals. The Akkadian period produced some of the most skillfully carved and iconographically varied seals. An early style with stocky well-defined forms was replaced by a mature, naturalistically modeled style. Seals in this style often depict balanced combats involving heroes, bull-men, bulls, lions, and water buffalo. There are also presentation scenes showing worshipers before deities and mythological scenes. Increasingly more common, cuneiform inscriptions, typically identifying the seal owner, are now enclosed within a frame. One of the finest cylinder seals belonged to a scribe of king Shar-kali-sharri (circa 2217 – circa 2193 B.C.E.). The extraordinary carving depicts a nude hero pouring liquid for a water buffalo. The scene is shown with a mirror image, the backs of the two animals supporting the inscription panel.

Presentation Scenes. With the Ur III period (circa 2112 – circa 2004 B.C.E.) uniform seals were produced, distinguished by a delicate carving already present in late Akkadian court seals. The iconography is restricted to combats, libations before plants (a fertility symbol), and

presentations to deities, or the deified king seated on a stool. It has been suggested that seal owners and rulers were given specific features in these presentation scenes. Ownership of such seals, which were highly standardized in their iconography and inscription formulae, seems to have been restricted to a class of high public officials.

Old Assyrian and Old Babylonian Seals, circa 2000 – 1595 B.C.E. In the first half of the second millennium B.C.E. different styles of cylinder seals existed contemporaneously across Mesopotamia. Early on, Old Assyrian merchant colonies were established in Anatolia by traders from the north Mesopotamian city of Ashur. These merchants documented their activities in cuneiform on clay tablets sealed with cylinders carved in a shallow, angular, and linear style; the iconography blends Mesopotamian and Anatolian subjects. In Mesopotamia the repertory consisted mainly of scenes with standing deities and the king, either

Nude heroes with water buffalo (top), seal of Ibni-sharrum, a scribe of Akkadian king Shar-kali-sharri (serpentine, height 1 1/2 inches), Akkadian; (bottom) seal owner's personal deity approaching Ishtar with lion, impression from the seal of seal cutter Ilak-nuid (height 1 5/8 inches), Akkadian (top: Louvre, Paris; bottom: Oriental Institute, Chicago)

Pink chalcedony seal (top, height 1 5/8 inches) and seal impression of a lion and winged horse fighting above a wingless foal, Middle Assyrian; seal impression (bottom) of an Assyrian official approaching Ishtar, with palm tree and goats (height 1 3/4 inches), Neo-Assyrian (both: British Museum, London)

robed and holding an offering or wearing a kilt and holding a mace. These Old Babylonian seals are typically made of hematite, a hard gray-black stone. Small symbols such as fish and dwarfs are characteristic features. From around 1750 B.C.E. the gradual increase in the use of the drill and cutting disc resulted in a deterioration of the style.

Kassite, Mitannian, and Middle Assyrian Seals. With the end of Hammurabi's dynasty around 1595 B.C.E. southern Mesopotamia came under the domination of the Kassites. Their seals fall into two main styles. One, a development of the late Old Babylonian style, is linear with a worshiper and/or a deity and symbols beside a lengthy inscription, often a prayer. The other is more modeled and naturalistic, with pastoral or mythological scenes. Across northern Mesopotamia and north Syria during the fifteenth and fourteenth centuries B.C.E., the Hurrian kingdom of Mitanni held sway. Throughout the kingdom and beyond, workshops produced inexpensive brightly colored seals made of sintered quartz, commonly referred to as faience. (The term *sintered* describes a mass of nonmetallic material that has been heated until it is fused. Faience is sintered material that has been glazed.) In Assyria, which became the new power in northern Mesopotamia as Mitanni declined, the cylinder seals consisted of shallow, linear carvings of fights between imaginary beasts. These were replaced in the thirteenth century by finely modeled animals beside trees, combats between a hero and real or imaginary animals, and rituals before symbols or deities. Much of this iconography continued in the repertory of the first millennium B.C.E.

Stamp Seals. During the Neo-Assyrian Empire (934–610 B.C.E.) and the Late Babylonian period (610–539 B.C.E.), cylinder seals began to be replaced with stamp seals. This change was largely related to the rapid spread of the Aramaic language, which could be written with just twenty-two characters in ink on parchment or papyrus. Such documents were most readily rolled and secured by string. A small lump of clay over the knotted string did not require a cylinder seal. Nonetheless, styles of cylinder seals can be identified during this period. A cut style and modeled style appeared across Mesopotamia. Differences between contemporary Neo-Assyrian and Neo-Babylonian carving cannot be clearly appreciated, but there are iconographic distinctions, such as different styles of garments and headdress. Favorite themes include hunts and hunting rituals, banquets, combats, processions of real and imaginary animals, worship of deities and symbols, and ceremonies beside the so-called sacred tree. The most common symbols—the spade of Marduk, the stylus of Nabu, the fish and goat-fish of Ea, the moon crescent of Sin on a pole, and the star of Ishtar—demonstrate continuity in imagery over three thousand years.

The Achaemenid Period. The administrators of the Achaemenid Empire (538–331 B.C.E.) maintained an anachronistic use of cylinder seals. Their wide range of iconographic influences suggests the extent of the empire and its foreign contacts, from Greece and Egypt in the west to India in the east. Early Achaemenid documents from Babylon have seal impressions that show continuity of Neo- and Late Babylonian worship scenes. The impressions of this period were followed by an increasing appearance of images of the royal hero—perhaps owing to a desire to emulate the Neo-Assyrian royal seal that showed an Assyrian king stabbing a rampant lion. One group of seals, in what is called the "Court Style," is similar in style to the Persepolis sculptures. On later tablets there is increasing use of stamp and cylinder seals in hybrid Graeco-Persian styles and, occasionally, in purely Greek style. Stamp seals and newly introduced metal finger rings with engraved almond-shaped bezels tended to be reserved for private, nonadministrative use. Their styles and iconography are similar to those of contemporary cylinders: especially a royal hero in combat with real or imaginary beasts. By the end of the fourth century B.C.E., the cylinder seal was virtually unused.

The Hellenistic Period (331 B.C.E.–129 B.C.E.). Following the death of Alexander and the Wars of the Successors (323–301 B.C.E.), Syria, Mesopotamia, and for a while, Iran, were ruled by one of Alexander's generals, Seleucus I (311–281 B.C.E.), and his dynasty. The Seleucids fostered a fusion of Greek and traditional native cultures. On engraved-metal finger rings and stone stamps with convex sealing surfaces classical Greek figures appear side by side with traditional Mesopotamian demons and monsters. The signs of the Babylonian zodiac, individually and in astrologically significant combinations, became popular motifs.

Legacy. Throughout the Parthian Empire (247 B.C.E.–224 C.E.), which at times included all of Iran and Mesopotamia, stamp seals were in wide use. These seals are difficult to date. It is clear from seal impressions found at Parthian sites that many seals were set into signet rings, probably made of metal, and were generally incised with an animal or plant motif. These motifs continued to be popular on the seals of the succeeding Sasanian Empire (224–651 C.E.), when both domed seals and seal-rings carved in hard colorful stones were popular. Ring bezels of carnelian or garnet were often carved with a portrait head and an inscription in Pahlavi.

Sources:

Dominique Collon, *First Impressions: Cylinder Seals in the Ancient Near East* (London: British Museum, 1987).

Henri Frankfort, *Cylinder Seals: A Documentary Essay on the Art and Religion of the Ancient Near East* (London: Macmillan, 1939).

Holly Pittman, "Cylinder Seals and Scarabs in the Ancient Near East," in *Civilizations of the Ancient Near East*, 4 volumes, edited by Jack M. Sasson (New York: Scribners, 1995), III: 1589–1603.

Ronald Wallenfels, *Uruk: Hellenistic Seal Impressions in the Yale Babylonian Collection* I. *Cuneiform Tablets*, Ausgrabungen in Uruk-Warka Endberichte 19 (Mainz am Rhein: Philipp von Zabern, 1994).

WOOD CARVING

Sources. Although wood from palms and trees such as tamarisk and poplar was used extensively in Mesopotamia for building and constructing furniture, larger or harder woods had to be imported. As a result good wood was always a scarce and desirable commodity. Rulers sent expeditions to bring back timber from the eastern Zagros Mountains or the mountains of Lebanon in the west. Modern scholars' lack of knowledge about wood carving is hampered because the climate of Mesopotamia creates an environment in which organic objects are rarely preserved. Occasionally, however, exceptional conditions have preserved evidence for the use of wood.

Uruk Period. Dating from the late fourth millennium B.C.E., a wooden chest or seat was found in the E-ana Precinct at Uruk. At each corner of the chest was an upright post capped in copper. Both the base and uprights were decorated with mosaic inlay. The chest was part of a large collection of objects, perhaps from a temple, that had been deliberately set on fire, possibly as part of a ritual. Because the chest did not burn completely, its wood became carbonized.

Early Dynastic Period, circa 2900 – circa 2340 B.C.E. A few wooden objects were preserved in the Royal Graves at Ur (circa 2600 – circa 2500 B.C.E.), including a large wooden chest, which the excavator interpreted as a wardrobe, found in the tomb of queen Pu-abi. Like the chest from Uruk it was decorated with mosaic, in this instance made of shell and lapis lazuli. In a later grave at Ur the excavator discovered the remains of a rectangular wooden table. The best surviving examples of wood carving from the third millennium B.C.E. are fragments from Ebla that perhaps came from chairs, a table, and possibly the door of a cupboard. Found in the royal palace, these fragments were preserved by a fire that destroyed the building (circa 2250 B.C.E.). The remains include a panel inlaid with shell that depicts a file of animals—an almost completely preserved bull, a lion, and another quadruped. Another carving from Ebla portrays a male figure holding an ax. He wears a long fleece-like robe, and his eyes are inlaid with shell. Possession of such wood carvings appears to have been restricted, at least in the third millennium B.C.E., to the higher levels of society. Indeed, texts sometimes make reference to gods being presented with wooden furniture.

The Levant and Anatolia. There are few surviving wooden objects from later periods of Mesopotamia. Furniture, presumably made of wood, is represented on seals, inlays, plaques, and stone reliefs. References in texts also allude to images of gods being fashioned from wood; the most important sculptures were overlaid with precious metals, but apparently none has survived. The best evidence for surviving wooden furniture after the third millennium B.C.E. comes from outside Mesopotamia, in sealed tombs at Jericho in the Levant (circa 1800 – circa 1650 B.C.E.), and from tumuli near the Phrygian capital of Gordion in central Anatolia (late eighth–early seventh century B.C.E.). The Phrygians produced some of the most beautiful examples of carved and inlaid wood from the ancient world. Herodotus reported that king Midas (738–696 B.C.E.) dedicated his throne as an offering at the sanctuary of Apollo at Delphi, in Greece. Herodotus claimed that it was "well worth seeing."

Source:

Georgina Herrmann, with Neville Parker, eds., *The Furniture of Western Asia Ancient and Traditional: Papers of the Conference held at the Institute of Archaeology, University College London June 28 to 30, 1993* (Mainz am Rhein: Philipp von Zabern, 1996).

SIGNIFICANT PEOPLE

BEROSSUS

EARLY THIRD CENTURY B.C.E.
HISTORIAN

Royal Historian. Berossus (perhaps *Bel-reushunu* in Akkadian) was a Babylonian priest, who wrote the so-called *Babylonian History* or *Babyloniaka* in Greek about 281 B.C.E. Dedicated to the Seleucid king Antiochus I (281–261 B.C.E.), these three books covered the history of Babylonia. Unfortunately, they are known incompletely, only from quotations by later authors. Berossus began by telling how Oannes (a half-fish, half-man creature) came from the sea and taught humans the arts of civilization. He then described how Marduk became the supreme god. In the second book, Berossus described ten legendary kings who ruled before the Flood and included a version of the Flood story. The final book, which is "historical" in the modern sense of the word, describes several Assyrian, Babylonian, and Persian rulers. The last event mentioned appears to have been the death of Alexander in 323 B.C.E.

Source:
Stanley Mayer Burstein, ed. and trans., *The Babyloniaca of Berossus,* Sources and Monographs. Sources from the Ancient Near East 1/5 (Malibu: Undena Publications, 1978).

ENHEDUANA

CIRCA TWENTY-THIRD CENTURY B.C.E.
POET

The Emperor's Daughter. In a profession dominated by men throughout Mesopotamian history, the earliest poet known by name is Enheduana, daughter of the Akkadian king Sargon (circa 2334 – circa 2279 B.C.E.). Her father appointed her high priestess of Nanna, the moon god, in the city of Ur. Ancient tradition credits her with the composition of a collection of forty-two "Temple Hymns," a hymn to the goddess Inana, and the autobiographical hymn known as the *Exaltation of Inana*. It is possible that, if Enheduana was indeed the author of the hymns, their composition was politically motivated to support the ambitions of her father, who united the independent Sumerian city-states under his rule.

Source:
William W. Hallo and J. J. A. van Dijk, *The Exaltation of Inanna,* Yale Near Eastern Researches, 3 (New Haven & London: Yale University Press, 1968).

ESAGIL-KINA-UBBIB

CIRCA ELEVENTH CENTURY B.C.E.
EXORCIST AND SCHOLAR

Author. Esagil-kina-ubbib identified himself as the author of the so-called *Babylonian Theodicy*, which must have been an important text among Mesopotamian scholars, as many cuneiform copies have been found. He describes himself as an incantation priest or exorcist, and, judging by his name, he may have been involved with E-sangil, the temple of Marduk in Babylon. The *Babylonian Theodicy* is cast as a dialogue between somebody who suffers injustice and a friend who tries to explain it in relation to the justice of the gods. It is an acrostic poem made up of twenty-seven stanzas of eleven lines each. Within each stanza all lines begin with the same sign. Read once and in order, the signs may be translated as: "I, Saggil-kinam-ubbib, the incantation priest, am an adorant of the god and the king."

Source:
W. G. Lambert, *Babylonian Wisdom Literature* (Oxford: Clarendon Press, 1960).

ILAK-NUID

CIRCA TWENTY-SECOND CENTURY B.C.E.
SEAL CUTTER

Skilled Artisan. Although many seal cutters are known by name from cuneiform texts, including ration lists, as a rule, none can be identified with his work. Thus, the seal cutter (Akkadian: *purkullum,* Sumerian: *bur-gul*) Ilak-nuid, who presumably carved the seal he dedicated as a gift to his personal deity, must have been a particularly important craftsman. The deity on this beautifully engraved cylinder seal is shown interceding, presumably on the seal cutter's behalf, before the great goddess Ishtar. The inscription on the seal is not reversed, suggesting that this seal was not intended for sealing but rather was a dedicatory object meant to be read directly by the goddess. No other information about Ilak-nuid may be found in any other source.

Source:
E. Porada, "Of Professional Seal Cutters and Nonprofessionally Made Seals," in *Seals and Sealing in the Ancient Near East,* edited by McGuire

Gibson and Robert D. Biggs, Bibliotheca Mesopotamica, 8 (Malibu: Undena Press, 1977), pp. 7–14.

KABTI-ILANI-MARDUK

CIRCA EIGHTH CENTURY B.C.E.
POET AND SCRIBE

Divinely Inspired. According to the concluding part of the *Poem of Erra and Ishum,* Kabati-ilani-Marduk was its author. It was highly unusual for an author to identify himself. Kabti-ilani-Marduk explained that the poem was revealed to him in a dream. In Mesopotamia, dreams were believed to have been sent by the gods. Kabati-ilani-Marduk claimed that he made no changes to the story, relaying only what the god had revealed to him.

Source:
Luigi Cagni, *The Poem of Erra,* Sources and Monographs. Sources from the Ancient Near East 1/3 (Malibu: Undena Press, 1977).

DOCUMENTARY SOURCES

The Descent of Ishtar into the Netherworld (Akkadian: Neo-Assyrian period, 934 – 610 B.C.E.)—In this retelling of a Sumerian-language composition, the goddess of sex and war decides to visit the underworld, knowing that even gods cannot escape once they enter. She passes through seven gateways, removing pieces of jewelry and clothing, symbols of her power, at each stop. Eventually, she comes before Erishkigal, queen of the underworld, who pronounces that, according to the rules, Ishtar must die. As a result, all sexual activity stops on earth and in heaven. The god of wisdom, Ea, fashions an asexual creature and gives it the food and drink of life. The creature carries the food and drink to the underworld and sprinkles it on Ishtar, who returns to life. Ishtar, however, has to find a replacement for herself in the underworld and eventually chooses her husband, the shepherd king Dumuzi, who is carried away by demons.

Dialogue Between a Man and his God (Akkadian: Old Babylonian period, circa 1894 – circa 1595 B.C.E.)—The poem starts with the advice that a man should take every opportunity to praise his god, but the young man cannot understand why his god is angry and letting him suffer misfortune. Despite undertaking all the rituals and prayers in the correct fashion, the man is still troubled. By the end of the poem, however, his constant weeping and cries for help are answered by his god, and his suffering is turned to joy.

Enmerkar and Ensuhkeshdanna (Sumerian: Ur III period, circa 2112 – circa 2004 B.C.E.)—Ensuhkeshdanna, the Lord of Aratta (a distant land that may have represented an actual locality on the Iranian plateau), requests that Enmerkar, the king of Uruk, acknowledge him as the favorite of the goddess Inana. Enmerkar refuses. A man from the city of Hamazu (a play on the Sumerian word *hamazi,* which means "may he learn") suggests a plan to make Enmerkar submit. A sorcerer from Aratta makes the cows and goats of the Sumerian city of Eresh withhold their milk. Twin shepherds ask the sun god Utu for help. The result is a fishing competition in which five animals caught in the river by the sorcerer are eaten by larger animals caught by a woman from Uruk. The sorcerer is thrown into the river, and Enmerkar is shown to be the superior.

Enmerkar and the Lord of Aratta (Sumerian: Old Babylonian period, circa 1894 – circa 1595 B.C.E.)—Enmerkar challenges the Lord of Aratta, requesting that the lord recognize Enmerkar as his overlord and provide exotic stones and metal to build the temple of Inana at Uruk. Enmerkar threatens the Lord of Aratta, and a spell of the god Enki is recited so that the citizens of Aratta will have to speak the same language as the rest of the world (that is, Sumerian). The Lord of Aratta agrees to comply if Enmerkar can solve a series of impossible tasks. Enmerkar outwits him three times. His invention of cuneiform writing and tablets is the proof of Enmekar's superior cunning.

Etana (Akkadian: Old Babylonian period, circa 1894 – circa 1595 B.C.E.)—The gods establish kingship and make Etana king of Kish. He builds temples, including one that contains a tree. A snake lives in the tree roots and an eagle in the crown. Although sworn to friendship with the snake, the eagle eats the snake's offspring. As a result, the eagle is thrown in a pit, from which he cries to Shamash, god of the sun and justice. Knowing that king Etana wants an heir, Shamash instructs Etana to save the eagle, which will help the king find the plant of birth. Etana helps the eagle leave the pit, and he flies with the king into the air. When they lose sight of the earth, the king begs the eagle to set him down, and the eagle does so. The end of the story is missing.

Kabti-ilani-Marduk, *The Poem of Erra and Ishum* (Akkadian: Neo-Assyrian period, 934–610 B.C.E.)—Marduk, the supreme god of Babylonia during the first millennium B.C.E., is described in this poem as remorseful about the great Flood, from which he saved a remnant of the earth's population and after which he introduced agriculture. The plague god Erra, who wants to destroy Babylon, looks on Marduk with contempt and complains about Marduk's appearance. Marduk replies that he had lost his glory by raising the Flood against humans. Because humans had neglected his cult, he has abandoned them to the forces of chaos. Erra advises Marduk to have his image refurbished and says that while Marduk does so, he, Erra, will sit in Marduk's place. After Marduk leaves to have his image restored by seven sages in the lower regions, Erra starts his reign of terror. The innocent and the guilty are slaughtered; the act is completed by Ishum, god of fire, and Erra is placated.

Lugalbanda and Enmerkar (Sumerian: Old Babylonian period, circa 1894 – circa 1595 B.C.E.)—Showing his cunning, Lugalbanda flatters the mythical Anzud bird, which offers him various gifts. Lugalbanda chooses the ability to run fast on condition that he does not reveal the secret to anybody. He soon reaches his brother Enmerkar's army besieging the city of Aratta. After a year of unsuccessful siege, Enmerkar needs a courier to deliver a message in which the goddess Inana in Uruk provides the means by which Aratta can be conquered. Lugalbanda is the only one of the brothers brave enough to volunteer to take this message. The others are angry with this upstart, but with his ability to run fast, Lugalbanda completes his mission. Aratta is conquered, and as a result Uruk is provided with precious stones and metals.

The Myth of Anzu (Akkadian: Old Babylonian period, circa 1894 – circa 1595 B.C.E.)—The Anzu, a bird-like creature, is born, and the supreme god, Enlil, appoints him as his guard. One day, as Enlil is bathing, Anzu steals the "Tablet of Destinies," which gives the holder power over the future. The gods are afraid or unwilling to battle Anzu, but Ea, god of wisdom, instructs the mother goddess to produce Ninurta. Gathering his weapons, Ninurta meets Anzu in battle and, after a dramatic fight, slays the wicked creature. Ninurta regains the "Tablet of Destinies" and apparently returns it to Enlil.

The Sumerian Sargon Legend (Sumerian: Old Babylonian period, circa 1894 – circa 1595 B.C.E.)—An official at the court of Ur-Zababba at Kish, Sargon has a dream that Ur-Zababba will drown and Sargon will succeed him. On learning of the dream, Ur-Zababba thinks it is Sargon who will drown but plans to have Sargon burned in a furnace just in case he is wrong. Because the gods favor him, Sargon escapes danger. Ur-Zababba then sends Sargon to the court of king Lugalzagezi at Uruk with a letter concealed in the world's first envelope (a clay cover for a clay tablet). The tablet instructs Lugalzagezi to kill Sargon. The end of the tale is missing, but presumably Sargon outwits Ur-Zababba.

Relief-carved limestone plaque (height 5 ½ inches) depicting the lion-headed eagle, Anzud, biting into the hindquarters
of a bison with a bearded human face, perhaps part of the façade at Ninhursanga Temple, Tell al-Ubaid,
circa 2500 – circa 2350 B.C.E. (University of Pennsylvania Museum of Archaeology and Anthropology)

COMMUNICATION, TRANSPORTATION, AND EXPLORATION

by RONALD WALLENFELS

CONTENTS

Sidebars and tables are listed in italics.

IMPORTANT EVENTS OF 3300-331 B.C.E.

3300*-3000* **B.C.E.**	• Uruk urban centers are established at sites in southern and northern Mesopotamia, Syria, Anatolia, and western Iran. Whether built on new foundations or on the sites of earlier towns, their well-constructed monumental buildings, regular networks of roads, and enormous settlement walls are the product of tremendous efforts in organization and labor.
2600*-2500* **B.C.E.**	• Jewelry and vessels made of imported precious stones and gold and silver are prominent among the grave goods interred in the Royal Graves at Ur. The stones include lapis lazuli from Afghanistan and long drilled biconical stone beads and bleached ("etched") carnelian beads, both distinctive products of the Indus Valley civilization.
2600*-2200* **B.C.E.**	• Chlorite vessels carved in the "Intercultural Style" are found widely scattered from Mari in Syria in the west to the Indus Valley in the east. Two centers of production are located near sources of the soft greenish stone at Tarut Island in the Persian Gulf and Tepe Yahya in south central Iran.
2334*-2193* **B.C.E.**	• Ships from Meluhha in the Indus Valley tie up at the quay in the city of Agade (Akkad).
2200*-2100* **B.C.E.**	• A local colony of Meluhhan merchants is noted in the state archives of the Third Dynasty of Ur. • A massive wall spanning the Euphrates and Tigris Rivers is built as part of an effort to prevent Amorite nomads from Syria from entering southern Mesopotamia.
1900*-1700* **B.C.E.**	• Merchants from the city of Ashur on the Tigris commission donkey caravans to transport finished textiles and tin to trading emporia in Anatolia, where the goods are exchanged for gold and silver.
1792*-1750* **B.C.E.**	• Hammurabi of Babylon is in direct control of the trade routes through northern and southern Mesopotamia, along which pass silver, gold, copper, tin, lapis lazuli, carnelian, exotic woods, and horses.
1749*-1712* **B.C.E.**	• The First Dynasty of the Sealand establishes itself in southernmost Mesopotamia, seizing control of the Persian Gulf trade from Babylon.

* DENOTES CIRCA DATE

IMPORTANT EVENTS OF 3300-331 B.C.E.

1390*-1295*
B.C.E.

- The "great kings" of Hatti, Mitanni, Assyria, and Babylonia exchange vast gifts of precious metals, stones, and wood with their Egyptian contemporaries. The Egyptian kings amass an archive of cuneiform correspondence with many great and petty rulers throughout the Near East.

1305*-1274*
B.C.E.

- Hittite king Muwatalli, fearing the political and military ambitions of Assyrian king Adad-nirari I, denies his request to visit the Amanus Mountains near the Mediterranean coast.

1243*-1207*
B.C.E.

- Assyrian king Tukulti-Ninurta I campaigns extensively in the mountains to the north and east of Assyria to secure trade routes that supply precious stones, tin, and horses.

858-824
B.C.E.

- At Imgur-Enlil (Balawat), Shalmaneser III builds monumental wooden-gate doors, each covered with eight decorated bronze bands illustrating his military activities; each band is 180 centimeters (nearly six feet) wide by 27 centimeters high (nearly one foot). Two similar sets of doors have been previously erected at the site by Shalmaneser's father, Ashurnasirpal II.

704-681
B.C.E.

- The Assyrian king Sennacherib moves his capital to Nineveh, which he rebuilds on a massive scale. The double wall surrounding the city is twelve kilometers long and has fifteen gates.

604-562
B.C.E.

- Nebuchadnezzar II rebuilds Babylon. The inner city—with its palaces, temples, and ziggurat—is surrounded by massive double walls fitted with nine gates, including the monumental Ishtar Gate, through which passes the broad stone-paved Processional Way. The temples in the city are lavishly refurbished with imported woods, stones, and precious metals. A bridge is built across the Euphrates River, which runs through the city.

538 B.C.E.

- The Persian king Cyrus II causes the flow of the Euphrates River, which passes through Babylon, to be diverted, permitting his troops to enter the city without opposition. Cyrus is hailed by the Babylonians as a liberator who has saved them from the neglectful rule of the last native king, Nabonidus.

331 B.C.E.

- Following his victory over the Persian king Darius III at Gaugamela, Alexander III (The Great) of Macedon sends word of his intention to enter Babylon peacefully. The city gates are thrown open at his approach.

* DENOTES CIRCA DATE

OVERVIEW

Communication and Locomotion. Communication and locomotion are two basic functions common to virtually all living creatures. Communication refers to the various ways in which organisms convey information to each other. Over the course of human evolution, these methods have included first noises and gestures, later intelligible speech, and still later, writing. Locomotion refers to the ways in which organisms move from place to place. Humans, naturally walkers and almost equally swimmers, learned to extend their range by riding on the backs of equids (donkeys, asses, and later horses) and oxen. They also learned to build and ride in vehicles—initially equipped with skids and later wheels—with equids or bovids harnessed to them. On the water, humans learned to propel floating objects by punting, paddling, rowing, sailing, and towing—first using found objects and later deliberately building watercraft of wood, bundles of reeds, or inflated animal skins.

Methods of Communication. Throughout most of human history, communication between individuals has relied on that most human of traits, articulate speech, supplemented by gestures and body language. The earliest representations of humans are so stylized that what few bodily gestures they display are virtually without meaning to the modern viewer, and little can be said of the nature of ancient speech, even after the initial invention of writing in southern Mesopotamia toward the end of the fourth millennium B.C.E. The earliest written proto-cuneiform inscriptions consisted of logograms (more-or-less abstract signs representing words) and numerals that were intended for maintaining complex accounting and bookkeeping records. Only after a period of several centuries did the signs begin to be adapted for rendering human speech by being assigned syllabic values allowing for phonetic writing. The earliest language recognizable in cuneiform is Sumerian, which is a language isolate (that is, it has no similarities with any other language, living or extinct). But toponyms (the names of rivers, mountains, and cities) and certain "culture" words (foreign words associated with imported materials and technologies) in these earliest legi-

ble texts reveal that the Sumerians were probably not the first and certainly not the only inhabitants of southern Mesopotamia. By the middle of the third millennium B.C.E., cuneiform had become sufficiently flexible so as to be used to record two Semitic languages, Akkadian and Eblaite, and, in the last quarter of the third millennium B.C.E., Hurrian, which is possibly related to modern languages of the Caucasus region. Before the end of the fourth millennium B.C.E., the concept of using ideograms, drawn symbols to record ideas and words, reached Sumer's neighbors in Egypt and southwest Iran (Proto-Elamites), where each developed its own system of writing. The writing system in use by the Harappan culture in the Indus Valley—the earliest evidence of which dates to shortly before the middle of the third millennium B.C.E.—may well have been stimulated by knowledge of the Proto-Elamite or Sumerian scripts communicated via long-distance trade.

The Spread of Writing. Cuneiform writing was adopted and adapted wherever Mesopotamian culture spread throughout the ancient Near East during the second and first millennia B.C.E. During the International Period in the fourteenth century B.C.E. the Akkadian language, written in cuneiform on clay tablets, was employed by the great kings in Egypt, Anatolia, North Syria, and Mesopotamia, as well as by the lesser princes of the southern Levant and Cyrus, regardless, for the most part, of their native tongues. These rulers regularly communicated with each other, expressing their desires and displeasure as they negotiated for prestigious exchanges of rich and exotic gifts or for military assistance. During the first millennium B.C.E., there was a steadily growing shift away from cuneiform toward the use of the simpler alphabetic writing systems of the Aramaeans and the Greeks, each of which was written in ink on prepared animal skins, papyrus, and pottery fragments. The simplicity of these writing systems brought about a dramatic increase in literacy, but because of the fragility of the writing media, few examples of these texts survive today.

Rivers and Roads. By the beginning of the Late Uruk period (circa 3300 B.C.E.), Mesopotamia was already crisscrossed by a system of well-traveled footpaths and roads and a network of natural and artificial waterways (canals). These roads and waterways enabled the Mesopotamians, who were blessed with fertile soil but few other natural resources, to seek out sources or suppliers of base and precious metals, semiprecious and hard building stones, hardwoods, and other exotica—allowing the ruling elite to display their wealth and power through buildings, furniture, and personal adornments. Over a period of more than three millennia, Mesopotamia directly or indirectly exported copious quantities of grain, dates, and textiles in exchange for—among much else—copper, tin, gold, and silver; lapis lazuli, carnelian, and diorite; cedar, cypress, juniper, and ebony; and ivory. Mesopotamia sat at the center of an economic world that at various times stretched from the Nile Valley and the eastern Mediterranean Sea in the west; eastward across Anatolia, Iran, and Afghanistan to the Indus Valley; and from Central Asia in the north to the Arabian Peninsula in the south.

Colonization and Exploration. The earliest and perhaps only evidence for large-scale colonization by Mesopotamians dates to the dawn of the historical period, circa 3300 B.C.E., when Late Uruk–culture urban centers were established at sites in southwest Iran, northern Mesopotamia, north Syria, and southern Anatolia. Little archaeological evidence has been unearthed at these sites to suggest that their residents were involved in any large-scale redirecting of local resources to Uruk itself, which is situated on the resource-poor southern alluvium. The residents of these colonies appear to have retained their southern cultural identities, even when situated close by native towns. On the other hand, the evidence of Meluhhan traders from the Indus Valley living in southern Mesopotamia at the end of the third millennium B.C.E. and of Assyrian merchants living in Anatolia early in the second millennium B.C.E. suggests that these communities became strongly acculturated.

Population Movements. Throughout the historical period, the military expansionist policies of the Akkadians, Babylonians, Assyrians, and Persians—whether within known or into uncharted territories—were stimulated by the desire for booty, plunder, and tribute, not colonization, and certainly not for exploration for its own sake. The policy of mass deportation of subject peoples exercised by the Assyrians and Babylonians during the first millennium B.C.E. served to redistribute peoples within existing urban centers rather than settle new centers. These policies ultimately weakened traditional Mesopotamian culture by widely dispersing speakers of the Aramaic language who wrote with the Aramaic script. With the coming of Alexander toward the end of the fourth century B.C.E. and the domination of the Near East by his Seleucid successors in the third and second centuries B.C.E., the systematic installation throughout the empire of retired Macedonian and Greek soldiers in newly founded Greek-style colonial cities became a significant factor in maintaining Graeco-Macedonian political ascendancy.

Costs of Communication. In the Sumerian legend of *Enmerkar and the Lord of Aratta*, Enmerkar, the semilegendary early third millennium B.C.E. ruler of the city of Uruk, learns by the end of the tale that in order to obtain the lapis lazuli and gold that he desires from the Lord of Aratta, ruler of a perhaps-mythical city situated far to the east, he must be willing to negotiate and offer goods of comparable value in exchange. Long-distance trade necessitated the building and maintaining of roads, along which a traveler might find safe and well-provisioned resting places. Canals needed to be dredged periodically to remove accumulated silt, and the natural tendency of a meandering river to abandon old channels needed to be regulated. Reliable and capable messengers and transporters were entrusted with purchasing and delivering goods. Kings devised laws and means to enforce them so that they could regulate trade and prevent abuses perpetrated by or against businessmen and their agents at the local level. International treaties provided regulation of trade across national boundaries. As the main repositories of the material wealth of the ruling elites, cities required protective walls and secure gates to regulate communication with the world beyond.

TOPICS IN COMMUNICATION, TRANSPORTATION, AND EXPLORATION

EXPLORATION AND LONG-DISTANCE TRADE

Prehistoric Exploration. It would appear to be an essential part of human nature to explore one's surroundings. As early as about 1.5 million years ago, tools belonging to the Oldowan tradition were being made by mankind's prehuman *Homo erectus* forebears. Originating in East Africa, these hominids migrated across Africa and then entered and spread across Asia and Europe. By about 500,000 years ago, tools of the Acheulian tradition had spread across Africa, Europe, and Asia as far east as India. Between circa 100,000 and circa 40,000 years ago, tools of the Mousterian tradition, made by *Homo sapiens,* were in use across the Old World.

Prehistoric Trade. Toward the end of the Paleolithic Period, following the end of the last Ice Age, bands of hunter-gatherers entered the Levant and Syria. The members of this Natufian culture settled in semipermanent villages, where they harvested local, naturally growing cereals by employing newly developed microlithic stone tools (typically made from small flakes of flint or obsidian). Natufian sites are often characterized by the presence of obsidian from Anatolia and of seashells most commonly coming from the Mediterranean Sea but also from the Red Sea; there are also some known examples from the Nile River and the Atlantic Ocean.

Obsidian. Obsidian is a hard, dark-colored volcanic glass capable of being made into sharp-edged tools. Obsidian from four Mediterranean island sources was shipped all over the central Mediterranean region in the most extensive long-distance trade network of its time. By circa 7000 B.C.E., obsidian from the island of Melos was being acquired by people who left remains in the Franchthi cave on the Greek mainland, implying some sort of early boat traffic. Obsidian found at Jarmo (circa 7500 – circa 6500

B.C.E.) in northern Iraq is three hundred miles from its source to the north.

Trade and Expansion. Beginning in the late sixth millennium B.C.E., the desire for survival at a level beyond mere subsistence may have been the motivation for the occupants of the southern Mesopotamian alluvial plain to establish centrally located towns, administered in part by the leadership of the local temples and set amid satellite rural villages. During this period, the peoples of the Ubaid culture (circa 5500 – circa 4000 B.C.E.) in southern Mesopotamia began to produce more grain, dates, wool, and woven goods than they themselves could consume. They may have begun to barter some of the excess for such locally unavailable raw materials as hardwoods, building stone, and copper. In time, the distinctive Ubaid painted pottery spread across northern Mesopotamia and Syria to the southern flanks of the Anatolian plateau, all along the flanks of the Zagros, and along the Arabian shore of the Persian Gulf. It is unclear whether this Ubaid "expansion" was motivated by any or all of such seemingly obvious economic factors as the desire to barter surplus goods in exchange for needed raw materials, the wish to maintain control over trade routes, or the hope to exploit for themselves resources lacking at home; other social factors may have come into play as well.

The Uruk Expansion. Beginning about 4000 B.C.E., a new culture emerged across southern Mesopotamia. By 3600 B.C.E. elements of this distinctive Uruk culture, named for the largest settlement of its type, existed at sites across an arc running from Susa in southwestern Iran northward along the Euphrates valley to Tell Braq in northern Syria and beyond into southeastern Turkey, as well as along the Tigris to Nineveh in northern Mesopotamia. The Uruk period is defined through its walled, well-ordered settlements—among them the world's first cities—

Ivory cosmetic-box lid (width 2½ inches) inlaid with lapis lazuli, from the tomb of Pu-abi at Ur, circa 2600 – circa 2500 B.C.E. (University of Pennsylvania Museum of Archaeology and Anthropology)

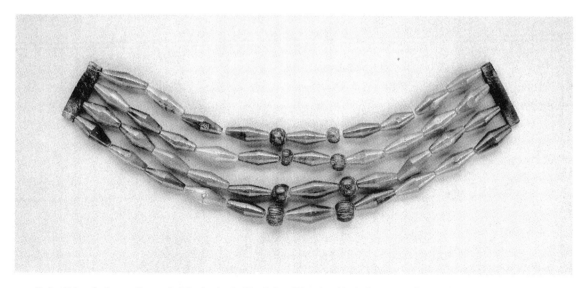

Belt of biconical carnelian and ribbed spherical lapis-lazuli beads with shale spacers (length 16 7/8 inches) from Ur, circa 2600 – circa 2500 B.C.E. (University of Pennsylvania Museum of Archaeology and Anthropology)

with elaborate monumental temples featuring sacred precincts. The period is also known for its monumental art, cylinder seals, mass-produced wheel-made and mold-made pottery, standardized units of measurement, accounting system (which later gave rise to writing), and extensive system of irrigation canals. Significant elements of the Late Uruk and immediately succeeding Jamdat Nasr (circa 3000 – circa 2900 B.C.E.) cultural assemblages—collections of material artifacts, including distinctive weapons, tools, utensils, and ceramics, that set one culture apart from another—have been identified in the Levant and in pre-Dynastic Egypt. Early scholarly assumptions that the Uruk expansion was motivated by the political or commercial interests of southern Mesopotamia do not appear to be substantiated by the archaeological evidence. There is no obvious evidence of conflict between the colonists and the local population; rather, they appear to have coexisted side by side, and at no Uruk colonies is there evidence for large-scale production, storage, or distribution of local resources directed toward the south. The expansion seems rather to have been driven by population growth sustained by agricultural and technological developments at home and a new social ideology reinforced by the ruling elite.

Trade across the Lower Sea. The author of the Sumerian legend *Enmerkar and the Lord of Aratta*, probably composed toward the end of the third millennium B.C.E. and preserved in copies from the early second millennium B.C.E., envisioned a period in history before the advent of long-distance trade. He described it as a time

> before the land of Dilmun yet existed . . . before commerce was practiced; before gold, silver, copper, tin, blocks of lapis lazuli, and mountain stone were brought down together from their mountains. (Black et al.)

The land of Dilmun, located in the Lower Sea (that is, the Persian Gulf), is generally identified with the island of Bahrain and the mainland opposite it on the Arabian Peninsula. Sumerian and Akkadian kings of the latter half of the third millennium B.C.E., whose economies were strongly centralized and dominated by temple and palace bureaucracies, wrote of how they exchanged Mesopotamian agricultural surpluses, textiles, and dairy products for such high-status luxury items as rare woods, ivory, semiprecious stones, and copper. Dilmun was not the producer of these goods but rather an entrepôt (a point of exchange), where goods from Mesopotamia were traded for exotica from Magan and Meluhha, lands further south along the Persian Gulf and beyond, perhaps as far away as the Indus Valley.

Magan. Magan is generally identified with the coastal regions of the Arabian Peninsula west and east of the Strait of Hormuz, across the present-day United Arab Emirates and Sultanate of Oman. During the third millennium B.C.E., Magan was the supplier to Mesopotamia of much-needed metals, stone, and exotic woods, either produced locally or trans-shipped from yet-further shores. Magan, the "land of copper," was probably the principal source of copper for the Sumerians. The Akkadian king Naram-Sin (circa 2254 – circa 2218 B.C.E.) and the city ruler of Lagash, Gudea (circa 2100 B.C.E.), both reported obtaining *esi*-stone, or diorite, from Magan for royal statuary. An Ur III (circa 2100 B.C.E.) text refers to an ivory tusk from Magan weighing 38 minas. Modern excavations in the region of ancient Magan have produced objects that are evidence of widespread contacts, including bronze objects made with tin that likely came from southern Afghanistan and an assortment of ivory and carved-stone objects, as well as ceramics, from Elam in southwest Iran, Bactria in central Asia, and Baluchistan and the Indus Valley in southern Asia. Mesopotamia appears to have lost direct contact with Magan at the end of the third millennium B.C.E.

Meluhha. In texts of the late third millennium B.C.E., Meluhha is called a land beyond Dilmun (Bahrain) and Magan (Oman). Meluhha was a source of gold, silver, exotic woods, and carnelian. Most scholars today agree that the sources of these materials in this period were the cities of the Harappan civilization in the Indus Valley of modern Pakistan and northwest India. Among the funerary deposits in the Royal Tombs of Ur (circa 2600 – circa 2500 B.C.E.) are many examples of distinctively Harappan exotica, including "etched" carnelian beads, long drilled biconical beads, and cosmetic containers made from seashells from the Arabian Sea or fashioned in gold and silver in the shapes of such shells.

Lapis Lazuli. As near as can be determined, all examples in the ancient Near East of lapis lazuli, the most highly prized of blue stones, originated in mines located in the Badakhshan district of modern Afghanistan, some 2,400 kilometers (1,500 miles) east of Mesopotamia. Examples of lapis lazuli are regularly reported from excavations of early fourth millennium B.C.E. sites in northern Mesopotamia; isolated earlier examples (late sixth millennium B.C.E.) have also been noted. The trade in lapis lazuli appears to have been interrupted early in the third millennium B.C.E. The resumption at the onset of the Early Dynastic II period (circa 2750 B.C.E.) may be marked in the epic of *Enmerkar and the Lord of Aratta*, in which Enmerkar, the ruler of Uruk, demands shipments of lapis lazuli, gold, and silver from the city of Aratta, presumably located nearer to the Badakhshan mines.

Carnelian. In ancient Mesopotamia, carnelian ranked second in popularity behind lapis lazuli as the stone of choice for manufacturing beads, amulets, and occasionally seals. In literature the two stones are often linked; in the *Epic of Gilgamesh* honey in a carnelian bowl and ghee (clarified butter) in a lapis-lazuli bowl are offered at daybreak to the sun god Shamash. Possible sources for carnelian included India, Iran, western Arabia, Oman, Anatolia, and Egypt. During the middle of the third millennium B.C.E.,

"Intercultural Style" cylindrical chlorite vessel with relief carving (diameter 7 inches), said to come from Khafaje, circa 2500 B.C.E. (British Museum, London)

the Indus Valley was the principal source of carnelian both as a raw material and in the form of finished beads. Among the most characteristic and widespread of the Indus-type beads from this period are long biconical beads drilled lengthwise for stringing and "etched" carnelian beads. To make an "etched" bead, linear or circular designs were painted on a bead with a bleaching agent; heating gave the carnelian a brilliant red color while the bleaching agent left behind a white surface design, perhaps intended to imitate naturally occurring eye designs on jasper. After long exposure to damp soils, the weakened stone in the bleached areas often fell out, leading early archaeologists to conclude mistakenly that the designs on the stones had been etched. Examples of bleached or "etched" carnelian beads, both Harappan exports and locally made imitations, have been excavated at mid to late third millennium B.C.E. sites in Central Asia, Iran, the Persian Gulf, and Mesopotamia. In jewelry from the Royal Graves at Ur (circa 2500 B.C.E.), long biconical carnelian beads and carnelian beads with bleached circular designs are often strung with gold beads and blue lapis-lazuli beads, creating a dramatic effect. The most westerly known examples of Harappan-style carnelian beads were recovered from a small jewelry hoard excavated from a late third millennium B.C.E. context on the island of Aegina, across from Piraeus, the port of Athens in Greece. In Mesopotamia during all periods, carnelian, as with all precious stones, was appreciated as much for its beauty as for its magical properties, which included protecting the wearer against paralysis of the right hand, hair loss, and black magic.

Base Metals. Mesopotamia lacks natural deposits of virtually every metal. Thus, metals found in Mesopotamia must have been imported, directly or indirectly, from a source elsewhere. Base metals were used to manufacture vessels, tools, and weapons at reasonable cost for more or less everyday use. Prior to the first millennium B.C.E., copper was the cheapest and most widely used metal in Mesopotamia. Foreign sources of copper included Oman, Iran, Anatolia, and Cyprus. During the late fourth and much of the third millennia B.C.E., copper with a high arsenic content was preferred because, when cast, it produces a beautiful silvery surface. By the end of the third millennium B.C.E., Mesopotamians were deliberately alloying copper with small amounts of tin to produce bronze. The tin they used probably originated in Afghanistan. Anatolia has also been suggested as a source for tin; however, the Assyrians of the early second millennium B.C.E. exported to Anatolia tin that they had previously purchased, presumably from Afghanistan via Iran. Anatolia did provide lead, a metal sought after for its softness and high density. Copper and bronze were largely replaced by iron during the first millennium B.C.E. Early modern studies suggested that the first iron used was meteoric in origin, but this view has come under considerable scrutiny of late. Iron ores occur widely in the lands surrounding Mesopotamia, but Anatolian sources seem to have been of greatest significance.

Precious Metals. Gold was imported into Mesopotamia in the form of nuggets, prepared as a powder, and cast in ingots. Cuneiform texts referring to the importation of gold rarely distinguish where the gold was mined from where it was trans-shipped to Mesopotamia. At different times in the history of ancient Mesopotamia, gold might have originated in Iran, Afghanistan, Anatolia, Egypt, or Nubia. Most silver in the ancient Near East was produced from ores mined in Anatolia; other sources include Iran and Egypt. Precious metals were also imported in the form of manufactured objects including all sorts of jewelry, vessels, and utensils. Such objects might also be made of electrum, an alloy of gold and silver that was both naturally occurring and man-made and is often difficult to distinguish from other, more-pure forms of gold.

The "Intercultural Style." Excavations at more than a dozen Mesopotamian sites—predominantly in the south but also at Mari on the middle Euphrates in Syria—have revealed imported carved-stone vessels and handled "weights" made of a soft greenish stone often identified as chlorite or steatite. These objects, which have been dated to the middle and latter half of the third millennium B.C.E., share a distinctive foreign style of carved decoration. The motifs rendered in this style include anthropomorphic figures with a characteristic physiognomy, snakes, felines, humped bulls, birds, scorpions, palm trees, and such geometric patterns as rosettes, mat weaves, and a running wavy pattern termed a "guilloche." Often the bodies of the figures show dense patterns of drill holes that were originally inlaid with other brightly colored stones. Obviously related pieces have also been discovered at sites along the Arabian coast of the Persian Gulf, and in southern Iran, Central Asia, and the Indus Valley. Two sites have been positively identified as places of manufacture, each located close to a local source of the raw material: the island of Tarut in the Persian Gulf near the modern Arabian city of Qatif and Tepe Yahya in south central Iran.

The "International Period." Cuneiform tablets belonging to a royal archive were excavated at Amarna in Egypt, the site of the capital city of Akhetaten, home

---

LETTERS FROM THE KING OF BABYLONIA

Among the nearly four hundred cuneiform tablets found in the Egyptian royal archives at Amarna (ancient Akhetaten) are records detailing the sometimes-lavish diplomatic gifts that the "great kings" gave each other. Some half dozen letters were exchanged between the Kassite Babylonian king Burna-Buriash II (circa 1359 – circa 1333 B.C.E.) and the Egyptian kings Amenophis III (circa 1390 – circa 1352 B.C.E.) and his successor Amenophis IV, better known as Akhenaten (circa 1352 – circa 1336 B.C.E.). Though these kings call each other "brother," the tone of the letters is at times anything but cordial, as in this letter from Burna-Buriash:

Because I (Burna-Buriash) was told the road is dangerous, the water is cut off, and the weather is hot, I did not send you (Akhenaten) many fine gifts. (Now) I have sent 4 minas (about 2 kilograms, or 4 pounds) of fine lapis lazuli as a gift to my brother, and I have sent five teams of horses to my brother. When the weather is good, future messengers who come will bring many fine gifts to my brother.... I have taken up a task and thus I wrote to my brother. Let my brother send me much fine gold so that I may use it for my task! And as for the gold that my brother sends, my brother must not leave it to any official. Let my brother's eyes inspect (it) and let my brother seal (it) and send (it) to me! As for the previous gold that my brother sent me—as if my brother did not inspect (it), just an official of my brother

sealed (it) and sent (it) to me—when I placed the 40 minas of gold which were brought to me in a kiln nothing *of value*(?) came out. (translated by author)

In response to the Babylonian king's letter, Akhenaten must have sent some gold, but obviously not in the quantity expected. Burna-Buriash complained bitterly:

Because my forefathers and your forefathers communicated in friendship, they sent fine gifts to each other and they did not withhold from each other (any) friendly request. Now, my brother has sent me 2 minas of gold as my gift. But now, (if) there is much gold, send me as much as your forefathers (sent)! But if there is scant gold send me half as much as your forefathers! Why did you send me (only) 2 minas of gold? Now my task I have undertaken and am carrying out in the temple is very great: Send me much gold! And as for you, anything you desire in my land, write me and it shall be brought to you! (translated by author)

Another tablet in the Amarna archive itemizes in more than three hundred lines of text quantities of objects made of gold, silver, and bronze, as well as textiles, stone vessels, and elephant ivory, sent to Burna-Buriash by Akhenaten. Unfortunately, none of the tablets in the Amarna archive is dated, so it is difficult to know whether this gift preceded or was in response to Burna-Buriash's many complaints.

Source: J. A. Knudtzon, *Die El-Amarna-Tafeln*, Vorderasiatische Bibliotek 2, 2 volumes (Leipzig, 1915).

Spouted gold cup (height 4 7/8 inches) found in Pu-abi's tomb at Ur; and part of a Tridacna shell carved in the form of a woman's head (height 2 1/2 inches), from Nimrud, circa ninth–eighth centuries B.C.E. (top: University of Pennsylvania Museum of Archaeology and Anthropology; bottom: British Museum, London)

to the late Eighteenth Dynasty king Akhenaten (circa 1364 – circa 1352 B.C.E.) and his wife, Nefertiti. The tablets record the direct correspondence between several Eighteenth Dynasty kings from circa the fourteenth century B.C.E. and their royal counterparts in Assyria, Babylonia, Mitanni, and Hittite Anatolia, as well as local princes in the Levant, Syria, and Cyprus. Several of the tablets itemize lavish exchanges of gifts by which the Egyptian and foreign kings demonstrated their wealth and power to each other. The items they exchanged might include ingots of gold, silver, and copper; a wide variety of precious stones and utensils made of gold, silver, or bronze; vessels filled with rare oils; and furniture made of rare woods, perhaps embellished with gold and ivory. A shipwreck found off the coast of Turkey, near Uluburun, demonstrates that, just a half century later (circa 1300 B.C.E.), international trade throughout the eastern Mediterranean basin continued to thrive. Perhaps a royal merchant ship, it carried some ten tons of copper ingots and about one ton of tin, the ingredients for making bronze. Other raw materials found in this shipwreck included ingots of glass, jars of terebinth resin, hippopotamus teeth, an elephant's tusk, ostrich eggshells, and ebony logs. The ship also carried a range of finished goods in smaller quantities, including storage jars packed with pottery from Cyprus, copper vessels, containers made of wood and ivory, glass beads, faience beads and drinking cups, and seashell rings. Among the personal effects of the crew were Mycenaean Greek weapons, pottery, seals, and jewelry. The variety of goods suggests that the ship made regular calls at ports throughout the eastern Mediterranean in Egypt, the Levantine coast, Syria, the Turkish coast, Cyprus, Crete, and Greece.

Carved Ivory. Throughout the ancient Near East, a variety of objects, including beads, seals, sculpture, and inlays for sculpture and furniture, were carved from ivory. A large artistic industry based on carved hippopotamus ivory was centered in the Levant during the third and second millennia B.C.E. Always produced for the luxury trade, carved-ivory objects might be inlaid with semiprecious stones and overlaid with gold leaf. During the first half of the first millennium B.C.E., elephant ivory became available to craftsmen in Syria and Phoenicia; whether this ivory was from some soon-to-become-extinct Syrian elephant or was imported from India or Africa remains unclear. Vast quantities of Syrian, Phoenician, and locally made carved-ivory decorations for chairs, footstools, and beds were discovered in the ruins of the Assyrian capital city of Kalhu. The various Syrian and Phoenician styles are readily distinguished from each other, but the respective artisans often relied on a similar pool of motifs, including sphinxes, griffins, heroic figures wearing Egyptian-like costumes and crowns, and various floral elements. As a general rule, the Phoenician carvings are slightly later in date (mid eighth through seventh centuries B.C.E.) and somewhat more "Egyptianizing" than the Syrian (ninth through mid eighth centuries B.C.E.). The imported material, both in the form of raw tusks and finished works, was likely shipped to Assyria as gifts and tribute or as booty seized by the Assyrians from their western neighbors. During the fifth and fourth centuries B.C.E., ivory from Ethiopia and the Indus Valley was worked by artisans in Lydia in western Anatolia and in Egypt, from which it reached the capitals of the Persian Empire.

Carved *Tridacna* Shells. Engraved shells made from the *Tridacna*, an Indo-Pacific giant clam, have been found at such Mesopotamian cities as Kalhu, Ashur, Babylon, and Uruk, in levels dating from the late seventh to the early sixth century B.C.E. During the eighth and seventh centuries B.C.E. the shells, obtained from the Red Sea, were incised with decorations on the back and interior perimeter by Phoenician craftsmen and were probably used as containers for cosmetics. The incised scenes depict natural and fantastic animals set among floral designs. The *umbo*—the tip of the valve hinge—was carved into the shape of the head of a human female or a bird. Although most commonly found throughout the Levant, carved *Tridacna* shells have been excavated from as far west as Vulci in Etruria, Italy, and at the Greek colony at Cyrene in Libya, to as far east as Susa in southwestern Iran.

Sources:

Robert J. Braidwood, *Prehistoric Men*, eighth edition (Glenview, Ill.: Scott, Foresman, 1975).

Paul Collins, *The Uruk Phenomenon: The role of social ideology in the expansion of the Uruk culture during the fourth millennium BC*, BAR International Series 900 (Oxford: Archaeopress, 2000).

C. C. Lamberg-Karlovsky, "The Archaeological Evidence for International Commerce: Public and/or Private Enterprise in Mesopotamia?" in *Privatization in the Ancient Near East and Classical World*, edited by Michael Hudson and Baruch A. Levine, Peabody Museum Bulletin, 5 (Cambridge, Mass.: Peabody Museum of Archaeology and Ethnology, Harvard University, 1996), pp. 73–97.

P. R. S. Moorey, *Ancient Mesopotamian Materials and Industries: The Archaeological Evidence* (Winona Lake, Ind.: Eisenbrauns, 1999).

D. T. Potts, "The Gulf: Dilmun and Magan," in *Art of the First Cities: The Third Millennium B.C. from the Mediterranean to the Indus*, edited by Joan Aruz with Ronald Wallenfels (New York: Metropolitan Museum of Art, 2003), pp. 307–308.

Cemal Pulak, "The Cargo of the Uluburun Ship and Evidence for Trade with the Aegean and Beyond," in *Italy and Cyprus in Antiquity: 1500–450 BC: Proceedings of an International Symposium held at the Italian Academy for Advanced Studies in America at Columbia University November 16–18, 2000*, edited by Larissa Bonfante and Vassos Karageorghis (Nicosia: Costakis and Leto Severis Foundation, 2001), pp. 13–60.

Rolf A. Stucky, *The Engraved Tridacna Shells*, Dédalo 19 (São Paulo: Museo de Arqueologia e Etnologia, Universidade de São Paulo, 1974).

Irene J. Winter, "Phoenician and North Syrian Ivory Carving in Historical Context: Questions of Style and Distribution," *Iraq*, 38 (1976): 1–22.

GATES AND DOORS

City Walls. By the end of the fourth millennium B.C.E. defensive walls were a regular feature of Mesopotamian cities. Immediately flanking the right (west) bank of the Euphrates in north Syria, the Late Uruk period (circa 3300 – circa 3000 B.C.E.) site at Habuba Kabira (south) was a well-planned rectangular city enclosed on its three exposed sides by rectilinear sun-dried mud-brick walls. Along the length of the walls, which were about 3 meters (10 feet) thick, were nearly fifty protruding square defensive towers; two gates set among the defensive towers along the western wall provided overland entry into the city, which was otherwise accessible only from the river. During the Early Dynastic I period (circa 2900 – circa 2750 B.C.E.) the wall enclosing Uruk, a city in southern Mesopotamia some thirty times the size of Habuba Kabira, was 9.5 kilometers (6 miles) long. Tradition, as preserved in the late second millennium B.C.E. composition *The Epic of Gilgamesh*, attributed the construction of the walls of Uruk to Gilgamesh, the legendary king of Uruk. Twice the narrator exhorts the listener/reader of the tale to "climb up onto the walls of Uruk and walk about, examine the foundation and inspect the brickwork," and see firsthand "if the brickwork is not kiln-fired brick." When Nebuchadnezzar II (604–562 B.C.E.) rebuilt Babylon, he completed the task begun by his father, Nabopolassar (625–605 B.C.E.), of surrounding the more or less rectangular city center—with its palaces, temples, and ziggurat—with a double wall more than 8 kilometers (5 miles) in length. Made of sun-dried mud brick, the outer wall—named *Nemitti-Enlil*, "(the god) Enlil is my support"—was almost 4 meters (13 feet) thick, while the inner wall—*Imgur-Enlil*, "(the god) Enlil granted (my prayer)"—was 6.5 meters (21.5 feet) thick. A road more than 7 meters (23 feet) wide ran between the walls, while beyond the outer wall, across a 20-meter-wide (66 feet) berm, lay a moat, 50 meters (165 feet) wide, connected at both ends to the Euphrates. The city at large lay behind another, outer ring of three walls, supplemented by a wide moat that stretched for 18 kilometers (11 miles). Nebuchadnezzar bragged that no arrow fired

---

THE CAPTURE OF BABYLON

The historian Herodotus, writing in Greek in the mid-fifth century B.C.E., recalled that when the Babylonians learned of the preparations by the Persian king Cyrus II to march on Babylon, they took to the field, attacked him, were defeated, and were forced to retire behind their defenses. However, they had taken the precaution of accumulating in Babylon a stock of provisions sufficient to last many years, and, in light of the city's massive defenses, they regarded the prospect of siege with indifference. But the Persians devised and executed a plan to take advantage of the city's fortifications, taking into account the fact that the Euphrates ran directly through the heart of the inner city:

Then somebody suggested or he (Cyrus) himself thought up the following plan: he stationed part of his force at the point where the Euphrates flows into the city and another contingent at the opposite end where it flows out, with orders to force an entrance along the river bed as soon as they saw that the water was shallow enough. Then, taking with him all his noncombatant troops, he withdrew to the spot where (the mythical Babylonian queen) Nitocris had excavated the lake, and proceeded to repeat the operation which the queen had previously performed: by means of a cutting he diverted the river into the lake—which was then a marsh—and in this way so greatly reduced the depth of water in the actual bed of the river that it became fordable, and the Persian army, which had been left at Babylon for the purpose, entered the river, now only deep enough to reach about the middle of a man's thigh, and, making their way along it, got into the town. If the Babylonians had learned what Cyrus was doing or had seen it for themselves in time, they could have let the Persians enter and then, by shutting all the gates which led to the waterside and manning the walls on either side of the river, they could have caught them in a trap and wiped them out. But as it was they were taken by surprise. The Babylonians themselves say that owing to the great size of the city the outskirts were captured without the people in the center knowing anything about it; there was a festival going on, and they continued to dance and enjoy themselves, until they learned the news the hard way.

In a cuneiform inscription on a clay cylinder from Babylon, Cyrus attributed his victory to the Babylonian god Marduk, who had chosen the Persian king after having searched for a righteous ruler to replace the last native Babylonian king, Nabonidus (555–539 B.C.E.):

Marduk, the great Lord, protector of his people, beheld with pleasure his (Cyrus') good deeds and his (Cyrus') upright heart, (and therefore) ordered him to march against his city Babylon. He made him set out on the road to Babylon going at his side like a real friend. His widespread troops—and number, like that of the water of a river, could not be established—strolled along, their weapons packed away. Without any battle, he made him enter his town Babylon, sparing Babylon any calamity. (Oppenheim)

Sources: Herodotus, *The Histories*, translated by Aubrey de Sélincourt, revised, with an introduction and notes, by A. R. Burn (Harmondsworth, U.K.: Penguin, 1954).

A. Leo Oppenheim, "Babylonian and Assyrian Historical Texts," in *Ancient Near Eastern Texts Relating to the Old Testament*, edited by James Bennett Pritchard, third edition with supplement (Princeton: Princeton University Press, 1969), pp. 265–317.

Bronze bands, originally numbering eight on a side, ornamenting the now-decomposed cedar doors of the gate to the palace of Shalmaneser III (858–824 B.C.E.) at Balawat (ancient Imgur-Enlil). Each band (approximately 10½ inches wide and 71 inches long) bears two registers of repoussé scenes (reliefs hammered from the back), with cuneiform captions, from military campaigns during the king's first ten years on the throne (British Museum, London).

from the outer wall could reach the inner defensive walls.

City Gates. People and goods had to be able to enter and leave a walled city. Under ordinary conditions and during times of siege, individuals could move in and out of the city through posterns, small, usually hidden, entrances to narrow, easily blocked tunnels through or beneath a city's walls. Yet, providing access for animal herds, transport vehicles, royal and religious processions, and, in wartime, large numbers of soldiers and their equipment demanded a substantially larger opening in the wall. City walls of stone and mud brick provided the best protection by being built as massively thick and tall as reasonably possible. However, a gate large enough to accommodate potentially large volumes of traffic and light enough to be opened and closed rapidly—even if it could be locked quickly and securely—created an inherent weakness in the defensive system and invariably became the focus of would-be attackers. Ancient-city planners faced the problem of how to build a strong, secure city gate that could provide necessary access yet withstand enemy attack. For large cities with long walls, the problem was compounded by the need for many gates distributed widely around the city. For example, the walls

of the seventh century B.C.E. Assyrian city of Nineveh were 12 kilometers (7.5 miles) long, necessitating the construction of fifteen gates. During the more than three thousand years of ancient Mesopotamian history prior to the Macedonian conquest (331 B.C.E.), a common solution developed, although with considerable differences in details of design and construction: a heavily fortified gatehouse variously straddling the city wall was located between a pair of defensive towers projecting from the wall. Set within the gatehouse, the main gate itself typically consisted of a pair of solid wooden doors heavily clad in thick metal sheets or bands. The doors, pivoting inward, were hung on gateposts, often capped with

metal, set between a stone threshold and a stone or wooden lintel. A heavy wooden or metal bolt secured the door leaves from within. The overall intention was to create a space that left an attacker as little opportunity as possible to approach the gate, or—failing that—to offer him as little room as possible to maneuver under cover when close to the gate, all the while allowing the defenders the greatest possible latitude to defend the doors and repel the assailants. The Ishtar Gate was the most spectacular of the nine city gates constructed at Babylon by Nebuchadnezzar II (604–562 B.C.E.). It was a double gate, reinforced with bastions, traversing the 17.5-meter-wide (58 feet) twin defensive walls that surrounded the

Detail of a modern reconstruction of the Ishtar Gate (height 47 feet), built by Nebuchadnezzar II (604–562 B.C.E.) as the principal entrance into Babylon. As with the original, the molded mud-brick core is clad in deep-blue glazed brick with alternating yellow and white striding serpo-dragons and bulls modeled in low relief (Vorderasiatisches Museum, Berlin).

CITY WALLS AND GATES IN OMENS

The Mesopotamians believed that the gods offered mankind omens, signs foretelling possible future events. Scattered throughout the omen series *Shumma alu ina mele shakin* ("If a city is set on a height"), one of the largest collections of unsolicited omens and their portended outcomes, are several that concern the fortification walls and main gate of a city.

[If a city]'s dump grows bishopweed, an enemy will surround that city's gate.

If an owl makes a nest in a hole in a city gate and fire spontaneously consumes the (temple) Bit Apsi—destruction of (the city of) Eridu.

If the parapet of a fortification-wall looks [like a monkey (but) you climb up the wall and] it is normal—destruction of (the city of) Nippur.

If the latch-hook of (all) the doors of the goddess's temple is persistently sticking, an enemy will approach the front of the city gate and cattle [. . .]

If the latch-hook of the goddess's temple has been lifted and changed position and latched, an enemy will [. . .] the city gate.

If lichen [. . .] on a city wall—dispersal of the city.

If lichen [. . .] on the city gate, that city gate will be closed.

If lichen is seen in the temple [. . .], that city's gate will be seized but not locked.

If a mongoose gives birth in the lower courses of the city gate—dispersal of the city.

If there are ants in the entrance to the city gate—restriction of access.

If a wild ox is seen in front of the city gate, an enemy will surround the city.

If bitches bark in the city gate, there will be pestilence in the land.

Source: S. M. Freedman, *If a City is Set on a Height: The Akkadian Omen Series Summa Alu ina Mêlê Šakin*, volume 1: Tablets 1–21, Occasional Publications of the Samuel Noah Kramer Fund, 17 (Philadelphia: University of Pennsylvania Museum, 1998).

central city. In its final form, this monumental gateway rose perhaps more than 23 meters (76 feet) in height and was clad in molded blue-glazed bricks decorated with dozens of striding bulls and long-necked dragons, symbols of the gods Adad and Marduk, respectively.

The City Gate as a Significant Public Space. In the epilogue to a late third millennium B.C.E. Sumerian-language law compilation, perhaps the end of the Laws of Ur-Namma (circa 2112 – circa 2095 B.C.E.), the curse on any despoiler of the inscription wishes, "May his city be a city despised by the god Enlil; may the main gate of his city be left open . . . ," that is, undefended. The city gate was significant in early second millennium B.C.E. laws concerning slavery: according to the laws of the city

of Eshnunna, slaves might not leave through the city gate without their owner (LE § 51), while a slave brought into the city would be kept safe for his or her owner (LE § 52). Hammurabi's laws (circa 1750 B.C.E.) imposed the death penalty on anyone allowing a slave to escape though the main city gate (LH § 15). Mesopotamian texts suggest that the area near a large city gate was a place for business. The gatekeeper collected taxes from merchants as they entered or left the city. Required to have witnesses for the validity of any transaction, businessmen could either bring their own to the gate or seek them from among the citizens present near the gate at the time. If it were required that a given transaction be recorded, scribes were also available at the gate. Judges might sit in the gate and hear grievances or take note of comings and goings. The area near a city gate also served for public proclamations and for the public display of the punishment of criminals.

Doors. An individual home might have a door made of woven reeds, or the door of a wealthier family might be made of wooden planks equipped with metal hardware. When a home with such a wooden door was sold, because its cost was not trivial, the contract might include specific clauses as to whether the door and its hardware would be removed from the house or remain with it.

Entrance Guardians. In addition to serving as a physical means of permitting or preventing communication between "inside" and "outside," gates and doors, by their nature as zones of transition, also required magical means of protection. Such liminal zones were envisioned by the Mesopotamians as magical boundaries across which spirits could pass into the everyday world. To combat such potential evil, magical apotropaic figurines might be buried beneath the doorway; pure barley flour might be sprinkled in front of the doorway; or clay plaques depicting scenes of sexual intercourse might be placed on the doorjamb. Entranceways to or within temples and palaces might be flanked by figures carved in the round or in relief. Gates and doors in first millennium B.C.E. Assyrian walls and palaces were guarded against evil by colossal human-headed bulls and human-headed lions that gazed with quiet strength at any who approached, and by winged genii posed as exorcists with bucket and sprinkler in hand blessing all who passed by. In Syria and the Levant, pairs of lions in the round, with jaws threateningly agape, were favored to protect temple and palace entrances. Further north, in the Hittite regions of north Syria and Anatolia, anthropomorphic deities in the round or in high relief often stood guard.

Sources:

Julia Assante, "Sex, Magic and the Liminal Body in the Erotic Art and Texts of the Old Babylonian Period," in *Sex and Gender in the Ancient Near East. Proceedings of the 47th Rencontre Assyriologique International Helsinki, July 2–6, 2001*, part 1, edited by Simo Parpola and Robert M.

Whiting (Helsinki: Neo-Assyrian Text Corpus Project, 2002), pp. 27–52.

Kay Kohlmeyer, "Habuba Kabira," in *The Oxford Encyclopedia of Archaeology in the Near East*, 5 volumes, edited by Eric M. Meyers (New York & Oxford: Oxford University Press, 1997), II: 446–448.

Amihai Mazar, "The Fortification of Cities in the Ancient Near East," in *Civilizations of the Ancient Near East*, 4 volumes, edited by Jack M. Sasson (New York: Scribners, 1995), III: 1523–1537.

Joan Oates, *Babylon* (London: Thames & Hudson, 1979).

Martha T. Roth, *Law Collections from Mesopotamia and Asia Minor*, second edition, Society of Biblical Literature, Writings from the Ancient World Series, volume 6 (Atlanta: Scholars Press, 1995).

Yigael Yadin, *The Art of Warfare in Biblical Lands in the Light of Archaeological Study*, 2 volumes, translated by M. Pearlman (New York, Toronto & London: McGraw-Hill, 1963).

LANGUAGES

Sumerian. It is most convenient to describe the peoples of Mesopotamia and the surrounding regions ethnolinguistically, that is, in terms of the group affinities they assigned both to themselves and to each other and the languages they spoke. Throughout much of the third millennium B.C.E., the Sumerians formed the dominant group among the population of southern Mesopotamia. Whence they came and when they entered Mesopotamia are much-debated questions to which there are at present no satisfactory answers. The language they spoke, Sumerian, is the oldest language for which there is evidence in the cuneiform writing system, which was developed in southern Mesopotamia toward the end of the fourth millennium B.C.E., not for the purpose of recording spoken language but rather for accounting and bookkeeping. The earliest texts are logographic, that is, each sign whether realistic or abstract in shape represents a whole word, and, in theory, can be read by a speaker of any language. Scholars continue to debate whether or not these earliest texts were in fact written by Sumerian speakers. Also debated is the process by which the writing system was adapted to convey spoken Sumerian through the representation of phonetic elements. Nonetheless, texts written by the mid-third millennium B.C.E. are unequivocally in Sumerian. A Sumerian-language poem set at the transition to Early Dynastic II times (circa 2750 B.C.E.), although composed many centuries later, attributes the first use of cuneiform to convey spoken language to the legendary Enmerkar, king of Uruk, during his protracted negotiations with the ruler of Aratta, a perhaps fabulous kingdom far to the east. Sumerian is a language isolate; that is, it shows no close affinities to any other known language, living or dead. Typologically, Sumerian is an ergative language, one in which the subjects of transitive and intransitive verbs bear distinctive case markers. It is also characterized as an agglutinative language, one in which strings of monosyllabic prefixes and suffixes (affixes) are attached to simple fixed bases serving as both verbs and nouns. Unlike Semitic and Indo-European languages, verbal and nominal bases in Sumerian are distinguishable only through syntax and the uses of different affixes. Two main dialects are known: Emegir, the main literary dialect, and Emesal, apparently reserved for a special group of priests and for direct speech among women or goddesses in literary texts. Sumerian appears to have ceased to be a living language by the beginning of the second millennium B.C.E., although as a didactic tool it remained the center of the school curriculum until the very end of the cuneiform writing tradition in the first centuries C.E.

Akkadian. Akkadian is generally acknowledged to be the earliest attested member of the Semitic family of languages, whose modern members include Arabic and Hebrew. Akkadian is an inflected language with three distinct verbal "tenses" conjugated for number and gender. Its nouns and adjectives are declined for number, gender, and case. During the more than two and a half thousand years for which there is evidence of its use, several distinct dialects of Akkadian appeared. Old Akkadian was the dialect of the texts associated with the empire ruled by the kings of Akkad (Agade), circa 2340 – circa 2200 B.C.E. During the Ur III period (circa 2112 B.C.E. – circa 2004 B.C.E.), the scribes returned to the use of Sumerian for royal inscriptions and administrative and legal documents. Nonetheless, there is some evidence during the Ur III period for a southern dialect of Akkadian akin to Old Babylonian, which became the pre-eminent dialect during the early second millennium B.C.E. In northern Mesopotamia, the Old Assyrian dialect is first observed in the tablets of the Assyrian merchant colonies. During the second half of the second millennium B.C.E., the Middle Babylonian dialect became the language of international communication, perhaps most extensively employed during the so-called International Period in the fourteenth century B.C.E., when Babylonian and Assyrian rulers—as well as those of the Hurrians, Syrians, Cypriots, and Canaanites—corresponded with the Egyptian kings of the latter part of the Eighteenth Dynasty. In some cases the local scribes, especially among the Canaanites, seem not to have been too well trained and wrote in distinctive mixtures of Akkadian and the local dialect. During the same period appeared Standard Babylonian, a purely literary dialect in which the Mesopotamian scribes attempted to reproduce the older, more-classical form of the language. Neo-Assyrian and Neo-Babylonian dialects evolved in the early first millennium B.C.E. but declined rapidly as spoken languages in the face of the spread of Aramaic, the Semitic language originally spoken in Syria. In the latter half of the first millennium B.C.E. Late Babylonian, used in royal inscriptions and legal and administrative texts, was almost certainly not spoken beyond a restricted circle of traditionally educated "priestly" scribes.

Hurrian and Urartian. The Hurrians began to appear in cuneiform references about 2400 B.C.E. These speakers of a non-Semitic, non-Indo-European language—perhaps related to those of the modern northeast Caucasus region—lived above the northern border of Mesopotamia in a broad area called *Subartu* in Akkadian and *Subir* in Sumerian. Their political power reached its zenith in the fifteenth and fourteenth centuries B.C.E. with the formation of the powerful kingdom of Mitanni, whose rulers were "great kings" on a par with their contemporary Egyptian, Hittite, Babylonian, and Assyrian counterparts. The capital city of Washukkani remains lost; hence, comparatively few Hurrian texts have been recovered. Nonetheless, cuneiform texts composed in Hurrian have been found in Egypt, throughout Syria, and in Anatolia. At the site of the ancient city of Nuzi on the periphery of northeast Mesopotamia, texts written in the Middle Babylonian dialect are mixed with Hurrian idiosyncrasies and filled with Hurrian personal names. In the thirteenth century B.C.E. the Assyrians established control in the region. During the first millennium B.C.E. the state of Urartu, whose rulers spoke a language closely akin to Hurrian, arose in the region from the upper Euphrates to Lake Van and Lake Urmia. For two centuries beginning in the ninth century B.C.E., the Urartians rivaled the Assyrians for dominance in the region, but by the end of the sixth century B.C.E., they had disappeared into obscurity, all their cities put to the torch.

Eblaite. The excavation of the archives at the site of ancient Ebla (modern Tell Mardikh) in north Syria brought to light several thousand cuneiform texts from circa 2400 – circa 2250 B.C.E., many written in a previously unknown Semitic language, which vies with Akkadian to be the oldest documented Semitic language. The majority opinion among scholars holds that the language spoken by the Eblaites was an archaic West Semitic dialect. (Later West Semitic dialects include Amorite, Hebrew, Phoenician, Aramaic, and Arabic.) However, a not insignificant minority of scholars holds that the Eblaite language is more akin to the East Semitic family, whose otherwise sole known member is Akkadian.

Amorite. Many of the rulers of the early second millennium B.C.E. Isin, Larsa, Old Assyrian, and Old Babylonian dynasties—and their contemporaries throughout Syria—bore names that, although Semitic, are not Akkadian. They represent one of the most important immigrant groups in the history of Mesopotamia, the Amorites. These tribes of pastoralists, ruled by chiefs, entered Mesopotamia from Syria (Akkadian *amurru* means "west") perhaps as a result of the deteriorating climate in the north at the end of the third millennium B.C.E. and the concomitant political weakness in the south. Gradually but systematically Mesopotamian cities were overrun by Amorites, who in their turn became completely assimilated into Mesopotamian urban cultural traditions. No texts have been identified as having been written in Amorite, although in the Akkadian-language texts from Mari in Syria, there are many West Semitic idiosyncrasies. The dialects of this language are known only through the analysis of the large corpus of personal names—some six thousand—preserved in late third and early second millennium B.C.E. cuneiform inscriptions.

Aramaic. A member of the West Semitic branch of the Semitic languages, Aramaic was originally spoken by the inhabitants of Syria who can be identified in Assyrian texts from as early as the end of the second millennium B.C.E. Vast numbers of Aramaean speakers, into the hundreds of thousands, became widely dispersed throughout Mesopotamia as a result of the policies of mass deportation implemented by conquering Assyrian armies during the first quarter of the first millennium B.C.E. The Aramaean deportees brought with them not only their language but also the simple twenty-two-character Levantine writing system, the *aleph-beth*, typically written in ink on papyrus, prepared animal skins, or pottery fragments *(ostraca)*. Together, Aramaic and the aleph-beth contributed significantly to the eventual extinction of both spoken Akkadian and the cuneiform writing system. During the reign of the Persian empire (539–331 B.C.E.) Aramaic became the most widely used imperial administrative language. Dialects of Aramaic survive to this day in isolated pockets of modern Iraq, Turkey, and Iran.

Arabic. The term *Arab* was used during the first millennium B.C.E. to describe the nomadic Semitic-speaking peoples of the Syro-Arabian desert, who were best known for their trade in aromatic resins and their use of camels. Early Mesopotamian evidence for the dialects of these peoples is found among a few personal names and town names recorded in Assyrian annals of the ninth through seventh centuries B.C.E. and in inscriptions written in the South Arabic script found at Ur and Nippur and dated to the seventh century B.C.E.

Other Mesopotamian Languages. Both Sumerian and Akkadian show evidence of having borrowed vocabulary, including place-names from one or more earlier and otherwise unknown languages in the region. Several Mesopotamian ethnolinguistic groups are known only from references to them in cuneiform texts or from personal names of members of these groups. The *Sumerian King List* records the names of twenty-one Guti kings, barbarian raiders from the Zagros Mountains, who were said to have brought about the final destruction of the Akkadian empire, circa 2200 B.C.E. Less than a century later, the last Guti king was defeated in battle by king Utu-hengal of Uruk; the Gutians were expelled shortly thereafter by king Ur-Namma of Ur (circa 2112 – circa 2095 B.C.E.). Another group, the Kassites, also appears to have entered Mesopotamia from the Zagros, this time filling the political vacuum created by the collapse of the First Dynasty of Babylon following a devastating Hittite raid on Babylon, circa 1595 B.C.E. The Kassites remained and established the longest-lived dynasty in Mesopotamia, some four hundred forty years in the conventional chronology, during which time they became, like the Amorites before them, thoroughly assimilated into Mesopotamian urban cultural traditions. And like that of the Amorites, their language is known only from the study of their personal names.

Iranian Languages. Beginning at the end of the fourth millennium B.C.E., a distinctive urban culture, termed "Proto-Elamite," arose immediately to the east of Sumer, centered on the city of Susa on the lowland plains of Khuzestan in southwest Iran. No doubt stimulated by their Sumerian neighbors, they developed a distinctive logographic writing system, which—along with other Proto-Elamite urban cultural notions—spread eastward across much of the Iranian plateau during the third millennium B.C.E. Toward the end of that millennium, the complex script was simplified, only to be abandoned and replaced by Old Akkadian–style cuneiform, permitting for the first time a vocalization of the Elamite language—yet another language isolate with no known cognates, ancient or modern. Cuneiform Elamite texts have been recovered only for sporadic intervals throughout the second and first millennia B.C.E. During the early first millennium B.C.E. western Iran was increasingly dominated by Indo-Aryan peoples, foremost among them the Medes, who partook of the destruction of the Assyrians at the end of the seventh century B.C.E. The Medes, whose power may have briefly extended into central Anatolia, were, in turn, overthrown by another Indo-Aryan group, the Persians, who went on to forge the greatest empire to date, stretching from Egypt and southeast Europe to western India. Both the Medes and the Persians spoke Indo-European languages; modern descendants of this group include all of the Romance, Germanic, Slavic, and Celtic languages of modern Europe, as well as Greek, Farsi in Iran, and Hindi in India. The Persians devised a unique cuneiform syllabary to render their Old Persian dialect alongside Akkadian and a late dialect of Elamite in trilingual display inscriptions on royal monuments of the sixth through fourth centuries B.C.E.

Anatolian Languages. The cuneiform archives found at Boghazköy (ancient Hattusa) in central Anatolia, dating to the second half of the second millennium B.C.E., contain writings in three different Indo-European languages: Hittite, Palaic, and Luwian. These texts also include evidence of Hattic, an older agglutinative language isolate. In addition to their use of cuneiform, the Hittites developed their own system of hieroglyphics, which they used on monumental reliefs and seals. Hittite hieroglyphic survived the destruction of the Hittite capital, circa 1200 B.C.E., and was used by Luwian speakers in southern Anatolia and the former Hittite vassal states in north Syria until the expansion of the Assyrian Empire into the region. In central Anatolia, the Phrygians eventually rose to dominance and rendered their distinct Indo-European language in an alphabetic script related to that of Greek. In the latter half of the first millennium B.C.E. several Indo-European lan-

guages—including Lycian, Lydian, and Carian—were spoken in western Anatolia and were written in various alphabets either similar to or directly derived from Greek.

Greek. Through the conquests of Alexander III (the Great) of Macedon and his successors toward the end of the fourth century B.C.E., the Greek language—a distinct branch of the Indo-European language family—and its associated alphabet were exported and established from southeastern Europe and Egypt in the west, across Anatolia, Mesopotamia, and Iran, to as far east as northwest India. The new dialect, termed the *koine glossa* ("common tongue"), was a simplified form of Attic, the standard dialect of the philosophers and orators. The *koine glossa* had been established by Alexander's father, Philip II (359–336 B.C.E.), as the official dialect of his court at Pella in Macedon. The impact of Greek in Mesopotamia in the last three centuries B.C.E. and the first two or three centuries C.E. was varied. On the one hand, among the several thousand individuals named in hundreds of surviving cuneiform archival documents from the period, only a handful appear to be native Babylonians who adopted Greek personal names. On the other hand, the lexical lists used to teach Sumerian and Akkadian cuneiform in the few remaining traditional Mesopotamian temple scribal schools often bear alphabetic Greek transliterations of the Sumerian and Akkadian cuneiform texts, better enabling the students to learn the pronunciation of these two extinct languages and their soon-to-be-extinct writing system.

Sources:

Israel Eph'al, *The Ancient Arabs: Nomads on the Borders of the Fertile Crescent 9th–5th Centuries B.C.* (Jerusalem: Magnes Press, Hebrew University / Leiden: Brill, 1982).

Ignace J. Gelb, *Computer-Aided Analysis of Amorite*, Assyriological Studies 21 (Chicago & London: Oriental Institute, University of Chicago, 1980).

Gelb, "The Language of Ebla in the Light of the Sources from Ebla, Mari, and Babylonia," in *Ebla, 1975–1985: Dieci anni di studi linguistici e filologic. Atti del Convegno Internazionale (Napoli 9–11 ottobre 1985)*, edited by Luigi Cagni (Naples: University Oriental Institute, Department of Asian Studies, 1987), pp. 49–74.

M. J. Geller, "The Last Wedge," *Zeitschrift für Assyriologie und vorderasiatische Archäologie*, 87 (1997): 43–95.

Gene B. Gragg, "Less-Understood Languages of Ancient Western Asia," *Civilizations of the Ancient Near East*, 4 volumes, edited by Jack M. Sasson (New York: Scribners, 1995), IV: 2161–2179.

John Huehnergard, *A Grammar of Akkadian*, third printing, corrected, Harvard Semitic Studies, no. 45 (Winona Lake, Ind.: Eisenbrauns, 2000).

David Langslow, "Languages and Dialects," in *Civilization of the Ancient Mediterranean: Greece and Rome*, 3 volumes, edited by Michael Grant and Rachel Kitzinger (New York: Scribners, 1988), I: 183–207.

M. C. A. MacDonald, "North Arabia in the First Millennium B.C.E.," in *Civilizations of the Ancient Near East*, 4 volumes, edited by Jack M. Sasson (New York: Scribners, 1995), II: 1355–1369.

H. Craig Melchert, "Indo-European Languages of Anatolia," in *Civilizations of the Ancient Near East*, IV: 2151–2159.

Marie-Louise Thomsen, *The Sumerian Language: An Introduction to its History and Grammatical Structure*, third edition, Mesopotamia, volume 10 (Copenhagen: Akademisk, 2001).

Serpentine cylinder seal (height 1 1/8 inches) and modern impression, belonging to Shu-ilishu, an interpreter of the Meluhhan language, circa 2254 – circa 2218 B.C.E. A small bearded figure, perhaps the seal owner, is seated on the lap of a goddess, to whom he turns and raises his right hand (Louvre, Paris). This Old Akkadian period seal may have been recut in antiquity because on other seals of this sort the seated figure is a child.

MERCHANTS

The Meluhhan Presence. References to Meluhha in texts dating to the third millennium B.C.E. are thought to indicate the region occupied by the Harappan civilization in the Indus Valley of modern Pakistan and India. Meluhha was said to be the source for exotic hardwoods, copper, tin, silver, and carnelian. The presence of certain distinctive objects among the grave goods found in the Royal Tombs at Ur (circa 2500 B.C.E.) is seen as a clear indication of commercial and/or diplomatic contacts between southern Mesopotamia and the Indus Valley. These objects include containers and vessels made from mollusk shells that are indigenous to the Arabian Sea and necklaces and belts strung with long biconical and "etched" carnelian beads. It has even been suggested that the bodies of several women found in the Great Death Pit at Ur were in fact those of Harappan ladies who accompanied the deceased, who is thought to be king Mesanepada, founder of the First Dynasty of Ur (circa 2600 B.C.E.), into the next world. Their headdresses with gold flowers and their necklaces with pendant gold leaves are not unlike the headdresses and necklaces depicted on Harappan figurines. Evidence from the last three centuries of the third millennium B.C.E. suggests the presence of Harappan merchants from Meluhha within Mesopotamia. Whether they were private businessmen or agents of some state entity in the Indus Valley is unknown. An inscription of Sargon of Akkad (circa 2334 – circa 2279 B.C.E.) refers to Meluhhan ships tied up at the quay of the capital city, Agade (Akkad). An inscribed Akkadian-period cylinder seal of unknown provenance identifies its owner as an interpreter of Meluhhan speech, while a locally made Harappan-like stamp seal from Ur bears a partially legible cuneiform inscription that might be the name or title of its presumed Meluhhan owner. Following the collapse of the Akkadian Empire, circa 2193 B.C.E., Meluhhan ships were still apparently calling on Mesopotamian ports. An inscription of Gudea, ruler of Lagash (circa 2100 B.C.E.), states that Meluhhan merchants brought wood and other raw materials directly to him. Archival texts dated in the reigns of the Ur III kings Shulgi (circa 2094 – circa 2047 B.C.E.), Amar-Suena (circa 2046 – circa 2038 B.C.E.), and Shu-Sin (circa 2037 – circa 2029 B.C.E.) suggest the existence of a village of by-then-long-acculturated Meluhhan colonists in the vicinity of Lagash. Early in the second millennium B.C.E., following the collapse of Indus Valley urban culture, the period of direct contact between the Indus Valley and lower Mesopotamia came to an end.

Assyrian Merchantmen. Discoveries at the site of the ancient city of Kanesh, modern Kültepe, in central Anatolia yielded the first extensive evidence of Mesopotamian merchants operating on their own behalf for the principal purpose of making a monetary profit. There, some 1,750 cuneiform tablets were found in private houses in the *karum* (literally: "the harbor"), the walled lower city. In all, some seventy archives—each containing from a few dozen to more than a thousand cuneiform tablets written in an archaic dialect of Assyrian—were found, most as they had been left at the destruction of the city circa 1830 B.C.E., with tablets in jars, baskets, wooden boxes, on shelves along walls, or stacked on reed matting. The tablets were archival texts, letters, and legal documents providing evidence of the business activities of the city's resident traders, who were predominantly foreigners from the city of Ashur on the Tigris River. From circa 1910 to circa 1830 B.C.E., and again from circa 1810 to circa 1740

A one mina (2 pounds 2½ ounces) green-stone weight (height 3¾ inches) with a cuneiform inscription identifying it as a Neo-Babylonian (sixth century B.C.E.) copy of the weight standard introduced by Shulgi, circa 2090 – circa 2047 B.C.E.; and a 2/3 mina (1 pound 7½ ounces) bronze-lion weight (height 2½ inches), inscribed in cuneiform and Aramaic, from Nimrud during the reign of Shalmaneser V (726–722 B.C.E.) (both: British Museum, London)

B.C.E., caravans of donkeys were loaded at Ashur with woolen textiles and tin and transported to Kanesh, where the goods as well as the donkeys were exchanged for currency—silver and gold bullion. From Kanesh the goods were further distributed across Anatolia. The tin and, for the most part, the textiles were imports into Assyria—the tin presumably from the east and the textiles from Babylonia to the south. Some textiles were also produced locally at Ashur specifically for the Anatolian trade. One merchant, Puzur-Ashur, wrote a letter to his wife, Waqqurtum, giving instructions regarding the kind and quantities of textiles he needed for his business dealings abroad:

> (Concerning) the fine cloth that you sent me, you must make cloth like that and send it to me. . . . Have one side of the cloth combed, but not shaved smooth: it should be close-textured. Compared to the textiles you sent me earlier, you must work in one pound of wool more per piece of cloth, but they must still be fine! The other side (of the cloth) must be just lightly combed: if it still looks hairy, it will have to be closeshaved, like *kutanu*-cloth (a common textile). As for the *abarne*-cloth which you sent me, you must not send me that sort of thing again. If you do want to do so, then make it the way I used to wear it. But if you don't want to make fine textiles—as I have heard it they can be bought in quantity over there (i.e., where you are); buy (them) and send them to me. One finished (piece of) cloth, when you make it, should be nine ells long and eight ells wide (4.5 by 4 m). (Veenhof, 1972)

Away on Business. The Assyrian merchants made two round trips a year via an overland route that probably covered on the order of 1,200 kilometers (750 miles) each way and took some five to six weeks to complete. Husbands left their wives at home and accompanied their caravans. Often these men settled in the emporia (trading centers) and corresponded with their wives, who were left behind. Some husbands paid scant attention to the needs of their wives and families back in Ashur. Some even took second wives and raised second families in Anatolia; others never returned home until their old age, leaving their wives lonely, ill, and at times, destitute. One such wife, Taram-Kubi, wrote her husband about her desperate situation and what she perceived to be his selfishness:

> You wrote to me as follows: "Keep the bracelets and rings that you have; they will be needed to buy you food." It is true that you send me half a pound of gold through Ili-bani, but where are the bracelets that you have left behind? When you left, you didn't leave me one shekel of silver. You cleaned out the house and took everything with you.
> Since you left, a terrible famine has hit the city of Ashur. You did not leave me one liter of barley. I need to keep on buying barley for our food. . . . Where is the extravagance that you keep on writing about? We have nothing to eat. Do you think we can afford indulgence? Everything I had available I scraped together and sent to you. Now I live in an empty house and the seasons are changing. Make sure that you send me the value of my textiles in silver so that I can at least buy ten measures of barley. (Michel; translated by Van De Mieroop)

Business and the Local Authorities. The Assyrian trade with Anatolia was quite profitable. Tin was sold in Kanesh at twice its purchase price in Ashur, and fine textiles were marked up as much as 300 percent. The local Anatolian ruler took a percentage of each donkey load as a tax payment for himself and had the right of first refusal to purchase another 10 percent of the textiles at a reasonable price. Nonetheless, the Assyrian merchants typically realized net profit margins of up to 100 percent per year. The Assyrians lived in their own commercial quarter, the *karum;* and the local ruler granted them the right to their own administrative and judicial authorities. The Assyrian merchants promised to abide by their business relationship with the local ruler and not attempt to avoid payment of taxes. Nevertheless, it appears that they engaged in smuggling in an effort to evade such taxes. In one letter three merchants warned an associate:

> As the orders of the *karum* (the trading authorities) are firm, your smuggling that you wrote about is not feasible, so we shall not write you about your smuggling. Make up your own mind! Do not rely on colleagues! Beware! (Larsen, 1988)

Sources:
Jonathan Mark Kenoyer, "The Indus Civilization," in *Art of the First Cities: The Third Millennium B.C. from the Mediterranean to the Indus,* edited by Joan Aruz with Ronald Wallenfels (New York: Metropolitan Museum of Art, 2003), pp. 377–381.

Mogens Trolle Larsen, *The Old Assyrian City-State and Its Colonies* (Copenhagen: Akademisk Forlag, 1976).

Larsen, "Old Assyrian Texts," in *Tablets, Cones, and Bricks of the Third and Second Millennia B.C.,* edited by Ira Spar, volume 1 of *Cuneiform Texts in the Metropolitan Museum of Art* (New York: Metropolitan Museum of Art, 1988), pp. 92–143.

Cécile Michel, *Correspondance des marchands de Kanish au début du IIe millénaire avant J.-C.,* Littératures anciennes du Proche-Orient, 19 (Paris: Cerf, 2001).

Simo Parpola, Asko Parpola, and Robert H. Brunswig Jr., "The Meluhha Village: Evidence of Acculturation of Harappan Traders in Late Third Millennium Mesopotamia," *Journal of Economic and Social History of the Orient,* 20 (1977): 129–165.

D. T. Potts, "Distant Shores: Near Eastern Trade with South Asia and Northern Africa," in *Civilizations of the Ancient Near East,* 4 volumes, edited by Jack M. Sasson (New York: Scribners, 1995), III: 1451–1463.

Marc Van de Mieroop, *A History of the Ancient Near East ca. 3000–323 B.C.* (Malden, Mass.: Blackwell, 2004).

Klaas R. Veenhof, *Aspects of Old Assyrian Trade and its Terminology,* Studia et Documenta, 10 (Leiden: Brill, 1972).

Veenhof, "Kanesh: An Assyrian Colony in Anatolia," in *Civilizations of the Ancient Near East,* 4 volumes, edited by Jack M. Sasson (New York: Scribners, 1995), II: 859–871.

MESSENGERS

Long-Distance Communication. Until writing was sufficiently well developed to convey accurately the spoken word, a message had to be memorized by a courier and, it was hoped, delivered verbatim to the recipient. In the Sumerian-language poem *Enmerkar and the Lord of Aratta*—written near the beginning of the second millennium B.C.E. but set at the period of transition from the Early Dynastic I to the Early Dynastic II period (circa 2750 B.C.E.)—a messenger is central to the ongoing contest between two city rulers vying for the attention of the goddess Inana. Enmerkar, the ruler of Uruk, chooses a messenger from among his troops, one who is "eloquent of speech and endowed with endurance." The messenger is told to go quickly to Aratta, a legendary city set far to the east of Uruk, and deliver Enmerkar's demands to the Lord of Aratta: "Messenger, by night drive on like the south wind! By day, be up like the dew!" On his arrival in Aratta,

---

UNWELCOME MESSENGERS

In 701 B.C.E. the Assyrian king Sennacherib launched an attack against the rebellious Levantine state of Judah, ruled over by Hezekiah from his capital at Jerusalem. According to the Hebrew Bible (II Kings 18), the Assyrian king, established at the city of Lachish, which his forces had just seized, sent to Jerusalem three of his highest-ranking officials, who demanded to speak with Hezekiah. When the three Assyrian officials were confronted outside the city walls, their spokesman, apparently speaking in Hebrew, said:

> Tell Hezekiah, thus said the Great King, the King of Assyria: "What makes you so confident? Do you think that plans and arming for war can emerge from empty talk? Look, on whom are you relying that you have rebelled against me? You rely, of all things, on Egypt, that splintered reed of a staff, which enters and punctures the palm of anyone who leans on it. And if you tell me that you are relying on the Lord your God . . . The Lord himself told me: Go up against that land and destroy it."

The Judaean officials pleaded with the Assyrians not to speak in Hebrew, but rather in Aramaic, the diplomatic language of the Assyrian Empire, so that the defenders on the walls might not understand the Assyrians' threats. But the Assyrian spokesman called out to the defenders on the wall in Hebrew:

> Hear the message of the great king, the king of Assyria: Thus said the king, "Do not let Hezekiah deceive you, for he cannot save you from me. And do not let Hezekiah have you put your trust in God by saying, 'God will surely save us,' and 'This city will not be handed over to the king of Assyria.'"

According to the Bible, Jerusalem was indeed saved miraculously:

> That night an angel of the Lord went out and struck down 185,000 in the Assyrian camp, and the following morning they were all dead corpses.

Source: Mordechai Cogan and Hayim Tadmor, *II Kings: A New Translation with Introduction and Commentary,* The Anchor Bible, volume 11 (Garden City, N.Y.: Doubleday, 1988).

---

the messenger announces himself and recites his master's demands word for word before the Lord of Aratta. The lord delivers a reply to the messenger, who—demonstrating his quick wit—presumes to answer it himself. The Lord of Aratta gives further instructions, whereupon the messenger returns quickly to Uruk. The messages that follow are in the form of riddles, which the messenger must convey back and forth. By the fourth trip, Enmerkar's message "was substantial, and its contents extensive. The messenger, whose mouth was heavy, was not able to repeat it." In response, Enmerkar takes a piece of clay and inscribes his message on it, thereby inventing the writing of letters on clay tablets and forever changing the role of the messenger.

Mar Shipri. The Akkadian term *mar shipri*, which first appeared in texts at the end of the third millennium B.C.E., may designate a "messenger," "envoy," "agent," "deputy," "ambassador," or "diplomat." His responsibilities ranged from conveying a simple memorized message, to carrying a tablet, to negotiating on behalf of his master. Women serving the same functions *(marat shipri)* on behalf of elite women are also known. Loyalty, trustworthiness, and speed were the *mar shipri*'s most desirable qualities. Messengers traveled on foot, by boat, or by wagon. Their journeys might take them through hostile territory, where they might be detained, interrogated, mistreated, robbed, or even killed. To alleviate such dangers, the messenger might also carry a tablet from his lord requesting safe passage; if such a request was granted, the messenger would be given an escort to accompany him through a given territory. On reaching his destination, the messenger had to gain admittance to the intended recipient. A foreign diplomat might need permission first to enter the city, then to enter the palace grounds, and finally to enter into the king's presence. Each step no doubt required the presentation of certain credentials, such as a tablet bearing the impression of the sender's personal seal. Once granted an audience, the messenger recited whatever message he had been given. Any tablet he might have brought was examined and read aloud and, if necessary, translated by a local scribe to corroborate the verbal message. A messenger of sufficient status would then be asked to expand on any issues raised by the recipient and perhaps even negotiate on behalf of his master. At his host's discretion, the messenger returned home with a reply. On the other hand, a messenger bearing ill tidings might well lose his life.

Securing the Message. The *Sumerian Sargon Legend* is an Old Babylonian–period (circa 1750 B.C.E.) account of

Cuneiform tablet (height 3½ inches) and envelope, one of two copies of an affidavit before the council of ancient Kanesh (Kültepe) in Anatolia. The envelope is inscribed "The (assembly of) the trading station of Kanesh granted us legal proceeding in this case. Before the 'Sword of (the god) Ashur,' we presented our testimony" and bears the seal impressions of two witnesses; circa 1910 – circa 1740 B.C.E. (Yale Babylonian Collection).

the events leading to the rise of Sargon of Akkad to power, circa 2334 B.C.E., as decreed by the gods, at the expense of his overlord Ur-Zababa, the king of Kish. Ur-Zababa learns of his fate through a dream that Sargon is forced to reveal to him. The king determines to circumvent his destiny by having Sargon killed. Ur-Zababa sends Sargon to the court of Lugal-zagesi, the king of Uruk, with a cuneiform tablet carrying instructions for the king of Uruk to kill its bearer. To ensure that Sargon does not learn of the contents of the letter, Ur-Zababa fashions an envelope of clay for the tablet:

> In those days, writing words on tablets certainly existed, but putting tablets into envelopes did not yet exist. King Ur-Zababa dispatched Sargon, the creature of the gods, to Lugal-zagesi in Uruk with a message written on clay, which would cause his own death. (Cooper and Heimpel)

The story is broken at this point, so it is not known how Sargon survived this plot. Most often, early examples of envelopes from the late third millennium B.C.E. bear the impression of the cylinder seal of the sender and perhaps the name of the addressee. Occasionally the envelope carries an abbreviated form of the letter it contains. The *Sumerian Sargon Legend* does not indicate whether Ur-Zababa's first envelope was uninscribed, or if it bore an inscription that did not convey the true contents of the letter.

Security during the First Millennium B.C.E. During the first millennium B.C.E., envelopes that were used to enclose contracts carried a verbatim copy of the enclosed document. Clay envelopes were still occasionally used to enclose letter orders on clay tablets in the Seleucid period, in the third century B.C.E. However, the widespread use of the Aramaic aleph-beth, inked on papyrus or on parchment or other kinds of prepared animal skins, necessitated new methods for securing the contents of messages. Most commonly, a document was rolled up and tied about with a string. The knot was enclosed within a small lump of clay (cretula), which might also be inscribed or bear the impressions of one or more seals. Because of the small size of the cretula, it was most convenient to use stamp seals, which became increasingly popular at the expense of the traditional cylinder seal, which was more appropriate for rolling over the broad surface of a tablet. However, on occasion, cylinder seals were used as stamp seals, leaving the impression of just a small portion of their full intaglio. During the Seleucid period, a unique method for enclosing inked documents emerged. Stamp seals, now typically engraved metal finger rings, were impressed onto a piece of clay that was wrapped entirely around the string that enclosed the document, giving the appearance of a napkin ring or a flattened ball (bulla) with the document passing through it. Only the cretulae and bullae have survived; the original papyrus or parchment documents have long ago been burned or turned to dust.

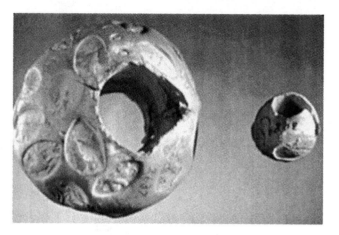

Spherical clay bullae with seal impressions, originally wrapped around rolled and tied parchment documents: (left) with forty impressions, diameter 2 1/8 inch; (right) with two impressions, diameter 3/4 inch, from Uruk, Seleucid period, third–second centuries B.C.E (Yale Babylonian Collection)

Courier Systems. When the Persian king Xerxes (485–465 B.C.E.) took his army into Greece, messages about his successful capture of Athens and his subsequent defeat in the naval battle at Salamis were dispatched via fast messengers *(piradazish)* to the capital at Susa. According to Herodotus of Halicarnassus, writing in Greek during the fifth century B.C.E., nothing in his day traveled faster than a Persian courier:

> The whole idea is a Persian invention, and works like this: riders are stationed along the road, equal in number to the number of days the journey takes—a man and a horse for each day. Nothing stops these couriers from covering their allotted stage in the quickest possible time—neither snow, rain, heat, nor darkness. The first, at the end of his stage, passes the dispatch to the second, the second to the third, and so on along the line. . . .

Herodotus erred in ascribing the invention of the horse-mounted courier system to the Persians. Such a system for the delivery of royal mail was already fully functioning across the Assyrian Empire during the ninth to seventh centuries B.C.E.

Persian Couriers. Many thousands of cuneiform clay tablets were excavated from the fortification walls at the royal Persian capital of Persepolis in Iran. Written in the local administrative language, Elamite, these texts are presumably a portion of a likely discarded royal archive. They are dated to the middle years (509–494 B.C.E.) of the reign of Darius I, and are concerned with the movement from place to place of huge quantities of commodities—such as grain, flour, wine, sheep, goats, and hides—and with their assignment for broad general purposes. Many of these records detail the apportionment of these supplies in the form of rations to the final consumer. Among these ration texts are hundreds of documents recording the disbursement of rations specifically to various state bureaucratic functionaries, who were about to travel to the far reaches of the empire. These travel rations were issued on a daily basis to guides, caravan leaders, and ordinary and fast messengers as they went about their business, journeying from the Persian heartland eastward to Central Asia and India, or westward to Babylonia, Lydia, and Egypt. Supply stations were apparently spaced at intervals of one day's journey along the main roads. The rations consisted predominantly of flour, supplemented by beer and wine. Fast riders rode special horses that were also allotted rations, on a monthly basis.

Rapid Communications. Mounted messengers in the employ of the Persian Empire (mid-sixth to mid-fourth centuries B.C.E.) may have been able to ride from the Aegean coast of Anatolia to the Persian capital within two weeks or less. However, classical sources describe even faster methods available to the Persians. Fire signals, referred to in cuneiform texts from the early second millennium B.C.E., were said to enable the Persian king to know important news from anywhere within his empire within a single day. Another story relates how guards stationed in the mountains of Iran rallied ten thousand archers within a single day, relaying their message by shouting across the valleys from mountain to mountain, a distance equal to a thirty-day journey.

Sources:

Jeremy Black, Graham Cunningham, Jarle Ebeling, Esther Flückiger-Hawker, Eleanor Robson, Jon Taylor, and Gábor Zólyomi, *The Electronic Text Corpus of Sumerian Literature,* The Oriental Institute, University of Oxford, 1998– <http://www-etcsl.orient.ox.ac.uk/>.

Jerrold S. Cooper and Wolfgang Heimpel, "The Sumerian Sargon Legend," *Journal of the American Oriental Society,* 103 (1983): 67–82.

David F. Graf, "The Persian Royal Road System," in *Continuity and Change: Proceedings of the Last Achaemenid History Workshop April 6–8, 1990, Ann Arbor, Michigan,* edited by Heleen Sancisi-Weerdenburg, Amélie Kuhrt, and Margaret Cool Root, Achaemenid History, volume 8 (Leiden: Nederlands Instituut voor het Nabije Ooste, 1994), pp. 167–189.

William W. Hallo, *Origins: The Ancient Near Eastern Background of Some Modern Western Institutions,* Studies in the History and Culture of the Ancient Near East, 6 (Leiden: Brill, 1996).

Richard T. Hallock, *Persepolis Fortification Tablets,* Oriental Institute Publications, volume 92 (Chicago: University of Chicago Press, 1969).

Herodotus, *The Histories,* translated by Aubrey de Sélincourt, revised, with an introduction and notes, by A. R. Burn (Harmondsworth, U.K.: Penguin, 1954).

Samuel A. Meier, *The Messenger in the Ancient Semitic World,* Harvard Semitic Monographs, 45 (Atlanta: Scholars Press, 1988).

Gary H. Oller, "Messengers and Ambassadors in Ancient Western Asia," in *Civilizations of the Ancient Near East,* 4 volumes, edited by Jack M. Sasson (New York: Scribners, 1995), III: 1465–1473.

Ronald Wallenfels, "Sealing Practices on Legal Documents from Hellenistic Uruk," in *Administrative Documents in the Aegean and their Near Eastern Counterparts. Proceedings of the International Colloquium, Naples, February 29–March 2, 1996,* edited by Massimo Perna (Turin: Paravia Scriptorium, 2000), pp. 333–348.

RECKONING TIME

Measuring Time. Three natural periodicities must have been evident to humans quite early in history: the rising and setting of the sun (day), the waxing and waning of the phases of the moon (lunar month), and the alternation of the stars in the night sky in concert with the changing seasons (solar year). Late in the fourth millennium B.C.E., with the advent of the ability to count abstractly beyond two or three, the period relations among the day, lunar month, and solar year must have become evident; the lunar month consists of either twenty-nine or thirty days, and the solar year consists of slightly more than twelve lunar months.

Naming Months and Years. During the Early Dynastic period (circa 2900 – circa 2334 B.C.E.) each city maintained its own system of naming months and years; the days of the month were numbered. Year names might refer to a military campaign, the building or restoration of a temple, the presentation of a special cult statue, the installation of a high priest or priestess, the construction of a city or defensive wall, or the excavation of a canal. During the reign of the Akkadian king Naram-Sin (circa 2254 – circa 2218 B.C.E.), the need to coordinate activities throughout the empire resulted in the systematizing of the calendrical system. Each year was named for a significant event that occurred in that year. Among the year names attested for Naram-Sin are:

> Year in which Naram-Sin received from the temple of Enlil the *mitum*-weapon.
>
> Year in which Naram-Sin destroyed Maridaban.
>
> Year in which the city wall of Agade (was built).
>
> Year in which (Tuta-napshum) the *en*-priestess of Enlil was chosen by means of omens.
>
> Year in which Naram-Sin reached the sources of the Tigris and the Euphrates and was victorious against Senaminda. (Sigrist and Damerow)

Until a name was chosen, each new year was called "The year after (the name of the previous year)." The ancient scribes maintained lists of official year names in their correct order. Without such lists, it would have been impossible to calculate the number of years that had elapsed between one year and any other. Unfortunately, no list of Akkadian year names has been discovered. The system of naming years after significant events continued in southern Mesopotamia through the end of the Old Babylonian Period (circa 1595 B.C.E.).

Dating by Regnal Years. Some existing evidence suggests that, toward the end of the Early Dynastic III period (circa 2400 B.C.E.), several Mesopotamian city-states were numbering their years in accordance with the length of time the local ruler had been on the throne. This system eventually came to replace the system of year names in Babylonia and remained in use until the early Seleucid period in the early third century B.C.E. Determining the length of time between one year and any other during a given reign is a simple subtraction problem. But determining time spans across reigns requires a king list naming the rulers in correct chronological order with the lengths of their reigns.

THE DIE OF YAHALI

The method of selecting officers for the annually appointed *limu*, or eponym office, seems to have varied throughout Assyrian history. For the century beginning with the reign of Shalmaneser III (858–824 B.C.E.), the order appears to have been relatively fixed with the king holding the office in the second year of his reign, followed by the commander-in-chief *(turtanu)*. The sequence thereafter was not rigid, but included three state ministers—the chief cupbearer *(rab shaqe)*, the palace herald *(nagir ekalli)*, and the chief steward *(masennu)*—followed by the governors of major cities within the empire. The exact order was apparently determined by the casting of lots, that is, by randomly drawing or throwing dice, each die *(puru)* bearing the name of the prospective officeholder. The nearly cubical (27 x 27 x 28 millimeter) clay die of the chief steward Yahali, who held the *limu*-office in 833 B.C.E. and again in 824 B.C.E., is inscribed in cuneiform and reads:

Ashur, the great lord! Adad, the great lord! (This is) the die of Yahali, the Chief Steward of Shalmaneser, king of Assyria; governor of the city of Kibshuni, the land of Qumeni, the land of Mehrani, the land of Uqi, (and) the land of Erimmi; chief of customs. In his eponoymy (assigned to him) by his die, may the harvest of Assyria prosper and thrive. Before Ashur (and) Adad, may he throw his die.

The Akkadian word *puru* is etymologically related to the name of the Jewish festival of Lots or *Purim*, its name reflecting the casting of lots to determine the most propitious day on which to carry out a pogrom against the Jews of the Persian Empire during the reign of king Xerxes (485–465 B.C.E.).

Sources: Alan R. Millard, *The Eponyms of the Assyrian Empire 910–612 BC*, State Archives of Assyria Studies, 2 (Helsinki: Neo-Assyrian Text Corpus Project, 1994).
Carey A. Moore, *Esther: A New Translation with Introduction and Commentary*, The Anchor Bible, volume 7B (Garden City, N.Y.: Doubleday, 1971).
K. Lawson Younger Jr., "The Die (*Pūru*) of Yahali (2.113I)," in *Monumental Inscriptions from the Biblical World*, volume 2 of *The Context of Scripture*, edited by William W. Hallo with K. Lawson Younger Jr. (Leiden & Boston: Brill, 2003), pp. 271–272.

Eponym Systems. Assyria, in northern Mesopotamia, employed an eponym dating system throughout its history, from the Old Assyrian period (circa twentieth century B.C.E.) through the fall of the Neo-Assyrian Empire (610 B.C.E.). In an eponym system, each year is named for an annually appointed high state officer called the *limu*-official. During the Neo-Assyrian period the *limu*-office rotated among the king, high palace officials, commanders of the army, and provincial governors. As with the system of year names, the eponym system demanded that accurate lists be maintained. Nineteen fragmentary Assyr-

ian eponym lists have been recovered, permitting their order to be established securely for the period 910–649 B.C.E. This system for naming years appears to have served as the model for the later annual Greek archonship and Roman consular dating schemes.

Dating by Era. The first true system of dating in which years are consecutively numbered beyond some significant starting point, regardless of reign, began in the Seleucid period during the early third century B.C.E. In 292 B.C.E., during the twentieth year of his reign, Seleucus I appointed his son Antiochus as coregent. Following the assassination of Seleucus in 281 B.C.E., Antiochus I was apparently faced with a dilemma: should he or should he not count the twelve years as coregent with his father toward the total length of his own reign, that is, should 280 B.C.E. be year one or year thirteen of his reign? Antiochus, perhaps because he took the throne as coregent with his own son Seleucus, obviated the problem by continuing his father's year count: 280 B.C.E. became year 32 of what later became known as the Seleucid Era. The system of dating by the year of the Seleucid Era spread across the ancient Near East and, while spawning imitators, remained in use for many centuries.

Sources:
William W. Hallo, "The Concept of Eras from Nabonassar to Seleucus," *Ancient Studies in Memory of Elias Bickerman*, special issue of *Journal of the Ancient Near East Society*, 16–17 (1984–1985): 143–151.

Hallo, "The Nabonassar Era and other Epochs in Mesopotamian Chronology and Chronography," in *A Scientific Humanist: Studies in Memory of Abraham Sachs*, edited by Erle Lichty, Maria deJ. Ellis, and Pamela Gerardi, Occasional Publications of the Samuel Noah Kramer Fund, 9 (Philadelphia: University Museum, 1988), pp. 175–190.

Alan R. Millard, *The Eponyms of the Assyrian Empire 910–612 BC*, State Archives of Assyria Studies, 2 (Helsinki: Neo-Assyrian Text Corpus Project, 1994).

Marcel Sigrist and Peter Damerow, "Mesopotamian Year Names: Neo-Sumerian and Old Babylonian Date Formulae," *Cuneiform Digital Library Initiative*, University of California at Los Angeles and the Max Planck Institute for the History of Science <http://cdli.ucla.edu>.

ROADS

The Earliest Roads. In ancient Mesopotamia, people and goods traveled either overland or by water. On land, people usually walked, while goods were likely to be carried on pack animals or in wheeled vehicles—wagons or carts—drawn by oxen or donkeys. A network of paths stretched across the countryside between trading centers. Whereas people and animals might be able to walk over quite uneven or steep terrain, wheeled vehicles, in regular use since the early third millennium B.C.E., required a surface free of obstructions, sufficiently firm for the wheels not to become stuck, and not too steep for a draft animal to pull its load. Thus, using wheeled transport required that paths be cleared of obstacles, leveled, and packed firm; and they had to be maintained in that condition. The trace of any path, especially one intended for wheeled vehicles, typically followed the natural terrain, limited by its grade, the locations of mountain passes and river fords, and the availability of water and food for man and beast.

The King of the Road. A frequent concern of Mesopotamian kings was the proper maintenance of the roads and the protection of travelers from wild animals and bandits. Grass growing on the roads was a sure sign of economic difficulties. In most periods corvée-labor (labor owed the state) from the local villages was responsible for road maintenance. Kings memorialized their support of road maintenance in year names and in poetry. Ur-Namma (circa 2112 – circa 2095 B.C.E.), the founder of the Third Dynasty of Ur, named one of his regnal years "The year Ur-Namma, the king, from below to above, put the road in order." His son and successor, Shulgi (circa 2094 – circa 2047 B.C.E.), realized the critical importance of maintaining the road system of his highly organized and highly centralized state. Among the self-laudatory poems he is credited with composing, one unabashedly describes his road-building accomplishments, which included re-establishing order on the roads to Nippur:

> Because I am a powerful man who enjoys using his thighs, I, Shulgi, the mighty king, superior to all, strengthened (?) the roads, put in order the highways of the Land. I marked out the double-hour distances, built there lodging houses. I planted gardens by their side and established resting-places, and installed in those places experienced men. Whichever direction one comes from, one can refresh oneself at their cool sides; and the traveler who reaches nightfall on the road can seek haven there as in a well-built city. (Black et al.)

Then, to demonstrate the quality of his road system and his own strength and endurance, Shulgi put his roads to good use:

So that my name should be established for distant days and never fall into oblivion, so that my praise should be uttered throughout the Land, and my glory should be proclaimed in the foreign lands, I, the fast runner, summoned my strength and, to prove my speed, my heart prompted me to make a return journey from Nippur to brick-built Ur as if it were only the distance of a double-hour. (Black et al.)

Shulgi's claim that "Truly I am not boasting!" is remarkable; Nippur is some 140 kilometers (90 miles), or nearly fifteen "double-hours," from Ur. A "double-hour" is equal to the distance one might walk at a moderate pace in two hours, some 10 kilometers (6 miles). The event was apparently memorialized in the fashioning of a statue of the king, perhaps in a running posture.

Imperial Road Systems. The Neo-Assyrian Empire (ninth-seventh centuries B.C.E.) was the largest and most centralized power to date. Its existence demanded an efficient and well-maintained road system for use by messengers and troops. The principal roads through the empire, the "royal" roads, were accurately measured and supplied with road stations, resting places for troops and other travelers. They also served as relay stations where messengers might obtain fresh horses. When the Persians became the masters of the ancient Near East (fifth-fourth centuries B.C.E.), they expanded the Assyrian road system. Perhaps the longest and best-known Persian royal road ran from Sardis, the former Lydian capital in western Anatolia, to the royal capital at Susa, in southwest Iran, a distance of some 2,400 kilometers (1,500 miles), which could be traversed in just ninety days. The fifth century B.C.E. historian Herodotus, who may well have traveled the road himself, described it thus: "At intervals all along the road are recog-

Polychrome glazed-relief brick panel (height 41 3/8 inches) depicting one of the 120 striding lions on the walls flanking the Processional Way leading to the Ishtar Gate, Babylon, sixth century B.C.E. (Louvre, Paris)

nized stations, with excellent inns, and the road itself is safe to travel by, as it never leaves inhabited country."

Processional Roads. As a royal road approached a capital city, such as the Assyrian capital cities of Dur-Sharrukin or Nineveh, the road might be paved with stone slabs. When Nebuchadnezzar II (604–562 B.C.E.) rebuilt Babylon he lavished great expense on reconstructing the main processional way, the *Ayy-ibur-shabu,* which led from the north, through the monumental Ishtar Gate, and on toward the great ziggurat E-temenanki. Excavated sections of the street reveal that the last 180 meters (600 feet) leading to the gate were at least 20 meters (66 feet) wide. The lower portions of the high defensive walls on either side of the street were decorated to a height of approximately 3 meters (10 feet) with polychrome glazed-brick tiles molded in relief. Depicted on the walls were some one hundred twenty striding lions between two bands of rosettes, one above and the other below the lions. In a royal inscription Nebuchadnezzar stated that he built up the road-bed of breccia and slabs of mountain-quarried limestone so high that the gates through which the street passed had to be rebuilt.

City Streets. Within a city, a system of streets served as a means of communication both within and between its various districts. Within residential areas, the streets were quite often narrow; frequently they were blind alleyways leading to homes. Wide city streets might run from the gates or the harbor to the major temples and administrative buildings. Processional streets were broad, straight, and paved with large stones.

Sources:

Michael C. Astour, "Overland Trade Routes in Ancient Western Asia," in *Civilizations of the Ancient Near East,* 4 volumes, edited by Jack M. Sasson (New York: Scribners, 1995), III: 1401–1420.

Jeremy Black, Graham Cunningham, Jarle Ebeling, Esther Flückiger-Hawker, Eleanor Robson, Jon Taylor, and Gábor Zólyomi, *The Electronic Text Corpus of Sumerian Literature,* The Oriental Institute, University of Oxford, 1998– <http://www-etcsl.orient.ox.ac.uk/>.

Douglas Frayne, "Šulgi, the Runner," *Journal of the American Oriental Society,* 103 (1983): 739–748.

Herodotus, *The Histories,* translated by Aubrey de Sélincourt, revised, with an introduction and notes, by A. R. Burn (Harmondsworth, U.K.: Penguin, 1954).

Jacob Klein, "Šulgi and Išmedagan: Runners in the Service of the Gods (SRT 13)," *Beer-Sheva,* 2 (1985): 7*–38*.

Joan Oates, *Babylon* (London: Thames & Hudson, 1979).

TRANSPORTATION BY LAND

Early Four-Wheeled Vehicles. The earliest evidence for wheeled vehicles in Mesopotamia is in the form of pictographic proto-cuneiform signs on clay tablets from Uruk, dated to the end of the fourth millennium B.C.E. Pulled by oxen, the vehicles appear to have been sledges equipped with a roofed superstructure. Rather than being dragged across the ground, they have been set on wheels or rollers. During the third millennium B.C.E., two- and three-dimensional representations of two-wheeled carts and four-wheeled wagons were typically depicted in military contexts. The four-wheeled vehicle termed a *battle car* was narrow, with low sides and high front breastwork topped by an open rail. The vehicle had solid composite-disk wheels pieced together from three boards; these wheels rotated on the ends of round axles fixed beneath the wagon. Two pairs of onagers, or wild asses, were yoked on either side of a low, straight, central draft pole and were controlled by lines from the driver to rings in the animals' noses. Behind the driver might stand a second man armed with an ax, sickle sword, or javelins. The battle car may have served as a mobile firing platform for the javelin thrower. On mosaics from Ur and Mari, the onagers are shown as if leaping over fallen enemy, but such depictions are likely an artistic convention. As the vehicle was in all probability neither fast nor particularly maneuverable, it likely more often served to transport officers to and from the battlefield and for public displays.

Two-Wheeled Vehicles. During the third millennium B.C.E., two distinct sorts of two-wheeled fighting vehicles were in use; strictly speaking, neither was a chariot in the accepted sense of the word. One of these vehicles, termed a *platform car,* is known from terra-cotta models; it was more or less a two-wheeled version of the four-wheeled battle car, in which a single rider could stand on the platform of the cart or sit on a small bench-like seat at the rear of the vehicle. The second kind of cart, known from stone relief plaques and three-dimensional models, has been termed a *straddle car,* because the driver sat or stood with his legs on either side of an extension of the yoke pole while his feet rested on the axle or on footrests just in front of it. The vehicle had no sides; a crossbar mounted on two uprights directly in front of the driver provided the only handhold as well as a place to mount a quiver of javelins. A straddle car represented on a plaque from Ur is drawn by four onagers and appears to have a leopard skin draped over the seat with a high saddle-like cantle at the rear. It must have been no mean feat for the driver to retain control of the speeding vehicle while hurling a javelin, thrusting a spear, or wielding an ax.

Chariots. The earliest representations of the true chariot began to appear early in the second millennium B.C.E. on cylinder seals and seal impressions from Kültepe (ancient Kanesh, the site of an important Old Assyrian trading colony) in Anatolia and, shortly thereafter, from Syria. Although superficially resembling the platform car, the early chariot must have been significantly faster and more maneuverable, and it gradually replaced both the platform car and the straddle car. Drawn by horses, which are capable of greater speed than onagers or oxen, the true chariot was equipped with spoked wheels spinning freely on the ends of a longer axle, probably mounted toward or at the rear of the box, an innovation that improved stability and permitted a wider carriage that could carry two riders side by side. The riders could stabilize themselves against a waist-high railing that enclosed both sides and the front,

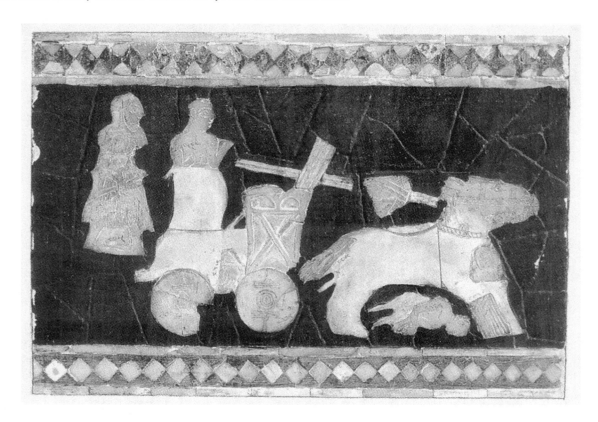

Four-wheeled battle car drawn by onagers (shell inlay, height 6¾ inches), Ninni-ZA.ZA Temple, Mari, Syria; and a modern model of a copper miniature straddle-car military vehicle with driver and team of four onagers (height 2¾ inches), from Tell Agrab in the Diyala region (top: National Museum, Damascus; bottom: Oriental Institute, Chicago)

Assyrian king Ashurnasirpal II (883–859 B.C.E.) on a lion hunt, drawing his bow while standing in a chariot pulled by a team of three galloping horses, alabaster relief panel (height 35 inches) from the wall reliefs of the North-West Palace at Nimrud (British Museum, London)

necessitating mounting the vehicle from the rear. During the second half of the second millennium B.C.E., the chariot achieved its full potential as a fighting vehicle and became the mainstay of fighting forces throughout the ancient Near East. The newest lightweight chariots, complete examples of which have been excavated from Egypt, were drawn by two horses controlled by reins attached to a mouth bit rather than a nose ring. The charioteer—equipped with shield, helmet, and scale corselet for protection—was armed with the latest technology, the powerful recurved composite bow, fashioned from layers of wood, horn, and sinew. In the first millennium B.C.E., changes in battlefield strategy, which included the introduction of the horse-mounted cavalry, reduced the effectiveness of the chariot in battle. As a consequence the chariot was increased in size and returned to its earlier function of transport and display. Nonetheless, Assyrian palace wall reliefs show the king, with drawn bow and arrow, standing in a speeding chariot during battle and ceremonial lion or bull hunts, the latter probably within the grounds of a royal game preserve. According to the Greek historian Xenophon, the Persian battle formations of the fourth century B.C.E. included scythe-chariots, so called for having scythes fitted to the axle trees and stretching out slantwise; other scythes protruded under the chariot seats, facing the ground, so as to cut through all they encountered.

Riding. Unlike a draft animal, which bears little if any of the weight of the vehicle it must pull, a ridden animal must bear the full weight of its rider. However, a ridden animal can proceed over terrain and up and down grades that would be impassable to animal-drawn sledges and wheeled vehicles. An Akkadian period (circa 2334 – circa 2193 B.C.E.) seal impression from Kish appears to show a javelin-wielding man seated bareback on an onager. The rider is seated astride the animal, his legs drawn up as if to grip better the animal's flanks. A seal impression from Kültepe (early second millennium B.C.E.) appears to show a rider seated sideways on some sort of packsaddle atop an equid. Evidence from the late third and early second millennia B.C.E. suggests the increasing frequency of riding various types of equids by officials and couriers; oxen continued in their role of mount. In the latter half of the second millennium B.C.E., the introduction of the horse and the mouth bit for control did not bring about a significant increase in riding, even in military contexts where the horse-drawn chariot was now dominant. The use of the ridden horse in warfare first became important when Assyrian troops on campaigns in the mountainous north and east were forced onto the backs of their horses; there they came into contact with the peoples of Transcaucasia, who have a tradition of horseback riding. During the ninth century B.C.E., Assyrian mounted troops operated in pairs; riding bareback at full gallop, one warrior drew his bow and shot his arrow while the second rider controlled the reins of both horses. By the seventh century B.C.E., improvements in reining permitted armored Assyrian mounted troops, armed with bows and arrows or spears, to function individually. As skilled as they were at harassing and raiding, Persian horsemen during the latter half of the first millennium B.C.E. were, despite their numbers, no match for true cavalry fielded by Alexander III (the Great) of Macedon, whose mounted troops were trained to function as a unit.

Pack Animals. The most commonly attested pack animal was the donkey, a domesticated descendant of the wild ass. It was able to carry considerable loads over terrain too difficult for wheeled transport or other pack animals, such as oxen or camels. During the Old Assyrian period (circa 1910 – circa 1740 B.C.E.), merchants used caravans of donkeys to carry goods from their home city of Ashur on the Tigris to the trading colony at Kültepe (ancient Kanesh), which lies at the crossroads of east-west and north-south routes on the Anatolian plateau, a journey of 1,200 kilometers (750 miles) that took five to six weeks. During the eighth century B.C.E. dromedaries (one-humped camels), which may have been domesticated by Arabian nomads by as early as the third millennium B.C.E., began to be used in caravans to transport incense and spices from southern Arabia to Mesopotamia, the Levant, and Syria. During the seventh century B.C.E., the Assyrians used camels as pack animals during military campaigns.

Sources:
Mary Littauer and J. H. Crouwel, *Wheeled Vehicles and Ridden Animals in the Ancient Near East* (Leiden: Brill, 1979).

Paula Wapnish, "Camels," in *The Oxford Encyclopedia of Archaeology in the Near East*, 5 volumes, edited by Eric M. Meyers (New York & Oxford: Oxford University Press, 1997), I: 407–408.

Xenophon, *Anabasis*, translated by Carleton L. Brownson, revised, with a new introduction, by John Dillery, Loeb Classical Library, 90 (Cambridge, Mass. & London: Harvard University Press, 1998).

Yigael Yadin, *The Art of Warfare in Biblical Lands in the Light of Archaeological Study*, 2 volumes, translated by M. Pearlman (New York, Toronto & London: McGraw-Hill, 1963).

TRANSPORTATION BY WATER

River Travel. The Tigris and Euphrates Rivers and the canals that connected them did more than just nourish the crops in the fields. They also provided an efficient means of transportation for individuals, military troops, and cargo, as well as for kings and statues of gods in religious ceremonies. Because the prevailing winds blow in the same direction as the river currents, sailboats were not widely used on the rivers and canals of Mesopotamia. Moving upstream could be accomplished only by paddling, rowing, punting, or towing the vessel. Such a journey might take four times as long as the comparable trip downstream. In some cases, it was actually preferable to transport goods via donkey caravan rather than by water.

An Early Model Boat. A terra-cotta model of a boat, approximately 26 centimeters (10 inches) long, was found in a burial at the site of ancient Eridu, near the ancient shoreline of the Persian Gulf. Eridu was the home of Enki, the Sumerian god of the freshwaters that lay beneath the surface of the earth.

A skin-covered boat propelled by four men with oars and a man fishing while seated on an inflated animal skin, drawing of a detail from an alabaster-relief panel, Southwest Palace of Sennacherib (704–681 B.C.E.) at Nineveh (drawing by T. Holland after Austen Henry Layard; from Joan Oates, *Babylon*, 1979)

Two Sumerian men paddling a boat, fragment of an alabaster-relief plaque (height 4 inches) from Fara (ancient Shuruppak), circa 2600 – circa 2500 B.C.E. (Vorderasiatisches Museum, Berlin)

Dating to the end of the Ubaid period, circa 4000 B.C.E., the model boat has a socket for a mast that presumably supported a sail and holes in the rim of its hull for rigging lines. The presence of late Ubaid-style pottery—which appears to have originated in southern Mesopotamia—at sites across northern Mesopotamia and north Syria, as well as at sites as far as 700 kilometers (450 miles) south of Eridu along the western shore of the Persian Gulf, suggests that the traders of Ubaid ware and its contents had some competency in sailing during the fifth millennium B.C.E.

Sumerian River Craft. A distinctive vessel with a high arched prow and stern is seen on cylinder seals of the Late Uruk period at the end of the fourth millennium B.C.E. One man aft, who kneels facing forward, propels the boat with a paddle while another man stands near the bow using a long punting pole with a bifurcated tip. A silver model of an elongated crescent-shaped boat, resembling a long canoe, was found at Ur in a royal grave, perhaps belonging to king Meskalamdug (circa 2500 B.C.E.). Inside the model, which is 64 centimeters (25 inches) long, but just 8 centimeters (5

inches) wide, are preserved five thwarts for the paddlers as well as their paddles with leaf-shaped blades. The fragment of a stone relief carving from Fara (ancient Shuruppak) shows two Sumerian men seated facing forward in the back of just such a boat, stroking their paddles in unison.

A Divine Riverboat. On cylinder seals of the Early Dynastic II and III periods (circa 2750 – circa 2340 B.C.E.), the man standing at the prow of the boat holding the punting pole is fused to the prow, creating a single bearded, anthropomorphic boat deity. Seated on a stool amidship is another divine figure wielding a long paddle with a leaf-shaped blade. This motif became the principal mythological subject on cylinder seals of the Early Dynastic II and III periods. A cylinder seal from the succeeding Akkadian period (circa 2340 – circa 2200 B.C.E.) depicts the seated god with rays emanating from his shoulders, thus identifying him as the sun god Shamash; presumably, the deity in the Early Dynastic seals is his Sumerian equivalent, Utu.

Other River Craft. Heavy loads—up to thirty-six tons— were transported downstream on rectangular rafts *(kalakku)*

Modern impression of a lapis-lazuli cylinder seal (height 1¾ inches) depicting a riverboat, perhaps made of bundled reeds, propelled by a punter and a paddler and transporting a Sumerian "priest-king," who stands before a bull supporting an altar on its back; from the "Sammelfund," a temple hoard at Uruk, circa 3000 – circa 2900 B.C.E. (Vorderasiatisches Museum, Berlin)

supported by inflated skins numbering from a few to many hundreds; they were then unloaded, dismantled, and returned upstream by donkey. People sat on individual inflated skins *(mashkaru)* for fishing or clutched them to the chest as an aid in swimming. Lighter traffic was carried out in small rowboats or coracles with wicker frames *(quppu)* made watertight by covering them with pitch or with skins. In the marshes, long bundles of reeds were lashed together to form boat-like rafts that were propelled by punting.

Regulating River Traffic. Rehearsing his credentials as a just king in the prologue to the Laws of Ur-Namma (circa 2112 – circa 2095 B.C.E.), the founder of the Third Dynasty of Ur claimed to have regulated the riverboat traffic on the banks of all rivers in the land. Although the specifics of Ur-Namma's code are lost, other late third millennium and early second millennium B.C.E. law codes are concerned with the loss of a boat by a renter who took it along a route other than one to which the owner agreed, as well as rental rates and establishing the right of way:

> If a boat under the command of a master of an upstream-boat collides with a boat under the command of a downstream-boat and thus sinks it, the owner of the sunken boat shall establish before god the property that is lost from the boat, and the master of the upstream-boat who sinks the boat of the master of the downstream-boat shall replace to him his boat and his lost property. (LH §240; Roth)

The potential volume of river traffic may be gauged by a letter sent by Ishbi-Erra to king Ibbi-Sin of Ur (circa 2028 – circa 2004 B.C.E.) requesting transport for some fifteen thousand tons of barley:

> You ordered me to travel (north) to Isin and Kazallu to purchase grain. . . . 72,000 gur of grain was brought—the entire amount of grain—inside Isin. . . . Because of the Martu (Amorites), I am unable to hand over this grain for

threshing. They are stronger than me, while I am condemned to sitting around. Let my lord repair 600 barges of 120 gur draught each; 72 solid boats, 20 . . . , 30 . . . , placing (?) 50 . . . and 60 (?) boat doors on the boats (?), may he also . . . all the boats. Let them bring it up by water, along the Kura and the Palishtum watercourses, to the grain heaps (?) that are spread out. And I myself intend to go and meet them (?). The place there where the boats moor will be under my responsibility. Let them load up huge amounts of grain (?), the entire amount of grain; it should reach (?) you. . . . I have at my disposal enough grain to meet the needs of your palace and of all your cities for 15 years. (Black et al.)

Ishbi-Erra was a vassal of Ibbi-Sin, the last king of the Third Dynasty of Ur during its period of greatest political turmoil. By stockpiling such an enormous quantity of grain at Isin, where he knew Ibbi-Sin would be unable to retrieve it, Ishbi-Erra was laying the foundation for his own rise to power. From Isin, where he established a new dynasty in southern Mesopotamia, Ishbi-Erra (circa 2017 – circa 1985 B.C.E.) went on to control the cities of Ur, Uruk, and Nippur, as well as the all-important roads leading to the Persian Gulf coast.

Sources:

George F. Bass, "Sea and River Craft in the Ancient Near East," in *Civilizations of the Ancient Near East,* 4 volumes, edited by Jack M. Sasson (New York: Scribners, 1995), III: 1421–1431.

Jeremy Black, Graham Cunningham, Jarle Ebeling, Esther Flückiger-Hawker, Eleanor Robson, Jon Taylor, and Gábor Zólyomi, *The Electronic Text Corpus of Sumerian Literature,* The Oriental Institute, University of Oxford, 1998– <http://www.etcsl.orient.ox.ac.uk/>.

Dominique Collon, *First Impressions: Cylinder Seals in the Ancient Near East* (London: British Museum, 1987).

Michael Roaf, *Cultural Atlas of Mesopotamia and the Ancient Near East* (New York: Facts on File, 1966).

Martha T. Roth, *Law Collections from Mesopotamia and Asia Minor,* second edition, Society of Biblical Literature, Writings from the Ancient World Series, volume 6 (Atlanta: Scholars Press, 1995).

TREASURES AND HOARDS

Buried Treasure. Excavations by archaeologists throughout the Near East have uncovered many caches of precious metals and stones, either in raw or manufactured form, that were deliberately hidden away in antiquity for safekeeping, but never retrieved by their owners. The contents of some of these "hoards" or "treasures" include heirlooms, objects demonstrably sometimes centuries older than suggested by the contexts in which they were found. In several cases the materials, methods of manufacture, and styles of decoration of the objects in the hoards indicate that these objects were imports from distant lands. Today, such collections are important evidence for reconstructing patterns of ancient long-distance transportation and trade.

Hoards of Silver. Throughout most of Mesopotamian history, silver was the primary means of exchange and payment. The silver might be in the form of rings, wires, ingots, or pieces cut from ingots; all these various objects and fragments were weighed out to determine payment. Standardized coinage, although introduced into Mesopotamia in the later sixth century B.C.E. during the Achaemenid period, did not come into wide circulation until the Seleucid period (312–129 B.C.E.), during which silver coins, called *staters*, were still weighed when they were used for purchases. Hoards of scrap silver, perhaps representing an individual's personal wealth or a jeweler's stock of raw materials, were buried for safekeeping and not recovered until modern times. Such hoards are known from sites in northern and southern Mesopotamia that

A lion-headed eagle ("Anzud") made of lapis lazuli, gold, bitumen, and copper alloy (height 5 inches)
from the "Treasure of Ur," Palace of Mari, circa 2500 – circa 2350 B.C.E.
(National Museum, Damascus)

Modern impression of a lapis-lazuli cylinder seal (height 1 5/8 inches) depicting the god Marduk standing between two mountains and holding two streams of water. The seal belonged to Kidin-Marduk, an official in the court of the Kassite Babylonian king Burna-Buriash II (circa 1359 – circa 1333 B.C.E.), and was part of a hoard of seals and beads found at Thebes in Greece, circa 1220 B.C.E. (Archaeological Museum of Thebes).

date to the Early Dynastic and Akkadian periods during the latter half of the third millennium B.C.E.—as well as an Old Babylonian period site at Larsa (first half of the second millennium B.C.E.), a Neo-Assyrian period site at Nippur (first half of the first millennium B.C.E.), and a hoard of bracelets, rings, and earrings in a pot within the ruins of a Kassite period (second half of the second millennium B.C.E.) building on the island of Bahrain.

Treasure of Ur. From time to time, archaeologists have recovered ancient collections of other precious objects of diverse origins that seem to have been intentionally hidden away. A container unearthed beneath the floor of a courtyard at Mari on the middle Euphrates was first taken to be a funerary jar. Inspection revealed a pendant and beads of lapis lazuli, beads of carnelian and gold, seals made of shell, and figurines of copper alloy and ivory. The distinctive blue stone lapis lazuli had been mined in eastern Afghanistan while the bright orange carnelian likely originated in western India. Among the objects was a lapis-lazuli bead inscribed with the name of Mesanepada, founder of the First Dynasty of Ur (circa 2600 B.C.E.). This bead—together with other lapis-lazuli and carnelian beads, similar to those found in the Royal Graves at Ur—led an early investigator to suggest that the hoard was a gift from the king of Ur to his counterpart at Mari. But more-recent studies have suggested that at least some of the objects in the collection originated at sites in northern Mesopotamia, the Diayala River valley, and the middle Euphrates valley, including Mari itself. It remains an open question how the hoard came to be accumulated and buried as it was.

Tôd Treasure. Four bronze caskets, inscribed with the name of the Twelfth Dynasty Egyptian king Amenenhat II (circa 1901 – circa 1867 B.C.E.), were found within the temple of Montu at Tôd, in Upper Egypt. They contained ingots of gold and silver, metal chains, and silver vessels, many crushed and folded, some showing Cretan parallels. There were also lapis-lazuli cylinder and stamp seals and amulets with stylistic connections to the Levant, north Syria, southern Mesopotamia, Iran, and possibly Bactria in Central Asia. The motifs and styles in which they were represented on the seals and beads indicate dates from as early as circa 2900 B.C.E. to as late as 1800 B.C.E. Although no one knows precisely how such a diverse body of material came to be assembled in Egypt, the general consensus of opinion holds that it represents a jeweler's stock buried for safekeeping and never recovered.

Vase à la Cachette. Two large painted clay jars excavated at Susa in southwestern Iran contained vessels of carved alabaster; copper and bronze vessels, tools, and weapons; gold, silver, and copper rings; gold beads; a tiny lapis-lazuli bead in the shape of a frog; and cylinder seals. The contents of the jars, which had been deposited during the two and a half centuries following circa 2400 B.C.E., were made over a five-hundred-year span. Their varied styles suggest connections between Susa and Mesopotamia to its west, as well as eastern Iran, the Persian Gulf, and the Indus Valley. The *vase à la cachette* appears to have belonged to a merchant, who buried it for safekeeping and never retrieved it.

Oriental Seals in Thebes, Greece. In a room belonging to a Mycenaean Greek building destroyed circa 1220 B.C.E., excavators discovered a substantial hoard of lapis-lazuli cylinder seals and beads together with a large number of agate beads. Nearby was found a second hoard of gold beads, lapis-lazuli objects, and pendants made of a dark blue paste imitating lapis lazuli. Thirty-three of the seals were originally manufactured in Mesopotamia and included examples of Akkadian (circa 2340 – circa 2200 B.C.E.), Old Babylonian (circa 1800 – circa 1600 B.C.E.), and Kassite, Mitannian, and Middle Assyrian (circa 1450 – circa 1250 B.C.E.) styles; of these, four were recarved in a Cypriot style. There were also eight cylinder seals in local Cypriot styles and a single Hittite-style cylinder seal (circa 1350 – circa 1250 B.C.E.). Among these seals one, according to its inscription, belonged to Hammi-Darab, king of Yaraguttim, a land perhaps in Syria, while another seal belonged to a high-ranking official in the court of the Kassite Babylonian king Burna-Buriash II (circa 1359 – circa 1333 B.C.E.). It has been suggested that the Kassite seals might originally have been seized as part of the booty taken by the Middle Assyrian king Tukulti-Ninurta I (circa 1243 – circa 1207 B.C.E.) from the temple of Marduk in Babylon. In an effort to counter hostile actions against Assyria by the Hittites in Anatolia and Syria, Tukulti-Ninurta may have attempted to establish relations with the Mycenaeans in Greece, who were also enemies of the Hittites.

Ur Coffin Hoard. Excavation of a plundered Persian-period grave (fifth to fourth centuries B.C.E.) at Ur revealed a clay coffin containing almost two hundred lumps of clay bearing impressions; most were from cylinder and stamp seals, but others were impressions of seal impressions on cuneiform tablets and of coins. The seal impressions included those of a seventh century B.C.E. Neo-Assyrian cylinder seal, eighth-fifth century B.C.E. Neo-Babylonian cylinder seals, fifth century B.C.E. Achaemenid cylinder and stamp seals, and fifth century Greek engraved gems and finger rings. Among the coin impressions was one of an Athenian tetradrachm, minted about 465–460 B.C.E., and those of coins from Aegae in Macedon (circa 485 B.C.E.) and Miletus (circa 500 – circa 430 B.C.E.). The presence of these impressions of Greek seals and coins in southern Mesopotamia demonstrates that Hellenism was already beginning to have an impact on the East well before the conquest of Alexander III of Macedon (331 B.C.E.). A recent opinion holds that the hoard, itself of no intrinsic value, had been accumulated by a seal engraver and represented designs he had chosen for study and perhaps inspiration, together with impressions of what might have been his own creations.

Sources:

Agnès Benoit, *"Vase à la cachette"* and "Cylinder seal with a contest scene, from the *vase à la cachette*," in *Art of the First Cities: The Third Millennium B.C. from the Mediterranean to the Indus*, edited by Joan Aruz with Ronald Wallenfels (New York: Metropolitan Museum of Art, 2003), pp. 302–306.

Nadia Cholidis, "The Treasure of Ur from Mari," in *Art of the First Cities: The Third Millennium B.C. from the Mediterranean to the Indus*, pp. 139–147.

Dominique Collon, "A Hoard of Sealings from Ur," *Archives et Sceaux du monde hellénistique: Archivi e Sigilli nel Mondo Ellenistico, Torino, Villa Gualino 13–16 Gennaio 1993*, edited by Marie-Françoise Boussac and Antonio Invernizzi, Bulletin de Correspondence Hellénique, supplement 29 (1996): 65–84.

P. R. S. Moorey, *Ancient Mesopotamian Materials and Industries: The Archaeological Evidence* (Winona Lake, Ind.: Eisenbrauns, 1999).

Edith Porada, "The Cylinder Seals Found at Thebes in Boeotia," *Archiv für Orientforschung*, 28 (1981): 1–78.

Porada, "Remarks on the Tôd Treasure in Egypt," in *Societies and Languages of the Ancient Near East: Studies in Honor of I. M. Diakonoff*, edited by M. Dandamaev (Warminster, U.K.: Aris & Phillips, 1982), pp. 285–303.

WRITING

Clay Tokens. It is widely, though not universally, accepted that the origins of writing in Mesopotamia lie in the use throughout the ancient Near East since the eighth millennium B.C.E. of small clay tokens used for counting. These counters were modeled from pieces of clay that were pinched between the fingers into simple geometric shapes: spheres, discs, cones, tetrahedrons, and rods. The tokens might be further modified by the use of incised lines, notches, punches, and appliqué pellets. It is believed that each distinct kind of token represented one unit, or some aggregate number of units, of some discrete entity in the Neolithic Near Eastern economy, for instance a sheep or goat, a loaf of bread, or a jar of barley or oil. Accounts were apparently maintained by placing one counter for each object, or each aggregate number of objects, in a leather or cloth bag that was tied with string. The string was secured by enclosing the knot within a piece of clay onto which a stamp seal, representing the authority of the accountant or another responsible party, might be impressed. After some four thousand years of use, a new type of token—the "complex token"—with a much wider variety of shapes and surface markings, appeared alongside the older plain tokens at Uruk and other culturally related sites, including Habuba Kabira (an Uruk colony in Syria) and Susa in southwest Iran. The appearance of the complex tokens more or less coincided with the monumental expansion of the E-ana temple, dedicated to the goddess Inana, at Uruk during its transformation into a city proper. Toward the end of the first half of the fourth millennium B.C.E., a new means of securing the tokens representing a given account appeared; the counters were enclosed within a clay envelope, a hollow clay ball over whose outer surface a cylinder seal was rolled. Occasionally, the outer sealed surface of an envelope was also marked with an impression of each token placed within the envelope, allowing the viewer to see the contents of the envelope without having to break it open. This act may be taken as the first step in the transformation of a three-dimensional token into a two-dimensional graphic symbol; that is, writing.

Clay Tablets. Beginning about the middle of the fourth millennium B.C.E. there appeared at sites along the major trade routes in Mesopotamia, Syria, and Iran small solid rectangular clay tablets. These tablets, about the size of the palm of a hand, bear on their slightly rounded surfaces cylinder-seal impressions and a limited repertoire of impressed signs that can be traced to token prototypes. In addition, the tablets bear ideograms, drawings incised

---

ENMERKAR INVENTS WRITING

Enmerkar, the legendary ruler of Uruk (Unug-Kulaba), engaged in a protracted rivalry with the ruler of Aratta, a mythical city far to the east of Mesopotamia. The two rulers send messengers back and forth with increasingly complex riddles for one another to solve and thereby demonstrate one ruler's superiority over the other. During the third exchange Enmerkar's instructions to his messenger are beyond the capacity of his memory:

His speech was substantial, and its contents extensive. The messenger, whose mouth was heavy, was not able to repeat it. Because the messenger, whose mouth was tired, was not able to repeat it, the lord of Kulaba patted some clay and wrote the message as if on a tablet. Formerly, the writing of messages on clay was not established. Now, under that sun and on that day, it was indeed so. The lord of Kulaba inscribed the message like a tablet. It was just like that. The messenger was like a bird, flapping its wings; he raged forth like a wolf following a kid. He traversed five mountains, six mountains, seven mountains. He lifted his eyes as he approached Aratta. He stepped joyfully into the courtyard of Aratta, he made known the authority of his king. Openly he spoke out the words in his heart. The messenger transmitted the message to the lord of Aratta:
"Your father, my master, has sent me to you; the lord of Unug, the lord of Kulaba, has sent me to you. . . . Enmerkar, the son of Utu, has given me a clay tablet. O lord of Aratta, after you have examined the clay tablet, after you have learned the content of the message, say whatever you will say to me, and I shall announce that message . . . to my king, the lord of Kulaba."
After he had spoken thus to him, the lord of Aratta received his kiln-fired tablet from the messenger. The lord of Aratta looked at the tablet. The transmitted message was just nails, and his brow expressed anger. The lord of Aratta looked at his kiln-fired tablet.

The "nails" on the tablet that were so inscrutable to the Lord of Aratta were the cuneiform wedges that composed the signs.

Source: Jeremy Black, Graham Cunningham, Jarle Ebeling, Esther Flückiger-Hawker, Eleanor Robson, Jon Taylor, and Gábor Zólyomi, *The Electronic Text Corpus of Sumerian Literature*, The Oriental Institute, University of Oxford, 1998– <http://www.etcsl.orient.ox.ac.uk/>.

---

with a sharp stylus and graphically depicting some of the complex tokens and perhaps the personal name of the proprietor. The incised drawings rapidly gave way to more-abstract symbols made by impressing into the clay the tip of a wedge-shaped stylus, producing the first proto-cuneiform tablets. (Cuneiform means "wedge-shaped.") Whether this step was the last in a series of evolutionary changes in an ever-increasingly complex accounting and bookkeeping system, or whether it represents an entirely new technology, invented as a system, remains to be determined. Clay tablets remained the preferred writing medium for the cuneiform system throughout its almost 3,500 years of use. Through much of that time period, cuneiform inscriptions were also incised on stone and metal surfaces, and—beginning in the middle of the second millennium B.C.E.—on wax-covered writing boards that could be "erased" and re-used.

Cuneiform. The signs on the earliest proto-cuneiform tablets are ideograms or logograms; that is, they are graphic symbols that represent nouns, a few basic adjectives, and perhaps some verbs for specific administrative actions; they do not represent grammatical elements, nor do they represent the sound of a word. Thus, the tablets can be "read"—that is, understood—by anyone initiated in the meanings of the signs, regardless of what language or languages that person speaks. Nonetheless, most scholars agree that the proto-cuneiform scribes spoke Sumerian. Because of gaps in the archaeological record, the precise steps in the path to recording natural language cannot be fully traced; nonetheless, by the middle of the third millennium B.C.E. cuneiform writing was becoming sufficiently flexible to capture spoken language, Sumerian first, and soon Akkadian, Eblaite, and Hurrian. The cuneiform writing system is a word-syllabic system in which a sign may represent either a whole word (logogram) or an individual syllable (syllabogram) within a word. Certain signs may also serve as determinatives, visual markers placed either before or after a given word, whether written logographically or syllabically, that serve to classify the word in question, such as a woman's name, an object made of wood, or a species of fish. Initially, the signs were arranged in rectangular cases that were read horizontally from right to left. In the earliest stages, the signs within each case were drawn randomly. In an innovation introduced during the reign of Eanatum of Lagash (circa 2500 B.C.E.), scribes began to write the signs in vertical columns within the cases in the order in which they were to be read and vocalized. Toward the middle of the second millennium B.C.E., the direction of reading and writing, together with the orientation of signs, was rotated ninety degrees counterclockwise so that the signs were read in horizontal rows from left to right. The Sumerian-Akkadian repertoire of signs proved sufficiently flexible to be used in rendering several Anatolian lan-

Sealed clay bulla (diameter approximately 2½ inches) with impressions recording the tokens inside, and the clay tokens it contained (each about ½ inch in length), from Susa, late fourth millennium B.C.E. (Louvre, Paris)

guages; Hurrian and Urartian; Iranian Elamite; as well as, on occasion, Aramaic. In the latter half of the second millennium B.C.E., the scribes at Ugarit in north Syria devised a completely new inventory of thirty cuneiform signs that were analogues to the Old Canaanite aleph-beth. Toward the end of the sixth century, the Persians devised a new cuneiform syllabary to render the Old Persian language in their royal inscriptions. Both the Ugaritic and Persian innovations proved transitory, but traditional cuneiform writing continued to be taught at a few Babylonian temple schools into the early centuries of the Common Era (C.E.).

Proto-Elamite. At the end of the fourth millennium B.C.E., the indigenous people of Susa in Khuzestan in southwestern Iran developed a writing system, apparently modeled on the proto-cuneiform system. Examples of proto-Elamite writing have been found distributed across the Iranian plateau. The signs appear to be logograms and numerals. Toward the end of the third millennium B.C.E., the complex script was simplified. Both forms of the script have so far eluded decipherment. The proto-Elamite script was abandoned and replaced by standard Akkadian cuneiform at the very beginning of the second millennium B.C.E.

The Aleph-Beth. The twenty-two-character West Semitic aleph-beth writing system appears to have developed among the Canaanites of the Levant during the last centuries of the second millennium B.C.E. Initially flexible in the orientation of its writing—like Egyptian hieroglyphs, from which is it thought to derive—the system eventually stabilized on being read from right to left. In its simplest form—as, for example, it was used by the Phoenicians—the graphemes, or signs, represent just the consonants, and the reader had to supply the vowels from context. Other users of the script, under specific condi-

tions, used as many as four of the graphemes to represent certain long vowels; modern scholars call graphemes used in this way *matres lectionis,* "mothers of reading." The Aramaic form of the script, written from right to left, was brought into Mesopotamia during the early centuries of the first millennium B.C.E. by the Aramaeans of north Syria, who were dispersed across Mesopotamia as a result of the Assyrian policy of mass deportation of captive peoples. Wall reliefs from eighth and seventh century B.C.E. Neo-Assyrian palaces clearly depict scribes writing with pen and ink on papyrus or prepared animal skins alongside traditional cuneiform scribes with stylus and clay tablet, or wax-covered writing board, in hand. Aramaic dockets (summary labels) appear penned or incised on cuneiform archival tablets throughout the latter half of the first millennium B.C.E. Examples of another aleph-beth, the South Arabic, dating from approximately the seventh century B.C.E., have been found in Mesopotamia at Ur and Nippur. Apparently an independent offshoot of the original proto-Canaanite script, the South Arabic script has twenty-nine letters and remained flexible with regard to the direction of writing, being written from left to right, right to left, and boustrophedon (Greek for "as the ox plows").

The Alphabet. The Greek alphabet, the first true alphabet with individual characters for consonants and all vowels, was developed from the West Semitic aleph-beth during the eighth century B.C.E. Although initially flexible in the orientation of its writing, the system stabilized at being read from left to right—the opposite of the aleph-beth. The Greek alphabet was brought into Mesopotamia in the wake of the conquests of Alexander III (the Great) of Macedon in 333–331 B.C.E. and the consequent spread of Hellenic culture and the Greek language.

Inscribed clay tablets: administrative tablet with impressed numerals and incised ideograms, southern Mesopotamia, late fourth millennium B.C.E.; and a cursive cuneiform copy of the *Sumerian Titles and Professions List,* a text used in scribal education, from Ebla, western Syria, circa 2250 B.C.E. (left: Louvre, Paris; right: Idlib Museum, Syria)

Assyrian scribes listing booty in cuneiform on a wax-covered writing board (front) and in Aramaic on a roll of prepared animal skin (behind), Southwest Palace, Nineveh, about 630–620 B.C.E. (British Museum, London)

Cuneiform tablet fragment (height 3 inches) with the legend of *Enmerkar and the Lord of Aratta,* Nippur, circa 1740 B.C.E.
(University of Pennsylvania Museum of Archaeology and Anthropology)

Detail (height 15 inches) from a Luwian hieroglyphic inscription of king Katuwa carved on a basalt doorjamb, Carchemish, circa 880 B.C.E.; and an Aramaic endorsement incised on an upside-down cuneiform tablet, Nippur, 423 B.C.E. (top: British Museum, London; bottom: University of Pennsylvania Museum of Archaeology and Anthropology)

A ROYAL WARNING

The Assyrian king Sargon II (721–705 B.C.E.) wrote a letter on a cuneiform tablet in response to a request by Sin-iddina, a royal official at Ur in Babylonia, cautioning him about the use of Aramaic script on parchment. The letter begins with the customary salutations:

Say to Sin-iddina: thus says the king. I am well, [you] can be glad. May the bread as well as the first-quality beer of the temple be good! May the guard of Ur and my temples be strong!

Sargon then recounts the words of an earlier letter from Sin-iddina, including a warning to the king and a request:

There are informers [. . . to the king] and coming to his presence; if it is acceptable to the king, let me write and send my messages to the king on Aram[aic] parchment sheets.

The king's response is unequivocal:

Why should you not write and send me messages in Akkadian? Really, the message which you write in must be drawn up in this very manner—this is a fixed regulation!

Source: Manfried Dietrich, *The Babylonian Correspondence of Sargon and Sennacherib*, State Archives of Assyria, volume 17 (Helsinki: Helsinki University Press, 2003), p. 5.

Hieroglyphics. Although objects with Egyptian hieroglyphics are known from excavations in Syria, the Egyptian writing system appears not to have had any impact in Mesopotamia. In fact, it is often argued that the Egyptian system was in some way modeled on the Mesopotamian, perhaps as a result of contacts made during the so-called periods of Uruk expansion in the latter half of the fourth millennium B.C.E. In Anatolia, Hittite, or more properly Luwian, hieroglyphics came into use during the second half of the second millennium B.C.E. The system survived the fall of the Hittite empire and continued in use during the early first millennium B.C.E. in southern Anatolia and north Syria until the Neo-Assyrian conquests of the ninth and eighth centuries B.C.E. In the eighth and seventh centuries B.C.E., the Assyrians themselves appear to have experimented briefly with hieroglyphics for certain royal inscriptions.

Sources:

Peter T. Daniels and William Bright, eds., *The World's Writing Systems* (New York: Oxford University Press, 1996).

Irving L. Finkel and Julian E. Reade, "Assyrian Hieroglyphs," *Zeitschrift für Assyriologie und Archeologie*, 86 (1996): 244–268.

Piotr Michalowski, "The Earliest Scholastic Tradition," in *Art of the First Cities: The Third Millennium B.C. from the Mediterranean to the Indus*, edited by Joan Aruz with Ronald Wallenfels (New York: Metropolitan Museum of Art, 2003), pp. 451–456.

Joseph Naveh, *Early History of the Alphabet: An Introduction to West Semitic Epigraphy and Palaeography* (Jerusalem: Magnes Press, Hebrew University / Leiden: Brill, 1982).

Hans J. Nissen, Peter Damerow, and Robert K. Englund, *Archaic Bookkeeping: Writing and Techniques of Economic Administration in the Ancient Near East*, translated by Paul Larsen (Chicago & London: University of Chicago Press, 1993).

Michael Roaf and Annette Zgoll, "Assyrian Astroglyphs: Lord Aberdeen's Black Stone and the Prisms of Esarhaddon," *Zeitschrift für Assyriologie und Archeologie*, 91 (2001): 264–295.

Benjamin Sass, *The Genesis of the Alphabet and its Development in the Second Millennium B.C.*, Ägypten und Altes Testament, 13 (Wiesbaden: Otto Harrassowitz, 1988).

Denise Schmandt-Besserat, *From Counting to Cuneiform*, volume 1 of *Before Writing*, 2 volumes (Austin: University of Texas Press, 1992).

SIGNIFICANT PERSON

TUKULTI-NINURTA I

CIRCA 1243 – CIRCA 1207 B.C.E.
KING OF ASSYRIA

The Middle Assyrian Kingdom. In the century after Ashur-uballit I (circa 1363 – circa 1328 B.C.E.) established the Middle Assyrian kingdom as a major international power on a par with the Egyptians, Hittites, Mittanians, and Babylonians, the Assyrians' need for imported raw materials grew dramatically. To secure access to supplies of copper, tin, lapis lazuli, and horses, the great warrior-king Tukulti-Ninurta I campaigned extensively in the mountains to the north and east, establishing control of access points to significant trade routes throughout the region.

Conflict with Babylon. Tukulti-Ninurta's success increased tensions between the Assyrians and their Kassite Babylonian neighbors to the south. The Babylonians, who needed access to the same raw materials, had once viewed Assyria as a breakaway vassal state. Thus, while Tukulti-Ninurta I was campaigning to his north, the Babylonian king Kashtiliash IV (circa 1232 – circa 1225 B.C.E.) advanced his troops north into Assyrian-controlled territory. From the Assyrian perspective, the Babylonian action violated a treaty that had been in effect for a half century. The Epic of Tukulti-Ninurta, several fragments of which were found on cuneiform tablets discovered in Ashur and in Nineveh, recounts how Tukulti-Ninurta, after exhausting all available procedures based on the abrogated treaty and with the approval of the gods—both Assyrian and Babylonian—achieved military victory over Kashtiliash. Kashtiliash was captured and brought to Ashur in chains; Babylon's wall was torn down, its temples looted, and the country annexed. A group of lapis-lazuli cylinder seals bearing dedicatory inscriptions to Marduk (the Babylonian national god), found

in the ruins of a Mycenaean building in Thebes in Greece, may have been among those looted from Babylon by the Assyrians. Tukulti-Ninurta may have then sent them as a royal gift to a Greek prince in an effort to obtain an ally against their common enemy, the Hittites of Anatolia.

A New Capital. When Tukulti-Ninurta assumed kingship over Assyria and Babylonia, as befit his new status, he founded a new capital city, Kar-Tukulti-Ninurta, just three kilometers (two miles) north of the old capital, Ashur, on the opposite, east, bank of the Tigris River. Babylonian influences are found in the architecture of Kar-Tukulti-Ninurta, in the deities worshiped there, and in the Akkadian and Sumerian literary compositions produced in Assyria during this period. He also adopted several somewhat outlandish titles including king of Babylonia, king of the land of the Sumerians and Akkadians, king of the upper and lower seas, and king of Dilmun and Meluhha. A Babylonian chronicle recounts how seven years after Tukulti-Ninurta assumed control of Babylon,

> Ashur-nasir-apli, son of Tukulti-Ninurta—who had carried out criminal designs on Babylon—and the officers of Assyria rebelled against him (Tukulti-Ninurta), removed him [from] his throne, shut him up in a room in Kar-Tukulti-Ninurta and killed him. (Grayson)

Almost a century passed before the Middle Assyrian kingdom had another strong king—Tiglath-pileser I (circa 1114 – circa 1076 B.C.E.), who was also its last.

Sources:

A. J. Brinkman, *Materials and Studies for Kassite History; Volume I: A Catalogue of Cuneiform Sources Pertaining to Specific Monarchs of the Kassite Dynasty* (Chicago: Oriental Institute of the University of Chicago, 1976).

Reinhard Dittmann, "Kar-Tukulti-Ninurta," in *The Oxford Encyclopedia of Archaeology in the Near East*, 5 volumes, edited by Eric M. Meyers (New York & Oxford: Oxford University Press, 1997), III: 269–271.

Albert Kirk Grayson, *Assyrian and Babylonian Chronicles*, Texts from Cuneiform Sources, 5 (Locust Valley, N.Y.: J. J. Augustin, 1975).

Amélie Kuhrt, *The Ancient Near East c. 3000–330 B.C.*, 2 volumes (London & New York: Routledge, 1995).

Edith Porada, "The Cylinder Seals Found at Thebes in Boeotia," *Archiv für Orientforschung*, 28 (1981): 1–78.

DOCUMENTARY SOURCES

The Amarna Archive (circa fourteenth century B.C.E.)—The state archive of the later kings of the Eighteenth Dynasty of Egypt was discovered in 1887 among the ruins of the ancient capital city of Akhetaten (modern Amarna). Among the nearly four hundred cuneiform tablets recovered from this source are letters from the kings of Babylonia, Assyria, Mitanni, and Hatti, and copies of some of the Egyptian kings' replies. The archive documents the exchange of lavish diplomatic gifts, at times including considerable quantities of luxury objects made of precious metals, semiprecious stones, hardwoods, and ivory. Other tablets in the archive document the declining political situation in the southern Levant, whose local princes were allied with the Egyptians and sought their help in the face of local rebellions. Several word lists and other scholarly tablets in the archive attest to the training of Egyptian scribes in the Akkadian language and cuneiform writing.

East India House Inscription (604–562 B.C.E.)—A large inscribed stone slab was discovered in the ruins of Babylon before 1801 and presented to the representative of the East India Company in Baghdad. In ten columns of text, the Babylonian king Nebuchadnezzar II describes in considerable detail how during his reign he rebuilt the cities of Babylon and Borsippa. Written in an archaizing Old Babylonian–like script, the inscription enumerates the temples the king refurbished, listing the names of the imported woods, stones and precious metals that were employed. It lavishes particular detail on the construction at Babylon of massive double walls, the great Ishtar Gate, and central Processional Way.

Enmerkar and the Lord of Aratta (circa 1750 B.C.E.)—This Sumerian-language tale, although set in the period of transition from the Early Dynastic I to Early Dynastic II period, circa 2750 B.C.E., was probably not composed until late in the third millennium B.C.E., with the earliest extant copies dating from the Old Babylonian period. The tale describes a time before commerce was practiced, before Dilmun (Bahrain) served to communicate exotica from overseas, and before gold, silver, copper, tin, lapis lazuli, and other stones were shipped from their mountain sources in the east. The plot focuses on the struggle for dominance between Enmerkar, the ruler of the city of Uruk in southern Mesopotamia, a land that produces grain and textiles, and the unnamed ruler of the city of Aratta, located across seven mountain ranges to the east, perhaps in eastern Iran, near the sources of the precious stones and metals that Mesopotamia lacks. In the course of their conflict, a messenger travels back and forth between the two cities conveying ever-more-complex memorized riddles, which the two rulers have devised to demonstrate the superiority of one over the other. When Enmerkar's message becomes too difficult for the messenger to memorize, the king devises a method (cuneiform) whereby his message can be written on a clay tablet to be read rather than memorized.

The Kültepe Archives (circa 1900 – circa 1700 B.C.E.)—Approximately seventeen thousand five hundred clay cuneiform tablets have been discovered in jars, boxes, and bags in the ruins of some seventy homes in the *karum*, the lower, commercial, city at Kültepe (ancient Kanesh) in Anatolia. The tablets—archival texts, letters, and legal documents—provide evidence of the presence of commercial traders from the city of Ashur, more than 1,500 kilometers to the southeast, who had taken up residence in the *karum* to oversee their import-export business. Many of the tablets bear the impressions of cylinder seals carved in a wide variety of styles: Assyrian, Syrian, and Anatolian. Twice a year Assyrian donkey caravans brought to Kanesh tin and textiles that were exchanged for gold and silver bullion, which was shipped back to Ashur.

Persepolis Fortification Archive (509–494 B.C.E.)—Thousands of cuneiform clay tablets written in Elamite were found in the fortification walls at Persepolis in Iran. These tablets document the movement within the Persian Empire of vast quantities of grain, flour, wine, sheep, goats, and hides. Ration texts in the archive provide evidence of state functionaries traveling from the Persian heartland eastward to Central Asia and India, or westward to Babylonia, Lydia, and Egypt. Many of the tablets bear the impressions of cylinder and stamp seals representing the individuals and offices mentioned in the documents, providing insight into the early development of Persian glyptic art.

Arched entrance to the Palace of Sargon II (721–705 B.C.E.), flanked by colossal human-headed
winged bulls, Khorsabad (photograph by M. Tranchand, 1850s)

SOCIAL CLASS SYSTEM AND THE ECONOMY

by KATHRYN SLANSKI

CONTENTS

Sidebars and tables are listed in italics.

IMPORTANT EVENTS OF 3300-331 B.C.E.

3300* B.C.E.

- By this date, southern Mesopotamia has experienced an "urban explosion" along the banks of the Tigris and Euphrates Rivers. Nascent urban centers have monumental architecture (temples), city walls, and public art.

- The cylinder seal has appeared alongside the older stamp seal as a means of indicating ownership and origin of commodities.

- Cities have spurred specialization and standardization of production. Using wheeled vehicles and donkeys, these cities engage in long-distance trade to exchange their surpluses for raw materials not available in Mesopotamia.

3300*-3100* B.C.E.

- Crafts manufacture, communal activities, and the "priest-king" are depicted on cylinder seals and relief carvings.

- Proto-cuneiform writing is developed in response to the need to keep economic records.

3100*-2500* B.C.E.

- City-states arise and flourish throughout southern Mesopotamia.

- A fully developed cuneiform writing system comes into widespread use for documenting the economic activities of the temple, which seems to control most resources of the land.

- An elite socio-political class creates rich burial sites such as the so-called Royal Tombs in the temple precinct of the city of Ur, which include luxury materials—including gold, silver, and semiprecious stones—obtained through long-distance trade.

2500*-2350* B.C.E.

- Temples continue to control most of the resources of Mesopotamia, using their agricultural surpluses and the products of their industrial weaving enterprises to support long-distance trading ventures.

- Palaces are built by a new socio-political and economic elite that challenges the power of the temple.

2350* B.C.E.

- Uru'inimgina, ruler of the city-state of Lagash, institutes social and economic reforms.

2334*-2279* B.C.E.

- Sargon of Akkad, a city in the north of Sumer (whose site remains undiscovered by modern archaeologists), conquers the southern city-states and establishes the world's first empire. Continually widening its borders to control trade routes with access to the natural resources lacking in Mesopotamia, Sargon imposes administrative unity throughout the land, in part by reforming the writing system and accounting procedures.

* DENOTES CIRCA DATE

IMPORTANT EVENTS OF 3300-331 B.C.E.

2112*-2095*
B.C.E.

- The founder of the Third Dynasty of Ur, Ur-Namma wrests free the city of Ur from domination by Uruk, following the expulsion of the Guti. He builds the first known temple ziggurat and is credited with writing the earliest collection of laws, which commemorates the securing and regulating of trade routes and standardizes the system of weights and measures.

2094*-2047*
B.C.E.

- Ur-Namma's son and successor, Shulgi, brings the Ur III state to its peak, instituting the *bala*-system, a far-reaching redistributive economy in which a state-run bureaucracy collects and allocates all goods and services. He also institutes reforms in the writing system and accounting procedures, further refines the system of weights and measures, and introduces a new calendar.

2094*-2004*
B.C.E.

- Under the Third Dynasty of Ur, the so-called Seafaring Merchants of Ur co-operate with the great institutions of the temple and palace to conduct trade with the civilizations on the northern shore of the Persian Gulf.

2010*-1595*
B.C.E.

- Old Assyrian long-distance trade flourishes with colonies established in Anatolia.

- The Old Babylonian kingdom continues the tradition of compiling law collections, which include stipulation of prices and interest rates. In order to re-establish socio-economic equilibrium in the land, Old Babylonian kings occasionally issue *misharum*-edicts, forgiving all debts.

1600*-1100*
B.C.E.

- The Kassite Dynasty is founded in Babylon. The age of the city-states is over, and the peace and prosperity of this period enables Babylonia to export its goods and its intellectual culture throughout the ancient world.

- In Babylonia, entitlement monuments (so-called *kudurru*) are created to commemorate transfers of land grants and purchases, acquisitions of temple prebends (rights to temple income), and resolutions of legal cases.

1450*-1350*
B.C.E.

- Family archives from the city of Nuzi, on the northeast periphery of Mesopotamia, document the practice of "purchase adoptions" to avoid restrictions against the sale of family property to nonrelatives.

1391*-1335*
B.C.E.

- A royal archive is compiled, at Amarna in Egypt, documenting the unprecedented magnitude of international diplomacy and trade among the kingdoms of Babylonia, Egypt, Hatti (Anatolia), Mitanni, and Assyria.

* DENOTES CIRCA DATE

IMPORTANT EVENTS OF 3300-331 B.C.E.

900*-612 B.C.E.

- The Neo-Assyrian Empire dominates the ancient Near East with unrivaled military technology, notably cavalry and horse-drawn chariots, requiring financial support from an ever-widening circle of tribute-paying vassals.

- The Neo-Assyrian Empire controls conquered populations and replaces its own labor force, which is perpetually on military campaign, through the large-scale deportation of populations from one region of the empire to another.

- Incorporation into the Neo-Assyrian Empire brings the economic advantages of a large market for goods and secure trade routes, but the tribute imposed by the Assyrians is devastating to many of its vassals, including the kingdoms of Israel and Judah.

625-605 B.C.E.

- Nabopolassar founds a dynasty in Babylon, wresting it free from its northern neighbor. He lays the foundation for the Neo-Babylonian Empire, which occupies the vacuum left by the Assyrians.

625*-500* B.C.E.

- Family-run financial "houses" flourish in ancient Babylonian cities such as Uruk, Ur, and Babylon; the archive of one such family, the Egibi, documents five generations of entrepreneurial activity.

612-609 B.C.E.

- A coalition of Babylonians, Medes, and perhaps Scythians sacks the Assyrian capital city of Nineveh in 612 B.C.E., beginning the final decline of the empire, which ends with the destruction of its army near Harran in Syria in 609 B.C.E.

604-562 B.C.E.

- Under Nabopolassar's son Nebuchadnezzar II, Babylonians continue the Assyrian policy of deporting conquered peoples. When the leaders of Jerusalem refuse to pay tribute to their new Babylonian overlords, the city is sacked, and much of its population is forcibly relocated to Babylon.

539 B.C.E.

- The Persian king Cyrus II (the Great) peacefully conquers Babylon, marking the end of Nabonidus's kingship and of native Babylonian rule. The once independent kingdom of Babylonia is encorporated into the Persian Empire.

331 B.C.E.

- Babylon opens its gates to Alexander III (the Great) of Macedon. For the next two centuries Mesopotamia is ruled by Alexander and his successors, the Hellenistic Seleucid dynasty, drawing Babylonia into a wider system of economic and cultural exchange.

* DENOTES CIRCA DATE

OVERVIEW

First Cities. Mesopotamia (ancient Iraq) was the setting for humankind's earliest complex civilization. Among the many ways by which social scientists measure civilization are the presence of political and social organizations such as government and religious hierarchies, specialization of labor, markets for the exchange of goods, achievements in the arts and sciences, and long-distance trade. These aspects of civilization are interdependent, and evidence for all of them is centered in the most significant development of complex civilization: the city. For many people to inhabit densely a small area—one mark of an urban center—there must be mechanisms that enable them to acquire the means of survival (food and water) and to live together peaceably (laws), as well as a system that maintains those mechanisms (government and bureaucracy). With some of the inhabitants producing enough basic foodstuffs for the whole population, primarily through farming and herding, others can specialize in crafts production, such as pottery making, textile weaving, and metalwork. The needs of the farmer to replace his broken plow, of the carpenter to obtain cloth for his daughter's marriage dowry, and of the weaver to procure grain for his family's bread leads to the establishment of markets, which then attract other producers and consumers. The function of the city as economic hub is paralleled by its role as a center for societal and political administration. While supplying the city with needed agricultural produce, people inhabiting the surrounding rural environs look to the center for economic, religious, and political leadership—each sector simultaneously depending on and supporting the other. The appearance of urban civilization in Mesopotamia cannot be traced to one single cause; rather it arose in response to multiple interrelated factors that together fostered the establishment and success of mankind's earliest cities. Nascent urban centers in the southern part of Mesopotamia provided opportunities and stimuli for further economic, religious, political, social, artistic, scientific, and technological achievements.

Geography and Environments. The basic requirement for the success of any civilization is a steady supply of food and water. All the pre-industrial civilizations of the world were fundamentally agricultural, with the majority of their members engaging in the production of food through farming crops and herding animals. The development of the Mesopotamian economy and social organization was rooted inextricably in geography and environment. The foremost physical features of Mesopotamia are its two great rivers: the Tigris and Euphrates; its two seasons: a hot, dry summer and a cool, rainy winter; its access to five great bodies of water: the Persian Gulf and the Black, Red, Caspian, and Mediterranean Seas; and its greatly differing physical regions in close proximity: alluvium, marsh, steppe, mountains, and desert. "The land," as Mesopotamia was called by its ancient inhabitants, can be divided into south and north, regions distinguished by one simple, yet all-important, difference: the south does not receive sufficient rainfall for agriculture, and the north does.

Natural Resources. Natural resources that were available to the early inhabitants of ancient Mesopotamia include the rich, fertile soil of the alluvium; reeds, fish, and birds found in the marshlands; animals and some hard stone found in the steppe and mountains. Bitumen, a naturally occurring black, sticky, tar-like substance, was used as an adhesive to waterproof boats and baskets made of reeds, as well as to inlay artworks with precious stones. At one time the Syrian Desert was inhabited by elephants and lions; elephants provided the precious luxury commodity of ivory, while the lion became as an important cultural icon for gods and kings. Mesopotamia was largely bereft of significant sources for hardwood and large, hard stones suitable for building; nor did the inhabitants have ready access to metals, metal ores, or precious stones. The most readily available and workable natural resource of Mesopotamia was mud from the banks of rivers and canals, which under the hot sun dried into hard and durable clay. Mesopotamians employed this resource ingeniously, forming mud into bricks for building, vessels for storing and transporting food and liquids, sickle blades for farming, and images of deities to worship and of demons to keep dangers away. The dead were buried in clay coffins; terra-cotta plaques advertised taverns; and clay pipes carried water for indoor plumbing in a palace. Last, and perhaps most important, damp, soft clay was fashioned into tablets on which the written records of Mesopotamia were inscribed.

Irrigation Agriculture. The south was the site of the earliest cities, founded in the fourth millennium B.C.E., and was viewed by ancient Mesopotamians in north and south alike as the older, more established of the two regions. In the third millennium B.C.E., the southern cities evolved into a patchwork of rival independent city-states, while sparse evidence for early civilization in the north seems possibly to suggest the emergence of small principalities there. It might be surprising that the earliest urban centers appeared in the southern part of Mesopotamia, where rainfall is insufficient to support agriculture. Yet, the soil of the alluvium, the flat plain created by the annual flooding of the Tigris and Euphrates Rivers, is extremely fertile, and the people who first settled there developed innovative irrigation techniques to provide the necessary water for raising crops. The economic value of a plot of land lay in its access to water, and fields were made long and narrow to maximize the number of plots that could border on a given watercourse. In addition to carrying water to farmlands, the canals also formed a transportation network that connected distant settlements and marked boundaries between distinct territories. Irrigation was not without its drawbacks. Over time, an irrigated field became exhausted of nutrients, its fertility compromised by the buildup of salts in the surface soil. Farmers developed techniques to combat this salinization, but the system was always fragile, and environmental crises, notably drought, had catastrophic consequences for Mesopotamian economy and society. Overall, however, the long-term success of southern Mesopotamian agriculture, together with herding, produced an economic surplus that allowed some members of the population to specialize in other sectors of the economy, such as crafts production, and provided the economic basis necessary for stable kingdoms and long-distance trade.

Labor and Technology. The need to co-ordinate labor in order to build and maintain irrigation canals may have been a factor that stimulated early development of political and social organization in southern Mesopotamia. An early Mesopotamian technological innovation, the seeder-plow, enabled ancient farmers to plant large areas with a low input of labor. Yet, the most critical time of the agricultural year, the harvest, which took place in the spring, required the participation of many laborers. The enduring agricultural orientation of Mesopotamian civilization accounts for the subjects of their earliest written records, which—although still imperfectly understood—seem to document quantities of agricultural products and to describe land and watercourses. The Mesopotamians' early development of the technology of writing enabled the creation of a complex bureaucracy that could oversee the organization of labor and other resources, keep track of economic production, and manage surpluses.

Economic Crossroads. The Tigris and Euphrates Rivers, their tributaries, and the network of canals connecting them served as a transportation system linking Mesopotamia with the Persian Gulf to the south, the Zagros Mountain region to the east, and overland routes across Syria to the Mediterranean Sea to the northwest. Evidence for long-distance trade among these lands, even long before the advent of writing, exists in the physical presence of natural materials and manufactured artifacts far from their original sources. As Mesopotamian urban civilization arose, so did the demand for resources available only outside that region. This demand, in combina-

tion with the local production of agricultural surpluses, fueled long-distance trade. Moreover, lying at the crossroads connecting these different regions, Mesopotamian cities—and the authorities governing them—profited financially from the river traffic. Sustained contact with different regions and cultures also stimulated developments in Mesopotamian civilization.

Redistributive Economy and Socio-Political Institutions. The economy of Mesopotamia evolved hand in hand with its political and social organizations, and it is unrealistic to try to consider developments in one area in isolation from the others. The oft-invoked model for the economy of Mesopotamia is the household, with reference to the work of Max Weber, a nineteenth-century C.E. socio-economic historian. According to this model, each of the "great institutions"—the temple and the palace—was organized as a household, with god or king, respectively, at its head. The resources of each temple or palace—including the land, the canals, the animals, and the labor of the individuals found there—were considered to belong to the head of the institution. This "owner" was served by a hierarchy of dependents, who worked the resources belonging to the household, and their production was collected by the household administrators. Members, or dependents, of the household received food, clothing, and other necessities, which were distributed to them by the administrators. Such a system is called a *redistributive economy,* and, in theory, each household was self-sufficient. Recent research has shown that private ownership and entrepreneurship also played a significant role and that the household model is inadequate to describe the complexities of Mesopotamian society and economy. Nonetheless, the model is useful for placing in context much of the documentary evidence from Mesopotamia, especially from the early periods (the third millennium B.C.E.) and from the south.

Social Hierarchy. During periods for which there is written evidence, Mesopotamian society seems to have consisted of freemen (who owned their own land or other means of production), dependents (who did not own land or means of production), and slaves (who were the property of other people). Men were heads of their households and held positions of power and authority throughout society. The normal family unit consisted of a married couple and their children. When a woman married, she moved from the house of her father to that of her husband, where she and their children lived under his authority. Regarding land, the normal route of inheritance was from father to a son or sons; at the time of her marriage a daughter was provided with a dowry in movable possessions that were equivalent in value to one inheritance share. Slaves were either foreigners captured in military activity, persons sold into slavery because of indebtedness, or individuals born into slavery. (Children of a slave belonged to that slave's owner.) On occasion, and in accord with Mesopotamian concepts of justice, kings decreed that all persons sold into slavery out of financial hardship be restored to their former free status. Distinctions were made between foreigners and native-born "sons of such-and-such a city," who might enjoy certain privileges. In other regards, native and foreign-born individuals were afforded the same rights before the law.

Private Property. In accordance with the Weberian household model of the great institutions, historians long assumed that all land in Mesopotamia was the property of only gods and kings. According to an emerging, more-balanced perspective, however, private persons also owned noninstitutional landholdings. In theory, land was inalienable; that is, it passed from father to son and could not be sold outside the family. In practice, individuals did buy and sell land, and they found ingenious ways to circumvent family ownership restrictions.

Trade and Finance. Evidence of local and long-distance trade in Mesopotamia exists from before the advent of writing. With the appearance of written records, the activities of merchants—individuals specializing in the procurement, transport, and sale of goods—are well documented. Having ready access to disposable capital, merchants and large institutions were in a position to make loans, which could be either interest or noninterest bearing. Silver and barley were the two standards by which the value of other commodities could be reckoned. Although in use within the Persian Empire, coins do not appear to have been used in Mesopotamia until the late fourth century B.C.E. Nonetheless, silver did serve as money throughout much of ancient Mesopotamian history; other commodities were valued according to their worth in silver (expressed in increments of weight).

Documentary Evidence. Mesopotamia is unique among ancient civilizations in the extent of its documentary evidence for social and economic history. Ancient Egypt, Greece, and China each had a writing system with which people recorded transactions (such as purchases, sales, wills, marriage gifts, and debt seizures), contracts (such as loans, marriages, business partnerships, and adoptions), legal proceedings (such as trials) and penalties, and internal business records (such as inventories and expenditures). Yet, the textual records of these societies were written on fragile materials such as papyrus, leather, parchment, paper, or silk, while the daily records of Mesopotamia were written on tablets made from clay. If buried below ground and thus protected from rain, wind, sun, and damage from animals (including man), inscribed clay tablets can survive for millennia. Hundreds of thousands of records relating to the everyday life and activities of Mesopotamians who lived as long as five thousand years ago have been preserved. All contracts and court records include lists of witnesses to a transaction or decision; typically they are listed by name, patronymic (father's name), and occupation. Witnesses were almost exclusively men, but a woman's name might appear when she was a direct participant in a transaction. When a group of tablets from the same time and place is assembled, the researcher can follow the names of individuals as they appear in the bodies of transactions and in witness lists, reconstructing the rise and fall of careers, fortunes, family business, and legal activities over generations—a method of research called *prosopography*. Taken individually, these records do not seem to offer much information and may not strike a modern reader as terribly interesting; even professional Assyriologists refer to them as "laundry lists." Yet, studied together, they constitute an elaborate sort of puzzle that, when viewed with the right kinds of questions in mind, has enabled researchers to begin to reconstruct humankind's earliest complex social-class system and economy.

Recovery of Documentary Evidence. Inscribed clay tablets arrive on a museum or university researcher's desk either after having been carefully unearthed in the course of a systematic scientific archaeological excavation or after having been looted from a site and purchased through the illicit, or "black market," trade in antiquities. When tablets are discovered during controlled excavations carried out by trained archaeologists, the spots where they are found are carefully recorded so that their ancient context—such as a palace archive or workshop, a temple, a school, or a personal library—may be reconstructed. Tablets found lying together in a storeroom, for example, might enable a scholar to trace the economic activity of a family business over a period of many years, perhaps even several generations. The contents of a palace archive can shed light on state-sponsored trade ventures, the revenue of state-owned lands, or the conscription of individuals for military service or for labor on state-sponsored construction projects. In contrast, tablets and other artifacts that have been looted from an ancient site—which are thus lacking provenance, or history of origin and ownership—have been separated from other pieces of the same puzzle. Ripped from the ground without any concern for their ancient physical context, these artifacts can tell a far-less-complete story than those recovered in the course of a controlled archaeological excavation.

Inherent Biases. There is evidence that Mesopotamians used cuneiform writing for a period of almost 3,500 years, and some three hundred thousand tablets are known. Yet, the textual record is incomplete and uneven in regard to time and place. Certainly, not every tablet ever written in antiquity has survived, nor have all of those that have survived been recovered. Because the scope of archaeological excavation is limited by available funding and expertise, archaeologists have tended to concentrate on high-profile buildings such as temples and palaces, which tend to achieve the highest physical elevation on the mound, or *tell*, the remains of an ancient city. While these buildings may yield an official archive that belonged to the palace or temple, the residential and business quarters of the city, where one might expect to find tablets, architecture, furnishings, tools, utensils, and garbage dumps—evidence relating to the social system and economic life of the middle and lower economic strata of the city—have received far less attention. Furthermore, little archaeological exploration has been conducted outside urban centers. Thus, the picture that the researcher bases on currently available evidence tends to be skewed toward urban centers, which developed in the south, and toward the view from the temple and palace—the urban elites at the top of the social and economic ladder.

TOPICS IN SOCIAL CLASS SYSTEM AND THE ECONOMY

AGRICULTURE

An Agricultural Civilization. Ancient Mesopotamia was fundamentally an agricultural civilization. By far, the great majority of people living there were engaged in some form of food production. Two technological innovations, canals that carried water to the fields and the seeder-plow—which in one pass broke up dry, hard turf and deposited seed—enabled ancient farmers to optimize their use of the alluvial plain, the fertile, flat area between the Tigris and Euphrates Rivers. The most important crops these farmers raised were cereals: barley and emmer, a form of wheat native to Eurasia. Legumes, chiefly lentils and hummus (chickpeas), and flax were also significant crops in the economy. Levees that formed along the banks of the canals were exploited for the cultivation of date palms, a valuable source of sugar and shade. Vegetables such as cucumbers, onions, and garlic, as well as spices, were raised beneath the shade canopy created by the palm orchards.

The Irrigation Regime. Cereal crops were planted in the fall and harvested in the spring. To the farmers' dismay, the rivers tended to flood in the spring, precisely when the harvest was most vulnerable. Mesopotamian irrigation agriculture required a short-term, but intense, input of labor for the spring harvest and periodically throughout the year to maintain the irrigation canals, which were likely to silt up. Field size was limited by the ability to irrigate, and fields tended to be long and narrow in order to maximize the number of farmers having access to a given watercourse. Intensive irrigation over many years led to salinization, or a build-up of salt, which reduced the fertility of the soil. Strategies developed by Mesopotamian farmers to combat salinization included rotating fields to let one lie fallow (unplanted) one year out of four, the cultivation of salt-resistant crops, and encouraging sheep or cattle to graze on and fertilize a field. A farmer's duties throughout the year are related in a didactic literary composition called *The Farmer's Instructions*, which enjoins the farmer to keep his tools sharp and clean, to perform tasks at the right times, and to be a good neighbor.

Labor Requirements. The specialized labor requirements of agriculture and irrigation may have contributed to shaping early Mesopotamian socio-political organization. The irrigation system—which required decision making and co-operation among individuals to plan, excavate, and maintain canals—may have been overseen by extended family or tribal networks. Reliance on these social structures lent them not

---

THE FARMER'S INSTRUCTIONS

The Farmer's Instructions is a third millennium B.C.E. agricultural manual written in Sumerian. While teaching an inexperienced farmer about good farming practices, the text also stands as a moral metaphor for how to lead a proper life.

Old Man Tiller instructed his son:

When you have to prepare a field for irrigation, inspect the levee, canals, and elevations which have to be opened.

When you let the floodwaters into the field, its waters should not rise there too high.
At the time the field emerges from the water, watch the spots with standing water in the field, it should be fenced.
Do not let the cattle herds trample it (anymore). . . .
Your implements should be ready. . . .
All necessary things for the field should be at hand. Carefully inspect your work.
The plow oxen should have backup oxen. . . .
When your field work becomes excessive, you should not neglect your work, so no one has to tell anyone: "Do your fieldwork!" . . .
When you have to reap the barley, do not let the plants become overripe.
Harvest at the proper time.

Source: Miguel Civil, *The Farmer's Instructions: A Sumerian Agricultural Manual*, Aula Orientalis-Supplementa 5 (Barcelona: Editorial Ausa, 1994), pp. 29–33.

Workers (at lower left and right) using a *shaduf* (a counterweighted water sweep with a bucket suspended from a rope at the end of a long pole) to lift water from one irrigation ditch to another; detail from a carved relief panel from Sennacherib's Palace at Nineveh, which also depicts (top) men dragging a colossal sculpture up a hill, 704-681 B.C.E. (British Museum, London)

only social but also political and economic authority. The agricultural regime, which required much labor only for short intense periods throughout the year, may have encouraged the development of the so-called great institutions, the palaces and temples, which were the large landholders and had the administrative infrastructure to summon and organize large labor forces. One response to the labor requirements of the system was the *corvée* (a French word meaning "forced labor"). Under the corvée system, residents of an area connected with an urban or provincial administrative center were obliged to contribute their physical labor to the state at specified times, generally one month during the year. The labor was typically dedicated to work on canals, in the fields, or on roads.

Agriculture and Ideology. Evidence dating to the third millennium B.C.E. suggests the existence of an ideology in southern Mesopotamia in which a city-state and its land were the property of its god or gods. Large parcels of farmland were thus understood to be "owned" by a deity and managed by the administrative bureaucracy of that god's temple. This ideology is articulated also in Mesopotamian mythology, particularly in stories narrating the beginnings of the cosmos and the creation of mankind. According to these myths, mankind's place in the universe is clear: he was created to dig canals and work the land in order to provide the gods' tables with food and drink. Although humans domesticated edible plants in the ancient Near East perhaps as early as 10,000 B.C.E.—some seven thousand years before they began to write down their thoughts in cuneiform on clay tablets—the cultivation and, moreover,

the processing of food occurred later and are regarded as integral parts of mankind's passage from surviving in the wild to living in a state of civilization. Indeed, bread and beer, the chief manufactured foodstuffs of ancient Mesopotamia, played key roles in cultic worship as well as on the family table, and the two comestibles were emblems for civilization itself. In the *Epic of Gilgamesh*, when the wild man Enkidu is served bread and beer for the first time, he is not just learning new table manners. The youth, who had grazed with the beasts of the steppe, is ingesting the definitive features of the Mesopotamian economy, and the meal itself constitutes a rite of passage that marks him henceforth as a *civilized* human being:

> They put bread before him,
> he squinted and he stared.
> Enkidu did not know how to eat bread,
> how to drink beer he had never been taught.
> The prostitute opened her mouth,
> Saying to Enkidu:
> "Eat the bread, Enkidu—the stuff of life;
> Drink the beer—the way of the land!"
> (translation after George)

It is no coincidence that several of the most vivid works of Mesopotamian art and literature make use of the theme of agriculture and its products. The Warka (Uruk) Vase, dating to circa 3300 – circa 3000 B.C.E., at about the time of the invention of proto-cuneiform writing, illustrates in carved-relief registers arrayed from bottom

Drawing of an ancient cylinder-seal impression on a clay tablet from Nippur. A man (center) is pouring seeds into the funnel of a seeder-plow drawn by a pair of humped-back oxen; Kassite period, reign of Nazi-Maruttash, circa 1307 – circa 1282 B.C.E. (drawing from Albert T. Clay, ed., *Documents from the Temple Archives of Nippur, Dated in the Reigns of Cassite Rulers*, 1912; impression: University of Pennsylvania Museum of Archaeology and Anthropology).

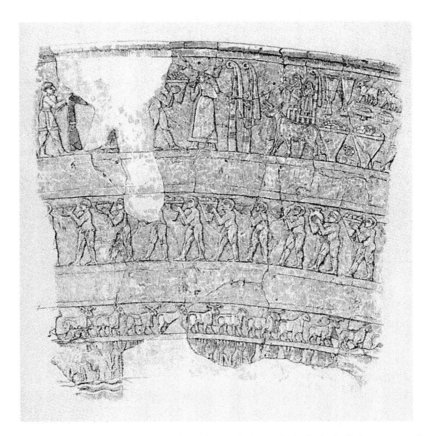

"Roll-out" of the relief carved on the alabaster Warka (Uruk) Vase (height 41¼ inches), depicting a procession culminating at center top with the presentation of offerings to the goddess Inana (or her chief priestess) standing before the gates of her temple (drawing from Elke Lindemeyer and Lutz Martin, *Uruk: Kleinfunde III,* Ausgrabungen in Uruk-Warka Endberichte, 9, 1993; vase: Iraq Museum, Baghdad)

to top, an ascending passage from water, to plants, to grazing rams and ewes, to men bearing baskets of foodstuffs, to a priest serving a goddess or priestess standing before the entrance to her temple. It is an elegant expression of Mesopotamian cosmic hierarchy, fundamentally grounded in agriculture and mankind's ability to cultivate plants and animals.

Sources:

Miguel Civil, *The Farmer's Instructions: A Sumerian Agricultural Manual,* Aula Orientalis-Supplementa 5 (Barcelona: Editorial Ausa, 1994).

Andrew R. George, *The Babylonian Gilgamesh Epic: Introduction, Critical Editions, and Cuneiform Texts,* 2 volumes (Oxford: Oxford University Press, 2003).

Susan Pollock, *Ancient Mesopotamia: The Eden that Never Was,* Case Studies in Early Societies (Cambridge: Cambridge University Press, 1999).

J. N. Postgate, *Early Mesopotamia: Society and Economy at the Dawn of History* (London & New York: Routledge, 1992).

Michael Roaf, *Cultural Atlas of Mesopotamia and the Ancient Near East* (New York: Facts on File, 1966).

ANIMAL HUSBANDRY

Wild and Domestic Animals. Along with agriculture, animals and animal products played a role in most households, as well as in larger, institutionally supported commercial enterprises, such as textile production and long-distance trade. Throughout Mesopotamian prehistory and history, wild animals such as fish, birds, and gazelles were hunted for food; their oils, plumage, hides, and horns were also put to use. Such animals seem also to have served as emblems for clans or tribes in southern Mesopotamia during the fourth and early third millennia B.C.E. Some exotic species, notably lions, which at one time inhabited the Syrian Desert, were symbols or emblems of gods and kings: Ishtar, goddess of love and war, was associated with the lion, and Neo-Assyrian palaces were decorated with monumental relief sculptures featuring the king engaged in a ritualized lion hunt. Evidence for early domestication of animals—especially sheep, goats, and dogs—dates to approximately 10,000 B.C.E., around the same time as the domestication of plants; the domestication of donkeys, chickens, horses, and camels came later. Domesticated ani-

mals represented an investment of resources that helped to shape the Mesopotamian economy, while the requirements of animal husbandry exerted influence on the development of the Mesopotamian social structure. Domesticated plants and animals were the basis of the economy, and the Mesopotamians were well aware of their foundational role in the evolution of Mesopotamian civilization. In a literary composition known as the *Disputation between Ewe and Wheat,* after the origin of the world is related, the two title characters debate which of them is the more important—a conflict reminiscent of the dispute between Cain and Abel in the biblical Book of Genesis. Whereas in the Bible, Abel's offering from his flocks is preferred to Cain's offering from his fields, the message of the Mesopotamian text is that Ewe and Wheat complement one another, and each is indispensable. Nevertheless, with intervention from the gods, Wheat is judged to "win" the dispute.

Domesticated Animals and Animal Products. Sheep, goats, and cattle provided milk, which was used to make cheeses, ghee (a kind of butter), and yogurt. Dairy products, legumes, and fish provided most of the protein in the Mesopotamian diet; meat was consumed only rarely and presumably was connected with celebratory or ceremonial occasions. Sheep and goats provided wool, which was woven into the textiles that were for all periods of Mesopotamian history the single most important good exported from southern Mesopotamia throughout the ancient Near East. Donkeys and oxen were used for plowing and seeding fields and for transporting goods. After about 1500 B.C.E., horses played an integral role in warfare. The Mesopotamians' horse-drawn chariots and the compound bows wielded by the charioteers were important technological advances. Horses (as well as chariots) became important prestige possessions sought after by Near Eastern kings, and the need to acquire more and more horses played a role particularly in the economic expansion of the first millennium B.C.E. Neo-Assyrian Empire. While deceased animals were an important source of hides for leather, bone for needles and other small fine tools, and—on occasion—meat, the greatest economic value of domesticated animals lay in the products and services they provided while alive rather than

Frieze of limestone and shell, set in bitumen within a copper-alloy frame (height 8 5/8 inches), depicting calves standing before their mothers (which are being milked), calves emerging from a reed hut, and workers processing milk into various dairy products; Temple of Ninhursanga, Tell al-Ubaid, reign of A'anepada of Ur, circa 2400 B.C.E. (Iraq Museum, Baghdad)

DISPUTATION BETWEEN EWE AND WHEAT

Disputations were a Sumerian literary genre in which two comparable entities were imagined to present arguments for the superiority of one over the other. The debate is typically set at a banquet after the participants have eaten and drunk. The final two lines of the *Disputation between Ewe and Wheat* are also known as an independent proverb in Sumerian.

When upon the Hill of Heaven and Earth
An had spawned the divine Godlings,—
Since godly Wheat had not yet been spawned or created with them,
Nor had the yarn of the godly Weaver been fashioned in the Land,
Not had the loom of the godly Weaver even been pegged out,
For Ewe had not yet appeared, nor were there numerous lambs. . . .

The people of those distant days
Knew not bread to eat,
They knew not cloth to wear;
They went about the Land with naked limbs
Eating grass with their mouths like sheep,
And drinking water from the ditches.

At that time, at the birthplace of the Gods,
In their home, the Holy Hill, they (the gods) fashioned Ewe and Wheat. . . .

Thus both Ewe and Wheat were radiant in appearance
And among the gathered people they caused abundance,
And in the Land they brought well-being. . . .
The storerooms of the Land they fill with abundance,
So that the barns of the Land are bulging with them.
Even in the home of the needy, who are crouching in the dust,
When they enter there, they bring about wealth.
Both of them, wherever they direct their steps,
Add to the riches of the household. . . .

They drank sweet wine,
They drank tasty beer;
And when they had drunk sweet wine
And sated themselves on tasty beer
They started a quarrel in the midst of the watered fields;
They held a wrangle in the Dining Hall.
Wheat calls out to Ewe:

"Sister, I am your better; I take precedence!
I am the most splendid of the jewels of the Land!
I give strength to the Chief Warrior
So that he fills the palace with awe,
And people spread his fame to the confines of the Land!
I am the gift of the Gods;
I am the strength of princes! . . .
I, I am wheat, the Holy Blade; I am Enlil's daughter (everywhere),
In the shacks, in the shepherds' huts,
Scattered over the plain,
What can you put against this? What can you reply? Answer me that!"

Thereupon Ewe replied to Wheat:
"Sister, what are you saying?
An, king of the Gods,
Made me descend from the holy and most precious place!
All the yarns of the divine Weaver, the splendor of Royalty, are mine! . . .
Also the watch over the elite troops is mine, as is the sustenance of the workers in the field,
And the water-skin of the refreshing drink and the sandals—all that is mine! . . .
And you are put in the oven, and taken out of the oven again.
When you are finally put on the table,
I come before you and you are behind!
Wheat, watch yourself!
You, just as I, are meant to be eaten. . . ."

Wheat replied to Ewe: . . .
"When your innards are taken away by the buyers in the market,
And your neck is wrapped with your very own loin-cloth,
One man says to another: 'Fill the measure with grain for my sheep!'"

Thereupon the god Enki spoke to the god Enlil:
"Father Enlil, Ewe and Wheat, both of them,
Should walk together! Of their combined metal, [the alloy] should never cease;
Yet of these two Wheat should be the greater! . . .
For whoever has gold, or silver, or cattle, or sheep,
Shall ever wait at the door of him who has grain, and so pass his days!"

Source: Hermann L. J. Vanstiphout, "Disputations," in *The Context of Scripture*, volume 1, edited by William W. Hallo, with K. Lawson Younger Jr. (New York & Leiden: Brill, 1996), pp. 575–578.

after their slaughter, and the owner of animals invested significant resources in keeping his animals healthy and in increasing the size of his flocks.

Semi-Nomadic Lifestyle. The domesticated animals most important to the ancient Mesopotamian economy were sheep and goats, which required green pasturage to survive and reproduce. Reproducing females provided milk for dairy products, and these mothers require steady supplies of food and water. In ancient times as now, lambing and calving took place in the spring, after which the flocks needed to be led north and west to higher and wetter lands that remain green throughout the summer. The requirement for mobility, the ability to pick up and take the animals for months at a time to locales where water and

Kids as offerings: carved-relief wall plaque with men bringing provisions, including a kid, to a banquet (limestone, height 7 7/8 inches), Sin Temple, Khafajah, circa 2600 – circa 2500 B.C.E.; and gypsum statue of a man carrying a kid (height 9 inches), Mari (left: Oriental Institute of the University of Chicago; right: National Museum, Aleppo)

pasturage were found, was contrary to the settled nature of an urban lifestyle. To meet this need, a pattern of settlement evolved in Mesopotamia whereby some members of a community, who were linked with settled members of the community by family ties or other association, spent the winter months of the year living in a settlement, village or city, and the summer months on the move with the flocks. Neither fully nomadic nor fully settled, these people led what is known as a semi-nomadic lifestyle, and although they appear in written sources less frequently than their settled urban counterparts, they were an integral part of the Mesopotamian economy and social structure.

Specialized Uses of Animals. Animals played a vital role in the Mesopotamian cult, which itself played a large part in the economy and social-class system. Within the framework of basic Mesopotamian religious belief, in which mankind was created to serve the gods and provide them with food and drink, animals were at the top of the hierarchy of sacrifices offered to the gods. The choicest animals of the flock were reserved for the gods' tables. The value of such offerings is demonstrated in the detailed descriptions of cuts of meat stipulated in written lists of cultic contributions. While in principle an animal was offered for the gods' table, in practice only a small portion was used for the sacrifice; for instance, blood was poured onto the ground before the image of the deity, or a piece of meat was "consumed" by fire. The remainder of the animal was carefully butchered and allocated to the temple staff and temple

offices. Shares in such socially prestigious offices ("prebends") became economically valuable. Prebends could be apportioned over the year; that is, one could serve as prebend for as little as one day. Prebends were handed down as part of an inheritance or, like movable property, might be bought and sold. The following passage is from a tenth century B.C.E. entitlement monument discovered in the temple to the sun god Shamash in the city of Sippar:

> (The king of Babylon established as follows):
> Allowance of the *sangu*-priest from the rams, the annual royal sacrificial offering:
> flesh of the loins, the hides,
> flesh of the back, the sinews,
> half the flesh of the viscera,
> half the flesh of the lungs,
> two knucklebones,
> one vessel of meat broth. . . . (Slanski)

A specialized cultic use of animals in Mesopotamia was in the art/science of extispicy, according to which a highly trained diviner examined the entrails of a sheep or goat sacrificed for this purpose. Such animals had to be of the highest quality and were extremely expensive; as might be expected, the remains of the animal went to the temple staff. Extispicy was a practice likely restricted to royalty and wealthy members of society.

Sources:
Mario Liverani, "Half Nomads on the Middle Euphrates and the Concept of Dimorphic Society," *Altorientalische Forschungen,* 24 (1995): 44–48.

Susan Pollock, *Ancient Mesopotamia: The Eden that Never Was,* Case Studies in Early Societies (Cambridge: Cambridge University Press, 1999).

J. N. Postgate, *Early Mesopotamia: Society and Economy at the Dawn of History* (London & New York: Routledge, 1992).

Michael Roaf, *Cultural Atlas of Mesopotamia and the Ancient Near East* (New York: Facts on File, 1966).

Kathryn E. Slanski, *The Babylonian Entitlement* narûs (kudurrus): *A Study in Form and Function,* ASOR Books, volume 9 (Boston: American Schools of Oriental Research, 2003).

Hermann L. J. Vanstiphout, "Disputations," in *The Context of Scripture,* volume 1, edited by William W. Hallo, with K. Lawson Younger Jr. (New York & Leiden: Brill, 1996), pp. 575–578.

CRAFT MANUFACTURE AND PRODUCTION

Technology. Technological innovation, principally in the area of agriculture, played a critical role in the development of crafts and other produced or manufactured goods. The introduction of the seeder-plow and other farming implements, such as metal sickles, allowed for the planting and harvesting of large fields without the need to maintain a large permanent labor force. This development had two significant impacts on manufacturing and production. By not having to grow their own sustenance, some members of the population were able to specialize in forms of production not related directly to producing food. These individuals became the craftsmen and artisans of Mesopotamia. Technological innovations in agriculture also enabled the large landowning institutions, the temple and the palace, to accumulate agricultural surpluses that they could then use for capital investments in specialized crafts production and in creating markets for their manufactured products through long-distance trade. The metalsmith is a good example of a specialized craftsman; his skills were not available in every household, and the products of his workshop were indispensable for the evolving technologies in farming, transportation, and warfare.

Main Areas of Production. Throughout Mesopotamian history, textiles were made mainly out of wool from sheep and, to a lesser extent, linen from flax. Each household made textiles on a small scale for the family's own use, and institutions produced them on a large scale for commercial ventures. Large-scale industrial production required a massive, permanent, trained workforce; temple factory records from the Ur III period (circa 2112 – circa 2004 B.C.E.) list more than six thousand workers, mostly women, along with their children. At all times throughout Mesopotamian history, textiles were the most economically significant area of production, followed by food processing (for example, beer brewing, bread baking, and cheese making), metalworking, and ceramics production. In general, crafts requiring imported materials probably were worked more in institutional settings, whereas production using domestic materials took place more often in private households.

Large-Scale, Institution-Sponsored Production. Production in the "public sector," the institutional households of temple and palace, is far better documented than production in the "private sector" (private or family households). Institutional production, collection, and redistribution of agricultural and manufactured goods during the period of the Ur III dynasty (circa 2112 – circa 2004 B.C.E.) is by far the best documented and represents the most bureaucratically organized system. The next-best-documented institutionally sponsored production took place in Babylonia in the seventh and sixth centuries B.C.E. Thanks to their ability to accumulate agricultural surpluses, institutions had capital to invest in large-scale projects and trading ventures, and they had access to imported resources. Large-scale production provided a setting for experimentation in new methods as well as the development of expertise within narrow areas of specialization.

INVOICE FOR A NEW GATE

An invoice for a gate in the tower of the city wall of Isin demonstrates how various sorts of craftsmanship and materials went into the manufacture of a single object. City walls were monumental defensive works punctuated at intervals by towers that provided lookout posts for sentries. The presence of monumental walls around a city indicates the need for military defense and the ability of leadership to organize necessary labor and materials; the kind of organization shown by the text below is just one small example. As public architecture, walls had an aesthetic as well as a practical function; thus, the components of the wall—such as a tower gate—were the product of high-quality materials and craftsmanship. The text is dated the thirty-third year of Ishbi-Erra's reign (circa 2017 – circa 1985 B.C.E.) over the city-state of Isin. (Ishbi-Erra served as a military general for the last king of the Ur III state before breaking away to found his own kingdom.)

1 door made of small boards:
its glue is 2/3 mina,
it is the work of the carpenters;
its white oxhides are 1 and 1/3,
its hairy oxhide is 1/3,
it is the work of the leatherworkers;
(its) bitumen is 15 sila,
its gypsum is 4 minas,
it is the work of the reedworkers;
for the gate of the tower of the wall of the city.
Sin-re'i, the mounted messenger (was) the conveyor.
Month III, day 11.
(King) Ishbi-Erra 33

Source: Marc Van de Mieroop, *Crafts in the Early Isin Period: A Study of the Isin Craft Archive from the Reigns of Isbi-Erra and Šū-Illisu* (Leuven: Departement Oriëntalistiek, 1987), p. 14.

Terra-cotta plaque (height 3 ¼ inches) depicting carpenter using an adz to fashion a chair leg; Isin-Larsa or Old Babylonian period, circa 2000 – circa 1600 B.C.E. (Louvre, Paris)

This expertise was then passed on to other members of the production workforce and must also be counted among the resources of the institution.

Crafts Production in the Ur III State. One unanticipated by-product of the Ur III bureaucracy was the accumulation of six to seven thousand administrative texts. Evidence from Ur III archives shows that bureaucrats charged with overseeing state-dominated production were constantly trying to standardize and classify production. One Ur III archive comprises the documents of a single administrator who was responsible for overseeing craftsmen working with wood and ivory, silver and gold, fine stones, copper, leather, rope, and reeds.

Expertise and Training. The transmission of expertise was primarily oral, although some cuneiform "manuals" have survived—including instructions for beer brewing, food preparation, glassmaking, perfume making, and horse training. Apprenticeship contracts are well known from the Neo-Babylonian period (mid-first millennium B.C.E.) and rarely from earlier periods. Most such agreements were probably made orally. There is some evidence that cities had established crafts quarters, which supports a hypothesis that craftsmanship was passed from father to son. Prosopographic studies of archival texts from the southern city of Uruk during the Neo-Babylonian (fifth century B.C.E.) and Seleucid (third–second centuries B.C.E.) periods demon-

strate the continuation of the practice of particular crafts—such as jeweler, leatherworker, smith, and builder—within given families over a period of three or more generations.

Sources:
Michael Jursa, *Prywatyzacja i zysk?: Przedsiebiorcy a gospodarka instytucjonalna w Mezopotamii od 3 do 1 tysiaclecia przed Chr* [Privatization or Profit? Entrepreneurs and Institutional Households in Mesopotamia from the Third to the First Millennium B.C.] (Poznan: Poznan Society for the Advancement of the Arts and Sciences, 2002).

Hans Martin Kümmel, *Familie, Beruf und Amt im spätbabylonischen Uruk: prosopographische Untersuchungen zu Berufsgruppen des 6. Jahrhunderts v. Chr. in Uruk*, Abhandlungen der Deutschen Orient-Gesellschaft, 20 (Berlin: Mann, 1979).

Marc Van de Mieroop, *Crafts in the Early Isin Period: A Study of the Isin Craft Archive from the Reigns of Išbi-Erra and Šū-Illišu* (Leuven: Departement Oriëntalistiek, 1987).

Hartmut Waetzoldt, "Compensation of Craft Workers and Officials in the Ur III Periods," in *Labour in the Ancient Near East*, edited by Marvin A. Powell, American Oriental Series, volume 68 (New Haven, Conn.: American Oriental Society, 1987), pp. 117–141.

ECONOMIC AND SOCIAL JUSTICE

Citizenship. While there are no Mesopotamian terms for "citizen" before the law nor any known declarations of citizens' rights, existing written texts indicate that distinctions were drawn between native-born "sons of the city" or "sons of the land" on the one hand and foreign residents on the other. In court records and ration lists, for example, the name of a foreign-born citizen appears with a notation regarding geographic origin, such as "Kassite" or "Elamite."

The king's first obligation seems to have been to his native-born subjects. According to a didactic literary composition known as *Advice to a Prince,*

> (If a king) denied due process to a citizen (literally "son") of (the Babylonian city of) Sippar, but granted it to an alien, (the god) Shamash, judge of heaven and earth, will establish an alien due process in his land, and neither princes nor judges will have regard for due process. (Foster)

Nonetheless, a passage from a thirteenth century B.C.E. Babylonian entitlement monument, which commemorates the royal affirmation of a permanent transfer of land and tax exemptions, indicates clearly that persons foreign and native born had the same rights before the law, "Whensoever in the future, be he Elamite, or Subarian, or Amorite, or Akkadian, officer, magistrate, who would come forward and litigate (regarding this transaction) . . ." (Slanski). While foreign residents seem to have enjoyed the same economic and social standing as native-born residents, several inscriptions from the second and first millennium B.C.E. attest to special economic privileges—chiefly exemptions from taxes and labor obligations—that were accorded to the "sons" of certain ancient cities, such as Babylon, Nippur, and Sippar. The *Edict of Ammisaduqa,* for example, refers to the special status of the "sons of Babylon," as does *Advice to a Prince.* The reasons for the granting of these privileges are not known, but they may be connected with the ancient religious importance of those cities or with the king's desire to cultivate support from their old established families.

Debt Slavery. Written records from Mesopotamia document an active practice of private and commercial lending. Loan contracts were executed with and without interest and were regularly drawn up with a penalty to the borrower who defaulted. When a head of household was not otherwise able to meet his debts, he might sell a member of his household—including himself—into slavery. Unlike chattel slaves, who were born into slavery or taken captive in foreign lands, debt slaves were contracted to serve for a predetermined period of time. The following paragraph from the Laws of Hammurabi (LH) describes the regular term for debt slavery during the Old Babylonian period (circa 1750 B.C.E.):

> If an obligation is outstanding against a man and he sells or gives into debt service his wife, his son, or his daughter, they shall perform service in the house of their buyer or the one who holds them in debt service for three years; their release shall be secured in the fourth year. (LH §117; Roth)

General Cancellation of Debts. Kings in southern Mesopotamia periodically issued decrees canceling all debts. The most complete surviving text of one of these decrees was issued by the Old Babylonian period king, Ammi-saduqa (circa 1646 – circa 1626 B.C.E.). It applied to loans executed legally and according to established lending practice. It seems that the moment such a decree was issued, a lender was no longer able to collect on his loans. In fact, stiff penalties were imposed on a lender who tried to collect after the king had issued his decree. Moreover,

THE EDICT OF AMMI-SADUQA

Ammi-saduqa (circa 1646 – circa 1626 B.C.E.) was the tenth ruler of the First Dynasty of Babylon and the great-great-grandson of Hammurabi. The text of his *misharum*-edict has been reconstructed from several fragmentary copies made by later scribes studying the inscription.

The tablet [that was read out loud to the people] listening, when the king established *misharum* ("equity," or "justice") for the land:

He (the king) in order to strengthen them and to treat them fairly, dissolved the debts of the farmers, the shepherds, the collectors of animal carcasses, the summer pasturers, and the tenant farmers of the palace. The collections officer may not make a claim against the palace. . . .

(A person) who has loaned silver to an Akkadian or an Amorite [as a loan] for interest or for a *melqetu*-loan and has executed a tablet (recording the loan), because the king has established *misharum* for the land, his tablet is void (literally, "broken"). [. . .] Barley or silver, that, according to the tablet, he (the creditor) may collect, he shall not collect. . . .

A creditor may not press the family (literally "house") of an Akkadian or an Amorite to whom he has made a loan; (if he) does press, then he will die. . . .

An Akkadian or an Amorite who has received barley, silver, or goods on consignment for a business trip, for safe-keeping, or as a loan without interest, his tablet shall not be voided (literally, "broken"); he shall pay according to the terms of his contract. . . .

Arrears of the porters, which had been given to the collections officer to collect, are dissolved; he shall not collect. . . .

A taverness of the summer pasturage region, who is paying silver, barley for brewing to the palace, because the king has established *misharum* for the land, the collections agent shall not make claims for their arrears.

A taverness who has loaned beer or barley; whatever she has loaned, she shall not collect.

A taverness or a merchant, who [records] in a sealed document false (information), shall die.

[If—a cit]izen (literally: "son") of Numhia, a citizen of Emut-balum, [a citizen of Ida]-Maraz, a citizen of Uruk, [a citizen of Isi]n, a citizen of Kisurra, [a citizen of Malgu]—an unpaid obligation has bound him, and [he has given hims]elf, his wife, [or his child] for silver, for distraint, [or for a pled]ge, [because the king has esta]blished *misharum* [for the land], (that person) is released; his return (to his family) is established. (translated by the author)

Source: Fritz R. Kraus, *Königliche Verfügungen in altbabylonischer Zeit,* Studia et Documenta ad iura orientis antiqui pertinentia, volume 11 (Leiden: Brill, 1984).

the decree released people who had been sold into debt slavery. It did not, however, include money that was loaned for the purpose of establishing a business partnership; such loans still had to be repaid according to the original contracts. While no such edict (called *andurar* in Sumerian and *misharum* in Akkadian) survives from Hammurabi's reign (circa 1792 – circa 1750 B.C.E.), references in his law-stele inscription indicate that he declared at least one *misharum*-edict early in his reign, as did his son and successors.

Socio-Economic Justice, or Equity. Derived from an Akkadian verb meaning "to be straight," the Akkadian term *misharum* may be translated in English as "justice" or "equity." Economic and social justice was conceived, therefore, as a "straightening out" of a situation that had somehow become "crooked," a return to a previous equilibrium that was equitable and just. In the Mesopotamian idea of social and economic justice every person was not expected to have the same access to resources and opportunities; rather the Mesopotamians believed that there existed an economic and social equilibrium in which each individual had his place. When that equilibrium was thrown off balance; that is, when its straight way was made crooked—as through extreme economic hardship—the king might act by decree to return society to its former equilibrium.

Limitations on State Power. Neither the king nor his officers had unlimited powers to claim economic resources or to conscript people into service, and both literary and archival texts bear witness to the righteous behavior of kings with respect to their subjects. According to *Advice to a Prince,*

> If a king does not heed justice, his people will be thrown into chaos, and his land will be devastated. . . . If he does not heed his advisor, his land will rebel against him. . . . If sons of Nippur are brought to him for judgement, but he accepts a present and improperly convicts them, the god Enlil, lord of the lands, will bring a foreign army against him to slaughter his army, whose prince and chief officers will roam the streets like fighting cocks. . . . If he takes silver from the sons of Babylon and adds it to his own coffers, or if he hears a lawsuit involving men of Babylon but treats it frivolously, the god Marduk, lord of heaven and earth, will set his foes upon him, and will give his property and wealth to his enemy. . . . (Lambert)

An inscription preserved on a twelfth century B.C.E. Babylonian entitlement monument says that a regional governor had expropriated a strip of land traditionally belonging to a temple:

> Farmland, of such-and-such an area, on the bank of the Tigris River, Gulkishar, king of the Sealand, delimited as the territory for the goddess Nanshe. . . .
>
> 696 years had passed, when, in the fourth year that Enlil-nadin-apli was king, Ekarra-iqisha, son of Ea-iddina, regional governor of Bit-Sin-magir, looked over the fields of Bit-Sin-magir of the province of the Sealand, and

trimmed off and returned to the province an area of that farmland.

> Nabu-shuma-iddina, *sangu*-priest of the gods Namma and Nanshe came with prayer and supplication before the king, his lord, Enlil-nadin-apli, and spoke to him as follows: "Our noble youth, pious prince, wise officer, one who reveres his gods—Regarding mistress Nanshe, eldest daughter of the god Ea, her border was not disturbed, her boundary marker was not removed. Now Ekarra-iqisha, regional governor of Bit-Sin-magir, has disturbed her boundary, has removed her boundary marker." (Slanski)

After the temple officials brought the governor's action to the attention of the king, the land was restored to the temple.

Sources:
Benjamin R. Foster, *From Distant Days: Myths, Tales, and Poetry of Ancient Mesopotamia* (Bethesda, Md.: CDL Press, 1995).

Fritz R. Kraus, *Königliche Verfügungen in altbabylonischer Zeit*, Studia et Documenta ad iura orientis antiqui pertinentia, volume 11 (Leiden: Brill, 1984), pp. 168–183.

W. G. Lambert, *Babylonian Wisdom Literature* (Oxford: Clarendon Press, 1960).

Kathryn E. Slanski, *The Babylonian Entitlement narûs (kudurrus): A Study in Form and Function*, ASOR Books, volume 9 (Boston: American Schools of Oriental Research, 2003).

ENTREPRENEURS

Private Business. The rich documentary sources relating to the Mesopotamian economy are inherently biased toward activities of the great institutions, the temple and the palace. By enabling administrators to record and predict activity in their various economic enterprises, the technology of writing was one of the tools that enabled large landholding institutions to achieve their high levels of productivity, and they employed large bureaucracies to maintain their financial records. Most of the surviving written sources at the economic historian's disposal come from the urban centers, which were dominated—socially, economically, and politically—by these institutions. With their monumental architecture, the physical edifices of temples and palaces also dominated the cities spatially, and the continued prominence of such structures in the archaeological remains of a city further contributes to the recovery of institutional written records. The most significant documentary sources for economic activity in the Pre-Sargonic period (circa 2350 B.C.E.), for example, are the 1,800 tablets from the archive of the temple of Ba'u in Girsu (modern Tello), the capital city of the state of Lagash, which provide a picture of a large institutional household engaged in multiple sectors of the economy: agriculture, animal husbandry, crafts manufacture, and long-distance trade. The evidence from this temple archive and others has tended to overshadow economic activity that is less well documented, and Mesopotamia has often been characterized as a "temple-state economy" in which all resources are owned and entirely managed by the temple. While the model of the institutional household continues to be valid for the productive activities of the temple or palace, it has become evident that the economy was also served by entrepreneurs, people external to the institutional households, whose activities, while not as prominently documented, were nonetheless vital to the long-lived success of the Mesopotamian economy.

Entrepreneurs and Entrepreneurship. An *entrepreneur* is defined as a person who organizes, operates, and assumes the risk for a business venture. He often plays the role of middleman, someone who fills a gap between the activities of a producer and a consumer—taking responsibility, for example, for the transportation and delivery of agricultural produce from outlying farms to the marketplace in the city or for the actual door-to-door collection of taxes owed the crown. In Mesopotamia, entrepreneurs are most evident in activities that took place outside the direct supervision of administrators of the temple or palace.

Shepherds as Entrepreneurs. The function of entrepreneurs in the Mesopotamian economy can be illustrated by an example of their activity in the sector of animal husbandry. The temple and palace generally owned large flocks of sheep and goats, which were not kept inside the city, where the institution was located, and had to be led great distances for adequate pasturage, returning to the city for shearing only once a year. The temple made a contract with a shepherd to take care of the flocks for the year. The contract typically included the number of animals entrusted to the shepherd, a projection of how many new animals would likely be born over the course of the year, and the amount of wool the shepherd was obligated to provide to the temple at the close of the contract year. At the end of the year, if fewer animals than the contract had stipulated were returned to the temple, the shepherd was obligated personally to make good the loss. If he could not pay from his own assets, he might have to commit himself or members of his family to the service of the institution. On the other hand, if he returned with more animals than expected, he could add the additional animals to his own flock; they were his profit from the venture. Because the shepherd took on the risk of managing the flock in exchange for the possibility of making a profit, he is, by definition, an entrepreneur. By contracting with the shepherd for a predetermined growth rate of the flock, the institution accepted a smaller margin of profit in exchange for reducing its risk of losses.

Limits of Institutional Accounting. The principles of interaction between institution and entrepreneur—as illustrated by the example of the temple contracting with the shepherd to manage its flocks—are essentially the same for other sectors of the economy: the institution set productivity goals that the entrepreneur agreed to meet. Deficits were charged to the entrepreneur, and surpluses constituted his profit. The internal redistributive system of an institutional household required careful bookkeeping, and Mesopotamian institutional accounting served what classical historian Moses Finley has termed (in regard to ancient Greece) a "police function": providing inventories of goods and identifying persons responsible for those goods. Keeping track of an institution's stores requires only the simple operations of addition and subtraction, and Mesopotamian accounting procedures were not equipped to predict future income by using the kind of statistical modeling used by modern accountants. The Mesopotamian models were arithmetically based, fairly simple, and suited the needs of the institution, which was always the stronger partner in any of its interactions with an entrepreneur. For example, in the case of a shepherd who contracted with the temple for the care of its flocks, no provision was made in the contract for the deaths of animals that died in circumstances where the shepherd was not at fault—as through accident, predator attack, illness, or other unforeseen calamity. Past records of the sizes of the flocks, as well as the experience of the administrator, would have provided some guidance as to what to expect for the next year, but the numbers in the contracts fail to take into account actual birth and death rates for the animals. Economic historian Michael Jursa has observed that the calculations used to predict the growth of the herd (or other forms of institutional income) amount to little more than wishful thinking: "the models had to simplify the complex realities considerably to make them appear controllable by the means at the bureaucrats' disposal. . . . There was no notion of 'probability' as we know it." Also, for the most part, the institutions had the power to set the terms of contracts, no matter how unfavorable they might be to their partners.

Entrepreneurship in the Third and Second Millennia B.C.E. In the third and second millennia B.C.E. entrepreneurs figured prominently in trade, especially long-distance trade. The so-called Seafaring Merchants of Ur, whose activity is particularly well documented circa 2000 B.C.E., were independent agents who took responsibility for transporting and selling the agricultural surplus and textiles produced by the Ur temples and using the proceeds to buy imported goods from Persian Gulf lands and transport them back to the city, where they were awaited by the temple administrators who had commissioned the deal. In taking on the temple's wares, the merchant also assumed the risks of the trade. For example, a ship could founder at sea, or the cargo could be seized by pirates. Some contracts did make provision for catastrophe and thus shared some of the risk between the institution and the entrepreneur. For the most part, however, the merchant took the risk of personal loss in exchange for the opportunity for personal profit. Because they had cash or consumables on hand in the course of executing trades, merchants could also make loans, another means by which they were able to take risks (lending money) in exchange for earning profits (through charging interest).

BABYLONIAN TOLL COLLECTOR

The city of Babylon lay on both sides of the Euphrates River, with the two parts of the city connected by one bridge. The governor of Babylon had the prerogative to collect tolls from boats passing under the bridge or mooring at its piers. Marduk-nasir-apli, a member of the entrepreneurial Egibi family, bought or leased these rights from the governor, probably in exchange for a fixed payment made in advance. According to this arrangement, Marduk-nasir-apli was to share the income from these tolls with the "guardians of the bridge." Instead of collecting the tolls himself, however, Marduk-nasir-apli and one of the other shareholders, Muranu, subcontracted the collection job to two other men, Bel-asua and Ubar, for a monthly payment of fifteen sheqels silver. The text of the contract for this complicated arrangement is dated the twenty-sixth year of Darius, or 495 B.C.E.:

The levy (of tolls) at the bridge and the harbor (from boats) going downstream and upstream, the [. . .] of Guzanu, governor of Babylon, which is at the disposal of Marduk-nasir-apli. A half share in the income from the bridge of Guzanu, governor of Babylon, which is (shared) with Muranu, son of Nabu-mukin-apli, Nabu-bullissu, son of Guzanu, as well as with Harisanu, Iqupu, (and) Nergal-ibni, guardians of the bridge. Marduk-nasir-apli and Muranu, son of Nabu-mukin-apli, descendant of Massar-elep-rukubi, have leased (it) to Bel-asua, son of Nergal-uballit, descendant of Massar-elep-rukubi, for a monthly payment of fifteen sheqels of white, medium-quality silver, of which one-eighth is alloy. Bel-asua and Ubar shall demand tolls from the boats that moor at the bridge. Bel-asua and Ubar shall not pass on the silver, the monthly income from the bridge that is due to Marduk-nasir-apli and Muranu, owners of a share in it, without (the consent of) Marduk-nasir-apli. Bel-asua and Ubar shall show to Marduk-nasir-apli and to the guardians of the bridge any written message that comes concerning the bridge.
Witnesses:
Nabu-ittanu, son of Ardiya, descendant of Sin-ili
Arad-Marduk, son of Mushezib, descendant of Sippe
Muranu, son of Bel-iddin, descendant of Sha-nashishu
Nabu-re'ushunu, son of Nabu-shuma-usur, descendant of Kanik-babi
Nidintu, son of Kalbaya, descendant of Shuhaya
Mushezib-Marduk, the scribe, son of Shuma-ukin, descendant of Babutu
Babylon: the 1st of Tashritu (the seventh month, i.e., September-October), the 26th year of Darius, king of Babylon, king of all the lands.
They (the participants) have taken one (copy of the document) each.

Source: Kathleen Abrams, *Business and Politics under the Persian Empire: The Financial Dealings of Marduk-nasir-apli of the House of Egibi* (Bethesda, Md.: CDL Press, 2004), pp. 465-466.

Financial Families in the First Millennium B.C.E. The best evidence for Mesopotamian entrepreneurial activity comes from Babylonia in the first millennium B.C.E., thanks in large part to texts from the private archive of the Egibi family in the city of Babylon. The archive probably once held some 2,500–3,000 tablets. Some 1,700 tablets have been identified as belonging to the archive, and most of them are now housed at the British Museum in London. Excavated illicitly by local inhabitants, the tablets were purchased on the antiquities market in the 1870s and 1880s. Thus, without any provenance information, the archive has been re-assembled by modern researchers on the basis of prosopographical, chronological, and geographical information within the texts on the tablets. The archive documents the financial dealings of five generations of the House of Egibi, during the reigns of Nebuchadnezzar II (604–562 B.C.E.) through Darius I (521–486 B.C.E.). The tablets tell the story of the rise of a nouveau-riche family that was unlike the traditional urban elite of the capital, whose wealth was based in large landholdings or positions in temple or palace bureaucracies. The first two generations of Egibi were commodities traders who bought large quantities of grain, dates, onions, and wool in the rural environs and then transported the goods by boat to markets in Babylon. Large building projects in the capital had attracted laborers and craftsmen, whom the palace supported with rations in consumable goods, which were purchased from traders such as the Egibi. Succeeding generations of the family then invested profits from this trade in the slave trade, agricultural management, and—most important—real estate.

The Fourth Generation of the Egibi Family. The eldest son of each generation directed the Egibi's financial business. The activities of the fourth generation, led by Marduk-nasir-apli, are represented with more than 429 tablets. The texts from the time of Marduk-nasir-apli document a high level of involvement with the temples and the palace of Babylon, as indicated by actual transactions or by the participation of individuals identified as institutional functionaries. Extremely varied in content, the tablets range from contracts to a guarantee of delivery of foodstuffs for a religious ceremony to a lease for the rights to collect tolls from boats passing the city bridge.

Sources:

Kathleen Abrams, *Business and Politics under the Persian Empire: The Financial Dealings of Marduk-nasir-apli of the House of Egibi* (Bethesda, Md.: CDL Press, 2004).

Michael Jursa, *Prywatyzacja i zysk?: Przedsiebiorcy a gospodarka instytucjonalna w Mezopotamii od 3 do 1 tysiaclecia przed Chr* (Poznan: Poznan Society for the Advancement of the Arts and Sciences, 2002).

Cornelia Wunsch, "The Egibi Family's Real Estate in Babylon (6th Century BC)," in *Urbanization and Land Ownership in the Ancient Near East*, edited by Michael Hudson and Baruch Levine (Cambridge, Mass.: Peabody Museum of Archaeology and Ethnology, 1999), pp. 391–419.

FAMILY AND HOUSEHOLD

Definitions. Evidence for reconstructing Mesopotamian social organization comes from a vast variety of written texts as well as from archaeological excavation of private houses and the architectural complexes of the great institutions, the temples and palaces. Social historians define *family* as persons related by blood or marriage, and *household* as persons living under the same roof. A married couple and their children constitute a nuclear family. If other relations—such as grandparents, aunts, uncles, and cousins—are included in the group, it constitutes an extended family. Family groupings that encompass even wider family ties are known as tribes or clans. Members of a nuclear family living together in one house constitute a family household, and extended family households are also possible. In Mesopotamia the temple and the palace were organized and functioned as households, even though their members might not have been related. Every household, family or institutional, shared the same general structure. At its head was an individual who held the authority for managing the household's assets and who was responsible for the well-being of its other members. In a Mesopotamian family household, the head was the senior adult male; that is, the father and husband, who was the holder of the family property. The head of the temple household was the god who "owned" the resources of the temple and to whom the temple and its personnel were dedicated. In Mesopotamian ideology, the chief administrators of the temple were the representatives of the deity and managed the temple resources on the god's behalf. The head of the palace household was the king, who also had a large staff to execute his decisions concerning the household and its resources. Thus, family and household structures played crucial roles in the Mesopotamian economy.

Urban Family Households. Textual and archaeological evidence from the third millennium B.C.E. indicates that the people who initially settled in Mesopotamian cities lived in extended family enclaves. Early legal contracts reveal that in these new and rapidly developing cities, neighbors were related. Sale documents from that time indicate that properties were owned by multiple family members rather than by individuals. Over time, the size and complexity of houses built in the cities decreased. Space was restricted in urban centers, and members of a growing extended family were forced to establish individual family households in other parts of the city. After the earliest settling of cities, for much of Mesopotamian history the basic building block of urban society seems to have been the simple or nuclear family: a married couple and their children—with or without additional relatives such as unmarried aunts and uncles or elderly grandparents. Children lived at home until marriage, at which point they founded their own family households. Because land was always subject to family ownership, however, ties of the extended family—tribal and clan affiliations—continued to be important in cities even though individuals did not live together in extended family households. The seemingly ageless custom of identifying persons according to their patrilineal descent—"Samsu-iluna, son of Hammurabi," for example—also helped to perpetuate clan and tribe affiliations even among people who did not live together.

Rural Family Households. While written evidence from rural areas is meager, people living outside Mesopotamian urban centers do occasionally appear in documents generated in cities. Extended family households were more likely in rural areas, where there were fewer restrictions on living space. Larger groupings, such as tribes or clans, were also more in evidence among nonurban nomadic or seminomadic people, with whom tribe or clan affiliation played a significant political and economic role. Tribe and clan affiliations appear in written economic documentation, for example, in dealings concerning livestock, whose urban-based owners would send them to outlying regions for pasturage under the supervision of nomadic or semi-nomadic herders. Evidence from Mari, a city on the middle Euphrates, indicates that herders usually had tribal or clan connections to the urban owners of livestock. At times, extended family affiliations provided the basis for urban political power, particularly in the early second millennium B.C.E., when people identified as Amorite (literally, "westerner") were able to establish ruling dynasties in several urban centers—the best known being Hammurabi's dynasty in Babylon (circa 1894 – circa 1595 B.C.E.). This pattern occurred again in the first millennium B.C.E., when first Aramaeans and then Arabs—both ethno-linguistic groups whose power lay in extended family structures outside the urban-centered traditional Mesopotamian elites—used the strength of their tribal support to achieve political power in the cities.

Institutional Households. At the head of the temple or palace hierarchy was the deity or the king, followed by administrators, cultic personnel or courtiers, soldiers, specialized craftsmen, and large numbers of manual laborers, mostly engaged in the agricultural enterprises of the institution but also in animal husbandry and building projects. Among institutional resources were also slaves, who were the property of the institution, and dependents, people something like the serfs of medieval Europe, who owned no means of production and worked the resources of the institution. In theory, the household was self-sufficient; that is, its members produced what they consumed. The household functioned by a principle of redistribution: consumable goods produced by members of the household employed in various activities with its resources were collected by a central administration and then distributed back to the household members. This kind of closed-circle system in Mesopotamia may be described according to the *oikos*-model, employing the Greek word for "house." (The word *oikos* is also echoed in the English word *economy*, which is derived from the Greek word *oikonomia*, literally "management of a household.") With its dependence on irrigation and the labor-saving device of the seeder-plow, the agricultural regime of southern Mesopotamia was most efficient when land was cultivated on a large scale. The ability of the largest landholders, the temples and the palaces, to produce agricultural surpluses enabled them to maintain large households and to invest their resources—including the labor of their dependents—on diversified economic activities. For much of Mesopotamian history, the temple and the palace were the major landholders and thus the major players in the economy.

Limitations of the *oikos* Model. Like any model for describing the real activities of an economy, the *oikos* model has its limitations. The closed circuitry of the model fails to consider the need and the ability of the institutions to exploit outside labor at peak times of the agricultural cycle, such as when the temple drew on village-based farming communities for labor at the harvest and the evolution of the corvée system, whereby the crown exacted monthly labor obligations from subjects outside of the palace household. Access to these external supplies of labor was key to the ability of the institutions to produce agricultural surpluses, which in turn were fundamental to their ongoing economic prosperity. The *oikos* model also fails to take into account relationships among various institutions, particularly that between the temple and the palace. After the third millennium B.C.E., it appears that the palace had increasing power to command the resources of the temple. Finally, the *oikos* model does not account for the activities of independent entrepreneurs or middlemen, such as merchants, who contracted with the institutions to take on the responsibilities and risks of overseeing and executing some of the institutions' activities in exchange for the opportunity to make profits.

Sources:

M. I. Finley, *Ancient History: Evidence and Models* (London: Chatto & Windus, 1985).

Michael Jursa, *Prywatyzacja i zysk?: Przedsiebiorcy a gospodarka instytucjonalna w Mezopotamii od 3 do 1 tysiaclecia przed Chr* (Poznan: Poznan Society for the Advancement of the Arts and Sciences, 2002).

J. N. Postgate, *Early Mesopotamia: Society and Economy at the Dawn of History* (London & New York: Routledge, 1992).

GREAT INSTITUTIONS: TEMPLE AND PALACE

The "Great Institutions." From prehistoric times, prior to circa 3300 B.C.E., until the end of ancient Mesopotamian civilization in the early centuries of the Common Era, two great institutions, the temple and the palace, played an integral role in the economy. The functions of these two institutions were greatly interdependent, and while the relative importance of each institution varied over time, evidence for the operations of the temple is both earlier and more extensive than that relating to the operations of the

palace. Moreover, the temple never completely lost its major position in the Mesopotamian economy.

The Temple. It is necessary to appreciate the ideology behind the temple in order to understand its significant—but not exclusive—role in the various productive, redistributive, and commercial sectors of the Mesopotamian economy. The word *temple* is expressed in Mesopotamian languages as "house of the god" (Sumerian: *e-dingir;* Akkadian: *bit ilim*), and evidence from as early as the third millennium B.C.E. indicates that the temple was organized as a large household with the deity at its head. As in any household, the head or owner of the household and its properties was served by a staff of personnel working in various capacities, all of whom were overseen by an administrative bureaucracy. As the landlord and owner of resources under its control, including the labor of persons dependent on it for support, the god was the ultimate owner of all temple products and profits. This vast enterprise was administered by the temple bureaucracy. Because records they generated are so prominent in the body of available evidence, modern economic historians once concluded that the Mesopotamian economy was dominated by the temple, giving rise to the characterization of ancient Mesopotamia as a "temple-state economy." Recent research, however, has modified the overall picture, and a less extreme view of the Mesopotamian economy has emerged, one in which the temple, the palace, and what might be called private enterprise each play a role.

Economic Role. As a major property owner, the temple was in a position to benefit from large-scale economic undertakings. The most complete picture from the third millennium B.C.E. is provided by an archive of some 1,800 inscribed tablets from the temple of the goddess Ba'u, a second-rank temple in the Sumerian city of Girsu, part of the larger city-state of Lagash. Dated to the first half of the twenty-fourth century B.C.E., the tablets detail the economic activities of the temple: cultivation of cereal crops, vegetables, and fruit trees; maintenance of irrigation systems; husbandry of sheep, goats, cows, and donkeys; and fresh- and saltwater fishing. Large-scale agriculture and animal husbandry enabled the temple to accumulate a surplus; that is, the temple produced more food, wool, and other products than it needed for the sustenance of its dependents. The surplus enabled the temple to devote some of its resources to specialized production and commercial ventures. The temple engaged in large-scale textile manufacturing, the most economically significant Mesopotamian commercial venture. Rations lists from the textile workshop of the Ba'u temple attest to a workforce of more than six thousand laborers, most of them women, along with children. The agricultural surplus also allowed the temple to invest in the infrastructure necessary for long-distance trade, such as large boats for transportation and warehouses for storage. Access to ready capital enabled the temple to fund long and expensive trading trips, and at

THE SUMERIAN KING LIST

Long-standing Sumerian tradition held that kingship was handed down from heaven; however, without warning or provocation, kingship might be removed from one city and bestowed on another. The *Sumerian King List* is apparently a composition from the period of the Third Dynasty of Ur (circa 2112 – circa 2004 B.C.E.), whose kings sought to legitimize their assumption of hegemony in southern Mesopotamia. The text is known from many Old Babylonian period (circa 1750 B.C.E.) copies, which are often at variance with each other. The list usually opens with kingship being handed down to the city of Eridu and passing to four other cities before "the flood swept over."

After the flood had swept over, and the kingship had descended from heaven, the kingship was in Kish.
In Kish, Gushur became king; he ruled for 1200 years. Kullassina-bel ruled for 900/960 years. Nangishlishma ruled for 670 years. Entarahana ruled for 420 years . . . , 3 months, and 3½ days. Babum . . . ruled for 300 years. Puannum ruled for 840/240 years. Kalibum ruled for 960/900 years. Kalumum ruled for 840/900 years. Zuqaqip ruled for 900/600 years. Atab (A-ba) ruled for 600 years. Mashda, the son of Atab, ruled for 840/720 years. Arwium,

the son of Mashda, ruled for 720 years. Etana, the shepherd, who ascended to heaven and consolidated all the foreign countries, became king; he ruled for 1500/635 years. Balih, the son of Etana, ruled for 400/410 years. Enmenuna ruled for 660/621 years. Melem-Kish, the son of Enmenuna, ruled for 900 years/1560 years. Barsalnuna, the son of Enmenuna ruled for 1200 years. Zamug, the son of Barsalnuna, ruled for 140 years. Tizqar, the son of Zamug, ruled for 305/1620 + x years. Ilku ruled for 900 years. Iltasadum ruled for 1200 years. Enmebaragesi, who made the land of Elam submit, became king; he ruled for 900 years. Aga, the son of Enmebaragesi, ruled for 625/1525 years.
23 kings; they ruled for 24510 years, 3 months, and 3½ days. Then Kish was defeated and the kingship was taken to E-ana.

Kish, as the first city to exercise kingship after the flood, retained its prestige: the title "King of Kish" came to mean "king of the world." Despite the seemingly fantastic lengths of the early kings' reigns, the list appears to have a kernel of historical actuality.

Source: Jeremy Black, Graham Cunningham, Jarle Ebeling, Esther Flückiger-Hawker, Eleanor Robson, Jon Taylor, and Gábor Zólyomi, *The Electronic Text Corpus of Sumerian Literature,* The Oriental Institute, University of Oxford, 1998– <http://www.etcsl.orient.ox.ac.uk/>.

---

times the temple acted as a "bank," granting loans, and as a charity, taking in the children of poor parents. The temple also used its accumulated surplus to finance other kinds of undertakings beyond the reach of family households, such as maintaining specialized workshops for artisans and craftsmen manufacturing luxury goods and everyday items from leather, wood, metal, and stone.

Emergence of the Palace. The nature of the economic—and political—relationship between the temple and the palace is still not clear for most periods of Mesopotamian history. The broad picture seems to be that the temple was the only major political and economic institution in prehistory. Archaeological excavations reveal construction during the mid to late third millennium B.C.E. of a new kind of building complex: a palace; that is, the physical residence of the king and his extended royal and bureaucratic household. The Early Dynastic II period (circa 2750 – circa 2600 B.C.E.) Palace A in the city of Kish—the earliest building identified as an example of monumental, secular architecture—had a massive entrance and decorated reception rooms with columns—features shared with later palaces built in other Mesopotamian cities. This new development in monumental architecture is evidence for the rise of secular leaders, and the appearance of royal inscriptions (circa 2400 B.C.E.) indicates the emergence and rise of kingship. Thereafter, the palace, as the locus for the king's authority,

took its place as a powerful institution separate from the temple. It would be a mistake, however, to consider kingship altogether secular; there was no such thing as the modern American principle of "separation of church and state." Ideologically, kingship was always closely connected with religious belief; the gods were believed to have chosen the kings, who reigned by the gods' grace. For three centuries, beginning with Naram-Sin of Akkad (circa 2254 – circa 2218 B.C.E.), Mesopotamian kings even went so far as to claim to be gods ruling on earth. Over time, as the power of the king grew, the palace claimed a sizable portion of the economy, income that might otherwise have gone to the temple, and it is clear that at times the palace had access to the temple's economic resources. The most enduring images of kingship depict the king as shepherd and as bringer of water, thus productivity, to the land—suggesting the roots of Mesopotamian royal ideology in the realm of animal husbandry and agriculture, the foundations of the Mesopotamian economy. Nevertheless, the temple consistently retained a significant role in Mesopotamian production and trade, and its economic role was never completely eclipsed by that of the palace.

Sources:
J. N. Postgate, *Early Mesopotamia: Society and Economy at the Dawn of History* (London & New York: Routledge, 1992).

Piotr Steinkeller, "The Administrative and Economic Organization of the Ur III State: The Core and the Periphery," in *The Organization of*

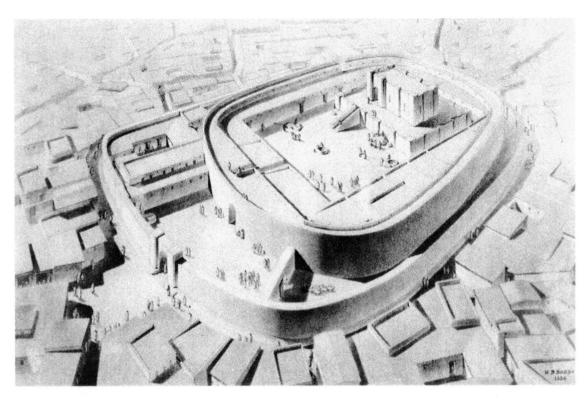

Artist's reconstruction of the Temple Oval at Khafajah. The temple complex, built on a bed of clean desert sand some twenty-six feet deep and covering an area of more than ¾ acre, was constructed during the Early Dynastic II period, circa 2700 – 2600 B.C.E. (drawing by H. D. Darby, from Pinhas Delougaz, *The Temple Oval at Khafājah*, Oriental Institute Publications, 53, 1940).

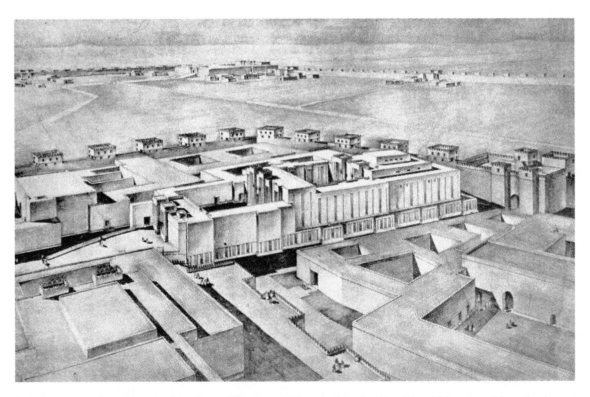

Artist's reconstruction of Assyrian king Sargon II's palace at Khorsabad (ancient Dur-Sharrukin) as viewed from the ziggurat across the fortified citadel to the distant city walls beyond, 721–705 B.C.E. (drawing by Charles Altman; from Gordon Loud, *Khorsabad II*, Oriental Institute Publications, 40, 1938)

Power: Aspects of Bureaucracy in the Ancient Near East, edited by McGuire Gibson and Robert D. Biggs (Chicago: Oriental Institute, 1987), pp. 19–41.

Marc Van de Mieroop, *Society and Enterprise in Old Babylonian Ur* (Berlin: Dietrich Reimer, 1992).

LONG-DISTANCE TRADE

Chronological and Geographic Scope. Evidence for long-distance trade goes back as early as the Neolithic period, with obsidian blades from the Lake Van region appearing in southern small-scale agricultural settlements and related burials. Other regions with which prehistoric Mesopotamians traded include Anatolia to the north, Iran and Afghanistan to the east, the Persian Gulf and as far as the Indus Valley to the southeast, and—via Syria and the Levant—the Egyptian Nile delta to the southwest. Although the cities of southern Mesopotamia had to import staples for everyday use, such as wood and tin for making bronze, written and archaeological evidence provides much more information about the trade in luxury goods.

Imports and Exports. Lacking indigenous sources for most metals, precious and semi-precious stone, wood, and most ivory, people living in Mesopotamia had to obtain them through direct or indirect trade with distant lands. The emergence of political and social hierarchies in southern Mesopotamia was concurrent with the establishment of stable, long-distance trade networks, which provided the raw materials necessary to make the luxury goods that signaled the socio-economic status of the new elites. Gold and ivory were obtained from Egypt; semi-precious stones such as blue lapis lazuli and red carnelian came from Afghanistan and the Indus Valley, respectively; silver and hard stone were imported from Iran; wood, aromatics, and spices came from the Levantine coast. In exchange for these raw materials, Mesopotamia exported fine wool and linen textiles, as well as reed mats. A picture of this moment in time, just before the widespread use of writing, can be compiled from the grave goods found in the elite burials at Ur, the so-called Royal Tombs of Ur (circa 2550 B.C.E.), which included luxury items made from imported gold, silver, and semi-precious stones.

Agents of Trade: Institutions and Merchants. The agents behind the long-distance trade network were the economic institutions of Mesopotamia, the temple and the palace, both of which co-operated with independent merchants, who contracted with the institutions to transport goods, chiefly by boat and donkey caravan. Thanks to their production of agricultural surpluses and their domination of the domestic textile industry, the institutions had the financial means to engage merchants for their journeys, as well as the capital to invest in transportation technology,

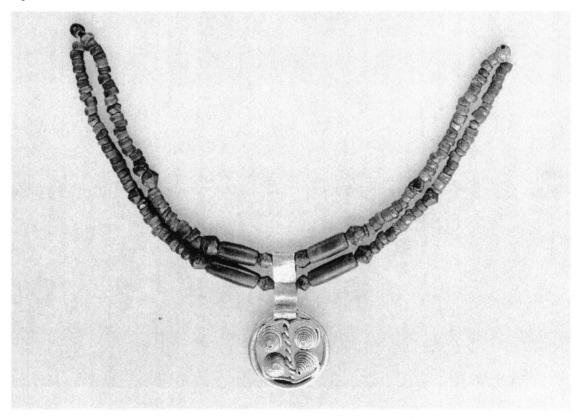

Modern stringing (length 5¾ inches) of imported lapis-lazuli and carnelian beads and a quadruple-spiral gold pendant, circa 2600 – circa 2500 B.C.E., found loose in the soil at Ur. The spiral pendant closely resembles an eastern Aegean or Anatolian type found at scattered locations across western and central Asia, but this example was made using a slightly different technique (University of Pennsylvania Museum of Archaeology and Anthropology).

such as larger, faster boats. The institutions also employed staffs of expert craftsmen and were thus in a position to requisition elite manufactured artworks using imported luxury materials. Records from two of the best-documented long-distant trade enterprises—the so-called Seafaring Merchants of Ur best documented for the Ur III and Isin-Larsa periods, circa 2100 – circa 1900 B.C.E., and the Old Assyrian Trading Colonies, circa 1900 – circa 1800 B.C.E.—indicate that trade operations were handed down from father to son and that merchant families, or houses, accumulated wealth over generations, which enabled them to invest their own capital in trading and banking ventures.

The Seafaring Merchants of Ur. In southern Mesopotamia, a seaborne trade is documented in texts from the city of Ur, which, in ancient times, had a port on the coast of the Persian Gulf. The Ur merchants sailed to the land of Dilmun, modern-day Bahrain, an island on which recent excavations have uncovered a port with trade links to places elsewhere on the shores of the Persian Gulf and as far east as the Indus Valley. This network is attested in prehistory and dates back as far as the sixth millennium B.C.E. This seaborne trade brought to Mesopotamia mother of pearl, aromatics, semi-precious stones, spices, and other luxury items. It also provided Mesopotamians with glimpses of Indus Valley culture in the form of distinctive Indus-style carved stamp seals. Artifacts provide evidence that this trade network dates back to prehistoric times, and it is well documented during the Ur III and Isin-Larsa periods (circa 2100 – circa 1900 B.C.E.). According to written records, the voyages were financed by a large number of investors, each of whom paid a small amount. The merchants who conducted the expeditions paid a 10 percent tax to the temple of the god Ningal, in addition to making voluntary gifts in thanks for a successful voyage. Thus, while the voyages were conducted by private traders, they were nonetheless made under the auspices of the temples and palaces. One import mentioned in particular in the written records was copper, whose origin was undoubtedly the mountains of ancient Magan, modern-day Oman.

Old Assyrian Trading Colonies in Anatolia. After the collapse of the Ur III state (circa 2004 B.C.E.) and the resulting end of the restrictions imposed by its stifling redistributive economic system, merchant families from the city of Ashur established trading colonies in Anatolia, the foremost of which was at Kültepe (ancient Kanesh), active from circa 1910 to circa 1830 B.C.E. and again from circa 1810 to circa 1740 B.C.E. Traveling distances of 1,200 kilometers (750 miles) from their home city, the Assyrian merchants led donkey caravans loaded with textiles from Babylonia and tin from Iran to the Anatolian plateau. There, they sold the textiles and tin—a requirement for making the alloy bronze—for gold and silver, which they then transported back to Ashur. Silver was re-invested in

---

CARAVAN EXPENSES

The following passage is from a letter written by an Old Assyrian merchant, reporting the expenses incurred along a segment of the trip from Ashur to Kanesh, which hosted a trading colony occupied by Assyrian merchant families resident in Anatolia. At its peak around 1910–1830 B.C.E., the Old Assyrian trade network transported Iranian tin and Babylonian woolen textiles by donkey caravan to Anatolia, where they were sold for silver and gold. This letter and others from the period document the day-to-day mechanics and expenses of running a long-distance-trade business and show that the system for collecting taxes, tolls, and other moneys along the trade route was as highly developed as the trade network itself.

From (the town of) Wahshushana until Shalatuwar we had to pay 0.96 kg of copper each for custom duties as well as for fodder for the donkeys and for (lodging at) inns. Furthermore, they charged (as a toll) for each donkey 0.17 kg at the bridge. 1 kg of copper was (the cost of) the fodder for the donkeys at Shalatuwar. We had to pay 1.25 kg until Burushattum. For each donkey they charged as toll 0.125 kg at the bridge. 0.75 kg was (the cost of) fodder for the donkeys and the food of the servant in Burushattum. I have given 1.25 kg of copper into the hand of Arwanahshu.

Considering these expenses, it is not surprising that some traders resorted to smuggling to reduce their overhead.

Source: Emin Bilgiç and Cahit Günbatti, *Ankaraner Kültepe-Texte III*, translated into German by Karl Hecker, Freiburger Altorientalische Studien Beihefte, volume 3 (Wiesbaden: Franz Steiner, 1995), no. 34.

---

procuring more textiles and tin for the next trip, but the merchant families hoarded their gold. Thanks to letters exchanged between merchants and family members managing the Ashur end of the business, modern scholars know that the trip took about six weeks each way. It has been calculated that each donkey carried a load weighing approximately 35 kilograms (77 pounds). One of the remarkable features of the enterprise is the apparent degree to which the Assyrian merchants assimilated into the local Anatolian culture while they were living there between trips; without the discovery of their letters, there would be no evidence of their presence so far from home.

Sources:

Joan Aruz and Françoise Demange, "Seals and Interconnections," in *Art of the First Cities: The Third Millennium B.C. from the Mediterranean to the Indus*, edited by Aruz with Ronald Wallenfels (New York: Metropolitan Museum of Art, 2003), pp. 407–413.

Wolfgang Heimpel, "Das untere Meer," *Zeitschrift für Assyriologie*, 77 (1982): 22–91.

A. L. Oppenheim, "The Seafaring Merchants of Ur," *Journal of the American Oriental Society*, 74 (1954): 6–17.

J. N. Postgate, *Early Mesopotamia: Society and Economy at the Dawn of History* (London & New York: Routledge, 1992).

Daniel T. Potts, "The Gulf: Dilmun and Magan," in *Art of the First Cities*, pp. 307–308.

Potts, *Mesopotamia: The Material Foundations* (London: Athlone Press, 1997).

Marc Van de Mieroop, "Gifts and Tithes to the Temples in Ur," in *DUMU-E₂-DUB-BA-A: Studies in Honor of Åke W. Sjöberg*, edited by Hermann Behrens, Darlene Loding, and Martha T. Roth, Occasional Publications of the Samuel Noah Kramer Fund, no. 11 (Philadelphia: Samuel Noah Kramer Fund, University Museum, 1989), pp. 397–401.

Klaas Veenhof, "Kanesh: An Assyrian Trading Colony in Anatolia," in *Civilizations of the Ancient Near East*, 4 volumes, edited by Jack M. Sasson (New York: Scribners, 1995), II: 859–871.

MONEY, PRICES, AND BANKING

From Barter System to Market. Before the rise of cities, individual households in Mesopotamia produced most of what they consumed. Within small villages and settlements, one household could trade or barter its goods with other households. In a simple barter transaction, participants exchange a product or service for a different product or service on terms both parties consider fair and equitable; that is, the good or service received is deemed worth the good or service given up. Over time, as individuals and individual households began increasingly to specialize in one of an ever-wider variety of goods and services, the network of exchange grew more complex. The brewer, for example, might seek to exchange his beer with a potter for storage jars; the potter, in turn, might seek to trade his wares for the services of the barber; the barber might seek to exchange a haircut and a shave for new blades from the metalsmith; and the metalsmith with a surplus of sickle blades might seek to obtain fine beer from the brewer for his daughter's wedding banquet. To facilitate such complex exchanges, markets developed, allowing groups of producers and consumers to meet simultaneously. Established markets stimulated further specialization and also attracted producers and consumers from other regions.

Weights and Measures. As markets evolved, systems of weights and measures were developed, enabling producers and consumers to set values for each other's products. In Mesopotamia, weights were typically fashioned out of stone in the shape of animals. A popular shape was a duck with its head reversed and resting on its back. After conquering and uniting southern Mesopotamia, king Sargon of Akkad (circa 2334 B.C.E. – circa 2279 B.C.E.) standardized the system of weights and measures throughout his new dominion. He and subsequent kings boasted of their efforts at standardization as a mark of the order and economic advancement that they had brought to the people under their rule. Ur-Namma (circa 2112 – circa 3095 B.C.E.), founder of the Ur III Dynasty, mentioned weights and measures in the prologue to his laws:

> I fashioned the copper *bariga*-measure and standardized it at 60 silas (liters). I fashioned the copper *seah*-measure and

> standardized it at 10 silas. . . . I standardized (all) the stone weights from the pure (?) 1 sheqel (weight) to the 1 mina (60 sheqel weight). I fashioned the bronze 1-sila measure and standardized it at 1 mina. (Roth)

King Shulgi (circa 2094 – circa 2047 B.C.E.), son and successor of Ur-Namma, reformed accounting procedures and the calendar, tools that played a role in the redistributive economy he established throughout his realm. Ensuring fair trade was a vital obligation of a king, as demonstrated by the Laws of Hammurabi (circa 1750 B.C.E.), in which a large number of measures are dedicated to regulating business transactions. One describes the penalty for a lender who used two different systems of weights and measures in order to cheat a borrower:

> If a merchant gives grain or silver as an interest-bearing loan, and when he gives it as an interest-bearing loan he gives the silver according to the small weight or the grain according to the small measure, but when he receives payment he receives the silver according to the large weight or the grain according to the large measure, that merchant shall forfeit all that he gave (as the loan). (LH gap § x; Roth)

Prices. The term *price* is defined as the quantity of money or goods asked for or given in exchange for something else. In general, price is an index of demand. Rising prices indicate increasing demand; likewise, falling prices indicate decreasing demand. Prices far higher than usual for basic foodstuffs, such as bread, may be an indicator of want or famine in the land. Prices can indicate the prosperity—or poverty—of the land, and stable prices are indicators of the stability of society and the economy. They are of concern, therefore, to rulers as well as their subjects, and prices of common goods are found in royal inscriptions as concrete illustrations of the health of the economy and the well-being of the people during a king's reign. The reforms of the Early Dynastic III period ruler of Lagash, Uru'inimgina (circa 2380 B.C.E.), list the prevailing prices of his day, as do the laws of the city of Eshnunna (circa 1770 B.C.E.), which open with a statement of what can be purchased for one sheqel of silver and for a measure of grain; this information is followed by the cost to hire certain services. The text also specifies interest rates for loans of silver and of grain. In hard times, such as during drought or a siege, highly inflated prices (expressed as the low purchasing power of the sheqel) appear in the textual record as indicators of the extent of the economic want the land is suffering. In the aftermath of the destruction of Akkad (circa 2200 B.C.E.), the narrator of *The Cursing of Agade* lamented:

> In those days, oil for one (silver) sheqel was only half a liter, grain for one sheqel was only half a liter, wool for one sheqel was only one mina, fish for one sheqel filled only a one ban measure—these sold at such prices in the markets of the cities! (Black et al.)

On the other hand, in the coronation prayer of the Assyrian king Ashurbanipal (668 – circa 627 B.C.E.), blessings for the new king and his reign included:

THE LAWS OF ESHNUNNA

The following passages are excerpted from the Laws of Eshnunna, a kingdom in northern Babylonia contemporary with the early part of the First Dynasty in Babylon (circa 1894 – circa 1595 B.C.E.) and conquered by Hammurabi as he expanded his kingdom to the north. The laws are preserved on three tablets that are later copies of the original, which—like other law collections—may have been inscribed on a stone stele for public display. The name of the ruler who wrote these laws, composed circa 1770 B.C.E., is not preserved. The provisions address a wide variety of situations (such as theft, fugitive slaves, marital rights, and vicious dogs) as well as economic and financial matters. Whatever king of Eshnunna wrote the laws, it is clear that his conception of justice for his people included fair treatment in economic matters.

300 silas (liters) of barley (can be purchased) for 1 sheqel of silver. 3 silas of fine oil—for 1 sheqel of silver. 12 silas of oil—for 1 sheqel of silver. 15 silas of lard—for 1 sheqel of silver. 40 silas of bitumen—for 1 sheqel of silver. 360 sheqels of wool—for 1 sheqel of silver. 600 sheqels of salt—for 1 sheqel of silver. 300 silas of potash—for 1 sheqel of silver. 180 sheqels of copper—for 1 sheqel of silver. 120 sheqels of wrought copper—for 1 sheqel of silver. (§1)

1 sila of oil . . . —30 silas is its grain equivalent. 1 sila of lard . . . —25 silas is its grain equivalent. 1 sila of bitumen . . . —8 silas is its grain equivalent. (§2)

A wagon together with its oxen and its driver—100 silas of grain is its hire; if paid in silver, 1/3 shekel is its hire; he shall drive it for the entire day. (§3)

The hire of a boat is, per 300-sila capacity, 2 silas; furthermore, [x] silas is the hire of the boatman; he shall drive it for the entire day. (§4)

20 silas of grain is the hire of a harvester; if paid in silver, 12 barleycorns (1/15 sheqel) is his hire. (§7)

15 silas is the hire of a sickle, and the broken blade (?) shall revert to its owner. (§9A)

10 silas of grain is the hire of a donkey; and 10 silas of grain is the hire of its driver; he shall drive it for the entire day. (§10)

The hire of a laborer is 1 sheqel of silver, 60 silas of grain is his provender; he shall serve for 1 month. (§11)

Per 1 sheqel (of silver), interest accrues at the rate of 36 barleycorns (= 20 percent); per 300 silas (of grain), interest accrues at the rate of 100 silas (= 33 percent). (§18A)

Source: Martha T. Roth, *Law Collections from Mesopotamia and Asia Minor,* second edition, Society of Biblical Literature, Writings from the Ancient World Series, volume 6 (Atlanta: Scholars Press, 1995).

With one sheqel of silver, may the resident of Ashur obtain 30 kur of grain!

With one sheqel of silver, may the resident of Ashur obtain 3 seahs of oil!

With one sheqel of silver, may the resident of Ashur obtain 30 minas of wool! (translation by the author, after Livingstone's edition)

During the period from the mid-seventh through the mid-first centuries B.C.E., texts now known as astronomical diaries—primarily records of the day-by-day observations of the positions of the sun, moon, and planets—also included data on the purchasing power of the sheqel for six basic commodities: barley, dates, mustard, cress, sesame, and wool. Typically, the diaries—whose entries can be dated precisely to the year, month, and day—list the commodity prices at the end of each month. Some, however, give the prices for the beginning, middle, and end of each month, while others chart virtually day-by-day fluctuations throughout the month.

Money and Coinage. Grain, usually barley, seems to have been the common standard by which the values of other commodities were originally reckoned. If payments, including wages, were made in a commodity other than barley (such as oil or beer), the value of the oil or beer was calculated according to its worth in barley, which was measured by volume. Over time, silver, measured in increments of weight, came to be more widely used as the standard of value. The basic unit of barley was the seah (Sumerian: *ban;* Akkadian: *sutu*), the equivalent of approximately ten liters (about ten quarts). The basic unit of silver, the mina (Sumerian: *mana;* Akkadian: *manu*), was about 480 grams (about 17 ounces); the mina was subdivided into 60 sheqels. Large payments, as for real estate or slaves, as well as investments in business partnerships, were generally made in silver, but smaller purchases could be made in silver as well. Mesopotamian texts express the concept "to sell" as "to give for silver." Whereas barley has an immediate, real value as a consumable good—to be eaten in some form or used for seed—silver does not; its worth lies in the fact that a person holding silver can use it to obtain other goods and services. In this way, silver functioned as money in ancient Mesopotamia. For this purpose, silver (and rarely gold) was fashioned into simple thin coils or rings that could be easily carried. Pieces were then clipped off the rings to measure out precise increments to be weighed on a balance. Silver served as money in Mesopotamia for at least two thousand years. Coins, the earliest of which were fashioned from electrum, first appeared circa 650 B.C.E. in Lydia in western Anatolia, apparently an innovation of the state to pay its mercenary soldiers. Coins came into popular use in Mesopotamia only after the arrival of Alexander III of Macedon in 331 B.C.E. In the Seleucid period (311–129 B.C.E.), despite the fact that coins were minted to specific values, cuneiform contracts recording large purchases, such

Basalt 30 mina weight (length 12 5/8 inches; weight 33 pounds, 4 ½ ounces) in the shape of a duck with its head resting on its back; from the palace of Eriba-Marduk, Chaldaean king of Babylon, circa 765 B.C.E. (British Museum, London)

as houses or slaves, still required that payment made in silver coin be weighed to determine its real value.

Borrowing and Lending. Large numbers of written texts from Mesopotamia are evidence of a lively commercial scene in which individuals and institutions entered into business partnerships and borrowed from institutions or other individuals. Loans could be either interest or non-interest bearing. The standard interest rate was 33 percent for a loan of barley and 20 percent for a loan of silver. To lend capital requires the existence of a surplus, and the temple at times served as a kind of bank; in times of economic distress, texts record that temples gave non-interest-bearing loans. Merchants (Sumerian: *damgar;* Akkadian: *tamkarum*) who came to have liquid capital on hand, also appear frequently in documents as lenders. If a borrower was not able to meet his loan obligations, he might be forced to sell himself or a member of his household into service to work off the debt. Debt slaves were obliged to serve for a proscribed period of time, but could be released before their terms were up if the king declared a general cancellation of debts.

Sources:

Sabina Franke, "Kings of Akkad: Sargon and Naram-Sin," in *Civilizations of the Ancient Near East,* 4 volumes, edited by Jack M. Sasson (New York: Scribners, 1995), II: 831–842.

Jacob Klein, "Shulgi of Ur: King of a Neo-Sumerian Empire," in *Civilizations of the Ancient Near East,* II: 843–858.

Alisdair Livingstone, *Court Poetry and Literary Miscellanea,* State Archives of Assyria, volume 3 (Helsinki: Helsinki University Press, 1989).

J. N. Postgate, *Early Mesopotamia: Society and Economy at the Dawn of History* (London & New York: Routledge, 1992).

Marvin A. Powell, "A Contribution to the History of Money in Mesopotamia Prior to the Invention of Coinage," in *Festschrift Lubor Matouš,* 2 volumes, edited by Bohuslav Hruška and G. Komoróczy, Assyriologia V (Budapest: Eötvös Loránd Tudományeggyetem, 1981), II: 211–243.

Powell, "Identification and Interpretation of Long Term Price Fluctuations in Babylonia: More on the History of Money in Mesopotamia," *Altorientalische Forschung,* 17 (1990): 95–118.

Martha T. Roth, *Law Collections from Mesopotamia and Asia Minor,* second edition, Society of Biblical Literature, Writings from the Ancient World Series, volume 6 (Atlanta: Scholars Press, 1995).

Alice Louise Slotsky, *The Bourse of Babylon: Market Quotations in the Astronomical Diaries of Babylonia* (Bethesda, Md.: CDL Press, 1997).

PROPERTY AND OWNERSHIP

Property and Society. There is no native Mesopotamian term for the concept of *property.* In the written documentation, fields, orchards, animals, houses, furniture, and slaves are identified by terms such as the "field of Gimillu, the divination priest," or the "ox of Enlil-bani, the metalsmith." No written treatise on the concept of property— whether private, communal, or state—has ever been discovered, and given the Mesopotamian disinclination to commit abstractions to writing, none is likely to be found. The majority of legal documents from Mesopotamia, however, are overwhelmingly concerned with the proper disposition of what modern people would call *property,* and thousands of written cuneiform tablets refer to customs— some of which may well predate the invention of writing and written texts—for ensuring legal, unchallengeable, and fair treatment of individuals with property claims. Concern with property, its preservation, and its use shaped not only the Mesopotamian legal tradition but also economic and social practice, notably the ability to sell and to buy land and to transfer property through marriage and inheritance.

Immovable and Movable Property. Property can be divided into two main categories: immovable (land, with or without houses or other buildings) and movable (such as slaves, animals, furnishings, jewelry, silver, gold, and textiles—including clothing, carpets, and wall hangings). The most valuable and durable property in Mesopotamia, an agricultural society, was farmland, and Mesopotamian texts distinguish between fields (Sumerian: *a-sha;* Akkadian: *eqlu*) and orchards (Sumerian: *kiri;* Akkadian; *kiru*). A field had access to water, a canal or river; typically it was bordered on one side by its water source. An orchard was far smaller than a field and was also characterized by proximity to a water source; it represented a long-term investment in the cultivation of trees, most commonly date palms, the primary source of sugar in Mesopotamia.

Ownership of the Land. In a civilization such as ancient Mesopotamia, whose survival was dependent on agriculture, social and economic practices evolved to ensure the continued cultivation of land. The irrigation system functioned most effectively when agriculture was conducted on a large scale, and throughout Mesopotamian history the great institutions, the temple and the palace, were landlords with vast holdings. Because such a large percentage of the surviving documentation comes from the archives of temple and palace, it was once thought that there was no, or little, private landownership in Mesopotamia. However, as new sources have become available from private family archives, scholars have begun to discover that private landownership was more extensive than was previously thought.

Property and the Family. Specific needs of the Mesopotamian agricultural regime may have played a role in shaping regional social structures. For example, if a man had three children and divided his estate among them at his death and if those three children each had three children of their own and divided the property among them again—and so on, the original estate would be divided into extremely small parcels before many generations had passed. While there were no laws prohibiting the alienation—that is, the buying and selling—of land, written records from Mesopotamia indicate a tendency against it. Measures were taken to keep land within a family and to keep it from being broken down into plots too small to be viable agriculturally. Some of the earliest written records, the so-called ancient *kudurrus* (circa 2300 – circa 2100 B.C.E.), provide evidence that for a field to be sold all male members of an extended family had to consent. The inscription on one of these artifacts, the Black Obelisk of Manishtushu (circa 2269 – circa 2255 B.C.E.), lists multiple sellers for each of various fields, all identified as "brother-owners" descended from the same grandfather. Customary inheritance practices also helped to keep property in the family. Equivalent shares of an estate—movable and immovable—were calculated according to the number of children, plus one. A daughter received her share of her father's estate in movable property as a dowry when

---

THE BLACK OBELISK OF MANISHTUSHU

Manishtushu (circa 2269 – circa 2255 B.C.E.) ruled the Mesopotamian empire conquered by his father, Sargon of Akkad. The inscription on the Black Obelisk, a stone, four-sided stele (about 1.5 meters tall) fashioned from black diorite (from the northern shore of the Persian Gulf) is a compilation of the king's land purchases from several families in central Mesopotamia. Several male relatives participated in each sale—an indication that land was not owned by an individual but rather by a family or clan and that the male members of the family had to agree to the sale for it to be legitimate. According to one field sale recorded on the obelisk,

Ilum-aha, son of Ilulu, the "colonel"
Watrum, son of Lamusa, the steward
Ayar-ilum, son of Pu-balum, the shepherd
Sin-alshu, son of Ayar-ilum, son of Pu-balum
UD-ISH (and) Zuzu, 2 sons of Ishtup-Sin, grandsons of Irrara
Ama-Sin, son of Ashi-qurud
Pu-Dagan, son of Allala
Warassuni, son of Mesi-ilim
Total, 10 men, brother-owners of the field.

Grand total 17 men, descendants of Mezizi
821 *iku* of land,
its price 2736.2.4 bushels of barley,
its value 1 sheqel silver per 1 bushel,
its silver (equivalent) 45 minas 36 2/3 sheqels of silver—
(this is) price of the field; 7 minas minus 9 1/2 sheqels silver—(this is) additional payment of the field.

Sources: Ignace J. Gelb, Piotr Steinkeller, and Robert Whiting, *Earliest Land Tenure Systems in the Near East: The Ancient* kudurrus, Oriental Institute Publications, 104 (Chicago: Oriental Institute, 1981).
J. N. Postgate, *Early Mesopotamia: Society and Economy at the Dawn of History* (London & New York: Routledge, 1992).

---

she married, left her father's household, and joined her husband's. Sons received shares in the remaining movable and immovable property, according to a formula by which the eldest son received two shares worth of the immovable property.

Adoption Sale. In ancient Nuzi, a city with a substantial Hurrian population on the northeast periphery of Mesopotamia (circa 1450 – circa 1350 B.C.E.), many tablets record a kind of "adoption-sale" transaction enabling individuals to accumulate land that presumably was not available for purchase. According to these *tuppi maruti*, or "tablets of sonship," a couple adopted a man as their son and heir; he promised to provide his adoptive parents with food, cloth-

Relief-carved archaic entitlement monument (so-called *kudurru*, gypsum, height 8 7/8 inches), circa 2900 – circa 2600 B.C.E., concerning a land transaction involving three houses, fields, and livestock. The Sumerian inscription names Ushumgal the *pab-shesh* priest and his daughter. Because of the difficulty in understanding such ancient Sumerian texts, the precise nature of the transaction is unclear (The Metropolitan Museum of Art, New York, Purchase, Funds from various donors, 1958).

ing, and other rations for the duration of their lives, and in return he inherited their property. These texts are easily distinguished from conventional adoptions, in which parents took the responsibility for raising and providing for a child and promised to name him as one of their heirs (or their sole heir). They also differ from cases in which parents who had no male issue adopted a son-in-law so that he would inherit their land and keep it in the family.

Property and the State. The state—that is, the palace—took measures to perpetuate the agricultural system and preserve landed property within traditional family holdings. King Hammurabi of Babylon (circa 1792 – circa 1750 B.C.E.) wrote to one of his officials ordering the restoration of family property that had been wrongfully seized. When Hammurabi asked, "When is a permanent property ever taken away?" he was referring to the established customary legal principle that land was the permanent property of a family. Though parallels are sometimes drawn between the Mesopotamian system of ownership and the feudal system of medieval Europe, all the land in Mesopotamia was not considered de facto property of the king. Rather, evidence from "entitlement monuments" of Babylonia from the

fourteenth through the seventh centuries B.C.E. indicates that not even the king could claim land without just cause. When, on occasion, kings did take land, they offered justifications such as creation of irrigation works, development of previously uncultivated land, or seizing land from an individual who had committed a crime.

Tenancy and Entitlements. Several statutes from the Laws of Hammurabi pertain to cultivation of land by people who had been granted the right to use land they did not own. "Crown lands" belonging to the palace were leased for a prescribed term to soldiers or others engaged in service to the king. Other landholders, notably temples, also leased land to tenant farmers. Tenants could be penalized or even lose the use of this land if they failed to meet certain production quotas or if they attempted to transfer it to other individuals. Tenants were protected by the crown, and penalties for taking away the land of a soldier or another tenant were severe. During the Kassite period in Babylonia (circa 1595 – circa 1155 B.C.E.), "entitlement monuments" (commonly, though erroneously, called "boundary stones," or *kudurru*) were introduced to commemorate permanent transfers of land to individuals. Unlike leases giving crown land to an individual for a limited time or his lifetime, the grants recorded on these monuments made the land the permanent property of the individual and his family in perpetuity. Rather than reverting to the state or another owner, it could henceforth be passed down to succeeding generations, theoretically without end.

Sources:

Ignace J. Gelb, Piotr Steinkeller, and Robert Whiting, *Earliest Land Tenure Systems in the Near East: The Ancient* kudurrus, Oriental Institute Publications, 104 (Chicago: Oriental Institute, 1981).

J. N. Postgate, *Early Mesopotamia: Society and Economy at the Dawn of History* (London & New York: Routledge, 1992).

Martha T. Roth, *Law Collections from Mesopotamia and Asia Minor*, second edition, Society of Biblical Literature, Writings from the Ancient World Series, volume 6 (Atlanta: Scholars Press, 1995).

Kathryn E. Slanski, *The Babylonian Entitlement* narûs (kudurrus): *A Study in Form and Function*, ASOR Books, volume 9 (Boston: American Schools of Oriental Research, 2003).

Piotr Steinkeller, *Sale Documents of the Ur III Period*, Freiburger Altorientalische Studien, volume 17 (Wiesbaden: Franz Steiner, 1989).

SOCIAL STATUS

Social Status and Property. In ancient Mesopotamia, social status seems to have been linked closely to ownership of property. Written records provide abundant evidence regarding transactions involving people of means, but these sources are biased toward privileged members of society who resided in urban centers, executed written contracts, and maintained private archives. Nonelite members of society undoubtedly also conducted economic transactions, but they were probably accomplished by verbal argreement and not written down.

Social Hierarchy. The clearest statement concerning Mesopotamian social hierarchy is found in the Laws of Hammurabi (circa 1750 B.C.E.), which provided for three separate—and unequal—tiers: the *awilum* (freeman), generally thought to be an individual owning his means of support; the *mushkenum* (dependent, or serf), who presumably did not own his means of earning a living and worked land owned by another; and the *wardum* (slave), who was the property of his owner. Outside this law collection, little is said about the relative status and privileges of the freeman and the dependent; the terms *awilum* and *mushkenum* do not occur regularly in administrative records, where one would expect to find information relating to individuals' niches in society and the economy. In fact, no one ever identified himself as *awilum* or *mushkenum*. As subjects of transactions, *wardu* (slaves) were bought, sold, and inherited, and slaves are identified as such in sale documents and other contracts.

Freemen. The basic social unit was the household, which usually consisted of parents and their children. The father was the head of the household. (He was called *en* in Sumerian and *belu* in Akkadian—words best translated as "lord" or "master," or in some contexts "owner.") The father was responsible for the family's land, their most important economic resource. Family land was passed on through the

generations from father to son, so Mesopotamian society can be described as *patrilineal.* The father was also responsible for his wife and children, and in texts he is referred to as his wife's "lord" or "master." He made decisions on the family's behalf, such as arranging the marriages of his children and disposing of the property his wife brought into the marriage as her dowry. He had authority to sell his wife and children into slavery, to divorce his wife, to adopt children and name them his heirs, and to disinherit his children, both biological and adopted.

Women. Most of the evidence bearing on the economic and social history of women pertains to their roles in marriage. Socio-economically, the point of marriage was to provide male heirs for family property. In Mesopotamia a woman married into her husband's family, and entered his household. Thus, in addition to being patrilineal, Mesopotamian society was also *patrilocal*. A woman's marriage was arranged by authority of her father, but both father and mother often appear as the contracting agents in marriage agreements. Parents could execute a marriage contract for their daughter even while she was an infant or a young girl. In most such cases, she continued to live in her father's home until she reached maturity, although some contracts stipulated that she move into the house of her contractual father-in-law, who would support her until the marriage to his son eventually took place. A father also provided his daughter with a dowry, movable property equivalent to her share in the inheritance from his estate. She took her dowry into her new household when she married, and her marriage contract stipulated how much—if any—control she might have over her dowry.

Women's Property. By and large, women did not own immovable property—that is, land. There were occasions when a head of household who had no sons designated his daughter as his heir, and under exceptional circumstances a father might give land to his daughter. According to a tenth century B.C.E. Babylonian entitlement monument, a father gave his daughter land on the occasion of her marriage. She married the son of a man to whom her father owed a debt, and it can be concluded that the marriage gift—in effect, the permanent transfer of land from one family to another—was the means by which the bride's father repaid his debt to the groom's father. In order to ratify the transfer, all the male members of the bride's family swore an oath acknowledging the gift—a legal means to ensure that no male family member could lay claim to this parcel of land that traditionally had been the property of the men in the bride's family.

Divorce and Second Marriages. Divorce was rare. It was usually executed by the husband and only if a wife had behaved in a way that was shameful to her husband or, most often, if she had not provided him with heirs. If a husband did divorce his wife for childlessness, he was enjoined not to send her away empty-handed but to return

AN ENTITLEMENT MONUMENT

The following text is inscribed on an entitlement monument from southern Mesopotamia and documents social and economic entanglements between two families over the course of several generations during the tenth century B.C.E. The monument was excavated by British archaeologists in the city of Sippar in the temple of Shamash, god of the sun and justice, around 1900. Today it is on display in the British Museum.

In the second year of king Ninurta-kudurri-usur (circa 986 B.C.E.), Arad-Sebitti, son of Atrattash, struck and killed with an arrow a [female sl]ave of Burusha, the jeweler, whom Bel-ilani-nasirshu had taken as wife.

Burusha, the jeweler, and Arad-Sebitti, son of Atrattash, pleaded the case before king Ninurta-kudurri-usur, and Ninurta-kudurri-usur said as follows to Arad-Sebitti: "Go and give seven persons to Burusha."

Arad-Sebitti did not have the persons to give, and Burusha affirmed the seven persons to his debt, and he became troubled about the per[sons?]

At the sealing of that sealed document (were present):

Sin-mushallim, son of Bu[   ]sha, mayor of the city of Isin. Ammennam, head officer of the king. Kashu-mukin-apli, son of Bazi, officer of the court. Kashu-shuma-iddina, son of Nazi-Marduk, vizier. Eulmash-nasir, son of Tunamissa, governor of the land. Nabu-tabni-bullit, son of Arad-Ea, provincial governor. Shamash-damiq, son of Asu-Marduk, *zazakku*-mayor of the settlement Kar-Marduk.
[Mon]th of Simanu, year two of king Ninurta-kudurri-usur.

(A field of) 3 (*kurru*) seed grain at the rate of 1 *iku* per 3 *sutu* (measured with) the large *ammatu*, district of the settlement Sha-Mamitu, bank of the canal Nish-qati-luda[ri], (its borders): upper long side, west, bord[ering] part of the same field; lower long side, east, adjacent to Bit-

Kidin-x, upper short side, south, adjacent to part of the same field; lower short side, north, adjacent to part of the same field.

(A field) that, in the fifth year of king Nabu-mukin-apli (circa 973 B.C.E.), Arad-Sebitti, son of Atrattash, in the city of his brothers, Kashshayya, the eldest son, Al-Larak-zer-ibni, Kashu-nadin-ahhe, Ninurta-apla-iddina, Ekallayya, Uzibiyya, Zer-ibni, the sons of Atrattash—sealed and gave, together with bridal gift and dowry, to Ilu-resh-damiq-sharbe, his daughter, wife of Shamash-nadin-shumi, [son] of Burusha, the jeweler.

Later on, in the twenty-fifth year of king Nabu-mukin-apli (circa 953 B.C.E.), Mar-biti-shuma-ibni, son of Arad-Sebitti, son of Atrattash, (said) thus: "The field which Arad-Sebitti, my father, sealed and gave to his daughter—I myself am (now) dying, and in the city of my brothers—Samardi, Babuti, Ahhu-shullim, Illatayyu, Ishnuku—I wish to seal and give to my sister."

Again, Mar-biti-shuma-ibni, in the presence of his brothers, sealed, swore an oath, and gave for all time the field to Ilu-resh-damiq-sharbe, wife of Shamash-nadin-shumi, daughter-in-law of Burusha, son of Apluti, the jeweler.

Whensoever, in future days, (if anyone) from among the brothers, sons, family, kin and relations of the House of Atrattash or any other person, who would be situated (in authority) over the House of Atrattash, would say: "Arad-Sebitti did not seal and give a three *kurru* seed-grain (field) from (the property of the) House of At[rattash] to Ilu-resh-damiq-sharbe, his d[aughter], daughter-in-law of Burusha, the jeweler" or: "Ma[r-biti-shuma-ibni] did not seal and give (it) to his sister, the wife of [Shamash-nadin-shumi], son of Burusha, the jeweler"—

May Anu, Enlil, and Ea, great gods of heaven and earth, [curse him] with a malevolent curse of no release! (translation by the author)

Source: Leonard W. King, *Babylonian Boundary-Stones and Memorial Tablets in the British Museum* (London: Trustees of the British Museum, 1912).

to her the value of the dowry she had brought from her father's house. Lack of heirs was also the usual circumstance under which a man took a second wife, a practice which appears in legal contracts only rarely. If his first wife were gravely ill and he took a second wife, a head of household was obligated to continue to support his ailing wife.

The Wife's Status. A wife had a particular legal status with certain socio-economic privileges, as indicated by a letter written by a Babylonian woman to the owner of her sister and her children, who had been sold into slavery during the reign of Kadashman-Turgu (circa 1281 – circa 1264 B.C.E.).

Because the king had recently declared the liberation of all native-born women, she demanded that her sister's owner free her and grant her the status of a wife. While a woman with the status of a wife was under her husband's authority, she was not his property and had certain privileges and rights. According to the Laws of Hammurabi (circa 1750 B.C.E.), a woman who could prove maltreatment by her husband would not be penalized and could take back her dowry and return to her father's house. Once her marriage ended through widowhood or divorce, a woman was free to "marry after her heart." Outside their roles as wives, women are found in surviving documents writing to the king, initiating and participating in lawsuits as defendants and witnesses, and on occasion taking part in business transactions.

Cloistered Women. During the Old Babylonian period (circa 1894 – circa 1595 B.C.E.) some daughters, seemingly of wealthy families, were dedicated as priestesses and entered a sort of cloister. In the city of Sippar the cloister, called the *gagum*, was attached to the temple of the sun god Shamash. These women, called *naditu*—literally, "women set apart"—took with them property equivalent to what would have been their dowries. Free to participate in commercial activity, some of the *naditu* amassed small and large fortunes, which, in most cases, reverted to their families when the women died.

Children. In the social hierarchy of the family, children were under the authority of their parents, and their father was responsible for making decisions that would affect their economic well being and their place in society. The strict family hierarchy is apparent in adoption contracts, which regularly included the following penalty provision: "If <name of child> says to his father: 'You are not my father,' or says to his mother: 'You are not my mother,' his father and mother shall beat him and/or sell him for silver, and/or disinherit him, and/or pour hot asphalt onto his head." The socio-economic status of children was determined by their sex. The eldest male child was the primary heir to the family property and responsible for performing the mortuary rituals that perpetuated the memory of deceased parents and ancestors and ensured them a good afterlife. These two functions were inextricably linked in a never-ending mutually beneficial cycle: land received from the family ancestors supported the next generation, who in return perpetuated the memory of the deceased ancestors. Daughters were an expense. They had to be supported while at home and provided with a dowry when they married. In families that did not derive their income from land—such as craftsmen or merchants—sons often seem to have followed their father into the family business. In times of economic distress, parents could and did sell their children—with males generally bringing higher prices than females. While this practice may appear heartless to modern people, selling a child to a family of means or to the temple was a way for impoverished parents to ensure that child's survival—and their own.

Chattel Slaves. Chattel slaves, individuals who were usually the lifelong property of other individuals and resided in the households of their owners, were different from debt slaves, who continued to live with their families and went into service for a set period of time to work off a debt. Male and female chattel slaves are documented in the records of family and institutional households. They could be bought, sold, bestowed as gifts (including marriage dowries), and disbursed as components of the inheritance from an estate. In general, children born to slaves were the property of the slaves' owners; such slaves were designated with a special term in Akkadian: *wilid bitim*, or "house-born." Slaves could marry free persons, and the Laws of Hammurabi include several provisions dealing with the social status and economic rights accorded children from such a union:

> If a slave of the palace or a slave of a commoner marries a woman of the *awilum*-class and she then bears children, the owner of the slave will have no claims of slavery against the children of the woman of the *awilum*-class.
> And if either a slave of the palace or a slave of a commoner marries a woman of the *awilum*-class, and when he marries her she enters (his) house . . . together with the dowry brought from her father's house, and subsequent to the time that they move in together they establish a household and accumulate possessions, after which the slave . . . should go to his fate (that is, die)—the woman of the *awilum*-class shall take her dowry; furthermore everything that her husband and she accumulated subsequent to the time that they moved in together shall be divided into two parts, and the slave's owner shall take half and the woman of the *awilum*-class shall take half for her children. (LH §§175–176; Roth)

Chattel slaves were also acquired from foreign lands, either as prisoners of war or abductees, and written records indicate that some merchants specialized in the slave trade. According to written evidence, slaves were rarely bound or chained, but instead wore a distinctive haircut, the *abbuttum*, that marked their slave status. Anyone who aided a fugitive slave—by removing the *abbuttum* or by any other means—was regarded as having stolen another man's property and dealt with severely. Within a family household, a wife who could not bear children could give a female slave to her husband as a concubine; the children of such a union would be regarded as her own. Similarly, a head of household could have children with a female slave belonging to him. In that case, he was permitted, but not required, to recognize such issue as his children, to grant them status as free persons, and to give them a share in his estate.

Temple Slaves. Temples owned slaves, receiving them as gifts or as foundlings left in the street. Ration lists indicate that male slaves performed heavy-duty agricultural labor on the extensive temple lands, such as working the fields, transporting heavy goods, or constructing and maintaining canals. Female temple slaves performed light agricultural work, but their most important task was helping with temple textile production.

Social Mobility and Manumission. Most of what is known about social mobility applies to slaves. *Wardum*, the Akkadian term for slave, is derived from the verb *waradum*, which means "to descend, go down"—a linguistic detail that gives a clue about the ancient Mesopotamian conception of slavery; that is, a slave was a person who had lost status. While kings could decree the return of all debt slaves to their former status, such decrees stipulated clearly that they did not apply to chattel slaves. Evidence of freeing chattel slaves dates from as early as the Ur III period, circa 2112 – circa

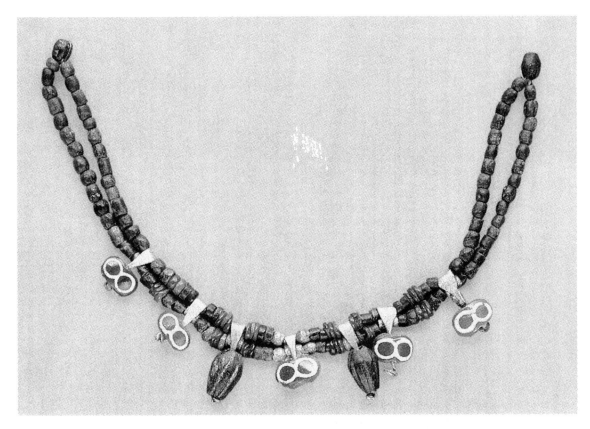

String (length 5½ inches) of imported lapis-lazuli, carnelian, and gold beads. The five pendant bleached-carnelian beads (often called "etched") are made in an Indus Valley tradition; from the Royal Graves at Ur, circa 2600 – circa 2500 B.C.E. (University of Pennsylvania Museum of Archaeology and Anthropology).

2004 B.C.E. All slaves could save money in order to buy their freedom, and a nonslave married to a slave could purchase his or her spouse's freedom. Children born to a freed slave were also free. An owner could grant his slave woman's freedom in order to marry her and give her the legal status of a wife, and the owner of a female slave who bore him children could—by publicly recognizing (literally, "naming") those children as his own—raise them from slave status and give them the right to claim a share of their father's property. Without such legal measures, any offspring a slave woman bore her owner were legally the owner's slaves rather than his children with rights to inherit. According to the Laws of Hammurabi, if a freeman had children with his wife as well as with a female slave and if during his lifetime he did not acknowledge the children of the slave as his offspring and heirs, at his death those children and their mother should be set free. Although these children did not receive a share in their biological father's estate, the children of the man's wife were prohibited from claiming them as slaves.

Sons of (the City). At certain times in both the Babylonian and Assyrian kingdoms, citizens of specific ancient cities were accorded special privileges, such as exemptions from taxation and labor obligations (corvée) otherwise due the palace. Eligibility seems to stem not only from one's place of residence, but from membership in one of the ancient families long established as scions of that city. After Shalmaneser V, king of Assyria (727–722 B.C.E.), suspended exemptions from paying straw and grain taxes for the ancient religious capital of Ashur, his successor, Sargon II, restored the privileges, sharply criticizing his predecessor. *Advice to a Prince*, a didactic Babylonian composition purporting to teach a monarch on how to enjoy a righteous and successful reign, advised:

> If he (the king) imposed a fine or imprisonment upon a "son" of Nippur, Sippar, or Babylon, the city where that fine was imposed will be razed to its foundations and a foreign foe will enter the place of imprisonment.
> If he called up the whole of Sippar, Nippur, and Babylon to impose forced labor on the peoples aforesaid, requiring of them service at the recruiter's cry, Marduk, sage of the gods, deliberative prince, will turn his land over to his foe so that the troops of the land will do forced labor for his foe. Anu, Enlil, and Ea, the great gods who dwell in heaven and earth, have confirmed in their assembly the exemption of these (people from such obligations). . . .
> If an officer or temple warden or royal administrator who holds wardenship of a temple in Sippar, Nippur, or Babylon, imposes forced labor upon them (the citizens aforesaid) for the temples of the great gods, the great gods will quit their sanctuaries in a fury, they will not enter their shrines. (Foster)

The reasons for granting these privileges are unknown. It may have been connected with the ancient religious importance of the cities in question or with the king's desire to cultivate support that the old established families of those cities could offer.

Sources:

John A. Brinkman, Review of *Symbolae iuridicae Martino David dedicatae, Journal of Near Eastern Studies,* 32 (1973): 159–160.

Benjamin R. Foster, *From Distant Days: Myths, Tales, and Poetry of Ancient Mesopotamia* (Bethesda, Md.: CDL Press, 1995).

Rivkah Harris, "The *naditu*-woman," in *Studies Presented to A. Leo Oppenheim, June 7, 1964* (Chicago: Oriental Institute, 1964), pp. 106–135.

Harris, "The Organization and Administration of the Cloister in Ancient Babylonia," *Journal of the Economic and Social History of the Orient,* 6 (1963): 121–157.

Leonard W. King, *Babylonian Boundary-Stones and Memorial Tablets in the British Museum* (London: Trustees of the British Museum, 1912).

Martha T. Roth, *Law Collections from Mesopotamia and Asia Minor,* second edition, Society of Biblical Literature, Writings from the Ancient World Series, volume 6 (Atlanta: Scholars Press, 1995).

Kathryn E. Slanski, *The Babylonian Entitlement* narûs (kudurrus): *A Study in Form and Function,* ASOR Books, volume 9 (Boston: American Schools of Oriental Research, 2003).

Slanski, "Middle Babylonian Period," in *A History of Ancient Near Eastern Law,* 2 volumes, edited by Raymond Westbrook, Handbuch der Orientalistik, volume 72 (Leiden: Brill, 2003), pp. 485–520.

Elizabeth Stone, "The Social Role of the *naditu*-woman in Old Babylonian Nippur," *Journal of the Economic and Social History of the Orient,* 25 (1982): 50–70.

Raymond Westbrook, "Old Babylonian Period," in *A History of Ancient Near Eastern Law,* pp. 361–430.

THE WORKFORCE

Sources of Information. Evidence about the Mesopotamian workforce comes from various bureaucratic documents, chiefly lists of workers and their compensation (rations or wages), as well as correspondence among administrators concerning the need for workers, problems with workers, or the release of workers from their duties. As with other aspects of the social and economic history of Mesopotamia, the conclusions of modern scholars are limited by the available source materials, which provide uneven documentation for different time periods and geographic locations. Consequently, the researcher must think in terms of individual case studies for particular times and places rather than draw general conclusions that apply to the entire span of Mesopotamian civilization. Two distinct groups of written documents have been particularly informative for reconstructing aspects of the early ancient Mesopotamian workforce: some 1,800 tablets dating to the Pre-Sargonic period (circa 2350 B.C.E.) from a temple in Girsu, the capital of the city-state of Lagash, and the tens of thousands of tablets generated by the bureaucracy of the Ur III state (circa 2112 – circa 2004), which seems to have functioned as an all-encompassing statewide household that collected and redistributed the production of its members. Records from the Old Babylonian period (circa 1894 – circa 1595 B.C.E.) document a system whereby citizens owed a month's labor to the crown every year.

Makeup of the Workforce. Information about the makeup of the workforce can be gleaned from the different categories in which individual laborers were grouped for administrative record keeping. Workers are distinguished in the written sources according to sex, age (adults, children, old men), social status (owners of their own means of production, dependents, slaves, prisoners of war, people of foreign origins), and physical ability (for example, blinded workers or those who work "full-output," "half-output," or even "one-quarter output"). Deceased workers are also listed and designated as such. The sources also include native distinctions that scholars still do not fully understand. Some of these categories overlap; for example, an individual worker classified as an old man in one text may well be grouped under "those who perform according to half-production" in another. Some sources suggest that at certain times adult male prisoners of war may have been blinded before they were put to work in the fields.

Compensation. Written sources indicate that workers were compensated for their labor with consumable goods for their basic sustenance—primarily grain, but also wool, oil, and occasionally fruits, vegetables, meat, and fish. For the most part, people received measured allotments of barley. Because the majority of the population was employed in some part of the agricultural sector and because barley was the chief crop, one can say that people were paid for their work "in kind." Rates of compensation varied according to the position held (degree of skill/experience), sex, and social status. The regular ration of barley for an adult man was reckoned at sixty liters per month.

The Temple Household in the Pre-Sargonic Period. The archives of the temple of the goddess Ba'u, the second-largest temple in Girsu, have yielded some 1,800 tablets spanning some thirty years, including the reign of Uru'inimgina (circa 2380 B.C.E.), a ruler well known for his social and economic reforms. While still not completely understood, these tablets provide a picture of the economic activities of a major institutional household. Some of these tablets are rations lists with different categories of people. The most important distinction is between men who were given the use of farmland to sustain their own households and others (men, women, disabled persons, and captives) who did not receive land. The usufruct (legal right to use) of temple land is one kind of prebend, and traditionally this right was inheritable. During the first seven to eight months of the year these men worked their land allotments and sustained themselves from the produce. The "men who receive (land) allotments" were given monthly barley rations only during the last four to five months of the year—the months when the agricultural cycle did not require their labor. Presumably, they owed their labor to the temple in exchange for the usufruct of the land they were allotted. When those fields did not require their labor, they worked for the temple and were compensated during those months with barley rations. Workers who did not receive land allotments worked for the temple and were given monthly rations year-round. Of particular interest are the workers in the temple weaving enterprise. The Ba'u temple employed a large number of women, who in temple lists are organized into work "gangs" of twenty, along with their children. Modern scholars do not know where the women came from, but in year seven of Uru'inimgina's reign, more than half of the women are identified as "(newly) purchased slaves." Women supervising work gangs and holding positions that required higher skills received more rations, as did women with more children than others.

Ur III Workers. Because of its micro-managed bureaucratic economic apparatus, the Ur III state left even more detailed evidence about its workforce than Pre-Sargonic Lagash. As for the Pre-Sargonic period, much information comes from written sources at Lagash, principally ration and wage lists, which identify workers according to age, sex, and job responsibility. State workers included men, women, and children. In general, individuals with greater responsibilities—or with the task of generating higher-quality products—received correspondingly greater compensation. By and large, the productive activities and system of compensation known from Pre-Sargonic Lagash seems to have continued into the Ur III period. What distinguishes the Ur III state from its predecessor is the ceaseless drive of the Ur III bureaucracy to document and standardize all aspects of economic activity. During the Ur III period, weaving continued to be a major temple enterprise, and one text records a payment of oil rations to 6,406 women weavers in the province of Lagash. In its agricultural enterprises, the Ur III state employed two categories of workers, "farmers" and "workers." Persons designated in the lists as "farmers"—who nonetheless seem to have lived in the cities—were considered permanent full-time agricultural workers. "Farmers" were compensated to sustain their households in one of three ways: by direct payments or "rations" of consumable goods, by allotments of land, or by opportunities to rent land from the institution on a sharecropping basis. As in Pre-Sargonic Lagash, during the months when they did not need to work the land, "farmers" could be put to work on other jobs for the state, such as canal and road maintenance. Some seventy-five texts from

INSPECTION OF THE UMMA FORESTERS

The following passages from a large clay tablet are excerpts from an evaluation of the workforce dedicated to collecting and processing wood and grass products in the province of Umma. Ration lists for the Umma foresters are attested only for the winter-spring season, during which the central administration of Umma provided them with barley and wool. During the rest of the year, they were likely working land that they held in prebend from the state in return for their foresting duties. The inspection was conducted under the authority of A'a-kala, governor of Umma, to determine how much barley and wool was needed to support the foresters during the next working season. There were thirty forests, divided into three groups of ten, each group under the supervision of a different foreman. The text lists sixty men and their ranks. (For example, A-class corresponds to foreman; B-class to head worker.) The text is dated to the twelfth month (she-kin-tar in Sumerian and addaru in Akkadian, the equivalent of February-March in the Julian calendar) of the eighth year of the reign of king Amar-Suena (circa 2046 – circa 2038 B.C.E.)—that is, February-March 2039 B.C.E.

Deceased: Urtarluh (replaced by) E'urbidug, A-class worker, the foreman,
Girni-ishag, C-class worker, his sons,

assigned to forest no. 1;
Dugani, M-class worker,
assigned to forest no. 2;
Ka-Shara, B-class worker,
Lugal-inim-gina, E-class worker, his son,
assigned to forest no. 3;
old: Ur-abba, (replaced by) Lu-Shara, B-class worker, his son,
assigned to forest no. 4;
deceased: Lugal-engur-da (replaced by) Lu-gina, B-class worker,
Ahu-waqar, D-class worker,
deceased: Lu-Shara (replaced by) Atanah, E-class worker, his sons
assigned to forest no. 5.

Their barley: 75 seahs to be alloted per month;
their wool: 4 mina to be alloted per year.

Inspection of the conscripted soldiers/workers of the forester (i.e., the overseer of the forest sector);
(under the authority of) A'a-kala, governor of Umma;
via Sagta-kugzu, the messenger,
Lu-Inanna, the messenger,
and Lu-Nanna, son of Ka-Shara.
12th month; year eight of Amar-Suena, king.

Source: Piotr Steinkeller, "The Foresters of Umma: Toward a Definition of Ur Labor," in *Labor in the Ancient Near East*, edited by Marvin A. Powell, American Oriental Series, volume 68 (New Haven, Conn.: American Oriental Society, 1987), text 41, pp. 107–110.

the province of Umma document the activities of the so-called Foresters of Umma, around sixty men employed in the gathering and processing of wood and grasses. Close study of the Umma foresters supports other, scattered evidence that sons succeeded their fathers in receiving the same land allotments for cultivation and the same task assignments for the off months of the agricultural year.

Obligatory State Service and the "Corvée." In texts from the Old Babylonian period, the Akkadian word *ilku* is used to designate different features of obligatory service. The word is applied to work performed on land held by a higher authority, work performed for a higher authority in exchange for the usufruct of land, delivery of part of the yield of such land as a tax payment to a higher authority (and—by extension—payment of money or manufactured objects in lieu of agricultural produce), and finally the land itself on which the *ilku*-service is performed. The expression *kasap ilki* (literally, "*ilku*-silver") denotes money that the holder of *ilku*-land could pay in lieu of performing his required service. The work obligation due the state varied. Individuals who apparently possessed the means to support themselves were obligated to work for only a short time and ostensibly were free to work for themselves for the rest of the year. Modern historians use a French word, *corvée* ("forced labor"), to designate such a system. Under the Mesopotamia corvée system, people designated as "workers" were summoned to perform physical labor for a monthlong period that was called their "turn." During their turn, workers were compensated in amounts of grain, oil, clothing, and other consumable goods, which the lists call "rations." These workers could also be hired to work at times other than their turn, in which case the compensation they received was designated not as "rations" but as "wages." The distinction may reflect the underlying ideology of the state as a household; that is, people working for the state (household) during their turn were considered members of the household and provided for accordingly, whereas people working for the state outside their turn were viewed as hired hands and paid according to services rendered.

Specialized Requirements. The origin of work obligations in return for usufruct of institutionally held land, as seen in the Pre-Sargonic and Ur III periods, and of the state corvée system of the later periods, may have been a response to the specialized requirements of the Mesopotamian agricultural regime. While many workers were needed only in certain times, such as during the harvest, the mouths of those workers needed to be filled year-round. The necessity of maintaining a pool of labor for the busy months may have motivated the development of state-run undertakings to make good use of that labor supply at other times. One large state-run operation, grain milling, drew workers from a variety of social backgrounds—including various professionals, dependents, squatters, and prisoners of war. Large-scale textile production, undertaken by temples in all periods and the palace (that is, the state) in some periods, demanded a permanent, year-round workforce of trained individuals.

Sources:

Igor M. Diakonoff, "Slave-Labor vs. Non-Slave Labor: The Problem of Definition," in *Labor in the Ancient Near East*, edited by Marvin A. Powell, American Oriental Series, volume 68 (New Haven, Conn.: American Oriental Society, 1987), pp. 1–3.

Kazuya Maekawa, "Collective Service in Girsu-Lagash: The Pre-Sargonic and Ur III Periods," in *Labor in the Ancient Near East*, pp. 49–71.

Maekawa, "Female Weavers and their Children in Lagash: Pre-Sargonic and Ur III," *Acta Sumerologica*, 2 (1982): 81–125.

J. N. Postgate, *Early Mesopotamia: Society and Economy at the Dawn of History* (London & New York: Routledge, 1992).

Piotr Steinkeller, "The Foresters of Umma: Toward a Definition of Ur Labor," in *Labor in the Ancient Near East*, pp. 73–115.

Hartmut Waetzoldt, "Compensation of Craft Workers and Officials in the Ur III Periods," in *Labour in the Ancient Near East*, pp. 117–141.

SIGNIFICANT PEOPLE

AMMI-SADUQA

CIRCA 1646 - CIRCA 1626 B.C.E.
KING OF BABYLONIA

Descendant of Hammurabi. Ammi-saduqa was the great-great-grandson of Hammurabi (circa 1792 – circa 1750 B.C.E.) and the penultimate ruler of the First Dynasty of Babylon. When Ammi-saduqa came to the throne, he was faced with a shrinking kingdom, whose deterioration had begun soon after the reign of Hammurabi's son and successor, Samsu-iluna (circa 1749 – circa 1712 B.C.E.).

Ammi-saduqa's *Misharum*-Edict. Few inscriptions are known from Ammi-saduqa's kingship, and he is chiefly remembered for issuing a *misharum*-edict. (The Akkadian word *misharum* means "justice" or "equity.") While references have been found to other Babylonian kings issuing such edicts, Ammi-saduqa's is the only *misharum* edict for which the (almost) complete text survives. The terms of his proclamation provided for the cancellation of debts and the release of persons sold into debt slavery. Ammi-saduqa's edict constitutes concrete evidence that Mesopotamian justice was conceived as an economic and social equilibrium in which each individual had his place.

Sources:

Fritz R. Kraus, *Königliche Verfügungen in altbabylonischer Zeit,* Studia et Documenta ad iura orientis antiqui pertinentia, volume 11 (Leiden: Brill, 1984).

Raymond Westbrook, "Old Babylonian Period," in *A History of Ancient Near Eastern Law,* 2 volumes, edited by Westbrook, Handbuch der Orientalistik, volume 72 (Leiden: Brill, 2003), pp. 361–430.

MARDUK-NASIR-APLI

CIRCA 550-543 - CIRCA 487 B.C.E.
BABYLONIAN FINANCIER

Babylonian Entrepreneurs. The Egibi were a financial family active in Babylon from the late sixth century through the fifth century B.C.E. Five generations are mentioned in surviving tablets from the family's financial archives, which document their rise from commodities traders in the first two generations to leading landholders and speculators in many different economic ventures.

The Fourth Generation. Born sometime between 550 and 543 B.C.E., Marduk-nasir-apli, nicknamed Shirku, was eldest son of the fourth generation. After his father died in 522 B.C.E., he inherited leadership of the family business and ran it until 487 B.C.E.—or roughly during the reign of Persian king Darius I (521–486 B.C.E.). Under his leadership, family business activities became increasingly involved with the institutions of Babylon, the temples and the palace, and their officials. The Egibi family archives, especially the texts from the time of Marduk-nasir-apli, include examples of the wide variety of financial entrepreneurship that was indispensable to the Mesopotamian economy.

Sources:

Kathleen Abrams, *Business and Politics under the Persian Empire: The Financial Dealings of Marduk-nasir-apli of the House of Egibi* (Bethesda, Md.: CDL Press, 2004).

Cornelia Wunsch, "The Egibi Family's Real Estate in Babylon (6th Century BC)," in *Urbanization and Land Ownership in the Ancient Near East,* edited by Michael Hudson and Baruch Levine (Cambridge, Mass.: Peabody Museum of Archaeology and Ethnology, 1999), pp. 391–419.

PU-ABI

CIRCA 2600-2500 B.C.E.
ELITE WOMAN OF UR

Unknown Role. One of the elite individuals buried in the Royal Tombs of Ur (circa 2600–2500 B.C.E.) was a slight woman, just under five feet tall, who was about forty years old at the time of her death. Her name, Pu-abi, is inscribed on a lapis-lazuli cylinder seal found near her body. No other inscriptions were found in the tombs. It has been suggested recently that she may have been the second wife of king Meskalamdug of Ur, who may have been buried in the adjacent tomb.

Elaborate Burial. Pu-abi's intact burial was discovered in 1928 by Sir Leonard Woolley. She was buried in a multi-chambered tomb that included gold and silver plates and cups, elaborate jewelry, full-size chariots with donkeys, and the bodies of many human attendants, including women outfitted as musicians and men equipped as soldiers and grooms. Semi-precious stones of lapiz lazuli and carnelian were worked masterfully into the ornate gold necklaces and headbands worn by Pu-abi and her female attendants. These materials, among others, are evidence of the existence of long-distance trade networks in the mid-third millennium B.C.E. and of the leading role of the city of Ur in that trade. The richness of her burial indicates that Pu-abi was an individual of high status at a time in Mesopotamia when religious, economic, and political elites were beginning to set themselves apart from the rest of the population.

Sources:
Julian Reade, "Assyrian King-Lists, The Royal Tombs of Ur, and Indus Origins," *Journal of Near Eastern Studies*, 60 (2001): 1–29.

Richard L. Zettler, "The Burials of a King and Queen," in *Treasures from the Royal Tombs of Ur*, edited by Zettler and Lee Horne (Philadelphia: University of Pennsylvania Museum, 1998), pp. 33–38.

Zettler, "The Royal Cemetery of Ur," in *Treasures from the Royal Tombs of Ur*, pp. 21–25.

DOCUMENTARY SOURCES

"Ancient *kudurru*s" (circa third millennium B.C.E.)—Small stone monuments and tablets commemorating land purchases in southern Mesopotamia; the inscriptions on these monuments are evidence that land was owned by family or kinship groups in the third millennium B.C.E.

Babylonian Entitlement Monuments (*kudurru*s) (circa 1374 – 648 B.C.E.)—Modest stone monuments commemorating the acquisition of permanent entitlements (land, tax, and labor exemptions, as well as temple prebends) and guaranteeing their perpetuity.

Drehem Archive (circa 2100 – circa 2000 B.C.E.)—A large number of extant tablets documenting aspects of the redistributive economy of the Ur III state. Drehem was the site of the collection center for animals in the redistributive system, which was established by king Shulgi (circa 2094 – circa 2047 B.C.E.).

Edict of Ammi-saduqa (circa 1640 B.C.E.)—a royal decree, or *misharum*-edict, in which king Ammi-saduqa of Babylonia ordered the cancellation of debts and the release of debt slaves. It is the most complete surviving *misharum*-edict. References to such edicts of other kings suggest that issuing such decrees may have been a regular tradition among southern Mesopotamian monarchs.

The Egibi Archive (circa 600 – circa 480 B.C.E.)—tablets from the archive of the Egibi family of Babylon, whose business dealings over five generations furnish a detailed picture of entrepreneurial activity in Babylonia during the Neo- and Late Babylonian periods.

Laws of Eshnunna (circa 1770 B.C.E.)—A collection of measures intended to promote equity in Eshnunna, a city-state in the Diyala River valley. Although the text also treats matters of injury and theft, its paramount concern is economic justice. The text opens with the prices of common goods and services and includes interest rates for loans of grain and silver.

Laws of Hammurabi (circa 1750 B.C.E.)—The longest and best known of the Mesopotamian law collections, inscribed on a monumental stone stele (almost 2 meters high) topped with a bas-relief of Hammurabi standing before Shamash, the sun god and god of justice. The text comprises 282 so-called laws framed by a prologue and an epilogue commemorating Hammurabi's righteous kingship. The laws create a picture of a three-tiered system of social hierarchy (freeman, dependent, slave) and include measures related to equitable financial dealings.

Murashu Archive (fifth century B.C.E.)—Tablets from the archive of an Achaemenid-period family financial house based in Nippur. Their chief business was giving credit to military colonists settled by the state to enable them to meet their tax obligations. In return, the family managed the colonists' agricultural activities in the environs of Nippur.

Old Assyrian Merchant Letters (circa 1900 – circa 1800 B.C.E.)—Letters exchanged between merchant families based in the Assyrian city of Ashur and their agents in the trading colony of Kanesh in Anatolia. The letters are evidence of a robust trade network, in which the Assyrians purchased Babylonian textiles and Iranian tin and transported them by donkey caravan to Anatolia, where they were sold for gold and silver that was carried back to Ashur and re-invested in the family business.

Reforms of Uru'inimgina (circa 2380 B.C.E.)—Measures instituted by Uru'inimgina, *ensi* (city ruler) of the city-state of Lagash, to correct systemic abuses committed by governing officials.

Royal Correspondence of Hammurabi of Babylon (circa 1750 B.C.E.)—Letters exchanged between king Hammurabi and his officers, evidence of the king's interest in the protection of rightful property claims and the fair treatment of his subjects as well as other concerns.

Sargonic Royal Inscriptions (circa 2300 B.C.E.)—Royal inscriptions commissioned by king Sargon of Akkad and his successors, to commemorate their conquest and rule over the first Mesopotamian empire.

POLITICS, LAW, AND THE MILITARY

by IRA SPAR

CONTENTS

Sidebars and tables are listed in italics.

IMPORTANT EVENTS OF 3300-331 B.C.E

3200* B.C.E.

- Cities begin to emerge, many in southern Iraq. Artworks depict city rulers in religious and ceremonial activities.

- Administrative records are written on clay with proto-cuneiform signs, indicating the need for a permanent form of financial record keeping.

- Large temples are built on platforms.

3200*-2900* B.C.E.

- External contacts and trade expand between Mesopotamian cities and neighboring centers in Iran, Syria, and Central Asia.

2900*-2350* B.C.E.

- Cuneiform (wedged-shaped) writing develops, representing the speech of the Sumerian inhabitants of the first cities.

- Sumerian city rulers build palaces and control temple estates.

- Conflicts develop between rival city-states. Two city-states, Umma and Lagash, clash repeatedly over control of land and water resources.

- Some cities expand into ministates controlling neighboring population centers.

2334*-2279* B.C.E.

- Sargon claims the throne and establishes the city of Akkad (or Agade) as the center of an Akkadian (Semitic) empire, stretching east into western Iran, west to the "Cedar Forest" and the Mediterranean Sea, and south through Sumer into the Persian Gulf.

2254*-2218* B.C.E.

- The Akkadian empire reaches its zenith under Sargon's grandson Naram-Sin, who claims divinity and has a temple built for himself in the middle of Akkad.

2100*-2000* B.C.E.

- The Akkadian Empire collapses as a result of internal unrest and foreign assaults from diverse foreign forces along its frontiers.

- Local rulers in southern Mesopotamia re-assert their rule. In the city-state of Lagash, commerce, trade, literature, and the arts flourish under the rule of its *ensi* (governor), Gudea.

- In the city of Ur, the rise of its Third Dynasty sparks a Sumerian cultural revitalization, with the development of new building projects and the implementation of a revised literary tradition. Its rulers establish an empire that is far smaller than the Akkadian Empire.

2004* B.C.E.

- The Third Dynasty of Ur falls when Elamites from western Iran sack the city of Ur.

* DENOTES CIRCA DATE

IMPORTANT EVENTS OF 3300-331 B.C.E

2000*-1800* B.C.E.

- In southern Mesopotamia a variety of smaller competing Amorite (western Semite) cities and kingdoms replace the Sumerian Ur III dynasty. Kings consider themselves the successors of the Sumerian dynasties. At first political power is centered in the city of Isin and later in the southern city of Larsa.

- In the north, Assyria emerges as a new political and economic center. Merchants from its capital city of Ashur travel to trading emporiums in Anatolia (modern Turkey), where they sell textiles and tin as well as the thousands of donkeys used to transport merchandise.

1792* B.C.E.

- Hammurabi comes to the throne and establishes the First Dynasty of Babylon as a regional power; the following year his forces defeat Isin.

1781* B.C.E.

- With the death of the Amorite ruler Shamshi-Adad I, who has controlled much of northern Mesopotamia, competing dynasties emerge with centers in the cities of Mari on the Euphrates in Syria and Babylon to the south.

1775*-1761* B.C.E.

- During the reign of Zimri-Lim the palace at Mari is rebuilt and decorated with wall paintings.

1763*-1761* B.C.E.

- Hammurabi defeats Larsa in about 1763 and Mari in 1761, ending the reign of Zimri-Lim.

1749*-1450* B.C.E.

- The southernmost portion of Sumer is dominated by the First Dynasty of the Sealand.

1595* B.C.E.

- Babylon and its kingdom fall to an Anatolian Hittite conqueror, Mursili I.

1595*-1200* B.C.E.

- After the Hittite withdrawal, Babylonia is seized and ruled by a Kassite dynasty, whose leaders may have originally come from the Zagros Mountains to the northeast of Babylon. The Kassites, who speak a language not related to any of the known language groups in the region, establish their political center at Dur-Kurigalzu, "fortress of Kurigalzu," where a ziggurat still stands. The Kassites rule for more than four centuries.

- Political stability encourages preservation of Babylonian and Sumerian literary traditions.

1500*-1350* B.C.E.

* DENOTES CIRCA DATE

- The Hurrian kingdom of Mitanni, located along the upper Habur River (a tributary of the Euphrates), controls territory from the Mediterranean to just east of the Tigris River in northern Mesopotamia. The Hurrians are in constant conflict with their Hittite neighbor to the north.

IMPORTANT EVENTS OF 3300-331 B.C.E

1390*-1327* B.C.E.

- A cuneiform archive at Amarna in Egypt includes correspondence between the Egyptians and the rulers of Mitanni, the Hittites, the Kassites, the Assyrians, and the small principalities of Syria, the Levant, and Cyprus.

1350*-1200* B.C.E.

- When Mitannian power begins to collapse, Assyrian hegemony emerges in northern Mesopotamia.

1243*-1207* B.C.E.

- Under the leadership of Tukulti-Ninurta I, Assyria defeats the Kassite ruler of Babylon. Tukulti-Ninurta seizes the statue of Marduk from its sanctuary and razes the walls of Babylon. He also fights successfully against the Hittites, whose empire collapses circa 1200 B.C.E.

1200*-935* B.C.E.

- Assyrian power waxes and wanes as the Aramaeans from north Syria press into northern Mesopotamia.

1157* B.C.E.

- The Kassite dynasty is replaced by the Second Dynasty of Isin, which rules until circa 1026 B.C.E.

934*-912 B.C.E.

- During his reign, Assyrian king Ashur-dan II campaigns extensively to the north, re-establishing an Assyrian presence in the region.

883-859 B.C.E.

- Ashurnasirpal II builds a new Assyrian capital at Nimrud (ancient Kalhu) and invites tens of thousands of guests to attend a banquet. During his reign he leads many military campaigns into foreign lands; the stone reliefs in his new palace depict his conquests and rituals in praise of his god, Ashur.

858-824 B.C.E.

- Ashurnasirpal's son Shalmaneser III expands the empire to the west.

853 B.C.E.

- Shalmaneser III fights against a coalition of Egyptian, Arabian, Ammonite, Israelite, and Phoenician forces at Qarqar on the Orontes River. Several battles later Shalmaneser claims victory against all his western enemies, which include the kingdom of Israel.

823-745 B.C.E.

- Assyria is in a period of weakness, fighting against various Aramaean and Urartean armies.

* DENOTES CIRCA DATE

IMPORTANT EVENTS OF 3300-331 B.C.E

744-727 B.C.E.
• Under Tiglath-pileser III the Assyrian empire continues to expand to the west and south.

722 B.C.E.
• Shalmaneser V (726–722 B.C.E.) of Assyria destroys the Israelite capital of Samaria and ends the kingdom of Israel.

721-705 B.C.E.
• Under Sargon II the Assyrian armies defeat Phoenician, Philistine, and Judaean forces. Sargon builds a new capital at Khorsabad (ancient Dur-Sharrukin) and decorates the walls of his palace with reliefs illustrating his victorious campaigns.

709 B.C.E.
• Sargon II becomes king of Babylon.

705 B.C.E.
• Sargon II dies in battle on the northern frontier.

704-681 B.C.E.
• Sargon's son Sennacherib fights to maintain the Assyrian empire. Though he besieges Jerusalem in 701 and destroys Babylon in 689 B.C.E., in comparison to those of his predecessors, Sennacherib's reign is one of relative peace. He constructs canals and aqueducts and builds a magnificent palace at Nineveh. He is murdered in a palace conspiracy by his sons.

680-669 B.C.E.
• Esarhaddon consolidates the Assyrian empire by imposing loyalty oaths on his vassals. He rebuilds Babylon and conquers Egypt but cannot retain control over it.

668-627* B.C.E.
• During his reign over Assyria, Esarhaddon's son Ashurbanipal assembles an enormous library of cuneiform ritual, literary, scholastic, and political tablets (which are discovered in the nineteenth century C.E.). His reign is filled with constant warfare and revolt.

664 B.C.E.
• During their reconquest of Egypt, the Assyrians sack Thebes.

651-648 B.C.E.
• Shamash-shum-ukin, who has ruled Babylon since 667 B.C.E., rises up against his brother, Ashurbanipal. The revolt is quashed in 648 B.C.E., when Shamash-shum-ukin sets his palace on fire and perishes in the flames.

626*-609 B.C.E.
* DENOTES CIRCA DATE
• Following the death of Ashurbanipal, his sons contend for the throne. Various cities pledge allegiance to the warring claimants, and confusion permeates Assyria.

IMPORTANT EVENTS OF 3300-331 B.C.E

616 B.C.E.

- Nabopolassar (625–605 B.C.E.), founder of the Neo-Babylonian dynasty, invades Assyria.

615 B.C.E.

- Medes from western Iran, allied with the Babylonians, attack the Assyrian heartland.

612 B.C.E.

- Allied armies of Babylonians, Medes, and possibly Scythians sack the Assyrian capital at Nineveh.

605 B.C.E.

- Nabopolassar's son and successor, Nebuchadnezzar II, defeats the Egyptians in battle at Carchemish on the upper Euphrates in Syria.

604-562 B.C.E.

- Nebuchadnezzar II rebuilds Babylon and constructs great temples, a ziggurat, a fortified palace, and a central paved processional way. The city gate is decorated with glazed bricks depicting bulls and dragons.

597 B.C.E.

- Nebuchadnezzar II conquers Jerusalem, loots its treasures, and exiles its leaders, placing a puppet ruler on its throne.

586 B.C.E.

- Nebuchadnezzar II destroys the city of Jerusalem and exiles much of its population.

555-539 B.C.E.

- The last king of the Neo-Babylonian dynasty, Nabonidus pays special attention to the cult of the moon god Sin, which leads to great internal dissension. He makes conquests in Arabia and lives for ten years in the oasis of Teima along an Arabian caravan route.

539-331 B.C.E.

- Persian rulers forge a new empire that exceeds in scope its Babylonian and Assyrian predecessors.

539 B.C.E.

- When Persian forces menace Babylon, the city surrenders without a battle to the Persian general, Gobryas. Nabonidus is taken prisoner.

538-530 B.C.E.

- Babylon is ruled by Cyrus II (the Great), who has reigned over Persia since 559 B.C.E. Cyrus allows Jewish exiles to return to their homeland, establishes a new royal center at Pasargadae in Iran, and builds palaces and irrigated gardens. He is killed while on a campaign to the east.

* DENOTES CIRCA DATE

IMPORTANT EVENTS OF 3300-331 B.C.E

525 B.C.E.

- Cyrus's son Cambyses II defeats the Saite dynasty, which has ruled Egypt since 664 B.C.E., and annexes Egypt.

522 B.C.E.

- Cambyses dies on his way to Syria to suppress a rebellion led by his brother Bardiya. The rebellion is finally put down by Darius I, who claims that Bardiya had been killed by Cambyses and that the leader of the rebellion was an imposter, Gaumata. Darius presents himself as a member of a bloodline parallel to that of Cyrus, with a common ancestor in one Achaemenes.

522-486 B.C.E.

- The Persian empire reaches its height under Darius I, who adds northwest India to the list of Persian conquests and extends his rule across the Hellespont into Thrace in 513 B.C.E. In Egypt he completes a canal linking the Mediterranean to the Red Sea. In Iran he builds palaces in the ancient city of Susa and establishes a new dynastic capital at Persepolis.

490 B.C.E.

- Darius's army is defeated by the Athenians at the Battle of Marathon.

485-465 B.C.E.

- During his reign, Xerxes, Darius's son and heir, tries but fails to establish Persian control over the Greek mainland.

480 B.C.E.

- The Greeks defeat Xerxes' Persian navy in a sea battle at Salamis.

479 B.C.E.

- Persian troops are defeated by a Greek army in a land battle at Platea.

465 B.C.E.

- Xerxes is murdered.

399 B.C.E.

- The Persians are driven out of Egypt; they contend with revolts for the next half century.

334-331 B.C.E.

- Alexander III (the Great) of Macedon defeats the Persians in battles at the Granicus River (334 B.C.E.), Issus (333 B.C.E.), and Gaugamela (331 B.C.E.).

331 B.C.E.

- Alexander enters Babylon and afterward declares himself king of Persia.

* DENOTES CIRCA DATE

OVERVIEW

The Priest-King. Urbanism began in Mesopotamia at the end of the fourth millennium B.C.E. At Uruk, the largest city in Mesopotamia, two great temples dominated the region. It has been proposed that the temple was at the center of a redistributive economic system. The head of the temple was an official who was called the *en* in Sumerian. While the exact nature of his functions and method of election is controversial, it appears that he also held a position of political authority. Scholars refer to the *en* as the "priest-king." At the beginning of the third millennium B.C.E., city-states began to expand in size and population. Royal ideology maintained that the main temple in each city was the residence of a particular god or goddess, a deity who acted as its protective patron. The temple administrator continued to act as the city ruler. The full range of his functions is unknown because no political texts survive from this period.

The Rise of Kingship. Myths and legends from the end of the third millennium B.C.E. describe a period of time, circa 2900 – circa 2340 B.C.E., during which some cities—having expanded into city-states with increased populations—came into conflict with neighboring population centers. Some of the leaders of these cities are described as war leaders. Documents from this period refer to both a temple and a "great house," or palace. The military ruler is called a *lugal*, or "big man," a term usually translated as "king." Other city rulers are referred to as *ensis*, a word for which there is no precise translation.

The First Empires. In the northern part of southern Mesopotamia, Sargon (circa 2334 – circa 2279 B.C.E.) founded a new dynasty, locating his capital city at Akkad (or Agade). As a result of his military successes, Sargon claimed kingship over all Sumer and Akkad and ended the independence of the Sumerian city-states. Sargon created a new centralized system of government. The former city-state rulers (*ensis*) became provincial governors. Taxes were imposed on conquered territories and used to support the central administration in Akkad. Internal opposition to Akkadian rule was constant, and these rebellious factions may have combined with foreign enemies to cause the decline in the dynasty. After a short period of political disruption and fragmentation of rule, a new dynasty emerged toward the end of the twenty-second century B.C.E. in the southern Mesopotamian city of Ur. The existing documentation does not describe territorial wars or offer any other explanation of how the city gained control over neighboring areas. Yet, the kings of Ur established centralized political control and called themselves "King of Sumer and Akkad." The dynasty existed for just over a hundred years, until it was destroyed by invading armies from the north and east. According to the *Sumerian King List*, "The very foundation of Ur was torn out."

Kingship in the Early Second Millennium B.C.E. After the collapse of Sumerian hegemony, centralized rule in Mesopotamia was replaced by independent city-states, competing dynasties, and tribal leaders. In the early part of the eighteenth century B.C.E.—during what is now called the Old Babylonian period (circa 1894 – circa 1595 B.C.E.)—Hammurabi (circa 1792 – circa 1750 B.C.E.) became the king of Babylon. Exerting political control over southern Mesopotamia, Hammurabi called himself the "shepherd" of his people, and cuneiform records indicate that he personally oversaw even minute details of the kingdom's administration. Ten years after his death, rebellion began in the land, but his dynasty continued to exist until circa 1595 B.C.E., when the Hittite king Mursili I (circa 1620 – circa 1590 B.C.E.) sacked Babylon.

Kassites and Hurrians. After the Old Babylonian period, two new political groups gained ascendancy in Mesopotamia: the Kassites in the south and Hurrians in the north. The Kassites originated in the Zagros Mountains to the east. Their social organization was based on tribal loyalties, but once the Kassites gained political control they appear to have become fully integrated into the older urban centers. The Hurrians, resident in northern Mesopotamia since at least the third millennium B.C.E., developed their own territorial kingdom known as Mitanni in northern Syria along the upper Habur River in the early fifteenth century B.C.E. Little is known of Mitanni political organization. The king of Mitanni exercised control of his territories through vassalage treaties made with local rulers. The Hurrians are best known for their use of horse and chariot, an innovation that changed the nature of warfare during the second half of the millennium. Their capital city, Washukanni, has not yet been discovered.

The Rise of Assyria. With the collapse of Mitannian power in the middle of the fourteenth century B.C.E.—the result of wars with the Hittites in Anatolia (modern Turkey)—Assyria, which had been a province under Mitannian rule, emerged as a territorial power. Royal annals document the wars of Assyrian kings as they transformed Assyria from a small state into a great power. Assyrian military campaigns were staged east to the land of Elam in southwestern Iran, north into Anatolia, south to Babylonia, west to Syria and the Levant, and ultimately, in the seventh century B.C.E., to Egypt. Many ethnic groups became part of the Assyrian Empire.

Assyrian Kingship. The Assyrian king ruled over a militaristic society. He was chosen from the military aristocracy and ruled for the benefit of the god Ashur. In theory the king led annual campaigns in search of territory and spoils. Conquered people were forced to serve in the Assyrian army, primarily as infantry. Conquered lands, such as those to the west of Assyria, were divided into provinces ruled by military governors, appointed puppet rulers, or local rulers charged with delivering tribute. Assyrian annals and palace wall reliefs describe an imperial policy designed to frighten enemies into submission. Leaders of cities that resisted Assyrian attack were impaled, beheaded, and flayed with their corpses left in front of their gates for public display. After conquest, entire populations of defiant cities were deported elsewhere within the empire; their territories were either left barren or resettled with population groups deported from elsewhere. The might of Assyria was frightening, and its rule exacted a heavy price; yet, Assyria did not impose its official cult or god on conquered populations.

The Fall of Assyria. Assyria was a highly centralized state, with an economy based primarily on agriculture. Conquest and tribute were necessary to support building projects and the elite. In the later part of the seventh century B.C.E. palace intrigue weakened central authority. Without a strong king the country was thrown into confusion. Babylon revolted, and imperial expansion had run its course. Tributary states began refusing to make annual payments and allied themselves with Babylon. For a decade following Nabopolassar's ascension to the throne in Babylon in 625 B.C.E., there was fighting around Assyrian strongholds in northern Babylonia. In 616 B.C.E. Babylonian armies marched along the Euphrates as far north as the Balih and along the Tigris to the Lesser Zab, where they unsuccessfully attacked Ashur. In 614 B.C.E. Medes from western Iran attacked central Assyria and utterly destroyed Ashur. Nineveh (and probably Kalhu) fell to a force of Babylonians, Medes, and perhaps Scythians in 612 B.C.E., while the remnants of the Assyrian army were destroyed in the vicinity of Haran, in Syria, in 609 B.C.E.

The Neo-Babylonian Empire. Nabopolassar's son, Nebuchadnezzar II (604–562 B.C.E.), extended Babylonian rule in the west, destroying Jerusalem in 586 B.C.E. and deporting large numbers of its population. His successors extended Babylonian conquest into southwest Anatolia and into the rich northern trading areas of Arabia. The royal archives of Babylon have not been discovered, so almost nothing is known about the administration of the Babylonian empire. Babylonia reached its greatest heights and greatest fame during the Neo-Babylonian dynasty (625–539 B.C.E.), the last native Mesopotamian dynasty to rule in the ancient Near East.

The Persian Empire. On 12 October 539 B.C.E., the kingdom of Babylon fell to an invading army led by Cyrus II, the king of the Persians and the Medes. He was succeeded by his son Cambyses II (529–522 B.C.E.), who conquered Egypt in 525 B.C.E. Following his death and the general insurrection that followed, Darius I (521–486 B.C.E.) seized power, expanded the empire into Libya, and obtained tribute from Nubia, the southern neighbor of Egypt. According to Greek sources, ambition and the search for precious metals led Darius into an unsuccessful invasion of Scythia, north of the Black Sea. Then, in revenge for a rebellion of Ionian Greek cities in western Anatolia, Darius invaded the Greek mainland, where he was defeated at the battle of Marathon in 490 B.C.E. His successor, Xerxes (485–465 B.C.E.), also led incursions into Greece, but he met with frustration and finally abandoned his efforts there. In spite of such defeats, the Persians created an enormous empire ranging from the Indus to Egypt and from Central Asia into northern Greece. The Persians governed their empire with great respect for indigenous population groups, local customs, and religious traditions. Under Darius, the empire was divided into "satrapies," or provinces, each ruled by a "satrap," or governor, who was nearly always a Persian nobleman. The satraps maintained order and provided the capital with tax revenues.

Alexander the Great and Successors. Between 334 and 331 B.C.E. Alexander III (the Great), king of Macedon, defeated Persian forces in a series of battles. He entered Babylon in 331 B.C.E. and afterward declared himself king of Persia. Alexander sought to legitimize his rule by continuing Near Eastern traditions. He rebuilt temples, called himself the son of the Egyptian god Amon, and made Babylon his capital. Furthermore, he and his Macedonian generals married Persian princesses. When he died in 323 B.C.E., he left no framework for continuing his ambition to merge Greek and Near Eastern cultures. With no one leader able to keep such a vast territory under his control, the empire disintegrated. For the next thirty-five to forty years, his generals struggled for possession of all, or parts, of the empire. In 312 B.C.E., Seleucus I Nicator ("the Victor"), a Macedonian companion of Alexander, was able to gain control over Syria, much of Anatolia, Mesopotamia, Iran, and Bactria toward the Indus Valley. Founding the Seleucid dynasty, he ruled until 281 B.C.E., establishing several capital cities, including Seleucia on the Tigris (circa 312 B.C.E.) in central Mesopotamia and Antioch on the Orontes (circa 300 B.C.E.) in Syria. The Seleucid empire continued under his successors with portions gradually being taken over, first by the Parthians of Iran in the mid-second century B.C.E. and then by the Romans in the first century B.C.E.

The Parthian and Sasanian Empires. In 141 B.C.E. the Parthians, who had gained control over the Iranian plateau about 260 B.C.E., seized control of Seleucia on the Tigris. Under their ruler Mithradates I (178–131 B.C.E.) they established a garrison at Ctesiphon on the Tigris, across from Seleucia. The Parthians, who successfully repelled several Roman incursions into northern Mesopotamia, were finally defeated in 224 C.E. by the Persian Ardashir I (224–240 C.E.), who founded the Sasanian dynasty. Ctesiphon became the capital of the new Persian Empire. The Sasanian Persians maintained control over the region until the Arab successors of Muhammad drove them from Mesopotamia in 637 C.E. and completed conquest of the empire in 651 C.E.

Social Justice. A Mesopotamian monarch was obligated to the gods to shepherd his people properly. Thus, when necessary, he was expected to bring about reforms. The earliest attested document of reform was issued by Uru'inimgina, the ruler of the city-state of Lagash around 2400 B.C.E. During the Old Babylonian period (circa 1894 – circa 1595 B.C.E.) some kings are known to have declared that, as the gods' trustee, they would restore order by reducing burdensome debt. In the prologue to his laws, Hammurabi (circa 1792 – circa 1750 B.C.E.) stated that it was his duty as the "pious prince, who venerates the gods, to make justice prevail in the land, to abolish the wicked and the evil, to prevent the strong from oppressing the weak." He also claimed that he quelled rebellion, guided his people, established justice, and enhanced the well-being of his people.

Law and Wealth and Class. Unlike modern law, law in the ancient Near East primarily protected the propertied interests of the elite. Both the military and the law were institutions of those in power and served to promote and protect wealth. Within the legal system, penalties varied in accordance with wealth and status. In the classic Old Babylonian legal collections, specific terms refer to distinct social classes. A member of the highest class of men (and on occasion women) who owned property was termed an *awilum.* A member of a lower status group was called a *mushkenum,* or commoner, while the lowest class was the slave population. Mesopotamian society, in the modern

sense of the term, did not constitute political communities with shared interests. Though ancient guilds and families voiced self-interest, there were no representatives of the public interest, no educational or welfare systems funded through taxes, and no other means of redistributing wealth. Enslaved war captives, their descendants, and other penal slaves were outside society. The poor, the handicapped, and foreign traders had limited rights and little or no political voice. In various degrees, women, and especially children—whose property value was in most cases considered minimal—were excluded from political participation and hence were given less legal protection than members of the upper class.

Mesopotamian Legal Collections. The earliest recorded compilation of laws is attributed to the Sumerian monarch Ur-Namma (LU), who ruled circa 2112 – circa 2095 B.C.E. Successive surviving major bodies of ancient Mesopotamian law include the Sumerian laws of king Lipit-Ishtar of Isin (LL), who ruled circa 1934 – circa 1924 B.C.E.; the Babylonian law collections of the city of Eshnunna (LE), which date from circa eighteenth century B.C.E., and of king Hammurabi (LH), who ruled circa 1792 – circa 1750 B.C.E.; Middle Assyrian Laws (MAL), circa fourteenth – circa eleventh century B.C.E.; and Neo-Babylonian Laws (LNB), from the sixth century B.C.E. Hittite laws (HL) were written in central Anatolia beginning in circa 1650 B.C.E. Beyond the Tigris and Euphrates Rivers, biblical collections of law from the early to mid first millennium B.C.E. are found in the biblical books of Exodus, Deuteronomy, and Leviticus. None of these legal collections is comprehensive. They omit many areas of law that presumably were well known and concentrate on difficult cases that may have been resolved in court cases. Written decisions, legal collections, contracts, and school copies of summaries of well-known cases are but a small portion of all Mesopotamian laws. Most disputes were resolved privately by heads of families in accordance with orally transmitted custom and tradition. Mesopotamian law did not distinguish between criminal and civil law. Almost all of what are today called crimes were considered private wrongs against propertied interests. Legal action was the prerogative of the offended party or their kin. Seeking recourse in court was a last resort. Cases that could not be settled amicably were brought before various sorts of judicial authorities: city elders, councils, assemblies, or a court composed of one or more judges. The king in the Old Babylonian period acted as the highest level of appeal.

Compensation for Harm. In Near Eastern legal traditions little attention was paid to moral culpability. The level of intent, planning, or negligence on the part of an offender determined the degree to which vengeance was meted out by the offended family. The court used similar criteria to determine the level of compensation. Murder not only took the life of a person, it also harmed a family's prestige. The victim's family had the right to expect suitable compensation for the loss of life, property, and honor. An appropriate recompense could take a drastic form under the rule of *lex talionis:* an eye for an eye, a life for a life. However, except for selected cases of regicide, treason, or murder that involved ritual pollution, the deceased person's next of kin normally negotiated a "blood-money" monetary payment and did not demand the manslayer's death.

Biblical Legal Tradition. Differing from the Mesopotamian legal tradition, biblical law is set within the framework of a religious re-interpretation of the history and traditions of ancient Israel. In Mesopotamia, the gods were the source of "truth," while the king was deemed responsible for justice. The king was lawgiver and final court of

appeal. In Israel the account of Israel's receipt of law from God was set in the wilderness at a time in its history when there was no king. Yahweh, Israel's God, gave Israel the law by speaking directly to the people. Yahweh was Israel's ruler, lawgiver, chief judge, and court of appeals. For Israel all law was religious law because it originated as a directive from the deity. If the people kept the word that God spoke directly to them, they would become their deity's "treasured possession" and be "a kingdom of priests and a holy nation" (Exodus 19:6). Holiness was an aspect of God and a condition people could achieve through adherence to law and the practice of ritual. Intentional violation of the law or ritual amounted to rebellion against God.

TOPICS IN POLITICS, LAW, AND THE MILITARY

CLASS AND SOCIETY IN ANCIENT NEAR EASTERN LAW

The Free Landed Class. Law is typically based on the values of the governing class; that is, those who own property have the greatest risk of loss and are thus in need of income protection. As the ancient Mesopotamian economy was primarily based on large-scale agriculture and animal husbandry, the elite comprised owners of land, houses, gardens, livestock, and slaves. Commerce and trade represented other major sources of income. In the Old Babylonian period (circa 1894 – circa 1595 B.C.E.) a member of the elite landowning class was referred to as an *awilum,* a noble or "a free person." In the later Neo-Babylonian period (625–539 B.C.E.) free citizens were called *mar bane.* Legal provisions gave this class rights and privileges that were not available to members of lower-status groups. Esteem among nobles was in accordance with their level of status within this class. For example, one of the provisions in the Laws of Hammurabi specifies: "If a free man should strike the cheek of a free man who is of status higher than his own, he shall be flogged in the public assembly with sixty stripes of an ox whip" (LH §202).

The Dependent Class. During the Old Babylonian period, the crown had vast holdings of land that produced income and tax revenue for the king's own use. A lower

class of commoners (Akkadian: *mushkenu;* singular: *mushkenum*) was a dependent population who lived on the king's land, owned livestock and occasionally slaves, and paid to the palace a portion of their yield. They may also have had military responsibilities. Commoners received special consideration in Old Babylonian law. Several provisions in the code protected their right to own slaves. One of them specifies: "If a man has harbored in his house either a lost male or female slave of the palace or a lost male or female slave of a commoner and has not brought (him or her) forth at the proclamation of the herald, the owner of that house shall be put to death" (LH §16).

Dependent-Class Status. Commoners were considered to be of lower social status than nobles. Their low income was derisively referred to in an Old Babylonian letter: "I am a member of the *awilum*-class, he is (only) a member of the *mushkenum*-class, how can he repay me a favor?" The Old Babylonian codes often contrast the status of the commoner to the status of the nobleman when referring to damages in personal-injury suits. Compensation for causing injury to a commoner was always considerably less than damages awarded to a nobleman for the same injury:

If a free man has knocked out a tooth of a free man of his own rank, they shall knock out his tooth. If he has knocked out a commoner's tooth, he shall pay one-third mina (twenty shekels) of silver. (LH §§200–201)

If a free man has struck the cheek of a(nother) free man who is of the same rank as himself, he shall pay one mina (sixty shekels) of silver. If a commoner has struck the cheek of a(nother) commoner, he shall pay ten shekels of silver. (LH §§203–204)

Women, Children, and Slaves. Women and children, even those of noble birth, were considered possessions of the master of the house and were thus of lesser status. Both male and female slaves, whether belonging to a member of the noble class, the commoner class, the palace, or the temple, were clearly distinguished as the lowest class. The laws also refer to specialized laborers and craftsmen. Unless they are specifically designated as possessing lesser status, it is commonly assumed that they belonged to the noble class.

Sources:

Jean Bottéro, *Mesopotamia: Writing, Reasoning and the Gods,* translated by Zainab Bahrani and Marc Van de Mieroop (Chicago: University of Chicago Press, 1992).

Muhammed A. Dandamaev, *Slavery in Babylonia: From Nabopolassar to Alexander the Great (626–331 B.C.),* revised edition, translated by Victoria A. Powell, edited by Marvin A. Powell and David B. Weisberg (De Kalb: Northern Illinois University Press, 1984).

COLLECTIONS OF LAWS

Law and Values. Values are a culture's standard for qualitative assessment and its guide for conduct. A society's formal and informal customs and institutions influence and are shaped by its values, which are not only embedded in its laws but are also influenced by them. Conditions of barter or market economies; rural or urban densities; patterns of cohabitation; clan, nuclear family, or kinship groups; political or hereditary military groups; polis or autocracy all define through permission and prohibition—acceptable and unacceptable conduct. Values also arise historically through resolutions of conflict, and they are stratified and justified in the narrative myths that ground the culture. Religious, moral, instrumental, political, or economic values are all embedded in a society's institutions and customs. As one of those institutions, the law defines and stabilizes those values, which are resident not only in the law but also in the language of the court. Ancient Near Eastern law seems to have been primarily oral and administered by heads of families. Written collections of laws did not appear until late in the third millennium B.C.E. It may be assumed that actions were to a great extent influenced by a regimen of custom; that is, common practice and precedent whose continuance acquired the force of law. The extant body of written decisions and legal collections, often called codes, are only a small portion of ancient Mesopotamian laws, many of which were never defined or organized according to principles and rules.

Modern Law. In the modern sense of the term, *law* is an institution of society that reaches into the economy, marriage relations, religion, and the other aspects of soci-

ety, regulating conduct by defining acceptable limits of behavior and the penalties for the infringement of those boundaries. Law may be embedded in the customs of the group, oral or written. Law is expected to be publicly available, so that those governed by it can know it, and to be enforced by the authority whose responsibility is the care of the community. Law is an indirect or direct expression by the body politic of the ways to achieve and maintain the common good. Beginning with the Romans, the law in Western society has been considered transcendent and unchanging, regardless of the historically changing institutions it governs. Modern law applies to all, regardless of wealth or status, and it implicitly or explicitly contains standards that are applied through legislation, policy, or judicial interpretation. The modern institution of law is usually designed to be comprehensive. It has a language of its own and its own traditions, which include precedent, established procedures, and a professional body of practitioners. Modern law is an expression of the modern state. The state or body politic was first acknowledged as an independent institution separate from religious authority in the late thirteenth and early fourteenth centuries of the Common Era (C.E.). In the modern state, consent of the governed validates elections of officials and their policies and the motions of representative bodies such as juries and legislatures. Hence, modern law—whether developed by courts, legislatures, or officials of government—is by definition publicly issued and known. Most of these assumptions about modern law do not apply to the laws of the Mesopotamians.

Ancient Near Eastern Law. In the ancient Near East, monarchs ruled with the consent of the city gods and as their representatives. Decisions of state were made with only minimal political limitations on the king's rule. There existed no concept of the autonomous individual and no independent legislature; hence, no consent was available or necessary for the promulgation of law. Lacking reference to many areas of contract and criminal law, Mesopotamian legal collections were not comprehensive digests of law, nor did they include any effort to elevate legal decision to the level of principle. Many were literary anthologies incorporating a compendium of legal decisions in knotty cases, as well as a king's royal boasts that he had maintained proper order. For example, the diorite stele on which Hammurabi had his laws inscribed was a monument of self-praise designed to bolster the monarch's claim to be the king of justice who established equity and order for his people.

Oral and Written Law. It is assumed that most ancient Near Eastern law was passed down orally, governing relations among and within families. Disputes over inheritance, contracts, or homicide were typically settled by the representatives of the family or clan. Only when disputes (usually over the transfer of property) could not be resolved by family members acting according to custom and tradi-

Tablet A (obverse) of the Middle Assyrian Laws from Ashur (height 12 5/8 inches), circa twelfth century B.C.E.
(Vorderasiatisches Museum, Berlin)

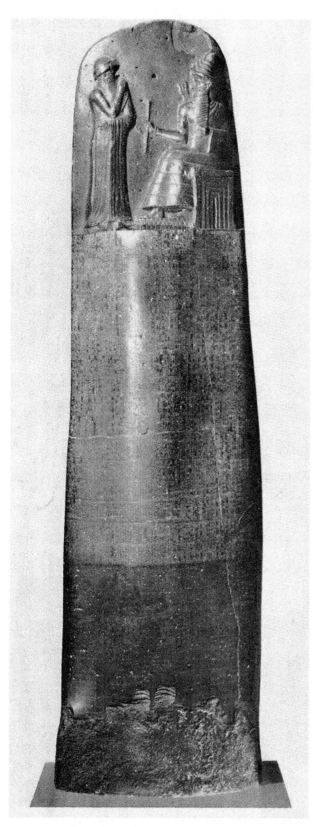

The Hammurabi Stele, erected in Sippar, circa 1750 B.C.E. (basalt, height 88 5/8 inches). At top Hammurabi stands before the seated god of justice, the sun god Shamash. Below, the laws are written in cuneiform and arranged in vertical columns. The stele was excavated from Susa, to which it was removed in the twelfth century B.C.E. (Louvre, Paris).

tion was it considered necessary to seek resolution through the courts. Since there were no professional legal practitioners in the ancient Near East, actions were brought by the litigants themselves and heard by a judge or panel of judges, who most likely decided issues according to a commonly accepted, orally transmitted standard rather than a written codified body of public law.

Positive Law. Mesopotamian law was positive law. That is, it was specifically created by the ruling authority. At present seven cuneiform legal collections are known. The Laws of Ur-Namma (circa 2112 – circa 2095 B.C.E.) and the Laws of Lipit-Ishtar (circa 1934 – circa 1924 B.C.E.) are written in Sumerian; the Laws of Eshnunna (circa eighteenth century B.C.E.), the Laws of Hammurabi (circa 1792 – circa 1750 B.C.E.), and the Neo-Babylonian Laws (sixth century B.C.E.) are written in Babylonian dialects of Akkadian; the Middle Assyrian Laws (circa fourteenth – circa eleventh century B.C.E.) are in an Assyrian dialect of Akkadian. Laws from ancient Anatolia, the Hittite Laws (beginning in circa 1650 B.C.E.), are written in Hittite.

Sources of Law. From the middle of the third millennium B.C.E. to the end of the first century C.E., many Mesopotamian legal documents have survived, including summaries of well-known court cases, trial records, contracts, agreements, dockets, deeds, and depositions. Thousands of legal records written in cuneiform on clay tablets document the legal traditions of the Sumerians, Babylonians, and Assyrians and also record the legal affairs of surrounding nations in the Near East, including the Hurrians in Syria and the Hittites in Anatolia. Additional legal information is found in letters, royal edicts, hymns, and school-exercise texts.

The Hammurabi Stele. The laws of the Babylonian king Hammurabi (circa 1792 – circa 1750 B.C.E.) were inscribed on a diorite stele more than seven feet in height, which was placed in the temple of Shamash, the god of justice, in the city of Sippar. Its intended audience was the gods and future rulers, as well as a larger audience that included those who felt wronged. The existence of school copies of the provisions on cuneiform tablets and of fragments of the code on other stelae—as well as a declaration in the prologue that Hammurabi "established truth and justice in the language of the land"—all suggest that the legal provisions of his code were probably publicly available in both written and oral form. The prologue is followed by a body of 282 legal provisions. Modern research has shown that the Laws of Hammurabi were not an ancient code (in the sense of the Napoleonic code) that was inclusive and used by jurists to determine guilt or innocence. The collection was instead a compilation of cases and edicts issued to demonstrate to gods and people that the monarch was a true king of justice. The text concludes with an epilogue in which the king claims that he has issued the laws, inscribed them on a stele, and made provision for them to be read aloud and serve as a standard of justice for future kings.

Cuneiform tablet of the Laws of Lipit-Ishtar, king of Isin (circa 1934 – circa 1924 B.C.E.). This Old Babylonian period (circa 1740 B.C.E.) copy (height 6 inches) was excavated from Nippur (University of Pennsylvania Museum of Archaeology and Anthropology).

Format. Most of the legal provisions in Mesopotamian legal collections are formulated in an academic style also used by scribes in divination and medical texts. Typically a legal provision describes a circumstance and then the sanction. In other words, "If a member of a status group does such and such, then the consequences will be the following." The first phrase of such a statement is called the *protasis,* and the second is the *apodosis.* It is thought that this formula was devised as a simple method of stating a principle that may have originated with a well-known case. Such cases may have arisen from unusual or contestable situations involving the extent of a defendant's liability. All extraneous circumstances that did not deal directly with the main subject matter were excised. Only a brief description of the circumstances remained and was then cast into a hypothetical *protasis-apodosis* formula—"if (a legal situation) . . . then (a legal prescription)"—which included the maximum penalty applicable to that case. In its final simplified form the nature of damages was clear.

Faulty Construction. The following example from the Laws of Hammurabi (LH) is a legal provision that may have derived from an actual case. The circumstances surrounding the case were summarized, the damages described, and the penalty stated:

If a builder constructed a house for a man, but did not make his work strong, with the result that the house that he built collapsed, and so has caused the death of the owner of the house, that builder shall be put to death (as the maximum penalty). (LH §229)

Expanding a Case. Following the presentation of this example, alternative circumstances and/or participants were then artificially constructed to form a small subsection on the legal issue being examined. Mesopotamian thought, in contrast to later Roman law, never clearly expounded categories of legal thought. Instead cases were piled on top of each other to illustrate contrasting aspects of a case without stating a general principle:

If (a builder constructed a house for a man but did not make his work strong with the result that) it has caused the death of a son of the owner of the house, they shall put the son of that builder to death (as the maximum penalty). If it has caused the death of a slave of the owner of the house, he shall give slave for slave to the owner of the house. If it has destroyed goods, he shall make good whatever it destroyed; also, because he did not make the house strong that he built and it collapsed, he shall reconstruct the house that collapsed at his own expense. (LH §§230–232)

Analogy in Laws. Analogies, as well as opposite sets of circumstances, were often employed to illustrate a legal point and develop new exemplars. To the modern mind what often appears to be a sudden jump in logic to an analogous or opposing circumstance appears confusing. While modern law develops principles to organize legal thought, ancient Near Eastern law merely continued to explore endless variations of circumstance. General principles were not deduced from observation; scholarship was based on practice, and knowledge was considered to be cumulative.

Exemplars. The exemplars found in the codes also avoid circumstances that would lead the verdict in an opposite direction. Ambiguity was not a part of a king's ideal statement of accomplishment. In a similar fashion, cases that vary from the norm were also not considered (for example, rape by a slave of another slave). Circumstances were limited to rare and unusual instances and not to an exhaustive list of hypothetical situations.

Contracts and Sales. Legal records of many sorts of property transfers were written on clay tablets inscribed with cuneiform signs. These documents include records of sales, exchanges, leases, and rentals. In order to establish title, contracts were drawn up regarding the sale of items such as real estate. Not all legal arrangements regarding property were recorded. Sales of commodities classified by weight, measure, or number, or sales of most *mobila*—movable goods of all kinds, including animals, furnishings, and garments—(except for slaves) were usually not recorded. If payment was made at the time of the transaction or if there existed no dispute over ownership, and if a written record of title was not required, no recording of the transaction occurred. The lack of a written record did not preclude the existence of some form of oral agreement that would lend legal validity to a transaction. In some instances, such as the necessity to formalize a marriage agreement, a verbal contract before witnesses must have been associated with some type of private ceremony or a symbolic act analogous to the modern practice of unveiling a bride at a wedding ceremony. Some of these acts are known; for example, a slave stepping over a pestle symbolized the transfer of property, or throwing a lump into a canal possibly represented the transitory nature of the land being purchased.

Sources:

B. L. Eichler, "Literary Structure in the Laws of Eshnunna," in *Language, Literature, and History: Philological and Historical Studies Presented to Erica Reiner,* edited by Francesca Rochberg (New Haven: American Oriental Society, 1987), pp. 71–84.

Martha T. Roth, "Mesopotamian Legal Traditions and the Laws of Hammurabi," *Chicago Kent Law Review,* 13 (1995): 13–39.

Ira Spar and Eva von Dassow, *Private Archive Texts from the First Millennium B.C.* Cuneiform Texts in the Metropolitan Museum of Art, volume 3 (New York: Metropolitan Museum of Art, 2000), pp. xiv–xxviii.

CRIME AND PUNISHMENT

Mesopotamian Laws of Homicide. In ancient Near Eastern law collections, laws regarding homicide are rare. In fact, except for a mention in the Sumerian laws of Ur-Namma (circa 2112 – circa 2095 B.C.E.)—"If a man commits murder, that man is to be killed"—Mesopotamian legal collections assume but do not clearly state that homicide was illegal. The Laws of Hammurabi (circa 1792 – circa 1750 B.C.E.) include no direct statement outlawing homicide. They include hypothetical examples of situations and circumstances that distinguished between intentional murder and various unintentional forms of homicide. The case of a wife who acted as an accessory to the murder of her husband is one of these hypothetical examples.

Homicide as a Property Offense. In the ancient Near East, where there was no criminal law in the modern sense, homicide was considered a civil, rather than criminal, offense. Civil law addresses the rights of private individuals and the legal proceedings concerning those rights; the appropriate remedy for civil offense is usually some form of compensation. Murder was primarily viewed as a private affair within the community, a civil offense against property. By intentionally shedding the blood of another individual, the murderer "stole property" that rightfully belonged to the victim and his immediate family. The crime was communal rather than individual, and the family of the perpetrator was expected to atone for it. The deceased's next of kin possessed the right to avenge their loss. The deceased's family also needed to retrieve the victim's corpse and ensure that it received a proper burial. If the victim's blood was not retrieved, it was feared that his ghost might become one of the "evil ones," the wandering dead, restless spirits troubled and roving, seeking to take revenge for their misery on the living.

Punishment by Revenge. It is not known what percentage of homicide cases were settled by private revenge. Sumerian legal and literary texts written circa 2100 – circa 1800 B.C.E. indicate that homicide and many other offenses were considered capital crimes and that the offenders could be subject to trial. At present the process and details of detention, trial, and execution are poorly understood. Individuals accused of capital offenses were brought to the "great house," where a trial took place. If convicted, the offender could receive the death sentence and be placed in a dungeon prior to execution. Little is known about the actual execution. According to a text from the Old Babylonian period (circa 1894 – circa 1595 B.C.E.), a slave who killed a member of the landowning class was put to death for the murder he committed: "Because he (the slave) threw the boy into the oven, you (the master) throw the slave into the furnace."

Compensation in Lieu of Execution. While the Old Babylonian codes do not deal directly with intentional homicide, they imply that the manslayer will be executed by the victim's next of kin. Later texts, beginning at the end of the second millennium B.C.E., indicate that the formulary of "an eye for an eye" meant capital punishment to be viewed as a maximum penalty. In most cases "execution" was not to be taken literally. A member of the landed class had the option of reaching a monetary settlement with the victim's next of kin. If a settlement was not reached, then the victim's relatives could petition the courts to impose the death penalty. Legal formulas stating that a monetary payment could be made in lieu of revenge developed in the later part of the second millennium B.C.E.

Middle Assyrian Laws of Compensation. The clearest legal description of compensation for spilled blood is found in Middle Assyrian laws (MAL) dating to the twelfth century B.C.E., wherein the deceased's nearest living relative could claim compensation for loss by negotiating a monetary settlement with the manslayer in lieu of spilled blood. If, however, a compensation settlement could not be reached, then the next of kin possessed the right to seek revenge by killing the blood shedder:

> If either a man or a woman (intentionally) entered another man's house and killed either a man or a woman, they shall give the murderers to the next of kin, and if he (the next of kin) chooses, he may spare them but take their property.... (MAL A §10)

> If one among brothers . . . took a life, they shall give him up to the next of kin; if he chooses, the next of kin may put him to death, or if he chooses, he may be willing to settle and take his share. (MAL B §2)

Murder, Pollution, and Execution. Spilling human blood within the confines of the temple was an action that polluted the home of the deity. The manslayer and the temple were both stained by the murder. The pollution produced by such murders endangered the efficacy of rituals and imperiled the welfare of the immediate community. Because the temple was an institution that served the great gods and protected the community through the enactment of rituals against demonic forces, such an offense threatened societal order. It could not be treated as a private crime to be satisfied by a monetary payment to the victim's family; it demanded expiation. Only execution of the offender would serve to sweep away the pollution. Similarly, the murder of a member of the royal house was considered an offense that created pollution imperiling the state at large. In a text written during the seventh century B.C.E., the Assyrian king Esarhaddon (680–669 B.C.E.) warned a vassal that if the crown prince, Ashurbanipal (who survived to rule Assyria in 668 – circa 627 B.C.E.), were killed during a rebellion, the vassal was obligated by the terms of the treaty to capture and put to death the instigators of the revolt. The execution of the rebel leader would avenge the death of the crown prince, by shedding blood for blood, and purge the land from the threat of rebellion by the rebel's descendants.

THE LAWS OF HAMMURABI

The following outline shows the areas of law covered in Hammurabi's legal code:

I. Basic Rules of Evidence and Testimony (§§1–5)

II. Property Law

    A. Theft

        1. Theft of Goods (§§6–13)

        2. Kidnapping (§14)

        3. Slavenapping (§§15–20)

        4. Theft of Private Property (§§21–25)

    B. Transfers and Forfeitures of Personal Property of a Public Servant (§§26–35)

    C. Impairment of Landed Property

        1. Fields (§§36–58)

        2. Tenant Laws (§§42–52)

        3. Damages to another's field (§§53–58)

        4. Orchards: (§§59–66)

            a. Tenant Laws

            b. Damages

        5. Houses (§§67–78)

        6. Not preserved (§§79–87)

    D. Loans and Safekeeping-Deposits (§§88–126)

III. Marriage and Family Law (§§127–194)

IV. Torts (Property Damage)

    A. Personal Injury Law

        1. Personal assault (§§195–214)

        2. Medical malpractice (§§215–225)

        3. Removal of Slave Marks (§§226–227)

        4. Personal Injury from Poorly Built Houses (§§228–233)

    B. Fees and Damages

        1. Boats (§§234–240)

        2. Oxen (§§241–256)

        3. Miscellaneous (§§257–260)

        4. Shepherds (§§261–267)

        5. Miscellaneous Rates of Hire §§ (268–277)

V. Slaves

    A. Purchases and Claims (§§278–281)

    B. Insolence (§282)

Source: Martha T. Roth, *Law Collections from Mesopotamia and Asia Minor,* second edition (Atlanta: Scholars Press, 1997).

Babylonian Laws of Unintentional Homicide. Babylonian law also treats homicide as injury to property. In cases of unintentional homicide—that is, when a person causes the death of another without any clear intent to do harm—the deceased's next of kin could seek damages for their loss of property. As opposed to suits that dealt with murder (that is, intentional homicide), the plaintiff's actions in most instances of unintentional homicide were brought without the option of revenge. Only in cases where the offender was considered to be criminally negligent did the victim's family have the option to put the offender to death. Babylonian laws of unintentional homicide are comparable to modern tort law, in which as a result of a private or civil wrong or injury, the court provides damages. Today, for example, in cases of death in automobile accidents or in claims for damages in medical-malpractice suits where there does not exist sufficient proof or evidence of intent for murder, damages are awarded to the plaintiff.

Tort Law. Instances of unintentional homicide are often grouped together in tort sections of Babylonian law collections. In tort cases the possible polluting consequence of property damage was not at issue; without intent, the assailant was not considered to be a manslayer, and there were no evil consequences to assess. Babylonian law centered on the amount of damages and subsequent level of personal-injury reward. The level of liability of the tortfeasor—the losing defendant—was therefore assessed together with a determination of the amount of remuneration due to the victim's family. By describing unintentional homicide in purely monetary terms, the law placed limits on the assailant's liability and thus protected the offender and his family from unbridled revenge or outrageous damage claims by the victim's next of kin.

Personal Injury Without Intent to Do Harm. Babylonian law examined the classic case of a fight to illustrate personal injury without premeditated intent to do harm. In the cases cited below two members of the propertied class became engaged in a brawl; blows were exchanged; and one of the combatants was hurt. The fight was not planned, and there existed no premeditated intent to do harm. Neither party was considered to be at fault, and thus no negligence was involved; liability was limited to physicians' fees:

> If a free man has struck a(nother) free man in a brawl and has inflicted an injury on him that free man shall swear, "I did not strike him deliberately," and he shall also pay for the physician. If he has died because of his blow, he shall swear (as before), and if it was a member of the propertied class, he shall pay one-half mina (30 shekels) of silver. (LH §§206–207)

Court Decision. The Babylonian court in the Case of a Brawl established lack of intent to cause personal injury by instructing the assailant to swear under oath that he did not intend to cause harm. By establishing first that there was no intent to do harm, the offender was cleared of a charge of aggravated assault. Without premeditation or intent to injure the other party, the offender was also not considered to be negligent in his actions, and his liability was limited to compensating the injured party for damages. The court, therefore, ordered him to pay only for his victim's doctor bills. If, however, the injured party died, then the assailant could compensate for the crime by paying a limited fee up to a maximum of 30 shekels of silver. There existed no evil and no pollution in this case, as death resulted from an unpremeditated blow.

Negligence. In the above case the court first established the circumstances under which the injury occurred (a fight) and found no intent to do harm. In a contrasting case, the law examined a different set of circumstances and came to a different conclusion. If a contractor's work was so shoddy that a house that he had built collapsed and caused the death of the head of the household, the builder was considered to be liable and the amount of damage was assessed on the basis of his culpable negligence: "If a builder constructed a house for a man, but did not make his work strong, with the result that the house that he built collapsed and so caused the death of the owner of the house, that builder shall be put to death" (LH §229). In this case the court determined that, even though it was not his intention to kill the owner of the house, the builder must have been aware that he was responsible for the safety of the household. As a result of his unsafe substandard work, an individual died. The builder should have inspected his work for defects and foreseen the dangerous consequences of poor workmanship. The court viewed his actions as constituting gross negligence in reckless disregard for the safety of the household.

Culpable Negligence. Given his culpable negligence in this matter, the court reasoned that the builder could be subject to revenge by the next of kin if a proper settlement was not reached. The court's ruling indicated that it did not think the builder intentionally designed the house to collapse; thus, he was precluded from a charge of intentional homicide. Nevertheless, the builder faced consequences that could potentially lead to his death if he did not agree to settle the suit. One may assume that the statement "that builder shall be put to death" acted as a powerful incentive to urge him to offer the deceased's family a proper settlement.

Damage to Property. Ancient Near Eastern legal tradition examined the issue of damage to property without clear intent to do harm in the Case of the Goring Ox. This case was well known in both Mesopotamia and the Hebrew Bible. It appears in the Laws of Eshnunna, the Code of Hammurabi, and in the biblical Covenant Code (Exodus 21–23). The Laws of Eshnunna (LE §53) examine negligence and liability by describing a case of nonnegligent civil injury. "A's" ox has gored "B's" ox, and "B's" ox has died. It is uncertain whether "B's" ox was vicious or incited "A's" ox to anger. There is also no indication that "A" was at fault. As neither party was liable, the law called for a division of damages. "B" therefore had the right to sue, but damages could be awarded only up to half of the value of the dead ox. By issuing a split decision, the court gave both parties due compensation so that both shared in their respective loss. "A" paid out 50 percent of the value of the dead ox, and "B" absorbed the rest. Here the assumption was made that the two animals involved in the incident were worth an equivalent amount of money. One may assume that if the animals had different market values then the owner's losses would have been subject to negotiation based on the principle of equity.

The Case of the Vicious Dog. In the Laws of Eshnunna (LE) the Case of the Goring Ox was followed by the Case of the Vicious Dog. After having been warned by the authorities to keep his dog penned up, the owner allowed it to roam loose. The dog bit a man and caused his death:

> If a dog is vicious and the local authorities have brought the fact to the knowledge of its owner, if nevertheless, he does not keep it in, and it bites a man and causes his death, then the owner of the dog shall pay out 2/3 mina (40 shekels) of silver. (LE §56)

The code examined this case to determine whether the owner of the dog was culpably negligent. Here the tortfeasor's liability was determined on the basis of the owner's prior knowledge of the special danger posed to the community by allowing his potentially vicious dog to wander at will. Once the owner has been forewarned, strict liability followed from the official notice.

The Case of the Collapsing Wall. The Code of Eshnunna also described a wall that was known to be likely to collapse. After the authorities informed him that his wall posed a public danger, the owner made no attempt to repair it. If the wall collapsed and caused the death of a passerby, then the owner's negligence bordered on being criminal:

> If a wall is threatening to fall and the local authorities have brought the fact to the knowledge of its owner, if nevertheless he does not strengthen his wall, (and) the wall collapses and causes a free man's death, then it is a capital offense (under) the jurisdiction of the king. (LE §58)

In the Case of the Vicious Dog, a pedestrian might be able to determine visually that a loose dog was vicious, but no warning was available for the danger of sudden death from a collapsing wall. By describing first the Case of the Goring Ox and by continuing with vicious dogs and collapsing walls, the legal tradition began with an instance of non-negligence and then moved into areas of culpable negligence arranged in order of increasing danger and liability. Even though the wall has caused the death of a nobleman, however, there is no mention of pollution or expiation—in contrast to the death of a member of the priest class murdered within the confines of the temple.

Laws of Hammurabi: The Case of the Goring Ox. The version of the Case of the Goring Ox in the Laws of Hammurabi begins with a case in which an ox accidentally killed a human being. The owner of the ox was not considered to be culpably negligent and was therefore not liable to a charge of contributory negligence. No indemnity was involved:

> If an ox, when it was walking along the street, gored a man to death, that case is not subject to claim. (LH §250)

HITTITE HOMICIDE LAW

The Hittites of central Anatolia adopted the cuneiform writing system and used it to write out their distinctive Indo-European language. A Hittite law composed around the fourteenth and thirteenth centuries B.C.E. specifically refers to monetary payments to be made to the immediate heir or legal representative of the victim's family:

> If anyone kills a man or a woman in a [quarr]el, he shall [bring him] for burial and shall give four persons, male or female respectively. He shall look [to his house for it (that is, the victim's heir is entitled to damages from the estate of the perpetrator)]. (HL §1)

In the *Edict of Telepinu*, written circa 1500 B.C.E., the Hittite king declared that compensation for homicide was the norm in his kingdom:

> A matter of blood is as follows. Whoever does blood, whatever the owner of the blood says: If he says, "Let him die!" he shall die. If he says, "Let him compensate!" he shall compensate. . . .

In a letter dated circa 1270 B.C.E., a Hittite king explained that the slaying of Babylonian merchants in Syria could be redressed only through compensation and that it was not customary for the Hittites to impose the death penalty for murder:

> (You write me that) merchants are being killed in the land of Amurru and in Ugarit—nobody kills (merchants) in Hatti (but that) they arrest the killer of the person and give notice to the companions of the murdered man, and his companions take the blood money for the murdered man, but they [let] the killer [live?] and only purify the city in which the person was killed—but if his companions do not want to accept the blood money, they may make the killer of that person [their slave?].

Sources: Harry A. Hoffner Jr., "Hittite Laws," in *Law Collections from Mesopotamia and Asia Minor*, by Martha T. Roth, second edition (Atlanta: Scholars Press, 1997), pp. 213–245.
Hoffner, *The Laws of the Hittites: A Critical Edition*, Documenta et Monumenta Orientis Antiqui, volume 23 (Leiden & New York: Brill, 1997).

THE CASE OF THE MURDERED TEMPLE PRIEST

A cuneiform tablet written in Sumerian and containing a record of a trial for murder was discovered in 1950 in an excavation in Iraq. The tablet does not contain the original trial record. It is a condensed summary and description of courtroom proceedings recorded for study and exposition in Mesopotamian schools. The text of the case describes a trial for murder that took place in the sacred temple city of Nippur during the reign of Ur-Ninurta (circa 1923 – circa 1896 B.C.E.) of Isin. Two men, Nanna-sig and Ku-Enlila, and a slave named Enlil-ennam were accused of killing Lu-Inana, a *nishakkum*-priest in the temple of Nippur. According to the record of the trial, the defendants had informed the victim's wife that they had murdered her husband, but the woman, Nin-dada, kept the identity of her husband's murderers a secret and did not notify the authorities. The case was brought before the king, who assigned the trial to be held before the judicial assembly at the temple of Nippur:

Nanna-sig, son of Lu-Suena, Ku-Enlila, son of Ku-Nanna the barber, and Enlil-ennam, slave of Adda-kalla, the orchardman murdered Lu-Inana, son of Lugal-uru the *nishakkum*-priest. After Lu-Inana, son of Lugal-uru had been killed, they (the murderers) told Nin-dada, daughter of Lu-Ninurta, wife of Lu-Inana, that Lu-Inana, her husband, had been murdered. Nin-dada, daughter of Lu-Ninurta, did not open her mouth, she covered it up (and kept silent). The case was taken to Isin before the king. King Ur-Ninurta ordered their case to be accepted for trial in the Assembly of Nippur.

The nine members of the court—Ur-Gula, son of Lugal-ibila; Dudu, the birdcatcher; Ali-ellati, the *mushkenum*; Puzu, son of Lu-Suena (possibly brother of the accused); Eluti, son of Tizkar-Ea; Shesh-kalla, the potter; Lugal-kam, the orchard keeper; Lugal-azida, son of Suen-andul; and Shesh-kalla, son of Shara-HAR—presented the case against the accused. They argued that the two men and the slave as well as the victim's wife were all guilty of murder and should be slain before the priest's chair (that is, symbolically in the presence of their victim).

(They) addressed (the assembly as follows): "As men who have killed a man they are not (fit to be) alive. The males (all) three of them and that woman before the (official) chair of Lu-Inana, son of Lugal-uru, the *nishakkum* priest, should be killed."

Two men in the assembly then spoke in defense of the victim's wife. They pleaded that, although the wife may have been an accessory to the murder, as a woman, she had little choice but to hide her knowledge of the crime. They implied that if she admitted knowledge of the crime she would have placed her own life in danger. Shuqalilum, the *erin-gal-gal* of the infantry of Ninurta, and Ubar-Enzu, the orchard keeper, addressed the assembly: "Nin-dada, daughter of Lu-Ninurta, may have killed her husband; but what can a woman do (under such circumstances) that she is to be killed?"

The elders of the Nippur assembly replied that the wife kept silent in order to cover the fact that she was having an affair with one of the murderers. If she admitted knowledge of the crime, they implied, she would have been acknowledging her affair. Rather than have her affair become public, the victim's wife conspired with her paramour and others to murder her husband. Her silence indicated her complicity. The elders concluded that the victim's wife acted as if she were an adulteress. In their view, she—more than any other person—was responsible for the death of her husband:

A woman who does not treasure her husband, she may surely be the type who would have had intercourse with a stranger, and he the stranger would then murder her husband. Should he the (paramour) then let her know that her husband had been killed—why should she then not keep silent about him? It is certainly she (more than anyone else) who killed her husband, her guilt is greater than (those who actually committed the crime).

Spilling human blood in the temple polluted the home of the deity. The manslayer and the temple were both stained by the murder, which endangered the efficacy of rituals and imperiled the welfare of the community, threatening societal order. It could not be treated as a private crime, satisfied by a monetary payment to the victim's family. The murderer's transgression exposed society to danger, and it demanded expiation. The Assembly of Nippur condemned Nanna-sig, son of Lu-Enzu, Ku-Enlilla, son of Ku-Nanna, the barber, Enlil-ennam, slave of Adda-kalla, the orchardman, and Nin-dada, daughter of Lu-Ninurta, wife of Lu-Inana, to death.

Sources: J. J. Finkelstein, "Sumerian Laws, YBC 2177," in *Ancient Near Eastern Texts Relating to the Old Testament*, edited by James Bennett Pritchard, third edition with supplement (Princeton: Princeton University Press, 1969), p. 542.

Thorkild Jacobsen, "An Ancient Mesopotamian Trial for Homicide," in *Toward the Image of Tammuz and Other Essays on Mesopotamian History and Culture*, edited by William L. Moran, Harvard Semitic Series, volume 21 (Cambridge, Mass.: Harvard University Press, 1970), pp. 193–214.

Indemnity. The code continues by describing circumstances that clearly warranted a charge of negligence. Instead of assuming that the ox simply became frightened and panicked in the street or that it gored an individual by accident, the tradition now describes the ox as a habitual gorer, a known menace to the public safety. Being aware of this ox's propensity to gore, the authorities warned its owner that his animal had to be kept penned and tied up at all times. If the ox were walked in the street, the owner was instructed to insure the public safety by padding the ox's horns.

> If a man's ox was a gorer and local authorities notify him that it was a gorer, but he did not pad its horns (or) control his ox, and that ox gores to death a free man, he (the owner) shall pay one-half mina (30 shekels) of silver. (LH §251)

Court Decision. The owner of the ox failed to either tether his animal or to pad its horns, and as a result the ox ran amuck and killed a nobleman. Under these circumstances the owner was certainly liable for damages. He wantonly disregarded the authorities' warning and therefore acted in reckless disregard for public safety. His actions, however, were not criminal in intent. The owner lost control of the animal in the street; he did not train the ox to be a gorer; that is, the owner probably thought that he could manage the animal when he let it out into the street.

Compensation for Loss of Property. In the Case of the Goring Ox, the family of the deceased was compensated for the loss of a human life. The value of the nobleman's life was quantified, and liability was limited to a maximum of fifty shekels of silver. As the owner of the ox earned his living in agriculture, he was allowed to keep the animal as a means of sustaining his livelihood.

Death of a Slave. The life of a member of the landowning class was deemed proportionally more valuable than that of a slave. If a slave were killed by a vicious dog or a goring ox, the owner of the dog or ox was obligated to pay only the replacement cost of the slave and nothing more:

> If it was a free man's slave (that was killed by the goring ox), he shall pay one-third mina (20 shekels) of silver. (LH §252)
> If (a vicious dog) bites a slave and causes its death, he shall pay 15 shekels of silver. (LE §57)

Theft in the Laws of Hammurabi. Rules regarding theft of valuable goods belonging to the temple or palace were treated as capital offenses (LH §6). The death penalty was also imposed for theft of a child (LH §14), breaking and entering (LH §§21–22), and theft of household furnishings taken during a fire (LH §25). Suspicion of theft was not determinative. The offender had to be caught in the act (that is, in the presence of witnesses) or in possession of another's goods (LH §9). Laws regarding common theft (LH §§259–260) were punishable by multiple restitution.

Babylonian and Biblical Laws of Assault. As in Babylonian legal codes, cases of personal injury are also treated as damage to personal property in the Hebrew Bible. All part of the ancient Near Eastern common legal tradition, three major cases are described in the Bible: accidental injury resulting from a brawl (Exodus 21:18–19), an accidental blow to a pregnant woman resulting in a miscarriage (Exodus 21:22), and accidental death from a goring ox (Exodus 21:28–35).

The Biblical Case of the Goring Ox. Some scholars have argued that the biblical version of the Case of the Goring Ox was based on knowledge of its Babylonian counterparts. In both instances the laws deal with wrongful damage: a situation in which an individual is not directly responsible for a death but is an accessory in a circumstance that led to the death of a man. In both examples, the law sought to establish the fact that knowledge of a potentially dangerous situation is a condition of liability. As in Babylonian law, the Bible also deals with the complex issue of the habitually goring ox, citing circumstances that parallel the Law of Eshnunna (§§53 ff) and the Laws of Hammurabi (§§250 ff):

> If, however, that ox has long been a gorer and its owner, though warned, has failed to guard it and it kills a man or a woman, the ox shall be stoned and its owner too shall be put to death. He (the owner) may redeem his life, however, by paying whatever ransom (*kofer*) is laid upon him. (Exodus 21:29)

In the biblical version of this case the owner is responsible for the actions of his ox. The law establishes the fact that the owner had already been told his animal had a propensity to gore and that the owner had chosen to ignore this warning. If the owner did not heed the warning and did not take adequate precautions, such as padding the ox's horns, he was subjecting the community to the peril of encountering a potentially homicidal animal. If the ox killed a man or a woman, the owner was not only criminally negligent but was an accessory to murder. In contrast to the Babylonian laws, in which the owner gets to keep the goring ox and pays a fine for damages, the Bible specifies that the ox is to be killed, and the death penalty is imposed on the criminally negligent owner. In the Bible, property can always be replaced, but a human life cannot.

The Biblical Rule of Ransom. Biblical law does indicate however, that the owner can redeem his life by paying a ransom—the only instance in the Bible in which a person sentenced to death can be ransomed by payment. Elsewhere, such penalties are expressly forbidden, even if a homicide is unintentional:

> You may not accept a ransom for the life of a murderer who is guilty of a capital crime; he must be put to death. Nor may you accept ransom in lieu of flight to a city of refuge.... (Numbers 35:31–32)

Expiation Payment. The *kofer*, or ransom payment, was an expiation offering, a ritual attempt to cleanse the guilt that lay on the sanctuary. This offering cannot be measured in pecuniary terms; it is not an award for damages to the victim's kin, but a payment to expiate sin. By paying a *kofer* the owner ransomed his life. In Israel, as a noble man or woman could not have a market price, the amount of the *kofer* could not be quantified but was determined by reckoning. If the ox's owner was not able to make payment, he could be sold as a slave (Exodus 22:2).

Inviolable Human Life. By describing the penalty for the death of a man or a woman in terms of the death of the ox and the payment of an offering by the owner, the Bible rejects the Babylonian concern over property indemnity and avoids the necessity of having to measure the value of a human life. Because it was inconceivable to place an assessment of value on an image of God, the value of the *kofer* was left purposely vague: "the owner may redeem his life by paying whatever is laid upon him" (Exodus 21:30).

Sources:
J. J. Finkelstein, *The Ox that Gored*, Transactions of the American Philosophical Society, volume 71, part 2 (Philadelphia: American Philological Society, 1981).

Samuel Greengus, "Law," in *The Anchor Bible Dictionary*, 6 volumes, edited by David N. Freedman (New York: Doubleday, 1992), IV: 242–252.

Moshe Greenberg, "The Biblical Grounding of Human Value," in *The Samuel Friedland Lectures, 1960–1966* (New York: Jewish Theological Seminary of America, 1966), pp. 39–52.

Claudio Saporetti, *The Middle Assyrian Laws* (Malibu, Cal.: Undena, 1984).

Raymond Westbrook, *Studies in Biblical and Cuneiform Law* (Paris: J. Gabalda, 1988).

Westbrook, ed., *A History of Ancient Near Eastern Law* (Leiden: Brill, 2003).

JUSTICE AND REFORM

Social Justice. In the modern world a socially minded leader faced with corruption and economic turmoil would declare that his or her political goal was "change," to give citizens and future generations a better life. The ancient Near Eastern worldview lacked this modern concept of ongoing progress. Reform meant the re-establishment of a past order in which each household operated without discord. Society was stratified, and the ordering of classes was considered normal; there existed little social mobility. Revolutionary transformation was unthinkable. A good society was one in which people in each class conducted themselves according to proper modes of behavior believed to have once existed in an idealized past. Change meant clearing away abuse and cleaning up economic dislocations; it did not imply social or political upheaval. In this view, society needed to return to the status quo by expelling those elements that interfered with good order.

Royal Reform. In order for a Mesopotamian monarch to fulfill his duty to the gods to shepherd his people properly, he was expected to bring about reform of abuses. Some rulers considered themselves reformers when they declared in royal pronouncements that they would fashion laws to make society more just and equitable. These kings maintained that they had a religious obligation as a trustee of their deity to protect their people and restore order so that the strong would not oppress the weak; widows and orphans would be cared for; and the poor would be released from their debts. The earliest attested reform document was issued by Uru'inimgina of Lagash, circa 2400 B.C.E. During the Old Babylonian period (circa 1894 – circa 1595 B.C.E.), some kings are known to have declared that, as the gods' trustee, they would restore order by reducing burdensome debt. In the prologue to his laws, Hammurabi (circa 1792 – circa 1750 B.C.E.) stated that as the "pious prince, who venerates the gods," he had a duty "to make justice prevail in the land, to abolish the wicked and the evil, to prevent the strong from oppressing the weak." He also claimed that he quelled rebellion, guided his people, established justice, and enhanced the well-being of his people. The ruler who claimed to have instituted equity called himself a *shar mesharim*, "king of justice."

Reform Edicts. During the Old Babylonian period, the king might issue periodic decrees that attempted to redress domestic economic problems and thereby proclaim himself to be a reformer who restored justice to the land. These releases, called *mesharum*-edicts, were issued at the king's accession or irregularly on an as-needed basis during the king's reign. The main focus of such edicts was to cancel existing debts, mainly agricultural loans. They provided relief for debtors bound into servitude, annulment of the debtor's sale of his property to pay off arrears, and cancellations of various unpaid land taxes and outstanding non-commercial loans. Their effectiveness as either propaganda or real attempts to alleviate economic hardship can be measured by the fact that some kings issued several of these edicts during their reigns.

Righteous Rule. According to a royal inscription attributed by scholars to the reign of Enlil-bani of Isin (circa 1860 – circa 1837 B.C.E.), the king provided food and proper housing for the inhabitants of the city of Nippur, perhaps because of dislocations caused by war. He also claimed to have acted on behalf of the citizens of Isin, his home city, by decreasing taxes, reducing burdensome compulsory-labor services (corvée), and restoring law and order. In addition, he maintained that he responded to complaints and reduced abuses of power by royal herdsmen. The king concluded that he established righteousness, banished evil and violence, and made justice prevail in Isin.

> O (god) Enlil . . . I established justice in Nippur and made righteousness prevail. As is done for sheep, I looked for food to eat, let them (the inhabitants of Nippur) eat fresh vegetables. The heavy yoke (of corvée) I removed from their necks. I settled them in a permanent settlement. After I had reestablished righteousness in Nippur (and) had pro-

THE EDICT OF AMMI-SADUQA

The tenth ruler of the First Dynasty of Babylon, Ammi-saduqa, who ruled circa 1646 – circa 1626 B.C.E., issued a reform edict that included many provisions referring to the cancellation of debts, a royal tradition that dated back to about 2400 B.C.E., when king Uru'inimgina of Lagash canceled obligations resulting from nonpayment of debt and slave status resulting from punishment for theft or murder. Ammi-saduqa's edict freed only citizens from debt obligations. Foreigners, prisoners of war, or house-born slaves were not affected by the decree. In Mesopotamian societies the concept of social justice existed to re-establish or restore the status of those citizens who fell into debt or servitude. Equality did not extend to all inhabitants of the land, and there existed no incentive to aid those born into poverty or slavery:

(This is) the tablet [of the decree that the land was ordered] to hear at the time that the king invoked a *mesharum* for the land. . . .

(Cancellation of arrears and promissory notes)

With respect to the arrears of the tenant farmers, the shepherds, the knackers (people who buy useless or worn out livestock and sell the meat or hides), their agreements, promissory notes and their payments are herewith remitted . . . the collector shall not dun their estate(s).

(Cancellation of interest-bearing debts)

Whoever has given barley or silver to an Akkadian or an Amorite on an interest-bearing basis, or on a *melqetum* basis, because the king has invoked the *mesharum* for the land, his document is voided, he may not collect the barley or silver on the basis of his document. . . .

(Legal protection against a creditor's suit)

A creditor may not sue against the house of an Akkadian or an Amorite for whatever he had lent him; should he sue for payment, he shall die.

(Exemptions)

(But) an Akkadian or an Amorite who has received barley, silver, or other goods either as merchandise for a commercial journey, or as a joint enterprise for the production of profit, his document is not voided (by the *mesharum* document); he must repay in accordance with the stipulations of his contract.

(Business agreements for profit not based on interest are still to be honored.)

(Similarly) if an Akkadian or an Amorite has received barley, silver, or other goods as an advance for use in a business enterprise for a profit, and had a document executed, the creditor stipulating in writing that at the expiration of the term (of the contract) the money would accrue interest, or if he made any additional stipulations, he (the debtor) shall not repay on the terms of the (added) stipulations, but shall repay only the principle. The supplementary stipulations upon the Akkadian or Amorite are remitted.

(Annulment of debtor and members of immediate family from debt-slavery)

If a debt has resulted in a foreclosure against a citizen of Numhia, a citizen of Emutbalum, a citizen of Idamaras, a citizen of Uruk, a citizen of Isin, a citizen of Kisurra, or a citizen of Malgium, which resulted in (the debtor) placing his own person, his wife or his children in debt servitude, or in placing them as collateral security for a loan—because the king has instituted the *mesharum* decree in the land, he is free; his release is established.

(Exemption)

If a houseborn slave woman or male slave of a citizen (of the above cities) . . . was sold or he was distrained for debt-service on a loan, or he was even left as collateral security on a loan, his release shall not be effected.

Source: J. J. Finkelstein, "The Edict of Ammisaduqa," in *Ancient Near Eastern Texts Relating to the Old Testament*, third edition with supplement, edited by James Bennett Pritchard (Princeton: Princeton University Press, 1969), pp. 526–528.

vided well-being (for the people) I also established righteousness and justice in Isin, the city which (the gods) An and Enlil entrusted to Ninisina (the patron goddess of Isin), provided well-being for the region.

The barley dues (to be delivered on the basis of field rentals), which so far have been one-fifth. I reduced indeed to one-tenth (of the yield). The subjects (*mushkenu*) I let serve (from now on) for only four days per month, and for the sheep and cattle of the places which (so far) were [permitted] to graze the field(s) [of the . . .] and because they (the persons affected) had therefore raised complaints—I have now indeed removed sheep and cattle of the palace from the furrows (with sprouting barley). And

raising a complaint I have declared to be taboo. I am a judge who loves righteousness. I destroyed evil and violence. I restored . . . the just man . . . (Renger)

Sources:

J. J. Finkelstein, "Ammisaduqa's Edict and the Babylonian 'Law Codes,'" *Journal of Cuneiform Studies*, 15 (1961): 91–104.

Finkelstein, "Some New *Misharum* Materials and Its Implications," *Studies in Honor of Benno Landsberger on his Seventy-fifth Birthday, April 21, 1965*, edited by Hans Gustav Güterbock and Thorkild Jacobsen, Assyriological Studies, no. 16 (Chicago: University of Chicago Press, 1965), pp. 233–246.

Johannes Renger, "Royal Edicts of the Old Babylonian Period: Structural Background," in *Debt and Economic Renewal in the Ancient Near East*, edited by Michael Hudson and Marc Van de Mieroop (Bethesda, Md.: CDL Press, 2002), pp. 139–162.

KINGSHIP

The *Sumerian King List*. The *Sumerian King List* is the main surviving document for understanding the early political history of ancient Mesopotamia. The text lists Mesopotamian rulers in order and gives the length of their reigns from the time kingship first appeared before the flood through the First Dynasty of Isin (circa 1794 B.C.E.). The first legendary kings are said to have reigned for thousands of years. Although the *Sumerian King List* claims that the kings all ruled consecutively, it can be shown that many ruled concurrently. The list was composed to support the Mesopotamian ideology that only one urban city and its divinely legitimized king ruled at any one time.

Royal Inscriptions. Royal inscriptions are one of the most important sources for reconstructing the political history of ancient Mesopotamia. The earliest ones, dating to the first part of the third millennium B.C.E., are found on votive objects dedicated to the gods and list only a royal name and title, such as "Enmebaragesi, king of Kish." As the uses of writing expanded, royal inscriptions began to include descriptions of political and military activities as well as royal building projects. During the first millennium B.C.E., Assyrian royal inscriptions focus on warfare. Reports of military campaigns began circa 1300 B.C.E. Assyrian annals of the first millennium B.C.E. include details on warfare and the spoils of war taken from the palaces, temples, and treasuries of conquered enemies. Amounts of tribute levied on defeated kings are also included. Neo-Babylonian royal inscriptions (625–539 B.C.E.) praise royal achievements, describing a broad range of construction activities, such as the creation and dredging of canals and the building of temples and palaces.

Royal Correspondence. Aspects of political history may also be found in cuneiform letters. Archaeologists have found several major palace archives that contain personal and state correspondence. One archive, from the royal palace of Mari on the middle Euphrates, dates to the nineteenth and eighteenth centuries B.C.E. and contains more than twenty thousand tablets. Mainly written between the palace and members of the court, the letters in this archive

Fragment of a diabase stone vessel (height 9 7/8 inches) with an image of a goddess, perhaps Nisaba, holding a cluster of dates, and a dedicatory cuneiform inscription attributable to the ruler Enmetena of Lagash, circa 2450 B.C.E. (Vorderasiatisches Museum, Berlin)

Two sides of the *Sumerian King List* inscribed in cuneiform on four faces of a clay prism (rectangular solid, height 7 7/8 inches), Old Babylonian period copy, circa 1740 B.C.E. (Ashmolean Museum, Oxford)

THE CURSING OF AGADE

Perhaps written within one or two generations after the fall of the city of Akkad (or Agade) and the concomitant collapse of its empire during the reign of Shar-kali-sharri (circa 2217 – circa 2193 B.C.E.), the poetic Sumerian text called *The Cursing of Agade* lays blame for the demise of Akkad on Shar-kali-sharri's father, Naram-Sin (circa 2254 – circa 2218 B.C.E.). In the poem Naram-Sin has a dream in which he sees Enlil, the chief god of the Sumerian pantheon, who had given kingship to Sargon (circa 2334 – circa 2279 B.C.E.), Naram-Sin's grandfather. Enlil is now determined to "not let the kingdom of Agade occupy a pleasant, lasting residence, that he would make its future altogether unfavorable, that he would make its temples shake and would scatter its treasures." In a vain effort to alter Enlil's pronouncement, Naram-Sin destroys the god's residence, the E-kur temple in Nippur. In revenge,

Enlil . . . the rising deluge that cannot be confronted . . . brought out of the mountains those who do not resemble other people, who are not reckoned as part of the Land, the Gutians, an unbridled people, with human intelligence but canine instincts and monkeys' features. Like small birds they swooped on the ground in great flocks . . . they stretched their arms out across the plain like a net for animals. Nothing escaped their clutches, no one left their grasp. Messengers no longer traveled the highways, the courier's boat no longer passed along the rivers. The Gutians drove the . . . goats . . . out of their folds and compelled their herdsmen to follow them, they drove the cows out of their pens and compelled their cowherds to follow them. Prisoners manned the watch. Brigands occupied the highways. The doors of the city gates of the Land lay dislodged in mud, and all the foreign lands uttered bitter cries from the walls of their cities. They established gardens for themselves within the cities, and not as usual on the wide plain outside. As if it had been before the time when cities

were built and founded, the large fields and arable tracts yielded no grain, the inundated tracts yielded no fish, the irrigated orchards yielded no syrup or wine, the thick clouds did not rain, the *mashgurum*-plant did not grow.

In unison, the great gods pronounced a terrible curse on the city:

". . . May your holy walls, to their highest point, resound with mourning! . . . May your pilasters with the standing protective-deities fall to the ground like tall young men drunk on wine! May your clay be returned to its *abzu* . . . ! May your grain be returned to its furrow . . . ! May your timber be returned to its forest . . . ! May the cattle slaughterer slaughter his wife, may your sheep butcher butcher his child! . . . May your prostitute hang herself at the entrance to her brothel! May your pregnant hierodules and cult prostitutes abort their children! May your gold be bought for the price of silver, may your silver be bought for the price of pyrite, and may your copper be bought for the price of lead! . . . May this make the city die of hunger! . . . May depression descend upon your palace, built for joy! May the evils of the desert, the silent place, howl continuously! . . . In your city that could not sleep because of the *tigi*-drums, that could not rest from its joy, may the bulls of (the moon god) Nanna that fill the pens bellow like those who wander in the desert, the silent place! May the grass grow long on your canal-bank towpaths, may the grass of mourning grow on your highways laid for wagons! . . . In your plains where fine grass grows, may the reed of lamentation grow! Agade, may brackish water flow where fresh water flowed for you! If someone decides, 'I will dwell in this city!', may he not enjoy the pleasures of a dwelling place! If someone decides, 'I will rest in Agade!', may he not enjoy the pleasures of a resting-place!" And before (the sun god) Utu on that very day, so it was!

Source: Jeremy Black, Graham Cunningham, Jarle Ebeling, Esther Flückiger-Hawker, Eleanor Robson, Jon Taylor, and Gábor Zólyomi, *The Electronic Text Corpus of Sumerian Literature,* The Oriental Institute, University of Oxford, 1998– <http://www-etcsl.orient.ox.ac.uk/>.

document a wide range of political, social, and economic activities as well as diplomatic relations between states. Some letters describe relations between the court and tribes living on the periphery. An archive found in the Egyptian city of Amarna includes correspondence between the kings of Egypt and their peers and vassals in the Near East during the fourteenth century B.C.E. Letters found in archives from the city of Ugarit in Syria (thirteenth century B.C.E.) and letters in the state archives of Assyria (seventh century B.C.E.) also provide important political, economic, and religious information.

Kingship in Sumer. According to Sumerian mythology, kingship descended from the heavens. Several texts main-

tain that the king was appointed as war leader by an assembly, but it is not known if he was elected by that body or if it just confirmed his status as a military commander. Sumerian rulers governed city-states, each dominated by a patron deity, who dwelt in the form of a statue in his or her residence, the temple. The temple owned large estates and employed farmers, fishermen, craftspeople, administrators, and individuals, some of whom were priests who oversaw cultic duties. The king also owned estates and was deemed responsible for managing and protecting the landed economy under his control. He was charged with ruling the city justly and efficiently. At the end of the fourth millennium B.C.E. and the beginning of the third, he was often

Limestone relief-carved plaque (height 18½ inches) from Tello (ancient Girsu), depicting the ruler Ur-Nanshe of Lagash (circa 2550 B.C.E.) and his children, each identified by name in the cuneiform inscription, as they accompany him (above) carrying a basket of bricks and (below) drinking at a banquet (Louvre, Paris)

depicted in art as a humble ruler with priestly duties. One of his titles, *en*, may refer both to his function as lord of his realm and to his role as "high priest." A dutiful king was expected to restore older holy places and administer the rites for his people. Another title, *lugal*, literally "big man," refers to his secular function as city ruler. In some cities the title *ensi* was associated with a local city ruler. The Sumerians used the epithet *sipa*, "shepherd," to refer to the king's role as administrative manager of the people under his rule.

Akkadian Kingship. During the middle of the twenty-fourth century B.C.E., the mantle of political power in southern Mesopotamia shifted from Sumerian city rulers to Semitic Akkadian rulers. The first king of the dynasty, Sargon (circa 2334 – circa 2279 B.C.E.), established his capital in the city of Akkad (or Agade). He boasted about the size of his army and the extent of his conquests, which included much of Syria to the north and west and the formerly independent Sumerian city-states to the south. Might and political power were the hallmarks of the new Akkadian rulers, who developed the first empire and called themselves "Kings of the Four Quarters of the World." Following his suppression of a general insurrection within the empire, Naram-Sin (circa 2254 – circa 2218 B.C.E.), Sargon's grandson and the fourth king of the dynasty, became the first ruler to claim that he was divine, calling himself the "strong god of Akkad." According to later legend, the gods withdrew their support of the dynasty, and it collapsed.

The Third Dynasty of Ur. Toward the end of the twenty-second century B.C.E. the Sumerian ruler Ur-Namma (circa 2112 – circa 2095) assumed the title king of Ur for himself and his new dynasty and refortified the city of Ur, which controlled large parts of the south. Soon adding "King of Sumer and Akkad" to their title, these kings no longer considered themselves rulers over just a single city-state. Under Shulgi (circa 2094 – circa 2047 B.C.E.), the second king of the dynasty, a huge bureaucracy was set up to gather animals sent as tax payments at a central distribution center and to allot them to temples. The major temples of the land were the chief beneficiaries of the

THE CORRESPONDENCE OF IBBI-SIN

A series of letters written in Sumerian and concerning the events surrounding the fall of the Third Dynasty of Ur during the reign of Ibbi-Sin (circa 2028 – circa 2004 B.C.E.) were a part of the regular school curriculum during the Old Babylonian period (circa 1894 – circa 1595 B.C.E.). Whether these letters are authentic is open to question, but they nonetheless appear to reflect the political situation that allowed Ishbi-Erra, a once trusted official of king Shulgi (circa 2094 – circa 2047 B.C.E.), to rebel successfully against his current overlord. Ibbi-Sin gave Ishbi-Erra twenty talents of silver with which to purchase grain. Ishbi-Erra wrote to the king that he bought all the grain in the land, enough to last fifteen years, and—because of the movements of hostile Amorites from the west—he placed the grain in the city of Isin for safekeeping. Ishbi-Erra then instructed the king to send six hundred boats to Isin to retrieve the grain, further counseling the king not to worry about the Elamite threat from the east. Ishbi-Erra also wrote that in the meantime, he would guard Isin and Nippur for the king. In an angry reply, the king accused Ishbi-Erra of overcharging him for the grain and demanded to know why a local commander had not faced the Amorites, these "puny men." Ibbi-Sin's fate was sealed when, in other correspondence, the king learned that Ishbi-Erra—"an ape which has descended from those mountain lands . . . an idiot, a seller of asafoetida . . . who is not of Sumerian origin . . . this man from Mari, with the understanding of a dog"—had successfully seized many cities in central Mesopotamia and installed governors loyal to him as the first king of the First Dynasty of Isin.

Source: Jeremy Black, Graham Cunningham, Jarle Ebeling, Esther Flückiger-Hawker, Eleanor Robson, Jon Taylor, and Gábor Zólyomi, *The Electronic Text Corpus of Sumerian Literature*, The Oriental Institute, University of Oxford, 1998– <http://www-etcsl.orient.ox.ac.uk/>.

invading armies from Elam in southwest Iran, who sacked Ur.

Babylonian Kingship. At the beginning of the second millennium B.C.E., following the collapse of the Third Dynasty of Ur, a Semitic civilization emerged, predominantly ruled over by Amorites. From north to south, Mesopotamia became a land of tribal leaders and city-states governed by city rulers. Except as it is preserved in personal names, the language of the new rulers, Amorite, was not recorded on any permanent medium. Sumerian as a spoken language appears to have died out, but it remained a language of learning in the schools. Some cuneiform inscriptions were still written in Sumerian, but more and more began to be written in a southern dialect of Akkadian, which modern scholars call Old Babylonian. The bureaucratic, centrally organized economy of the Ur III state with its large temple estates also did not survive. The kings of the competing dynasties of Isin (circa 2017 – circa 1794 B.C.E.) and Larsa (circa 2025 – circa 1763 B.C.E.) did, however, continue the Ur III tradition of divine kingship, until they were overthrown by Hammurabi of Babylon (circa 1792 – circa 1750 B.C.E.). The Babylonian king continued to govern with the assent of his gods, and the title "shepherd" was also used. A new concept originating in

Fragment of a basalt victory stele (height 22½ inches) naming Akkadian king Naram-Sin, from Pir Hussein in Anatolia (Eski Şark Museum, Istanbul)

kings' largess. Ur-Namma and his successors rebuilt temples to the major Sumerian deities throughout the cities of Sumer and Akkad and thereby won the support of their priests. Although the rulers of the Third Dynasty of Ur conceived of themselves simply as pious rulers, beginning with Shulgi, they too—like the previous Akkadian kings Naram-Sin and Shar-kali-sharri (circa 2217 – circa 2193 B.C.E.)—were deified during their own lifetimes. The kingdom collapsed during the reign of Ibbi-Sin (circa 2028 – circa 2004 B.C.E.), who faced disloyal subordinates, the infiltration of seminomadic Amorites from Syria, and

Cylinder seal (hematite, height 1 1/8 inches) and modern impression showing a goddess leading the seal owner, Ilum-bani, before the young deified king Ibbi-Sin (circa 2028 – circa 2004 B.C.E.), who is seated and wearing a flounced garment befitting his divine status (The Metropolitan Museum of Art, New York, Gift of Martin and Sarah Cherkasky, 1988)

this period was the idea of kingship based on descent from a deceased common ancestor.

Assyrian Kingship. For most of the period from circa 1300 until the late seventh century B.C.E., Assyria was the dominant military power in the ancient Near East. The king appears to have been chosen from among an elite group of the military aristocracy. He ruled as the regent of the god Ashur, but he was subject to assassination if the elite thought he had neglected his duties or undertaken actions that did not serve the well-being of the state. In Assyria the king—like his Babylonian, Hittite, and Egyptian contemporaries—adopted the title "Great King" and ruled over a territorial state called the "Land of Ashur." The land was divided into provinces and ruled by governors drawn from among the elite families at Ashur, the capital city. The vast empire was bonded together through the governors' religious obligations to supply offerings to the central temple in the city of Ashur.

The King of Justice. Both Assyrian and Babylonian kings were held responsible for upholding justice in their lands. The king was expected to protect his people from foreign and domestic harm. Royal documents frequently boast of the king's military accomplishments. An Assyrian text called *Advice to a Prince* indicates that the king was responsible for his acts and was subject to divine punishment if he failed to heed justice and uphold the divine standards expected by the gods:

If the king has no regard for due process, his people will be thrown into chaos, and his land will be devastated. If he has no regard for the due process of his land, Ea, king of destinies, will alter his destiny and misfortune will hound him. (Foster)

Bronze dedicatory statuette from Larsa, with gold foil on hands and face (height 5¾ inches), king Hammurabi (circa 1792 – circa 1750 B.C.E.) kneeling in adoration, probably before a deity (Louvre, Paris)

Divine Blessing for Just Rule. If the Assyrian king followed the desires of his god and upheld justice, he would be praised and the gods would provide bounty. A letter written to an Assyrian king indicates that prosperity and good times were the result of the king's good judgment and caring rule:

> Good health to the king, my lord! May the gods Nabu and Marduk very much bless the king, my lord. . . . The reign is good, (its) days are righteous (and) the years (are ones of) justice; there are copious rains, abundant floods, (and) a fine rate of exchange; the gods are appeased; there is much reverence to god (and) the temple abound in riches; the great gods of heaven and earth have become revered again in the time of the king, my lord. The old men dance, the young men sing, the women and girls are happy and joyful; women are married, adorned with earrings; boys and girls are brought forth, the births thrive. The king, my lord, has revived the one who was guilty (and) condemned to death; you have released the one who was imprisoned for many years. Those who were sick for many days have got well, the hungry have been sated, the parched have been anointed with oil, the needy have been covered with garments. (Parpola)

Sources:

André Finet, "Typologie des lettres des archive «royales» de Mari," in *Cuneiform Archives and Libraries. Papers read at the 30ᵉ Rencontre Assyriologique Internationale. Leiden, 4–8 July 1983*, edited by Klaus R. Veenhof (Istanbul, Turkey: Nederlands Historisch-Archaeologisch Instituut te Istanbul, 1986), pp. 153–159.

Benjamin R. Foster, *Before the Muses: An Anthology of Akkadian Literature*, 2 volumes (Bethesda, Md.: CDL Press, 1993).

W. G. Lambert, "Kingship in Ancient Mesopotamia," in *King and Messiah in Israel and the Ancient Near East, Proceedings of The Oxford Old Testament Seminar*, edited by John Day, Journal for the Study of the Old Testament Series 270 (Sheffield, U.K.: Sheffield Academic Press, 1998), pp. 54–69.

William L. Moran, ed. and trans., *The Amarna Letters* (Baltimore: Johns Hopkins University Press, 1992).

A. Leo Oppenheim, *Ancient Mesopotamia: Portrait of a Dead Civilization*, revised edition, completed by Erica Reiner (Chicago: University of Chicago Press, 1977).

Simo Parpola, ed., *Letters from Assyrian and Babylonian Scholars*, State Archives of Assyria, volume 10 (Helsinki: Helsinki University Press, 1993).

J. Nicholas Postgate, *The First Empires* (Oxford: Elsevier-Phaidon, 1977).

Postgate, "Royal Ideology and State Administration in Sumer and Akkad," in *Civilizations of the Ancient Near East*, 4 volumes, edited by Jack M. Sasson (New York: Scribners, 1995), I: 395–411.

THE LEGAL SYSTEM

Lawsuit Procedures. In modern legal systems, criminal law is separated from civil law, and two state actions may be taken against the offender. That is, a suspect may be convicted in criminal court and sentenced to a jail term, and then, in a civil court, the injured party can sue for monetary damages. In Mesopotamian law almost all crimes were considered private wrongs against property interests. Legal action against the offender was thus the responsibility of the injured party or his next of kin. If the claim could not be settled privately, the injured party brought the case to court and argued it personally. (There were no lawyers.)

Public Responsibility. Although crime in Mesopotamia was not considered an action against the interests of the state, local authorities were nevertheless responsible for the welfare of citizens. The Laws of Hammurabi (circa 1792 – circa 1750 B.C.E.), for example, held that a governor was responsible for the breach in the public order when the authorities did not apprehend a thief. In such instances the city and governor were required to compensate the victim:

> If a man is caught in the act of robbery, that man shall be put to death. If the robber has not been caught, the robbed person shall set forth the particulars regarding his lost property in the presence of a god, and the city and governor, in whose jurisdiction the robbery was committed, shall make good to him his lost property. If a life (was lost during the robbery), the city and governor shall pay one mina (sixty shekels) of silver to the family (of the deceased). (LH §§22–24)

The Legal System. If a dispute between two Babylonians could not be privately adjudicated, it was referred to one or more levels of judicial authority. On the lowest level, a case could be heard by a local council, then by judges or by a court, and on the highest level a case could be appealed to the king. No appeals to the king are known to have occurred in Assyrian society.

The Courts. Cases were heard by local courts of city elders, councils, or city and residential assemblies. In the Old Assyrian period (circa 2000 – circa 1780 B.C.E.) commercial affairs were regulated by the merchants of the city. Provincial civil and military officials also on occasion functioned as judges. Priests had their own collegium courts, which usually oversaw oaths or ordeals for evidentiary purposes. All courts, except for the royal court and the assemblies, were composed of judicial panels of three to six men.

Local Courts. Local courts dealt with most cases of civil and criminal concern. Litigation regarding theft and property—such as conflicts over sale, inheritance, and location of land boundaries—were common. Actions brought by merchants are well documented in testimony heard before the "harbor authorities" during the Old Assyrian period. The king, governor, and mayor also heard a large variety of cases. The king acted as the highest court of appeal, especially in cases of official misconduct. Capital cases, including murder trials, were referred to the king for assignment of venue. Royal judges and officials heard serious cases involving homicide, treason, and adultery. In the Neo-Babylonian and later Persian periods (seventh–fourth centuries B.C.E.) kings appointed royal officials to oversee temple activities. Temple officials in turn served on town assemblies and acted as local judges.

THE KING AS JUDGE

In addition to his administrative, religious, and military roles, the king also rendered verdicts in disputes. One difficult case, Three Ox-Drivers from Adab, recorded in Sumerian on a tablet dating to the beginning of the second millennium B.C.E., concerns the dilemma of three friends faced with a lack of water:

There were three friends, citizens of Adab, who fell into a dispute with each other, and sought justice. They deliberated the matter with many words, and went before the king.

"Our king! We are ox-drivers. The ox belongs to one man, the cow belongs to one man, and the wagon belongs to one man. We became thirsty and had no water. We said to the owner of the ox, 'If you were to fetch some water, then we could drink!' And he said, 'What if my ox is devoured by a lion? I will not leave my ox!' We said to the owner of the cow, 'If you were to fetch some water, then we could drink!' And he said, 'What if my cow went off into the desert? I will not leave my cow!' We said to the owner of the wagon, 'If you were to fetch some water, then we could drink!' And he said, 'What if the load were removed from my wagon? I will not leave my wagon!' 'Come on, let's all go! Come on, and let's return together!'"

"First the ox, although tied with a leash(?), mounted the cow, and then she dropped her young, and the calf started to chew up(?) the wagon's load. Who does this calf belong to? Who can take the calf?"

The king did not give them an answer, but went to seek advice from a cloistered lady. Her response is not fully preserved.

When the king came out from the cloistered lady's presence, each(?) man's heart was dissatisfied. The man who hated his wife left his wife. The man . . . his . . . abandoned his . . . . With elaborate words, with elaborate words, the case of the citizens of Adab was settled.

Source: Jeremy Black, Graham Cunningham, Jarle Ebeling, Esther Flückiger-Hawker, Eleanor Robson, Jon Taylor, and Gábor Zólyomi, *The Electronic Text Corpus of Sumerian Literature*, The Oriental Institute, University of Oxford, 1998– <http://www-etcsl.orient.ox.ac.uk/>.

Judges. Judges were leading members of the community. They might be professionals or citizens chosen because of their familiarity with the case at hand. Judges were responsible for investigating cases, summoning witnesses, determining guilt, and, where relevant, assessing liability and establishing the degree of compensation. Decisions were probably not made in accord with any single written body of law; rather they were likely based on the discretion of the judges in accord with oral precedent. As leading citizens, their judgment was most likely respected and accepted. Judicial behavior was regulated by law;

acceptance of a bribe or failure to properly carry out duties were considered serious offenses that could lead to removal from office or imposition of a stiff fine.

Courtroom Procedures. Little is known about courtroom procedures. Trials were open affairs held in public spaces. The plaintiff's case was heard first. Both parties presented documentary evidence, and—when available—witnesses were called on to confirm testimony or establish fact. Before testifying, witnesses were required to take an oath. Oath taking was a serious affair. Oaths could be sworn on or before a symbol of a god. The individual taking an oath was often required to touch a divine object—such as the dagger of the god Ashur, the dog of the god Gula, the weapon of the god Marduk, the spear symbol of the goddess Ishtar, the divine hand of the mother goddess Dingirmah, or the pruning saw of the sun god Shamash—and swear by the "life of the god (or goddess)." The symbol was an actual object housed in the temple of the god and rented to the court as a source of income for the temple authorities. The god's symbol was brought to the court for the oath-taking ceremony. Oaths could also be sworn by "the life of the king." Perjured testimony was regarded as a sin, and a false declaration taken in the name of a god or goddess was rife with the possibility of divine or human wrath. Human sanctions could include smearing the offender's head with hot bitumen or cutting off his tongue and hand. False testimony given under oath in a case involving life was considered a capital offense. Divine vengeance could be even worse. The sacred and the profane were thus intertwined as part of court procedure.

The River Ordeal. In serious cases involving charges of homicide, treason, sorcery, adultery, or theft of temple property, where there existed disputed testimony or where the court had no grounds for determining truth, the case was remanded to the river god for discovery. The god acted as a divine judge and determined guilt or innocence. According to a Sumerian hymn to the god Nungal, the river ordeal left the just ones alive and chose the evil ones by drowning them. Literary texts state that in practice not everyone was allowed to die. If the accused began to drown, a mooring pole was extended, and the guilty party was dragged out of the river and placed in custody in a dungeon-like room. The Laws of Hammurabi include the following provisions:

If the finger was pointed at the wife of a man because of another man, but she has not been caught while lying with the other man, she shall throw herself into the river for the sake of her husband. (LH §132)

If a man brought a charge of sorcery against (another) man, but has not proved it, the one against whom the charge of sorcery was brought, upon going to the river, shall throw himself into the river, and if the river has then overpowered him, his accuser shall take over his estate; if the river has shown that man to be innocent and he has accordingly come forth safe, the one who brought the charge of sorcery

Helmet of Meskalamdug, king of Ur, made of sheet gold with relief decoration and shaped like an elaborately braided royal hairdo (height 8 5/8 inches), from the Royal Tombs of Ur, circa 2600 B.C.E. (Iraq Museum, Baghdad)

against him shall be put to death, while the one who threw himself into the river shall take over the estate of his accuser. (LH §2)

The King of Justice, a Neo-Babylonian text from the sixth century B.C.E., includes a detailed description of the river ordeal:

A man charged a man with murder but did not prove it. They were brought before him (the king) and he ordered them (to be taken) above (the city of) Sippar, to the bank of the Euphrates, before Ea, king of the depths, for trial. The troops of the guard, keeping both under close surveillance all night, lit a fire. At daybreak, the prince, governor, and troops assembled as the king commanded, and took their places around them. Both went down (and) . . . the river. Ea, king of the depths, in order to [. . .] his royal beloved (and) in order to see justice [done, did] what always had . . . [The first] . . . he had to jump in, he (the river god) brought him safely t[o the bank]. The one who had charged him with murder sank in the water. From morning until noon no one saw him nor was aught heard of [him]. As for the troops of the guard, who had stood

around them at the riverbank from evening until day-bre[ak], their hearts sank and they set out to search [. . .], "What shall we report? How shall we answer the king?" When the king heard, he was furious at the troops. A courier was coming and going. "Did you not watch over the man? Has he gotten across the river and lain down in the open country?" Since none saw him at any time, they could not answer. Anxious boat(?) riders went along the river, bank to bank, checking the edge. When high noon came his corpse rose up from the river. He had been struck on the head, blood was running from the ears and nostrils. The top of his head was burned, as if with fire, his body was covered with sores. The people saw, and spoke (? of it) in reverence; all the world was borne down with awe. The enemy, the wicked one, and the hostile betook themselves into hiding. (Foster)

Witnesses. Eyewitnesses were essential for convicting a criminal. Hearsay or rumor did not qualify as evidence. The Middle Assyrian Laws (circa fourteenth – circa eleventh century B.C.E.) refer to a case of suspected adultery. Without the testimony of witnesses, the accused could not be convicted. The case was remanded to the god for a decision on the basis of the river ordeal: "If a free man has said to another free man: 'People have lain repeatedly with your wife,' since there were no witnesses, they shall make an agreement and go to the river (for the water ordeal)" (MAL A §17). Witnesses were also necessary to validate agreements. In marriage contracts, for example, the groom's father was listed as the first witness to guarantee the inheritance rights of his unborn grandchildren. His presence as a witness presumably also insured that there would be no mix-ups regarding the rights of his other sons' children who might dispute the allocation of their grandfather's money.

Imprisonment. Since Mesopotamian law did not distinguish between criminal and civil offenses, all crimes were actions that caused damage to private property, not offenses against the state. (Even treason was considered to be an offense against the royal family.) There were no state prisons or penitentiaries. Incarceration (usually under conditions of forced labor) existed only as a place of detention. Imprisonment for a capital offense was a grisly affair. According to the Sumerian *Hymn to Nungal*, a person incarcerated

> does not recognize his fellow men, they have become strangers. A man does not return the password of his fellow men, their looks are so changed. The interior of the House gives rise to weeping, laments, and cries. Its brick-walls crush the evil-ones but give birth to honest men. The angry hearts spend there the days in weeping and laments. . . . No one wears clean clothes in my dusty House. My House falls, like some drunkard, upon the man. He is listening for snakes and scorpions in the darkness of the House. (Black et al.)

Punishment. In Sumerian and Babylonian law written during the period circa 2100 – circa 1600 B.C.E., punishment for theft and homicide was stated in terms of a maximum sentence. In the codes, execution of the offender was primarily applied to injuries sustained by the *awilum* (property-owning) noble class in cases of homicide, theft of property, kidnapping, adultery, rape of a betrothed girl, fraud, purchase without witness, false accusation, and special circumstances including incest, death of a commoner's wife or daughter following unlawful distrainment, and breach of military orders.

Execution. Although the Laws of Hammurabi constantly refer to execution, there was no official state executioner. In fact, no word exists in Akkadian for executioner or for a person who mutilates another's body (as in "an eye for an eye"). It is now assumed that the injured party or the victim's legal representative or next of kin had the right to take proper and necessary action. In cases where the court needed to apply punishment the actual process remains unknown. In cases where the guilty party clearly intended to do harm, or where the possibility of death was great and where witnesses were present at the scene of the crime, the injured party possessed the right of immediate revenge. Private execution or imposition of sanctions was left to the wronged party.

Revenge. Causing the death of an offender was instant revenge, but this action precluded any monetary compensation. If the wronged party or next of kin wanted compensation from the manslayer, thief, or adulterer, they could seek a monetary settlement for any of these offenses either through private negotiations or through legal action. Though the ultimate penalty for crimes of intent, such as theft, against members of the landholding class was death, the available documentary evidence seems to indicate that in practice thievery was punished by payment of a monetary fine. In fact, the penalty for most capital offenses (except in cases of regicide or murder within a temple) was some sort of monetary payment. The amount of compensation demanded by the family of the manslayer's victim is not stated in extant texts; no guidelines were given. Common law and societal limits of acceptable behavior acted to quantify the judgment. In instances where the victim's kin could not reach agreement with the manslayer, they could use the threat of execution to force settlement.

Sources:
Jeremy Black, Graham Cunningham, Jarle Ebeling, Esther Flückiger-Hawker, Eleanor Robson, Jon Taylor, and Gábor Zólyomi, *The Electronic Text Corpus of Sumerian Literature,* The Oriental Institute, University of Oxford, 1998– <http://www-etcsl.orient.ox.ac.uk/>.

G. R. Driver and John L. Miles, *The Babylonian Laws,* 2 volumes (Oxford: Oxford University Press, 1952, 1955).

Benjamin R. Foster, *Before the Muses: An Anthology of Akkadian Literature,* 2 volumes (Bethesda, Md.: CDL PRess, 1993).

Tikva S. Frymer-Kensky, "The Judicial Ordeal in the Ancient Near East," dissertation, Yale University, 1977.

Remko Jas, *Neo-Assyrian Judicial Procedures,* State Archives of Assyria Studies, volume 5 (Helsinki: Neo-Assyrian Text Corpus Project, 1996).

J. N. Postgate, "Laws and the Law," in his *Early Mesopotamia: Society and Economy at the Dawn of History,* revised edition (London: Routledge, 1994), pp. 275–291.

WARFARE

City Walls. At the beginnings of urbanism in ancient Mesopotamia, city walls were constructed for defense from enemies and for the protection of livestock. Animals were driven inside the walls at night to provide safety from marauders and predators. Massive city walls signaled the might and wealth of the ruler. The *Epic of Gilgamesh* ends with praise for the city walls, whose foundations were made of kiln-fired brick. Siege warfare was a frequently employed military strategy, and texts mention battering rams. Kings boasted that victory was achieved after a city was taken and its walls destroyed. According to an Old Babylonian text that contains excerpts from older inscriptions:

> Sargon, king of Agade, was victorious over Ur in battle, conquered the city and destroyed its wall. He conquered Eninmar, destroyed its walls, and conquered its district and Lagash as far as the sea. He washed his weapons in the sea.

Incised limestone inlays (height 4 1/8 – 5 1/2 inches), from the Royal Palace at Ebla, circa 2250 B.C.E.: (top left) soldier spearing an opponent through his jaw; (top right) soldier plunging a sword at an opponent on the ground; (bottom left) soldier carrying two severed heads and perhaps a folded battle net on a stick over his shoulder; (bottom right) soldier grasping the leg of an inverted nude opponent (Idlib Museum, Syria)

He was victorious over Umma in battle, [conquered the city, and destroyed its walls]. (Frayne)

At the end of the third millennium B.C.E. the inhabitants of the city of Ur were besieged by invading Amorites. A great wall was built to keep them away from major population centers. Nonetheless, the country eventually fell to the invaders. It is not known if the wall was dismantled at that time.

Conflict between Lagash and Umma. During the Early Dynastic period (circa 2900 – circa 2340 B.C.E.) populations increased and city-state leaders competed for control of arable lands. Between cities lay steppes, arid, treeless tracts used for hunting and herding. Modern scholars have speculated that the climate in the region may have become drier during this period, leading to even more competition for natural resources. City leaders became increasingly more militaristic and possibly more secular. Two of the leading southern city-states, Lagash and Umma, became embroiled in a border conflict. The war was described in ideological terms as a dispute between the patron deities of each city. From the point of view of the Lagash authors of a text describing the conflict, the chief god, Enlil, had drawn the borders between the two cities, but the rulers of Umma, upstream from Lagash, had "ripped out the stele (that marked the borders) and marched unto the plain of Lagash." According to this text, after the boundaries had been re-established, the men of Umma again illegally occupied land. The text continues:

> If the man of Umma, in order to carry off the fields crosses the boundary channel of Ningirsu (patron deity of Lagash) and the boundary channel of Nanshe (a Lagash goddess), be he a man from Umma or a foreigner, may Enlil destroy him, may Ningirsu after casting his great battle-net, place his hands and feet upon him. May the people of his own city, after rising up against him, kill him in the midst of his city! (Van de Mieroop)

A battle scene depicting heavily armed Lagash troops preparing for battle against Umma is preserved on a monument known as the Stele of the Vultures. The war dragged on for one hundred fifty years apparently without a clear resolution.

Weapons. Third millennium B.C.E. stelae celebrating victory in war depict the king armed with bow and arrow. One monument, the Stele of the Vultures, shows three sorts of heavily armed warriors: soldiers wearing thick leather helmets and holding axes over their shoulders, another contingent carrying adzes, and a third forming a phalanx, with each man holding a large rectangular leather shield embossed with metal studs. The soldiers carry copper-tipped spears in their hands. A shell plaque from Mari on the middle Euphrates depicts a man carrying a spear and holding a large wicker shield. The shield, which curves above his head, provides head-to-toe protection. Beginning at the end of the second millennium B.C.E., metal weapons

Incised limestone inlay (height 5 5/8 inches), from the Royal Palace at Mari, circa 2600 – circa 2300 B.C.E., depicting two soldiers, one with a spear and shield (perhaps made of bundled reeds), the other firing a bow and arrow. At top is the falling body of a naked enemy (Museum of Deir ez-Zor, Syria).

whose blades were sharpened on both sides were used for cutting and slashing. Swords were not employed during the third millennium B.C.E.; smelted iron was not available, and iron was needed to produce a weapon with a sharpened edge. Daggers made of copper or bronze were used instead. Slings, throwing sticks, nets, maces, and clubs were also employed in warfare during the third millennium B.C.E. A gold helmet was excavated from the grave of Meskalam-dug, who was king of Ur during the Early Dynastic IIIA period (circa 2600 – circa 2500 B.C.E.). It was probably produced for a ceremonial purpose. Gold daggers have also been found in the royal graves.

Chariots. Wheeled vehicles that might loosely be termed chariots were used in war and in ceremonies. One side of the so-called Standard of Ur, a wood box with inlaid panels excavated from the mid-third millennium B.C.E. Royal Cemetery at Ur, shows four-wheeled battle wagons carrying a driver and either a spear-wielding warrior or a warrior with battle-ax in hand. A quiver for the spears is located in the front of the vehicle. The battle wagons are drawn by four onagers (Asian asses). (Horses did not appear in the region until the end of the third millennium B.C.E.) The vehicle must have been extremely heavy; its

Fragment of a limestone relief plaque (height 5 1/8 inches) from Ur, circa 2750 – circa 2600 B.C.E., depicting a two-wheeled straddle car drawn by a team of four onagers. In battle the driver, who is shown walking behind the cart and holding the reins, would have sat with his legs on either side of the saddle-like seat (University of Pennsylvania Museum of Archaeology and Anthropology).

Fragment of a gypsum wall relief from the North Palace of Ashurbanipal (668 – circa 627 B.C.E.) at Nineveh. In the upper two registers, large, horse-drawn Assyrian chariots each carry a driver, archer, and two shield bearers, and are led by a mounted archer. At the bottom, Elamite prisoners await their fate (Louvre, Paris).

wheels were made of solid timber, and rotated behind linchpins on solid axles fixed to the underside of the carriage. This kind of vehicle was relatively slow and unwieldy. It was most likely a status object used primarily for display rather than actual combat. A two-wheeled battle cart is depicted on a slightly earlier stone plaque from Ur. In the Sumerian myth *The Return of Ninurta to Nippur*, the god's shining chariot—with defeated enemies hung on the crosspiece of the yoke—is described as inspiring terrible awe. The true lightweight horse-drawn chariot did not appear until the middle of the second millennium B.C.E.

Troops. It is not known if Mesopotamian kings of the third millennium B.C.E. maintained professional armed forces. Prior to Roman times, war was a seasonal activity. In emergencies any adult able-bodied male was conscripted into the armed forces. King Sargon of Akkad (circa 2334 – circa 2279 B.C.E.) claimed that 5,400 soldiers ate bread before him. Shulgi of Ur (circa 2094 – circa 2047 B.C.E.), stated that a unit of his spearmen was formed from among the male citizens of Ur. Chariot riders—men who could afford the cost of animals, equipment, and carriage—were among the elite. The foot soldier was the mainstay of the armed forces. Military uniforms are not evident in the preserved pictorial remains, which do show, however, that units of different status and ethnic background wore different styles of dress.

Spoils of War. After their defeat, cities were plundered. The king reserved a portion of the booty for himself, while another portion was presented as gifts to the shrines of the gods. Victorious forces are known to have desecrated temples and stolen or destroyed cult statues and decorative items. The bodies of defeated foes are described in myths as being heaped in mounds after battle. Reliefs show the enemy, stripped of all clothing, lying dead on the battlefield. Others are bound with their elbows tied behind their backs. Prisoners of war could be held for ransom, employed in forced labor, or resettled. Male prisoners of war might be blinded and enslaved; some worked carrying buckets filled with water for irrigation of fields and gardens. Young women were assigned to work in weaving mills and temples. In the Neo-Babylonian period (625–539 B.C.E.)—when there was a great need for labor to construct canals, roads, temples, and palaces—most prisoners of war were settled on the land as palace workmen or were presented by the kings to the temples to be employed as temple workmen.

Old Babylonian Period Warfare. In the Old Babylonian period (circa 1894 – circa 1595 B.C.E.) the king granted state land to selected members of the elite, who in return served in the army. Others worked state-owned land to satisfy their obligation to provide royal service. The army was composed of many units, some formed from various ethnic groups. New innovations in chariot equipment—such as the development of the mouth bit—allowed for greater control but battle still meant the clash of two infantries. Letters mention contingents of three hundred men and armies of between ten thousand and sixty thousand. Most warfare consisted of raids on outposts or caravans. Old Babylonian legal codes indicate that soldiers who refused to go on military campaigns were to be put to death. If a soldier hired someone to take his place, he could also be killed. Captured prisoners of war could be ransomed by relatives.

Warfare in the Later Second Millennium B.C.E. (circa 1600 – circa 1000 B.C.E.). The most significant changes in the methods of warfare came about as the result of the introduction of the true chariot, a horse-drawn lightweight vehicle with two spoked wheels. The vehicle carried two men, the driver and an archer armed with a composite bow. Perhaps originally intended as a hunting vehicle, it quickly became adapted to warfare as a mobile firing platform. At the height of their popularity, chariots were in use from Greece in the west, to Egypt, across the Near East, to India.

The Neo-Assyrian Period (934 – 610 B.C.E.). In the first millennium B.C.E. iron succeeded bronze and other copper alloys as the major metal for weapons and armor. Reliefs and archaeological finds attest to changes in chariot design. In the late eighth century B.C.E. some Assyrian chariots had eight-spoked wheels and carried as many as four men, such as monarch, driver, bowman, and shield bearer. Some chariots carried leaders shooting with bow and arrow. Development of the bridle made it possible for cavalry to develop independent of chariotry. Since saddles and stirrups were not yet in use, a rider sat on a horse blanket and employed his weaponry. In one battle the Assyrian king Shalmaneser III (858–824 B.C.E.) faced an enemy who was said to have had twelve hundred chariots and an equal number of cavalrymen. In the middle of the seventh century the cavalry had become a major battle weapon, while chariots were mostly used in ceremonial contexts, such as royal hunts. The majority of soldiers were infantrymen. The army had units of various sizes; the basic unit was a company consisting of fifty men under the command of a captain called the "Head of the Fifty," or "The Head of the Company." Troops wore protective gear. The lower orders of men wore leather in battle; higher-ranking troops were clothed in armor with overlapping metal scales. Professional corps of soldiers wore pointed metal helmets. Foreign troops—often allied with the Assyrians by terms of treaty—wore their native dress. Although scholars caution that royal inscriptions are laudatory texts rather than objective records, inscriptions indicate that armed forces might have numbered into the hundreds of thousands. Annual campaigns led by the Neo-Assyrian kings or by their commanders were commonplace. They began in the spring, once the winter rains had ceased.

Fragment of a wall relief (height 71 5/8 inches) from the Southwest Palace at Nineveh, showing a portion of the victory of Ashurbanipal (668 – circa 627 B.C.E.) over the Elamites at the Battle of Til-Tuba. In the lower half the Assyrians drive the Elamites to the right toward the river Ulai. Above, Assyrians execute Elamite prisoners (British Museum, London).

Wall relief (height 42 7/8 inches), from the Center Palace at Nimrud, depicting Tiglath-pileser III's assault on a walled town in the mountains (perhaps in Anatolia). At right an officer fires his bow from behind a wicker shield, providing cover for the wheeled battering ram. On the left, spearmen scale a ladder onto the walls, from which dead defenders fall. Captives are beheaded at bottom or impaled at top right (British Museum, London).

Assyrian Royal Annals. Royal annals written in Akkadian at the court of the Assyrian kings are the most important historical source for reconstructing Assyrian conquests during the first part of the first millennium B.C.E. Beginning in the thirteenth century B.C.E. they provide accounts of annual military campaigns. A major problem in assessing their historical accuracy is that the annals magnify achievements and distort historical events in the king's favor. They are addressed to the gods and most likely to posterity, and they include royal boasts designed to show that the king was governing in rapport with the will of the gods. Considerations of fact and objectivity are secondary to emphasis on military success and royal achievement. The annals are filled with hyperbole and gross exaggerations of booty, tribute, and numbers of enemy fatalities; yet, they also include valuable and often vivid descriptions of ancient warfare. Ashurnasirpal II (883–859 B.C.E.) dramatically recounted a military advance into a mountainous region:

> The (enemy) troops were frightened (and) took to a rugged mountain. Since the mountain was exceptionally rugged I did not pursue them. The mountain was as jagged(?) as the blade of a dagger and therein no winged bird of the sky flew. Like the nest of the *udinu*-bird their fortress was situated within the mountain which none of the kings my fathers had penetrated. For three days the hero (the king) explored the mountain. His bold heart yearned for battle. He ascended on foot (and) overwhelmed the mountain. He smashed their nest (and) scattered their flock. I felled 200 of their fighting men with the sword (and) carried off a multitude of captives like a flock of sheep. With their blood I dyed the mountains red like wool, (and) the rest of them the ravines (and) torrents of the mountain swallowed. (Grayson)

King Sennacherib of Assyria (704–681 B.C.E.) described in vivid detail a battle with the Elamites in 691 B.C.E.:

> At the command of the god Ashur, the great Lord, I rushed upon the enemy like the approach of a hurricane. . . . I put them to rout and turned them back. I transfixed the troops of the enemy with javelins and arrows. . . . I cut their throats like sheep. . . . My prancing steeds, trained to harness, plunged into their welling blood as into a river, the wheels of my battle chariot were bespattered with blood and filth. I filled the plain with the corpses of their warriors like herbage. (Luckenbill)

In 646 B.C.E. Ashurbanipal (668 – circa 627 B.C.E.) sacked the Elamite city of Susa, describing its destruction in his annals:

> I tore out the raging wild bull-(figures), the attachments of the gates; the temple of Elam I destroyed so that they ceased to exist. I counted their gods and goddesses as powerless ghosts. Into their hidden groves into which no stranger goes, whose bounds he does not enter, my battle troops penetrated, beheld its hidden (place), burnt it with fire. The burial places of their early (and) later kings, who had not feared Ashur and Ishtar, my lords, (and) who had

made my royal predecessors tremble, I devastated, I destroyed (and) let them see the sun; their bones I removed to Assyria. I laid restlessness on their spirits. Food-offerings (to the dead) and water-libations I denied them. For the distance of one month (and) 25 days, I devastated the region of Elam. Salt and cress I sowed over them. (Streck)

Ashurbanipal brought the severed head of the Elamite king back to Assyria, where it was displayed in public: "I, Ashurbanipal, king of Assyria publicly set up the head of Teumman, king of Elam, opposite the towers of the city-center." Scenes depicting soldiers with the severed heads of the enemy were also carved on the walls of Assyrian palaces.

Siege Warfare. Under the Assyrians, siege warfare became highly developed. Faced with strong enemy garrisons and well-fortified walls, ramps, and ramparts, Assyrian engineers developed new innovative forms of attack. Special battering rams mounted on enclosed wheeled platforms—like primitive tanks—were used to batter walls. Archers ensconced in turrets on top of these machines shot at defenders atop walls. In turn the enemy tried to burn these machines by throwing lit torches at their wooden frames. They also attempted to loop chains around a battering ram and pull it from its machine. While the battering ram attacked from one direction, Assyrian warriors scaled ladders placed against walls. They also built earthen ramps to the tops of defensive ramparts so that a battering ram could be pushed up a ramp and used on the upper portion or top of a wall. Diggers burrowed under walls to weaken or collapse them. Fires were set at wooden gates while defenders shot arrows, threw spears, dropped rocks, and poured scalding liquids on the attacker below. If all else failed, the Assyrians prolonged the siege until the inhabitants capitulated or starved.

Prisoners of War. The Assyrian annals and palace reliefs also depict the Assyrian treatment of defeated foes. They describe in graphic terms how enemies were slaughtered en masse, hung on stakes, flayed, or blinded. Hands, heads, or lower lips were cut off for the purpose of counting the numbers of dead. From the eighth century B.C.E. onward the Assyrian kings practiced a policy of mass forced deportations. The deportees were made to gather up what baggage they could carry and travel on foot. They were resettled hundreds of miles from their native territories. Such cruelty had a decided psychological effect on surrounding peoples. On hearing of such acts of terror, many chose to surrender rather than offer resistance.

Sources:
Jerrold S. Cooper, *Reconstructing History from Ancient Inscriptions: The Lagash-Umma Border Conflict*, Sources from the Ancient Near East, volume 2, fasc. 1 (Malibu, Cal.: Undena, 1983).

Robert Drews, *The End of the Bronze Age: Changes in Warfare and the Catastrophe ca. 1200 B.C.* (Princeton: Princeton University Press, 1993).

Douglas Frayne, *Sargonic and Gutian Periods (2334–2113 B.C.)*, The Royal Inscriptions of Mesopotamia: Early Periods 3 (Toronto: University of Toronto Press, 1993).

Albert. K. Grayson, *Assyrian Royal Inscriptions*, 2 volumes (Wiesbaden: Harrassowitz, 1972, 1976).

Mary A. Littauer and J. H. Crouwel, *Wheeled Vehicles and Ridden Animals in the Ancient Near East* (Leiden: E. J. Brill, 1979).

Daniel D. Luckenbill, *The Annals of Sennacherib* (Chicago: University of Chicago Press, 1924).

Bustenay Oded, *Mass Deportations and Deportees in the Neo-Assyrian Empire* (Wiesbaden: Reichert, 1979).

J. N. Postgate, "War and Peace," in his *Early Mesopotamia: Society and Economy at the Dawn of History*, revised edition (London: Routledge, 1994), pp. 241–259.

Jack M. Sasson, *The Military Establishment at Mari*, Studia Pohl 3 (Rome: Pontifical Biblical Institute, 1969).

Maximilian Streck, *Assurbanipal und die letzten assyrischen köige bis zum untergang Niniveh's* (Leipzig: J. C. Hinrichs, 1916).

Marc Van de Mieroop, *A History of the Ancient Near East, ca. 3000–323 B.C.* (Malden, Mass.: Blackwell, 2004).

SIGNIFICANT PEOPLE

ASHURNASIRPAL II

883-859 B.C.E.
KING OF ASSYRIA

Empire Builder. Ashurnasirpal II, son of Tukulti-Ninurta II (890–884 B.C.E.), was the founder of a revitalized and expanded Neo-Assyrian Empire. He was renowned for his military might, conquests of foreign lands, hunting, and building activities—all aspects of the ideal Assyrian king. He was a master of military tactics, and his annual campaigns caused fear and destruction to those who opposed him. Conquered peoples were forced to pay tribute and contribute men to his corvée (forced labor service imposed on conquered peoples). His campaigns are documented in inscriptions and in monumental reliefs that decorated his palaces. By the end of the seventh century B.C.E., his successors dominated the entire ancient Near East, from Egypt to the land of Urartu in the north to the Persian Gulf in the south.

Ideology of Empire. During the tenth century B.C.E., one of the predecessors of Ashurnasirpal, Ashur-dan II (circa 934–912 B.C.E.), developed the ideology of Assyrian rule, claiming that his imperial conquests were but a resumption of control over territories that rightly belonged to the Assyrian realm. Thus, all opposition to Assyrian rule was characterized as revolt. Ashur-dan campaigned as far as the mountains to the north of Assyria and to the northwest into Anatolia, a source of crucial metals. In the west, his forces waged war against the Aramaeans, and in the east they fought for control of the Zagros foothills. They also made forays into Babylonia. Ashur-dan set a pattern that was followed by succeeding Assyrian kings. Conquered regions were incorporated into the realm; tribute was imposed; alliances were established; and new fortified centers were constructed.

Northern Campaigns. Ashurnasirpal continued his predecessor's practice of regular military campaigns, mounting at least fourteen major incursions during his twenty-five-year reign. He received huge amounts of tribute, both from defeated cities and as gifts of homage and friendship from those not wishing to oppose his might. The king's campaigns took him to the north into southeast Anatolia, where he pacified and plundered the opposition. One of the local rulers who had formed an alliance with Ashurnasirpal's father was assassinated in 879 B.C.E., and Ashurnasirpal avenged the murder. He made the local leaders pay tribute and took several princesses into his harem as well as their dowries. Assyrian colonists were settled in southeast Anatolia. In the city of Tushan, Ashurnasirpal erected a stone statue of himself and had it inscribed with a list of his northern conquests. As a result of his northern offensive, many of the small states in the regions of southeast Anatolia, Upper Mesopotamia, and northern Syria provided rich gifts and manpower to the Assyrian king for the duration of his reign.

Southern Campaigns. Ashurnasirpal encountered opposition from political centers to his south. Uprisings occurred in cities in the Babylonian region, submissive since the time of his predecessors. The first rebellion occurred in 883 B.C.E. The king put down the revolt and exacted heavy tribute, but he had to return to the area in the next year. A revolting city was captured; its walls were razed; and the city was plundered. Revolts continued to occur in the following years, and according to the annals, when the area was finally pacified, heavy tribute was imposed.

Western Campaigns. Ashurnasirpal campaigned to the west four times. When his troops reached the Euphrates they crossed the waters on rafts. Many cities submitted without a fight and offered lavish presents. When he reached the Mediterranean he ceremonially washed his weapons in the sea. He was regaled with exotic presents from the Phoenician cities, including monkeys and sea creatures as well as rare woods from equatorial Africa. The king cut down tall trees and transported them back to Assyria for use in constructing temples.

Building Activity. Much of the wealth Ashurnasirpal received from his campaigns was invested in building up the city of Kalhu (modern Nimrud), originally inhabited in the third millennium and enlarged by Shalmaneser I (circa 1273 – circa 1244 B.C.E.). Ashurnasirpal rebuilt the city, employing large numbers of laborers from the Assyrian corvée and deportees from conquered territories. Hundreds of acres in size, the city was surrounded by a mud-brick protective wall. For the new city Ashurnasirpal had a canal dug, a zoo created, and orchards planted with a wide variety of imported, native, and exotic trees and vines. Ashurnasirpal built an enormous palace as his primary residence, as well as a temple, other palaces, and a ziggurat dedicated to Ninurta, the city's patron deity. He also constructed or rebuilt new temples for many other gods of the realm. The city remained the capital of the empire until the end of the eighth century. To celebrate the rebuilding of his capital Ashurnasirpal threw an enormous banquet, inviting dignitaries from regions as far away as Iran, Anatolia, and Phoenicia. Inscribed on a royal stele, the record of the celebration describes with great relish the elaborate preparations for the event and the choice foods that were served. After a long list of dishes prepared for the banquet, the king presented a list of his honored guests.

The North-West Palace. Today, Ashurnasirpal's primary residence, the largest and most important palace built on the site of Kalhu, is called the North-West Palace. Rooms in the palace were found lined with large stone slabs bearing reliefs and inscriptions praising the exploits of the king. Originally painted in bright colors, the reliefs depict royal campaigns, hunts, and rituals. Huge, winged, human-headed bulls and lions symbolically protected the entrances to the palace and its doorways. In 1989 an archaeological expedition conducted by the Iraqi Department of Antiquities and Heritage uncovered within the palace the tombs of

three Assyrian queens who lived in the eighth century B.C.E. The spectacular finds in the tomb chamber include jewelry, vessels, and ornaments, many made of gold.

Sources:

Mogens Trolle Larsen, *The Conquest of Assyria: Excavations in an Antique Land, 1840–1860* (London & New York: Routledge, 1996).

Samuel M. Paley, *King of the World: Ashur-nasir-pal II of Assyria 883–859 B.C.* (New York: Brooklyn Museum, 1976).

DARIUS I

521-486 B.C.E.
KING OF PERSIA

The Persians. The Persians were a cattle-herding group who moved from Central Asia into Iran at the end of the second millennium B.C.E. and formed an independent political unit following the collapse of Elamite power in the mid-seventh century B.C.E. They spoke Old Persian, a member of the Indo-European language family. The founder of the Persian Empire was Cyrus II (the Great), who, after achieving dominance in Iran, conquered Babylon in 539 B.C.E. Darius I, a member of the Achaemenid royal family in Iran, came to power, under circumstances that remain unclear, following the death of Cyrus's son Cambyses II on his return from his successful conquest of Egypt. Darius's ascent to the throne was greeted by widespread rebellion, which he ruthlessly crushed.

Empire. With his own house in order, Darius began a series of conquests aimed at expanding his control. He conquered parts of northwest India and led his forces into the lands of the Scythians north of the Black Sea. Forays to the west brought him into contact with east Greek (Ionian) colonies in western Anatolia. Faced with continual revolt by Ionian cities (499–494 B.C.E.) and defeated on the plains of Marathon in Greece in 490 B.C.E., Persian forces temporarily retreated but retained control of the city-states in Macedonia, Thrace, and around the Bosporus Straits. Darius also retained power over Egypt. He reorganized his realm into twenty provinces, or satrapies. Each province was governed by a satrap who was responsible for the collection of taxes, military matters, and civil affairs. In some areas garrisons were under the control of commanders appointed by and responsible to the king. The satrap was usually a wealthy aristocrat who may have been a close relative of the king, and he modeled his administration on that of the "Great King." Monumental royal inscriptions were typically trilingual, written in Old Persian, Elamite, and

Akkadian. The administrative language of the empire was Aramaic, which was widely used throughout the realm.

Persepolis. Darius commissioned the building of a new dynastic capital at Persepolis in the province of Fars, the homeland of the Achaemenids. The reliefs on the stairway of his Apadana, or audience hall, depict the king, his court, and delegates of his empire bringing him gifts. The reliefs represent the Achaemenid ideal of a harmonious, culturally diverse kingdom of peoples ruled by a benevolent king who cares for the welfare of his people. Darius also built palaces in the ancient city of Susa and at Babylon. Persepolis was burned by Alexander III (the Great) of Macedon in 331 B.C.E.

Sources:

Pierre Briant, *From Cyrus to Alexander: A History of the Persian Empire,* translated by Peter T. Daniels (Winona Lake, Ind.: Eisenbrauns, 2002).

Ilya Gershevitch, ed., *The Median and Achaemenian Periods,* volume 2 of *The Cambridge History of Iran* (Cambridge: Cambridge University Press, 1985).

A. T. Olmstead, *History of the Persian Empire* (Chicago: University of Chicago Press, 1948).

NEBUCHADNEZZAR II

604-562 B.C.E.
KING OF BABYLON

Accession of the King. Following the destruction of Assyrian military power at the end of the seventh century, a new Babylonian dynasty inherited the mantle of the Assyrian empire. The founder of the Neo-Babylonian dynasty (often called the "Chaldean" dynasty) was Nabopolassar (625–605 B.C.E.). He was succeeded on the throne by his son Nebuchadnezzar II, who reigned for forty-three years. Nebuchadnezzar continued his father's claims to the lands of northern Syria by campaigning in the region eight times. Once Assyrian control over this area had disappeared, Syria and the Levant were hotly contested. Small states such as Judah and city-states such as the Mediterranean port of Tyre were caught between the military ambitions of the Babylonians and the Egyptians. In 605 B.C.E., while still crown prince, Nebuchadnezzar routed the Egyptian forces in a battle for control of the Syrian garrison at Carchemish. Four years later, his army reached the Egyptian frontier.

Attacks on Judah. Nebuchadnezzar's control over Syria and the Levant was continually threatened by rebellions of small states and by their alliances with Egypt. In 597 B.C.E. he marched against Jerusalem and "carried off from there all the treasures of the House of the Lord and the treasures of the royal palace; (and) he stripped off all the golden decorations in the Temple of

the Lord" (II Kings 24:13). King Jehoiachin, his wives, the nobility, commanders of the army, and all the troops, together with craftsmen and smiths (II Kings 24:14–15), were deported to Babylon. Only the poor were left in the city. After the puppet ruler, Zedekiah, Jehoiachin's uncle, rebelled, Nebuchadnezzar moved against Jerusalem in 588 B.C.E. In 586 B.C.E. Jerusalem fell; the city was burned, its walls torn down, and the Temple looted. The last remnants of the population were deported, leaving only the poorest on the land to tend the fields and vineyards.

Domestic Rebellion. Nebuchadnezzar's own records present a picture of domestic peace and tranquility. But hints of rebellion emerge from private records. A legal record written in 594 B.C.E. reveals that a member of the elite broke a solemn loyalty oath to his king and may have planned, or been a part of, a revolt. The traitor, Baba-aha-iddina, was convicted of treason by the assembly and sentenced to death. A portion of his property was confiscated and donated to the temple of the god Nabu.

Law. Although school copies of the Laws of Hammurabi continued to be made during the first millennium B.C.E., no new law codes from the period are preserved. Nebuchadnezzar referred to himself as a "King of Justice," but only a small collection of laws dealing with aspects of family law and property is attributed to his reign. The beginning and end of this legal collection are missing.

Babylon. Nebuchadnezzar's inscriptions stress his pride in the rebuilding of Babylon, which became his most renowned achievement. The city was one of the largest in the ancient Near East, covering an area of more than three square miles. To the fifth century B.C.E. historian Herodotus of Halicarnassus, the city surpassed in splendor any city in the known world. It was surrounded by huge double walls with many finely decorated gates. The Euphrates River ran north to south through the city, dividing it into two parts. A stone bridge in the middle of town allowed passage between the eastern and western districts. The city was filled with impressive temples, shrines, paved streets, and palaces.

Ziggurat. Dominating Babylon at its center near the river was the massive ziggurat E-temenanki ("House of the link between Heaven and Underworld"). Begun in the second millennium B.C.E., the structure had been repaired several times by his predecessors. Nebuchadnezzar raised the height of the terrace, enlarged the outer wall to the north, and provided for water drainage into a nearby canal. At the conclusion of his work, the temple tower stood seven stories in height. According to Herodotus, the uppermost part, the dwelling of the city's god, Marduk, was adorned with blue-glazed enameled bricks made to imitate the appearance of the heavens. Staircases led from ground level to the top of the tower. This building may have inspired the story about the biblical Tower of Babel.

Temples. Nebuchadnezzar continued his father's work of rebuilding, enlarging, and embellishing the temples of Babylon. He succeeded in making the city "a wonder" after its partial destruction by Assyrian armies in the seventh century B.C.E. Nebuchadnezzar claimed to have begun work on sixteen temples in the city of Babylon and many more in twelve other cities throughout his realm. In some temples he made shrines "shine like a bright day" by adorning their interiors with gold. Other temples were decorated with silver, gold, and precious stones. Processional streets leading to the temple were covered with glazed bricks. Weavers were commissioned to make rich garments of dyed wool for the statues of the gods.

The Ishtar Gate. At Babylon, a broad processional street led to the monumental Ishtar Gate, located in the north wall of the city. On its dedicatory inscription, the king wrote that the gates of his city were "made of (glazed) bricks with blue stone on which wonderful bulls and dragons were depicted. I covered their roofs by laying majestic cedars lengthwise over them. I hung doors of cedar adorned with bronze at all the gate openings. I placed wild bulls and ferocious dragons in the gateways and thus adorned them with luxurious splendor that people might gaze on them in wonder."

The Hanging Gardens of Babylon. According to classical writers, the Hanging Gardens of Babylon were one of the Seven Wonders of the Ancient World. The Greek geographer Strabo, writing in the first century B.C.E., said that these gardens were planted with many large trees. Another first century B.C.E. classical writer, Diodorus Siculus, maintained that the gardens were four hundred feet wide by four thousand feet long and more than eighty feet high. However, no such gardens are mentioned in any Babylonian inscriptions, and no clear archaeological remains of them have been found. The Assyrian king Ashurnasirpal II (883–859 B.C.E.) recorded that he planted gardens at Kalhu and filled them with trees imported from distant lands. Even more dramatic were the gardens built by Sennacherib (704–681 B.C.E.) at Nineveh. It is not impossible that in later antiquity the gardens in one great city of Mesopotamia became confused with massive building projects in another.

Sources:

Ronald H. Sack, *Images of Nebuchadnezzar: The Emergence of a Legend* (Selinsgrove, Pa.: Susquehanna University Press, 1992).

D. J. Wiseman, *Nebuchadrezzar and Babylon* (Oxford & New York: Published for the British Academy by Oxford University Press, 1985).

SARGON OF AKKAD

CIRCA 2334 – CIRCA 2279 B.C.E.
KING OF AKKAD

Origins. Sargon, the first ruler of the Akkadian Dynasty, was of humble origin. The *Sumerian King List* says his father was a gardener and does not include his personal name. Another source says his father was a certain La'ibum, a name that may be associated with a skin disease. Sargon's *Birth Legend*, of uncertain origin, indicates that he never knew his father. According to this folktale, his mother, an *entu* (high) priestess, found it necessary to hide her infant. She set the child in a reed basket sealed with bitumen to make it watertight. The basket was placed in a river and floated away. Akki, a drawer of water, rescued the child and reared him as his son, teaching him to be a gardener who raised dates. The goddess Ishtar/Inana took a liking to the boy and granted him her love.

The Cupbearer. According to a Sumerian tale, Sargon became the cupbearer to Ur-Zababa, king of the northern city of Kish. Ur-Zababa became frightened by his dreams. At that time Sargon also had a dream during which he groaned and gnawed the ground. Ur-Zababa heard about his cupbearer's distress and addressed him: "Cupbearer, was a dream revealed to you in the night?" Sargon answered his king: "There was a young woman, who was as high as the heavens and as broad as the earth. She was firmly set as the base of a wall. For me, she drowned you in a great river, a river of blood." Ur-Zababa ordered that Sargon be thrown into the chief smith's molten bronze vat. But Sargon's goddess, Inana, apprised him of the plot, and he apparently escaped, although the end of the story is fragmentary.

Rise to Kingship. Sargon's name (Akkadian Sharru-kin) means "the king is legitimate," suggesting that "Sargon" was not his birth name and that, in fact, he was a usurper. According to the *Sumerian King List*, Sargon built a new capital city at Agade and ruled there for the next fifty-five years. The site of Agade has yet to be discovered; some archaeologists speculate that it was located near modern-day Baghdad.

Conqueror. Sargon campaigned throughout the lands of Sumer and Akkad and beyond. In all, he claimed to have conquered to the west as far as the Mediterranean and to the northwest as far as central Anatolia to protect Akkadian trade routes. He penetrated northeast into Assyria, east into the lands of the Elamites, and south as far as Dilmun (modern Bahrain) in the Persian Gulf. In his later years revolts broke out, possibly under the leadership of Lugal-zagesi of Uruk. According to one legend Sargon crushed the revolts, attacked and laid waste the city of Uruk, destroyed its wall, defeated

Lugal-zagesi and his fifty governors (the rulers of smaller Sumerian city-states), and took Lugal-zagesi prisoner, bringing him in a neck stock to the gate of Enlil. Sargon appointed local rulers from regions as far away as Mari on the upper Euphrates to *ensis* (city-state rulers) in Elam, all of whom served him as the king of the land. He also installed members of his family to high positions, most notably his daughter Enheduana as high priestess of the moon god at Ur. Other posts were filled by men who owed their primary allegiance to the king rather than to tribal or city loyalties. Sargon thus forged the first real empire in the ancient Near East, but intrigue and assassination prevailed in his royal court. Sargon's sons were both murdered by their courtiers, and Shar-kali-sharri (circa 2217 – circa 2193 B.C.E.), his great-grandson, also met a violent end. Anarchy ensued at the end of the dynasty, and the *King List* asks, "Who was king; who was not king?"

Sources:

Brian Lewis, *The Sargon Legend: A Study of the Akkadian Text and the Tale of the Hero Who Was Exposed at Birth* (Cambridge, Mass.: American Schools of Oriental Research, 1980).

Mario Liverani, ed., *Akkad, the First World Empire: Structure, Ideology, Traditions* (Padua: Sargon, 1993).

UR-NAMMA

CIRCA 2112 – CIRCA 2095 B.C.E.
KING OF UR

Rise to Kingship. At the end of the twenty-second century B.C.E. in Sumer, the city of Uruk was ruled by king Utu-hengal. Utu-hengal had expelled the hated Guti from the land and ruled the city of Ur through his governor, Ur-Namma, who may have been the king's brother or son. At the death of Utu-hengal, who may have drowned while fishing, Ur-Namma ascended the throne and began a new dynasty that is today known as the Third Dynasty of Ur. Linking himself with the past glories of the city of Uruk, Ur-Namma claimed to be the elder brother of the legendary Gilgamesh, king of Uruk and a son of the goddess Ninsun ("the Lady of the Wild Cow"). According to the official ideology, the god Enlil assisted Ur-Namma and brought order to the "rebellious and hostile lands." Enlil also "made Sumer flourish in joy, in days filled with prosperity."

Builder of Temples. Ur-Namma embarked on a massive building program in honor of the city's patron deities, the moon god Nanna and his consort Ningal, who was regarded as the mother of the sun god Utu, the lord of justice. He raised a great mud-brick platform in Ur and placed upon it a large ziggurat, whose function is unknown. It was undoubtedly associated with religion, and its height, reaching in stages toward the heavens, may be connected with the homes of the gods. Ur-Namma also built ziggurats in religious centers at Eridu, Uruk, and Nippur. Ziggurats continued to be built at major Mesopotamian centers well into the Seleucid period (311–129 B.C.E.). Ur-Namma also built temples dedicated to the gods Enlil and Ninlil at Nippur, the holy city of the Sumerians. The construction of the E-kur, the foremost of these temples, with its brick terrace inlaid with gold and lapis lazuli, may have been initiated to win the political favor of the Nippur priesthood. Other temples were constructed throughout Sumer as well as in cities to the north in the land of Akkad. During the fourth year of his reign Ur-Namma was invested with the title King of Sumer and Akkad.

The Good Shepherd. Ur-Namma boasted that he was a good shepherd who cared for his people. He made the desert roads passable, reconstructed the quays for overseas commerce, rebuilt walls destroyed by the Guti, and made the land secure from outside invasion. Calling himself the "faithful farmer," he cultivated the fields with oxen and built irrigation works that allowed for greater crop production.

The Laws of Ur-Namma. Ur-Namma also described himself as a social reformer, one who upheld justice, prosecuted the thief and criminal, and cared for the poor. As far as is presently known, he was the first monarch to collect legal precedents from his realm and issue a collection of laws. Written in Sumerian, these laws were phrased in a conditional ("if-then") form that was later used in Babylonian, Assyrian, Hittite, and Hebrew legal collections. The laws of Ur-Namma were collected within a literary framework of prologue and epilogue (not preserved), a structure repeated in the later Sumerian laws of Lipit-Ishtar, in the code of Hammurabi, and in the Covenant Code of Israel (Exodus 21–23).

Death of Ur-Namma. Ur-Namma married a daughter to the *ensi* (ruler) of Anshan in Iran, a political maneuver meant to secure trade and treaty with an eastern neighbor. Despite his abilities as a diplomat and his desire to avoid war, Ur-Namma died from a wound in the field of battle. A description in a hymn of his burial rites and the beautifully wrought, precious-metal objects buried with him closely resembles discoveries made by Sir Leonard Woolley in the earlier royal tombs of the kings of the First Dynasty of Ur. The hymn describes how Ur-Namma was buried with his donkeys and chariots and how he had elaborate gifts to present to the gods in order to enter the desolate world of the dead.

Sources:

Jeremy Black, Graham Cunningham, Jarle Ebeling, Esther Flückiger-Hawker, Eleanor Robson, Jon Taylor, and Gábor Zólyomi, *The Electronic Text Corpus of Sumerian Literature*, The Oriental Institute, University of Oxford, 1998– <http://www-etcsl.orient.ox.ac.uk/>.

Piotr Steinkeller, "The Administrative and Economic Organization of the Ur III State: The Core and the Periphery," in *The Organization of Power: Aspects of Bureaucracy in the Ancient Near East*, edited by McGuire Gibson and Robert D. Biggs, second edition, corrected (Chicago: Oriental Institute of the University of Chicago, 1987), pp. 19–41.

DOCUMENTARY SOURCES

Hittite Laws (circa 1650 – circa 1200 B.C.E.)—Discovered in the Hittite capital city of Hatusha (modern Boghaz-köy) in the central Anatolian highlands, these laws are written in Hittite, an Indo-European language, on clay tablets using standard Middle Babylonian cuneiform signs. Originally composed during the Hittite Old Kingdom (circa 1650 – circa 1500 B.C.E.), the laws were revised several times and recopied in cuneiform over the next three centuries. In contrast to Mesopotamian law, the Hittite code lists both secular and cultic offenses (a practice that has more in common with biblical law). Many provisions set forth in the text are identified as revisions of an earlier version of the law. Stylistically, the laws are composed in accordance with Sumerian and Babylonian legal traditions, but they reflect the customs and values of a people living outside Mesopotamia.

Laws of Eshnunna (circa eighteenth century B.C.E.)—During the early second millennium B.C.E., the city of Esh-nunna was a major power center in the Diayala River valley until it was conquered by Hammurabi of Babylon (circa 1792 – circa 1750 B.C.E.). The ruler Dadusha of Eshnunna probably promulgated this first preserved collection of laws written in Akkadian, the language of many of the Semitic inhabitants of southern Mesopotamia. This text includes no epilogue and only a brief prologue. This compendium comprises fifty-nine extant sections that deal with hire or lease of property, burglary, theft, marriage, divorce, adoption, sexual offenses, loans and pledges, sale of property, and bodily injury. The text is known only from school exercise tablets. Some scholars have speculated that the document was composed for an unknown purpose differing from that of those collections of laws with a prologue and epilogue (such as the Laws of Ur-Namma, Lipit-Ishtar, and Hammurabi).

Laws of Hammurabi (circa 1750 B.C.E.)—The best-known and most-extensive body of ancient Near Eastern law was compiled during the later years of the reign of Hammurabi of Babylon (circa 1792 – circa 1750 B.C.E.).

The most complete copy is preserved on an imposing black diorite stele excavated at Susa in Iran, where it had been taken in antiquity, probably from Sippar; dozens of copies and extracts are also known. Written in Akkadian, this collection appears to have been based in part on legal precedents found in earlier law collections. The stele contains 282 laws as well as a lengthy prologue and epilogue. Provisions deal with legal procedures, property laws, marriage and family law, torts, and slaves. The prologue—which stresses the gods' choice of Hammurabi as ruler, his achievements as protector of his people, and his piety—appears to be a hymn of praise rather than an introduction to legal precedents. It extols the king, describing his success in protecting his people from external threat, his pledge to care for the weak and poor, and his building activities on behalf of the patron deities of the cities of his realm. The epilogue praises the king as a military leader and shepherd of his people who brings peace and justice to the land.

Laws of Lipit-Ishtar (circa 1934 – circa 1924 B.C.E.)—Lipit-Ishtar was the fifth ruler of the First Dynasty of Isin in southern Babylon. Written in Sumerian, this collection comprises a prologue, a body of laws, and an epilogue. Its legal provisions deal with agricultural offenses, fugitive slaves, false accusations, property obligations, marriage and inheritance, and injuries to hired draft animals. Only two fragments of the original stone stele have been found; the main body of the laws has been reconstructed from later school tablets.

Laws of Ur-Namma (circa 2112 – circa 2095 B.C.E.)—This earliest surviving law collection is ascribed to Ur-Namma, the first ruler of the Third Dynasty of the southern Mesopotamian city of Ur. This royal composition, written in Sumerian, comprises three sections: a prologue, a body of laws, and an epilogue. The collection includes more than thirty provisions, many imperfectly preserved. Its stipulations deal with sexual offenses, marriage and divorce, bodily injury, false testimony, and agriculture. While the original stone stele of the laws has not yet been discovered, many later copies written on clay tablets have been found, indicating that this collection was a canonical text, considered a "classic" worthy of copy and continued study.

Middle Assyrian Laws (circa fourteenth – circa eleventh century B.C.E.)—At the beginning of the twentieth century C.E. German archaeologists digging at ancient Ashur along the Tigris River discovered fourteen tablets in a gatehouse. Called today the Middle Assyrian Laws, this collection dates from the eleventh century B.C.E. but includes sections that were probably formulated as far back as the fifteenth or fourteenth century B.C.E. Some scholars believe that these laws were written as a legal handbook for judges. The Middle Assyrian Laws comprise more than 120 provisions with no prologue or epilogue. One text (Tablet A) contains laws regarding women with provisions that are much harsher than those in Babylonian law. Married women were required to wear head veils and were subject to physical abuse. A husband had the right to mutilate his wife and castrate or kill her lover if he so desired. Unlike Babylonian law, Middle Assyrian laws gave a woman no rights to inherit her husband's property. Other tablets deal with slaves, land and agriculture, sale, theft, boats, and accusations of blasphemy. Even though the Assyrians continued to dominate Mesopotamia militarily and economically until the end of the seventh century B.C.E., no Assyrian collection of laws from the first millennium is known. Appeals for justice were made to court officials, and no Assyrian courts of law are known to have existed.

Neo-Babylonian Laws (circa sixth century B.C.E.)—The latest preserved Mesopotamian collection of laws—known from only one school text, now in the British Museum—was probably written during the reign of king Nebuchadnezzar II (604–562 B.C.E.). The text deals with marriage, inheritance, and agricultural matters. The function of this legal collection is unknown.

The Sumerian King List (circa 1750 B.C.E.)—This work is known from many Old Babylonian school copies, no two of which are alike. The latest versions of the text purport to list in order Mesopotamian rulers and the length of their reigns from the time kingship first appeared before the flood through the fall of the First Dynasty of Isin (circa 1794 B.C.E.). The king list may have originally been composed by the kings of the Third Dynasty of Ur (circa 2112 – circa 2004 B.C.E.)—a version from the reign of Shulgi (circa 2094 – circa 2047 B.C.E.) is known—in support of the ideology that only one Mesopotamian city and its divinely legitimized king ruled at any one time.

CHAPTER SEVEN

LEISURE, RECREATION, AND DAILY LIFE

by KAREN NEMET-NEJAT

CONTENTS

Sidebars and tables are listed in italics.

IMPORTANT EVENTS OF 3300-331 B.C.E.

2600*-2500* **B.C.E.**

- The grave goods placed in the Royal Cemetery of Ur during this period are a rich store of Sumerian clothing, headgear, banquet scenes, jewelry, cosmetic containers, musical instruments, and gaming boards.

2254*-2218* **B.C.E.**

- On his victory stele king Naram-Sin is depicted wearing sandals.

1792*-1750* **B.C.E.**

- The legal code of king Hammurabi of Babylon includes penalties for builders of poorly constructed houses.

1750* **B.C.E.**

- Scribes record thirty-five recipes on three tablets, which in modern times become known as the "Yale Culinary Tablets."

1400*-1000* **B.C.E.**

- A series of perfume recipes is attributed to a woman.

934-610 **B.C.E.**

- During the Neo-Assyrian period kings build royal roads, straighten and widen various streets, and establish zoos, libraries, museums, and botanical gardens.
- Assyrian kings hunt lions, elephants, ostriches, bulls, and other large beasts.

883-859 **B.C.E.**

- During his reign Assyrian king Ashurnasirpal II builds a new palace and royal gardens in his capital at Kalhu (modern Nimrud) and stages a ten-day banquet to celebrate their completion.

750*-700* **B.C.E.**

- An elaborate funeral banquet is held for a Phrygian king.

704*-681* **B.C.E.**

- Assyrian king Sennacherib abandons his father's capital at Dur-Sharrukin to build his "Palace without Rival" at Nineveh, which he rebuilds and greatly enlarges.

649-547 **B.C.E.**

- Living for more than a century, Adad-guppi, the mother of Babylonian king Nabonidus, attributes her longevity to her piety and simple lifestyle.

* DENOTES CIRCA DATE

OVERVIEW

Location and Lifestyle. Between circa 3300 and 331 B.C.E. many ethno-linguistic groups lived both contemporaneously and successively across the length and breadth of Mesopotamia. Despite ethnic variations, however, factors such as geography, climate, and availability of natural resources—coupled with Mesopotamia's strongly conservative urban traditions—ensured that some aspects of daily life remained much the same over the entire period.

Housing. Because wood and stone suitable for building were scarce in Mesopotamia, while mud was readily available on the banks of rivers and canals, houses were usually constructed of sun-dried mud bricks. The extensive use of wood was reserved for the wealthy. In urban areas workshops and housing for the rich and the poor could be found together in the same neighborhood.

Food and Drink. Bread and beer made from barley were the staples of the Mesopotamian diet. Mesopotamians also used millet, emmer wheat, and rye to make bread, which was usually unleavened. They supplemented their steady diet of bread and beer with vegetables, dairy products, meat, poultry, eggs, and fish. Only the wealthy ate mutton, beef, and goat. Surviving texts describe elaborate royal banquets.

Furniture. Furniture designs differed according to time, location, and wealth of the owner. Since it was usually made from wood and other organic materials, most ancient Mesopotamian furniture has decomposed over time. A few examples have survived, but most of what modern scholars know about ancient Mesopotamians' tables, chairs, stools, and beds comes from artworks and ancient texts.

Clothing, Hairstyles, and Grooming Aids. Information about clothing styles comes from surviving art objects and lists of qualities of textiles. Clothing was usually made from flax and wool, and styles changed over time. Many Mesopotamians did not wear shoes, even in battle. There were some exceptions, however. For example, high-ranking Assyrians and Babylonians of the first millennium B.C.E. are depicted wearing sandals or slippers. Most Assyrian soldiers are shown without shoes, but

some wear calf-high boots. Footwear was made from cowhide and goat's leather. Hairstyles also changed over time. Sometimes most men seemed to shave their heads while others wore their hair long. Women usually had long hair. In some periods they typically wore their hair braided and on top of their heads; later the most common style seems to have been a large bun on the back of the head. Women also decorated their hair with bands, hair nets, and hairpins. Sometimes they wore wigs adorned with jewelry. Men, women, and children wore jewelry, both in life and death. Texts describe jewelry and jewelry workshops that created and repaired jewelry for people and gods. Toiletries and grooming aids have been found in homes of the wealthy. They include unguents for the body and hair, kohl (blue eye shadow), combs, tweezers, and mirrors.

Board Games and Toys. Board games, some of which are still played today, have been excavated at various sites. Often these games include dice and pieces to be moved on the board. Children's toys were frequently miniature versions of objects used by adults, including weapons such as slingshots, bows and arrows, and boomerangs or throw sticks, as well as small pieces of furniture that children used while playing "house" with their dolls or toy animals. Other toys included tops, rattles, jump ropes, and hoops.

Entertainment. Dancing was part of the entertainment at religious festivals, as was music, which was also performed at banquets and various public occasions. Musicians played string, wind, and percussion instruments. The Mesopotamians also had horns, but they were used for communication, especially in military settings, not for entertainment. On some public occasions literary works were performed. For example, *Enuma elish,* the Babylonian creation myth, was recited at the Babylonian New Year's festival.

Hunting and Other Sports. Mesopotamian kings often engaged in hunting. A successful hunt was thought to be proof that the gods favored the ruler, thus demonstrating the legitimacy of the king's reign. Assyrian kings staged elaborate hunts in which they killed lions and bulls. Not much is known about organized sports in ancient Mesopotamia. Balls have been found at various sites, but not the rules for the games played with them. Surviving artworks and texts provide evidence that the Mesopotamians also engaged in individual sports such as wrestling, boxing, and juggling.

Gardens. In ancient Mesopotamian cities, land was often enclosed and irrigated to create gardens or parks. Lavish palace gardens and parks were status symbols throughout the Near East. Temples had gardens in which to grow food offerings for the gods, and the homes of the upper classes included gardens in which vines, fruit trees, and vegetables might be grown.

TOPICS IN LEISURE, RECREATION, AND DAILY LIFE

BANQUETS

Occasions for Banquets. In ancient Mesopotamia rulers held banquets to celebrate military victories and successful hunts. During the first half of the third millennium B.C.E., banquets were held in connection with agrarian festivals, while, in the mid second millennium B.C.E., the Hittites in Anatolia celebrated a banquet in connection with their Sacred Marriage rite. In the first millennium B.C.E. the practice of holding a funeral banquet appears to have entered Mesopotamia from Egypt. Artworks usually depict banqueters sitting down, but on occasion they are shown standing. Beginning in the mid-seventh century B.C.E., reclining at a banquet became increasingly popular, spreading from Syria eastward into Mesopotamia and westward into Anatolia and the Greek world.

Early Banquets. A late fourth millennium B.C.E. seal impression on a door sealing from Choga Mish in southwest Persia shows a seated figure being offered a vessel by a standing figure. Behind him are a variety of other vessels and musicians playing a harp, a drum, and clappers. During the third millennium B.C.E., banquet scenes were often depicted on cylinder seals and impressions, votive plaques, inlays, and sculptures. Banquet guests drank beer through long tubes from large jars and wine, perhaps made from dates, from small cups. One of the mosaic panels on the Standard of Ur, excavated from the Royal Graves at Ur (circa 2600 – circa 2500 B.C.E.), depicts a banquet, which may have taken place after a battle depicted on another panel on the Standard. The banquet also seems to have religious overtones. The principal figure, perhaps the king, and six other seated men

Assyrian king Ashurbanipal (668 – circa 627 B.C.E.) reclining, and his wife (seated), celebrating his victory over the Elamites, whose king's head dangles from a tree at left; alabaster relief (height 22 inches), North Palace, Nineveh (British Museum, London)

A ROYAL FUNERARY BANQUET

Banquets were given for the dead as well as the living. Excavations near the ancient Phrygian city of Gordion in Anatolia—at an enormous, fifty-three-meter-high, three-hundred-meter-diameter burial tumulus, dating to the eighth century B.C.E.—uncovered a wooden burial chamber that was initially said to be the grave of king Mita (the rich and famous king Midas of Greek legend), although that attribution is now considered doubtful. The deceased, a man aged sixty to sixty-five, was laid out on a thick pile of dyed textiles in a massive four-poster bed surrounded by beautiful pieces of furniture, as well as cauldrons, ladles, jugs, bowls, and bronze and pottery vessels, some of which contained residues of food. Chemical analysis revealed that the menu for the funerary feast, which may have accommodated as many as one hundred guests, included a spicy stew of lentils and barbecued sheep or goat and a beverage made from a mixture of grape wine, barley beer, and honey mead. Leftovers and dirty dishes were placed in large cauldrons and left in the burial chamber.

Source: Patrick E. McGovern and others, "A funerary feast fit for King Midas," *Nature*, 402 (December 1999): 863–864.

holding drinking cups are attended by four men while a lyre player and singer provide entertainment.

A Ten-Day Feast. In an inscription on a stone block placed near his throne room, the Assyrian king Ashurnasirpal II (883–859 B.C.E.) commemorated a banquet celebrating the opening of his new palace and royal gardens in the capital city of Kalhu (modern Nimrud). At this ten-day feast, he hosted Ashur (the Assyrian national god) and the other gods of his country, together with 69,574 human guests, including 47,074 men and women from all over his kingdom; 5,000 delegates from Suhu, Khindana, Khattina, Hatti, Tyre, Sidon, Gurguma, Malida, Khubushka, Gilzana, Kuma, and Musasir; 16,000 inhabitants of Kalhu from all walks of life; and 1,500 palace officials. The menu included vast quantities of cattle, calves, sheep, lambs, stags, gazelles, ducks, geese, doves, fish, jerboa, eggs, bread, beer, wine, pickled and spiced vegetables and fruits, oil, salted seeds, pomegranates, grapes, pistachios, garlic, onions, honey, rendered butter, milk, cheese, dates, and olives. Ashurnasirpal concluded his inscription with the boast that he had provided his guests with the means to clean and anoint themselves, did them due honors, and sent them home healthy and happy.

A Private Celebration. One carving among the many reliefs that decorate the palaces of the Assyrian king Ashurbanipal (668 – circa 627 B.C.E.) at Nineveh shows the king celebrating after his victory over the Elamite king Teumman, whose capital was at Susa in southwest Iran. In the midst of a beautiful tree-lined garden, in the shade of a vine trained on an arbor overhead, Ashurbanipal reclines on a couch. This relief is the earliest depiction of such a posture in ancient Mesopotamian art. With a blanket thrown over his legs, he holds a flower in his left hand and lifts a cup with his right. Facing him, his queen, also holding a flower and drinking cup, sits stiffly in a high-back throne decorated with ivory inlays. Incense burners, fan bearers, and musicians flank the banqueters as birds sit or fly about in the trees. Dangling from a high branch in one tree is the severed head of Teumman.

Sources:
Dominique Collon, *Ancient Near Eastern Art* (London: British Museum Press for the Trustees of the British Museum, 1995).

Collon, "Banquets in the Art of the Ancient Near East," in *Banquets d'Orient*, Res Orientales, 4 (Bures-sur-Yvette, France: Groupe pour l'étude de la civilisation de Moyen-Orient / Louvain: Peeters, 1992), pp. 23–29.

Louis Francis Hartman and A. Leo Oppenheim, *On Beer and Brewing Techniques in Ancient Mesopotamia*, supplement to the *Journal of the American Oriental Society*, no. 10 (Baltimore: American Oriental Society, 1950).

Henri Limet, "The Cuisine of Ancient Sumer," *Biblical Archaeologist*, 50 (1987): 132–147.

A. Leo Oppenheim, "The Banquet of Ashurnasirpal II," in *Ancient Near Eastern Texts Relating to the Old Testament*, edited by James Bennett Pritchard, third edition with supplement (Princeton: Princeton University Press, 1969), pp. 558–560.

Jane M. Renfrew, "Vegetables in the Ancient Near East," in *Civilizations of the Ancient Near East*, 4 volumes, edited by Jack M. Sasson (New York: Scribners, 1995), I: 192–202.

BOARD GAMES AND TOYS

Games. At ancient sites in the Near East, archaeologists have excavated board games consisting of playing boards and various objects that were thrown or moved. At Ur the dice were tetrahedrons. Their faces were not marked, but each die had its vertices shaved flat, with two of the four corners decorated or inlaid in some way to make them stand out. When rolled, each die had a fifty-fifty chance of coming up "marked" or "unmarked." Later dice, probably of Indian origin, have been found at sites throughout Mesopotamia and have been dated to all periods. Made of bone, clay, stone, and even glass, they had the numbers one through six incised on them. Other thrown objects included knucklebones, throw sticks, and stones. Playing pieces came in various shapes, including circles, cones, and pyramids. Texts refer to them as dolls, birds, and dogs.

Twenty-Squares. Played by the rich and the poor, twenty-squares was a racing game for two people using seven black and seven white counters, which were moved according to the roll of the dice. Several twenty-squares boards owned by rich people were found in the Royal Cemetery of Ur (circa 2600 – circa 2500 B.C.E.). Among them was a board inlaid with a mosaic of shell, bone, lapis lazuli,

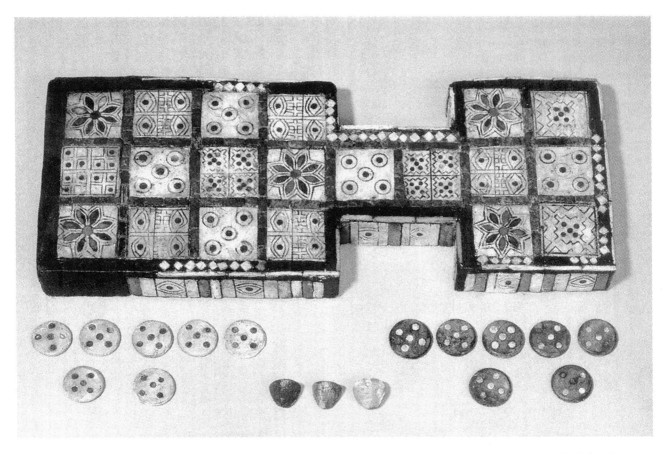

Restored game board with shell, limestone, and lapis-lazuli inlays (length 11 7/8 inches); fourteen shale, shell, and lapis-lazuli gaming pieces (diameter 7/8 inch each); and three tetrahedral dice; all from the Royal Cemetery of Ur, circa 2600 – circa 2500 B.C.E. (British Museum, London)

and red limestone. During the reign of the Assyrian king Sargon II (721–705 B.C.E.), guards of the palace at Khorsabad may have passed their time playing the game of twenty-squares on a game board scratched into the pedestal of one of the two bull colossi guarding the gates. Some board games bearing the imprimatur of the Assyrian king Esarhaddon (680–669 B.C.E.) have been found in his palace.

Senet. One of the most popular games found throughout the ancient Near East became known as *senet* in Egypt. Archaeological evidence of the game has been found at sites dating from prehistoric times through the Hellenistic period. In Egyptian the word *senet* means "to pass" or "to go by." The rules have not been discovered. Apparently, two players throwing dice each moved four differently shaped game pieces around the board, which typically had thirty squares, although the number varied.

Other Games. The rules for "Pack of Dogs" have survived. Two lots boards, one connected with the twelve signs of the zodiac, have the rules of the game on their reverse sides. Eighty-four sections were drawn on the ground, and pieces called the eagle, raven, rooster, swallow, and another unidentified bird were moved according to the roll of the dice. This game is still played by women in the Jewish community of Cochin in southern India, where the game is called Asha.

Toys. Some toys were miniatures of the weapons used by adults, such as slingshots, bows and arrows, and boomerangs or throw sticks. Other toys included spinning tops, rattles, jump ropes (sometimes called "the game of Ishtar"), pucks and mallets, and hoops. Like their modern counterparts, Mesopotamian children liked to play "house" or "grown-up," using dolls and toy animals as well as miniature furniture such as tables, beds, and stools. Model vehicles—including miniature carts, wagons, chariots, and ships—have also been found. It is not clear, however, whether all were toys for children or objects associated with cultic-magical rituals, such as gifts to the gods.

Sources:

Paul Collins, "Game board and fourteen gaming pieces," in *Art of the First Cities: The Third Millennium B.C. from the Mediterranean to the Indus*, edited by Joan Aruz with Ronald Wallenfels (New York: Metropolitan Museum of Art, 2003), p. 101.

Wolfgang Decker, *Sports and Games of Ancient Egypt*, translated by Allen Guttmann (New Haven & London: Yale University Press, 1992).

Irving J. Finkel, *Ancient Board Games* (London: Welcome Rain, 1998).

William W. Hallo, "Games in the Biblical World," in *Avraham Malamat Volume*, edited by Shmuel Ahituv and Baruch A. Levine, Eretz-Israel Archaeological, Historical and Geographical Studies, 24 (Jerusalem: Israel Exploration Society, 1993), pp. 83–88.

Anne D. Kilmer, "Games and Toys in Ancient Mesopotamia," in *Actes du XIIe Congrès International des Sciences Prehistoriques et Protohistoriques*, 4 volumes, edited by Juraj Pavúk, Union Internationale des Sciences Prehistoriques et Protohistoriques (Bratislava: Institut Archéologique de l'Académie Slovaque des Sciences, 1993), I: 359–364.

Karen Rhea Nemet-Nejat, *Daily Life in Ancient Mesopotamia*, Daily Life through History (Westport, Conn.: Greenwood Press, 1998).

Michael Roaf, *Cultural Atlas of Mesopotamia and the Ancient Near East* (New York: Facts on File, 1966).

CLOTHING

Materials. Mesopotamian sculptures, reliefs, and cylinder seals show that clothing was worn for modesty and protection against the elements, as well as to indicate status. In these surviving artworks men are shown more often than women and children, and members of the elite are depicted more often than workers. The first information about clothing comes from the end of the fourth and the beginning of the third millennia B.C.E. with the beginning of sculpture and writing. During this period some garments appear to have been made of dressed animal skins, including sheep, goat, and leopard. Sheep wool and goat hair were spun into yarns that were woven into cloth; linen was made from flax. Low-quality felt made from sheep or goat wool was used for shoes, linings, and cushions. By the middle of the third millennium B.C.E., the manufacture of textiles was a major industry in ancient Mesopotamia. By the early second millennium B.C.E. dyes were used; reversible fabrics were manufactured; and clothes were adorned with decorative needlework. In all periods textiles were traded and given as royal gifts.

Clothing in the Third and Second Millennia B.C.E. In Sumerian art of the third millennium B.C.E. votive figurines usually depict men wearing nothing but ankle-length skirts. The skirts may be tufted or smooth with a fringe along the bottom. Women—and, on occasion, men—wore a tufted garment that draped over the left shoulder and under the right armpit, leaving the right arm free. Sumerian soldiers are occasionally shown wearing a hooded cloak over a knee-length fringed skirt. During the Akkadian period (circa 2334 – circa 2183 B.C.E.) men wore robes draped over one shoulder or kilts of pleated and draped material with intricately knotted fringes at the hems and edges. Women continued to wear a wrapped garment that was draped over one shoulder. Men are sometimes shown with a garment draped over both shoulders to form a V-shaped neckline. Short-sleeved dresses, some with rounded necklines, were introduced. From the Ur III period (circa 2112 – circa 2004 B.C.E.) through the Old Babylonian period (circa 1894 – circa 1595 B.C.E.) clothing styles for men and women were basically the same. Men sometimes used the fringes of their garments instead of cylinder seals

DRESSING FOR THE NETHERWORLD

In the Sumerian-language myth of *Inana's Descent to the Netherworld*—known from many copies dating to the Old Babylonian period (circa 1894 – circa 1595 B.C.E.)—Inana, the goddess of love, decides for reasons not stated in the text to visit her sister Ereshkigal, the queen of the Netherworld. In preparation for her descent, Inana puts a crown and wig on her head, lapis-lazuli stones around her neck, ornaments on her breast, and a gold ring on her hand. She then wraps herself in a garment of ladyship, and lastly, applies kohl to her eyes. These, and other emblems of her rank, Inana has to yield in turn before she may proceed through each of the seven gates in the Netherworld. In a later Akkadian-language adaptation of this myth known as *The Descent of Ishtar into the Netherworld*—best known from copies found in the library of the Assyrian king Ashurbanipal (668 – circa 627 B.C.E.) at Nineveh—Ishtar, the goddess of love and war, similarly enters the Netherworld. The variations in the regalia discarded at the gates in this version seem to reveal a different fashion consciousness. Ishtar wears a great crown, ear pendants, necklaces, breast ornaments, a girdle of birthstones on her hips, clasps around her hands and feet, and a breechcloth around her body. There is no mention of the goddess's eye makeup.

Sources: Samuel Noah Kramer, "Inanna's Descent to the Nether World," in *Ancient Near Eastern Texts Relating to the Old Testament*, edited by James Bennett Pritchard, third edition with supplement (Princeton: Princeton University Press, 1969), pp. 52–57.
E. A. Speiser, "Descent of Ishtar to the Nether World," in *Ancient Near Eastern Texts Relating to the Old Testament*, edited by James Bennett Pritchard, third edition with supplement (Princeton: Princeton University Press, 1969), pp. 106–109.

to make seal impressions on contracts. After about 1400 B.C.E., Assyrian men and women wore fringed lengths of fabric wrapped around the body and held in place by a belt with long tassels that hung down between the wearer's legs. They also wore kilts on occasion, sometimes under robes. An Assyrian woman would not have gone out in public without a veil.

Clothing in the First Millennium B.C.E. Assyrian art objects and lexical texts listing words relating to clothing and various qualities of textiles provide evidence that by the first millennium B.C.E. fashions had changed. A man might wear one or more short-sleeved, fitted tunics, which were knee-length and belted at the waist. A person of high status, such as an official or military officer, also wore a wool or linen cloak in blue, red, purple, and white. In addition to the cloak, people sometimes wore an overgarment that had no armholes and was put on over the head.

Sumerian clothing: Lugal-dalu, king of Adab, in a wrapped tufted skirt (limestone, height 30¾ inches), circa 2600 – circa 2350
B.C.E.; and a woman wrapped in plain garment draped over her left shoulder (limestone, shell, and lapis lazuli,
height 9¾ inches), Nippur, circa 2600 – circa 2500 B.C.E. (left: Eski Şark Museum, Istanbul; right:
The Metropolitan Museum of Art, New York, Rogers Fund, 1962)

Nudity. Sculptures and cylinder seals from the late fourth millennium B.C.E. suggest that nudity, especially of the "priest-king," was associated with ritual activity. From the third millennium B.C.E. on, prisoners of war were often depicted as naked, a symbol of their humiliation. During their military campaigns, the Assyrians stripped conquered people of their clothing. One text describes how a conquered population was so impoverished that they were reduced to wearing clothing made of papyrus, the ancient equivalent of paper.

Footwear. In artworks from all periods most people are barefooted, even in battle. From the late fourth millennium through the fifth century B.C.E., people from the mountainous regions of Iran and Anatolia wore ankle-high boots with upturned toes. On his victory stele, king Naram-Sin of Akkad (circa 2254 – circa 2218 B.C.E.) is depicted wearing sandals. During the first millennium B.C.E. high-ranking Assyrians and Babylonians wore sandals or slippers. Although most Assyrian soldiers are depicted without shoes, some wear calf-high

Statue of Puzur-Ishtar II, governor-general of Mari, circa 2000 B.C.E., wearing a round cap with horns on the brim and a wrapped garment with long fringes (height 69 inches), found at Babylon (head: Vorderasiatisches Museum, Berlin; torso: Archaeological Museum, Istanbul)

Assyrian king Shalmaneser III (858–824 B.C.E.), right center, greeting king Marduk-zakir-shumi I of Babylon. The kings and their courtiers are wearing sandals and garments distinctive of their ranks (alabaster relief, height 9¾ inches), Fort Shalmaneser, Nimrud (Iraq Museum, Baghdad).

Delegations of dignitaries dressed in their national costumes: (top) from Bactria, leading a camel, and from Susa, with lions; (second row) from Babylon, leading a bull, and from Syria; (third row) from Syria, leading draft horses, and from Armenia, with a horse; and (bottom), from Iran, Persians (with tall crowns) and Medes; Apadana terrace facade, fifth century B.C.E., at Persepolis, Iran

Nude priest offering a vessel and cup for a libation before a standard with bulls' feet (shell, height 3 inches), Ur, circa 2600 – circa 2350 B.C.E.;
and nude prisoners of war in the custody of an Akkadian soldier, with a weapon on his shoulder (olivine-gabro, height 18¼ inches),
circa 2334 – circa 2279 B.C.E., excavated from Susa, where it was taken in the twelfth century B.C.E.
(left: British Museum, London; right: Louvre, Paris)

Two vessels in the shape of boots with upturned toes (baked
clay, height 4 3/8 inches), similar to examples excavated
from Kültepe, circa eighteenth century B.C.E.
(Vorderasiatisches Museum, Berlin)

boots, presumably made of leather. Artworks depict only
a few examples of women's footwear. Libbali-sharrat,
the queen of Ashurbanipal (668 – circa 627 B.C.E.), is
shown wearing slippers. Shoes were fashioned from
cowhide when it was available. Goat's leather may have
been used for the upper part of boots that covered the
lower leg. Sinews and tendons were used as laces and
thread.

Sources:
Carol Bier, "Textile Arts in Ancient Western Asia," in *Civilizations of the
   Ancient Near East*, 4 volumes, edited by Jack M. Sasson (New York:
   Scribners, 1995), III: 1567–1588.

Dominique Collon, "Clothing and Grooming in Ancient Western Asia,"
   in *Civilizations of the Ancient Near East*, I: 503–515.

Samuel Noah Kramer, *The Sumerians: Their History, Culture and Character*
   (Chicago & London: University of Chicago Press, 1963).

Karen Rhea Nemet-Nejat, *Daily Life in Ancient Mesopotamia*, Daily Life
   through History (Westport, Conn.: Greenwood Press, 1998).

Marten Stol, "Private Life in Ancient Mesopotamia," in *Civilizations of
   the Ancient Near East*, I: 485–501.

Young girl holding a mirror, between seated man and woman, basalt funerary stele, Maraş, circa 700 B.C.E.
(Archaeological Museum, Istanbul)

COSMETICS AND PERFUMES

Grooming Aids. In private homes and graves of the wealthy, archaeologists have found toiletries such as pots of unguents for the body and hair, as well as wood or ivory combs and tweezers and mirrors fashioned from copper, silver, and even gold. The reflective surface of the mirror was usually made from highly polished bronze.

Cosmetics. Archaeologists have also found shells containing kohl (blue eye shadow) in private homes and graves. In general, however, evidence relating to cosmetics is meager. It is known that women used them to enhance the appearance of their eyes and complexions. White, red, yellow, blue, green, and black pigments in cockle shells were found in graves at the Royal Cemetery at Ur (circa 2600 – circa 2500 B.C.E.). Some sources refer to cosmetics, but the texts are difficult to interpret. A second millennium B.C.E. myth about Inana, the Sumerian goddess of love, describes her preparations for descent to the underworld. She daubs

Cosmetic containers: (top) gold, in shape of a cockle shell (length 3 1/8 inches), Royal Graves, Ur, circa 2600 – circa 2500 B.C.E.; and (bottom) glazed ceramic (heights 2 3/4 inches and 1 7/8 inches), Babylon, circa twelfth–eleventh centuries B.C.E. (top: University of Pennsylvania Museum of Archaeology and Anthropology; bottom: Vorderasiatisches Museum, Berlin)

her eyes with an ointment called "Let him come, let him come"—a clear indication that even in ancient times eye makeup was considered sexy. Eye cosmetics were made from antimony paste and applied with a carved ivory pin. Rouge is also mentioned in lexical lists. The Sumerian word for *rouge* is literally "gold paste," and the Akkadian word is literally "red pigment of the face."

Perfumes. In Mesopotamia the production of aromatic substances became a major industry. Perfumes were used for medicine, magic, and rituals, as well as grooming. Perfume makers were often women. In fact, one series of recipes from the Middle Assyrian period (circa 1400 – circa 1000 B.C.E.) for making perfumes is attributed to a woman.

Sources:

Dominique Collon, "Clothing and Grooming in Ancient Western Asia," in *Civilizations of the Ancient Near East,* 4 volumes, edited by Jack M. Sasson (New York: Scribners, 1995), I: 503–515.

Erich Ebeling, *Parfümrezepte und kultische Texte aus Assur* (Rome: Pontificium Institutum Biblicum, 1950).

Karen Rhea Nemet-Nejat, *Daily Life in Ancient Mesopotamia,* Daily Life through History (Westport, Conn.: Greenwood Press, 1998).

Nemet-Nejat, "Women in Ancient Mesopotamia," in *Women's Roles in Ancient Civilizations: A Reference Guide,* edited by Bella Vivante (Westport, Conn.: Greenwood Press, 1999), pp. 85–114.

J. N. Postgate, *Early Mesopotamia: Society and Economy at the Dawn of History* (London & New York: Routledge, 1992).

Diane Wolkstein and Samuel Noah Kramer, *Inanna, Queen of Heaven and Earth: Her Stories and Hymns from Sumer* (New York: Harper & Row, 1983).

ENTERTAINMENT

Dance. Dancing was depicted in Mesopotamian artworks before circa 3000 B.C.E., but most images of dancers date from circa 2000 – circa 1000 B.C.E., and few occur after circa 1000 B.C.E. Dancers performed in religious rituals and on occasions such as weddings and harvest festivals. Dancers performed alone, in pairs, and in groups. Men and women did not dance together. Instead they took turns. Sometimes one group sang while the other danced. Dance steps included jumping and leaping, kneeling and bending, and dancing on one's toes. Line dancers and circle dancers were usually women. Men performed a squat dance (something like the well-known folk dance performed by Russian cossacks), a foot-clutch dance in which the dancer hopped on one leg while holding up the other leg in front or behind his body, and a whirling dance similar to that of Islamic "whirling dervishes." Dancers sometimes performed on platforms or tables. In cultic festivals entertainers danced and sang. They might be in costume, masked, or naked. Ordinary people also danced during magic healing rituals. Palaces and temples employed dancers, as well as instrumentalists and singers.

Music. Instrumental musicians and singers were also featured at royal and religious festivals, appearing along with snake charmers, bear trainers, and jesters. Instrumentalists may have accompanied dancers or singers as well as reciters of epics and myths. Sometimes musicians are shown dancing. Instrumentalists and singers

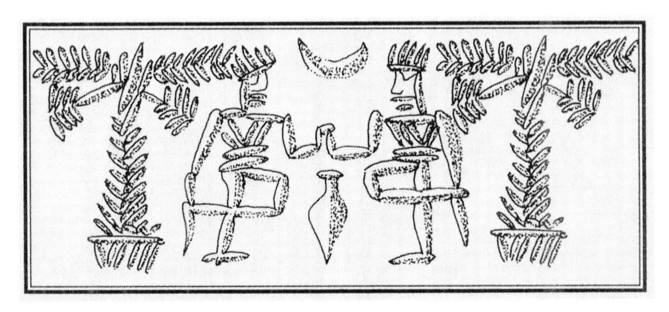

Two men performing a foot-clutch dance, drawing after the impression of a bitumen cylinder seal (height 1 inch), Susa, circa 1750 B.C.E. (drawing by Ronald Wallenfels; seal: Louvre, Paris)

Seated figure of the singer Ur-Nanshe (gypsum, height 10¼ inches), Mari, circa 2600 – circa 2350 B.C.E.; and a female singer clutching her throat, detail from an alabaster relief at the Southwest Palace of Nineveh, 668 – circa 627 B.C.E.
(left: National Museum, Damascus; right: British Museum, London)

were depicted in Neo-Assyrian military scenes, accompanying the army as they marched into battle.

Singers. Singers were both male and female. Their repertoire consisted of religious and secular works. Texts mention solo singers and choirs. Sometimes captured women were trained to become singers.

Songs. Songs were central to religious ceremonies and rituals in the ancient Near East. The earliest known composer of religious songs was Enheduana, the priestess of the moon god Nanna and the daughter of Sargon of Akkad (circa 2334 – circa 2279 B.C.E.). A Middle Assyrian text of circa 1100 B.C.E. lists more than three hundred Sumerian and Akkadian songs in more than thirty categories. The complete texts for some songs have survived, while only the opening line exists for others. Second millennium B.C.E. tablets from Babylonia, Assyria, and Ugarit in Syria described music theory, naming the nine strings of the harp and using a heptatonic (seven-note) scale. A libretto and score for a psalm praising the moon goddess Nikkal was

found complete at the site of thirteenth century B.C.E. Ugarit. Complete scores have also been found.

Musical Instruments. Mesopotamians played musical instruments from the string, wind, and percussion families. Mesopotamians also had trumpets, but they used these instruments from the horn family for communication, as in battle, not as musical instruments. In the string family, harps and lyres, as well as a few examples of lutes, have been found at ancient sites throughout the Near East. Mesopotamians also played single and double pipes, wind instruments. Circular drums ranged in size from a small hand drum to a standing drum about four to five feet in diameter. A large kettledrum was beaten in the temple courtyard during eclipses of the moon. Performers generally used small handheld drums and other percussion instruments, including cymbals and rattles.

Recitation of Written Works. Some written compositions were performed on public occasions. For example, the Babylonian creation myth, *Enuma elish,* was

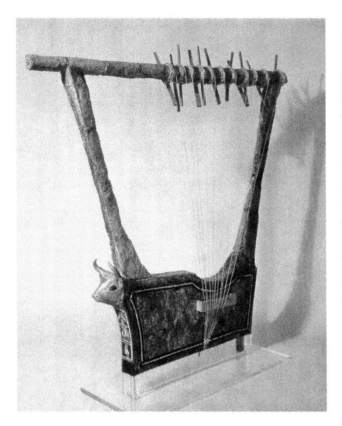

Silver lyre (height 41¾ inches), Royal Graves, Ur, circa 2600 – circa 2500 B.C.E.; and seated harp player (stamped terra-cotta plaque, height 5¼ inches), perhaps from Eshnunna, early second millennium B.C.E. (left: British Museum, London; right: Iraq Museum, Baghdad)

Nude lute player, terra-cotta relief, circa fourteenth century B.C.E.; and double-flute player, tambourine player, and dancing men with psalteries (similar to zithers), fragment of a relief-carved Syrian ivory box (height 2 5/8 inches), Nimrud, ninth–eighth centuries B.C.E. (left: Louvre, Paris; right: British Museum, London)

Cult scene with a large vertical drum (top), fragment of a relief on a steatite vessel, Tello (ancient Girsu), circa 2100 B.C.E.; and a boxing match, with men playing a kettle drum (bottom), terra-cotta relief, Larsa, circa 1894 – circa 1595 B.C.E. (top: Louvre, Paris; bottom: British Museum, London)

recited at the *akitu*-festival, or New Year's festival, at Babylon, and its battle scene may have been re-enacted. Other texts include instructions that they be recited as part of particular religious rituals. Each city had its own rites and honored particular gods.

Narration. Some compositions addressed their audience directly. For example, the narrator of the *Epic of Gilgamesh* speaks directly to the tablet reader and anyone listening to him, praising the accomplishments of king Gilgamesh and asking his audience to examine Gilgamesh's monuments, that is, the temple, the city wall, and the lapis lazuli tablet buried as part of the foundation deposit in the wall.

Dialogues. Dialogues such as the *Babylonian Theodicy* (circa eleventh century B.C.E.) and the *Dialogue of Pessimism* (first millennium B.C.E.) may also have been performance pieces since they are written in the form of scripts for two actors. In the *Babylonian Theodicy*, a brooding piece that echoes parts of the biblical book of Job, a sufferer and his friend discuss why the gods allow man to suffer. A series of exchanges between a master and his servant, the *Dialogue of Pessimism* is a more humorous examination of the purpose of life. When the master suggests a plan of action, the servant obsequiously agrees with him. When the master proposes doing the exact opposite, the servant agrees with him again. Only at the end of the dialogue does the servant express his own opinions about life and his master. Other dialogues feature exchanges between characters such as Summer and Winter, the Pickaxe and the Plough, the Date Palm and the Tamarisk. These contests end with judgments and reconciliations in which the contestants leave as good friends.

The Audience. In some cases, scholars can only speculate about the size and makeup of audiences for performances of literary works; that is, whether these works were performed only before the royal court or for the general public. Certainly, however, these literary compositions show an awareness of the tastes and standards of their time.

Sources:

Mark E. Cohen, *The Cultic Calendars of the Ancient Near East* (Bethesda, Md.: CDL Press, 1993).

Anne D. Kilmer, "Music and Dance in Ancient Western Asia," in *Civilizations of the Ancient Near East*, 4 volumes, edited by Jack M. Sasson (New York: Scribners, 1995), IV: 2601–2613.

Kilmer and others, "Musik," *Reallexicon der Assyriologie*, 8 (1995–1997): 463–469.

Karen Rhea Nemet-Nejat, *Daily Life in Ancient Mesopotamia*, Daily Life through History (Westport, Conn.: Greenwood Press, 1998).

FOOD AND DRINK

Bread. The Mesopotamians based their diet on barley, from which they made unleavened bread and beer. (It has been noted that eating only barley could lead to severe vitamin deficiencies.) They also used other grains—including millet, emmer wheat, and rye—to make bread or cereal. They ground grain with portable millstones and then mixed the flour with water (usually without any leavening agent) to produce various kinds of breads. In the grave of queen Pu-abi (circa 2500 B.C.E.) in the Royal Cemetery at Ur, archaeologists found pieces of unleavened bread made from finely ground flour. Breads were described as first quality, ordinary, black, or white.

Flavored Breads. Breads were also made by beating in fats such as sesame oil, lard, mutton "butter," and fish oil. Occasionally, flavoring was added to the oils to disguise the fact that the hot climate of Mesopotamia had made them rancid. Sometimes honey, ghee (clarified butter), sesame, milk, fruit juice, cheese, or fruit were added to the dough. Of course, only the highest-quality breads and cakes were deemed fit for the king's table.

Beer. Mesopotamians made beer from malted barley (barley seeds that have been permitted to sprout); they did not have hops. Beer was an important part of the daily diet and is included on the ration lists for palace workers, who received the equivalent of from one quart to one gallon of beer per day, depending on their importance. In taverns, people drank beer from a common vat, usually through drinking tubes with small perforated holes on the ends to act as strainers to remove solids from the beer. Beer could be made all year round.

Wine. Unlike beer, wine could be made only once a year, when the grapes ripened. There are no surviving texts describing how wine was manufactured. When it was kept in a sealed jar, wine had a longer shelf life than beer. A wine jar typically held several gallons. Wine was described as an expensive and rare commodity, produced in the dry-farming agricultural areas to the north and west of Babylonia. Many wines were named for their place of origin; even in the mid first millennium B.C.E., wine was referred to as "mountain beer," or "bright wine like the uncountable waters of the river." Though wine consumption increased over time, it continued to be a luxury item, served only to the gods and the wealthy. Tablets from eighth century B.C.E. Nimrud (ancient Kalhu) describe the wine ration for the royal household as less than a half pint per person. Around 1800 B.C.E., women ran wineshops. Some priestesses were prohibited from entering them on penalty of death. Other grape products included grape juice, wine vinegar, and raisins.

Dairy Products. The Sumerians also drank milk from cows, goats, and ewes. Milk soured quickly in the hot climate of southern Mesopotamia. Ghee (clarified butter) was less perishable than milk. Sumerians also made a round, chalky cheese that could be transformed back to sour milk by grating it and adding water. There were many other kinds of cheese as well, including a white cheese (for the king), "fresh" cheese, and flavored, sweetened, and sharp cheeses. Other dairy products included yogurt and butter.

Storm god (height approximately 13 feet) holding ears of grain and clusters of grapes being adored by Warpalawas,
king of Tuwana, rock relief, circa 730 B.C.E., at Ivriz, Turkey

Modern impression of a chalcedony cylinder seal (height 1¼ inches), depicting a man milking a goat, circa 2600 – circa 2350 B.C.E.
(from James B. Pritchard, *The Ancient Near East in Pictures*, 1969)

From the Persian period on, sheep's milk was made into a kind of cottage cheese.

Meat. Mutton, beef, and goat were expensive meats. The gods and the king were given large portions of them. Among the many reforms and innovations introduced during the reign of king Shulgi of Ur (circa 2094 – circa 2047 B.C.E.) was the establishment of Drehem (ancient Puzrish-Dagan), a huge redistribution center in the vicinity of Nippur for livestock and animal products. Tens of thousands of cuneiform administrative tablets document the movement of several hundred thousand animals through the site each year. Animals were delivered alive as taxes from the provinces and redistributed to temple and palace personnel in Nippur and, apparently, in Ur and Uruk. Some animals were dead on arrival, and this fact too was noted in the documents. A letter from Old Babylonian period Mari (circa eighteenth century B.C.E.) on the middle Euphrates mentions an ox intended as a palace offering that was so fat it could not stand. There was no taboo against the consumption of pork; pig bones are found throughout the ancient Near East, particularly in areas with wet climates. During the third millennium B.C.E. pigs were tended in large herds; the food they scavenged was supplemented by barley feed. Fatty meat was prized but in short supply, so pork was valued. Horseflesh was also eaten, and dogs were fed dead asses. Geese and ducks were raised for meat and eggs. In the first millennium B.C.E. the chicken was brought to Mesopotamia from Persia.

Fish. The rivers and canals of Mesopotamia, as well as the seas beyond, were filled with many species of fish, turtles, and eggs, which were an important source of protein. Fishermen worked in teams using large nets or individually using smaller nets or lines and hooks. Nets were typically woven from plant fibers. Hooks were made of metal or bone. Small pieces of netting found attached to terra-cotta sinkers at Khafaje were dated circa 2700 B.C.E.; two copper barbed hooks found at Ur were dated circa 2600 B.C.E. Fish were also raised in fish ponds or reservoirs. The catch might be sold alive or preserved by salting and drying. As with any food, fish was an appropriate sacrifice for the gods. At Eridu, large quantities of fish bones were discovered on the floor of the late Ubaid-period temple (circa 4200 B.C.E.). These bones are likely the remains of offerings to the local deity, who in historical times was Enki (Ea), the wise creator god and the god of the underground body of fresh water (*apsu*). Strings of fish, "the wealth of the *apsu*," continued to be offered to the gods in the first millennium B.C.E. The Assyrian king Sennacherib (704–681 B.C.E.) "threw into the sea a golden fish (and) a golden crab with a (model of a) gold ship (as an offering to Ea)."

AN OLD BABYLONIAN RECIPE

One of the three known culinary tablets from the Old Babylonian period (circa 1750 B.C.E.), now at Yale University, comprises twenty-five simple recipes for broths made from a variety of meats and vegetables. Unfortunately, the precise meaning of some technical terms and names for ingredients is not known.

To prepare *amursanu*-pigeon in broth

Slaughter the pigeon, soak it in hot water, and pluck it. Wash with cold water and skin the neck . . . cut out the ribs . . . remove the gizzard and pluck (that is, the heart, liver, and lungs) . . . split and peel the gizzard. Cut open and chop the intestines.

To prepare the broth, put the bird, gizzard, pluck, intestines . . . head, and a piece of mutton in a cauldron and heat . . . Remove from heat, wash with cold water and wipe carefully. Sprinkle with salt and place all ingredients in a pot. Prepare water; add a piece of fat with grizzle removed, vinegar as required . . . "groats," leek and garlic mashed with onion. . . . Let simmer.

When cooked, pound and mash together to add to the dish leek, garlic, *andahshu*, and *kisimmu* . . . or mashed and pounded *baru*. . . . Remove the pigeon from the pot, wipe . . . roast the legs, covered with dough, at high heat. . . .

When everything is cooked, remove the meat from the fire, and before the broth cools . . . serve it accompanied by garlic, greens and vinegar. The broth can also be eaten later, by itself. Carve and serve.

Source: Jean Bottéro, *Textes culinaire Mésopotamiens = Mesopotamian Culinary Texts*, Mesopotamian Civilizations, volume 6 (Winona Lake, Ind.: Eisenbrauns, 1995), p. 12.

Vegetables and Fruits. Soups were thickened with a flour base made of chickpeas, lentils, barley flour, or emmer flour. Members of the onion family—including leeks, shallots, and garlic—were part of the ancient Mesopotamian diet. Lentils, chickpeas, a variety of lettuces, cabbage, summer and winter cucumbers (described as either sweet or bitter), radishes, beets, and a kind of turnip were eaten raw or boiled in water. Some fruits were also eaten raw. Fruits commonly grown in Mesopotamia included dates, apples, pears, grapes, figs, quinces, plums, apricots, cherries, mulberries, melons, and pomegranates.

"Infernal Cuisine." During the first millennium B.C.E. there was a professional known as the *aluzinnu*, a sort of clown or buffoon. When asked what he could do, he replied that nothing of the craft of the incantation-priest

Drawing of an Assyrian gypsum wall relief (height 19½ inches) depicting an Assyrian fishing in a pond, Nineveh, 704–681 B.C.E. (drawing by Austen Henry Layard, 1849; British Museum, London)

(*ashipu*) escaped him—whereupon he burned down the house he was fumigating. When asked about what dishes he would like to prepare or taste, his replies included "Mule dung with garlic, and chopped straw with sour milk" and, "as a warm dish, donkey bowels stuffed with dog excrement and fly specks."

Methods of Cooking. Breads, cakes, meats, and soups all required cooking. Meat could be cured, dried, roasted, boiled, and "touched with fire." Fish was described as "touched by fire" and "placed upon the fire." Both phrases may refer to broiling over glowing coals. Some breads were also cooked in the coals, and a grill was used for cooking over the flames. Stews and soups were cooked in pots placed on the fire. The Sumerians used several kinds of ovens, including a clay oven. The oven might be located within the house or in the courtyard.

Cooking and Serving Utensils. Many words for cooking pots, made of clay or metal, have survived. Cooking utensils included a copper frying pan and a sieve pot. Pots were made with small handles through which a rope could be passed to hang them out of the reach of rats and mice. Ladles were common cooking utensils. A mortar and pestle made of baked clay or stone was used for pounding some cereals and legumes. Hand mills made from imported volcanic stone, some dating back to the prehistoric period, have been found in private homes. Food was served from copper or wooden bowls and earthenware jugs or pots. Plates, bowls, and cups were made of pottery, wood, metal, or stone. Jars came in various sizes. The designs of eating and drinking vessels varied greatly over time. Earthenware and metal drinking flasks were used, as were forks, knives, and spoons. A large number of single-pronged bone

DANIEL AND THE PRIESTS OF BEL

In the Greek and Latin translations of the biblical book of Daniel appears a brief additional tale that ridicules the practice of presenting daily food offerings to the statues of the gods. According to this story, each day the statue of Bel (Marduk) in the temple in Babylon was presented with twelve bushels of the finest flour, forty sheep, and more than fifty gallons of wine. The prophet Daniel, a confidant of king Cyrus II (538–530 B.C.E.), determined to demonstrate to the naive king that in fact the temple staff of seventy priests and their families—not the deity—consumed the daily offerings. After the offering table had been set, Daniel ordered that ashes be sprinkled throughout the temple, whereupon the king closed and sealed the temple doors. When the temple doors were unsealed and opened the next day, footprints in the dust—those of the priests and their families—were seen leading from a hidden door to the offering table from which all of the previous night's offerings had been taken. Infuriated by the deception, the king ordered the arrest and execution of the priests and their families and then permitted Daniel to destroy the statue of the god and its temple.

In reality, the king would have been completely aware of the fact that the priests consumed the daily food offerings in the temple; in fact, the rights to portions of these offerings—temple prebends—were for centuries bought and sold among the members of the Babylonian priestly elite. The biblical author's intent was to offer an object lesson supporting the prohibition against idolatry.

Source: Carey A. Moore, *Daniel, Esther and Jeremiah: The Additions*, The Anchor Bible, volume 44 (Garden City, N.Y.: Doubleday, 1979).

forks have been discovered at Godin Tepe in west central Iran. Knives, with blades made of bronze or iron, were common. Spoons were made of bitumen, metal, wood, terra-cotta, and occasionally ivory. These utensils were probably used for preparation and serving; people usually picked up their food with their hands or with a piece of bread.

Food Preservation and Storage. Many foods were preserved. Cereals were easy to keep in pottery vessels. Legumes could be dried in the sun. A variety of fruits were pressed into cakes. Fish and meat were preserved by salting, drying, immersion in oil, and smoking. Ice was brought from the highlands and stored in icehouses for cooling beverages. Storage containers ranged from small wooden or leather cases to large wooden chests. Two particular sorts of wooden crates were used for vegetables. Some storage containers were made from reeds, which were sometimes waterproofed with bitumen.

The Yale Culinary Tablets. Three Old Babylonian period tablets in the Babylonian Collection at Yale University include thirty-five different recipes for dishes probably meant for the elite and the gods. Many of the dishes are cooked in water with fat added. Whether these dishes are broths, soups, sauces, or vegetable porridges is not stated in the tablets. Meat broths are often identified by the kind of animal from which the meat in the broth came: venison, gazelle, goat, kid, lamb, or ram; organ meat, including liver and spleen, is often used. Several different kinds of birds, such as doves and francolins, are also used. Various mineral, plant, and animal products are used as seasoning. Some recipes specify their geographical or cultural origin, for example, "Elamite" or "Assyrian." The recipes range from simple

Men (inside tent and outside) preparing food near a fortification wall, detail from an alabaster wall relief, Nineveh, 668 – circa 627 B.C.E. (Iraq Museum, Baghdad)

Obverse (front) of a cuneiform tablet (height 6½ inches) with recipes for twenty-one kinds of meat broth and four kinds of vegetable broth, circa 1700 B.C.E. (Yale Babylonian Collection)

meat and vegetable broths to more complex dishes, which use a wide variety of ingredients and additional cooking techniques. Some of the recipes recommend "side dishes" and garnishes. Since only scribes were able to read and write, these recipes would have had to be read to the cook. Furthermore, the recipes do not include the amounts of ingredients or cooking times; perhaps this information was learned by observation and oral instruction.

Cooks. The Yale Culinary Tablets mention professional cooks, identifying them as "the great cook" and "the chief cook." As a mark of his status, one chef had a seal presented to him personally by the king. Little work was done by women in royal kitchens.

Food for the Gods. The Sumerians bragged about their advanced skills of cookery and considered their cuisine superior to that of desert nomads, whom the Sumerians believed were uncivilized. Modern scholars are unable to evaluate their culinary skills, however, because the only rations lists that have survived are those for meals served to the gods (and later eaten by the temple staff). According to the ritual texts, the gods (and presumably most people) ate twice a day, early in the morning and at sunset.

Food for Ordinary People. In a text describing a student's schooldays, a mother gives her son two bread rolls. The ration lists for workers from about 2000 B.C.E. noted that working women received half the rations of working men (forty to sixty liters of barley). Old Babylonian lists of food rations show that people of lower status received fish; meat was reserved for the upper class.

Sources:
Robert McCormick Adams, *Heartland of Cities: Surveys of Ancient Settlement and Land Use on the Central Floodplain of the Euphrates* (Chicago: University of Chicago Press, 1981).

Jean Bottéro, *The Oldest Cuisine in the World: Cooking in Mesopotamia,* translated by Teresa Lavender Fagan (Chicago & London: University of Chicago Press, 2004).

Bottéro, *Textes culinaire Mésopotamiens = Mesopotamian Culinary Texts,* Mesopotamian Civilizations, volume 6 (Winona Lake, Ind.: Eisenbrauns, 1995).

Erich Ebeling, *Tod und Leben nach den Vorstellungen der Babylonier* (Berlin & Leipzig: De Gruyter, 1931).

Louis Francis Hartman and A. Leo Oppenheim, *On Beer and Brewing Techniques in Ancient Mesopotamia,* supplement to the *Journal of the American Oriental Society,* no. 10 (Baltimore: American Oriental Society, 1950).

Brian Hesse, "Animal Husbandry and Human Diet in the Ancient Near East," in *Civilizations of the Ancient Near East,* 4 volumes, edited by Jack M. Sasson (New York: Scribners, 1995), I: 203–222.

Samuel Noah Kramer, *The Sumerians: Their History, Culture and Character* (Chicago & London: University of Chicago Press, 1963).

Armas Salonen, *Die Fischerei im alten Mesopotamien* (Helsinki: Suomalainen Tiedeakademia, 1970).

Marten Stol, "Private Life in Ancient Mesopotamia," in *Civilizations of the Ancient Near East,* 4 volumes, edited by Jack M. Sasson (New York: Scribners, 1995), I: 485–501.

FURNITURE

Household Furniture. Household furniture differed over time, location, and economic status of the owners. Like modern furniture, ancient Mesopotamian furniture was usually made from wood and other organic materials that decomposed. Fine furniture might be inlaid with other rare woods or ivory. Furniture designs in the third and second millennia B.C.E. were similar. Early second millennium B.C.E. texts from Mari include detailed descriptions of how royal furniture was made.

Seating. Constructed in many shapes and sizes from a wide variety of woods, chairs had legs, backs, and sometimes arms. They were often painted. Stools were made as early as the third millennium B.C.E. and were used by lower-class workers. Some stools had crossed legs and could be folded up. Padded armchairs, sedan chairs, and thrones were also made. Chair seats were covered with leather, palm fiber, rushes, or felt. Some chairs had loose linen slipcovers. One Assyrian king, Ashurbanipal (668 – circa 627 B.C.E.), was depicted reclining on a couch, which

PHRYGIAN FURNITURE

Excavation of the four monumental burial tumuli at the site of Gordion, the ancient capital of the Phrygian kingdom in central Anatolia, yielded the remains of more than fifty pieces of wooden furniture. In tumulus MM—once thought to have contained the remains of the late eighth century B.C.E. king Mita (king Midas of Greek legend)—was found a three-legged boxwood banquet table, constructed from forty major components, all joined with mortise and tenon. The walnut top was inlaid with pieces of juniper cut in a wide variety of geometric patterns.

Phrygian furniture design and craftsmanship were still highly regarded in the fifth century B.C.E., when Herodotus of Halicarnassus mentioned a throne donated by Midas and still on display in the sanctuary at the shrine in Delphi in Greece. Of the throne, Herodotus remarked, "Midas presented the royal throne from which he used to give judgement; it . . . is well worth seeing."

Sources: Herodotus, *The Histories,* translated by Aubrey de Sélincourt, revised, with an introduction and notes, by A. R. Burn (Harmondsworth, U.K.: Penguin, 1954).
Elizabeth Simpson, "Phrygian Furniture from Gordion," in *The Furniture of Western Asia, Ancient and Traditional: Papers of the Conference held at the Institute of Archaeology, University College London June 28 to 30, 1993,* edited by Georgina Herrmann with Neville Parker (Mainz am Rhein: Philipp von Zabern, 1996), pp. 187–209.

Relief-carved Syrian ivory chair back (height 21 inches), Fort Shalmaneser, Nimrud, ninth – mid-eighth centuries B.C.E.; and
Sennacherib on a throne with three rows of gilded bronze or ivory supporting figures, pine-cone feet, and footstool,
detail from a wall relief at his palace in Nineveh, 704–681 B.C.E. (both: British Museum, London)

Ashurnasirpal II on backless throne and footstool, carved wall relief (height 7 feet 9 inches), North-West Palace, Nimrud, 883–859 B.C.E.;
and attendants carrying a backless throne, carved-gypsum wall relief (height 9 feet, 4¾ inches), Khorsabad, 721–705 B.C.E.
(left: British Museum, London; right: Iraq Museum, Baghdad)

may have been made in Phoenicia or Syria, whose crafts-men decorated furniture with carved ivory inlays.

Tables. Artwork and texts from the third millennium B.C.E. reveal that Mesopotamians of that period ate their meals at tables and tray tables. Tables, models of tables, and illustrations of tables on reliefs have survived from the first millennium B.C.E. in Assyria. Tables were typically made of wood and sometimes decorated with metal or ivory inlays. They often had three legs so they would be stable on uneven ground.

Beds and Bedding. Beds were usually made of a frame and supporting base of wood. Rope, interwoven reeds, or metal strips woven in a crisscross pattern were sometimes used to support the mattress, which might be stuffed with wool, goats' hair, or palm fibers. Linen sheets, cushions, and blankets might be placed atop the mattress. Not every-body owned a bed. The poor slept on mats made from straw or reeds.

Floor Coverings. Tablets refer to bedside mats on the floor. Palaces may have had carpets. Limestone slabs in the palaces of the Assyrian kings Sennacherib (704–681 B.C.E.) and Ashurbanipal (668 – circa 627 B.C.E.) at Nineveh were carved to imitate carpeting.

Sources:
Elizabeth Simpson, "Furniture in Ancient Western Asia," in *Civilizations of the Ancient Near East*, 4 volumes, edited by Jack M. Sasson (New York: Scribners, 1995), III: 1647–1661.

Marten Stol, "Private Life in Ancient Mesopotamia," in *Civilizations of the Ancient Near East*, I: 485–501.

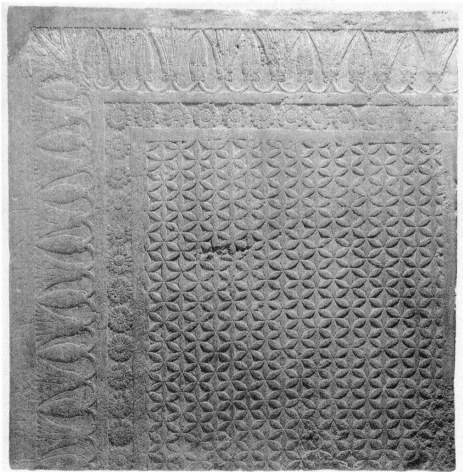

Model bed with nude female lying on textured surface (terra-cotta, length 4¾ inches), unprovenanced, circa 1894 – circa 1595 B.C.E.;
and detail of a carved-stone imitation carpet, throne-room doorsill, North Palace, Nineveh, circa 645–640 B.C.E.
(top: Ashmolean Museum, Oxford; bottom: British Museum, London)

Paradise garden laid out by Sennacherib (704–681 B.C.E.) in Nineveh. Water spilling from an aqueduct (upper right) flows into irrigation channels with trees growing along their sides; at the top of the hill stand a pavilion (center) between a stele depicting the king (left) and a columned hall (right); carved-stone wall relief (width 48 inches), North Palace of Ashurbanipal, Nineveh, 668–circa 627 B.C.E (British Museum, London).

THE HANGING GARDENS OF BABYLON?

The fourth century B.C.E. Babylonian priest Berossus described "The Hanging Gardens of Babylon" in his *Babylonaica*, written to explain the culture of Mesopotamia to the Seleucid masters of Babylonia. According to Berossus, the Babylonian king Nebuchadnezzar II (604–562 B.C.E.) created the Hanging Gardens to please his wife, who longed for the mountainous areas of her native Media in Iran. The Hanging Gardens became one of the "Seven Wonders" of the ancient world. However, there are no references to such a garden among Nebuchadnezzar's many building inscriptions or among the references to Babylon in the fifth century B.C.E. *Histories* by Herodotus of Halicarnassus, who claimed to have visited the city less than a century after Nebuchadnezzar's reign. In a corner of one of Nebuchadnezzar's palaces, archaeologists found an underground crypt, where a three-shafted well in one of the cellars may have been some kind of hydraulic lifting system—perhaps the water source of the Hanging Gardens—but no archaeological finds have provided compelling evidence for the existence of the Hanging Gardens. Recent scholars have suggested that late-classical writers may have confused the vast building activities of Nebuchadnezzar at Babylon with those of the earlier Assyrian king Sennacherib (704–681 B.C.E.) at Nineveh, which did, in fact, possess a vast artificial garden.

Sources: Stanley Mayer Burstein, *The Babylonaica of Berossus*, Sources and Monographs, Sources from the Ancient Near East, volume 1, fascicle 5 (Malibu, Cal.: Undena Publications, 1978).

Stephanie Dalley, "Nineveh, Babylon and the Hanging Gardens: Cuneiform and Classical Sources Reconciled," *Iraq*, 56 (1994): 45–58.

Irving L. Finkel, "The Hanging Gardens of Babylon," in *The Seven Wonders of the Ancient World*, edited by Peter A. Clayton and Martin Price (London & New York: Routledge, 1988), pp. 38–58.

GARDENS AND PARKS

Irrigated Land. In ancient Mesopotamia, Persia, and Egypt, a garden or park was enclosed irrigated land containing collections of cultivated plants and animals. Several early Sumerian kings were said to be gardeners. A tablet from Babylon names the vegetables and herbs in the garden of the Neo-Babylonian king Merodach-baladan II (721–710 B.C.E.). Wealthy Mesopotamians grew vines, fruit trees, and vegetables in gardens watered by pools and ponds. Ration lists included food for gardeners, who sometimes lived in cottages within the gardens they tended. Information about gardens comes from texts that list staples grown for temples or palaces. Laments for the destruction of cities bemoan the loss of material things considered essential for civilized life, including gardens as well as houses, palaces, and temples.

Royal Gardens. Palace gardens were status symbols for kings throughout the Near East. Assyrian kings bragged that large parts of their cities were set aside for parks and the irrigation works necessary for raising the plants and animals they brought from distant lands. The Assyrian king Tiglath-pileser I (circa 1114 – circa 1076 B.C.E.) boasted:

> I carried off the following trees from the lands: cedar, boxwood, oak from Kanesh (in Anatolia), these trees from the countries (I have conquered), I planted them in the gardens of my country. . . . (Luckenbill)

Royal parks are represented in Assyrian palace wall reliefs. Sennacherib (704–681 B.C.E.) was proud of the plazas, fields, gardens, and botanical and zoological park in his capital at Nineveh.

Temple and Kitchen Gardens. Temple gardens provided fresh offerings for the gods. Unfortunately, evidence about them is scant. At the Temple of the New Year's Festival at Ashur, rows of planting pits for shrubs and trees were cut into the rock of the inner courtyard and the surrounding area. Records of Assyrian kings described temple gardens. Some houses in the ancient Near East had a central courtyard that might contain a garden. In the third millennium B.C.E. and later, gardens were often planted with date palms, and in their shade—sheltered from the intense sunlight, strong winds, or sandstorms—smaller fruit trees, vegetables, and herbs were grown. The gardens were located close to or within settlements and near rivers and canals for irrigation. Workers drew water by hand from these sources, or from wells and ponds, and used it to water the plants.

Sources:

Miguel Civil, *The Farmer's Instructions: A Sumerian Agricultural Manual,* Aula Orientalis-Supplementa 5 (Barcelona: Editorial Ausa, 1994).

Daniel David Luckenbill, *Ancient Records of Assyria and Babylonia,* 2 volumes (Chicago: University of Chicago Press, 1926, 1927).

James D. Muhly, "Ancient Cartography," *Expedition,* 20, no. 2 (1978): 26–31.

Karen Rhea Nemet-Nejat, *Daily Life in Ancient Mesopotamia,* Daily Life through History (Westport, Conn.: Greenwood Press, 1998).

Mirko Novák, "The Artificial Paradise: Programme and Ideology of Royal Gardens," in *Sex and Gender in the Ancient Near East, Proceedings of the XLVIIᵉ Rencontre Assyriologique Internationale, Helsinki, July 2–6, 2001,* 2 volumes, edited by Simo Parpola and R. M. Whiting, Compte Rendu du Rencontre Assyriologique Internationale, 47 (Helsinki: Neo-Assyrian Text Corpus Project, 2002), II: 443–460.

Joan Oates, *Babylon* (London: Thames & Hudson, 1979; revised, 1986).

Michael Roaf, *Cultural Atlas of Mesopotamia and the Ancient Near East* (New York: Facts on File, 1966).

Martha T. Roth, *Law Collections from Mesopotamia and Asia Minor,* second edition, Society of Biblical Literature, Writings from the Ancient World Series, volume 6 (Atlanta: Scholars Press, 1995).

Georges Roux, *Ancient Iraq* (London: Allen & Unwin, 1964).

H. W. F. Saggs, *Civilization before Greece and Rome* (New Haven & London: Yale University Press, 1989).

HAIRSTYLES AND HEADGEAR

Hair Care. People at all levels of ancient Mesopotamian society anointed their bodies and hair with oil. It softened the skin, which became easily irritated and chapped by the dry atmosphere, and destroyed vermin in the hair.

Third Millennium B.C.E. Hairstyles. Artworks from the Early Dynastic period (circa 2900 – circa 2340 B.C.E.) often show men with their heads shaved, but some are depicted with long hair. Women wore their

---

PU-ABI'S JEWELRY

The Royal Cemetery of Ur, which was excavated by Sir Leonard Woolley in the late 1920s, is a valuable source of information on Mesopotamian jewelry of the Early Dynastic period. Some of the most impressive objects were found in the tomb of queen Pu-abi (circa 2500 B.C.E.). She wore an elaborate headdress of long gold ribbons, wreaths of gold, carnelian, and lapis-lazuli beads, and a gold hair comb tipped with golden rosettes. Large gold crescent-shaped earrings were woven into her hair or wig near her ears. Fifty strands of strung carnelian, agate, lapis lazuli, silver, and gold beads may have been decorations on a cape. Around her waist was a broad belt of gold, carnelian, and lapis-lazuli beads. She wore ten gold rings on her fingers. Three lapis lazuli cylinder seals, one with the queen's name on it, lay near her body. Pu-abi went to eternity surrounded by attendants, grooms, and guards. Ten of the women, all wearing elaborate gold headdresses, earrings, and necklaces, may have been singers and musicians.

Source: Richard L. Zettler and Lee Horne, eds., *Treasures from the Royal Tombs of Ur* (Philadelphia: University of Pennsylvania, Museum of Archaeology and Anthropology, 1998).

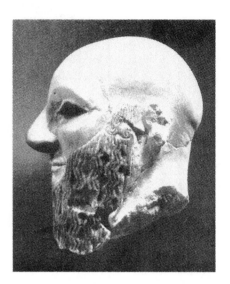

Hairstyles and headgear: (top) man from Eshnunna, circa 2900 – circa 2600 B.C.E.; woman, perhaps from Eshnunna, circa 2600 – circa 2350 B.C.E.; man from Mari, circa 2350 B.C.E.; (bottom) woman from Girsu, circa 2100 B.C.E.; man, possibly a eunuch, from Khorsabad, 721–705 B.C.E.; man from western reaches of the Assyrian Empire, 721–705 B.C.E. (top left: Iraq Museum, Baghdad; top center and bottom left: Louvre, Paris; top right: National Museum, Aleppo; bottom center and right: British Museum, London)

hair long, braided and piled on top of the head, with either a net or scarf to hold the hair in place, and a pleated headdress. They also wore jewelry in their hair. Sometimes women wore wigs.

Late Third through Mid-Second Millenia B.C.E. In the Akkadian, Neo-Sumerian, and Old Babylonian periods, men were either shaved bald or wore their hair and beards carefully waved. A woman often wore her hair in a large bun that reached from the top of the head to the nape of the neck. Women also decorated their hair with bands, hairnets, and hairpins.

First Millennium B.C.E. Assyrian reliefs show most men with full beards and mustaches waved and curled at the ends. Some men are depicted beardless and may be eunuchs. Priests, doctors, and slaves wore distinctive hairstyles. A potion and an incantation were used to treat graying hair. Gods, royalty, soldiers, and religious personnel wore headdresses indicating their status or ritual functions.

Sources:

Dominique Collon, "Clothing and Grooming in Ancient Western Asia," in *Civilizations of the Ancient Near East*, 4 volumes, edited by Jack M. Sasson (New York: Scribners, 1995), I: 503–515.

Georges Contenau, *Everyday Life in Babylon and Assyria*, translated by K. R. and A. R. Maxwell-Hyslop (New York: St. Martin's Press, 1954).

J. N. Postgate, *Early Mesopotamia: Society and Economy at the Dawn of History* (London & New York: Routledge, 1992).

Queen Pu-abi's headdress (gold, lapis lazuli, and carnelian),
from the Royal Graves at Ur, circa 2600 – circa 2500 B.C.E.
(University of Pennsylvania Museum of
Archaeology and Anthropology)

HOUSING

Neighborhoods. Residential areas of cities were crowded with houses, workshops, and shrines. Rich and poor people lived in the same neighborhoods. The house of an important official could be next to the house of a poor worker or a workshop for a craftsman such as a copper-bronze smelter. Residential areas were connected by a network of streets and alleys. Streets were uneven because, as houses were rebuilt on previous foundations, parts of the streets had to be raised to reach their doors. Clay models of houses have been recovered from several sites throughout the ancient Near East, where they may have served as votive offerings; no one style of house can be considered typical.

Materials. Ancient Mesopotamian houses were constructed from materials still used in Iraq today. Walls were made of sun-dried mud bricks, whose shapes and sizes changed over time. Clay and chopped straw were put into molds and left to dry in the sun. The finished walls were then covered with plaster, variously made from mud, lime, or gypsum. Houses often shared a common wall. A stone foundation might underlie the walls. Bitumen and lime were used to waterproof the foundation.

Housing for the Rich and the Poor. Rich people's houses were often large with rooms opening onto a square central courtyard. If there was a second story, it duplicated the plan of the ground floor, and the building had extra-thick foundation walls for support. Ordinary peasants lived in simple one-story buildings containing one or two rooms with little furniture. Some bricks were baked in ovens, which made them harder than sunbaked bricks, but the scarcity of wood and other fuels made oven-baked bricks expensive, and they were mostly used for religious and government buildings. Often painted red to frighten away evil spirits, doors were usually made of wood and set in a wooden frame. Small apotropaic figures meant to ward off evil were buried beneath the outer door or inside the house, along the walls, in lavatories, and, especially, in the bedroom.

Housing Construction and the Law. Houses built from sun-dried brick sometimes collapsed as a result of long exposure to wind and rain. Included among the Laws of Hammurabi (circa 1792 – circa 1750 B.C.E.) are several sections dealing with the possibly tragic consequences of shoddy house construction:

> If a builder constructs a house for a man but does not make his work solid, and the house that he constructed falls

---

OLD BABYLONIAN UR

The most vivid picture of Old Babylonian life (circa 1894 – circa 1595 B.C.E.) comes not from the city of Babylon itself, but from Sir Leonard Woolley's excavation at Ur of private two-story courtyard houses. The names of homeowners can be determined from cuneiform tablets found in their ruins. No. 1 Broad Street (Woolley fancifully named streets from his Oxford schooldays) contained hundreds of exercise tablets written by the students of Igmil-Sin. No. 1 Old Street belonged to Ea-nasir, a major figure in the copper trade. No. 14 Paternoster Row was a restaurant with a wide window opening onto the street; a brick counter immediately inside presumably displayed the cooked dishes of the day. The kitchen contained a bread oven and a solid brick range for cooking meat over charcoal braziers.

Source: Joan Oates, *Babylon* (London: Thames & Hudson, 1979; revised, 1986).

CITY LIFE

Following the death of his father during a military campaign, the Assyrian king Sennacherib (704–681 B.C.E.) chose to abandon Sargon II's capital at Kuyunjik (ancient Dur-Sharrukin) and build his "Palace without Rival" at Nineveh, the ancient cult city of the goddess Ishtar. The city was enclosed within a wall some 12 kilometers (7 miles) in length pierced by fifteen gates.

Mesopotamian cities, regardless of size, were both divided and united by streets and canals. Sennacherib had buildings pulled down to let light into alleys and narrow streets, enlarged the city squares, and straightened and widened various streets to create a main ceremonial avenue paved with limestone blocks. Although people apparently could build their homes where and according to whatever plan they wanted, Sennacherib was adamant that they be kept away from the king's highway:

> In days to come, there should be no narrowing of the royal road as I had steles made which stand facing each other. I measured the width of the royal road, which was fifty-two cubits. . . . Should (anyone of) the people living in that city . . . tear down his old house and build a new one, and the foundation of his house encroaches upon the royal road, they shall hang him upon a stake over his (own) house. (Luckenbill)

Sennacherib's building inscriptions provide a detailed description of Nineveh, which coincides with the archaeological data. It was a city filled with plazas, fields, gardens, and a large botanical and zoological park next to the palace. The park was irrigated, and the excess water from the canal system was fed into an area that created a man-made swamp for canebrakes, water birds, and wild pigs. Sennacherib also gave the citizens of Nineveh plots of two acres on which to plant orchards.

Sources: Daniel David Luckenbill, *Ancient Records of Assyria and Babylonia*, 2 volumes (Chicago: University of Chicago Press, 1926, 1927).
John Malcolm Russell, *Sennacherib's Palace without Rival at Nineveh* (Chicago: University of Chicago Press, 1991).
Russell, *The Writing on the Wall: Studies in the Architectural Context of Late Assyrian Palace Inscriptions* (Winona Lake, Ind.: Eisenbrauns, 1999).
H. W. F. Saggs, *Civilization before Greece and Rome* (New Haven & London: Yale University Press, 1989).

down and causes the death of the homeowner, that builder shall be killed.
If it causes the death of a son of the homeowner, they shall kill a son of that builder.
If it causes the death of a slave of the homeowner, he shall give a slave of equal value. (LH §§ 229–231; Roth)

Three bird-headed apkallu-figurines, probably part of a collection of seven such apotropaic (evil-averting) figures that were placed in a brick receptacle in the floor of a house (height 4¾–5 inches), Neo-Assyrian, ninth–seventh centuries B.C.E.
(British Museum, London)

Floors and Roofs. Floors in the homes of the well-to-do were covered in thick plaster made either from mud or lime, polished smooth and decorated with red or black. The poor had dirt floors. The ancient Mesopotamian house was typically inhabited by ants, cockroaches, reptiles, scorpions, lizards, and beetles. The roof was an integral part of the house and was used for sleeping during the summer. The roof was usually made from planks of date-palm wood, brushwood, or matting covered with mud plaster.

Light. Windows, when present, were openings covered with clay or wooden grills to provide ventilation and natural light. Otherwise, indoor lighting was provided by oil lamps.

Lavatories. As early as the third millennium B.C.E., palaces had lavatories, a platform above a pit or drain, sometimes with a seat made of bitumen for comfort. Each lavatory had a large pitcher with water for cleaning the body and flushing away the waste. Some also had a pottery dipper. Similar toilets are found in the Near East today. The homes of the rich might have bathing rooms with tubs, stools, jars, and a mirror. All lavatories and bathing rooms had drains leading to a main sewer, which was approximately one meter high and covered with baked bricks. The poor urinated and defecated outdoors, in orchards and in fields within or outside the city walls.

Sources:
Michael Roaf, "Palaces and Temples in Ancient Mesopotamia," in *Civilizations of the Ancient Near East*, 4 volumes, edited by Jack M. Sasson (New York: Scribners, 1995), I: 423–441.

Martha T. Roth, *Law Collections from Mesopotamia and Asia Minor*, second edition, Society of Biblical Literature, Writings from the Ancient World Series, volume 6 (Atlanta: Scholars Press, 1995).

Elizabeth C. Stone, *Nippur Neighborhood*, Studies in Ancient Oriental Civilization, no. 44 (Chicago: Oriental Institute of the University of Chicago, 1987).

Votive offering in the form of a house (terra-cotta, height 16½ inches), said to be from Salamiyya, near Hama, Syria,
circa 2900 – circa 2350 B.C.E.; and model of a house with a circular wall (lightly fired clay, diameter 24½ inches),
from a private house at Mari, circa 2900 – circa 2500 B.C.E. (left: National Museum,
Aleppo; right: National Museum, Damascus)

HUNTING

The Sport of Kings. A king who was a successful hunter proved that the gods favored him and that his power was therefore legitimate. The earliest known artworks depicting royal hunts date from the Late Uruk period (circa 3300 – circa 3000 B.C.E.). On the so-called Lion Hunt Stele, a large relief-carved boulder, a king is shown slaying lions with a spear and a bow and arrows. On a cylinder seal from the same period, a king hunts bulls with a bow and arrows.

Assyrian Royal Hunts. The Assyrian kings were renowned for hunting lions, elephants, ostriches, wild bulls, and other beasts, particularly large, aggressive species. Tiglath-pileser I (circa 1114 – circa 1076 B.C.E.) claimed that he killed 4 wild bulls, 10 elephants, and 920 lions. A relief at the palace of Ashurnasirpal II (883–859 B.C.E.) depicts him hunting lions and bulls from a chariot. The Assyrian royal hunt often took place in royal game parks.

Ashurbanipal's Hunt. The Assyrian king Ashurbanipal (668–circa 627 B.C.E.) held carefully staged lion hunts. From a booth above a wooden cage, a servant raised a door and released a lion, which was first attacked by dogs and beaters. The beaters' job was to drive the lion toward the king, who killed it from his chariot using a spear or a bow and arrows. Sometimes, as on his official seal, Ashurbanipal is shown on foot, killing the lion by holding his mane and thrusting a sword into his prey. (The depiction of the king using a sword to slay a rampant lion was a common motif on Neo-Assyrian royal stamp seals.) When Ashurbanipal's hunt was over, he poured a libation over the dead lions to atone for killing them and appease their angry spirits. He also recited a speech attributing the success of the hunt to his patron goddess. The popularity of this sport is apparent from information preserved on tablets and from the many life-like hunting scenes carved on Assyrian palace walls.

Sources:

Suzanne Herbordt, *Neuassyrische Glyptik des 8.–7. Jh. v. Chr.*, State Archives of Assyria Studies, volume 1 (Helsinki: Neo-Assyrian Text Corpus Project, 1992).

Michael Roaf, *Cultural Atlas of Mesopotamia and the Ancient Near East* (New York: Facts on File, 1966).

H. W. F. Saggs, *The Greatness That Was Babylon: A Sketch of the Ancient Civilization of the Tigris-Euphrates Valley*, revised and updated edition (London: Sidgwick & Jackson, 1988).

SPORTS

Ball Games. Little evidence relating to Mesopotamian sports has survived from the ancient Near East. Clay and faience balls have been excavated, but the rules for the games played with them are not clear. In the *Epic of Gilgamesh*, king Gilgamesh wears out the young men by playing a kind of human polo, riding on their backs while hitting a puck with a stick.

Individual Sports. Aside from the royal hunt, sports were often ritualistic. Seals and sculpture show wrestling and boxing matches between real and mythical creatures. A ritual text from Mari (circa eighteenth century B.C.E.) describes wrestlers, gymnasts, and jugglers performing in

Scenes from Assyrian royal hunts (top): in two registers, king Ashurbanipal (668 – circa 627 B.C.E.) on foot stabbing and shooting lions and on horseback spearing lions (relief-carved stone slab, height 65 3/8 inches); and details from a lion hunt (bottom), a dead lion and wounded lioness, North Palace, Nineveh (British Museum, London)

Offering stand in the form of twin vessels balanced on the heads of a pair of nude wrestlers (copper alloy, height 3 7/8 inches), Tell Agrab, circa 2650 B.C.E.; and boxers wearing knee-length skirts (stamped terra-cotta plaque, height 4 3/4 inches), unprovenanced, circa early second millennium B.C.E. (left: Iraq Museum, Baghdad; right: Louvre, Paris)

the Temple of Ishtar. Gymnasts appear on reliefs in Anatolia. In the *Epic of Gilgamesh*, king Gilgamesh and his comrade Enkidu engage in a wrestling match. At Ugarit in western Syria, circa 1500 – circa 1200 B.C.E., the god Baal was depicted as a sportsman who is accomplished at wrestling, running, throwing the javelin, and hunting with a bow. In both Akkadian and Ugaritic, the phrase "to bend the knee" means to admit defeat in a sport. In Hittite Anatolia, circa 1600 – circa 1200 B.C.E., wrestling, boxing, running, jousting, and weight throwing were connected with rituals.

Sources:

Piotr Bienkowski, "Sport," in *Dictionary of the Ancient Near East*, edited by Bienkowski and Alan Millard (Philadelphia: University of Pennsylvania Press, 2000), p. 276.

Karen Rhea Nemet-Nejat, *Daily Life in Ancient Mesopotamia*, Daily Life through History (Westport, Conn.: Greenwood Press, 1998).

SIGNIFICANT PERSON

ADAD-GUPPI

649-547 B.C.E.

QUEEN MOTHER

The Secret to Longevity. In her funeral stele, Adad-guppi claimed to have lived 104 years. During that time, she witnessed the fall of the Assyrian Empire and the establishment of a Babylonian Empire by Nabopolassar (625–605 B.C.E.) and Nebuchadnezzar II (604–562 B.C.E.). The wife of Nabu-balassu-iqbi, a "learned counselor," she lived long enough to see her son Nabonidus (555–539 B.C.E.) sit on the Babylonian throne, after the murderous intrigues that cut short the lives of Nebuchadnezzar's immediate successors. Her inscription, found on the bottom of a paving step at the north entrance to the Great

Mosque in Harran in Syria, was originally her funeral stele, which stood in the E-hulhul, the temple dedicated to the moon god Sin. In the inscription, written in the first person, she attributed her longevity to her piety and simple lifestyle: "I am Adad-guppi, the mother of Nabonidus, king of Babylon, who worships Sin, Ningal, Nusku and Sadarnunna, my personal gods, whose godheads I have constantly sought after since my youth. . . . In order to satisfy my (personal) god and goddess, I did not put on fine wool clothing, nor jewels, nor silver and gold, nor a new garment, nor would I anoint myself with perfumes and sweet oil. I wore a torn garment. My clothing was sackcloth. . . ."

Source:

Paul-Alain Beaulieu, *The Reign of Nabonidus King of Babylon 556–539 B.C.*, Yale Near Eastern Researches, 10 (New Haven: Yale University Press, 1989).

DOCUMENTARY SOURCES

Adad-guppi's Funerary Stele (649–547 B.C.E.)—Written in the first person, this inscription by the mother of Assyrian king Nabonidus (555–539 B.C.E.) attributes the queen mother's longevity to her piety and simple lifestyle.

Ashurnasirpal's Banquet Stele (883–859 B.C.E.)—This inscription on a stone block placed near the throne room of king Ashurnasirpal II in the Assyrian capital city of Kalhu commemorates a banquet given to celebrate the opening of his new palace and royal gardens. The text describes in detail the vast quantities of food and drink provided for consumption by all the gods of the land

and 69,574 invited guests from throughout the realm and all walks of life.

Inana's Descent to the Netherworld (Old Babylonian period)—This second millennium B.C.E. Sumerian-language myth about Inana, the Sumerian goddess of love, describes the items of clothing, jewelry, and makeup she puts on as she prepares for her descent to the underworld.

Yale Culinary Texts (Old Babylonian period)—Now at Yale University, these three second millennium B.C.E. tablets include thirty-five recipes for the sort of foods that might have been served to the gods or eaten by wealthy Mesopotamians.

THE FAMILY AND SOCIAL TRENDS

by KAREN RHEA NEMET-NEJAT

CONTENTS

Sidebars and tables are listed in italics.

IMPORTANT EVENTS OF 3300-331 B.C.E.

3200* B.C.E.

- The *Titles and Professions List,* a text used for teaching scribes proto-cuneiform, the oldest form of writing, is created in Uruk.

2334*-2279* B.C.E.

- During his reign, Akkadian king Sargon appoints his daughter Enheduana high priestess of the moon god Nanna at Ur, a move designed to consolidate his political and religious power.

2094*-2047* B.C.E.

- During his reign, king Shulgi of the Third Dynasty of Ur institutes major reforms in the school curriculum.

1770* B.C.E.

- The Laws of the city of Eshnunna include sections on marriage contracts, child care, adoption, divorce, and sexual offenses.

1750* B.C.E.

- The legal code compiled toward the end of Babylonian king Hammurabi's reign (circa 1792 – circa 1750 B.C.E.) includes laws addressing medical malpractice, marriage, adoption, adultery, divorce, inheritance, and family relationships.

- Cloistered priestesses are allowed to marry but are not permitted to have children. The best-known cloister is in the city of Sippar.

1445*-1350* B.C.E.

- Free women at Nuzi are active in the economy and in the courts. When their husbands grant permission, women in business perform the same jobs as men and are considered their legal equals.

1400*-1050* B.C.E.

- A tablet of Middle Assyrian laws has fifty-nine clauses relating to women, who are granted fewer rights than women elsewhere and at other times in Mesopotamia. The laws also prescribe harsh punishments for prostitutes and homosexuals.

480*-420* B.C.E.

- In his *Histories,* Herodotus of Halicarnassus includes details about the culture and family life of Babylon, which he claims to have visited during his travels.

* DENOTES CIRCA DATE

OVERVIEW

Mesopotamian Culture. In its broadest definition, Mesopotamia encompasses an enormous area from the shores of the Persian Gulf north along the alluvial plain dissected by the Tigris and Euphrates Rivers and their tributaries to their respective headwaters in the mountainous regions of southern Anatolia and western Iran. During the three millennia from about 3300 to 331 B.C.E. the region was inhabited by a wide variety of ethnic groups, each with their own customs and traditions, speaking a polyglot of often unrelated languages; some were wandering nomads, others permanent residents of villages, towns, and cities. Nonetheless, Mesopotamia's agricultural, urban, and literary traditions, some with roots deep in the prehistoric period, tended to level the differences among contemporary ethnic groups and create a remarkable, though certainly not absolute, level of uniformity throughout the period.

Family Life. Mesopotamian marriages were usually monogamous. The bride was expected to be a virgin, and society disapproved of divorce. The father was the head of the family for his entire life. His wife's chief role was bearing children. Having sons was particularly important because the eldest son was expected to care for his parents in old age, perform the appropriate rituals after they died, and care for the family graves. Infant mortality was high, and many women died in childbirth. Every city had its own customs concerning inheritance. Typically, the eldest son inherited the largest share of the father's estate. In ancient Mesopotamia the Akkadian term designating a widow (*almattu*) also referred to a poor woman. Widows and destitute or homeless girls were protected by the charity of a righteous ruler.

Education. Writing began in Mesopotamia circa 3200 B.C.E. in response to the need to keep accurate records of the movement and storage of vast quantities of commodities and of the people handling them. Trained scribes were required to keep the records. Detailed information about scribes' education comes from the many surviving later school tablets, particularly from the Old Babylonian period (circa 1894 – circa 1595 B.C.E.), when students studied at a school called an *eduba*, "tablet house." Only fairly wealthy families could afford to send their sons to such schools. Most people could not read or write.

Archives and Libraries. Institutions and individuals amassed archives and libraries. Many of these "tablet rooms" were located in palaces, at places where they would be useful for accounting and reference, such as near a palace entrance for registering goods entering or leaving, adjacent to a royal audience room, or close to a workshop, kitchen, or warehouse. Small personal libraries have been unearthed at archaeological sites dating to every time period of Mesopotamian history. The library amassed by the Assyrian king Ashurbanipal (668 – circa 627 B.C.E.) was especially impressive. He sent agents all over Mesopotamia to find works for his library at his capital in Nineveh.

Sexual Practices. Clay figurines, cylinder seals, and clay and lead plaques depicting erotica have been found in the ruins of ancient temples, tombs, houses, and taverns throughout the Near East. Prostitution, homosexuality, lesbianism, transsexuality, and sexual dysfunction are described in the ancient texts. The Babylonians had a laissez-faire attitude toward alternative lifestyles, but Middle Assyrian law called for castration of homosexuals.

Women's Roles. After she married, a wife's dowry was controlled by her husband and his family. Women from rich families, however, were sometimes given gifts separately from their dowries and were allowed to manage the money generated from those possessions. Some women were educated. There are records of female scribes, some the daughters of scribes. An Old Babylonian tablet lists female scholars, diviners, physicians, performers, and artists. At Sippar, the religious cloister for women had a thriving business operation run by the priestesses.

TOPICS IN THE FAMILY AND SOCIAL TRENDS

CHILDBIRTH AND CHILDREN

Prenatal Care. Death in childbirth and infant mortality were common. The average number of children born to a husband and wife is unknown, but typically two to four children per family survived early childhood. Women sought protection for themselves and their unborn infants through the magical powers of amulets, herbal potions, rituals, and incantations. During the first millennium B.C.E. a pregnant woman might wear an amulet shaped like the head of the dog-faced demon Pazuzu to chase away the goddess Lamashtu, the daughter of the sky god Anu. Represented as having the head of a lion, the teeth of a donkey, naked breasts, a hairy body, stained hands, and long fingers and fingernails as well as bird talons, Lamashtu was believed to slip into the house, where she might cause a miscarriage or a crib death. She was also thought to kidnap babies from their wet nurses. If a woman became ill during pregnancy, woolen material was thoroughly soaked with a magical potion and placed in her vagina twice daily. This treatment was applied in addition to anointing and bandaging.

Childbirth. Mesopotamian medical texts describe "female problems" related to pregnancy and childbirth. There were many treatments for a woman with complications after childbirth. Midwives helped a woman during delivery, and female relatives might also be present. During childbirth, a woman was given tree bark to chew; her stomach was massaged with an ointment; and a magic rolling pin was rolled over her body. Myths and incantations were recited, including the *Epic of Atrahasis*. In this tale, the god Enlil has decided to flood the earth and rid it of mankind because their noise is disturbing to the gods. Ea, the god of wisdom, helps to save Atra-hasis and his family, who ride out the flood in a boat Atra-hasis has built. After the flood Ea instructs the goddess Nintu to create three new classes of human beings whose existence will keep the earth from becoming overpopulated (and noisy) again: women unable to bear children; babies who are snatched by demons during childbirth; and priestesses who remain celibate. A magical medical incantation called *A Cow of Sin* was recited. It describes the moon god Sin's consort, who is in the form of a cow and having a difficult delivery. Anu, the chief god, eases her labor by rubbing her with oil and "waters of labor pangs" (that is, amniotic fluid). The incantation concludes, "Just as Maid-of-the-Moon-God gave birth easily, so may this girl in labor give birth."

Labor and Delivery. The dangers of childbirth are described in an elegy constructed as a series of dialogues between a husband and wife and their prayers to the mother goddess, who remains unmoved:

"Why are you adrift, like a boat, in the midst of the river,
Your rungs in pieces, your mooring rope cut?"
". . . The day I bore the fruit, how happy I was,
Happy was I, happy my husband.
The day of my going into labor, my face became darkened,
The day of my giving birth, my eyes became clouded.
With open hands I prayed to the Lady of the gods (the mother goddess)
You are the mother of those who have borne a child, save my life!"
Hearing this, the Lady of the gods veiled her face (saying),
". . . Why do you keep praying to me?"
[My husband, who loved me], uttered a cry,
"Why do you take from me the wife in whom I rejoice?"
". . . [All] those [many] days I was with my husband,
I lived with him who was my lover.
Death came creeping into my bedroom:
It drove me from my house,
It tore me from my husband. . . ." (Reiner)

Many Sumerian and Akkadian rituals were recited during pregnancy and delivery, sometimes to save a child stuck in the womb and free the baby to the waiting midwife.

The woman having a difficult delivery . . . is in great difficulty. The baby is held fast. . . . she who is creating a child

Mother with a child at her breast, upper half of a terra-cotta figurine (height 2 inches), Babylon, circa sixth-fifth centuries B.C.E. (Vorderasiatisches Museum, Berlin)

is shrouded in the dust of death. Her eyes fail, she cannot see; her lips are sealed, she cannot open them. . . . She wears no veil, she has no shame. "Stand by me, . . . O merciful Marduk! Now am I surrounded with trouble. Reach out to me! Bring forth that sealed up one (the baby), creature of the gods, as a human creature; let him come forth! Let him see the light!" (Lambert)

Birth Abnormalities. The omen series *Shumma izbu,* "If a malformed newborn," is a collection of birth abnormalities dating back to the Old Babylonian period (circa 1894 – circa 1595 B.C.E.). The series was widely copied, with exemplars found at Boghazköy (ancient Hattusa) in central Anatolia, at Ugarit in western Syria, and throughout Assyria and Babylonia. It lists deformities such as a child born with only one foot, Siamese twins, and a hermaphrodite. Some deformities listed are "theoretical," including newborns with two, three, four, and five heads. A malformed infant was viewed as an evil

omen. First, a ritual was performed, and then the baby's body was thrown into a river. Omen collections and magical texts carefully describe infant and childhood diseases, but medical texts, which prescribe treatments, do not mention them.

Nursing. A newborn baby might starve to death if its mother was unable to produce milk. Rich people could hire wet nurses, but a child of a poor family died if its mother could not nurse it. A proverb suggests a remedy: "Intercourse brings on lactation." Children were nursed for two or three years. Lactation was a means of birth control because women are relatively infertile while nursing. An infant slept in a basket. As the baby became older, its mother or nurse carried it in a sling. The birth of a boy was considered a blessing. Ridding the family of an unwanted child through infant exposure was probably practiced more often with daughters than with sons.

THE BIRTH LEGEND OF SARGON

The story of the birth of king Sargon of Akkad (circa 2334 – circa 2279 B.C.E.) has been called his autobiography or his legend. He was the illegitimate son of a priestess who was not permitted to have children. His name—which means "the king is legitimate"— suggests, in fact, that he was a usurper. He achieved his status because the goddess Ishtar fell in love with him. Bearing similarities with the biblical story of Moses in chapter 2 of Exodus, the *Birth Legend of Sargon* is known from fragments of Neo-Assyrian and Neo-Babylonian copies dating to the first millennium B.C.E. and found respectively at Nineveh and Dilbat.

I am Sargon, the mighty king, king of Akkad,
My mother was a priestess. I did not know my father.
My uncles lived in the hills.
My city is Azupirnu, which is on the banks of the Euphrates.
My mother, the priestess, became pregnant and gave birth to me in secret.
She put me in a reed basket and pitched the top with bitumen.
She left me to the river, so I could not come up.
The river carried me, it brought me to Akki the water-drawer,
Akki, the water-drawer took me in and raised me.
Akki, the water-drawer, appointed me to be his gardener.
While I was working in the orchard, (the goddess) Ishtar fell in love with me.
I ruled as king for fifty-four years.
I was lord and ruled the black-headed people (mankind). . . .

Source: Benjamin R. Foster, "The Birth Legend of King Sargon of Akkad," in *The Context of Scripture*, volume 1, edited by William W. Hallo, with K. Lawson Younger Jr. (New York & Leiden: Brill, 1996), p. 461.

Lullabies. The ancient Mesopotamians believed human "noise" made the gods angry and caused them to do evil. Mothers sang lullabies to stop babies from crying. These lullabies, which originated from incantations, were meant to keep the gods, as well as the baby, calm:

Little one who lives in the dark chamber (that is, the womb),
You really did come out here, you have seen the [sunlig]ht.
Why are you crying? Why are you fretting?
Why did you not cry in there?
You have disturbed the household god, the bison (-monster) is astir, (saying)
"Who disturbed me? Who startled me?"
The little one disturbed you, the little one startled you.
Like wine tipplers, like a barmaid's child,
Let sleep fall upon him! (Foster)

Raising Children. Little is known about how Mesopotamian children were reared. Judging by surviving statues of divinities and contracts between parents and children, however, emotional bonds between children and their parents were strong. Gods were referred to as either father or mother. Babylonian and Assyrian lists describe the stages of the human life cycle as a child at the breast, a weaned child, a child, an adolescent, an adult, and an elderly person.

Sources:
Jeremy A. Black and Anthony Green, *Gods, Demons and Symbols of Ancient Mesopotamia: An Illustrated Dictionary* (Austin: University of Texas Press, 1992).

Benjamin R. Foster, *Before the Muses: An Anthology of Akkadian Literature*, 2 volumes (Bethesda, Md.: CDL Press, 1993).

W. G. Lambert, "A Middle Assyrian Medical Text," *Iraq*, 31 (1969): 28–39.

Karen Rhea Nemet-Nejat, *Daily Life in Ancient Mesopotamia*, Daily Life through History (Westport, Conn.: Greenwood Press, 1998).

A. Leo Oppenheim, *Ancient Mesopotamia: Portrait of a Dead Civilization*, revised edition, completed by Erica Reiner (Chicago: University of Chicago Press, 1964).

Erica Reiner, *Your Thwarts in Pieces, Your Mooring Rope Cut: Poetry from Babylonia and Assyria* (Ann Arbor: Horace H. Rackham School of Graduate Studies, University of Michigan, 1985).

Wolfram von Soden, *The Ancient Orient: An Introduction to the Study of the Ancient Near East*, translated by Donald G. Schley (Grand Rapids, Mich.: Eerdmans, 1994).

Niek Veldhuis, *A Cow of Sin*, Library of Oriental Texts, volume 2 (Groningen: Styx, 1991).

EDUCATION FOR DOCTORS

Exorcists and Physicians. Writing in the fifth century B.C.E., Herodotus of Halicarnassus made the following observations about the practice of medicine in Babylonia:

They have no doctors, but bring their invalids out into the street where anyone who comes along offers the sufferer advice on his complaint, either from personal experience or observation of a similar complaint in others. Anyone will stop by the sick man's side and suggest remedies which he has himself proved successful in whatever the trouble may be, or which he has known to succeed with other people. Nobody is allowed to pass the sick person in silence; but everyone must ask him what is the matter. (*Histories*)

This statement was untrue. As early as the third millennium B.C.E. there were two sorts of medical practitioners: the exorcist (Akkadian: *ashipu*), whose cures were magical, and the physician (Akkadian: *asu*), whose cures were basically medical. Some illnesses were believed to have natural causes, such as overexposure to heat or cold, overeating, eating spoiled food, or drinking too much of an alcoholic beverage. A disease, however, was believed to be caused by a demon in punishment for a patient's sin. The exorcist's job was to identify the sin and cast out the demon. Sometimes the exorcist and the physician used each other's practices and

Cuneiform tablet (reverse, height 4 inches) with Sumerian medicinal prescriptions, Nippur, circa 2100 – circa 2000 B.C.E.
(University of Pennsylvania Museum of Archaeology and Anthropology)

worked together. Little is known about how doctors were educated, but medical knowledge was apparently passed down from father to son. An early-second-millennium B.C.E. tablet refers to a woman doctor. A first-millennium B.C.E. tablet refers to an eye doctor, and veterinarians are also mentioned in Mesopotamian sources. As symptoms, prognoses, and treatments for diseases were recognized, they were organized into texts for exorcists and physicians. The Babylonians also recorded patients' hallucinations and their meanings.

Texts for Exorcists. Diagnostic texts dealt with omens, signs seemingly unrelated to the patient's illness that might be revealed to the exorcist as he went to the patient's house. These omens served as predictions of whether the patient would recover or die. These texts also included lists of symptoms and related prognoses about the course the disease would follow. Incantations were used to exorcize the demon, and foul substances were administered as enemas, emetics, and inhalants to purify the body. Remedies were prescribed for specific demons. For example, in the case of epilepsy, the exorcist ordered the patient to place "the little finger of a dead man, rancid oil, and copper into the skin of a virgin goat; you shall string it on a tendon of a gerbil and put it round his neck, and he will recover."

Texts for Physicians. Medical books for physicians link symptoms with appropriate medications. These texts include extensive lists of herbal remedies, some of recognized medicinal value, and they often include ingredients and methods for preparing medicines. Therapeutic medical texts identify and prescribe treatments for many kinds of illnesses, among them intestinal obstructions, headaches, tonsillitis, tuberculosis, typhus, lice, bubonic plague, smallpox, rheumatism, eye and ear infections,

MURSILI'S ILLNESS

The Hittite king Mursili II came to the throne in the latter half of the fourteenth century B.C.E., after his brother Supiluliuma I died in a plague brought back from the Levant by his soldiers. Confronted with widespread disease and revolt, the young king seems to have lost his voice. In modern terms, this physical symptom could be seen as an obvious manifestation of emotional stress, but the Hittites consulted an oracle, which attributed the king's malady to the displeasure of the storm god in Kummanni, a city in a southern province of the Hittite Empire:

Thus says His Majesty Mursili, Great King: I was driving to the ruined town (belonging to Kunnu) when a storm came up. On top of this, the storm-god repeatedly thundered frightfully so that I became afraid. Speech became small in my mouth and came out of me only sparingly. I had put this matter completely out of my mind when years later it began to come to me repeatedly in a dream. In a dream the hand of the god touched me so that my mouth went to the side. So I instituted an oracular inquiry, and the storm-god of (the town of) Manuzziya was indicated. I consulted the storm-god of Manuzziya by oracle, and it was indicated that I should give him a substitute ox, roasted in the fire, and also roast some birds. I consulted the oracle further concerning the substitute ox, and it was indicated that I should give it in its (proper) place in the Land of the town of Kummanni in the temple.

Mursili appears to have obtained relief by placing his hands on the ox, sending it and other gifts to the god, and then performing other sacrifices at home.

Source: Gary Beckman, "The Aphasia of Murshili II," in *Civilizations of the Ancient Near East*, 4 volumes, edited by Jack M. Sasson (New York: Scribners, 1995), III: 2010.

The Mesopotamians were largely uneducated about human anatomy and physiology. The organs were considered the seats of various emotions or intelligence. Because of a religious taboo against dissecting human corpses, the Mesopotamians' knowledge of human anatomy was derived from what they observed while cutting up animals used in divination and food preparation. Skeletal remains from as early as 5000 B.C.E. show evidence of trephination, the removal of parts of the scalp and skull bone, usually to relieve headaches and epilepsy or treat a fractured skull. The Laws of Hammurabi (circa 1792 – circa 1750 B.C.E.) dealing with surgeons' fees and penalties for botched treatments provide clues about some of the other sorts of operations a surgeon was taught to perform. Some surgery was simple, such as lancing boils. Surgeons also set broken bones, treated wounds, and even operated on eyes. The penalty for surgical errors could be mutilation and even death. In less serious cases of malpractice the surgeon was expected to return the patient's fee.

Knowledge of Mental Illness. Medical practitioners were also taught about mental illnesses. Texts mention that the royal family of Elam in southwest Iran seemed to suffer particularly from mental illness. Other texts mention the psychological basis of sexual impotence. Omen literature interprets dreams of falling, flying, and walking around naked. One text explains that if a man dreams about being naked in public, "troubles will not touch this man"; if a man dreams of committing "bestiality with a wild beast, his household will become prosperous."

Sources:

Benjamin R. Foster, *Before the Muses: An Anthology of Akkadian Literature*, 2 volumes (Bethesda, Md.: CDL Press, 1993).

Samuel Greengus, "Legal and Social Institutions," in *Civilizations of the Ancient Near East*, 4 volumes, edited by Jack M. Sasson (New York: Scribners, 1995), I: 469–484.

Herodotus, *The Histories*, translated by Aubrey de Sélincourt, revised, with an introduction and notes, by A. R. Burn (Harmondsworth, U.K.: Penguin, 1954).

A. Leo Oppenheim, *The Interpretation of Dreams in the Ancient Near East* (Philadelphia: American Philosophical Society, 1956).

Erica Reiner, *Your Thwarts in Pieces, Your Mooring Rope Cut: Poetry from Babylonia and Assyria* (Ann Arbor: Horace H. Rackham School of Graduate Studies, University of Michigan, 1985).

E. K. Ritter, "Magical Expert (= *āšipu*) and Physician (= *asû*): Notes on Two Complementary Professions in Babylonian Medicine," in *Studies in Honor of Benno Landsberger on his Seventy-fifth Birthday, April 21, 1965*, edited by Hans Gustav Güterbock and Thorkild Jacobsen, Assyriological Studies, no. 16 (Chicago: University of Chicago Press, 1965), pp. 299–321.

Martha T. Roth, *Law Collections from Mesopotamia and Asia Minor*, second edition, Society of Biblical Literature, Writings from the Ancient World Series, volume 6 (Atlanta, Ga.: Scholars Press, 1995).

Georges Roux, *Ancient Iraq* (London: Allen & Unwin, 1964).

H. W. F. Saggs, *Civilization before Greece and Rome* (New Haven & London: Yale University Press, 1989).

tuberculosis, diarrhea, colic, gout, and venereal diseases such as gonorrhea. In time, physicians began to use remedies that were related in shape or color to the disease. For example, jaundice was treated with yellow medicine. Some sources also mention contagious diseases, as in this letter written by Zimri-Lim, king of Mari (circa 1776 – circa 1761 B.C.E.), to his wife, Shibtu:

I have heard that the lady Nanname has become ill. She was in contact with many people of the palace. She meets many women in her house. Thus, give exact orders that no one should drink from the cup from which she drinks, no one should sit where she sits, no one should sleep in the bed where she sleeps. She should not meet with many women in her house. This disease is contagious. (Roux)

Training for Surgeons. Surgeons probably learned by training and observation rather than from textbooks.

Marten Stol, "Private Life in Ancient Mesopotamia," in *Civilizations of the Ancient Near East*, 4 volumes, edited by Jack M. Sasson (New York: Scribners, 1995), I: 485–501.

EDUCATION FOR SCRIBES

Origins of Writing. Beginning around the eighth millennium B.C.E., Mesopotamians used small clay tokens to represent units or aggregate units of various entities such as animals or jars of grain. Around the middle of the fourth millennium B.C.E., more-complex methods were developed to keep track of the ever-increasing numbers of sheep and cattle and the vast quantities of grain and other commodities entering and leaving temple-owned farms and warehouses. The most significant of these developments, appearing about 3200 B.C.E., was proto-cuneiform, the world's first writing system. Mesopotamians wrote on clay tablets with a stylus made from a reed that was trimmed to form a round, pointed, or sloping end. These writing materials were readily available in the river valleys of southern Mesopotamia. At first, signs were incised into the surface of the clay, but soon they were created by impressing the stylus into the surface, leaving the characteristic wedge-shaped marks called *cuneiform* (from the Latin word *cuneus,* "wedge"). Proto-cuneiform writing included numerals and ideograms (pictographic and abstract signs) representing nouns, a few adjectives, and perhaps some verbs denoting administrative actions. No grammatical elements are indicated, and the signs can, in theory, be read in any language. In fact, although it is generally accepted that the scribes spoke Sumerian, these early tablets cannot be used to prove this assumption.

Earliest Scribal Training. Most tablets from the Late Uruk period, from about 3200 B.C.E. on, are administrative accounts or economic records. Some, however, are lists of words denoting officials, commodities, and animals. The earliest evidence for a formal system of education, these lexical lists were used to train young scribes, who had to learn to copy them accurately. Lexical lists continued to be the basis of scribal education until the end of the cuneiform tradition in the early centuries of the Common Era.

School tablet with an exercise in copying cuneiform signs (diameter 2¾ inches), Nippur, circa 1900 – circa 1600 B.C.E. (University of Pennsylvania Museum of Archaeology and Anthropology)

Early Dynastic Developments. During the Early Dynastic period (circa 2900 – circa 2340 B.C.E.), cuneiform writing evolved to become sufficiently flexible that scribes could begin to record spoken language, principally Sumerian. Before the end of the third millennium B.C.E., they could also use cuneiform to record Akkadian, Eblaite, and Hurrian. With this newfound freedom of expression, scribes began to compose poetic texts glorifying the gods, heroes, and rulers. Few of these early texts survived the radical reforms introduced by Shulgi (circa 2094 – circa 2047 B.C.E.), the second king of the Third Dynasty of Ur. New texts lauding his dynasty and other new compositions were used in schools that trained loyal bureaucrats.

The *Eduba*. During the Old Babylonian period (circa 1894 – circa 1595 B.C.E.), the school was called the "tablet house" (Sumerian: *eduba*). Its day-to-day operation is well documented by the many surviving student/teacher exercises, lexical lists, essays on school life, and examinations. Students studied with the "expert" or "father of the tablet house." A dean, called "supervisor of the tablet house," enforced the rules and regulations. Teaching assistants were called "older brothers." Their jobs were to write new tablets for the students to copy, to check the students' work, and to listen to memorized lessons. Other members of the faculty included "the man in charge of Sumerian" and "the man in charge of drawing." Mathematics was taught by the "scribe of accounting," the "scribe of measurement," and the "scribe of the field." Finally, there were men in charge of attendance and discipline, including a "man in charge of the whip." Students were punished for poor class work and penmanship, sloppiness of dress, speaking without permission, not speaking Sumerian with the Sumerian instructor, and a variety of other offenses. When the student finished school, he became a scribe (literally, a "tablet writer"). As an institution, the *eduba* does not appear to have survived the end of the Old Babylonian period. In succeeding periods education seems to have become a private matter, carried out in the home of a master teacher.

Curriculum. Central to the instructional curriculum at the *eduba* was the study of two languages: Akkadian, the scribes' native tongue, and Sumerian, which had become extinct as a spoken tongue before the end of the third millennium B.C.E. but remained the traditional language of learning. Teaching methods included memorization, dictation, writing new lessons, reviewing old ones, reading aloud from a written document, and spelling. Students learned signs and vocabulary through syllabaries (lists of syllabic signs) and lexical lists. Some tablets have the teacher's copy on one side and the student's work on the other. Other tablets range from beginners' copies to those of the advanced student, whose work looks like the teacher's. The lexical lists included botanical, zoological, geographical, and mineralogical terminology; they also provided important tools

---

AN OLD BABYLONIAN RIDDLE

Sumerian riddles and proverbs were copied by students studying in the *eduba* to become scribes. This riddle was found at Ur on a school tablet written circa 1750 B.C.E.

(What is) a house with a foundation like heaven,
A house which like a . . . vessel has been covered with linen,
A house which like a goose stands on a (firm) base,
One with eyes not opened has entered it,
One with open eyes has come out of it?
Its solution: the school.

Source: Å. W. Sjöberg, "The Old Babylonian Eduba," in *Sumerological Studies in Honor of Thorkild Jacobsen on his Seventieth Birthday June 7, 1974*, edited by Stephen J. Lieberman, Assyriological Studies, no. 20 (Chicago & London: University of Chicago Press, 1976), pp. 159–179.

---

for the study of grammar, bilingual and trilingual dictionaries, and legal and administrative terms. After developing a command of the basics, a student learned to take dictation and to write prose and poetry. In mathematics instruction, students learned about multiplication, reciprocals, coefficients, balancing of accounts, administrative accounting, and how to make all kinds of pay allotments. They also studied surveying, including how to divide property and delimit shares of fields. Finally, the well-rounded student learned to sing and play musical instruments. Not every scribe completed the full curriculum.

Students. Literacy was highly regarded, but most Mesopotamians could not read or write. The kings Shulgi (circa 2094 – circa 2047 B.C.E.) and Ashurbanipal (668–circa 627 B.C.E.) were possibly the only Mesopotamian rulers who were literate. Only wealthy families could afford to educate their sons. Administrative documents from about 2000 B.C.E. list about five hundred scribes, as well as the names and occupations of their fathers. Their fathers were members of what today might be termed the "upper middle class": governors, ambassadors, temple administrators, military officers, sea captains, important tax officials, priests, managers, accountants, and scribes. Other surviving documents mention poor orphan boys adopted by generous patrons and sent to school. There is only one reference to a female scribe studying in the *eduba*. However, there were female scribes among cloistered priestesses at Sippar, and at Mari women scribes, probably slaves of the harem, were occasionally part of a princess's dowry. Some celibate priestesses may have devoted themselves to scholarship.

School Days. Boys began their studies at the *eduba* between the ages of five and seven years and continued until they became young men. The school day lasted from sunrise to sunset. There is no information about vacations. One pupil described his monthly schedule:

My days of freedom are three per month,

Its festivals are three days per month.

Within it, twenty-four days per month

(Is the time of) my living in the tablet house. They are long days. (Saggs)

Examinations. Examinations were administered before an assembly of masters by a scribe in the courtyard of the tablet house. Students were tested on a vast body of knowledge. A school essay called "A Failed Examination" lists questions on correct sign forms; secret meanings of Sumerian words (cryptography); translation from Sumerian to Akkadian and Akkadian to Sumerian; three Sumerian synonyms for each Akkadian word; Sumerian grammatical terminology; conjugation of Sumerian verbs; various types of calligraphy and technical writing; and writing Sumerian phonetically. Examinees were also expected to understand the technical language of priests and other professions, such as silversmiths, jewelers, herdsmen, and scribes. They had to know how to make an envelope and seal a document. They were also tested on mathematics, division of fields, and allotting rations, as well as their ability to play various musical instruments, sing all kinds of songs, and conduct a choir. "A Failed Examination" begins with the teacher speaking kindly to his student, addressing him as "my son," and with the student bragging about his knowledge:

Come, my son, sit at my feet. I will talk to you, and you will give me information! From your childhood to your adult age you have been staying in the tablet-house. Do you know the scribal art that you have learned?

What would I not know? Ask me, and I will give you the answer. (Landsberger)

A series of questions follows, beginning with easy ones and continuing with more-difficult ones. The student failed his exam and blamed his teacher.

Careers for Scribes. Students who passed their examinations found jobs in the service of palaces, temples, private estates, and other institutions. They worked in positions such as royal scribe, district scribe, military scribe, land registrar, scribe for laborer groups, administrator, public secretary to a high administrative official, accountant, copyist, inscriber of stone and seals, ordinary clerk, astrologer, mathematician, or professor of Sumerian.

Sources:

Samuel Noah Kramer, *The Sumerians: Their History, Culture and Character* (Chicago & London: University of Chicago Press, 1963).

Benno Landsberger, "Scribal Concepts of Education," in *City Invincible: A Symposium on Urbanization and Cultural Development in the Ancient Near East Held at the Oriental Institute of the University of Chicago,* December 4–7, 1958, edited by Carl H. Kraeling and Robert M. Adams (Chicago: University of Chicago Press, 1960), pp. 94–123.

Piotr Michalowski, "The Earliest Scholastic Tradition," in *Art of the First Cities: The Third Millennium B.C. from the Mediterranean to the Indus,* edited by Joan Aruz with Ronald Wallenfels (New York: Metropolitan Museum of Art, 2003), pp. 451–456.

Karen Rhea Nemet-Nejat, *Daily Life in Ancient Mesopotamia,* Daily Life through History (Westport, Conn.: Greenwood Press, 1998).

Hans J. Nissen, Peter Damerow, and Robert K. Englund, *Archaic Bookkeeping: Earliest Writing Techniques of Economic Administration in the Ancient Near East,* translated by Peter Larsen (Chicago & London: University of Chicago Press, 1992).

Laurie E. Pearce, "The Scribes and Scholars of Ancient Mesopotamia," in *Civilizations of the Ancient Near East,* 4 volumes, edited by Jack M. Sasson (New York: Scribners, 1995), IV: 2265–2278.

Georges Roux, *Ancient Iraq* (London: Allen & Unwin, 1964).

H. W. F. Saggs, *Everyday Life in Babylonia & Assyria* (London: Batsford / New York: Putnam, 1965).

Å. W. Sjöberg, "The Old Babylonian Eduba," in *Sumerological Studies in Honor of Thorkild Jacobsen on his Seventieth Birthday June 7, 1974,* edited by Stephen J. Lieberman, Assyriological Studies, no. 20 (Chicago & London: University of Chicago Press, 1976), pp. 159–179.

C. B. F. Walker, *Cuneiform* (London: Published for the Trustees of the British Museum by British Museum Publications, 1987).

THE FAMILY UNIT

Patriarchy. Documents from as early as circa 2100 B.C.E. indicate that the Mesopotamian family was patriarchal; that is, the father was head of the family for his entire life, and descent was traced from fathers through sons. The father's importance is shown in the Laws of the Babylonian king Hammurabi (circa 1792 – circa 1750 B.C.E.): "If a son hits his father, they shall cut off his hand." Referred to as a "house," the family was nuclear, not extended; that is, the family unit included only a man, his wife, and their children. Grandparents, as well as adult brothers and sisters and their offspring, had their own family units. The husband was expected to "build a house." Each family worshiped one particular god, a personal deity who intervened on the family's behalf with the major gods.

Children. Sons and daughters lived in their father's home until they married. To satisfy a debt, the father could give his slaves or any members of his family to his creditors, a practice known as "debt slavery." The father could redeem them later, but he was not obliged to do so. When the father died, unmarried children became the responsibility of the oldest son, the executor, or the state. A son was expected to support his parents when they became old and to perform the appropriate rituals when they died. If children were young when their father died, their mother might be given the power of "fatherhood," a practice documented by a mid-second-millennium B.C.E. text from Nuzi on the periphery of northeast Mesopotamia.

Adoption. In general, not having children was unacceptable to Mesopotamians. A man whose wife was barren could have children by a surrogate, or a couple with

Deported Elamites: (top) several men and a woman walking as children ride in an ox-drawn cart; (bottom) women, one with a child on her shoulders, and men being driven forward by an Assyrian soldier; gypsum wall relief (height 38¼ inches), Palace of Ashurbanipal, Nineveh, 668 – circa 627 B.C.E. (Louvre, Paris)

no male heir could adopt an abandoned, unwanted new-born. Such children were described as "left to the dog" because they were sometimes left to die in the streets, where dogs were likely to eat them unless passersby decided to save them and perhaps adopt them. Older children could be adopted if the adoptive parents reimbursed the birth parents for their expenses in feeding and raising the children. Records of these transactions resemble sales agreements. Some childless families freed slaves and adopted them as sons. Even an adult could decide to enter another family. Adoptive parents agreed that the adopted child would be their heir even if they later had natural children.

Names. A baby was named soon after birth. Many Akkadian personal names reveal the family's feelings about the newborn and also acknowledge a deity. For example, a baby might be named Nidinti-Bel, "gift of (the god) Bel"; Nabu-apla-iddina "(the god) Nabu gave me an heir"; or Sin-ahhe-eriba (Sennacherib), "(the moon god) Sin replaced for me the brothers (that died)."

A foundling might be named Suqayya, "the one of the street." In addition to a personal name, each man or woman was identified by his or her father's name; that is, "so-and-so, the son (or daughter) of so-and-so." In some cases where paternity was in doubt, especially among slaves, the child was given the mother's name instead. In the first millennium B.C.E., the naming system became more complex. A free citizen was described as "so-and-so, the son of so-and-so (the patronymic), the descendant of so-and-so (the family name)." Sometimes an occupational title was given in addition to or in place of the family name. Slaves were never given a family name.

Sources:
Karen Rhea Nemet-Nejat, *Daily Life in Ancient Mesopotamia*, Daily Life through History (Westport, Conn.: Greenwood Press, 1998).

J. J. Stamm, *Die akkadische Namengebung*, Mitteilungen der Vorderasiatisch-Aegyptischen Gesellschaft, volume 44 (Leipzig: J. C. Hinrichs, 1939).

Marten Stol, "Private Life in Ancient Mesopotamia," in *Civilizations of the Ancient Near East*, 4 volumes, edited by Jack M. Sasson (New York: Scribners, 1995), I: 485–501.

MARRIAGE AND DIVORCE

Love. Like all people throughout time, ancient Mesopotamians fell in love and described this kind of emotion in myths about such divine lovers as Dumuzi and Inana or Nergal and Ereshkigal. Texts also refer to depression over rejection. To make the objects of their attention return their love, men or women prayed to a god or used a magic spell. Some magic rituals promised that, if the man performed them, "this woman will speak to you whenever you meet her, she will be powerless to resist and you can make love to her." If he quarreled with his lover, a man might also resort to charms or spells, including one that promised "with this charm she will not sleep alone; she will be loved."

Marriage Contracts. Marriages were usually monogamous. Prior to a marriage, representatives of the two families, usually the fathers, drew up legal documents to define their respective property rights. The law codes addressed various aspects of marriage. The following extracts are from a law collection drawn up by a king of the city of Eshnunna, located on the banks of the Diyala River, a major tributary of the Tigris, and dated to circa 1770 B.C.E.

> If a man marries the daughter of another man without the consent of her father and mother, and moreover does not conclude the nuptial feast and the contract for her father and mother, should she reside in his house for even one full year, she is not a wife.
>
> If he concludes the contract and the nuptial feast for her father and her mother and he marries her, she is indeed a wife; the day she is seized in the lap of another man, she shall die, she will not live. (LE §§27–28; Roth, 1995)

If the groom died or changed his mind, his father had the right to insist that the bride be given to another of his sons, if one were unmarried and of age. For a marriage to be valid, the engagement was announced; the bride's family paid a dowry, and the groom's family paid a bride price; then the bride moved to her father-in-law's house, and sexual intercourse took place between the bride and groom. The bride price and the dowry could be paid in installments until the first child was born. At that time the remainder of both payments had to be paid, finalizing the marriage contract and giving the woman the legal rights of a "wife." The following marriage contract, witnessed and sealed in Borsippa on 28 May 550 B.C.E., is typical:

> Nadin, son of Lusi-ana-nur-Marduk, descendant of Ili-bani, promises to marry Kabta, daughter of Nabu-shum-ishkun, descendant of Ili-bani.
> Nabu-shum-ishkun voluntarily has promised to Nadin: . . . (an) orchard, including the fallow area . . . (and) Inba, the slave, a bed, two chairs, a table, three bronze goblets, a bronze bowl, one copper cooking vessel, and one lamp—in total, ten household objects. . . . (Roth, 1989)

A WOMAN'S VIRTUE QUESTIONED

When a woman's virginity was challenged, the court might call on her to speak on her own behalf. A letter from Old Babylonian–period Mari includes a young woman's testimony in defense of her honor:

The "wife" of Sin-iddinam declared as follows: Before Sin-iddinam took me (in marriage), I had agreed with [the wish of] father and son. When Sin-iddinam had departed from his house, the son of Asqudum sent me the message "I want to take (marry) you." He kissed my lips, he touched my vagina—his penis did not enter my vagina. Thus I said: "I will not sin against Sin-iddinam."

Source: Marten Stol, "Private Life in Ancient Mesopotamia," in *Civilizations of the Ancient Near East*, 4 volumes, edited by Jack M. Sasson (New York: Scribners, 1995), I: 485–501.

Bride Price. Paying the bride price, a considerable sum of silver in the Old Babylonian period (circa 1894 – circa 1595 B.C.E.), was an act of good faith that ensured the groom's right to the bride. The bride price was equal in value to the dowry.

Dowry. The same as a written contract, the dowry was promised or given by the bride's agent and accompanied the bride to her husband. It typically consisted of household utensils, silver rings (a form of ancient coinage), slaves, and even fields. In addition to these items, dowries in later periods included goods such as furniture, textiles, and jewelry. A husband combined his wife's property with his own assets. Old Babylonian dowries were often itemized. A document was drawn to specify that the bride's father "sent it and her into the house of A, her father-in-law, for B, his son." While a woman's dowry increased her husband's property holdings, it reduced her own family's estate.

The Wedding. Little is known about Mesopotamian marriage ceremonies. The marital vows—"You are my husband," and "You are my wife"—can be reconstructed from words used in a divorce: "You are not my husband," and "You are not my wife." Wedding parties in wealthy families could go on for days or weeks. The groom and his family gave the bride and her family gifts such as food for the prenuptial and wedding parties, as well as clothing, jewelry, and other valuables. The bride arrived at the wedding celebration wearing a veil, which the groom removed. In Babylonia a woman did not wear a veil once she was married, but in Assyria all women, except for slaves and prostitutes, were veiled.

Living Arrangements. Girls often married young, in their early teens. Assyrian texts describe brides who were

Seated couple embracing, dedicatory statue from the Inana Temple at Nippur, gypsum with shell and lapis-lazuli
eyes inlayed in bitumen, circa 2900 – circa 2600 B.C.E. (Iraq Museum, Baghdad)

only "four half cubits high (about three feet)." Sometimes a young bride continued to live in her father's house. Consummation might not occur right away, but the groom, who was typically about ten years older than his young wife, was permitted to visit her at her parents' house in order to consummate the marriage and might live there with his bride for a while. This phase of a marriage was referred to as "calling at the house of the in-law." Dowry lists often include a bed in which to consummate the marriage.

Virginity. A young woman was expected to remain a virgin until she married. She had a group of male "friends" called "best men," who were expected to protect her from danger, safeguard her chastity, and display the "bloody sheet" from the marriage bed after her wedding night. Penetration of the vagina was the standard used to determine whether a woman was a virgin. The law code of Babylonian king Hammurabi (circa 1792 – circa 1750 B.C.E.) addresses the issue of a bride's compromised virginity:

If a free man selects a bride for his son and his son carnally knows her, after which he himself (the father) then lies with her and they seize him in the act, they shall bind that man and cast him into the water.

If a man selects a bride for his son and his son does not yet carnally know her, and he himself then lies with her, he shall weigh and deliver to her 30 shekels of silver; moreover he shall restore to her whatever she brought from her father's house, and a husband of her choice shall marry her. (LH §§155–156; Roth, 1995)

Polygamy. With few exceptions, a man could have only one wife. The Laws of Hammurabi allowed the husband to take a second wife, if his first wife was incapacitated. He could not divorce his first wife, however, and had to support her for the rest of her life. According to both law and custom, a barren wife could have a slave girl bear children for her. Under the law this surrogate's children were considered the wife's children. A barren wife could also adopt a woman such as her sister and allow that woman to marry her husband. If he married a celibate priestess, the second wife was often her sister. In Assyria, where the status of women was low, a man could elevate a concubine to wife by covering her in a veil (which was worn by a married woman). A Middle Assyrian law explains: "If a man veils his concubine, he shall have five or six of his comrades present, and he shall veil her in their presence, he shall say, 'She is my wife.' She is (then) his wife." A concubine who became a wife, like any wife, had to be veiled in public. An ordinary concubine not in the company of her master's wife could not be veiled, but she was expected to wear a veil when she accompanied the legal wife in public. The status of a concubine-wife remained secondary, and, if the legal wife bore sons, they, not the concubine's children, inherited the father's estates. If a secondary wife were chosen from among the family's slaves, she was expected to continue serving the legal wife, performing duties such as carrying her chair when she went to the temple and assisting her in her toiletries.

Adultery. The Laws of Hammurabi include a case in which a wife took a lover and encouraged him to murder her husband. The wife's punishment was death by impalement (§153). In Middle Assyrian Law, if a cuckolded husband formally accused his wife and her lover, there were several courses of punishment:

> If the woman's husband kills his wife, then he shall also kill the man; if he cuts off his wife's nose, he shall turn the man into a eunuch and they shall lacerate his entire face; but if [the husband wishes to release] his wife, he shall [release] the man (MAL A §15; Roth)

Divorce. Divorce was rare, usually initiated by the husband, and social stigma was attached to it. The grounds for divorce were usually the wife's adultery or infertility. However, a childless marriage did not automatically result in divorce. A marriage contract sealed before five witnesses and a scribe in the city of Opis on 21 April 564 B.C.E. provides terms for divorce:

> Nabu-ah-iddin, son of Apla, spoke of Dalili-eshu, son of Arba-ila, spoke, saying, "Would you give me Banat-Esagil, your daughter, the young woman that she might be my wife?" Dalili-eshu agreed and gave Banat-Esagil his daughter, the young woman to be his wife.
>
> If at any time Nabu-ah-iddin, releases Banat-Esagil and marries another, he must give her (Banat-Esagil) six minas of silver and she can go where she wants.
>
> If Banat-Esagil is found with another man, she will die by an iron dagger.
>
> They swore on the life of Nabu and Marduk, their gods, and on the life of Nebuchadnezzar, the king, their lord, not to contravene (this agreement). (Roth, 1989)

Penalties for Divorce. If a husband divorced his wife, he had to return his wife's property and sometimes pay a fine. When a woman was divorced, the hem of her robe was cut, a symbolic reversal of knotting the bride payment

---

THE VEIL AND THE PROSTITUTE

Middle Assyrian Law identified which women must and must not be veiled. A married woman had to be veiled in public, but slave women and prostitutes were strictly forbidden from this practice. The penalty for a prostitute caught wearing a veil was severe:

Whoever sees a prostitute veiled shall seize her, he shall secure witnesses, and bring her before the entrance of the palace. They shall not take her jewelry, but the one who seized her shall take her clothing. Fifty strokes he shall beat her and they shall pour liquid pitch on her. . . . (MAL A §40)

The law further stipulated that a man who sees a prostitute or slave woman wearing a veil and does not detain her shall receive the same punishment, and the person who reports him to authorities shall be given his clothing as a reward.

Source: Martha T. Roth, *Law Collections from Mesopotamia and Asia Minor*, second edition, Society of Biblical Literature, Writings from the Ancient World Series, volume 6 (Atlanta, Ga.: Scholars Press, 1995).

---

in her robe. Many marriage contracts from the Old Babylonian period (circa 1894 – circa 1595 B.C.E.) specify that the wife cannot divorce her husband, and mandate that, if she leaves him, she will receive the sort of severe punishment usually reserved for adultery, such as drowning in the river, being pushed from a tower, being impaled, or being sold into slavery. In other cases, if a woman said she wanted a divorce, she could be turned out of her husband's home penniless and naked. The circumstances of a divorce were determined by whether the wife had sons. If she had no sons, the husband's family did not care if she went back to her father's house or elsewhere. Some Late Babylonian marriage contracts (seventh through third centuries B.C.E.), however, allowed either the husband or the wife to divorce and fined each an equal amount. Middle Assyrian Laws (circa 1400 – 1050 B.C.E.) specified that, if a woman's husband deserted her without providing for her or leaving sons who could support her, she could take another husband after five years. If her first husband then returned, he could not reclaim her unless he had been away for reasons beyond his control, such as being captured in battle. In such cases, however, the first husband had to find a replacement wife for the second husband.

Sources:
W. G. Lambert, *Babylonian Wisdom Literature* (Oxford: Clarendon Press, 1960).

Karen Rhea Nemet-Nejat, *Daily Life in Ancient Mesopotamia*, Daily Life through History (Westport, Conn.: Greenwood Press, 1998).

Martha T. Roth, *Babylonian Marriage Agreements 7th–3rd Centuries B.C.*, Alter Orient und Altes Testement, volume 222 (Kevelaer: Butzon & Bercker / Neukirchen-Vluyn: Neukirchener, 1989).

Roth, "The Dowries of the Women of the Itti-Marduk-balāṭu Family," *Journal of the American Oriental Society*, 111 (1991): 19–37.

Roth, *Law Collections from Mesopotamia and Asia Minor*, second edition, Society of Biblical Literature, Writings from the Ancient World Series, volume 6 (Atlanta, Ga.: Scholars Press, 1995).

PROPERTY AND SUCCESSION

Inheritance. Patterns of inheritance varied by time and place. Each city had its own customs. For the most part, the eldest son received a larger share of his father's estate than his brothers; for example, he might be left two of the shares instead of one; an extra proportion, at least 10 percent, of the total assets; or a choice of what part of the estate his share might comprise while his brothers drew lots for their shares. Inheritance might include land, houses, furniture, slaves, and animals, as well as religious and military duties. During the second millennium B.C.E., in some peripheral areas such as Nuzi in northeast Mesopotamia and Emar in Syria, a daughter was treated the same as a son in the eyes of the law and could inherit a share of her father's estate.

The Estate. The estate was physically divided after the father's death so the married brothers could set up independent households. The oldest son might be left the family home because of his duties to maintain the family graves, which were often beneath the house. Burying the

---

PROOF OF PATERNITY

In a patrilineal system, property is divided among the surviving sons or the closest related male line. The children of a man whose brother died without heirs therefore stood to inherit from their uncle's estate. Sometimes uncles became greedy and disputed the paternity of a baby born after a brother's death. Three tablets from Emar on the Euphrates in Syria include an attempt to forestall actions that might prevent a man's children from inheriting his estate. One or both footprints of each child—two boys and one girl, apparently triplets—were impressed on tablets next to the seals of the witnesses. For example, written around and across one footprint are the words: "Foot(print) of Ishma-Dagan, the son of Satamma, son of Karbi, a man from the city of Satappa. The seal of Dagan-belum. The seal of Lahe. The seal of Aya-damqat."

Source: Erle Leichty, "Feet of Clay," in *DUMU-E₂-DUB-BA-A: Studies in Honor of Åke W. Sjöberg*, edited by Hermann Behrens, Darlene Loding, and Martha T. Roth, Occasional Publications of the Samuel Noah Kramer Fund, no. 11 (Philadelphia: Samuel Noah Kramer Fund, University Museum, 1989), pp. 349–356.

---

dead beneath the family's house was practiced in various parts of Mesopotamia from Early Dynastic times (circa 2900 – circa 2340 B.C.E.) through the Old Babylonian period (circa 1894 – circa 1595 B.C.E.). Cemeteries were also found within and outside cities. In some periods, in order to maintain the revenue it produced, real estate was not divided. If the family home was large enough for each brother to have separate family quarters in it, the house was divided. Sometimes the division of the family house resulted in such small rooms that people could not live in them. In these cases some people transferred ownership of tiny uninhabitable rooms to other family members in "paper transactions."

Wills. Even though a will might favor the eldest son, bequests to others could be made as well. The father could also disinherit family members, but this decision required validation by the court, which could modify or revoke a father's action if it found that the father acted either quickly or unfairly. Because sons of a deceased brother inherited their father's share of the grandfather's estate, uncles sometimes questioned the paternity of a son born after his father's death. The resolution to a case of disputed paternity is found in a tablet from Nippur during the reign of Samsu-iluna (circa 1749 – circa 1712 B.C.E.) during the Old Babylonian period:

> Ninurta-ra'im-zerim, son of Enlil-bani, approached and faced the court officials and judges of Nippur (testifying): "When I was in the womb of Sin-na'id, my mother, Enlil-bani, my father, died before (my mother) gave birth to me. Habannatum, my paternal grandmother, informed Luga, the chief herdsman, and Sin-gamil, the judge, (and) she sent a midwife and delivered me. When I grew up, in the 20th year of Samsu-iluna . . ." (The uncles testified:) "Ninurta-ra'im-zerim is not the son of Enlil-bani." . . . The court officials and the judges investigated the case. They read the earlier tablet with the oath. They questioned their witnesses, and discussed their testimony. In this regard, thus was their testimony: "We know that Ninurta-ra'im-zerim is the child of Enlil-bani," they said. (Leichty)

Gifts. During his lifetime the head of the household could give gifts that were not later considered part of the family estate. The Laws of Hammurabi (circa 1792 – circa 1750 B.C.E.) cover this situation:

> If a man awards by sealed contract a field, orchard, or house to his favorite heir, when the brothers divide the estate after the father goes to his fate (dies), he (the favorite son) shall take the gift which the father gave to him and apart from that gift they shall equally divide the property of the paternal estate. (LH §165; Roth)

Such gift giving also protected daughters so that they might receive a proper dowry. Also, if the father died before a dowry was executed, the sons had to give a share of the estate to their sister.

Widows. The Akkadian term *almattu* designated not only a widow in the modern sense of a woman whose husband has died but also any married woman who had no financial support from a male member of her family. Such a woman was in need of legal protection and could even contract a second husband or enter a profession. A woman who had children was granted control of her dowry when her husband died, and it went to her biological sons and daughters when she died. A widow could not inherit from her husband's estate if she had no children, and when she died, her dowry became the property of her brothers and their descendants. However, her husband could set aside property for her before he died. If a husband died before his wife and left no will, his widow was allowed to live in his house, and their children had to support her. A widow could run her husband's business by herself, but, if she remarried, she lost this right. Contracts from Emar, a city on the Euphrates in western Syria, describe a symbolic act performed by a widow leaving her late husband's family to remarry. She placed "her clothes on a stool" and left without taking any of her possessions.

Priestesses. If a girl became a priestess, her brothers were obligated to support her. They managed the dowry she took with her to the temple or cloister, and when she died, they or their descendants inherited her estate. This practice conserved the family estates. However, the priestesses of Marduk (the patron god of Babylon) kept their dowries, and their brothers were not permitted to claim their estates. Sometimes a priestess adopted another priestess or a slave and left her property to that person instead of her brothers. The slave could be emancipated with the condition that the slave take care of the priestess in her old age and carry out the burial rites.

Sources:

F. R. Kraus, "Von Altmesopotamischen Erbrecht," in *Essays on Oriental Laws of Succession,* Studia et Documenta, volume 9 (Leiden: Brill, 1969), pp. 1–57.

Erle Leichty, "Feet of Clay," in *DUMU-E₂-DUB-BA-A: Studies in Honor of Åke W. Sjöberg,* edited by Hermann Behrens, Darlene Loding, and Martha T. Roth, Occasional Publications of the Samuel Noah Kramer Fund, no. 11 (Philadelphia: Samuel Noah Kramer Fund, University Museum, 1989), pp. 349–356.

Karen Rhea Nemet-Nejat, *Cuneiform Mathematical Texts as a Reflection of Everyday Life in Mesopotamia,* American Oriental Series, volume 75 (New Haven: American Oriental Society, 1993).

Nemet-Nejat, *Daily Life in Ancient Mesopotamia,* Daily Life through History (Westport, Conn.: Greenwood Press, 1998).

J. N. Postgate, *Early Mesopotamia: Society and Economy at the Dawn of History* (London & New York: Routledge, 1992).

Martha T. Roth, *Law Collections from Mesopotamia and Asia Minor,* second edition, Society of Biblical Literature, Writings from the Ancient World Series, volume 6 (Atlanta, Ga.: Scholars Press, 1995).

SEXUAL PRACTICES

Erotica. Erotic clay figurines, cylinder seals, and plaques graphically depicting positions for sexual intercourse and sensual pleasure have been found throughout

Nude couple on a bed; modern impression made from a mold (length 4 7/8 inches), unprovenanced, circa 1900 – circa 1600 B.C.E. (Vorderasiatisches Museum, Berlin; photograph by Julia Assante)

the Near East at the sites of ancient temples, tombs, houses, and taverns. Terra-cotta plaques from the Old Babylonian period (circa 1894 – circa 1595 B.C.E.) and lead plaques from the Middle Assyrian period (circa 1400 – 1050 B.C.E.), in particular, illustrate a variety of erotic subjects, providing information about Mesopotamian sexual practices.

Intercourse. The most common position for sexual intercourse was "the missionary position." Some sources describe intercourse with the woman on top of the man, which is perhaps the context for the Amorite saying "You

"Woman at the window" (height 4 3/8 inches), from the North-West Palace, Nimrud, about ninth–eighth centuries B.C.E.
Perhaps a sacred prostitute, the woman is wearing an Egyptian-style headdress, and the window is over a balcony
supported by columns depicted in relief in a south Syrian-style ivory furniture inlay
(British Museum, London).

be the man, let me be the woman." A sexual omen in the series *Shumma alu,* the encyclopedic corpus of omens taken from events in people's everyday lives, compiled in the seventh century B.C.E., warns that in this position, the "woman will take his vigor (and) for one month (a variant has 'one year'), he will not have a personal god." Old Babylonian–period clay plaques commonly depict intercourse with the man standing and penetrating the woman from behind.

Menstruation. A menstruating woman was said to be "hit by the weapon" and was released from her daily work for the six days of her period. During this time she was regarded as unclean, and a man who touched her was also considered unclean for six days.

Contraception. Omen texts also mention anal intercourse between husband and wife, which may have been used as a form of contraception. Priestesses, who were not supposed to bear children, are said to have practiced anal

intercourse to avoid pregnancy. They were also reputed to have contraceptives, possibly herbs and charms, to "keep their wombs intact."

Abortion. One medical text provides a prescription for abortion, called "to drop her fetus." These apparent abortion remedies consist of eight ingredients to be added to wine for a woman to drink on an empty stomach.

Prostitution. Some plaques seem to portray prostitutes leaning on the town walls, where they commonly lived and worked. Prostitutes dressed to attract business. An Assyrian text describes an undergarment that a prostitute untied to prepare herself for clients. She also wore a special leather jacket. Religious prostitutes—males, females, and eunuchs—were associated with some temples, more often in Babylonia than in Assyria. Phoenician ivory furniture inlays from the first millennium B.C.E. portraying a woman at the window have been found in Assyria, Syria, and ancient Israel. Art historians typically interpret this motif as representing the Phoenician goddess Astarte, or her votary, luring men to serve the goddess by sexual union. Herodotus of Halicarnassus reported that, in the fifth century B.C.E., every native Babylonian woman "must once in her life go and sit in the temple of Aphrodite (i.e., Ishtar), and there give herself to a strange man." Alewives ran taverns where men drank, listened to music, and had sex with prostitutes. The taproom walls were decorated with clay plaques of erotic scenes. The alewife's social position is not clear. One tavern that has been excavated had small rooms off the main hall. Within each small room was a hole in the ground that held a special vessel for drinking beer.

Homosexuality. Mesopotamian texts from the third millennium B.C.E. and later, refer to male homosexuality. Lesbian practices were rarely mentioned. Sodomy occurred between men and between men and boys. During the latter half of the second millennium B.C.E., Babylonians did not condemn sodomy or other homosexual practices, but male prostitutes were either despised or considered laughable. While the Babylonian policy toward homosexuality was relatively tolerant, during the Middle Assyrian period (circa 1400 – 1050 B.C.E.) homosexuality was severely punished. According to Middle Assyrian Law,

> If a man sodomizes his comrade and they prove the charges against him and find him guilty, they shall sodomize him and they shall turn him into a eunuch (that is, castrate him). (MAL A §20; Roth)

Some priests in the cult of Ishtar were homosexuals known for their skills in dancing and cross-dressing.

Eunuchs. Eunuchs, men who had been castrated, were common. They served at the court and became high officials, a practice that continued up to the nineteenth century C.E. in the Turkish and Persian Empires.

Though not all courtiers and officials were eunuchs, kings liked to put eunuchs in charge of districts because no family claims would create conflicting loyalties. In the Middle Assyrian period eunuchs worked in the harems. Eunuchs whose sex organs were removed as a punishment were rare. Instead they were castrated as boys to prepare them for lucrative government careers. Some small percentage of males failed to develop normally and were considered eunuchs. In Assyria many of them are thought to have become prostitutes.

Sexual Dysfunction. Impotence and premature ejaculation are mentioned in various sources. Impotence was treated by performing rituals and using particular ointments and aphrodisiacs. No treatment for premature ejaculation is included in surviving sources.

Sources:
Julia Assante, "Sex, Magic and the Liminal Body in the Erotic Art and Texts of the Old Babylonian Period," in *Sex and Gender in the Ancient Near East. Proceedings of the 47th Rencontre Assyriologique International Helsinki, July 2–6, 2001*, 2 volumes, edited by Simo Parpola and Robert M. Whiting (Helsinki: Neo-Assyrian Text Corpus Project, 2002), I: 27–52.

Karen Rhea Nemet-Nejat, *Daily Life in Ancient Mesopotamia*, Daily Life through History (Westport, Conn.: Greenwood Press, 1998).

Martha T. Roth, *Law Collections from Mesopotamia and Asia Minor*, second edition, Society of Biblical Literature, Writings from the Ancient World Series, volume 6 (Atlanta, Ga.: Scholars Press, 1995).

WOMEN'S ROLES

The Position of Women. In a hymn to the goddess Gula (the patron of doctors and healing), the stages of a woman's life were described as follows: "I am a daughter, I am a bride, I am a spouse, I am a housekeeper." Once she was married, a woman's most important role was to bear children, especially sons. A tablet of Middle Assyrian Laws (circa 1400 – circa 1050 B.C.E.) has fifty-nine clauses relating to women.

Women in the Third Millennium B.C.E. Mesopotamian women were never equal to men before the law. The position of women in the early Sumerian city-state was higher than in later periods, perhaps because goddesses were important in Sumerian religion. Later, during the reign of king Sargon (circa 2334 – circa 2279 B.C.E.), the Akkadians continued Sumerian religious observances. Sargon appointed his daughter Enheduana high priestess of the moon god, Nanna, at Ur, a position which succeeding kings filled with royal princesses for the next five hundred years. A gifted poet, Enheduana is the first author whose name is known. She wrote religious and personal poetry in Sumerian, using traditional Sumerian literary forms. Thirteen hundred lines of her poetry have survived. Her poetry was catalogued, studied, and copied in Mesopotamian scribal schools. Many succeeding kings emulated Sargon by appointing their daughters to high religious positions.

Women in the Second Millennium B.C.E. During the mid-second millennium B.C.E. free women at Nuzi, a

---

THE DIVINE ALEWIFE

The divine alewife Siduri appears in the Old Babylonian version of the *Epic of Gilgamesh*, where she offers these words of advice to Gilgamesh before he undertakes his final journey in search of eternal life:

When the gods created mankind,
they fixed Death for human beings,
and retained Life in their own hands.
Now, you, Gilgamesh, let your stomach be full!
Rejoice day and night,
make a party of each day,
dance in circles day and night!

Source: Maureen Gallery Kovacs, *The Epic of Gilgamesh* (Stanford: Stanford University Press, 1989).

ENHEDUANA'S BANISHMENT

Late in the reign of Sargon (circa 2334 – circa 2279), her father, as revolts spread throughout his empire, Enheduana, the chief priestess of the moon god Nanna, was driven from office and fled the city of Ur. In a poem to the goddess Inana, she lamented her situation:

Verily I had entered my holy *giparu* at your behest,
I, the high priestess, I, Enheduana!
I carried the ritual basket, I intoned the acclaim.
(But now) I'm placed in the lepers' ward, I, even I, can no
   longer live with you!
They approach the light of day, the light is obscured about
   me,
The shadows approach the light of day, is covered with a
   (sand)storm.
My mellifluous mouth is cast into confusion.
My choicest features are turned to dust.

Source: William W. Hallo and J. J. A. van Dijk, *The Exaltation of Inanna,* Yale Near Eastern Researches, volume 3 (New Haven: Yale University Press, 1968).

Mesopotamian provincial town with a substantial Hurrian population, were active in the economy and the courts. In Nuzi a wife could be involved in business activities with her husband's permission. When they were permitted to engage in business, women performed the same jobs as men. They were considered the legal equals of men and could sue and be sued in cases related to landownership. One free woman of Nuzi owned at least six towns. Elsewhere, widows who were responsible for minor children could be involved in economic activities. As head of such a family, a widow could inherit and administer the family estate. Though a woman had no control over her dowry, a woman from a rich family might be given silver or other precious metals apart from her dowry. She was allowed to keep whatever profit she made from investing or lending these assets. During different periods, the property a woman built up by herself was described as in her "hand," "tied in the corner of her garment," or "in her basket." Middle Assyrian Laws permitted widows to cohabit with a man without a formal marriage contract, but after two years, she legally became that man's wife (MAL A §34).

Female Scribes. The kings of the Ur III Dynasty (circa 2112 – circa 2004 B.C.E.) were praised in songs written by their queens. Lullabies for the crown prince, long songs to the king, and laments were also written by female scribes. Though most scribes were men, there were woman scribes in Old Babylonian Sippar and Mari, some of them daughters of male scribes. At least ten female scribes are known to have worked in Mari. Nine of them were slaves, women of low status who received small rations. Sometimes slave scribes were given to princesses as part of their dowries. One fragment of an Old Babylonian vocabulary text lists female scribes as scholars. There were also female equivalents of diviners, physicians, performers, and artists. All these female professionals were considered secondary to males in the same jobs, and women were paid less.

Cloistered Women. Priestesses were wealthy women who lived in cloisters. Except for priestesses of Shamash (the sun god), these women were not allowed to marry, and even the women who served Shamash were celibate and bore no children. According to the Laws of Hammurabi (§§144–147), these priestesses gave their husbands female slaves to provide children. Cloisters were established in the Old Babylonian period. The best known was in Sippar, where the cloister staff included managers, officials, scribes, laborers, and female personal slaves. A wealthy family might send one daughter with a considerable dowry consisting of houses, fields, orchards, and household slaves. In return, her family expected her to pray for them. In Sippar the cloister also functioned as an entrepreneurial institution. Female scribes recorded business transactions for the members of the cloister. Priestesses took part in various business activities, such as buying, selling, and leasing fields. The many records of such transactions reveal that the priestesses at Sippar were talented businesswomen.

Sources:

Benjamin R. Foster, "The Birth Legend of King Sargon of Akkad," in *The Context of Scripture*, volume 1, edited by William W. Hallo, with K. Lawson Younger Jr. (New York & Leiden: Brill, 1996), pp. 518–521.

Karen Rhea Nemet-Nejat, *Daily Life in Ancient Mesopotamia*, Daily Life through History (Westport, Conn.: Greenwood Press, 1998).

Nemet-Nejat, "Women in Ancient Mesopotamia," in *Women's Roles in Ancient Civilizations: A Reference Guide*, edited by Bella Vivante (Westport, Conn.: Greenwood Press, 1999), pp. 85–114.

Martha T. Roth, *Law Collections from Mesopotamia and Asia Minor*, second edition, Society of Biblical Literature, Writings from the Ancient World Series, volume 6 (Atlanta, Ga.: Scholars Press, 1995).

Marten Stol, "Private Life in Ancient Mesopotamia," in *Civilizations of the Ancient Near East*, 4 volumes, edited by Jack M. Sasson (New York: Scribners, 1995), I: 485–501.

SIGNIFICANT PEOPLE

ENANATUM

CIRCA MID TWENTIETH CENTURY B.C.E.
HIGH PRIESTESS OF UR

King's Daughter. The kings of the First Dynasty of Isin went to great lengths to justify their claim to kingship. Following the example of Sargon of Akkad two centuries earlier, the fourth king of the dynasty, Ishme-Dagan (circa 1953 – circa 1935 B.C.E.), installed his daughter Enanatum as the high priestess at Ur, where she was charged with the task of rebuilding the ancient temple. It has been suggested that she was responsible for the preservation of a stone disk bearing an inscription and image of Sargon's daughter Enheduana, the first high priestess of the moon god at Ur.

Source:
R. McHale-Moore, "The Mystery of Enheduanna's Disk," *Journal of the Ancient Near Eastern Society*, 27 (2000): 69–74.

HAMMURABI

CIRCA 1792 – CIRCA 1750 B.C.E.
KING OF BABYLON

Conqueror and Lawgiver. When Hammurabi first came to the throne, he ruled a small area around the city of Babylon—including the nearby cities of Kish, Sippar, and Borsippa—he was the subject of the king Rim-Sin of Larsa. In his thirtieth regnal year Hammurabi defeated Rim-Sin and seized control of much of central and southern Mesopotamia. Two years later, circa 1760 B.C.E., Hammurabi gained control of Eshnunna, the dominant city in the Diyala River valley, and further north, the city of Ashur on the Tigris. These conquests gave him control over the trade routes to and from the Iranian plateau. In the following year, to gain control of the trade routes to the west, Hammurabi attacked Mari on the middle Euphrates, eventually tearing down its walls. This conquest made him the sole and undisputed master of Mesopotamia, a kingdom his successors were unable to retain. Hammurabi was greatly revered in future generations, who read, studied, and recopied his law code, royal inscriptions, and royal correspondence. A substantial portion of his law code is devoted to marriage and family law.

Source:
Amélie Kuhrt, *The Ancient Near East c. 3000-330 B.C.*, 2 volumes (London & New York: Routledge, 1995).

DOCUMENTARY SOURCES

A Cow of Sin (Akkadian: second half of the second millennium B.C.E.)—Known from five manuscripts from Hittite, Middle Assyrian, and Neo-Assyrian sites, this incantation for a woman during childbirth includes magical ceremonies and medical prescriptions. In this story the moon god falls in love with his beautiful cow and inseminates her. As she is giving birth, the moon god in heaven hears her cries and sends two spirits to help ease her labor pains. The calf is named "Milk Calf," and the incantation ends, "Let the child come out rapidly and see the light of the sun."

Laws of Eshnunna (Akkadian: circa 1770 B.C.E.)—The date formula written in Sumerian on the incomplete tablet of these laws suggests that they date to the reign of Dadusha, king of the city of Eshnunna, located on the Dyala River. The composition is similar to royal *mesharum*-edicts, enacted at irregular intervals to cancel private debts in order to provide for economic reforms. The Laws of Eshnunna set price and wage standards for services and equipment and grain interest rates. Other examples concern renter's liability, agricultural matters, theft, pledges, deposits and loans, silver and grain values for basic goods and equipment, sexual offenses, the goring ox, and runaway slaves.

Laws of Hammurabi (Akkadian: circa 1750 B.C.E.)—Compiled toward the end of Hammurabi's forty-two-year reign (circa 1792 –circa 1750 B.C.E.), the laws of Hammurabi are the most complete surviving legal code. Based on earlier traditions, this body of laws comprises 282 laws, as well as an introduction and a conclusion. The cases deal with promises, debts, loans, sales and rentals, marriage, rates for hire, adoption, assault, and the goring ox.

Middle Assyrian Laws (Akkadian: circa fourteenth – circa eleventh century B.C.E.)—The Middle Assyrian Laws are a series of more than a dozen tablets copied in the eleventh century B.C.E. from originals dating as far back as the fourteenth century B.C.E. With the exception of a Neo-Assyrian fragment excavated at Nineveh, all were excavated at Ashur. The laws are not part of a single code. Together they include a variety of legal provisions covering a wide range of situations. Tablet A focuses on women as principles and victims in issues of theft, assault, sexual conduct, inheritance, marriage, divorce, veiling, witchcraft, pregnancy, and rape.

The Poor Man of Nippur (Akkadian: 701 B.C.E.)—In this Babylonian poetic-satirical folktale set in the city of Nippur during the Old Babylonian period, a poor man takes revenge on the mayor who wronged him. Copies of the poem include a dated example from Sultantepe and a fragment from Ashurbanipal's library in Nineveh. The poor man, Gimil-Ninurta, trades his only garment for a nanny goat. He presents the goat to the mayor of the city, hoping the mayor will provide him with a meal and clothing. The mayor accepts the goat and has it slaughtered, but then throws Gimil-Ninurta out, giving him only a bone and gristle to eat and third-rate beer to drink. Gimil-Ninurta connives to take his revenge on the mayor on three different occasions, each time "thrashing him from head to toe."

Shumma alu ina mele shakin (Akkadian: circa seventh century B.C.E.)—The subjects of this omen series, whose Akkadian title may be translated, "If a city is set on a height," are taken from seemingly ordinary events in people's everyday lives. Tablets 103–106 list omens taken from observations of human sexual practices and familial relations.

Titles and Professions List (circa 3200 B.C.E.)—Lexical lists were at the core of the curriculum for training scribes in all periods of cuneiform use. Copies of this particular list are known from the earliest phase of proto-cuneiform writing at Uruk, circa 3200 B.C.E. The list continued to be copied virtually unchanged, except for the sign forms, in every period until the Old Babylonian period in the first half of the second millennium B.C.E., when new lexical lists were devised. This text lists titles, names of professions, and functional designations in an order and sequence determined by rank. It seems to show the actual administrative situation at archaic Uruk in the late fourth millennium B.C.E.

RELIGION
AND PHILOSOPHY

by IRA SPAR

CONTENTS

Sidebars and tables are listed in italics.

IMPORTANT EVENTS OF 3300-331 B.C.E.

3200* B.C.E.

- Writing is developed in southern Mesopotamia.

2900*-2600* B.C.E.

- Uruk is ruled by the postdiluvian legendary kings Enmerkar, Dumuzi, Lugalbanda, and Gilgamesh.

- Real-estate transactions are inscribed on stone.

2500* B.C.E.

- Myths, hymns, incantations, and wisdom texts are recorded on tablets in the Sumerian cities of Fara (ancient Shuruppak) and Abu Salabikh.

- The first royal inscriptions are recorded at Kish.

2350*-2150* B.C.E.

- Myths about Semitic gods and legends about Akkadian rulers are possibly composed during this period.

- Sumerian, Akkadian, and Eblaite literary and magical texts are preserved in a royal archive at Tell Mardikh (ancient Ebla) in Syria. The earliest known Semitic letters and ritual tablets are written at Ebla.

2100*-2000* B.C.E.

- A period of Sumerian literary creativity takes place during the Third Dynasty of Ur. The *Sumerian King List* and probably Sumerian legends of the early kings of Uruk are recorded. Royal hymns, temple hymns, and hymns to the gods are written.

- The first surviving reference to the celebration of the Akitu festival, the "Festival of the Sowing of Barley," dates to this period. It is held at the beginning of spring during the first month of the year.

1800* B.C.E

- Antediluvian rulers are added to the *Sumerian King List.*

1800*-1600* B.C.E.

- Although the Sumerian language is probably no longer spoken, Sumerian literature is studied and edited in the Old Babylonian school *(edub'a)*. Hymns, rituals, prayers, and magical texts—mainly in Sumerian—are created for use in temples and palaces. Myths, proverbs, fables, literary letters, and wisdom literature are also copied and preserved. Akkadian translations of Sumerian words begin to appear in school copies of lexical texts.

- Akkadian literary, religious, and poetic texts increase in number. Babylonian versions of the *Epic of Gilgamesh* and the *Myth of Atra-hasis* are developed.

1750* B.C.E.

- The local god Marduk is elevated to supreme god of Babylon.

* DENOTES CIRCA DATE

IMPORTANT EVENTS OF 3300-331 B.C.E.

1600*-1150* B.C.E.

- Mesopotamian literary and religious texts written primarily in Akkadian continue to grow in number and evolve under the Kassite dynasty. Sumerian religious texts are copied; some are translated line by line into Akkadian, creating new bilingual Sumerian-Akkadian compositions.

- The scribe Sin-leqe-unnini edits a new version of the *Epic of Gilgamesh*, which later becomes the standard version of that work.

1100* B.C.E.

- *Enuma elish*, the Babylonian myth of creation, is composed.

1000*-612 B.C.E.

- Aramaic becomes the lingua franca of Mesopotamia, with Akkadian becoming a language of scholarship.

800*-700* B.C.E.

- The Babylonian myth *Erra and Ishum* is composed by the scribe Kabti-ilani-Marduk.

668-627* B.C.E.

- During the reign of Ashurbanipal, king of Assyria, a great collection of cuneiform scholastic and religious tablets is gathered and placed in a royal library in Nineveh. Scribes copy traditional religious texts, primarily those created during the second millennium B.C.E. The largest group of tablets in the library is omen texts. Lexical texts, scholarly lists of words and signs, are the second largest body of tablets. Incantations and prayers, many of which are bilingual with line-by-line translations of Sumerian into Akkadian, are the third largest body of texts. The library also includes medical texts, literary compositions, and commentaries.

- Collections of literary and scholastic texts also are assembled in temple libraries.

- Specialized collections of incantations and medical texts are maintained by exorcists and priests.

331 B.C.E.-224 C.E.

- Greek is adopted as the language of the upper class.

* DENOTES CIRCA DATE

OVERVIEW

History. Mesopotamian civilization existed for more than three millennia. The religious system founded by the Sumerians at the end of the fourth millennium B.C.E. continued for more than a thousand years until it merged with the Semitic religions of the Babylonians and Assyrians. In this incarnation it lasted for another two thousand years, still retaining characteristics of its Sumerian ancestry. Throughout the millennia, the changing world of the gods represented differing political configurations of monarchy and unquestioned political power. Within this context enduring questions about mankind's existence and its relationship to divinity were raised, and a variety of mythological responses was proposed.

Theological Questions. The theologians of ancient Mesopotamia sought to interpret the world around them. Questions abounded about the origins of evil, the beginnings of the universe, the nature of the gods, and the ills of everyday life. There were no clear answers to these questions. The only certainty for the Mesopotamians was that everything in the world was controlled by the supernatural. The ebb and flow of life and the events of history were understood for the most part as an unending sequence of divine approval or disapproval of mankind's conduct. An individual who followed the proper path was, according to the official theology, rewarded by the gods with prosperity, good health, and a long life. But, those who angered the gods by violating their rules, willfully or otherwise, suffered divine retribution. Cursed for their crimes, attacked by evil spirits, and dogged by misfortune, these individuals suffered grievously for their misdeeds.

Relationship to the Gods. Religious thinkers never questioned the superiority of the gods. They recognized that the gods, like rulers, were inscrutable and unpredictable and that one had to live with their judgments. According to the theology of the cult, the gods needed mankind to make divine lives more pleasant, just as a ruler needs servants to supply comfort. Thus, even if the gods became angry with mankind and caused distress, illness, or misfortune, there was always hope that requests through prayer, hymns, rituals, and sacrifices would soften their attitudes and cause them to relent. Rituals filled with flattery, good food, pomp, and song were thought to appeal to the gods' sympathetic inclinations.

Revelation. What sort of life and events the gods determined for mankind was a difficult question for Mesopotamians to answer. Unlike the deity of ancient Israel, Mesopotamian gods did not reveal themselves to mankind. Instead, they allowed divination specialists glimpses into the future by communicating encoded signs that could be accessed through observations of animals' entrails, humans' unusual behaviors or dreams, and celestial bodies and meteorological phenomena. If these signs were properly understood, the events they foretold could be averted through prayer, penitence, and appropriate rituals.

Admonitions. Writers throughout the ancient Near East saw no distinction between the sacred and the secular. Rules of conduct were designed to pertain to all areas of life. Mesopotamian scribes copied out admonitions, words of wisdom addressed by a father to a son. These directives, which instructed a son to worship his god and operate within prescribed behavioral boundaries, were directed toward maintaining the status quo, so as not to upset the order that the gods had determined for mankind. If followed, this path would bring the individual into harmony with the divine order and lead to success and a prosperous life.

Suffering of the Righteous. Mesopotamian theologians asked if piety would yield its own reward. They observed that some people suffer for no reason other than having been forsaken by a personal god. To probe further would mean to ask troubling questions about the motivations of the gods. Only prayer to one's god could heal one's ills. Sumerian and Babylonian theology had no satisfactory answer for the problem of human suffering. If the gods chose not to forgive a person's transgressions, neither magic, sacrifice, nor prayer would be of any use.

Law and Religion. While Babylonian religious thinkers described history as a sequence of moral crimes and divine punishments, Mesopotamian legal thinkers recognized that for society to be ordered and to function for the benefit of its inhabitants and gods, penitential prayers and cultic incantations were not by themselves sufficient; laws were necessary to set limits and regulate behavior. Rulers who called themselves kings of justice developed laws and proscribed certain actions as illegal. Legal systems were developed to maintain and advance a country's economic and political stability and at the same time to proscribe behavior that, under the common ethic, was believed to be offensive to the gods. Law in accord with the gods' desires was merely one way to make life better, to obtain security, and to achieve prosperity.

Temples. The temple was the center of religious practices. It was the home of the god and the deity's family. Each city had a temple dedicated to its main god and other temples for lesser deities. The god ate and conducted affairs in the temple. A table (altar) was set up for meals. The god slept in a house (temple), and its rooms served the needs of family and servants. A boat was moored at a quay, prepared to take the deity on journeys to neighboring temples. The god was represented in the temple by a statue made of wood, plated with gold, and inset with precious stones. The temple raised livestock on its lands, fish in its fisheries, and food crops on its fields; various products were made in its workshops. Income from temple industries paid for the pomp and ceremony needed to support the gods and the temple staff. One of the ruler's main tasks was to build temples, keep others in good repair, and contribute funds for their operation.

Hellenism and Mesopotamian Religion. When Alexander III (the Great) of Macedonia (336–323 B.C.E.) conquered the land between the two rivers in 331 B.C.E., he encountered strange, exotic practices largely unknown to the Greeks. During the centuries that followed, old rituals continued to be practiced. Libraries of lamentation singers and exorcism specialists that have been recovered from the third and second centuries B.C.E. include traditional songs, prayers, and rituals in the Sumerian and Akkadian languages. Ancient texts and rituals continued to be used in the cult of the gods down to at least the first century B.C.E. Astronomical tablets were still being copied in the first century of the Common Era (C.E.). Yet, encounters with Greek thought caused a revolution in thinking and feeling. Eventually, the old gods faded away; old myths and rituals were no longer understood; and cuneiform writing came to an end. Ancient Mesopotamian thought survived in only a few fragments. It may be found in mythological parallels in the Hebrew Bible, in some Talmudic-period rabbinical practices, in divine names incorporated into later religions, in the astral religions of the Hellenistic world, and in obscure references in Greek writings.

TOPICS IN RELIGION AND PHILOSOPHY

THE CULT

Destiny. In the Mesopotamian worldview, the powers granted to the gods were considered essential for maintaining the cosmic and world orders against the constant threat of demonic chaos. The gods were said to control and be controlled by an ill-defined design, some sort of powerful and ever-present law of nature to which they had to conform. However, just as the ruler was in charge of even the smallest areas of his administration, so too the gods had to oversee the functioning of all life on earth, lest man and the demons destabilize the world. The gods' directives to mankind were not easy for humans to grasp. They had to be deciphered through techniques of divination.

Divination. In Mesopotamia the gods gave signs of their intent through events. Man sought to learn what the future held by identifying and interpreting signs in the world around him. Some signs were communicated through strange happenings on earth and in the sky, others through everyday events. The Babylonians were renowned for their practice of the art of divination, in which a symptom or an observation was used to foretell a possible future event. The prediction might herald good fortune, disaster, or doom. Elaborate collections of omens (records of phenomena that when interpreted foretold the future) were systematically compiled in order to provide possible signs of the gods' intentions and as a research base for deducing the meanings of new occurrences. Some omens were based on observation of unusual phenomena. Mundane occurrences, such as the sight of a lizard on a wall, could also be ominous warnings. Ordinary people could not be expected to interpret divine signs; only professional practitioners could understand them. During the first half of the first millennium B.C.E. most diviners worked as independent consultants to the royal courts and temples.

Consultants to Kings. Kings made use of various kinds of diviners to protect themselves and their kingdoms from the possible wrath of angry gods who may have been displeased with their actions, whether intentional or unintentional. But a king's misguided actions might not incur divine displeasure without warning. The king would be given preliminary notice in the form of portents, dreams, oracles, or visions sent as signs of divine displeasure. If these divine signals were heeded and correctly interpreted, the ruler could identify his mistake and avoid punishment by atoning for his actions through penitence, prayer, or ritual.

Dream Omens. If they wished, the gods could forewarn people of their intentions by announcing future actions in dreams, which were explained through the practice of oneiromancy (dream interpretation). A series of dream-omen tablets was compiled for use by dream interpreters. Contents of bad dreams are described in an eleven-tablet omen series called *Ziqiqu*, a "dream book" that treated dreams about drinking, eating, cannibalism, eating dung, erotica, flying, and incest. Two of the tablets describe exorcist rituals to ward off the consequences of dreams that predict illness or disaster. Other rituals were designed to protect against ominous dreams.

Directives from Gods. Mesopotamians regarded some dreams as directives from the gods. Some such dreams are recorded in mythological texts. In one version of the Gilgamesh story, the god Ea reveals to the Flood hero in a dream that the gods want to destroy mankind. A different sort of text tells how Gudea, the city governor of Lagash (circa 2100 B.C.E.), dreamed that his personal god directed him to build a temple. In the Sumerian version of the *Sargon Legend*, Ur-Zababa, the king of Kish (circa 2340 B.C.E.), has a dream about his impending assassination.

> Ur-Zababa was sleeping (and dreaming) in the holy bed-chamber, his holy residence. He realized what the dream was about, but did not put into words, did not discuss it with anyone.... After five or ten days had passed, king Ur-Zababa ... became frightened in his residence. Like a lion he urinated, sprinkling his legs, and the urine contained blood and pus. He was troubled, he was afraid like a fish floundering in brackish water. (Black et al.)

The cupbearer Sargon also has a dream:

> It was then that the cupbearer of Ezina's wine-house, Sargon, lay down not to sleep, but lay down to dream. In the dream, holy Inana drowned Ur-Zababa in a river of blood. The sleeping Sargon groaned and gnawed the ground. When king Ur-Zababa heard about this groaning, he was brought into the king's holy presence, Sargon was brought into the presence of Ur-Zababa (who said:) "Cupbearer, was a dream revealed to you in the night?" Sargon answered his king: "My king, this is my dream, which I will tell you about: There was a young woman, who was as high as the heavens and as broad as the earth. She was firmly set as the base of a wall. For me, she drowned you in a great river, a river of blood." (Black et al.)

If the king received a communication from the gods in the form of a dream or vision, he consulted with specialists who were believed capable of interpreting for him the gods' intent. Dream interpreters were often women. Some specialists were of great renown.

Prophecy. Some chosen individuals received messages from the supernatural realm in the form of visions or inspirations. At present, information about these revelations is limited to examples from two periods and areas: the city of Mari in the eighteenth century B.C.E. and Assyria during the reign of king Esarhaddon (680–669 B.C.E.). It is uncertain if these prophecies represented the interests of political or religious groups, or if they were spontaneous personal outpourings. In Assyria, the prophecies were pronounced in the name of the divinity. In Mari an official reported to king Zimri-Lim (circa 1776 – circa 1761 B.C.E.) that a prophet came to him and spoke about a vision concerning the restoration of a great door, possibly a door of a temple:

A BIBLICAL DREAM INTERPRETER

According to the Bible, Daniel, because he was considered able to interpret the gods' wishes, became an adviser to Belshazzar, who ruled Babylon as co-regent while his father, Nabonidus (555–539 B.C.E.), was in Arabia. In this tale, Nebuchadnezzar is not literally the king's "father" but rather his "ancestor" Nebuchadnezzar II (604–562 B.C.E.). The queen addressed Belshazzar as follows:

There is a man in your kingdom who has the spirit of the holy gods in him; in your father's time, illumination, understanding, and wisdom like that of the gods were to be found in him, and your father, King Nebuchadnezzar, appointed him chief of the magicians, exorcists, Chaldeans, and diviners. Seeing that there is to be found in Daniel (whom the king called Belteshazzar) extraordinary spirit, knowledge and understanding to interpret dreams, to explain riddles and solve problems, let Daniel now be called to tell the meaning [of the writing on the wall]. (Daniel 5:11–12)

Modern restoration of an inlaid panel depicting the slaughter or sacrifice of a goat; ivory, shell, red limestone, and schist set in a modern frame (height 8½ inches), Mari, Syria, circa 2600 – 2250 B.C.E. (National Museum, Aleppo)

[A certain] prophet came to find me, some time ago, concerning the restoration of the Great Door. He was all upset, and he said to me: "Undertake this work!" At present, the very day when I am sending my lord the present tablet, he came back to tell me, forcefully: "If you do not restore this door, there will be piles of bodies, and you will never escape the consequences!" This is what he said to me. (Bottéro, translated by Durand)

Celestial Omens. The fate of the king might also be determined through divination of astrological phenomena by a specialist who consulted a reference guide of some seventy tablets titled *Enuma Anu Enlil*, "When (the gods) Anu (and) Enlil." A significant body of correspondence exists from the first millennium B.C.E. that attests to the inquiries to diviners made by kings at the royal court. Although many civilizations believe that astronomical occurrences portend disaster, Babylonian and Assyrian diviners thought that signs emanating from the gods could augur both good or evil. A specialist apprised the king of the portents resulting from his observations of celestial and meteorological phenomena. The first part of the series includes predictions derived from lunar phenomena, such as the appearance of the moon, the shape of horns, halos, conjunctions, and especially eclipses. The next group of tablets deals with solar phenomena including halos, colors, and solar eclipses. An example of a solar omen is: "If the Sun rises and when it

becomes visible its light appears darkish, there will be rebellion in the land; an enemy will plunder the country." Another group investigates meteorological phenomena such as thunder, lightning, rainbows, and winds. The final section comprises omens concerning planets and fixed stars. References in the Bible attest to Israel's contempt for these magical practices of Babylon's astrologers.

Terrestrial Omens. Predictions of events associated with daily-life occurrences were compiled in a series called *Shumma alu ina mele shakin*, "If a City is Set on a Height." The series comprised more than one hundred tablets containing some ten thousand omens, including some derived from events associated with the site of a city, the construction of a house, and the appearance of fungi or phantoms. Other omens deal with human sexual practices, with washing oneself, and with predictions derived from the movements of animals, reptiles, and birds. One section concerns omens associated with the construction of a well. If, for example, a man opened a well in the sixth month of the year, "the man's son will die."

Omens of Abnormal Birth. The standard version of the omen collection dealing with abnormal births was inscribed on a series of twenty-four tablets titled *Shumma izbu*, "If a Malformed Newborn." The omens derived from observations of unusual or bizarre features of newborn animals and humans. If, for example, a ewe gives birth to (its young who looks like a) lion and it has five heads, one head (that looks like) a lion, one head (that looks like) a dog, one head (that looks like) a pig, one head (that looks like) an ibex, and one head (that looks like) a gazelle: in that year the city will suffer a defeat; an enemy will take its valuable possessions. (Leichty)

Liver Omens. According to the Mesopotamian way of thought, the gods—especially the sun god Utu (Akkadian: *Shamash*)—were believed to have encoded messages to mankind and hidden them inside the entrails of sheep, especially the liver. Practitioners were employed by kings and temples to sacrifice sheep, study their entrails, and decode the gods' words. These procedures are called extispicy. In order to practice their professions systematically, these diviners compiled reference guides to the interpretation of sheep organs. A typical entry took this form: "If an organ has the following appearance or shape, then the following events might occur." The last part of the formulation often referred to predictions about one's fortune, such as "the king will die," or "the enemy will be defeated." The practice of extispicy was the main Mesopotamian means of consulting the wishes of the gods. It was transmitted to Italy, where it continued to be used by the Etruscans and later the Romans.

Popular Omens. Most individuals who wished to know whether or not their lives or health would improve but were unable to afford the expense of slaughtering animals, sought less expensive forms of prognostication. One method, called lecanomancy, involved studying the configurations of oil when it was poured onto water. Other practices included observation of the patterns of smoke that emerged from a censer (libanomancy) and the casting of dice with omens inscribed on each of its sides. Observance of unusual phenomena could also portend immediate or future danger. If a person on waking found a scorpion in his lap or if a wolf appeared within the city, a diviner, magician, or other specialist was needed to interpret its meaning. Divination omens appear in the Bible. In I Samuel 20:20, for example, there is a reference to shooting arrows and observing the place where they land. Arrow divination is also mentioned in early Islamic sources.

Menologies. Mesopotamian life was filled with concerns that ill fate might result from taking actions in certain months or on certain days. A group of texts called "menologies" lists selected days of a certain month that are either propitious or unfavorable for a given action. Some days, for example, were suitable for marriages or for shaving, while on other days one should take care not to utter a prayer. The first day of the lunar year was "an ill fated day . . . the doctor must not touch them. Nor will the diviner formulate a divinatory decision. This day is not suitable for whoever wishes to achieve his desires. Neither fish nor leeks should be eaten, under risk of misfortune." In a letter to an Assyrian king, an astrologer reported that his prediction

FORBIDDEN MAGIC

Terms referring to magical practices are found throughout the Hebrew Bible. The Book of Deuteronomy preserves a particularly detailed and specialized technical vocabulary that sheds light on contemporary practices of the ancient Near East that came to be rejected by the Israelites:

When you enter the land that the Lord your God gave to you, you shall not learn to imitate the abhorrent practices of those nations. Let there not be found among you one who makes his son or daughter pass through the fire, an augur, a soothsayer, a diviner, a sorcerer, one who casts spells, one who consults ghosts or familiar spirits, or one who calls up the dead. (Deuteronomy 18: 9–11)

Source: Brian B. Schmidt, *Israel's Beneficent Dead: Ancestor Cult and Necromancy in Ancient Israelite Religion and Tradition* (Winona Lake, Ind.: Eisenbrauns, 1996), pp. 179–190.

depended on the month of the year; another astrologer warned the king not to go through the door of his palace when Mars was in a certain position. These concepts of an ill-fated day still survive in modern-day practices such as observing certain prohibitions on Friday the thirteenth.

Apotropaic Rites. To prevent an ill omen from becoming a reality, various types of rituals were performed. Some rituals were recorded as appendices to the omen series, allowing the diviner to try to prevent the portended calamity. Other rituals intended to offset the prediction were called *Namburbu,* "Undoing of Such-and-Such an Evil." *Namburbu* typically included an incantation akin to a prayer addressed to a god, as well as a rite in which evil was transferred to a disposable object.

Shamash, king of heaven, and earth, judge of things above and below,
Light of the gods, leader of mankind, who acts as judge among the great gods!
I turn to you, seek you out:
Among the gods, grant me life;
May the gods who are with you grant me well-being.
Because of this dog who urinated on me, I am in fear, worried, terrified.
If only you make the evil (portended by) this dog pass by me,
I will readily sing your praise! (Farber)

Spells. A wide variety of magical spells dealt with daily life situations. Some, such as the *Shaziga* rite to restore male potency, probably had a psychological effect on the patient that resulted in increased sexual desire for a male unable to maintain an erection. Other spells dealt with dangers that might result from fire, a scorpion sting, a rabid dog, a sty in one's eye, or the cries of a baby.

Cultic scenes on a carved-relief wall plaque (limestone, height 9 inches) found in the Gipar, residence of the High Priestess of the moon god Nanna at Ur, circa 2500 – 2300 B.C.E.: (bottom) a nude man pouring out a libation before a stylized temple façade is accompanied by two women and a man carrying a sacrificial animal, and (above) the same man, with three identically cloaked women, pours out a libation before a seated deity with a horned crown (British Museum, London).

Cultic Rituals. Because the gods were held to control the universe, they were able to make the country powerful and prosperous or to make it suffer disaster. To ensure the well-being of the country, ritual performances in temples took place regularly. Some were practiced daily or monthly, while other rituals were for seasonal festivals or in response to happenings of dangerous import. The purpose of all rituals was to keep the gods in good humor: fine meals were provided as part of the rituals; cultic songs were sung or chanted to flatter the gods and to obtain what humans wanted. Rituals were used to gratify and manipulate the gods, not as exercises in human devotion or to inculcate piety in the masses. Thus, only the priests and occasionally members of the ruling class participated, and the human population in general was not allowed in temples, though they did share in the spirit of major seasonal festivals.

Religious Specialists. The many rituals needed for devotions, sacrifices, and cult to appease the gods necessitated an extensive clergy. There exist titles for more than thirty different sorts of religious personnel who served the gods. The *ashipu* was an exorcist, a specialist in ritual incantations and conjurations; the *baru* ("seer") dealt with extispicy and lecanomancy. Other specialists dealt with the interpretation of dreams and clairvoyance. Additional cultic personnel accompanied rituals with music and song.

Hymns. Those in positions of power can become used to the benefits of office, and enjoy exaltation, flattery, and constant reminders of their superiority. Hymns of praise were addressed to the major gods of the pantheon and also to rulers. They were sung by male *(naru)* and female *(nartu)* singers, who accompanied themselves on musical instruments. The words of the hymn are not just words of glorification or mystical devotion. Mesopotamian gods were transcendent, distant, haughty, undependable, and capricious. They inspired fear and reverence rather than love. Hymns express praise in order to ensure the gods' benevolence for the person, land, and sovereign. A Sumerian hymn to the god Ninurta describes his awesome powers:

The warrior, the lordly son of Enlil, Ninurta, the fierce bull, fit to be a prince, the hero, the rigorous judge, king . . . of the gods, the butting bull, placing his foot on the rebel lands. . . . Like the new moon he comes forth over the people. . . . He holds in his hand a scepter of shining precious metal, and the true crown of An is placed on his head. Like (the son god) Utu he comes forth over the cypresses; like (the moon god) Nanna he stands over the high mountains. (Black et al.)

A hymn to the goddess Ishtar lauds her beauty and charms:

Sing of the goddess, most awe-inspiring goddess
Let her be praised, mistress of people, greatest of the Igigi
    gods. . . .
She is the joyous one, clad in loveliness,
She is adorned with allure, appeal, charm.
Ishtar is the joyous one, clad in loveliness,
She is adorned with allure, appeal, charm.
In her lips she is sweetness, vitality her mouth,
While on her features laughter bursts to bloom.
She is proud of the love charms set on her head,
Fair her hues, full ranging, and lustrous her eyes. (Foster)

Sources:

Robert D. Biggs, *ŠÀ.ZI.GA: Ancient Mesopotamian Potency Incantations,* Texts from Cuneiform Sources, volume 2 (New York: J. J. Augustin, 1970).

Jeremy Black, Graham Cunningham, Jarle Ebeling, Esther Flückiger-Hawker, Eleanor Robson, Jon Taylor, and Gábor Zólyomi, *The Electronic Text Corpus of Sumerian Literature,* The Oriental Institute, University of Oxford, 1998– <http://www-etcsl.orient.ox.ac.uk/>.

Jean Bottéro, *Religion in Ancient Mesopotamia,* translated by Teresa Lavender Fagan (Chicago: University of Chicago Press, 2001).

Mark E. Cohen, *The Canonical Lamentations of Ancient Mesopotamia,* 2 volumes (Bethesda, Md.: CDL Press, 1988).

Cohen, *The Cultic Calendars of the Ancient Near East* (Bethesda, Md.: CDL Press, 1993).

Walter Farber, "Witchcraft, Magic, and Divination in Ancient Mesopotamia," in *Civilizations of the Ancient Near East,* 4 volumes, edited by Jack M. Sasson (New York: Scribners, 1995), III: 1895–1909.

Benjamin R. Foster, *Before the Muses: An Anthology of Akkadian Literature,* 2 volumes (Bethesda, Md.: CDL Press, 1993).

Ulla Jeyes, *Old Babylonian Extispicy: Omen Texts in the British Museum,* Uitgaven van het Nederlands Historisch-Archaeologisch Instituut te Istanbul, no. 64 (Istanbul: Nederlands Historisch-Archaeologisch Instituut te Istanbul, 1989).

Ulla Koch-Westenholz, *Babylonian Liver Omens* (Copenhagen: Carsten Niebuhr Institute of Near Eastern Studies, University of Copenhagen, 2000).

Erle V. Leichty, *The Omen Series Šumma Izbu,* Texts from Cuneiform Sources, volume 4 (New York: J. J. Augustin, 1970).

A. Leo Oppenheim, *The Interpretation of Dreams in the Ancient Near East* (Philadelphia: American Philosophical Society, 1956).

Simo Parpola, *Assyrian Prophecies,* State Archives of Assyria, volume 9 (Helsinki: Helsinki University Press, 1997).

Ivan Starr, *The Rituals of the Diviner,* Bibliotheca Mesopotamica, volume 12 (Malibu, Cal.: Udena Publications, 1983).

Starr, ed., *Queries to the Sungod: Divination and Politics in Sargonid Assyria,* State Archives of Assyria, volume 4 (Helsinki: Helsinki University Press, 1990).

The Gods. In Mesopotamian thought the gods were represented in terms of human stereotypes. Their personalities, instincts, needs, minds, morality, feelings, weaknesses, and powers were as diverse as those of humankind. Unlike humans, however, they possessed eternal life and superhuman powers. While not coterminous with astral phenomena—the stars, sun, and moon are not themselves gods—the gods were conceived as animators and controllers of the heavens and the forces of nature. They brought heat and light through command of the sun, and they established the seasons through power over the moon. In addition, hidden divine forces with no perceptible image were assumed to make the grain grow and multiply and to cause animals to mate and reproduce. A Sumerian hymn to the god Enlil describes the great powers that the god possessed.

Without the Great Mountain Enlil . . . the carp would not . . . come straight up(?) from the sea, they would not dart about. The sea would not produce all its heavy treasure, no freshwater fish would lay eggs in the reedbeds, no bird of the sky would build nests in the spacious land; in the sky the thick clouds would not open their mouths; on the fields, dappled grain would not fill the arable lands, vegetation would not grow lushly on the plain; in the gardens, the spreading trees of the mountain would not yield fruits. (Black et al.)

Attributes of the Gods. The great gods were described as possessing an awe-inspiring radiance (Akkadian: *melammu*), a sort of supernatural luminosity that glowed on their heads and bodies as a magnificent and terrifying sheen. Their beings were filled with power that evoked terror in mankind. There was no way to describe them clearly without recourse to associations with the forces of nature. Gods were, therefore, likened to real or imaginary fear-inspiring animals—such as the fierce bull, lion or lioness, wild ox, and dragon—or to natural phenomena such as the flood, storm, thunder, or mighty mountain. Most of the principal gods were masculine and had one or more consorts; some goddesses were thought to possess great powers and were important in the cult. Gods also had divine families.

Representations of the Gods. In the art of the Early Dynastic period (circa 2900 – circa 2340 B.C.E.), Mesopotamian deities were pictured with human forms for the first time. They could also be represented by animals that to the ancients conveyed one of a god's qualities, such as the dog for the goddess Gula, or by symbolic objects, including a plow for Ninurta, the god of agriculture. The personality of a god was thought to reside in its cult statue, which underwent a series of rituals, such as the "Opening of the Mouth" and "Washing of the Mouth," enabling the statue to be imbued with the divine presence. Statues were typically made of wood. Their hands and faces were covered with precious metals; their eyes and beards were inlaid with precious

Symbolic representations of deities on one side of a limestone entitlement monument (so-called *kudurru*, height 25 5/8 inches) found at or near Sippar. (In the second register from the bottom, Gula, goddess of healing, sits next to her dog.) The protection of these deities is invoked in the cuneiform inscription on the other side (not shown), a charter granted by Babylonian king Nebuchadnezzar I (circa 1125 – circa 1104 B.C.E.) for military services (British Museum, London).

stones. Texts provide details of gods' appearances down to the last details of hair, eyes, and sexual parts.

The Gods' Behavior. The gods behaved like humans and had the same wants and needs. Like people, the gods desired large houses, luxurious clothing, sex, and good food and drink. In the Sumerian myth *Inana and Enki,* the god Enki becomes drunk and carelessly relinquishes control over the *me,* the gods' power to regulate the cultural artifacts of urban civilization. Some gods are rational; others act based on whim, selfishness, and emotion. In the *Epic of Gilgamesh,* the goddess Inana, attracted by the semi-divine but mortal hero's good looks, proposes a sexual liaison. After Gilgamesh rejects her advances, the goddess pouts and fumes, demanding that Anu, her father, release the Bull of Heaven to punish Gilgamesh's insolence. Myths also deride the gods' weaknesses, including their fickle decisions. How else, it was thought, could one account for man's hardships?

Fear of the Gods. The gods were supreme figures: transcendent, awesome, and distant—not close to man as in modern religions. Admired, revered, and feared, they were masters and lords. They might show kindness, but they were not loved. Their presence did not inspire happiness; it caused anxiety and fright. When Gilgamesh awakens from a nightmare, he asks his friend Enkidu, "Why am I so disturbed? Did a god not pass by? Why does my flesh tingle? My friend, I had a dream, And the dream I had was very disturbing." One did not seek a god in order to be in its presence; instead one directed a prayer to a god to express admiration, offer praise, and obtain protection from undesirable forces.

The Divine Plan. Mesopotamian philosophy asserted that the gods possessed a divine design for mankind, which resides in the gods' inaccessible minds, incomprehensible to humans. In contrast to biblical religion, the gods of the Mesopotamians never reveal their plan to man. They act capriciously; their ways are impenetrable. A Babylonian poet cogently expressed these thoughts in a composition called *The Babylonian Theodicy:*

> The plans of the gods are as far from us as the center of heaven:
> To understand them properly is impossible; no one can understand them. (Lambert)

Mankind and the Gods. In *Ludlul bel nemeqi,* "Let me Praise the Lord of Wisdom (that is, Marduk)," a Babylonian theologian explored the reasons for the suffering of the righteous. The poet expressed his frustration and despair, knowing that man was merely mortal, unable to decipher the will of the gods:

> I wish I knew that these things were pleasing to one's god!
> What is proper to oneself is an offense to one's god,
> What in one's own heart seems despicable is proper to one's god.
> Who knows the will of the gods in heaven?

Stone tablet (height 11½ inches) with cuneiform text and carved relief celebrating Babylonian king Nabu-apla-iddin's
restoration of the temple of the sun god Shamash at Sippar, during the early ninth century B.C.E. The king
(second from left) stands before an altar with the god's disc emblem and a monumental statue
of Shamash seated beneath a canopy (British Museum, London).

Who understands the plans of the underworld gods?
Where have mortals learnt the way of a god? (Lambert)

Immortality. Only the gods, including the demons, were thought to be immortal. Mankind was doomed to live a short life, cursed by disease, illness, accident, and old age. In mythology only a few gods were ever said to have died. They were slain in battle, and in each instance their beings became a part of another entity. The rebellious god Qingu in the creation epic *Enuma elish* and the minor god We in the *Epic of Atra-hasis* were both killed, only to be incorporated into newly created humans as different parts of human nature. Never-ending life was granted to only a few select humans. In the *Epic of Gilgamesh,* the survivors of the flood, Uta-napishti and his wife, were made immortal and sent to live on an island at the end of the world. The hero Gilgamesh sought everlasting life, but even though he was partly divine he was not able to escape death.

Gods and History. According to Mesopotamian theology, the gods managed the world and predetermined historical events. Defeat in war, for example, could be explained as divine retribution for the king's crimes. According to the Sumerian composition *The Cursing of Agade,* when Naram-Sin (circa 2254 – circa 2218 B.C.E.), king of the city of Agade (or Akkad), desecrated the E-kur, the holy shrine of the god Enlil, the deity responded by causing the uncivilized Gutian tribes from the nearby Zagros Mountains to attack the land. Swarming like locusts, they destroyed cities, desolated fields, and ravaged the land:

Enlil, the roaring(?) storm that subjugates the entire land, the rising deluge that cannot be confronted, was considering what should be destroyed in return for the wrecking of his beloved E-kur. He lifted his gaze toward the Gubin mountains, and made all the inhabitants of the broad mountain ranges descend(?). Enlil brought out of the mountains those who do not resemble other people, who are not reckoned as part of the Land, the features. Like small birds they swooped on the ground in great flocks. Because of Enlil they stretched their arms out across the plain like a net for animals. Nothing escaped their clutches, no one left their grasp. Messengers no longer traveled the highways, the courier's boat no longer passed along the rivers. The Gutians drove the trusty(?) Goats of Enlil out of their pens and compelled their cowherds to follow them. Prisoners manned the watch. Brigands occupied the highways. The doors of the city gates of the Land were covered with mud, and all the foreign lands uttered bitter cries from the walls of their cities . . . As it had been before the time when cities were built and founded, the large fields and

Fragment of a limestone stele (height 46 ½ inches), Babylon, perhaps eighth century B.C.E. An Assyrian king (right)
is standing before Adad, the storm god, and Ishtar, the goddess of war and sexual love; divine emblems
fill the upper field (Eski Şark Museum, Istanbul).

Gypsum relief carving (height 18½ inches) with an Assyrian warrior god, perhaps Ashur, standing on the back of a winged horned lion, Ashur, seventh century B.C.E. (Vorderasiatisches Museum, Berlin)

arable tracts yielded no grain, the inundated fields yielded no fish, the irrigated orchards yielded no syrup or wine, the thick clouds(?) did not rain, the *mashgurum* plant did not grow. (Black et al.)

Polytheism. Mesopotamian religious thinkers never developed a concept of exclusive monotheism, the existence of one and only one god. The official religion included a bewildering number of local, city, state, and heavenly deities, all of whom had supernatural and transcendent qualities. This polytheistic system tolerated and even encouraged the existence of a diversity of gods. By the end of the third millennium B.C.E. the Sumerians claimed there were 3,600 deities. Wars of religion, characteristic of peoples with monotheistic belief systems, were unknown in the ancient Near East. The condemnation of false faiths and insistence on dogmatic belief was unknown in a world of religious pluralism.

City Gods. The cosmological deities who ruled earth, sea, and sky were considered the greatest of the gods. By the second quarter of the third millennium B.C.E., each polity was thought to have its own patron deity who could install and depose rulers. Among the Sumerian cities in southern Mesopotamia, the city of Ur was home to the moon god Nanna; the city of Eridu was associated with Enki; Larsa and Sippar shared the sun god Utu; Uruk was the center for worshiping the sky god An as well as Inana, "The Lady of Heaven." Nippur, considered a holy city, was home to Enlil, the god who ruled the heavens. Some deities were worshiped in several local cults. Each god had his or her own temple in his or her capital city.

Syncretism. At the end of the third millennium B.C.E., religious traditions began to merge. Sumerian divinities became identified first with the gods of the Semitic-speaking

Akkadians and then—following the fall of the Third Dynasty of Ur, circa 2004 B.C.E.—with those of the West Semitic Amorites. Some of the older gods of the Sumerians became known by the Akkadian forms of their names. For example, An, the sky god, was called Anu, and in the Semitic mythology he became a distant deity. Other deities were merged with Semitic counterparts. Enki retained his role as a god of wisdom and had a close relationship with humanity; he was referred to as Ea. Nanna (also called Suen), the moon god, was referred to as Sin; Utu, the god of justice, was venerated by the Babylonians, who called him Shamash; and the goddess Inana became Ishtar. The Semites found no local god who could be equated with the supreme god Enlil, so his name remained unchanged. Many of the older subordinate Sumerian gods lost their significance, while Marduk, who was a city god associated with the then minor city of Babylon, was elevated in importance as Babylon rose in prominence.

Assyrian Gods. In Assyria the god Ashur, who was at first the god of the city of Ashur, became a national god. As the power and extent of Assyrian domination grew in the later part of the second millennium B.C.E., Ashur became an imperial god of state and empire, depicted as supporting the Assyrian army and the ever-growing Assyrian territory. During the height of Assyrian conquests in the first part of the first millennium B.C.E., Ashur was equated in mythology and ritual with the Babylonian national god, Marduk. Even such symbols of the Babylonian deity as Marduk's snake-dragon were transferred to Ashur. Assyrian kings incorporated the god's name into their own: Ashur-nasir-apli (Ashurnasirpal), "Ashur-who-protects-the-heir"; Ashur-bani-apli (Ashurbanipal), "Ashur-is-the-creator-of-the-heir"; and Ashur-ahhe-iddina (Esarhaddon), "Ashur-gave-me-sons." However, the peoples of the conquered provinces of the Assyrian Empire were not required to worship Ashur.

The Hierarchy of the Pantheon. Babylonian theologians of the second millennium B.C.E. devised a method of expressing the supremacy of certain gods within the pantheon. In accordance with the Mesopotamian concept of classifying phenomena, each of the major Babylonian deities was assigned a number in the writing system. Anu, the chief deity, was represented by the number 60; Enlil, the god of the earth, was number 50; Ea, the god of wisdom, was 40; Sin, the god of the moon, was 30; Shamash, the sun god, was 20; 15 was associated with Ishtar and 6 with Adad, the god of the storms.

Genealogy. In mythology the great gods were conceived of as having descended from each other. Various parallel and often contradictory traditions associated with different cities or priesthoods existed at the same time. Thus, according to one tradition, Enlil, one of the most important gods in the pantheon, was the offspring of An, while in another tradition he was a descendant of the gods Enki (Lord Earth) and Ninki (Lady Earth).

Monotheistic Tendencies. As the Babylonians assumed political supremacy over large parts of Mesopotamia, they began to reduce the number of gods. Many of the large number of deities that existed during the period of Sumerian dominance fell from prominence, were amalgamated into one deity, or they were equated with Semitic gods. Instead of the thousands of Sumerian deities, the Babylonians worshiped a pantheon of twelve or thirteen major gods. In hymns, some gods are represented as aspects of one of the major deities. An example of this new theology is found in the concluding section of the Babylonian creation epic *Enuma elish*, which refers to the chief deity Marduk and praises him with fifty different names that represent characteristics of particular gods. This syncretistic theology made it possible for many prayers to be largely interchangeable. Babylonian texts of the first millennium B.C.E. elevated certain deities with exaltations such as "Trust in Nabu, trust in no other god but Nabu." Other documents refer to "the god" or "the goddess" while never denying the existence of the pantheon.

Personal Gods. In addition to the great pantheon of gods, who had little daily contact with most ordinary people, individuals also worshiped a personal god. These deities were on a more intimate basis with the individual. Personal gods were viewed as divine parents who guarded and watched over their children. Personal gods sought to prevent wickedness but could not control man's actions and acted as advocates who could intercede with the great gods on behalf of the worshiper. In a prayer to the personal god of his family a worshiper sought his deity and requested protection from evil and help in thriving and living to old age.

> . . . O my god, where are you?
> You who have been angry with me, turn towards me,
> Turn your face to the pure godly meal of fat and oil,
> That your lips receive goodness. Command that I thrive,
> Command (long) life with your pure utterance.
> Bring me away from evil, that through you, I be saved.
> Ordain for me a destiny of (long) life,
> Prolong my days, grant me (long) life! (Foster)

Death. Death was the inevitable fate of mankind, and the gods did not "make known the days of death." Immortality was reserved only for gods. According to the theology embedded in the *Epic of Gilgamesh*, any attempt by man to achieve eternal life would be in vain. In contrast to the Egyptian concept of a bountiful afterlife for the righteous, the Mesopotamian view was that the deceased faced a horrid, gloomy existence in the Netherworld.

The Netherworld. In some religions there exists life after death in heaven or in a region where justice prevails, and the righteous fare better than the wicked. In ancient Mesopotamia all the dead—except for the unburied, who became angry spirits that caused torment and terror among the living—were believed to reside in a "Land of No Return." This Netherworld, behind locked gates and beneath the freshwater ocean under the earth,

Lower half of a statue of a *lahmu* (known from other depictions to be a bearded male figure with long curly hair, nude except for his belt). He is seated with his legs around a socket for a standard (hollow-cast copper alloy, base 27½ inches in diameter), found at Bassetki, near the Turkey-Iraq border. In the accompanying cuneiform inscription Akkadian king Naram-Sin (circa 2254 – circa 2218 B.C.E.) described his deification in his own lifetime (Iraq Museum, Baghdad).

was a dreary place where the dead existed in a residual form as a spirit or ghost. With light available only when the sun god visited, and without water, the dead resided in the dark and had only dust to eat. They had no hope of liberation or resurrection of the body. All were naked and, with only a few exceptions, suffered the same miserable existence. There was no separation or elevation of the just. Only proper burial could ameliorate the harsh treatment one received in the Netherworld. Existence among the dead could become more tolerable only if one's surviving relatives provided offerings of food, drink, and oil. Libations were poured to the dead through clay pipes located at funerary sites. This belief that the dead needed support contributed to the idea that one should have a large family to provide sustenance for one's spirit after death. Cremation was never practiced because of the belief that those who die in fire suffer the worst fate: no longer possessing a spirit left to be buried.

Sources:

Bendt Alster, ed., *Death in Mesopotamia: Papers Read at the XXVIe Rencontre assyriologique internationale*, Mesopotamia, volume 8 (Copenhagen: Akademisk Forlag, 1980).

Jeremy Black, Graham Cunningham, Jarle Ebeling, Esther Flückiger-Hawker, Eleanor Robson, Jon Taylor, and Gábor Zólyomi, *The Electronic Text Corpus of Sumerian Literature*, The Oriental Institute, University of Oxford, 1998– <http://www-etcsl.orient.ox.ac.uk/>.

Jean Bottéro, *Mesopotamia: Writing, Reasoning and the Gods*, translated by Zainab Bahrani and Marc Van de Mieroop (Chicago: University of Chicago Press, 1992).

Bottéro, *Religion in Ancient Mesopotamia*, translated by Teresa Lavender Fagan (Chicago: University of Chicago Press, 2001).

Jerrold S. Cooper, *The Curse of Agade* (Baltimore: Johns Hopkins University Press, 1983).

Benjamin R. Foster, *Before the Muses: An Anthology of Akkadian Literature*, 2 volumes (Bethesda, Md.: CDL Press, 1993).

W. G. Lambert, *Babylonian Wisdom Literature* (Oxford: Clarendon Press, 1960).

A. Leo Oppenheim, *Ancient Mesopotamia: Portrait of a Dead Civilization*, revised edition, completed by Erica Reiner (Chicago: University of Chicago Press, 1964).

EVIL AND SIN

Moral Precepts. Mesopotamian society never developed a clearly stated set of divinely revealed moral precepts like the Ten Commandments. Yet, Mesopotamian collections of laws express wrong actions in accord with an unstated moral consciousness. In the ancient Near East, improper conduct included a large canvas of unacceptable behavior: reprehensible actions, misdeeds, and intentional and inadvertent cultic sins. Morally correct and ritually proper behaviors were considered as two sides of the same coin. A person who committed a moral offense or a criminal action, or who accidentally touched an impure object, was considered to have sinned against his or her god. The gods were equally angered by crime, false oath, consumption of ritually impure food, inadvertent contact with an unclean person, or oppression of a widow or orphan. All these transgressions were human violations (Sumerian: *nam-tag*) or trespasses against the divine order.

Sin. According to one myth, the Babylonian creation epic *Enuma elish*, humans were created by the gods from clay mixed with the blood of a rebellious god. Men and women (as opposed to animals) were therefore blessed with the ability to think, but they also possessed an inclination to disobedience and error. There existed no single universal term for sin; rather a series of terms signified offenses of different weights. Serious violations of the proper order (Akkadian: *arnu*) or even inadvertent transgression that deviated from the moral rules of proper conduct (Akkadian: *ikkibu*) were considered abominations to the gods. Akkadian *egitu* were sins of negligence or carelessness. *Ikkibu* originally referred in Akkadian to taboo

actions, but later it became a more general term referring to secular actions such as lying and stealing. Human actions were observed and monitored by the gods. Repelled by a person's actions, one's personal god could depart. "How long will you (my personal god) neglect me, leave me unprotected?" lamented the "Babylonian Job." Without protection from one's personal god, an individual was liable to the attacks and ravages of demons. Evil spirits—irrational, unpredictable, and life threatening—were released by one's misdeeds to beset the transgressor. If people followed the proper course of life, the gods rewarded them, and the nation thrived. If they sinned and if the demons were released to attack and plague man, the entire community could experience disorder and even disasters such as plague, earthquake, fire, and invasion, while individual sinners were punished with disease, various forms of failure, and even death.

Unintentional Sins. In the theology of Mesopotamia the gods punished people for their improper actions even if they were unintentional. However, as the gods' actions were unpredictable, one never knew if they were angered by one's transgressions or if they were indifferent. It was thought that if one suffered a reversal of fortune, disgrace, illness, or mishap, the gods had to be the cause. The birth of an unwanted or perhaps disabled child led some parents to name such offspring *Mina-arni*, "What is My Sin?" Even if one knowingly did nothing wrong, one's troubles were interpreted as the result of an unintentional action that had offended a deity. Inadvertent infractions could include such minor activities as stepping in the wrong place or breaking a reed in the marshes. In a hymn to

Both sides of a pink limestone relief-carved plaque (height 4 7/8 inches), Nimrud, seventh century, B.C.E. On the front (left) the demon Pazuzu peers over the top while the demon Lamashtu (from whom Pazuzu protects pregnant women) is kneeling on a collapsing donkey and holding serpents while suckling a pig and a hound. The back (right) depicts Pazuzu's winged scaly body with lion's feet and a snake-headed phallus (Iraq Museum, Baghdad).

the god Marduk an ancient poet expressed the view that all people at one time or another commit sins:

> Who is he that . . . has not sinned?
> Who is he so watchful that has incurred no sin?
> Which is he so circumspect that has committed no wrong-doing?
> People do not know their invisible faults,
> A god reveals what is fair and what is foul. (Foster)

Ancestral Sins. The wrath of the gods could also descend on an innocent person who had committed neither intentional nor unintentional sins. The gods were believed to have long memories and to punish an individual for iniquities committed by parents or ancestors. The deity Marduk could be both fierce and forgiving. In a prayer addressed to Marduk a servant begged forgiveness for the misdeeds of his kin:

> Absolve my guilt, remit my punishment,
> Clear me of confusion, free me of uncertainty,
> Let no guilt of my father, my grandfather, my mother, my grandmother, my brother, my sister, my family, kith, or kin
> Approach my own self, but let it be gone! (Foster)

Demons. Demons were thought to be the agents of the great gods, sent to punish mankind for their misdeeds. They might include angry ghosts (Akkadian: *etemmu*) of the deceased, who could haunt people's dreams, or evil spirits (Akkadian: *utukku lemnutu*), who tormented the living with illness. Other demons acted completely without control and often against the will of the gods. These illegitimate demons attacked mankind at any time or in any situation. *Lamashtu* demons were known for their attacks on pregnant women and infants. *Lilu* demons were young men who had died unmarried; they entered houses looking for the spouses they were never able to find in life. If an afflicted person was abandoned by his personal protective spirit and overcome by evil demons and if he did not know what had offended the gods, he had to turn to ritual and magic to ward off attacks and counter calamity.

Divine Punishment. In a world ruled by authoritarian leaders, unjust or arbitrary punishment was not uncommon. In a similar manner personal misfortune might not be the result of sin or misguided actions but instead the result of a capricious decision by a god or demon. The sufferer in the poem *Ludlul bel nemeqi*, "Let me Praise the Lord of Wisdom," claims to be righteous. He realizes that he has committed an offense against the deity, but he does not know what he has done wrong. Crime and moral transgression, breaches in the common code of conduct, and even inadvertent contact with things considered to be magically impure could cause divine punishment. But the righteous sufferer in *Ludlul bel nemeqi* can find no cause for the gods' punishment.

RITUAL TO EXPEL A SPIRIT

There were many methods to prevent an attack by a ghost or demon, including wearing an amulet, making a representative figurine, drinking a magic potion, making an offering, and reciting an incantation to exorcise the unwanted spirit. The following excerpts from a first millennium B.C.E. magical text describe part of a ritual and incantation:

If a ghost has seized a man (and) continually follows him or if an *alu*-demon or a *mukil resh lemutti*-demon has seized him, or generic evil continually seizes him or [pursues him], you take dirt from an abandoned town, dirt from an abandoned house, dirt from an abandoned temple, dirt from a tomb, dirt from foundations(?), dirt from an abandoned canal, (and) dirt from a road. You mix (them) together with ox blood. You make a figurine of generic evil. You clothe it with the skin of a lion. You thread carnelian (and) put it on its neck. You provide [it] with a waterskin and give it travel provisions.

. . . For three days, (by) day, the exorcist . . . sets up a censer (filled with burning) juniper before Shamash; by night, he scatters emmer flour before the stars of the night. For three days, before Shamash and the stars, he repeatedly recites (the following) over it: "Ghost (or) whatever is evil—from this day forward, you are extracted from the body of so-and-so, son of so-and-so; you are expelled; you are driven away and banished. The god who put you in place, the goddess who put you in place—they have removed you from the body of so-and-so, son of so-and-so, the patient."

. . . "I am so-and-so, son of so-and-so; I kneel in exhaustion. For me, whom an obligation has bound as a result of the anger of god and goddess, an *utukku*-demon, a *rabisu*-demon, a ghost (and) a *lilu*-demon have weighed out paralysis, convulsions, limpness of the flesh, vertigo, arthritis (and) insanity, and daily they cause me to have convulsions. Shamash, you are the judge and I have brought you my life. I kneel for judgment of the case concerning the sickness which has seized me. Judge my case; make a decision about me. Until you cause my case to be decided, you shall not give [a decision] for [any other] case. After you have caused my case to be decided, (and after) my obligation has let me go (and) fled [from] my body, wherever I put my trust, let (those) gods come to agree with what you say. [May the heavens be pleased with] you; may the earth rejoice in you."

Source: Jo Ann Scurlock, "Death and the Afterlife in Ancient Mesopotamian Thought," in *Civilizations of the Ancient Near East*, 4 volumes, edited by Jack M. Sasson (New York: Scribners, 1995), III: 1883–1893.

He suffers social rejection. His friends abandon him. His family recoils from his presence, and even his slave mocks his former position. In the end his only answer is to assume that the gods acted without any justifiable motive. Convinced that the gods were ultimately benevolent, the sufferer, like the biblical Job, believes that his only recourse is to submit to his deity and offer praise:

My (personal) god has forsaken me and disappeared,
My goddess has failed me and keeps at a distance.
The benevolent angel who (walked) beside me has
    departed,
My protecting spirit has taken to flight, and is seeking
    someone else.
My strength is gone; my appearance has become gloomy;
My dignity has flown away, my protection made off. . . .
. . . I have become a slave. . . .
If I walk the street, ears are pricked (up). . . .
My friend has become foe. . . .
In his savagery my comrade denounces me. . . .
My slave has publicly cursed me in the assembly.
When my acquaintance sees me, he passes by on the other
    side.
My family treats me as an alien.
The pit awaits anyone who speaks well of me,
While he who utters declamation of me is promoted . . .
I have no one to go at my side, nor have I found a helper. . . .
    (Lambert)

Pessimism. Babylonian theologians sought explanations for mankind's suffering and woe, but they had no satisfactory answer. They recognized that the gods wished them to render homage, to provide them with goods and services, and to offer prayer. It was expected that once these duties had been fulfilled, the gods would respond with favor. But in practice it was apparent that the gods did not always do so. There could be no moral justification for an attack by demons. The thief could prosper; crime could pay; and the strong did oppress the weak. To solve this dilemma, the theologians declared that the gods created both good and evil and that one had to adjust to life in an unjust world. Thus, even if one were pious, devoted to one's god, and kept all of the divine ordinances, the gods could still bring disgrace and torment. In the *Babylonian Theodicy,* a sufferer complains to a friend that he lives in a crazy topsy-turvy world, one in which piety and devotion are not rewarded:

Just one word would I put before you.
Those who neglect the god go the way of prosperity,
While those who pray to the goddess are impoverished and
    dispossessed.
In my youth I sought the will of my god;
With prostration and prayer I followed my goddess.
But I was bearing a profitless corvée as a yoke.
My god decreed instead of wealth destitution.
A cripple is my superior, a lunatic outstrips me.
The rogue has been promoted, but I have been brought
    low. (Lambert)

Sources:
Benjamin R. Foster, *Before the Muses: An Anthology of Akkadian Literature,* 2 volumes (Bethesda, Md.: CDL Press, 1993).

W. G. Lambert, *Babylonian Wisdom Literature* (Oxford: Clarendon Press, 1960).

Karel van der Toorn, *Sin and Sanction in Israel and Mesopotamia: A Comparative Study* (Assen, Netherlands: Van Gorcun, 1985).

EXORCISM AND MAGIC

Sickness. For the theologian, sickness was a perplexing matter. Minor illness was attributed to random occurrences that all humans suffer, but serious health problems were attributed to external, supernatural forces. Each person was protected by a personal god or goddess, but because of unforeseen circumstances or sin, one's god could flee, leaving the unprotected individual vulnerable to attack by demons, ghosts, and other evil forces. Healers needed to determine if a "Hand of a Ghost" or an unknown human agent, such as a witch, had caused illness. Treatment was in the hands of the *asu,* "physician," and the *ashipu,* "magician or exorcist." Each had a role in healing the sick, and they often worked together to treat difficult cases. The physician prescribed salves and potions, and the magician battled the demons with spells, incantations, amulets, and rituals to exorcise evil forces.

Diagnosis. Not all sickness was believed to have been caused by misdeeds. One could be injured in a fight or simply be sick with a cold. A letter to the king of Assyria informed him not to be alarmed; his present illness was merely the result of a seasonal bug that had been going around:

To the king, my lord: your servant Marduk-shakin-shumi. Good health to the king, my lord! May Nabu and Marduk bless the king, my lord!

Concerning the chills about which the king, my lord wrote to me, there is nothing to be worried about. The gods of the [king] will quickly cure it, and we shall do whatever is relevant to the matter. [It is] a seasonal illness; the king, my lord, should not [wor]ry (about it). (Parpola)

If the *ashipu* believed that the "Hand" of a god or ghost has caused suffering, he could consult with a tablet series entitled *Enuma ana bit marsi ashipu illaku,* "When the Exorcist goes to the House of a Sick Person." This document includes a lengthy list of symptoms and a prognostication. For example,

If (the patient) is stricken at his head, and he is afflicted by one attack after the other, and his face is (alternately) red and greenish; whenever he has an attack, his mind becomes deranged, and he has convulsions: (It is the) grip of the *lamashtu*-demon—his days may (still) be long, but (eventually) he will die. (Farber)

Incantations. It was commonly understood that to keep demons and ghosts at bay it was necessary to employ magic and hope that the recitation of spells or incantations would repel evil forces. Entreating demons to flee and take away their evil, incantations were performed by specialists trained in the cultic arts, who also used rituals to expel the evil and effect cures. The series *Uttuku lemnutu,* "The Evil Udug-Demons," includes a detailed description of a group of *udug* demons known as the "evil seven."

They are seven, they the seven,
They are seven in the springs of the depths,

Modern impression of an Akkadian-period cylinder seal, circa 2334 – circa 2193 B.C.E. The sun god Shamash, with rays emanating from his shoulders, is shown with a plow, while an anthropomorphic boat deity holds a punting pole. They are led by another deity and a sphinx (a human-headed lion), perhaps on their nightly journey through the underworld. The sun god's consort is seated at right (Iraq Museum, Baghdad).

They are seven, adorned in heaven.
They grew up in the springs of the depths, in the cella.
They are not male, they are not female,
They are drifting phantoms,
They take no wife, they beget no son.
They know neither sparing of life nor mercy,
They heed no prayers nor entreaties.
They are steeds that grew up in the mountains,
They are the evil ones of Ea,
They are the prefects of the gods.
They loiter in the side streets to make trouble on the highway.
They are evil, they are evil!
They are seven, they are seven, they are twice seven!
Be conjured by heaven, be conjured by the netherworld!
(Foster)

Incantations against Illness. Many incantations deal with a wide variety of conditions, such as impotency, headache, fever, eye disease, misshapen fetuses, misery, excessive anger, and flatulence. An incantation against toothache explains that this affliction originates from a worm placed in the mouth by the gods. The cure is to extract the tooth:

After Anu created heaven,
Heaven created earth,
Earth created rivers,
Rivers created watercourses,
Watercourses created marshes,
Marshes created the worm.
The worm came crying before Shamash,
Before Ea his tears flowed down,
"What will you give me, that I may eat?"
"What will you give me, that I may suck?"

"I will give you a ripe fig and an apple."
"What are a ripe fig and an apple to me?"
"Set me to dwell between teeth and jaw,
that I may suck the blood of the jaw,
that I may chew on the bits of (food) stuck in the jaw."
(Foster)

Conjurations. Some incantations were directed against illness caused by witchcraft. If a person had a terrifying dream, the nightmare was thought to have been sent by a demonic witch. Burning was necessary to ward off the evil. The magical tablet series *Maqlu*, "Burning," includes incantations and rituals directed against witches and witchcraft. A ceremony was performed beginning in the night and ending the next morning. The exorcist met the afflicted patient in his home and began the ritual with an invocation to the gods of the night. Later a representation of the witch and other objects were burned in a brazier. The remains were then stirred, and water was poured over the smoldering embers. The rite of burning and dousing with water was intended to destroy evil magically and quell the witch's life force. Acts performed at dawn included ritual cleansing and throwing an edible representation of the witch to dogs.

***Shurpu* Incantations.** In the incantation series called *Shurpu*, "Burning (away the curse)," misfortune is ascribed to a victim's intentional or unintentional sins. When the sufferer did not know what he had done to bring on his affliction, he recited a long list of misdeeds with the hope that it would include his relevant offense. The list includes serious offenses such as murder, robbery, and adultery, as well as lesser offenses such as eating prohibited foods, gossiping, lying, and showing lack of respect for family members. Incantations were designed to purify the sinner ritually. For example,

> Incantation. Be it released, great gods,
> god and goddess, lords of absolution . . .
> his sins are against his god, his crimes are against his goddess,
> He has eaten what is taboo to his god,
> He is full of contempt against his father, full of hatred against his elder brother,
> He despised his parents, offended the elder sister,
> gave with small (measure) and received with big (measure),
> he said "there is," when there was not,
> he said "there is not," when there was;
> he pointed his finger accusingly behind the back of his fellow man; who calumniated, spoke what is not allowed to speak; who as a witness, caused wicked things to be spoken; who caused the judge to pronounce incorrect judgment,
> who scorned his god, despised his goddess,
> he used an untrue balance, but did not use the true balance,
> he took money that was not due to him, but did not take money due to him,
> he disinherited the legitimated son and did not establish (in his rights) the legitimated son. . . .
> He entered his neighbor's house,
> had intercourse with his neighbor's wife,
> shed his neighbor's blood,
> took his neighbor's clothes,
> and did not clothe a young man when he was naked. . . .
> His mouth is straight, but his heart is untrue,
> when his mouth says "yes" his heart says "no"
> altogether he speaks untrue words. (Reiner, 1958)

***Shurpu* Rituals.** In *Shurpu* the offender sought to rid himself of sin by transference of the evil to materials such as wool, an onion, or part of a date. The object was held in the sufferer's hand while the ritual took place. Purification resulted from the destruction of the object by ritual burning, which released the sufferer from the evil spell.

> Just as this flock of wool is plucked apart and thrown into the fire, (and just as) the Firegod consumes it altogether,
> just as it will not return to its sheep,
> will not be used for the clothing of god or king.
> May invocation, oath, retaliation, questioning,
> the illness which is due to my suffering, sin, crime, injustice and shortcomings, the sickness that is in my body, flesh and veins, be plucked apart like this flock of wool, and may the Firegod on this very day consume it altogether.
> May the ban (curse) go away, and may I (again) see light (!) (Reiner, 1958)

Purification. Mesopotamian litanies include a long list of *mamitu*, lesser offenses against the gods. They include inadvertent contact with unclean people or objects, accidentally touching an accursed man while crossing the street, stepping in dirty water, walking on nail clippings or armpit shavings, stepping on old shoes with holes in them, touching an object associated with black magic, inadvertently brushing against a person with a skin disease, breaking promises, releasing confidential information, and speaking intemperately. The sufferer sought relief from his ills by appealing to his gods and goddesses for purification from misdeeds. The following excerpt from a collection of texts known as *Lipshur Litanies* describes some offenses and the sufferer's call for absolution:

> May the tamarisk tree purify me . . .
> may the pure river water carry away my sin!
> O, Shamash, you are supreme judge of the great gods,
> whether, while I was walking in the street, an accursed man touched me,
> whether, while I was crossing the square,
> I stepped upon (someone's dirty) washwater which did not drain away,
> whether I have walked on nail-parings, (or) armpit shavings,
> or shoes with holes in them, (or) a tattered belt,
> (or) a leather bag with (material for) black magic, or scales (from a person afflicted with skin disease), (all these) things unlucky for human beings,
> let it be released for me, let it be absolved for me!
> O, Shamash, if I have been neglectful today in your presence, if I have committed grievous sins,
> let it be released for me, let it be absolved for me!
> (Through) all my sins, all my errors, all my crimes
> may the unbeliever learn from my example,
> who was neglectful, who committed grievous sins against his god and his goddess
> I have made promises, but changed my word, I had people put their trust in me, but did not give,
> I did unfitting things, my mouth was full of improper words, I repeated confidential information,
> . . . I am dazed . . . I do not know where I am going,
> the sins and crimes of mankind are more numerous than the hair of its head;
> I tread upon my sins, my errors, my crimes that are heaped up like chaff,
> let it (the evil) be released from me, let it be absolved from me! . . .
> O Shamash, I prostrate myself before you (asking you) to judge my cause, wipe out my sins, drive away my errors, direct me on the right way
> O Shamash may the angry heart of my god and my goddess be pacified
>
> Oh Shamash, you are the supreme judge, you bring justice to the land,
> . . . I have sinned against my god, I have sinned against my goddess. (Reiner, 1956)

Purification Rites. Purification rites were held in ancient Near Eastern temples and palaces. Their purpose was to cleanse those affected by pollution resulting from transgressions, sin, or exposure to demons. Buildings also had to be cleansed after contact with impure substances or polluted people or to rid them of evil effects from earthquakes or eclipses. Purification was needed to make rites effective. Liquids such as water and oil were used in ceremonies that involved washing and bathing. Specialized priests performed the ceremonies. During the Babylonian New Year's Festival, an executioner was ordered to behead a sheep. The sheep's body was used to wipe away pollution and purify the temple. An exorcist then threw the polluted carcass into the river, whose flowing waters magically carried away its impurities.

Sources:

I. Tzvi Abusch, *Mesopotamian Witchcraft: Toward a History and Understanding of Babylonian Witchcraft Beliefs and Literature,* Ancient Magic and Divination, no. 5 (Leiden: Brill Styx, 2002).

Walter Farber, "Witchcraft, Magic, and Divination in Ancient Mesopotamia," in *Civilizations of the Ancient Near East,* 4 volumes, edited by Jack M. Sasson (New York: Scribners, 1995), III: 1895–1909.

Benjamin R. Foster, *Before the Muses: An Anthology of Akkadian Literature,* 2 volumes (Bethesda, Md.: CDL Press, 1993).

Markham J. Geller, *Forerunners to Udug-hul: Sumerian Exorcistic Incantations* (Stuttgart: F. Steiner, 1985).

Jørgen Læssøe, *Studies on the Assyrian Ritual and Series "Bit Rimki"* (Copenhagen: Munksgaard, 1955).

Guido Majno, *The Healing Hand: Man and Wound in the Ancient World* (Cambridge, Mass.: Harvard University Press, 1975).

Simo Parpola, *Letters from Assyrian and Babylonian Scholars,* State Archives of Assyria, volume 10 (Helsinki: Helsinki University Press, 1993).

Erica Reiner, *Astral Magic in Babylonia,* Transactions of the American Philosophical Society, volume 85, part 4 (Philadelphia: American Philosophical Society, 1995).

Reiner, "Lipšur Litanies," *Journal of Near Eastern Studies,* 15 (1956): 129–149.

Reiner, *Šurpu: A Collection of Sumerian and Akkadian Incantations,* Archiv für Orientforschung, supplement 11 (Graz, 1958).

Reiner, *Your Thwarts in Pieces, Your Mooring Rope Cut: Poetry from Babylonia and Assyria* (Ann Arbor: Horace H. Rackham School of Graduate Studies, University of Michigan, 1985).

MORALITY

Piety. In the ancient Near East, a pious person was one who told the truth, avoided blasphemy, gave charity, and avoided controversy. These actions by themselves were nevertheless insufficient without constant devotion to sacrifice and prayer. These concepts were expressed in a series of Wisdom texts. In one text, *Counsels of Wisdom,* a wise man instructs his "son" about piety.

> Every day worship your god
> Sacrifice and benediction are the proper accompaniment of incense
> Present your free-will offering to your god,
> For this is proper toward the gods.
> Prayer, supplication, and prostration
> Offer him daily, and you will get your reward
> Then you will have full communion with your god. (Lambert)

Moral Code. The modern maxim "Don't rock the boat" was an idea expressed throughout Mesopotamian history. One sought to live a cautious quiet life without discord, aspiring to success without change. This pragmatic approach to life is included in the earliest known piece of Wisdom literature, the *Instructions of Shuruppak,* dating to around 2600 B.C.E. In this collection a father gives his son practical advice and moral precepts—what modern people would term a "code of proper conduct"—standards of action providing guidelines for a family-centered, urban, civilized society ruled by a monarch. A son is advised to seek success; to avoid undue risk; to pay attention to the authority of parents, law, gods, and ruler; and to seek lasting rather than temporal values. The following are excerpts from this text:

> You should not steal anything. . . . You should not break into a house. . . . A thief is a lion, but after he is caught, he will be a slave. My son you should not commit robbery, you should not cut yourself with an axe. . . .
> You should not sit alone in a chamber with a married woman.
> You should not travel during the night: it can hide both good and evil.
> You should not have sex with your slave girl: she will chew you up (?).
> You should not curse strongly: it rebounds on you.
> You should not drive away a debtor: he will be hostile towards you.
> My son, you should not use violence (?) . . . You should not commit rape on someone's daughter; the courtyard will learn of it.
> With your life you should always be on the side of the warrior; with your life you should always be on the side of Utu (the god of Justice).
> The palace is like a mighty river: its middle is goring bulls; what flows in is never enough to fill it, and what flows out can never be stopped.
> You should not pass judgment when you drink beer.
> Heaven is far, earth is most precious, but it is with heaven that you multiply your goods, and all foreign lands breathe under it.
> You should not buy a prostitute: she is a mouth that bites. You should not buy a house-born slave: he is a herb that makes the stomach sick. You should not buy a free man: he will always lean against the wall. You should not buy a palace slave girl: she will always be the bottom of the barrel (?). You should rather bring down a foreign slave from the mountains, or you should bring somebody from a place where he is an alien; my son, then he will pour water for you where the sun rises and he will walk before you. He does not belong to any family, so he does not want to go to his family; he does not belong to any city, so he does not want to go to his city.
> You should not speak arrogantly to your mother; that causes hatred for you. You should not question the words of your mother and your personal god. The mother, like Utu, gives birth to the man; the father, like a god, makes him bright (?). The father is like a god: his words are reliable.

Hoard of twelve carved-stone votive statues (height of tallest, 28 inches), circa 2900 – circa 2600 B.C.E., all but one with inlaid eyes. Found beneath the floor near an altar in a sanctuary of the Abu Temple at Tell Asmar (ancient Eshnunna), where they were perhaps buried after the chapel was remodeled, the figures probably once stood before a cult image and prayed on behalf of their donors (Iraq Museum, Baghdad, and Oriental Institute, Chicago).

The instructions of the father should be complied with. (Black et al.)

The *Moral Canon*. The moral injunctions of Mesopotamians parallel the prohibitions and precepts of many of their neighbors. There existed in Sumerian, Babylonian, and Hittite civilizations a common body of ethics resembling in part that found in Hebrew and Christian scriptures. In contrast to later biblical theology, however, there did not exist any uniform moral code. A section of an omen collection called by scholars the *Moral Canon* comprises sayings about praiseworthy conduct that are similar in many respects to the sayings called the Beatitudes in the Christian scriptures (Matthew 5 and Luke 6):

If he says "I am poor," he will become rich.
If he says "I am weak," he will become strong.
If he says "I am powerful," he will become small.
If he says "I am a hero," he will be shamed.
If he is impetuous, he will not obtain what he wishes.
If in his heart he wants mortification, he will prosper.
If he is surrounded by wealth, he will let go of everything, he will die soon.
If their heart is troubled, it will rejoice, it will light up.

If he is sick in his heart, he will be answered in his inmost desires.
If his heart is in the dark, he will rejoice.
If in his heart he weeps constantly, . . .
If he asks himself, "Why should I keep it up?" he will rejoice.
If he is in joy, a depression will seize him.
If he says all the time "When shall I see? When shall I see?" his days will become longer.
If there is too little for him, he will prolong his life, he will have sufficient food.
If everything goes well for him, either death or poverty will come.
If his health is good, a serious disease will overtake him.
If he is just, and nevertheless things go wrong, later on things will go better.
If he speaks according to justice, he will have a good recompense.
If he is just, he will see light.
If he is flattered, he will not obtain . . .
If he is always praised, he will remain well.
If he loves what is good, only goodness will follow him all the time.
If he has a great heart, he will reach old age.
If he is endowed with fear (of god?), he will be victorious.

If he is merciful, he will die in abundance.

If he does favors, people will do favors to him.

If he is limpid in his heart, he will find honor.

If he is pure . . .

If "yes" and "no" follow in good order in his mouth, hunger will go from his granary.

If he is tranquil in his heart . . .

If he is concerned about helping others, the gods will follow him all the time. (Buccellati)

Moral Texts in the Hellenistic Period. Even as late as the first century B.C.E., after the conquest of the Near East by Alexander III (the Great) of Macedon (336–323 B.C.E.), inscriptions written in Greek still expressed values and ethics that can be shown to have roots in Mesopotamian texts. A Greek foundation inscription found in Asia Minor describes the revelation of a man called Dionysus who dreamt that the god Zeus gave him commandments to be observed by all visitors to his sanctuary. The instructions require strict observance of moral injunctions and ritual purity in order to prevent the desecration of holy sites; misdeeds angered the gods, endangering the health of the individual and the purity of the sanctuary. All who entered the shrine of Zeus were instructed to swear to obey the following injunctions:

Not to rob

Not to murder

Not to steal anything

Be loyal to the sanctuary

If somebody commits (a transgression) or plans (to commit one), he shall not be allowed to, and it will not be kept silent, but they will make it known and punish him.

A man shall not lie with a strange woman except for his wife . . . not with a boy and not with a virgin.

A man or woman who has committed one of these transgressions shall not enter this sanctuary, for here great gods sit (on their seats) who keep watch against these transgressions and will not tolerate transgressors. . . . The gods shall pardon the obedient and grant them blessings, and they will hate those who transgress (against the commandments) and impose upon them great punishments. . . . The men and women who are certain of their uprightness shall touch the inscribed pillar every month and year at the time of offering sacrifices. (Weinfeld)

Sources:

Bendt Alster, *The Instructions of Suruppak: A Sumerian Proverb Collection,* Mesopotamia: Copenhagen Studies in Assyriology, volume 2 (Copenhagen: Akademisk Forlag, 1974).

Alster, *Proverbs of Ancient Sumer: The World's Earliest Proverb Collections,* 2 volumes (Bethesda: CDL Press, 1997).

Giorgio Buccellati, "Ethics and Piety in the Ancient Near East," in *Civilizations of the Ancient Near East,* 4 volumes, edited by Jack M. Sasson (New York: Scribners, 1995), III: 1685–1696.

W. G. Lambert, *Babylonian Wisdom Literature* (Oxford: Clarendon Press, 1960).

Moshe Weinfeld, *Deuteronomy 1–11: A New Translation with Introduction and Commentary,* The Anchor Bible, volume 5 (New York, London, Toronto, Sydney & Auckland: Doubleday, 1991).

MYTHS—CREATION

Myths. In ancient Mesopotamian religion there existed no single source of revelation. Theologians sought to explain and justify the existence of mankind, its institutions, and the cosmos through the development of myths. Their explanations varied with time and place, and many differing traditions came to exist side by side. Theologians viewed each myth as offering its own insight. Knowledge was cumulative. There existed no Bible, no orthodoxy, and no canonical compilation of theological insight. Each myth reflected its own, often independent, tradition.

Creation Myths. In the modern world people look for natural causes to explain matters as diverse as human conflict or the movement of stars in the heavens. War is the result of conflicts of interest; physical disease has organic origins; psychological factors influence emotions; and science is used to explain the motion of celestial bodies. The ancient Near Eastern world explained such things as results of the actions of deities. Illness derived from an attack by demons; historical events such as defeat in war were interpreted as divine retribution for improper actions; and creation was an activity of the gods, who made both the world and mankind. Just as humans were expected to serve their earthly rulers without question, so too humankind was created to serve the gods.

Sumerian Myths of Creation. Little is known about the myths written in Sumerian during the early part of the third millennium B.C.E. No single Sumerian story describes creation; the existence of the gods is simply assumed. There was no conception of a beginning void, an unimaginable starting place like the one described in Genesis. The powers of the cosmos were thought to have existed throughout eternity, originating—according to one version of a god list—from the goddess Namma, a deity of the subterranean waters, "who gave birth to the Universe." Heaven and earth (sometimes conceived as being male and female) are the creation of the god Enlil, the head of the Sumerian pantheon. The author of one poorly preserved myth, whose title is unknown, expresses his belief that heaven and earth were already separated before the existence of the gods Enlil and his spouse, Ninlil. Another text, written in the city of Ur at the end of the third millennium B.C.E., explains that in its beginnings the earth was dark; there existed no light or vegetation, and no water emerged from the deep. In the Sumerian myth *Gilgamesh and the Netherworld,* the formation of the world by the gods An and Enlil is described as a result of separation of the parts of the universe, which were initially all mixed together.

Procreation. Just as humans bear offspring as the result of sexual intercourse, in some texts the process of divine creation is represented by a male god impregnating another deity or a part of nature. Yet, in other texts divinities and mankind are created by the modeling of clay. In the Sumerian tale called *The Debate between Summer and Winter,* the god Enlil impregnates the mountains to create the seasons, which, in turn, provide the conditions for agriculture and procreation of plants and animals:

> He copulated with the great hills, he gave the mountain its share. He filled its womb with Summer and Winter, the plenitude and life of the Land. As Enlil copulated with the earth, there was a roar like a bull's. The hill spent the day at that place and at night she opened her loins. She bore Summer and Winter as smoothly as fine oil. He fed them pure plants on the terraces of the hills like great bulls. He nourished them in the pastures of the hills.
>
> Enlil set about determining the destinies of Summer and Winter. For Summer founding towns and villages, bringing in harvests of plenitude for the Great Mountain Enlil, sending laborers out to the large arable tracts, and working the fields with oxen; for Winter plenitude, the spring floods, the abundance and life of the Land, placing grain in the fields and fruitful acres, and gathering in everything—Enlil determined these as the destinies of Summer and Winter. (Black et al.)

Origins of Mankind. The origins of mankind are addressed in the Sumerian poem *The Hymn to the Hoe*, a composition that compares the creation of man to the growth of plants. After the god Enlil has separated heaven from earth and earth from heaven, he causes the human seed to sprout forth like a plant from the soil at a sacred place called "Where Flesh Came Forth." Humans are then assigned their role as providers for the gods. Another Sumerian poem, *The Disputation between Ewe and Wheat*, includes a description of primeval earth as initially barren. People ate grass as if they were sheep, for wheat or bread did not yet exist; and they went about naked, because without ewes and goats, there was no weaving, cloth, or clothing.

The World Order. Ancient thinkers pondered the question of how the earth came to be ordered. One explanation is given in the Sumerian myth *Enki and the World Order*. Enki, one of the main deities in the Sumerian pantheon, is assigned responsibility for the organization of the

Striding *mushhushu*, a horned serpo-dragon, the emblematic animal of the god Marduk; unglazed molded brick (height 51 1/8 inches), from the earliest phase of the Ishtar Gate built by Nebuchadnezzar II (604-562 B.C.E.) at Babylon

world, including the fates of the land of Sumer, the foreign lands, and the Tigris and Euphrates Rivers. In order to manage his work he entrusts various gods with specific responsibilities, such as management of the twin rivers and marshes, the sea, rains, irrigation and crops, construction and architecture, wildlife on the high plain, herding of domestic animals, oversight of the whole of heaven and earth, and woman's work. Goddesses are assigned tasks of overseeing birthing, tending to the god An's sexual needs, metalwork, demarcation of boundaries and borders, preparation of meals for the gods, and fishing. According to *Enki and the World Order*, the world is administered by the gods as if it were a kingdom run by a ruler who delegates authority from the top.

Birth of Mankind. Other Sumerian myths address issues of disorder in the world. The myth *Enki and Ninmah* begins after heaven and earth have already been separated. At that time, after the gods have procreated, there is a shortage of food, and minor gods are assigned to the task of producing food by farming. To do so they have to undertake the burdensome job of digging and dredging the canals. The work is so difficult that the junior gods complain and finally decide to rebel. The senior god Enki, fast asleep at the time, is roused from his slumber and, realizing the need for a creative solution, he decides to create humankind. The goddess Namma is asked to knead clay from the fresh waters that lie under the earth and place it in her womb. She gives birth to the first humans, who then take up the burden of working the soil and creating produce.

Origins of Disabilities. The second part of the myth *Enki and Ninmah* deals with the origins of humans whose various disabilities make them unable to find productive employment. In this myth, Enki and the goddess Ninmah become inebriated at a banquet and challenge one another to a contest. The goddess begins by creating crippled and disabled people and challenging Enki to provide for their welfare. Enki responds by assigning them professions in which each person's infirmity becomes an asset, so they can be independent and earn their own living. For example,

> Enki looked at the man who cannot bend his outstretched weak hands, and decreed his fate: he appointed him as a servant of the king. . . . Enki looked at this one, the one born as an idiot, and decreed his fate: he appointed him a servant of the king. . . . Enki looked at the one who could not hold back his urine and bathed him in enchanted water and drove out the *namtar* demon from his body. (Black et al.)

Enki then challenges Ninmah. He molds clay and places it in the womb of a woman, creating a being unable to function. Ninmah is confounded and cannot find a suitable profession for this being. The myth concludes with the exclamation that Ninmah is not the equal of the great Enki.

Enuma Elish. Babylonian poets incorporated stories about the creation of man and the world in texts designed to justify and glorify kingship. The Babylonian creation epic *Enuma elish*, "When on high," illustrates the way in which Marduk obtained his position as the chief god of Babylon and reveals the nature of the unchallenged power of the Babylonian ruler. The story begins with the existence of an immense expanse of sweet (*apsu*) and salt (*tiamat*) waters that existed before the universe and the first gods came into being. This watery chaos may echo an older Sumerian tradition about descent of the gods from the goddess Namma, a deity of the subterranean waters. Out of the mingling of these primeval waters, the gods emerge in pairs. Like young children, the gods are rambunctious, so upsetting the god Apsu that he decides to destroy the young deities. The clever god Ea comes to their rescue and kills Apsu. Described as perfect and unequaled, the god Marduk is born to Ea and his wife Damkina. Marduk, as a leader of the younger generation, is selected by the gods as their commander. He becomes their supreme leader and champion, defending the lesser deities against the fury of the goddess Tiamat, who has become upset at all the noise and commotion caused by the younger generation and determined to avenge the slaying of her husband, Apsu. Armed with an array of winds Marduk heroically battles Tiamat, a symbol of the old order. After killing the goddess, Marduk needs to dispose of the corpse, so he splits it in two like a dried fish and fashions the upper part as heaven and the lower part as earth. Afterward, he creates the constellations and the netherworld. He also makes the sun and moon come forth, organizes the calendar, and is given the authority to care and provide for the sanctuaries necessary for worship of the gods. Finally, Marduk, thankful for the benefits granted by the gods and their submissiveness to his rule, decides to ease their burden by creating man from the blood of a slain rebellious god. The myth employs this episode to explain that man was created both to sustain the gods and to release them from their menial labors. The same story also provides a rationale for the rebellious nature of mankind. Marduk gives the gods new roles by assigning them to various positions in heaven and on earth. In the next episode of *Enuma elish*, Marduk demands that the gods build him a capital city, Babylon, and in it his temple, E-sangil, where he will dwell and administer the affairs of the gods. In gratitude to Marduk, the gods comply. They prostrate themselves before him, pledge obedience to their unquestioned leader and commander, and confirm his kingship in the Council of Gods. The myth continues with the gods pronouncing the fifty names of Marduk, each an aspect of his power and character. *Enuma elish* concludes with a reiteration of its main political theme: Marduk, the victor, the absolute ruler, "defeated Tiamat and took kingship."

Sources:

Jeremy Black, Graham Cunningham, Jarle Ebeling, Esther Flückiger-Hawker, Eleanor Robson, Jon Taylor, and Gábor Zólyomi, *The Electronic Text Corpus of Sumerian Literature,* The Oriental Institute, University of Oxford, 1998– <http://www-etcsl.orient.ox.ac.uk/>.

Benjamin R. Foster, *Before the Muses: An Anthology of Akkadian Literature,* 2 volumes (Bethesda, Md.: CDL Press, 1993).

Foster, *From Distant Days: Myths, Tales, and Poetry of Ancient Mesopotamia* (Bethesda, Md.: CDL Press, 1995).

Thorkild Jacobsen, *The Harps that Once . . . : Sumerian Poetry in Translation* (New Haven: Yale University Press, 1987).

Jacobsen, *The Treasures of Darkness: A History of Mesopotamian Religion* (New Haven: Yale University Press, 1976).

Samuel Noah Kramer and John Maier, *Myths of Enki, The Crafty God* (New York & Oxford: Oxford University Press, 1989).

MYTHS—DEITIES

Enlil. Enlil was one of the chief gods of the Sumerian and Babylonian pantheons. His spouse is Ninlil, who is also called Sud in a Sumerian myth. His offspring include the goddess Inana (the Queen of Heaven) and the gods Ishkur (a storm god, known in Babylonian sources as Adad), Nanna/Suen (a moon god, called Sin in Akkadian), the twins Nergal and Meslamtaea (underworld deities), Ninurta (principally a god of war also known as Ningirsu), Pabilsag (whose associated constellation was later identified by the Greeks as Sagittarius), Nuska (Enlil's minister, who was also a god of fire), Utu (the sun god, known as Shamash in Akkadian), Zababa (a war god), Ennugi (the canal inspector), and Ninazu (an underworld god).

Enlil and Ninlil. A tale of rape and marriage, the Sumerian myth of *Enlil and Ninlil,* known from copies written in the Old Babylonian period (circa 1894 – circa 1595 B.C.E.), opens with Enlil spotting the young, beautiful goddess Ninlil bathing in the pure canal. He approaches and propositions her with offers of kisses and love, but the goddess demurs, explaining that she is young and innocent and does not know how to kiss. Furthermore, if her parents found out that she has had an affair they will punish her. Nevertheless, Enlil perseveres. He hugs her, kisses her, and finally impregnates her. When Enlil's rape of Ninlil is reported in the assembly of the gods, Enlil is declared to be "unclean" and banished from the city. Enlil is taboo, his offense a crime. Despite the impropriety of Enlil's advances, however, Ninlil, now pregnant, endeavors to stick by his side, determined to be with him and to bear him children. When Enlil tries to get away, she follows him. Enlil then disguises himself and tricks her into sleeping with him several more times. The myth ends with praise to the mother Ninlil, who has conceived Enlil's children, and with a celebration of Enlil as bringer of fertility and prosperity. The story implies that even though Enlil raped and deceived Ninlil, she continued to follow him to fulfill her craving to be a wife and produce children. The story also implies that even though he wronged Ninlil and became an outcast, Enlil was never permanently barred

Molded-clay relief plaque (height 4 inches) depicting a goddess with a child's head emerging from each shoulder and holding a suckling baby to her breast, probably Nintu as the "Lady of Births." The emaciated figures on either side sit beneath symbols of the goddess; unprovenanced, Isin-Larsa or Old Babylonian period, circa 2000 – circa 1600 B.C.E. (Iraq Museum, Baghdad).

from returning to civilization. According to one interpretation, Enlil was god of earth and god of the moist winds of spring. The myth explains Enlil's disappearance at the end of the long dry summer and his return in the spring to bring fertility and productivity to nature.

Enlil and Sud. The Sumerian myth *Enlil and Sud,* known from copies written in the Old Babylonian period (circa 1894 – circa 1595 B.C.E.), relates the story of the young god Enlil's search for a wife. The poem describes Enlil's infatuation with the beautiful young Sud (another name for Ninlil), his courtship, and subsequent marriage. The story opens with Enlil, the great god of heaven, searching for a wife. He spots Sud, a young inexperienced girl full of charm and delight, in the street in front of the house of her mother, the goddess Nisaba. Enlil assumes that she must be a disreputable woman or else she would not be alone in the street. Taken with her beauty, Enlil offers to rehabilitate her, give her proper clothing, and

Modern impression of a black serpentine cylinder seal (height 1¼ inches), unprovenanced, Akkadian period, circa 2334 – circa 2279 B.C.E. The god, Ea (seated), with streams of water at his shoulders, is approached by his two-faced vizier, Usmu, who leads a male figure (presumably the seal owner) carrying a kid as an offering; behind them is an attendant with a pail (Yale Babylonian Collection).

make her a lady. Sud is confused by the directness of his advances and is taken aback by his disrespectful speech. She tries to brush him off, but Enlil persists, saying that he wants to express his love for her. Shocked by Enlil's brash behavior, Sud turns away and enters her house. Enlil, however, does not give up. He instructs his emissary Nuska to go immediately to the girl's house laden with bridal gifts and to ask Sud's mother for the hand of her daughter. Nuska arrives and, in the name of Enlil, asks the goddess for the hand of her daughter. The great goddess is flattered that Enlil wishes to marry her daughter and responds that the message gladdens her heart. Enlil's behavior toward her daughter will be forgotten; proper amends have been made; and she will gladly become his mother-in-law.

Enlil's Wedding. Enlil now prepares for the wedding, sending great gifts of meats, cheeses, fruits, nuts, gold, silver, and topaz. After the wedding the finest perfumes are poured over Sud, and Enlil makes love to his wife. He then sits on his throne, blesses her, and decrees that she will be known as "Nintu, the Lady-who-gives-Birth." Nintu is then placed in charge of all the secrets pertaining to women. Like her mother, the grain goddess, Sud becomes a great fertility goddess and is given another name, Ninlil ("Lady of Full-grown Wheat"). She is also made mistress of the scribal arts. Ending with praise for Enlil and Ninlil, the story illustrates the Mesopotamian view that a woman's role was to be both fertile and the manager of her husband's household.

Enki. The Mesopotamian god called Enki in Sumerian and Ea in Akkadian was considered the god of the subter-

ranean fresh waters, called the *abzu* in Sumerian (Akkadian: *apsu*). In Sumerian and Akkadian mythology he is a wise and clever deity and determiner of destinies. Associated with magic and incantations, he is described in some stories as the son of An, the sky god. Other myths depict him as the offspring of Enlil, while at other times he is the issue of the goddess Namma. In art, Enki is depicted as a water god, shown with streams of water flowing over his shoulders to the ground. As a provider of fresh water, he was considered to be favorable to mankind.

Enki and Inana. A Sumerian myth called *Enki and Inana*, known from copies written in the Old Babylonian period (circa 1894 – circa 1595 B.C.E.), revolves around an attempt by Enki's daughter Inana, the goddess of sex and love, to visit her father in his temple at Eridu, so that she can obtain greater powers through possession of the *me* (pronounced "may"). The *me* are the divine powers and wisdom, the norms underlying all facets of human civilization, including religion, government, morality, warfare, family and society, art, economy, technology, and crafts. Inana receives the *me* from her father while he is drunk and successfully brings them to her home city of Uruk, in spite of Enki's attempts to stop her and retrieve the powers. The story may represent a mythological justification for the transfer of regional hegemony over the land of Sumer from the city of Eridu to the city of Uruk at the beginning of the Early Dynastic Period (circa 2900 – circa 2340 B.C.E.).

Erra. The underworld god Erra was associated with warfare, anarchy, and plague. His activities are known mainly from an Akkadian myth called *Erra and Ishum*, pre-

Cuneiform clay tablet with the myth of Enki and Ninhursanga (height 5 inches), from Nippur, Old Babylonian period, circa 1740 B.C.E. (University of Pennsylvania Museum of Archaeology and Anthropology)

served in copies produced during the first millennium B.C.E. The myth deals with the sources of violence and explores issues arising from the gods' dislike of any human actions that upset the equilibrium between humans and deities. The myth describes the Seven, a group of terrifying demons who serve as Erra's assistants and when needed are employed to crush mankind. Erra takes control of the heavens and earth and denigrates man's malevolent actions. He orders all the enemies of Babylon to fight each other to the end, so that only Babylon will remain to rule. The Seven are sent to devastate Babylon's enemies. Led by the god Ishum, they obliterate the cities and their wildlife. The myth expresses Babylonian attitudes toward the hostile and violent nature of its enemies.

Inana. Known as Ishtar in Akkadian, Inana, "The Lady of Heaven," was a goddess of war and fertility and the most important female deity in the Sumerian and Akkadian pantheon. In most stories, she is described as the offspring of the moon god Nanna and his consort Ningal. Her brothers included the sun god Utu and the storm god Ishkur. She was also the sister of Ereshkigal, queen of the Netherworld and goddess of death and gloom. Inana had no permanent spouse, but in most myths she was linked to the shepherd god Dumuzi. According to most accounts, she did not have any children, but the warrior god Shara may be an exception. In Sumerian myths she is depicted as an assertive female—powerful, sexual, independent, petulant, selfish, and naive.

Inana and Dumuzi. Dumuzi, known as Tammuz in the Bible (Ezekiel 8:14), was a fertility god. In the sacred marriage ceremony in which Sumerian kings were ritually married to the goddess Inana, Dumuzi was identified as Ama-ushumgal-ana, a reference to the date-palm bud, a symbol of fertility and growth. It was believed that the sexual union of Dumuzi and Inana produced new life and prosperity. In songs accompanying the sacred marriage ceremony, Inana chooses Dumuzi, a passive shepherd-king, to be her husband. She is attracted by his beauty and views him as a good provider. Beginning with the Third Dynasty of Ur (circa 2112 – circa 2004 B.C.E.), the ritual featured a marriage, either real or symbolic, of the king representing Dumuzi and a female partner or statue representing Inana.

Inana's Descent to the Netherworld. The second millennium B.C.E. Sumerian myth *Inana's Descent to the Netherworld* describes the goddess's journey to and return from the "Land of No Return." In this myth Inana attempts to take control of the Netherworld, the domain of her sister Ereshkigal. When her plan fails, she is turned into a corpse and hung on a hook like a slab of meat. While she is trapped in the Netherworld, the earth withers. The minister Ninshubur approaches the gods Enlil, Nanna, and Enki, begging for their intervention to save the goddess. Understanding the gravity of the situation, the wise god Enki fashions figures that sneak into the Netherworld and

sprinkle life-giving waters on the goddess, bringing her back to life. Before Inana can leave, she is told that she will have to provide a substitute for herself. Demons escort her from the Netherworld and locate the festively dressed Dumuzi seated on his throne. When Inana finds out that her husband has been enjoying himself in her absence, she becomes furious that he has not been mourning her death. The goddess then gives permission for the demons to make Dumuzi her substitute in the Netherworld. The end of the myth is fragmentary and difficult to understand. Inana asks Dumuzi's sister, the goddess Geshtinana, to take her brother's place in the Netherworld for half of each year. A shorter Akkadian version of the myth, *The Descent of Ishtar into the Netherworld*, dates to the latter half of the second millennium B.C.E. A copy of this text was found in the library of the Assyrian king Ashurbanipal (668–627 B.C.E.) at Nineveh.

Ninhursanga. Ninhursanga was a Sumerian mother goddess. An early second millennium B.C.E. Sumerian tale, *Enki and Ninhursanga*, describes a sacred land called Dilmun, in which "the raven was not yet cawing, the partridge not cackling. The lion did not slay, the wolf was not carrying off lambs, the dog had not been taught to make kids curl up, the pig had not learned that grain was to be eaten." Before the advent of human civilization this land is virginal and pristine, a place where there is no disease, no death, and no old age. The latter part of the story revolves around Enki, the mother goddess Ninhursanga, and their offspring and descendants whom Enki has impregnated. One descendant, the spider goddess Uttu, has Enki's semen removed by Ninhursanga. From this seed grows eight plants, which Enki devours, causing him great pain. Ninhursanga then heals Enki and gives birth to eight divinities. The composition ends with Enki assigning destinies to each of his offspring.

Sources:
Jeremy Black, Graham Cunningham, Jarle Ebeling, Esther Flückiger-Hawker, Eleanor Robson, Jon Taylor, and Gábor Zólyomi, *The Electronic Text Corpus of Sumerian Literature*, The Oriental Institute, University of Oxford, 1998– <http://www-etcsl.orient.ox.ac.uk/>.

Luigi Cagni, *The Poem of Erra*, Sources and Monographs, Sources from the Ancient Near East, volume 1, fascicle 3 (Malibu, Cal.: Undena Press, 1977).

Miguel Civil, "Enlil and Ninlil: The Marriage of Sud," *Journal of the American Oriental Society*, 103 (1983): 43–66.

Benjamin R. Foster, *Before the Muses: An Anthology of Akkadian Literature*, 2 volumes (Bethesda, Md.: CDL Press, 1993).

Thorkild Jacobsen, *The Harps that Once . . . : Sumerian Poetry in Translation* (New Haven: Yale University Press, 1987).

Samuel Noah Kramer and John Maier, *Myths of Enki, The Crafty God* (New York & Oxford: Oxford University Press, 1989).

Yitzhak Sefati, *Love Songs in Sumerian Literature: Critical Edition of the Dumuzi-Inanna Songs* (Ramat Gan, Israel: Bar-Ilan University Press, 1998).

Diane Wolkstein and Samuel Noah Kramer, *Inanna, Queen of Heaven and Earth: Her Stories and Hymns from Sumer* (New York: Harper & Row, 1983).

MYTHS—FLOOD

Flood Myths. Stories about a great flood are known from many civilizations, both ancient and modern. The first written mention of a great deluge is found in Sumerian literary sources dating to the end of the third millennium B.C.E. Some versions of the *Sumerian King List* include a list of eight kings of five cities from the beginnings of kingship to the time of the flood. The last antediluvian ruler was a sage named Ziusudra ("Life of Distant Days"), who in other Mesopotamian sources is called Atra-hasis ("Exceedingly Wise") or Uta-napishti ("I Found Life"). The king list continues in the postdiluvian era with semi-historical and historical rulers. Because it is possible to approximate the regnal dates of known historical kings on the list, scholars have deduced that the Sumerians believed the flood to have been a localized event dating to early in the third millennium B.C.E.

The Sumerian Flood Myth. The annual spring flooding of the Tigris and Euphrates Rivers, or possibly changes in ancient sea levels, may have given rise to stories about the beginnings of the Flood. Unfortunately, no Sumerian version of the flood myth survives from the third millennium B.C.E. A *Sumerian Flood Myth* dating to the beginning of

the second millennium B.C.E. begins after the gods have created the black-headed people (the Sumerians) and animals that have multiplied everywhere, lowered kingship from heaven, and assigned gods to rule over the main cities of the land of Sumer. At this point, the tablet on which the text was written is broken. When the story resumes, the gods have given an order to destroy mankind, possibly as a result of displeasure with mankind's deeds or as a result of man having multiplied like the animals. A storm begins, and a great flood sweeps over the land for seven days and seven nights. Only Ziusudra survives the flood in his ark, together with animals and the "seed of mankind." When the floodwaters recede, Ziusudra disembarks on land and is granted eternal life by the gods An and Enlil. He then settles overseas in the faraway land of Dilmun, where the sun rises.

The Epic of Atra-hasis. Sumerian stories of the flood probably influenced the creation of later Babylonian versions. In the myth known to the ancients as *Enuma ilu awilum,* "When the gods were (like) men," the hero is called Atra-hasis. This myth begins before the creation of mankind, at a time when the junior gods, the Igigi—on the orders from the higher gods, the Anunnakki—have the task

Cuneiform clay tablet with the Sumerian flood story (height 4 inches), from Nippur, Old Babylonian period, circa 1740 B.C.E. (University of Pennsylvania Museum of Archaeology and Anthropology)

of configuring the earth by digging rivers, canals, and marshes. Feeling exploited, the Igigi deities complain about the difficulty of their work and decide to revolt. They put down their tools and march in protest to the dwelling of the senior god Enlil, the chief god of the earth. In order to resolve their complaints, Enki suggests that the gods create humans to relieve the junior gods of their burden. The birth goddess is summoned, and she creates man out of clay. Clay may have been chosen because, like mankind's bones, it dries out when it becomes old and ultimately turns to dust. At first, mankind is not subject to death. Since humans can reproduce, however, an explosion of the human population occurs. Enlil becomes greatly disturbed by events on earth. The noise of mankind is so overwhelming that he cannot obtain his needed rest. An aloof deity with little concern for humankind, Enlil decides that the creation of humanity was a mistake, an error to be remedied by a drastic solution. In order to decrease the numbers of mankind, Enlil orders a plague, but the god Ea intervenes on behalf of man and tells the hero Atra-hasis to placate the plague god with offerings. After the plague ends, the human population does not diminish but becomes more numerous than before. Enlil decides he must take action. He orders the rain to stop and reduces the food supply, inducing famine. Again, Ea comes to the aid of mankind, and rain ends the drought. Frustrated that his designs are not working, Enlil decides to bring about a flood to destroy all mankind. This time Ea advises Atra-hasis to build a boat, roof it over, and make it waterproof with pitch. Animals and family board the ark as the weather changes. Just as the bolt is slid to close the ark, the storm begins. For seven days and nights it rages. After the flood subsides, Atra-hasis makes a sacrifice to the gods. When Enlil sees the vessel, he becomes enraged and demands to know how man survived. Enki once again says that he was responsible for saving life. At the end of the story, Enlil decides that only Atra-hasis and his wife will be granted eternal life. As for the rest of mankind, their days will henceforth be numbered, and human population will be controlled through the creation of women who do not bear children.

The *Epic of Gilgamesh*. A better-preserved and more-detailed version of the Flood story, possibly composed at the end of the second century B.C.E., is found on Tablet 11 of the Babylonian *Epic of Gilgamesh*. In this version of the story, the gods decided to bring about a flood to destroy mankind. The hero, here named Uta-napishti, son of Ubar-Tutu of the city of Shuruppak, tells Gilgamesh how he was forewarned by the god Ea, who told him to abandon his property and wealth and build a ship. Uta-napishti built an ark, six decks high, and waterproofed it with pitch. He then loaded onto the ship everything he owned, including all his gold and silver, and sent aboard his animals, family, and artisans. Uta-napishti had the hatch sealed by a boatman and gave the man his palace and all his remaining goods as a going-away gift. The next morning the storm began. For six days and seven nights the wind blew, and the Deluge flattened the land. On the seventh day the storm ended, and the ocean grew calm. Uta-napishti scanned the horizon. His boat had run aground on a mountainside. After seven days he let loose a dove, which returned because there was no other place to land. He then sent forth a swallow, but it too returned. Finally, he released a raven, which—because the waters had receded—found food and did not return. Uta-napishti then made an offering to the gods. Enlil was seized with anger when he saw that people had survived. Calmed by Ea, Enlil came inside the boat, where he decreed that from then on only Uta-napishti and his wife would be like gods, endowed with eternal life. The two were sent to settle far away, in a land where the rivers flow forth.

Gilgamesh and the Bible. The Gilgamesh version of the Flood myth, with several major differences, parallels the biblical accounts found in Genesis 6:5–8:22. The biblical versions, probably composed during the first half of the first millennium B.C.E., begin with Israel's God, Yahweh, taking account of mankind's wickedness and regretting that he created man. He instructs Noah, the only human with whom he finds favor, to build an ark, providing him with its exact dimensions. Noah, in one version, is instructed to take into the ark pairs of animals, male and female, as well as birds of every kind, and every variety of creeping thing. Noah also places on board his wife, his sons, and his daughters-in-law. The Flood lasts for forty days, and all existence on earth is destroyed, except for Noah and those with him in the ark. When the ark finally comes to rest on Mount Ararat, Noah opens the hatch and releases a raven, which returns, and then a dove, which also returns. Days later he releases the dove once again. This time the dove returns with an olive leaf in its bill, showing that the flood waters are beginning to subside. Seven days later, when Noah again releases the dove, it does not return. The biblical account concludes with Noah making an offering to God Yahweh, and Yahweh sealing a covenant with Noah in which he promises never again to destroy the world as a result of mankind's evil.

Comparison of Biblical and Babylonian Versions of the Flood. In several of its details, such as the setting forth of birds, the biblical story closely parallels the Babylonian Gilgamesh story. Yet, the biblical version also includes theological elements not found in any of the Mesopotamian versions. In Genesis, the Flood results from man's evil rather than from overpopulation. In the aftermath of the Flood, instead of limiting man's days or granting the hero immortality, Yahweh promises never again to destroy his creation. He favors Noah and his family with divine blessing and tells them to "be fruitful and multiply, and fill the earth."

Berossos's Flood Myth. The latest Mesopotamian version of the Flood story was written in Greek by Berossos, a priest of the god Marduk, in about 275 B.C.E. The original composition, now lost, is preserved only in a version copied by the fourth-century C.E. Church historian Eusebius. In this story, the Flood hero is called Xisouthros, an obvious Hellenized rendering of the Sumerian hero Ziusudra's name. The Greek god Kronos appears to Xisouthros in a dream and tells him that mankind will be destroyed by a flood. The hero is ordered to dig a hole and bury all the writings in the city of Sippar. He is then to build a boat and fill it with his kin, friends, birds, and animals. The description of the flood is not preserved in Eusebius's copy. After the flood subsides, Xisouthros sends forth some of the birds on the vessel, who find no food or place to rest and come back. A few days later the hero lets out the birds again, and they again return to the ship, their feet covered in mud. The third time they are sent forth, they do not return. Seeing now that the boat is moored on a mountain, Xisouthros disembarks and makes a sacrifice to the gods. Soon he and his family disappear, leaving behind those who have stayed on the boat. A voice tells the survivors that Xisouthros, his wife, and the boat pilot will henceforth dwell with the gods. The others are told to return to Babylon, rescue the buried writings from Sippar, and pass them on to mankind. The survivors obey, and after digging up the writings, they found many cities and shrines and re-establish Babylon.

Sources:

Jeremy Black, Graham Cunningham, Jarle Ebeling, Esther Flückiger-Hawker, Eleanor Robson, Jon Taylor, and Gábor Zólyomi, *The Electronic Text Corpus of Sumerian Literature*, The Oriental Institute, University of Oxford, 1998– <http://www-etcsl.orient.ox.ac.uk/>.

Stanley Mayer Burstein, *The* Babylonaica *of Berossus*, Sources and Monographs, Sources from the Ancient Near East, volume 1, fascicle 5 (Malibu, Cal.: Undena Publications, 1978).

Benjamin R. Foster, *Before the Muses: An Anthology of Akkadian Literature*, 2 volumes (Bethesda, Md.: CDL Press, 1993).

Foster, ed. and trans., *The Epic of Gilgamesh* (New York: Norton, 2001).

Andrew R. George, trans., *The Epic of Gilgamesh: The Babylonian Epic Poem and Other Texts in Akkadian and Sumerian* (London: Allen Lane, 1999).

Thorkild Jacobsen, *The Harps that Once . . . : Sumerian Poetry in Translation* (New Haven: Yale University Press, 1987).

W. G. Lambert, Alan R. Millard, and Miguel Civil, *Atra-ḫasīs: The Babylonian Story of the Flood, with the Sumerian Flood Story* (Winona Lake, Ind.: Eisenbrauns, 1999).

MYTHS–HEROES

Adapa. In Babylonian tradition, Adapa was known as a wise man or sage from the early Sumerian city of Eridu. The myth of Adapa, a Babylonian composition, explores the topic of humankind's mortality, explaining mankind's limited life span as well as commenting on human anger and rage. The myth opens with a description of Adapa as a wise, ritually observant servant of the god Ea. One day while Adapa is out fishing, a south wind comes up and capsizes his boat. He is thrown overboard and spends the day "in the home of the fish." Wet and angry, he curses the wind, and the power of his spell breaks its wings. The wind is incapacitated; for seven days there is no wind over the land. Annoyed, the supreme god Anu summons Adapa to appear before him. When he arrives for his audience with Anu, Adapa declines an offer of food and drink, a rite of hospitality reserved for visiting deities, not realizing that accepting Anu's offering would give him eternal life. Anu laughs at the sage's naiveté and asks him why he does not eat or drink. Adapa answers that Ea has advised him in the ways of heaven and that he is merely following that god's instructions. Anu then explains that he had offered eternal life and that by refusing Adapa will be returned to earth to live as a mortal.

Etana. Another Babylonian myth tells of an episode in the life of Etana, a legendary king who ruled in the Sumerian city of Kish after the flood. The story revolves around a folktale about the interaction among an eagle, a serpent, and Etana. Etana comes to the aid of the eagle,

Serpentine cylinder seal (height 1 ½ inches) and modern impression, depicting at the right a man seated on the back of an eagle, perhaps representing an otherwise unknown earlier Akkadian version of the myth of Etana and the Eagle; unprovenanced, Akkadian period, circa 2334 – circa 2193 B.C.E. (British Museum, London)

Drawing of a sculpted stone relief depicting a half-man half-fish *apkallu*, or "sage," a semi-divine exorcist—perhaps Adapa who brought the fruits of civilization to mankind—one of a pair blessing passersby at the entrance to the Ninurta temple, Nimrud, reign of Ashurnasirpal II, 883–859 B.C.E. (drawing by Austen Henry Layard; British Museum, London)

which is imprisoned in a pit for killing the serpent's offspring. In return for his assistance the eagle promises to help the childless king find the mythical plant of fertility. Etana mounts the bird, and they ascend to the heavens. The preserved part of the story ends with Etana's return from his flight. The tablet is broken in key spots, and it is not known if Etana's quest for the plant of birth is successful. Another text, however, refers to a son who succeeds him as king of Kish.

Sources:
Benjamin R. Foster, *Before the Muses: An Anthology of Akkadian Literature*, 2 volumes (Bethesda, Md.: CDL Press, 1993).

Michael Haul, *Das Etana-Epos: Ein Mythos von der Himmelfahrt des Königs von Kiš*, Göttinger Arbeitshefte zur altorientalischen Literatur, 1 (Göttingen: Seminar für Keilschriftforschung, 2000).

Shlomo Izre'el, *Adapa and the South Wind: Language Has the Power of Life and Death*, Mesopotamian Civilizations, 10 (Winona Lake, Ind.: Eisenbrauns, 2001).

RELIGIOUS PRACTICE

Purpose of Life. In the Mesopotamian worldview, the gods were so distant from man that, even one who lived a proper righteous life could never count on the gods to ensure prosperity or happiness. All people had to fend for themselves, provide for their families, and seek their own pleasures. In the *Epic of Gilgamesh*, the hero arrives at a tavern located at the ends of the earth. There the mysterious female tavern keeper Siduri advises him to abandon his search for immortality and enjoy what life and families have to offer:

> Gilgamesh, where are you wandering?
> You will not find the life for which you are searching.
> When the gods created man,
> They allotted death for mankind,
> Keeping life for themselves.
> Gilgamesh, let your belly be full,
> Make merry by day and by night.
> Make a feast of rejoicing every day.
> By day and by night, dance and play.
> Let your clothing be clean and fresh.
> Your head be washed, your body bathed in water.
> Look to the child who clutches your hand,
> Let your wife enjoy herself in your lap.
> This is the fulfillment of man! (Foster)

The Cult. According to the theology preserved in myth, man had both to attend to his own needs and to give service to the cult. Humans were created to be servants to the gods and were expected to provide them and their families with a lifestyle of luxury and ease. To maintain, treat, clothe, feed, and honor the gods in accordance with their exalted rank, temples were created as homes for the deity. Called in Sumerian *e-gal*, "Great House," the temple was a center of worship, a seat of judicial assembly, and a place of ceremony and ritual. It was also a part of a complex that could include workshops and a temple tower or ziggurat, whose rites and purpose remain largely unknown. A cult statue of the god, accompanied by images of his family and companions, was placed in the cult room, a room in the temple "which knows no light." Statuettes presented by worshipers to intercede on the supplicant's behalf stood on benches or offering tables before the divine presence.

Temple Personnel. The care and feeding of the gods required an extensive retinue of cooks, millers, bakers, carpenters, metalworkers, butchers, weavers, laundry workers, and cleaners, among others. Many of these workers probably lived on temple grounds; others came to the temple from their nearby homes. Most priests lived within the temple compound. The highest-ranking priest was the *shangu*, who had both administrative and religious duties. The *kalu* were cantors who chanted laments; the *naru* and *zammeru* were singers; the *pashishu* poured liquids as part of anointing ceremonies; the *ramku* sprinkled purification waters; and the *erib-biti*, "One who Enters the Temple," had access to restricted areas. There were many other kinds of specialized priests and priestesses. The high priestess, the *entu*, was chaste—as was the *naditu*, who lived and worked in a sort of cloister. These women were highly educated; some wrote beautiful poetry that has been preserved on clay tablets. Scribes kept accounts of temple income and expenditures.

Sacrifice. An important element for the comfort of the gods and their families was a house in good repair. Good meals, clothing, and ritual entertainment had to be provided to ease the gods' work burden and keep them in good cheer. The cult image of the god was presented with breakfast in the morning and a large sumptuous meal in the evening. According to a ritual text, the table (that is, the altar) was set with gold vessels filled with various kinds of beer, wine, and food. An alabaster vase was filled with milk. Emmer wheat and barley were used to make loaves of bread for the gods. Dates were served, and cakes were prepared. Sacrificial meat dishes were made from sheep, oxen, rams, and calves. Ducks and various varieties of birds, as well as ostrich and duck eggs were also served. Cult statues were bathed, groomed, perfumed, dressed in cloths, and bedecked with jewelry. Texts from later periods indicate that the king was served whatever foods the god did not finish.

Journeys. In modern times, heads of state travel to meet with other political leaders. Their journeys may be social or diplomatic. Leaders may seek approval for political activities or attempt to cement alliances. In ancient Mesopotamia the statues of the gods also made state visits, transported either in chariots or in barges from their temples to the residences of other gods. During the third millennium B.C.E., the moon god Nanna-Suen's journey from his home in Ur to the temple of his father, Enlil, in Nippur, one hundred and fifty kilometers away, was recorded in the *Myth of Nanna-Suen's Journey to Nippur*. After a short introduction, the text describes Nanna-Suen's preparation of a special barge worthy of a state visit. The boat is built of reeds, pitch, rushes, and cypress, cedar, and fir woods. It is then loaded with gift offerings of animals, birds, and fish. During the course of its journey, the barge stops at six towns before finally docking at Nippur. Nanna-Suen disembarks and, aware of proper etiquette, asks the doorkeeper to admit him to the temple. Once in the presence of his father, Nanna-Suen presents gifts, and the great god reciprocates with sweet cakes, fine bread, fine beer, and syrup. On Nanna-Suen's departure, Enlil grants his son's request that there be prosperity in his home city of Ur. Nanna-Suen then returns to Ur. This myth shows that gods, like kings, had both ceremonial and political responsibilities. The tale may have its roots in either a political or a religious alliance between Ur and the holy city of Nippur.

Ceremonial Acts. In Mesopotamian thought the entire universe was filled with awesome divine powers that controlled both humankind and nature. Royalty and the elite sought to shield themselves from harm by cultic performance. The proper performance of cultic acts and rituals was believed to placate the gods and ensure that they supported one's endeavors. To secure well-being, various rituals and accompanying formulas were performed in the temple on a daily, monthly, seasonal, and annual basis. Typical cultic activities included the performance of cultic songs, incantations, and spells. Rituals involved priests, royalty, and occasionally members of the elite. Entrance into the temple was restricted. As the residence of the god, the temple was not considered a place of public assembly or a center of popular devotion. The populace participated only during major seasonal festivals.

The New Year Festival. The Babylonian festival honoring the New Year, known as the *akitu* festival, was celebrated from the first day to the twelfth day of the New Year. During the course of a ritual ceremony held in the city of Babylon, the statue of the god Marduk was brought in a great procession into a ceremonial house (the *akitu*) located outside the city wall. During the ceremony, the king, as the representative of the people, participated in a purification ritual. He received a strong slap to the face; if it brought tears, it acted to expiate sin. The Babylonian myth of creation, *Enuma elish*, was recited during the ritual in honor of the god Marduk. Other rites celebrated during the festival include those marking the spring barley harvest and the enthronement of the monarch. New Year's ceremonies with differing rites are attested from the end of the third millennium B.C.E. and were celebrated in other Sumerian and Babylonian cities.

The Rite of the Substitute King. Cuneiform texts refer to the rite of a substitute king, who was installed when portents predicted a crisis or the violent death of the monarch. The replacement king, like the scapegoat in the Bible and Babylonian incantation documents, was supposed to attract evil and its consequences onto his body. This rite was first recorded in the Old Babylonian period (circa 1894 – circa

Hypothetical reconstruction of the interior of the Cult Room of the Archaic Ishtar Temple, level G, at Ashur,
including objects excavated from the temple area, circa mid-late third millennium B.C.E.
(drawing by Walter Andrae; Vorderasiatisches Museum, Berlin)

1595 B.C.E.), when the ruler of Isin had a substitute installed as king. At the end of his term, the replacement king was killed, taking the evil omen with him to the "Land of No Return" and theoretically freeing the real king and his realm from potential harm. The most important source of information about the ritual dates to the reign of the Assyrian king Esarhaddon (680–669 B.C.E.), who feared the consequences that might befall him because of ominous predictions in omens. When his specialist priest determined that the ruler's life was in danger, the real king was hidden away and the substitute placed on the throne. No one, including the king, could avoid the destiny determined by the gods, but if necessary steps were taken, rituals could temporarily avert fate.

Sacred Marriage Ceremony. A ritual performance in Mesopotamian temples was enacted between two lovers, the goddess Inana and the god Dumuzi. It was believed that the sexual union between the pair, referred to in love poems and hymns dating to the Ur III and Old Babylonian periods, would produce new life and prosperity. During the course of the ritual, it is thought that the king represented Dumuzi. The identity of the female partner in the rite is unknown, but it has been assumed that she was a priestess. However, she may have been represented by a statue, in

which case the ceremony was performed only symbolically. As part of the ceremony, the goddess bathed and a bed was set up for her and her lover. The king and goddess united, and after the sacred union people brought food and offerings to the temple. The ceremony concluded with a banquet, hymns, and sacred music sung in honor of the goddess. Some of the songs celebrated the erotic nature of the couple's union:

As I set my eyes upon that place,
My beloved man met me,
Took his please of me, rejoiced alone in me;
The brother (i.e., Dumuzi) brought me into his house,
And laid me down upon a bed dripping with honey.
My precious sweet, when lying next to my heart,
Time after time, making tongue, time after time,
My brother of beautiful eyes, did so fifty (times),
Like a powerless person I stood there for him,
Trembling from below, I was dumb silent for him there.
With my brother, placing (my) hands upon his hips.
With my precious sweet, I spent the day there with him.
(Sefati)

Lamentation Prayers. In contrast to modern prayer, which expresses an individualized outpouring of expressive feeling, most Mesopotamian prayers were associated with rituals and sound distant and emotionless to the modern ear. During the second and first millenniums B.C.E. several sorts of lamentation prayers were sung in a special dialect of Sumerian known as Emesal. The *balag*, named after the string instrument that accompanied the recitation of the prayer, is a lament over the destruction of the god's temple. Many *balag* prayers also include long songs of praise for the gods. An *ershemma*, a song that was accompanied by a drum called the *shem*, contains litanies and prayers for "soothing the heart" of a god. The *ershemma* was sung by the *kalu* during the performance of a ritual. *Balags* often end with an *ershemma* accompanied by the playing of the *shem* drum. A *shuilla* (literally: "raising the hands") was in the form of a long litany, which could include a petition to assuage the anger of the deity. It was often recited in rituals associated with processions of the gods. A prayer called *ershahunga* (literally: "lamentations to soothe the heart") includes a lamentation describing the worshiper's suffering and a request on behalf of the petitioner for his welfare. In general, all these prayers sung in the Emesal dialect were designed to avert a god's anger and entice his favor through the recital of the lamentation.

Lamentation Prayers and Rituals. *Balags, ershemmas,* and *ershahunga* laments were recited to the gods on the occasion of rebuilding all or part of a damaged or destroyed temple. The prayer was designed to calm the gods' anger at having their home damaged or destroyed. The *kalu* also performed Emesal songs and prayers during apotropaic rituals to avert enemy attacks or to protect troops and animals against demonic attacks that could cause disease. These special prayers were also performed in rituals to avert a calamity predicted by a sign or omen.

Personal Prayers. The few surviving examples of personal prayer are filled with feeling and emotion, in contrast to ritual prayer, which was permeated with flattery and fear. Petitioners implored their god for aid and relief from disease, depression, and other ills. They requested that their god allow them to find happiness and peace of mind. Prayers were believed to work because most gods, like good rulers, were thought to be concerned with the welfare of the people. King Esarhaddon of Assyria addressed the following prayer to his personal god:

I have done good for the gods and for men, for the living and for the dead. But then, why do illness and sadness, difficulties and prejudice continue to plague me? Discord in the land, complaining in my palace, troubles and failures of all sorts are constantly against me! Illness of the body and the heart have completely shriveled me up. I spend my time sighing and complaining. Even the day of the Great Feast I remain in despair. . . . O my god, reserve such a fate for the impious, and allow me to find happiness once again! How long are you going to abuse me so and to treat me as one who respects neither gods nor goddesses. (Bottéro)

Penitential Prayers. Most prayers addressed to the gods of heaven and earth were similar in tone to official requests made to one's king or superior. As such, they include little religious sentiment. A few prayers explore the psychology of man's fear of the gods, as well as the moral stain and physical and emotional distress that result from sin. While it is difficult to ascertain if sin was regarded simply as a misguided action or as something that profoundly affected the psyche, it is known that Mesopotamians believed the resultant guilt could be resolved through performance of prayer and ritual, rather than through clearly expressed pleas for forgiveness, a concept that was not developed in Mesopotamian religious thought. A penitent sufferer expressed his feelings in this especially poignant prayer.

Who has not been negligent, which one has committed no sin?
Who can understand a god's behavior?
I would fain be obedient and incur no sin.
Yes, I would frequent the haunts of health!
Men are commanded by the gods to act under curse.
Divine affliction is for mankind to bear.
I am surely responsible for some neglect of you.
I have surely trespassed the limits set by the god.
Forget what I did in my youth, whatever it was.
Let your heart not well up against me,
Absolve my guilt, remit my punishment,
Clear me of confusion, free me of uncertainty . . .
O warrior Marduk, absolve my guilt, remit my guilt! (Foster)

Sources:

Jean Bottéro, *Religion in Ancient Mesopotamia,* translated by Teresa Lavender Fagan (Chicago: University of Chicago Press, 2001).

Mark E. Cohen, *The Canonical Lamentations of Ancient Mesopotamia,* 2 volumes (Bethesda, Md.: CDL Press, 1988).

Benjamin R. Foster, ed. and trans., *The Epic of Gilgamesh* (New York: Norton, 2001).

Andrew George, trans., *The Epic of Gilgamesh: The Babylonian Epic Poem and Other Texts in Akkadian and Sumerian* (London: Allen Lane, 1999).

A. Leo Oppenheim, *Ancient Mesopotamia: Portrait of a Dead Civilization,* revised edition, completed by Erica Reiner (Chicago: University of Chicago Press, 1964).

Yitzhaq Sefati, *Love Songs in Sumerian Literature: Critical Edition of the Dumuzi-Inanna Songs* (Ramat Gan: Bar-Ilan University Press, 1998).

SIGNIFICANT PEOPLE

ASHURBANIPAL

668 – CIRCA 627 B.C.E.
KING OF ASSYRIA

The Royal Library. Digging in mounds of ancient Assyria during the 1840s, the British explorer Austen Henry Layard discovered a library of some thirty thousand fragments of cuneiform tablets, which had been preserved because they were baked in the conflagration that swept the city when it was sacked in 612 B.C.E. When pieced together these fragments constitute a royal library of more than two thousand tablets. The library also originally included three hundred wooden and ivory writing boards covered with a thin layer of wax and inscribed with cuneiform texts. The cuneiform texts are no longer preserved.

Tablet Acquisition. The tablets in the library were acquired during the reign of Ashurbanipal, king of Assyria. The monarch, one of the few Mesopotamian rulers who claimed to be literate, ordered his courtiers to search for copies of texts throughout the realm. Tablets and writing boards were taken, sometimes by force, from temples, other royal libraries, and private collections. Ashurbanipal ordered that complete editions of omen series, rituals, lexical texts (lists of signs or words), and literary texts be assembled. No new compositions were commissioned. Commentaries to explain the meaning of older traditional texts were also found in the library.

The Scholar's Collection. The collection was not assembled to be used as a lending library. It was a private library for the professional use of the king's advisers. As the gods' trustee, the king had to manage his realm in accord with their wishes, but without divine direction; the gods were unfathomable, "like a sealed beer-barrel." Thus, the tablets in Ashurbanipal's library were a royal reference guide to provide insight into the supernatural. If used properly, they would allow the scholars and priests resident in his court to communicate with the gods and maintain the tenuous rapport that existed between man and god.

Library Use. The king was not perfect. He was human. (Only a few Mesopotamian kings ever claimed to be divine, and none of these rulers lived in the first millennium B.C.E., when great libraries were founded.) The king's mistakes, whether intentional or unintentional, could be interpreted by the gods with prejudice and could provoke divine displeasure or anger. Such misguided actions (which modern people call sins) would not be punishable without warning. The king would be given preliminary notice in the form of portents, dreams, oracles, and visions sent as premonitions of divine displeasure. If these divine signals were correctly interpreted through the texts found in the library, the ruler could identify his mistake, avoid punishment by atoning for his actions, make sacrifices to appease the gods, and instruct his exorcists to prepare rituals to avoid calamity.

Sources:

Simo Parpola, ed., *Letters from Assyrian and Babylonian Scholars*, State Archives of Assyria, volume 10 (Helsinki: Helsinki University Press, 1993).

Olof Pedersén, *Archives and Libraries in the Ancient Near East, 1500–300 B.C.* (Bethesda, Md.: CDL Press, 1998).

SHULGI

CIRCA 2094 – CIRCA 2047 B.C.E.
KING OF UR

King of Ur. As the ruler of Ur, Shulgi built on the foundation established by his father Ur-Namma (circa 2112–2095 B.C.E.), continuing to build and refurbish temples, encourage trade, and pursue military conquest. Basking in his success, Shulgi declared himself a god, a status that rulers in Mesopotamia had not claimed since the fall of the Sargonic empire in the previous century.

Patron of Learning. Following in his father's footsteps, Shulgi traced the origins of his dynasty back to the early legendary kings of the city of Uruk. Under his patronage, literary compositions about the epic monarch Lugalbanda, whom Shulgi claimed as his father, and the hero Gilgamesh, whom he claimed was his brother, were put into a final form. These compositions, as well as legends about Enmerkar, another early ruler of Uruk, were probably used as foundation myths to glorify the dynasty. Shulgi was featured in literary letters and may have been a patron of Wisdom literature. He also either commissioned or supported the creation of new hymnal compositions praising the gods and goddesses of his realm.

School Reforms. Shulgi—or a member or members of his administration—introduced major reforms of the school curriculum. During his reign, scribes no longer copied the large corpus of old Sumerian myths and literary compositions created during the first part of the third millennium B.C.E., a body of work that now exists only in fragmentary form. It cannot be determined if this restructuring of Sumerian scholarship had ideological or religious roots. In the place of the old myths and compositions appeared a new form of literature, the royal hymn, which lauded the accomplishments of the dynasty and its rulers. In these hymns Shulgi claimed that he was able to speak all five of the languages spoken in his realm and that he had achieved excellence as a musician. He was also the only king during the third millennium B.C.E. who claimed to be literate.

Sources:
Jeremy Black, Graham Cunningham, Jarle Ebeling, Esther Flückiger-Hawker, Eleanor Robson, Jon Taylor, and Gábor Zólyomi, *The Elec-* *tronic Text Corpus of Sumerian Literature*, The Oriental Institute, University of Oxford, 1998– <http://www-etcsl.orient.ox.ac.uk/>.

Jacob Klein, *Three Šulgi Hymns* (Ramat Gan, Israel: Bar Ilan University Press, 1981).

SIN-LEQE-UNNINI

CIRCA 1600-1150 B.C.E.
SCRIBE

Scribe and Scholar. Sin-leqe-unnini, whose name means "O Moon God, Accept my Prayer," was a renowned wise man and scholar. In a text found in Ashurbanipal's library, Sin-leqe-unnini is credited as the author of the standard. Babylonian version of the *Epic of Gilgamesh*. A later tradition, dating to the second millennium B.C.E., claims that he was an early third millennium contemporary of Gilgamesh. By placing the scholar in the distant past— even though the available evidence indicates that he lived during the period of the Kassite dynasty, circa 1600–1150 B.C.E.—the tradition attested to his greatness. Many hundreds of years later, in the Hellenistic period, there were scribes at Uruk copying scholarly and scientific texts and recording private business transactions who regarded him as an ancestor.

Sources:
W. G. Lambert, "Ancestors, Authors, and Canonicity," *Journal of Cuneiform Studies*, 11 (1957): 1–14.

Lambert, "A Catalogue of Texts and Authors," *Journal of Cuneiform Studies*, 16 (1962): 59–77.

Ira Spar and Lambert, eds., *Literary and Scholastic Texts of the First Millennium B.C.*, volume 2 of *Cuneiform Texts in the Metropolitan Museum of Art* (Winona Lake, Ind.: Eisenbrauns, forthcoming 2004), pp. xvi–xix.

DOCUMENTARY SOURCES

Berossos, *Babylonaika* (Greek: circa 275 B.C.E.)—A history of Babylon by a priest of Marduk. Parts of the work that survive as excerpts in Greco-Roman sources include a description of an epic struggle between the gods, culminating in the victory of Marduk; references to ten legendary kings who ruled before the Flood; and a history of the Flood itself.

Counsels of Wisdom (Akkadian: late second – early first millennium B.C.E.)—A collection of moral exhortations expressed by a father to his son. The work includes advice on improper speech, avoidance of disputes and improper companions, reverence for the gods, and charity for the poor.

The Cursing of Agade (Sumerian: early part of the second millennium B.C.E.)—This work was one of the most-popular Sumerian literary compositions in the Old Babylonian period. The date of its composition is unknown. The text includes a narrative and theological interpretation of the rise and fall of the third millennium B.C.E. Akkadian dynasty (circa 2334 – circa 2193 B.C.E.) and empire, whose fate is related to the favor and wrath of the great god Enlil.

The Instructions of Shuruppak (Sumerian: circa 2600 – circa 2500 B.C.E.)—This collection of precepts, maxims, admonitions regarding proper conduct, and practical advice is addressed by Shuruppak to the Sumerian flood hero Ziusudra ("Long Lived").

Lipshur Litanies (Akkadian: edited in the first millennium B.C.E.)—These litanies are a collection of incantations in which many lines end with the refrain *lipshur* ("may he undo, absolve"). The text includes rituals to remove a curse, prayers against sins and curses, and invocations to the gods. Many litanies include phrases similar to those in the series *Shurpu.*

Ludlul Bel Nemeqi (Akkadian: late second millennium B.C.E.)—This poem about a righteous sufferer dates to the Kassite period of Mesopotamian history. Composed on four tablets, it describes the physical sufferings and social ostracism endured by a noble named Shubshi-meshre-Shakkan. Dealing with the divine power of the gods and human guilt, the poem ends with praise for the redeeming power of the god Marduk.

Maqlu (Akkadian: edited in the first millennium B.C.E.)—An eight-tablet collection of almost one hundred Akkadian incantations concerning the effects, on a sufferer, of various types of witchcraft, together with rituals to rid the body of evil magic. The title, *Maqlu,* means "Burning."

Moral Canon (Akkadian: edited in the first millennium B.C.E.)—The name *Moral Canon* has been applied by scholars to sections of a first millennium B.C.E. collec-

tion of physiognomic omens in the series titled *Shumma alamdimmu,* "If a figure." The omens refer to features of the body and speech as well as to moral qualities.

Myth of Atra-hasis (Akkadian: circa seventeenth century B.C.E.)—This composition, written on three tablets, comprised in its original form about 1,245 lines of poetry. The text begins with the formation of the world by the gods and continues with the creation of humankind. The last part of the composition deals with the decision by the gods to destroy the world with a flood in order to contain a human population explosion. The tale ends with measures to control population by limiting the life span of humans and the creation of certain groups of women who could not bear children.

Shurpu (Akkadian: edited in the first millennium B.C.E.)—*Shurpu,* "Burning away the curse," is a nine-tablet collection of incantations that attributes personal misfortune to an offender's transgressions. The victim's offenses result in divine punishment. The incantations are meant to purify the sinner of his misdeeds. The second tablet of the series includes a long list of sins.

Utukku lemnutu (Bilingual Sumerian/Akkadian: third-first millennium B.C.E)—This sixteen-tablet incantation series dates in its earliest surviving form to Sumerian texts written in the mid-third millennium B.C.E. Bilingual copies of the text with an Akkadian translation of the Sumerian incantations are attested beginning in the late Old Babylonian period (seventeenth century B.C.E.). A full bilingual edition is known from Ashurbanipal's library (seventh century B.C.E.) at Nineveh. The incantations deal with the attacks of demons and ghosts and intervention by the gods Ea and Marduk both to protect and to heal an afflicted person.

CHAPTER TEN

SCIENCE, TECHNOLOGY, AND HEALTH

by ALICE LOUISE SLOTSKY

CONTENTS

Sidebars and tables are listed in italics.

IMPORTANT EVENTS OF 3300-331 B.C.E.

3300*-2100*
B.C.E.

- The Mesopotamians compose the world's first mathematical tables and problem texts.

- Mesopotamian economic and mathematical tablets include the earliest evidence of a metrological numeration system for determining the exact relations among various units of length, area, volume, and weight.

- Mesopotamians develop a sexagesimal (base 60) number system and introduce a place-value notation system.

- For the first time stars and constellations are given names, such as the Bull (Taurus), the Lion (Leo), and the Scorpion (Scorpio).

- Mesopotamians write the world's first medical texts and prescriptions.

2112*-2095*
B.C.E.

- The ziggurat of Ur-Namma is built at Ur, marking a new treatment of elevation in architectural construction.

1950*-1600*
B.C.E.

- Scribal schools across Mesopotamia produce many mathematical tables and problem texts, the main source of knowledge about Mesopotamian mathematics. These works demonstrate the Mesopotamians' knowledge of such complex operations as multiplication, division, roots, powers, reciprocals, co-efficients, linear and quadratic equations, geometrical constructions, and "Pythagorean" numbers. The best-known text of this kind shows that the Mesopotamians knew what is commonly called the "Pythagorean Theorem" one thousand years before Pythagoras.

- The concept of zero is known but not yet written; it is represented by an open space.

- During the reign of king Ammi-saduqa of Babylon (circa 1646 – circa 1626 B.C.E.), scholars begin to observe and record the appearances and disappearances of the planet Venus in the sky.

- Lunar and solar omens, including eclipse omens, are based on observations of celestial phenomena.

- The linear zigzag function is used in a mathematical model to measure variations of periodic functions.

1200*-1000*
B.C.E.

- Celestial omens are compiled into the series *Enuma Anu Enlil*.

- The two-tablet astronomical compendium *MUL.APIN* is written.

- The medical omen series *SA.GIG* is edited and catalogued.

- The therapeutic medical tablet *DUB.Ú.HI.A* lists symptoms with their cures.

747-734
B.C.E.
* DENOTES CIRCA DATE

- Regular eclipse reports begin in the reign of king Nabonassar of Babylon. They include tables of eclipses and eclipse possibilities.

IMPORTANT EVENTS OF 3300-331 B.C.E.

668-627*
B.C.E.

- *Enuma Anu Enlil,* the primary source of Mesopotamian celestial omens for modern scholars, is copied for the library of Assyrian king Ashurbanipal.

- Scholars send "letters and reports" to the Assyrian kings.

652 B.C.E.

- The first preserved astronomical diary is written, but the tradition of writing these texts probably began a full century earlier.

604-562
B.C.E.

- During his reign, Babylonian king Nebuchadnezzar II builds the E-temenanki, the largest ziggurat to date.

538-331
B.C.E.

- The Babylonians use the earliest written sign for zero.

- There is regular use of the nineteen-year cycle of intercalations long before the "Metonic Cycle" is implemented. Intercalation, the periodic insertion of an extra month, is necessary to keep the year of twelve lunar months in step with the agricultural solar year.

- The zodiacal reference system is invented and used to keep track of the movements of the moon and the five visible planets.

410 B.C.E.

- The earliest preserved proto-horoscope is written. In this new genre of astrological text, all planetary positions are calculated, not observed.

399*-300*
B.C.E.

- Attention turns from observational to mathematical astronomy.

- The mathematical models System A and System B are constructed to describe and predict lunar, solar, and planetary periodic movements.

- Ephemerides (tables of computed daily positions of the sun, moon, and planets) and procedure texts, which contain directions for the calculation of the ephemerides, are written.

- The *na*-gauge is used to measure changes in the level of the Euphrates River.

* DENOTES CIRCA DATE

- Zero begins to be represented in writing by a word divider sign.

OVERVIEW

Ancient Science. The seeds of modern science are evident in the scholarly pursuits of ancient Mesopotamia; however, what modern people think of as "science" was not a concept that the Mesopotamians would have understood. They observed the physical and material world about them and kept records of natural phenomena. They systematically organized their knowledge, compiled compendia of facts by topic, and made inventories of these collections. They thought of themselves as learned experts in one or more disciplines, and they perceived their function as descriptive and interpretive. Yet, they had no interest in experimentation or in stating and testing hypotheses. Their approach was empirical rather than theoretical.

Modern Science. Modern scholars must be careful to distinguish between the exact sciences and the ancients' investigations of the natural world. Looking at the night sky does not fall into the realm of "astronomy." Only after regular observation of the sun, moon, and planets was established in the second millennium B.C.E. did the written record of astronomy begin, and it was not until the emergence of mathematical astronomy in Mesopotamia during the latter half of the first millennium B.C.E. that the science of astronomy itself was born.

The "Science" of Divination. The use of observations to make predictions about the future fit the Mesopotamian worldview. They believed that the gods sent signs as warnings of events to come and that only trained specialists could use divination to interpret the signs, or omens. To tell what the gods predicted, these experts consulted texts that paired omens with associated possible outcomes. These texts were compiled by generations of scholars who systematically observed and recorded phenomena and the events they seemed to announce. In celestial divination, scholars watched and documented astronomical and meteorological phenomena and matched them to related predictions in age-old collections. As they became knowledgeable about the celestial events, they also became curious about their timing and circumstances. Thus, celestial divination provided a solid background for the mathematical astronomy they developed later. Odd as it seems,

the road from celestial divination, which seems mere superstition to modern people, to abstract and theoretical astronomy was not long.

The "Science" of Medicine. The practice of medicine straddled the scientific and magical worlds. The origins of sickness were not considered to be natural occurrences. Illness was interpreted as a supernatural intrusion from outside the body, either a punishment sent by the gods for some sin or misdeed or the work of demons or sorcerers. Cures, however, could be brought about by magical or "scientific" means, sometimes used in tandem. Two different kinds of medical practitioners treated illness. The exorcist diagnosed illnesses according to handbooks of symptoms (the "scientific" part of his job) and then used magic spells and incantations to bring about cures. The physician prescribed medications of great complexity, also recorded and collected in "scientific" texts, but at the same time he might arrange for offerings to the gods or recitations of incantations as the medicines were applied. Medical "science," therefore, was a mix of herbal medicine and magic. Trained and skilled experts had a large body of "scientifically" collected diagnostic and pharmaceutical sources at their disposal.

Influences. The origins and early development of astronomy and mathematics took place in ancient Mesopotamia. These scholarly disciplines played a major role in Babylonian political and religious life. They had a profound effect on contemporary neighboring civilizations, as well as on all subsequent cultures of the world. So many later efforts in the exact sciences are descended in direct line from the theoretical astronomy of the late first millennium B.C.E. and—principally through this astronomy—Mesopotamian mathematics. In no other area has the influence of ancient Mesopotamia been more important.

Contributions. Mesopotamians made lasting contributions to astronomy and mathematics. They devised the sexagesimal (base 60) number system and sexagesimal fractions (preserved as the hour/minutes/seconds of time and degree/minutes/seconds of angle), place-value notation in written numbers, the first zero, the concept commonly known as the "Pythagorean Theorem," number theory, algebraic equations, and the degree as the basic unit of angular measure. They invented the luni-solar calendar (preserved in the Jewish calendar, which was adapted from the Babylonian). They defined certain parameters, such as the mean length of the synodic month (the length of time for one complete cycle of the moon's phases, that is, from one first visibility of the moon to the next), and the length of the year. They knew and used period relations of celestial bodies (mathematical relations stating that s intervals or events of one kind equal t intervals or events of another kind; for example, 235 lunar months equal 19 solar years). They kept observational records and computed mathematical ephemerides (tables of astronomical events, each computed at regular intervals). They created a zodiacal reference system, methodology in theoretical astronomy, constellation names, and proto-horoscopes, which—unlike the horoscopes cast by ancient Greek and Roman astrologers—stated astronomcal facts at the time of birth but did not make predictions about the future based on these facts.

TOPICS IN SCIENCE, TECHNOLOGY, AND HEALTH

ASTRONOMY

The Babylonian View of the Universe. There are limited and conflicting views of the universe in ancient Mesopotamian cosmology. One envisioned a six-level universe with three heavens and three different "earths": the heaven of the stars, two additional heavens above the sky, the earth, the underground waters of Apsu, and, beneath it, the underworld of the dead. The most common perception of the universe, however, was three-fold. The heavens included everything above the ground. They were where the birds fly, the winds blow, the clouds float, as well as where the moon and the five visible planets drift among the fixed stars and—above them—the Upper Heavens where the gods reside. Below the heavens was the earth, where humankind live. Below the earth lay a body of fresh underground water and, below that, the underworld of the dead. Presumably the earth was considered to be flat, as the only surviving Mesopotamian world map (the so-called Babylonian Map of the World) shows a flat circular disk. It depicts the inhabited world within a large circle entirely surrounded by water, beyond which are triangular uncharted regions, the rest of the world.

The Beginning of Regular Recorded Astronomical Observations. The movements of the sun and of the celestial bodies in the night sky had been keenly observed since earliest times. It was not until the seventeenth century B.C.E. that regularly written astronomical records began to be kept in Mesopotamia. There are earlier references in Mesopotamian sources to astronomical phenomena, such as eclipses; and there are lists of stars and constellations, which were first named by the Sumerians in the third millennium B.C.E. Nevertheless, the observations of the planet Venus recorded at the time of king Ammi-saduqa of Babylon (circa 1646 – circa 1626 B.C.E.) are the earliest known written records of regular observations of the moon and the planets.

Astronomical Observation and Divination. These early observations of the rising and setting times of the planet Venus were cast into an omen framework and used to make predictions about possible future events on earth. This use of observational data to forecast future possibilities was entirely consistent with ancient Mesopotamian thinking. In their worldview, the gods used events in the natural world as divine signs to warn mankind of possible happenings in the future. Astral omens could signal some outcome for the state; that is, the king, the country, or the city. Other kinds of omens might predict imminent vicissitudes for ordinary individuals. The signs sent by the gods could be observed by anyone, and their ominous meanings could affect anybody, but only the trained specialist could interpret the effects of a circumstance revealed by means of a sign. Through divination the signs were interpreted, and the will of the gods was made known.

Record Keeping and Signs. In the second millennium B.C.E., there was little difference between purely descriptive nonmathematical "astronomy" and the "science" of celestial omens. Data were accumulated for divinatory purposes. Divination was a highly respected scholarly pursuit for the intellectual elite of Assyria and Babylonia.

Celestial Divination. Celestial divination provided the astronomical background for the later growth of mathematical astronomy in Mesopotamia. Celestial omens were based on a variety of observed astral or meteorological events. Some of these omens concerned weather-related events, such as thunder, lightning, rain, wind, hail, rainbows, or cloud formations. Others included such optical events as halos, flashes of light, or the color and brightness of constellations. Still others included specifically lunar and planetary phenomena, such as first and last visibilities of heavenly bodies, conjunctions of planets and stars (the time when two heavenly bodies are at the same celestial longitude), and eclipses. In a typical astral omen, the celestial event is described in the *protasis* (the subordinate "if" clause of a conditional sentence), while the *apodosis* (the main "then" clause of that sentence) predicts some corresponding earthly event for the king or state.

Textual Evidence. The first suggestion of the practice of celestial divination, such as the observation of an eclipse followed by the death of a king, goes back to the late third millennium B.C.E. Solid textual evidence for the first celestial omens comes later, in the Old Babylonian period (circa 1894 – circa 1595 B.C.E.). The bulk of celestial-omen material is even later, mostly from the Neo-Assyrian period (circa 934 – 610 B.C.E.), when celestial divination was the prime means of forecasting possible events for the king. Extispicy, the time-honored technique of predicting the future by examining the entrails of sacrificial animals, was not abandoned; sometimes it was used with celestial divination when there was uncertainty about the interpretation of an ominous astral event. Extispicy always had the advantage that it could be performed whenever it was needed, and it was considered well tested and proven. Still, celestial divination became the most prevalent form of divination toward the end of the Assyrian Empire.

Celestial Omen Series. Celestial omens began to be collected into series as early as the beginning of the second millennium B.C.E., and this practice continued into the first millennium B.C.E. The earliest known are the Old Babylonian lunar and solar omens, such as the eclipse omens of circa 1700 B.C.E. These astral omens were forerunners of those later organized into the major series of celestial-omen tablets, known today, as in antiquity, as *Enuma Anu Enlil*—"When (the gods) Anu (and) Enlil." These series are the primary sources of Mesopotamian celestial omens.

Enuma Anu Enlil. The title of this series comes from the *incipit*, the opening words, of its mythological introduction, which credits the gods Anu, Enlil, and Ea with the creation of the order of heaven and earth in the uni-

verse. *Enuma Anu Enlil* was probably first compiled around 1000 B.C.E. The tablets continued to be copied, and new omens were added, even after the seventh century B.C.E. Most of the surviving tablets are copies made during the reign of Assyrian king Ashurbanipal (668 – circa 627 B.C.E.) in his library at Nineveh. The series comprises observations of the moon and sun, especially eclipses; planets and stars; and weather and earthquakes. These natural occurrences were linked to forecasts about the king, affairs of state, and the fate of the kingdom in general. Typically, these omens would be stated in the form "If *x* occurs in the sky, then *y* will occur on earth." The series consisted of at least seventy tablets, originally containing some 6,500–7,000 omens. In modern times they were organized into four sections: lunar omens, solar omens, weather omens, and omens about stars and planets.

The *Venus Tablet*. Tablet 63 of *Enuma Anu Enlil*, the so-called *Venus Tablet of Ammi-saduqa*, with its fifty-nine omens, is the best-known tablet in the series. It contains an observational record of the appearances and disappearances of Venus during the reign of the Old Babylonian king Ammi-saduqa (circa 1646 – circa 1626 B.C.E.), linking these phenomena with possible consequences on earth:

Clay cuneiform tablet with an astronomical diary for the thirty-seventh regnal year of the Babylonian king Nebuchadnezzar II (568 B.C.E.), with data for months I–III on the obverse (top) and months X–XII on the reverse (bottom); compiled in 567 B.C.E., probably at Babylon (Vorderasiatisches Museum, Berlin)

(If) in month XI, 15th day, Venus disappeared in the west; it stayed away in the sky for three days, and in month XI, 18th day, Venus became visible in the east, (then) springs will open, Adad will bring his rain, Ea his floods, (and) a king will send messages of reconciliation to a(nother) king.

(If) In month VIII, 11th day, Venus disappeared in the east; it stayed away in the sky two months, 7 days, and in month X, nineteenth day, Venus became visible in the west: (then) the harvest of the land will prosper. (Reiner and Pingree, 1975)

The sequence of observations in these tablets has tempted many a scholar to attempt a chronology for the Old Babylonian period. The obstacles are many, including the choice of data to use and the arbitrary intercalation, or insertion, of extra months into the calendar at this time. Conflicting interpretations of observations in Tablet 63 have resulted in different views of Old Babylonian dating. There are three common proposals, and others are possible. The Low Chronology puts the beginning of Ammi-saduqa's reign at 1582 B.C.E., the Middle Chronology places the event at 1646 B.C.E., and the High (or Long) Chronology points to 1702 B.C.E. Although the Middle Chronology, which dates the end of Hammurabi's reign at 1750 B.C.E., is the most commonly used as a matter of convention, including throughout this volume, scholars continue to disagree about which of these three chronologies, if any, to use.

Scholars' Letters and Reports to Assyrian Kings. The omens of *Enuma Anu Enlil* were well known to, and regularly consulted by, the experts in celestial divination who served the Neo-Assyrian kings of the late eighth and seventh centuries B.C.E. Their correspondence—now called "letters and reports"—shows that these scholars, living in cities all over Assyria and Babylonia, made regular observations of astral phenomena, interpreted their meanings according to the omen compendia, and sent observations, predictions, and advice to the king at court. For example, the Babylonian scribe Munnabitu wrote to one of the later Neo-Assyrian kings during the first half of the seventh century B.C.E.:

> If on the 16th day the moon and sun are seen together: one king will send messages of hostility to another; the king will be shut up in his palace for the length of a month; the step of the enemy will be set towards his land; the enemy will march around in his land victoriously. . . . The king must not be negligent about these observations of the moon; let the king perform either a *namburbi* or some (other) ritual which is pertinent to it. (Hunger)

The kings depended on such communications to undertake state and religious activities at propitious times, to avoid bad portents by the performance of the appropriate rituals, and to keep themselves, their families, and their kingdom safe and well.

MUL.APIN (The *Plow Constellation*). Another astral compendium connected with celestial omens is the two-tablet Assyrian series *MUL.APIN*, likely composed around the beginning of the first millennium B.C.E. *MUL.APIN* is more astronomical in character than *Enuma Anu Enlil*. It sets out rules for the intercalation of months in an ideal and schematic 12-month, 360-day calendar and provides a prediction scheme for the risings and settings of planets. Its six catalogues of stars provide a reference system for the identification of Mesopotamian constellations. One catalogue describes the division of the fixed stars and planets into three paths on the eastern horizon, over which they and the moon rise: the northernmost path of Enlil, "Lord Wind," the divine ruler of Earth and its inhabitants; the central path of Anu, god of the sky; and the southernmost path of Ea, god of fresh underground waters. *MUL.APIN* also has shadow lists for equinox and solstice days, and for those days it lists weights of water to be used in a water clock to measure time intervals during the day and night.

Observational Astronomy in the First Millennium B.C.E. After some seven to eight centuries of descriptive astronomy, scholars turned their attentions to what would today be classified as true astronomy. For the first time, there is evidence of regular and continuous record keeping of astronomical observations in chronological sequence. Clear proof of such record keeping is provided by the "astronomical diaries," the earliest datable to 652 B.C.E. There are compelling arguments, however, that diaries were likely being written a full century earlier, in the reign of the Babylonian king Nabonassar, who ruled from 747 to 734 B.C.E. First, there are eclipse reports and tables of eclipses and eclipse possibilities from this time. Second, the astronomer Claudius Ptolemy, working in Alexandria circa 130–175 C.E., wrote that he had access to continuous astronomical records from the time of Nabonassar on, but nothing from before that time. In book 3 of his *Almagest*, Ptolemy wrote: "The beginning of the reign of Nabonassar is the era beginning from which the ancient observations are preserved down to our own time." Ptolemy certainly used these Mesopotamian observations in his own work. The last datable astronomical diary comes from 61 B.C.E., demonstrating that Babylonian astronomers continued to compose these texts for at least six, and most likely seven, centuries. If diaries were still being written up to the time of the last datable cuneiform text in the mid first century C.E., the tradition of diary writing was maintained eight centuries, not only under native Mesopotamian rulers but also under the succeeding Achaemenid Persians, Hellenized Macedonians, Seleucids, and Arsacid Parthians.

Astronomical Diaries. "Astronomical diaries" is the modern name given to the collection of day-by-day accounts of celestial and meteorological phenomena once housed in a vast but still undiscovered astronomical archive in Babylon. The basic format of a diary was fixed. A half-year diary covering either the first or last half of a Babylonian year had six sections, seven in an intercalary year, each

ALEXANDER'S INVASION

A fragment of an astronomical diary from 331 B.C.E. makes a brief reference to the presence of Alexander III (the Great) of Macedon in Babylonia. Alexander defeated the last of the Achaemenid Persian kings, Darius III, at Gaugamela, near the ruins of Nineveh, on the first of October in that year and then headed south, entering Babylon without resistance.

That month, from the 1st to [. . . .] came to Babylon saying, "Esangila (temple) [. . . .] On the 11th, in Sippar an order of Al[exander . . . . ". . .] I shall not enter your houses." On the 13th, [. . .] to the outer gate of Esangila and [. . . .] On the 14th, these Ionians (Greeks) a bull [. . . .] short, fatty tissue [. . . .] Alexander, king of the world, [came in]to Babylon [. . . hor]ses and equipment of [. . . .] and the Babylonians and the people of [. . . . .] a message to [. . . .]

Alexander's plan to rebuild Babylon and make it the capital of his newly won empire ended with his death there just eight years later at the age of thirty-two. A passage in an astronomical diary for 8 September 323 B.C.E. laconically reports:

[Month V, ...] . . . . The 29th, the king died; clouds [. . . .]

Source: Abraham Joseph Sachs and Hermann Hunger, *Astronomical Diaries and Related Texts from Babylonia*, volume 1: *Diaries from 652 B.C. to 262 B.C.* (Vienna: Österreichische Akademie der Wissenschaften, 1988), pp. 179, 207.

velocities around the sun. The point in a planet's orbit when its apparent motion changes to retrograde motion is called the first stationary point, and the point where it resumes "forward" motion is termed its second stationary point. A planet is said to be in "opposition" when it is 180 degrees from the sun.) Observers also wrote down detailed accounts of local weather conditions by night and day, because these had an impact on visibility. Eclipses were dated and described; equinoxes and solstices were recorded; and dates of rising and settings of the bright star Sirius were noted. An observational passage for November 271 B.C.E. includes the following information:

Month VIII. . . . Night of the 1st, clouds crossed the sky. The 1st, in the afternoon, clouds crossed the sky. Night of the 2nd, the moon was 1½ cubits behind Jupiter, the moon being one cubit high to the north. The 2nd, Mer[cury's first appearance in the east in Libra? . . .]. Night of the 3rd, very overcast, lightning, thunder, rain . . . gusty wind. The 3rd, clouds crossed the sky, it thundered, rain shower. Night of the 4th, overcast, rain, but the sandal was not removed. . . . (Sachs and Hunger)

(The reference to the sandal means that the rain was not heavy enough to cause sticky mud to remove one's sandals.) Meteors and comets were mentioned, including what is now known to have been Halley's comet in February 234 B.C.E., September/October 164 B.C.E., and August 87 B.C.E. At the end of the daily observations, there was a final statement about the last appearance of the moon, a measurement of the interval between moonrise and sunrise, and then a recapitulation of planetary positions at the end of the month. Then there was a list of the market values of the same six commodities (barley, dates, mustard, cress, sesame, and wool) and measurements of the changes in the water levels of the Euphrates. Finally, there might be some anecdotal historical information. The diaries occupy a unique position in the study of ancient history. In sheer bulk, continuity, detail, and kind of information, they are unmatched. Most importantly, because of the astronomical content of the diaries, particularly the continuous attention to the changing position of the moon, it is possible to date these texts confidently to the day, when they can be dated at all. Thus, any evidence extracted from them—whether astronomical, meteorological, economic, or historical—can be dated with certainty.

Goal-Year Texts and Almanacs. The diaries were used not only to preserve an astronomical record but in the last centuries of the first millennium B.C.E. (in the Seleucid and Parthian periods) to provide material for the construction of tables of eclipses and other chronologically arranged lunar and planetary phenomena. The diaries were also the source of two other kinds of astronomical texts, "goal-year texts" and "almanacs." The goal-year texts, composed from at least 236 B.C.E. on, predicted the behavior of the moon and planets for some given year, the

spanning one lunar month. Each monthly unit was filled with almost daily observations, made almost exclusively in Babylon. The major emphasis was on the behavior of the moon, by far the swiftest of all the "planets," and the lunar month was the basic unit of the Mesopotamian calendar and the construction of each diary. The diary began with what was considered to be the beginning of the new month, the first visibility of the new moon at sunset. This observation was followed by a statement about the length of the preceding month; that is, whether the first sighting of the new moon was seen on the thirtieth evening (meaning the previous month had twenty-nine days) or on the thirty-first (meaning the previous month had thirty days). Next the observers recorded the monthly progress of the moon among the stars and the planets, the first and last appearances of planets, stationary points, and oppositions; and time intervals of various phenomena, which helped the astronomers predict the date on which the next month would begin. (When viewed from the earth, the planets appear to speed up, slow down, and change direction of travel—a phenomenon called "retrograde motion"—as a result of the differences between the earth's and the planets' goal year. They presented data derived from the diaries that antedated the goal year by some astronomically significant period, such as a period of eight years for Venus to complete its travel from a given starting point on the ecliptic back again to that same point. (The *ecliptic* is the great circle that is the apparent orbit of the sun among the stars.) Scribes could pick an appropriate year in the past, find the diary data for that year, and list the phenomena expected to occur in the following goal year. These texts, being based on the periodic character of planetary and lunar behavior, show that period relations of recurring phenomena of the moon and five planets (Jupiter, Venus, Mercury, Saturn, and Mars) were well known to Babylonian astronomers of this time. Later, these became a fundamental notion in Babylonian theoretical astronomy. In fact, Otto Neugebauer has called them "the very backbone of Babylonian mathematical astronomy." In mathematical terms, period relations state that s intervals or events of one kind equal t intervals or events of another. For example, 235 lunar months equal 19 solar years (the so-called Metonic Cycle). For a planet, the period relations state that x number of phenomena of one kind equal y number of revolutions around the ecliptic. For example, 391 like phenomena of Jupiter occur in 36 revolutions around the ecliptic. The sun travels one complete revolution of the 360 degrees of the ecliptic in a year (the definition of a year), and for each cycle by Jupiter from one appearance of a phenomenon to the next of the same kind, the sun travels once around the ecliptic plus the increase in longitude Jupiter makes for that cycle. This period then can be translated into years by stating that 391 such phenomena take 391 times around the ecliptic plus 36 more revolutions. The "period relations of Jupiter" would then be 391 + 36 = 421 years. Derived from goal-year texts, almanacs predicted month-by-month lunar and planetary phenomena: beginning of the month planetary positions; dates of entry into a zodiacal sign; dates of solstices and equinoxes; dates of Sirius risings and settings; and eclipses. Normal Star almanacs gave dates when planets moved into certain positions among the stars near the ecliptic that were used as reference points to give the position of the moon and planets.

Mathematical Astronomy. Around the mid-first millennium B.C.E., after more than a millennium and a half of systematic observation of celestial phenomena and the collection of celestial omens, a new kind of astronomy developed in Babylonia. Scholars began to create original methods of calculation to find solutions for what had become the main focus of scholarly endeavor, the prediction of astronomical phenomena. For the moon, the Babylonians were interested in the dates of the new and full moon, the lunar visibilities near these phases, times and magnitudes for eclipses, and the lengths of the months. For the planets, they wished to predict appearances and disap-

pearances, stations and oppositions. The new strategies were mathematical and computational. The basic elements of the new methodology were the sexagesimal (base 60) number system and place-value notation; period relations; the 19-year luni-solar cycle (19 solar years = 235 lunar, or synodic, months); the "Saros cycle" of eclipse possibilities (in 223 synodic months, approximately 18+ years, there are 38 eclipse possibilities with the average interval of 5+ months between eclipses); the planetary periods, the number of years it took a planet to complete a cycle from one appearance of a particular phenomenon to the next of the same kind; and a zodiacal reference system.

The Zodiacal Reference System. The zodiac is defined as an imaginary belt of the celestial sphere extending about eight or nine degrees on either side of the ecliptic (the apparent orbit of the sun among the stars); within the zodiacal belt occur the apparent paths of the moon and planets. It is likely that sometime in the mid fifth century B.C.E. Babylonian astronomers invented a reference system of zodiacal signs. The astronomers divided the ecliptic into twelve equal thirty-degree segments, or "signs" (each named for a different ecliptical constellation), through which the moon and planets travel. Each sign could be further subdivided into twelve microzodiacal signs to enable observers to further refine a planet's position. This zodiacal system became the basic reference for Mesopotamian astronomers and, later, for all Babylonian mathematical astronomy. Before this time, the so-called Normal Stars, a group of more than thirty-one stars near the ecliptic and on the zodiacal belt, served as reference points for the movement of the moon and the planets. During the Seleucid period (311–129 B.C.E.), the Babylonian signs of the zodiac, both individually and in astrologically significant combinations, became popular as designs for personal finger-ring intaglios.

Ephemerides. Beginning in the fourth century B.C.E., theoretical astronomical texts began to be composed in scholarly centers at Babylon and at Uruk. There are some four hundred to five hundred of these tablets, many surviving only in small fragments. These texts fall into two categories. Some present dates and a particular function necessary to compute *ephemerides*, successive phenomena of the moon, or the planets, which, for planets, might include the dates and times of first and last visibility, opposition, and stationary points. The rest are lunar or planetary procedure texts, which give directions for calculating the ephemerides. Nowhere are the theories that underlie the instructions stated. They have been reconstructed by modern scholars using the ephemerides and procedure texts. Two broad categories of Babylonian astronomy emerged: lunar and planetary theory. Intrinsic in this work are "System A" and "System B." These theoretical texts underscore the valuable contribution of the Babylonians to the science of astronomy.

Two halves of a clay cuneiform tablet with an astrological text and captioned depictions of constellations and planets:
on the obverse (top), Leo walking on the back of the Hydra and an eight-pointed star (left) representing Jupiter;
on the reverse (bottom, left to right), Corvus pecking at the tail of the Hydra, an eight-pointed star,
Mercury, and Virgo holding an ear of grain; Uruk, Seleucid period, early second century B.C.E.
(top: Vorderasiatisches Museum, Berlin; bottom: Louvre, Paris)

Fragment of a clay cuneiform tablet with an astrological text and captioned depictions of constellations and the moon, Uruk, Seleucid period, second century B.C.E. The full moon stands between the seven stars of the Pleiades (left) and Taurus (right). The "man in the moon" is a male deity holding a lion upside down by its hind leg (Vorderasiatisches Museum, Berlin).

System A and System B. Two kinds of mathematical models were used to describe and predict the periodic movements of the moon, the sun, and the planets, none of which travels at a constant velocity. These arithmetical models are distinguished by modern scholars as "System A" and "System B." They differ in the way in which they treat the velocity of celestial bodies as they travel around the ecliptic. In System A, the ecliptic is divided into zones inside which phenomena, or events, of celestial bodies progress in steps of different velocities. In System A, for example, the sun is assumed to travel through the ecliptic with two distinct velocities throughout the year, a constant value of 30 degrees per month in its travel from Virgo 13 to Pisces 27 and a constant value of about 28 degrees per month (28;7,30 in sexagesimal numbers) from Pisces 27 back to Virgo 13. The ecliptic is thus divided into two parts, a fast arc and a slow arc, or two steps. System A, therefore, can be described as a step-function scheme. In contrast, System B assumes that velocity can be characterized as a linear zigzag function in which a variable is reduced to an arithmetic progression alternately increasing and decreasing by a constant amount in successive intervals of time between some fixed maximum and minimum values. System A was designed to calculate variable quantities from one initial value, such as a sequence of longitudes for a corresponding sequence of dates from one starting point. System A was useful, for example, for finding the changing positions in longitude as a celestial body progressed from some particular phase to the next phase of the same kind.

In the case of a planet, the model could be used to compute the longitudes as the planet traveled from one synodic phenomenon to the next same phenomenon, for example, from one first stationary point to another. System B was useful for describing deviations from mean values of solar, lunar, and planetary movements, such as the length of the month. System A, with its use of the step function, is the earlier of the two models and a fresh innovation designed to fit the requirements of the new computational astronomy. System B was constructed soon after, relying on the linear zigzag function, which had already been devised as early as the Old Babylonian period to describe variations of daylight; later it was used in *Enuma Anu Enlil* for the prediction of two periodic functions: the time within a month that the moon was visible at night and the variation of the increment of this time over the course of the year. Recycled into System B, the linear zigzag function served in an innovative way to describe periodic phenomena. Both models are ingenious in the way they are able to separate and describe, one by one, any single component of more complex astronomical phenomena and then combine them again to make predictions. The creation of such mathematical models for numerical predictions of astronomical phenomena is one of the finest Babylonian accomplishments.

Transmission of Babylonian Mathematical Astronomy. The surviving astronomical tablets come almost exclusively from three sites: Nineveh, Babylon, and Uruk. The library of Ashurbanipal at Nineveh was destroyed in 612 B.C.E. Texts from Uruk cease about 150 B.C.E., about

Zodiacal signs in ancient seal impressions of engraved-metal finger rings (average length ¾ inch); top: ram (Aries), twin gods Nabu and Nergal (Gemini), crab (Cancer); middle: balance (Libra), scorpion (Scorpius), centaur-archer god Pabilsag (Sagittarius); bottom: goat-carp (Capricornus), water god Ea (Aquarius), swallow and fish on a string (Pisces); Uruk, Seleucid period, third-second centuries B.C.E. (Libra: Vorderasiatisches Museum, Berlin; all others: Yale Babylonian Collection)

the time southernmost Babylonia was seized by the Parthians from Iran. However, the astronomers at the astronomical center of Babylon, which eventually fell to the Parthians as well, continued to write tablets into the first century C.E. By this time, Babylonian astronomical knowledge had spread and was used throughout the Hellenistic world. Certainly, much of Babylonian astronomy underlies the work of the astronomer Ptolemy in the *Almagest*, written circa 150 C.E. Ptolemy used sexagesimal fractions, the degree as the basic unit of angular measure, and the zodiacal reference system—all inventions of Babylonian astronomers. He also used Babylonian observations of celestial phenomena, including eclipses that went back to those recorded in the reign of Nabonassar; Babylonian parameters, such as the value for the mean synodic month, the length of the year, and period relations for the moon and planets; and Mesopotamian constellation names. His knowledge of Babylonian astronomy likely came from the works of the astronomer Hipparchus, who worked in Rhodes, circa 150–125 B.C.E., and who not only used Babylonian observations and parameters but also had access to their mathematical techniques for prediction. The mathematical astronomy of the Babylonians has recently been found on papyrus fragments from Roman Egypt. The astronomy of the Greek and Roman world may well have been inspired by the Babylonian conception that it was possible to build astronomical models for prediction purposes.

Sources:

Asger Aaboe, *Episodes from the Early History of Astronomy* (New York, Berlin & Heidelberg: Springer, 2001).

John Britton and C. B. F. Walker, "Astronomy and Astrology in Mesopotamia," in *Astronomy Before the Telescope*, edited by Walker (London: Published for the Trustees of the British Museum by the British Museum Press, 1996), pp. 42–67.

Richard I. Caplice, *The Akkadian Namburbi Texts: An Introduction*, Sources from the Ancient Near East, volume 1, fascicle 1 (Los Angeles: Undena, 1974).

Wayne Horowitz, *Mesopotamian Cosmic Geography*, Mesopotamian Civilizations, 8 (Winona Lake, Ind.: Eisenbrauns, 1998).

Hermann Hunger, ed., *Astrological Reports to Assyrian Kings*, State Archives of Assyria, volume 8 (Helsinki: Helsinki University Press, 1992).

Hunger and David Edwin Pingree, *Astral Sciences in Mesopotamia* (Leiden & Boston: Brill, 1999).

Hunger and Pingree, *MUL.APIN: An Astronomical Compendium in Cuneiform*, Archiv für Orientforschung, Beiheft 24 (Horn, Austria: Berger, 1989).

Ulla Jeyes, "The Act of Extispicy in Ancient Mesopotamia: An Outline," *Assyriological Miscellanies*, 1 (1980): 13–32.

Ulla Koch-Westenholz, *Mesopotamian Astrology* (Copenhagen: Museum Tusculanum Press, 1995).

Otto Neugebauer, *The Exact Sciences in Antiquity*, second edition (Providence: Brown University Press, 1957).

Neugebauer, *A History of Ancient Mathematical Astronomy*, 3 volumes (Berlin & New York: Springer, 1975).

Neugebauer, ed., *Astronomical Cuneiform Texts: Babylonian Ephemerides of the Seleucid Period for the Motion of the Sun, the Moon, and the Planets*, 3 volumes (London: Published for the Institute of Advanced Studies, Princeton, N.J., by Lund Humphries, 1955).

A. Leo Oppenheim, *Ancient Mesopotamia: Portrait of a Dead Civilization*, revised edition, completed by Erica Reiner (Chicago: University of Chicago Press, 1977).

Oppenheim, "Divination and Celestial Observation in the Last Assyrian Empire," *Centaurus*, 14 (1969): 97–135.

Simo Parpola, ed., *Letters from Assyrian and Babylonian Scholars*, State Archives of Assyria, volume 10 (Helsinki: Helsinki University Press, 1993).

Erica Reiner, *Astral Magic in Babylonia*, Transactions of the American Philosophical Society, volume 85, part 4 (Philadelphia: American Philosophical Society, 1995).

Reiner with David Edwin Pingree, *Enūma Anu Enlil. Tablet 63: The Venus Tablet of Ammisaduqa*, part 1 of *Babylonian Planetary Omens*, Bibliotheca Mesopotamica, volume 2, fascicle 1 (Malibu, Cal.: Undena, 1975).

Reiner with Pingree, *Enuma Anu Enlil, Tablets 50–51*, part 2 of *Babylonian Planetary Omens*, Bibliotheca Mesopotamica, volume 2, fascicle 2 (Malibu, Cal.: Undena, 1981).

Reiner and Pingree, *Babylonian Planetary Omens*, part 3 (Groningen: Styx Publications, 1998).

Francesca Rochberg, *Babylonian Horoscopes* (Philadelphia: American Philosophical Society, 1998).

Francesca Rochberg-Halton, *Aspects of Babylonian Celestial Divination: The Lunar Eclipse Tablets of Enūma Anu Enlil*, Archiv für Orientforschung, Beiheft 22 (Horn, Austria: Berger, 1988).

Rochberg-Halton, "Elements of the Babylonian Contribution to Hellenistic Astrology," *Journal of the American Oriental Society*, 108 (1988): 51–62.

Abraham Joseph Sachs and Hermann Hunger, *Astronomical Diaries and Related Texts from Babylonia*, volumes 1–4 (Vienna: Österreichischen Akademie der Wissenschaften, 1988–2002).

W. H. van Soldt, *Solar Omens of Enuma Anu Enlil: Tablets 23 (24) – 29 (30)* (Istanbul: Nederlands Historisch-Archaeologisch Instituut Te Istanbul, 1995).

Ivan Starr, *The Rituals of the Diviner* (Malibu, Cal.: Undena, 1983).

Starr, ed., *Queries to the Sungod: Divination and Politics in Sargonid Assyria*, State Archives of Assyria, volume 4 (Helsinki: University of Helsinki Press, 1990).

Ronald Wallenfels, "Appendix I: Zodiacal Signs among the Uruk Tablet Seal Impressions in the Yale Babylonian Collection," in his *Uruk: Hellenistic Seal Impressions in the Yale Babylonian Collection I. Cuneiform Tablets*, Ausgrabungen in Uruk-Warka Endberichte 19 (Mainz am Rhein: Verlag Philipp von Zabern, 1994), pp. 153–157.

THE CALENDAR

The Babylonian Luni-Solar Calendar. The Mesopotamian calendar was a luni-solar calendar, based on the lunar month and the solar year and day. The basic unit was the month, which began on the evening of the first sighting of the new moon. It lasted twenty-nine or thirty days, depending on when the first crescent of the moon became visible again. There is no evidence for a thirty-one-day month, so it is likely that if thirty days had passed since the previous first visibility, a new month was begun even if weather conditions prevented sighting of the crescent. By the fifth century B.C.E., the beginning of the month could be determined by computation, but cuneiform texts suggest that actual observations of first visibility were still relied on well into the Seleucid period

(311–129 B.C.E.). The year began in the spring, in the month of Nisannu (comparable to March/April). Of course, the calendar of lunar months did not stay in line with the solar year. Twelve revolutions of the moon around the earth (twelve lunar, or synodic, months) are about eleven days shorter than the solar year, the time it takes the sun, moving eastward, to make a full revolution of travel from its starting point and back again. Thus, Mesopotamians had the problem of keeping the twelve-lunar-month year in step with the solar agricultural year, so that the seasons fell at more or less the same point of the calendrical year every year.

Intercalation. From at least the late third millennium B.C.E., when it was felt that the seasons had become sufficiently displaced from the calendar, a thirteenth, or intercalary, month was added to the year at any time. Somewhat later, in the early second millennium B.C.E., only months VI and XII were intercalated. This step was taken according to royal command or on the advice of temple officials. From about 500 B.C.E. on, a nineteen-year cycle of intercalations began to be used consistently. This cycle is often attributed to the late fifth-century Greek astronomer Meton of Athens, and it is commonly called "the Metonic Cycle," but it was known and used by the Babylonians long before his time. In this scheme, additional months were added according to specific guidelines, and the pattern was repeated every 19 years, or 235 months. The traditional Jewish calendar was taken from the Mesopotamian calendar, the only difference being that the Babylonian year began in the spring, while the Jewish year begins in the fall. Most Jewish month names are similar to their first millennium B.C.E. Babylonian counterparts.

Procedure for Intercalation. The 19-year cycle of intercalations called for the addition of 7 intercalary months throughout every period of 19 years. The 19 years were composed of 12 years with 12 months each plus 7 years with 13 months each. These 7 years with intercalary months were made up of 6 years with a second month XII, called Addaru II, and 1 year with a second month VI, known as Ululu II.

Sources:

Asger Aaboe, *Episodes From the Early History of Astronomy* (New York, Berlin & Heidelberg: Springer, 2001).

John Britton and C. B. F. Walker, "Astronomy and Astrology in Mesopotamia," in *Astronomy Before the Telescope*, edited by Walker (London: Published for the Trustees of the British Museum by the British Museum Press, 1996), pp. 42–67.

Richard A. Parker and Waldo H. Dubberstein, *Babylonian Chronology: 626 B.C. – A.D. 75*, Brown University Studies, volume 19 (Providence: Brown University Press, 1956).

Francesca Rochberg, "Astronomy and Calendars in Ancient Mesopotamia," in *Civilizations of the Ancient Near East*, 4 volumes, edited by Jack M. Sasson (New York: Scribners, 1995), III: 1925–1940.

Ronald Wallenfels, "30 Ajjaru 219 SE = 19 June 93 BCE," *Nouvelles Assyriologiques Brèves et Utilitaires* (1992): 37, no. 46.

DIVINATION

The "Science" of Divination. Signs of all kinds, solicited or unsolicited, might be sent by the gods. In the case of a solicited omen, a professional diviner (Akkadian: *baru*) examined a condition that he had deliberately provoked. By doing so, he could ask the gods to answer specific questions or inquire about the advisability of undertaking some action. If the answer was negative, the plan was postponed, and the diviner made another attempt at divination at what he hoped was a more propitious time.

Solicited Omens. Extispicy was an especially important means of soliciting omens. The entrails (the liver, lungs, or colon spiral) of a slaughtered young sacrificial animal (usually a sheep, sometimes a goat) were inspected and interpreted by the diviner. The signs and their associated portents were consistently written down, and eventually they were collected into omen series. Livers modeled in clay were marked with various characteristics and inscribed with their related predictions. Extispicy was used from the mid-third millennium B.C.E. on, and over time it developed into an advanced discipline with its own vocabulary of technical words for the entrails and a catalogue of their many different markings. Other means of soliciting omens included lecanomancy (the observation of the patterns formed by oil blobs dropped onto water), libanomancy (the observation of the behavior of smoke from incense), belomancy (the observation of arrows shot into the air), cledonomancy (the analysis of chance responses or remarks overheard in a crowd), and, rarely, necromancy (calling up the spirits of the dead).

Unsolicited Omens. Other forms of divination involved observation of naturally occurring events, such as signs seen in the sky. They were the domain of other kinds of diviners: the exorcist (Akkadian: *ashipu*), and, in later times, a scholar (Akkadian: *tupsharru*). Observing unprovoked omens gradually became more widespread, and celestial divination eventually surpassed extispicy in popularity, surviving even after the end of Mesopotamian civilization. Also important among unsolicited signs were teratological omens (monstrous births among animals), terrestrial omens (a huge range of strange everyday occurrences), hemerological and menological omens (favorable and unfavorable days for undertaking certain plans), prognostic omens (predictions of the course and outcome of diseases), and physiognomic omens (predictions derived from the appearance and behavior of individual people). Augury (the observation of birds) and oneiromancy (the interpretation of dreams) were also practiced. All branches of divination had their own specialized practitioners.

Longevity of the Tradition. Divination was used in all periods of Mesopotamian history. It was practiced in the service of kings to guide them in important decisions about military campaigns, temple building, court appointments, and many other matters. It was also used by people of lesser

Clay model of a sheep's liver (height 5¾ inches) used by divination priests as an aid to making predictions. Cuneiform inscriptions indicate omens associated with blemishes at various marked positions; probably from Sippar, Old Babylonian period, circa 1900–1600 B.C.E. (British Museum, London).

rank to investigate the future or to find an answer to a particular question.

The Nature of Omens. A sign from a god, such as an eclipse, was believed to forecast the same good or bad fortune in all future days. Once a sign was observed and had been followed by a specific event, this sign, whenever it was seen again, was thought to indicate a similar future event. The sign did not have any influence on or in any way cause the coming event. It was just a warning; if x occurred, it was expected that y would follow. Scribes wrote down such signs and their indications, compiling tablet upon tablet of omens, which only they, as specialized diviners, had been trained to interpret. When x happened again, scholars consulted these compendia of omens to see what outcome, y, might be on the way.

Divination and Prevention. The portended events detected by divination were not inevitable. If the signs were properly read and interpreted, magical or other appropriate steps might be taken to avert the potential consequences. One measure was the performance of apotropaic rites by an exorcist. Intended to ward off evil, these rites took many different forms, each designed to take care of specific and different evil portents. If the origin of the evil was unknown, the exorcist could resort to the generic "rite against all evil." For eclipses, one of the most perilous and fearful of events, there were several preventive measures. One was a ritual that called for the continuous and rapid beating of a bronze kettledrum.

The Substitute King Ritual. For eclipses that specifically forecast the death of the king, there was a special remedy, the "substitute king ritual," in which a man was selected to take the place of the king, thereby assuming the fate predicted for the true king. He was usually some flawed individual, perhaps a condemned criminal, who, while he had no power, wore the real king's clothes, sat on the throne, and listened as the bad omen predicting his impending death was recited. Meanwhile, the real king, addressed as "farmer" to disassociate him from his royal station, remained in seclusion and underwent a purification process. At the end of the period for which the omen was considered valid, usually one hundred days, the substitute king was put to death.

Omen Series. Omens were recorded and eventually organized into collections, or series. Over time, they were copied and recopied, edited and revised, shortened or amplified. Each of the many branches of divination had its own omen manual for diviners to consult. All omens, no matter what their themes, were phrased in identical form. All were expressed as a conditional sentence consisting of two clauses: the *protasis* "if x happens," and the *apodosis* "then y will happen." In omen collections, every conceivable protasis, whether possible or not, was considered. For example, there are omens about lunar eclipses that cannot possibly occur on the eighteenth to twenty-first days of the Babylonian lunar month. One reason for the inclusion of such impossible situations can likely be the systematic way in which omens were organized into collections. Whenever gaps occurred in the scheme, they were filled by omens deliberately created to make the arrangement complete. Omen series became increasingly more detailed, and series contain runs of certain themes, such as an event happening on selected days of the month, or on each and every day of the month, or a phenomenon occurring in all four common colors. There was an ever-present contrast between right and left. In extispicy it might be the right and left side of the liver, or in celestial divination perhaps the left and right side of eclipse shadows. Other opposites might be above and below, in front of and behind, bright and faint, sunrise and sunset, on time and late or early. When there was more than one event in the protasis, there were clear guidelines: a good sign combined with a good sign predicted a good outcome; good combined with bad meant a bad result; bad combined with bad had a good portent.

Spread of the Babylonian Tradition. The history of divination in Mesopotamia is a long one. Although the observation and interpretation of divine signs warning of future events must have begun earlier, omens were written down and copied from at least the last third of the third millennium into the first century C.E. Divination was an accepted means of predicting future events, and it was the work of learned professionals. The corpus of omens was respected as a scholarly source to be referred to and quoted throughout the ages. It is not surprising that divination texts make up the largest single category of recovered Akkadian literature. Mesopotamian divination, and especially celestial omens, spread to neighboring kingdoms in the mid-second millennium B.C.E. Omens were copied in Mari, Emar, Alalah, Qatna, and Ugarit in Syria; Hazor in the upper Galilee; Hattusa in Anatolia; Nuzi on the northwest periphery of Mesopotamia; and Susa in southwest

Iran. Inside Mesopotamia, the astronomical omen series *Enuma Anu Enlil* was still being copied in the Achaemenid and Hellenistic periods, and experts in charge of astronomical observations acquired a special name: "Scribe of *Enuma Anu Enlil*," a title that survived into the second century B.C.E. These long-lived Mesopotamian celestial omens were undoubtedly the source for similar omens found in Egyptian, Indian, and Greek sources. From Egypt, there is a demotic papyrus preserving two Achaemenid texts that include counterparts to Babylonian examples. Babylonian astronomical knowledge, as well as celestial and terrestrial omens, was transmitted to India from the mid-first millennium B.C.E. on; Greek omens in Babylonian style were composed by someone now known as Pseudo-Petosiris. From these sources, Mesopotamian omens spread to the Far East, to Islam, and to medieval Europe. Where the Mesopotamian omen tradition was not adopted or adapted, it was treated with contempt; divination was forbidden in ancient Israel and scorned in the Hebrew Bible.

From Celestial Divination to Mathematical Astronomy. As a scholarly pursuit, celestial divination in Mesopotamia provided a solid background for the composition of other observational astronomical texts and especially for the mathematical astronomy that developed later. Astronomers and astral diviners became masters of scholarly investigation. As they regularly observed and recorded astronomical and meteorological phenomena and matched their observations to related predictions from collections of omens, they began to be interested in the timing and circumstances of astronomical events in themselves. From the omen series *Enuma Anu Enlil* alone, it is apparent that by end of the second millennium B.C.E. and the beginning of the first, scholars were aware of the periodicity of planetary and other celestial phenomena; they were curious about the possibilities of the predictability of their cycles; and they were engaged in finding mathematical methods to do just that. Their efforts to measure intervals between certain celestial phenomena for prediction purposes is just one example of this new interest. The scholars, by observing eclipses and their various aspects, gathered knowledge that would stand them in good stead when later they began to construct eclipse theory. And in measuring some periodic deviations from mean-time intervals of phenomena, they developed tools such as the linear zigzag function, which was useful later in their mathematical astronomy.

Personal Celestial Divination. Until the end of the fifth century B.C.E., astronomy and astral omens were the concern of the king and the country in general but not the province of his subjects. It was not until the Achaemenid period (538–331 B.C.E.) that the use of celestial omens expanded to include predictions, based on astronomical phenomena at the time of birth, about the future lives of common people. These personal celestial omens describing the position and phenomena of one or more planets or fixed stars at birth are now termed "nativity omens." Personal proto-horoscopes also emerged. Unlike nativity omens, they do not normally give predictions about the future life of a child; yet, they might include nativity omens. While the terms "nativity omens" and "proto-horoscopes" bring to mind the pseudo-science of modern astrology, the recording of celestial omens at the time of birth, which were considered signs from the gods, is quite different from what modern people think of as astrology or even what the ancient Greeks thought it was.

Proto-Horoscopes. Thirty-two Babylonian-style proto-horoscopes are known, ranging in date from 410 B.C.E. to 69 B.C.E., near the virtual end of cuneiform writing. Technically, because Babylonian proto-horoscopes do not contain predictions based on planetary positions and zodiacal signs, these texts are not identical to Hellenistic and Roman horoscopes. Classical horoscopes use a far richer collection of significant data, and their validity is derived from Aristotelian physics and Hellenistic cosmology rather than from signs from the gods. Rather than forecasting the future, Babylonian proto-horoscopes merely state certain astronomical facts at the time of birth or, in a few cases, time of conception. Following the date, and perhaps the time of day, of the child's birth or conception are the positions of the planets, all at one point in time. These data cannot be observational and must have been computed. They follow a fixed order: the moon, sun, Jupiter, Venus, Mercury, Saturn, and Mars. Sometimes the planetary positions are described by degree within a zodiacal sign, but more often than not the zodiacal sign is given alone. There also might be statements about the length of the month (twenty-nine or thirty days); measurements of time intervals such as sunrise to moonset or moonrise to sunrise; eclipses, including those not visible in Babylon; equinoxes and solstices; and the conjunction of the moon with reference stars. The following is a proto-horoscope for someone born on 7 September 140 B.C.E.:

> Year 172 (Seleucid Era) Arsaces was king.
> [Ululu (month VI)] 30 (were the days of the previous month), night of the 13th . . . evening watch,
> In his hour (of birth), the moon was in Pisces,
> the sun in Virgo, Jupiter in Sagittarius, Venus in Libra
> Mars in Gemini, Mercury and Saturn
> which had set were not visible. They were with the sun.
> That month, moonset after sunrise on the 14th, last lunar visibility on the 28th,
> That year, (autumnal) equinox was on the 2nd of Tashritu (month VII). (Rochberg, 1998)

Sources:

Hermann Hunger and David Edwin Pingree, *Astral Sciences in Mesopotamia* (Leiden & Boston: Brill, 1999).

Ulla Jeyes, "The Act of Extispicy in Ancient Mesopotamia: An Outline," *Assyriological Miscellanies*, 1 (1980): 13–32.

Ulla Koch-Westenholz, *Mesopotamian Astrology* (Copenhagen: Museum Tusculanum Press, 1995).

A. Leo Oppenheim, *Ancient Mesopotamia: Portrait of a Dead Civilization*, revised edition, completed by Erica Reiner (Chicago: University of Chicago Press, 1977).

Simo Parpola, ed., *Letters from Assyrian Scholars to the Kings Esarhaddon and Assurbanipal*, part 2, Alter Orient und Altes Testament 5/2 (Kevelaer: Butzon & Bercker, 1983).

Erica Reiner, *Astral Magic in Babylonia*, Transactions of the American Philosophical Society, volume 85, part 4 (Philadelphia: American Philosophical Society, 1995).

Francesca Rochberg, *Babylonian Horoscopes* (Philadelphia: American Philosophical Society, 1998).

Francesca Rochberg-Halton, "Benefic and Malefic Planets in Babylonian Astrology," in *A Scientific Humanist: Studies in Memory of Abraham Sachs*, edited by Erle Leichty, Maria deJ. Ellis, and Pamela Gerardi, Occasional Publications of the Samuel Noah Kramer Fund, no. 9 (Philadelphia, 1988), pp. 323–328.

Ivan Starr, *The Rituals of the Diviner* (Malibu, Cal.: Undena, 1983).

MATHEMATICS

Mathematical Cuneiform Tablets. The history of mathematics begins with ancient Babylonian mathematics recovered by modern scholars from cuneiform texts. These texts are plentiful and can be found in museums, collections, and libraries all over the world. They are the product of the Mesopotamian scribal schools, where mathematics was an intrinsic part of the curriculum. Whereas surviving astronomical tablets come almost exclusively from just three sites—Nineveh, Babylon, and Uruk—mathematical cuneiform texts come from many different locations across Mesopotamia. With the exception of a small number of school exercise texts from the late third millennium B.C.E., most mathematical tablets fall into two periods of Mesopotamian history. The earlier group comes from the Old Babylonian scribal schools of the first half of the second millennium B.C.E., and the later texts were composed by the Late Babylonian scholars working in the astronomical archive in Babylon and the Resh temple at Uruk in the last centuries of the first millennium B.C.E. Nothing can be said about mathematics during the large gap in time between these two distinct groups, other than that no mathematical texts have been found for this time span—almost certainly the result of the vagaries of preservation and recovery. From the texts that have survived, modern scholars can see how the Mesopotamian number system worked; how they computed numerical quantities as diverse as interest on loans and lengths, widths, and areas; and how they solved mathematical problems. Babylonian mathematics was made up of arithmetic, elementary algebra, number theory, and geometry. As in astronomical texts, theories were never stated, and there are no texts setting forth mathematical rules. For example, they knew and used the concept of the "Pythagorean Theorem" a millennium before Pythagoras's birth in the sixth century B.C.E., but they never wrote it down as a principle or offered proof. The underlying procedure for solving problems, however, can be found by modern scholars in the details of the solution.

The Number System. The Mesopotamian system of numbers has two distinguishing characteristics. It is, first of

PLACE-VALUE NOTATION

The sexagesimal number system is based on sixty and uses place-value notation. Thus any numeral x can represent itself, or itself multiplied by sixty ($x \cdot 60$), or by sixty squared ($x \cdot 60^2$), and so on, depending on the place position of the digits. Similarly, the same numeral can represent itself divided by sixty ($x/60$), or divided by sixty squared ($x/60^2$), and so on. Context alone determines the correct reading. For example,

$$1,25,30 = 1 \cdot 60^2 + 25 \cdot 60 + 30 = 3600 + 1500 + 30 = 5130$$

$$1,25;30 = 1 \cdot 60 + 25 + {}^{30}\!/_{60} = 85\ \tfrac{1}{2}$$

$$1;25,30 = 1 + {}^{25}\!/_{60} + {}^{30}\!/_{3600} = 1\ {}^{153}\!/_{360}$$

Source: Asger Aaboe, *Episodes From The Early History of Mathematics* (Washington, D.C.: Mathematical Association of America, 1964), pp. 8–9.

all, a sexagesimal system; that is, it uses a base of 60; second, it uses place-value notation so that the place position of a digit in the representation of a number is crucial. In sexagesimal numbering, a digit can be any number from 1 to 59, so even signs made up of two characters, such as 25, represent one sexagesimal digit. Moving a digit one place to the left or right signifies a change in its value by a factor of sixty. When one moves a digit one place to the left, its value becomes sixty times as large, so it must be multiplied by sixty. If a digit is moved two places, it must be multiplied by sixty squared. Similarly, if a digit is moved one place to the right, it must be divided by sixty. The principle is the same as in the modern decimal system, but in that system a digit is multiplied or divided by ten instead of sixty. The idea that the value of a digit varies according to the position it occupies in the entire representation of a number allowed for an easy and economical way of writing large numbers. Using multiplication, division (performed by multiplying by the reciprocal $1/x$), addition, and subtraction, this system was a vast improvement over the earlier purely additive system, in which all the individual values contained in a representation of a number were added together to determine the aggregate value.

Sexagesimal Fractions. Like the modern decimal system, the sexagesimal number system was used to write both whole numbers and fractions. Modern people are used to thinking of the decimal fraction 1/8 as 0.125 where the 1 is 1/10; the 2 is 2/100 or $2/10^2$, the 5 is 5/1000 or $5/10^3$. In the Babylonian system, the units place, when zero (the 0 in 0.125), was not indicated as such in the cuneiform, and there was no decimal point, or anything like one. Sexagesimal fractions were determined by their position, that is,

their place value. When one reads numbers in cuneiform, one determines their place value by context. Then modern scholars write them with the units place followed by a semicolon and the remaining digits separated by commas to show that they are fractions. For example, the number of days of a synodic (lunar) month in the nineteen-year cycle is 29;6,22,58 . . . in sexagesimal numbers. This number is equal to 29 days plus 6/60, $22/60^2$, and $58/60^3$. Sexagesimal fractions were a most useful invention, because, with multiplication and reciprocal tables at hand, the work of arithmetical computations was greatly reduced. The Babylonian number system, with its place-value notation and sexagesimal system, was the linchpin of Babylonian mathematics and mathematical astronomy. It was also an important tool in later Greek and Roman astronomy. The Babylonian system of expressing fractions was later used by astronomers, such as Hipparchus (second century B.C.E.) and Ptolemy (second century C.E.), when dealing with complicated calculations with fractions. Even today, hours and time and degrees and angle are subdivided in sexagesimal fractions.

Babylonian Numerals. Two basic signs were used to write all Babylonian numerals. One was a vertical wedge, which could represent 1 or 60; multiples of the vertical wedge were used to produce the digits 2 through 9. The other fundamental sign was a corner wedge ("Winkelhaken"), which was equal to 10; multiples of this wedge were used to produce the numerals for 20, 30, 40, and 50. These signs could be combined to produce all of the numerals from 1 to 59; then the vertical wedge, which had been used for 1, became equal to 60. The reading of 1 or 60, or for that matter, 1/60, can be determined only by context. There were special signs for 100

CUNEIFORM NUMERALS

The numerals employed by cuneiform scribes to express numbers may be traced directly back to the sexagesimal numerals of the earliest proto-cuneiform tablets at the end of the fourth millennium B.C.E. As exemplified by the typical Old Babylonian period (circa 1894 – circa 1595 B.C.E.) numerals

below, in the sexagesimal cuneiform system every number from 1 to 599 can be written with the correct relative placement of combinations of just two types of wedges, the vertical wedge for digits and the corner wedge ("Winkelhaken") for tens. Additional signs were used for 600 and 3600.

1	10	40	90
2	11	50	100
3	12	60	110
4	13	61	120
5	20	62	121
6	21	70	130
7	22	71	131
8	23	72	180
9	30	80	600
			3600

In nonmathematical texts special numerals represent 100 and 1000:

100, 200, 300, 1000, 3000, 3333

In both mathematical and nonmathematical texts from the Seleucid and Parthian periods during the last three centuries B.C.E., a sign formerly used as a word separator occasionally came to represent "zero":

0

Source: John Huehnergard, *A Grammar of Akkadian* (Atlanta: Scholars Press, 1997), pp. 235–237.

A TABLE OF MULTIPLICATION

The following table text for the principle number 9 shows how multiplication was done in the sexagesimal, or base 60, number system.

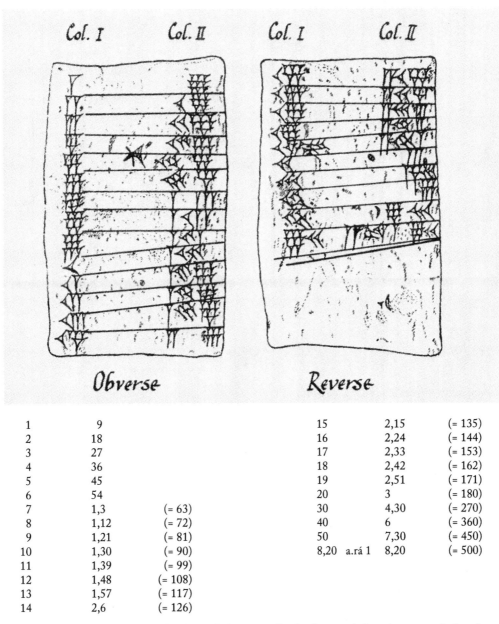

1	9	
2	18	
3	27	
4	36	
5	45	
6	54	
7	1,3	(= 63)
8	1,12	(= 72)
9	1,21	(= 81)
10	1,30	(= 90)
11	1,39	(= 99)
12	1,48	(= 108)
13	1,57	(= 117)
14	2,6	(= 126)

15	2,15	(= 135)
16	2,24	(= 144)
17	2,33	(= 153)
18	2,42	(= 162)
19	2,51	(= 171)
20	3	(= 180)
30	4,30	(= 270)
40	6	(= 360)
50	7,30	(= 450)
8,20 a.rá 1	8,20	(= 500)

On the front (obverse) and the back (reverse) of this Old Babylonian school tablet, cuneiform signs are written in two columns. In the left-hand column of the obverse are the signs for 1 through 14, and on the reverse, 15 through 19 (here written "20 minus 1" instead of the more usual "10 plus 9"), then 20, 30, 40, 50, and 500. In the right-hand column (beginning on the obverse and continuing on the reverse) are the numbers 9, 18, 27, 36, 45, 54, 63, and so on, each 9 times the number opposite it in the left-hand column. In order to get 63, for example, the vertical wedge and the three that follow must be read 1,3 or 1 · 60 + 3 = 63. The following lines would be 1,12 = 72; 1,21 = 81; and so on.

In the fourteenth line, the two vertical wedges and a 6 must be read 2,6 or 2 · 60 + 6; then 2,15 = 135 and 2,51 = 171. The next line must read 180, so the three vertical wedges must be read 3 · 60 = 180. This numeral might have been written 3,0 = 3 · 60 + 0 = 180 had the Babylonians in this period used a sign for zero at the end of a line, but they did not, so it must simply be assumed. The last line reads "8,20 times 1 (=) 8,20" or 500 · 1 = 500; this line is the "catch line," the first line of the next multiplication tablet in the series.

Source: Asger Aaboe, *Episodes From The Early History of Mathematics* (Washington, D.C.: Mathematical Association of America, 1964), p. 7.

TABLE OF RECIPROCALS

On tablets with tables of reciprocals the signs are arranged in two columns. At first glance, it appears that the numbers in column i on the left, all less than sixty, all factors of some power of 60, when multiplied by values in the right column, yield a product of 60 or a power of 60 (for example, 2 · 30 = 60; 3 · 20 = 60). However, there is another way to explain the use of this table. The reciprocal of column i ($1/x$ where x's are the values in column 1) is equal to the value in column ii on the right (y) divided by 60, or an appropriate power of 60, or $y/60^n$, where n = 1, 2, 3, ... Thus, $1/x = y/60^n$ or ½ · 60 = 30.

i	ii	x		y
𒐖	𒌍	2	(1/2 · 60 =)	30
𒐗	𒌋𒌋	3	(1/3 · 60 =)	20
𒐘	𒌋𒐙	4	(1/4 · 60 =)	15
𒐙	𒌋𒐖	5	(1/5 · 60 =)	12

(and so on)

Column ii therefore gives the reciprocals of column i. If one thinks of time and angle; that is, hours/minutes, degrees/seconds, the meaning is clear: 1/2 hour = 1/2 · 60 minutes = 30 minutes. This division descends from the Babylonian system. Larger, more extensive, reciprocal tables include reciprocals of regular and irregular numbers. Some tablets have a section of reciprocals followed by a collection of consecutive mathematical tables. A reciprocal table followed by a series of related multiplication tables, which in turn are followed by tables for squares or square roots, suggests that the table texts were intended to perform the operations of multiplication, division, and fractions.

Source: Asger Aaboe, *Episodes From The Early History of Mathematics* (Washington, D.C.: Mathematical Association of America, 1964), p. 10.

economic and metrical texts show variations in the writing of numbers in different times and places.

The Concept of Zero. Once a system of place-value notation is used, it becomes desirable to indicate the absence of a value in a particular position so that units of 60, or 60^2, or 60^3, and so on (in a sexagesimal number system) are not missing. A symbol standing for "nothing" was a necessity to show the absence of anything in a particular position in a number. In the Old Babylonian texts, zero was assumed but not written; that is, it was represented by an open space in the middle of a number. At the end of a number, it was omitted, leaving it to the reader to assume an empty place. For example, 180 was written with three vertical wedges each equal to 60. (In another context those same vertical wedges could be read as 3.) In this way, 3 · 60 = 180, and they chose this practice instead of alternatively writing (3 · 60) + 0 = 180. In texts from the fourth century B.C.E. on, a cuneiform sign previously used to separate words in a line of text began to be used to signify nothing in place of the empty space. The Babylonian zero arrived late in the history of Babylonian mathematics; nevertheless it was the first in world history. At a later date, a zero for the base-ten system was developed in India; similarly, the Maya in Central America developed a zero for their base-twenty system.

Table Texts. The Mesopotamian mathematical tablets are of two kinds: table texts and problem texts. They were arranged in fixed sequences of mathematical operations, and some were designated as tablets within a series. The table texts are characterized by columns of numbers that are related to each other in some way: products, reciprocals, squares, square roots, cubes, and cube roots. Table texts were the means by which all computations were calculated. There are no tables of division. Instead, reciprocal tables were used for this function. The reciprocal of a number x is $1/x$. Instead of dividing by x, the Mesopotamians multiplied by $1/x$, using the reciprocal tables of $1/x$. A large number of such tables has survived from both the Old Babylonian period and the Seleucid period (311–129 B.C.E.). Other table texts include "Pythagorean" Numbers, co-efficient lists, compound interest, and price equivalencies.

Problem Texts. Problem texts contain one or more problems. The problems on a given tablet may have the same theme or yield the same answer and typically become progressively more difficult. There are many different kinds of problems in these texts. There are solutions to first and second degree equations, cubic and quadratic equations, and arithmetic progressions. The scribes and students correctly computed areas and volumes of simple polygons and solids. They calculated interest rates and worked out construction problems. Some of the problems obviously had no practical value, such as those adding areas to lengths. They were included for intellectual exercise. Some problem texts demonstrate that the Mesopotamians used the so-called

(a vertical wedge followed by an horizontal wedge) and for 1000 (a combination of the corner wedge representing 10 and the sign for 100); so 10 did play a role, perhaps as an auxiliary base. Although 100 might be expressed as 1,40 (60 + 40) instead of by the sign for 100, and 19 might be written (20 - 1) rather than with one corner wedge for 10 and nine vertical wedges for 9, mathematical and astronomical texts used the sexagesimal system in a consistent manner, but

A MATHEMATICAL PROBLEM

This Old Babylonian school tablet shows a problem dealing with the ratio of the length of the diagonal of a square to the length of its side. It demonstrates that the Babylonians knew that the length of the diagonal of a square is equal to the length of its side multiplied by the square root of two ($\sqrt{2}$), and it shows that they had an excellent approximation of the value of $\sqrt{2}$.

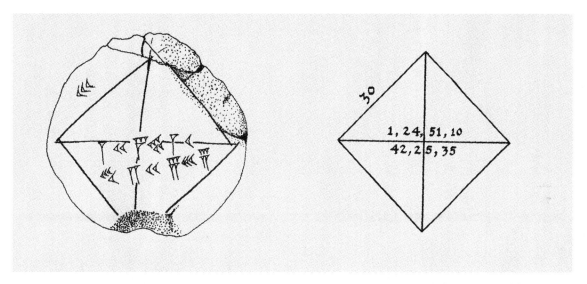

Three numbers are inscribed:

a = 30, the length of the side of the square

b = 1,24,51,10

c = 42,25,35, the length of diagonal

It can be shown that $c = a \cdot b$ if b and c are written with semicolons in their correct places in order to show place-value notation and thereby differentiate whole numbers from fractions:

b = 1;24,51,10 (= $1 + 24/60 + 51/60^2 + 10/60^3$)

c = 42;25,35 (= $42 + 25/60 + 35/60^2$)

That is, 30 · 1;24,51,10 = 42;25,35

Using the "Pythagorean Theorem," $c^2 = 2\,a^2$, and $c = a\sqrt{2}$, the value of b can be shown to be close to $\sqrt{2}$:

$(1;24,51,10)^2$ = 1;59,59,38,1,40

Therefore b is a very good approximation of $\sqrt{2}$.

Source: Asger Aaboe, *Episodes From The Early History of Mathematics* (Washington, D.C.: Mathematical Association of America, 1964), pp. 26–27.

Pythagorean Theorem a thousand years before Pythagorus's birth. These texts showed that they knew that the length of the diagonal of a square is equal to the length of its side multiplied by the square root of two ($\sqrt{2}$), using an excellent approximation in sexagesimal numbers to $\sqrt{2}$. A text now known as Plimpton 322 suggests fifteen solutions, in whole numbers, some quite large, to the "Pythagorean" equation: $a^2 + b^2 = c^2$; that is, the square of the hypotenuse (longest side) of a right triangle (c) is equal to the sums of the squares of the two remaining sides (a and b). The use of place-value notation was crucial. In fact, both the table texts and problem texts make sense today only if the number signs (that is, the digits) change their value with their place notation. The goal of the problems on the problem tablets was always a numerical answer. Procedures and proofs were never stated, instead examples were given.

Cryptography. Numerals could also stand for words and phrases or divine and geographical names in omen, astro-

CRYPTOGRAPHY

Cuneiform scribes could use numerals to stand for syllables, words, and phrases. Such numerals most commonly served as a form of shorthand, but they might also be deliberately employed to conceal the true meaning of the text. As a shorthand for divine names, the practice was in use from the late third millennium B.C.E. through the end of cuneiform writing in the early Common Era (C.E.), with some gods represented by more than one numeral, particularly in different periods of time. Typically the name of a god was written with a numeral preceded by the cuneiform sign read *dingir*, Sumerian for "god," and rendered in modern transliterations as a superscripted letter *d*. The following is a list of numerals for some of the gods:

^{d}1 = Ea, god of subterranean fresh waters.

^{d}10 = Adad, storm god.

^{d}15 = Ishtar, goddess of love and war; planet Venus.

^{d}20 = Shamash, god of justice, sun god, the sun.

^{d}21 = Anu, sky god, sky, the heavens.

^{d}30 = Sin, moon god, the moon.

^{d}40 = Ea (see ^{d}1)

^{d}50 = Enlil, god of the wind, the wind.

^{d}60 = Anu (see ^{d}21)

The cardinal directions could be rendered numerically; the cuneiform sign IM is Sumerian for "wind."

IM.1 = south

IM.2 = north

IM.3 = east

IM.4 = west

Similarly, the left and right sides of a person or an object could be rendered:

2,30 (= 150) = left

15 = right

Sources: Jeremy A. Black and Anthony Green, *Gods, Demons and Symbols of Ancient Mesopotamia: An Illustrated Dictionary* (Austin: University of Texas Press, 1992).
Laurie E. Pearce, "Cuneiform Cryptography: Numerical Substitutions for Syllabic and Logographic Signs," dissertation, Yale University, 1982.

lennium B.C.E. through the end of cuneiform writing in the early Common Era (C.E.). Some gods were represented by more than one numeral, especially in different periods of time. The numeral representing the god's name was preceded by the Sumerian sign *dingir*, "god," for example, dingir 30 (conventionally written ^{d}30), for the moon god Sin.

Sources:
Asger Aaboe, *Episodes From The Early History of Mathematics* (Washington, D.C.: Mathematical Association of America, 1964).

Jens Høyrup, "Babylonian Mathematics," in *Companion Encyclopedia of the History and Philosophy of the Mathematical Sciences*, 2 volumes, edited by I. Grattan-Guiness (London: Routledge, 1994), I: 21–29.

Høyrup, *Lengths, Widths, Surfaces: A Portrait of Old Babylonian Algebra and Its Kin* (New York & Heidelberg: Springer, 2002).

Karen Rhea Nemet-Nejat, *Cuneiform Mathematical Texts as a Reflection of Everyday Life in Mesopotamia*, American Oriental Series, volume 75 (New Haven: American Oriental Society, 1993).

Otto Neugebauer and Abraham Joseph Sachs, eds., *Mathematical Cuneiform Texts*, American Oriental Series, volume 29 (New Haven: American Oriental Society/American Schools of Oriental Research, 1945).

Laurie E. Pearce, "Cuneiform Cryptography: Numerical Substitutions for Syllabic and Logographic Signs," dissertation, Yale University, 1982.

Eleanor Robson, *Mesopotamian Mathematics, 2100–1600 B.C.: Technical Constants in Bureaucracy and Education* (Oxford: Clarendon Press, 1999).

MEDICINE

Illness and Treatment. Illness in ancient Mesopotamia was perceived as an intrusion from outside the body by an evil spirit or demon, who was believed to invade and occupy the body because of divine displeasure or a witch's sorcery. Treatment consisted of offerings to the god who may have caused the ailment; magic spells, incantations, and rituals; and, at the same time, medicinal remedies. Rivers were often the locus of the cure, for it was believed that the evil would be carried away in the rushing waters. Written evidence for Mesopotamian medical knowledge spans at least two thousand years. It may be characterized as a kind of folk medicine based on magic and herbal medicine. Possessing special knowledge and skills, its practitioners would today be called lay doctors. Copious documentation shows how concerned Mesopotamians were about their health and how responsibly their medical practitioners cared for them. Doctors had to be remarkably keen in observing symptoms and shrewdly intelligent in matching diagnoses and treatments to symptoms. As with all other scientific pursuits, a huge body of well-organized scholarly lore was at their disposal, and these diagnostic and pharmaceutical treatises are a valuable contribution to the history of medicine.

Medical Practitioners. There were two kinds of professional medical practitioners: the exorcist (Akkadian: *ashipu*), who, after making a diagnosis, cast magic spells and recited incantations to restore the sick person to health; and the physician (Akkadian: *asu*), who prescribed medications as a remedy. At times their functions overlapped.

nomical, land, and medical texts. This use of cryptography reached its peak in the first millennium B.C.E., especially during the Seleucid period. Numerals were used as shorthand for divine names, in particular, from the late third mil-

Bronze Lamashtu amulet (height 5 ¼ inches), Neo-Babylonian, eighth–seventh century B.C.E.. At bottom, a Pazuzu drives the evil Lamashtu toward offerings at right. In the middle, a sick man on a bed is flanked by fish-apkallu performing exorcism rites. To the right and above them are protective lion-headed demons and symbols of the major gods. A three-dimensional Pazuzu head peers over the top; his body is engraved on the back of the amulet (Louvre, Paris).

Sometimes the exorcist and the physician worked in tandem. One was not deemed superior to the other.

The Exorcist. The role of the exorcist was both diagnostic and magical; he was internist as well as exorcist. He had to examine the patient and ascertain the symptoms of the illness, then interpret them in order to determine the cause. He had to identify the god or evil spirit who had brought on the attack, or he had to discover what sin or error the patient had committed to bring on his present state. Then, he tried to bring about a cure by driving out the evil spirit with the appropriate magic spells and charms.

The Physician. The role of the physician was medical. A specialist in herbal remedies, he was responsible for preparing and applying medications, which consisted of plants and plant products—including resins, spices, seeds, fruits, roots, leaves, branches, bark, and gums—and of minerals such as salt (sodium chloride) and saltpeter (potassium nitrate). These plants and minerals were made into poultices for external application or mixed with beer or honey to be taken by mouth or inserted internally. Incantations were recited and ritual offerings were made by the physician as the medications were applied.

Medical Texts. A large number of medical tablets, as well as some pictorial representations—such as a bronze plaque of exorcists treating a supine patient—have been recovered, so the practice of medicine in Mesopotamia is well documented. Written sources—including medical texts, literary texts, letters, and extispicy material—reveal that the ancient Mesopotamians knew a great deal about their bodies, sickness, and medical treatments. They recognized and treated hundreds of different diseases, such as eye diseases, skin rashes, stomach ailments, toothaches, and earaches. They dealt with the medical conditions of conception, pregnancy, and childbirth. They were knowledgeable about herbal and pharmaceutical treatments. Among the medical works are therapeutic texts and diagnostic texts, including diagnostic omens, physiognomic omens, and rituals and incantations. These works provide detailed information about the art and science of medicine in ancient Mesopotamia. On the other hand, little is known about unassisted home medicine, for which there is far less evidence.

Therapeutic Medical Texts. Among the earliest, if not the first, pieces of written evidence for the practice of medicine are tablets filled with prescriptions. The earliest example, recovered from Nippur, was written in Sumerian during the Third Dynasty of Ur (circa 2112 – circa 2004 B.C.E.). This tablet, although damaged, preserves fifteen prescriptions; the afflictions they were intended to treat are not clear. Other therapeutic texts are filled with lists of medical symptoms and instructions for the preparation and application of appropriate medications to cure the symptoms. A good example is the tablet named *DUB.Ú.HI.A*, writ-

ten about 1000 B.C.E. This text categorizes symptoms by disease and gives detailed instructions (such as chopping, grinding, mixing in beer, or blending with oil) for the preparation of ingredients into the correct medicines. The application of each preparation (potion, salve, or lotion) is also specified. Magic, especially astral magic, was often an element of the cure. To make a medicine more effective, the ingredients might be set out in the night to absorb the powers of the stars and planets or gathered from plants growing over graves.

Diagnostic Medical Texts and Diagnostic Omens. The diagnostic medical texts identify diseases based on their symptoms and give the corresponding prognoses for recovery or death. They do not deal with treatments. The medical omen collection *SA.GIG*, "symptoms," is a large compendium of forty tablets. It includes diagnostic and prognostic omens that predict the course and outcome of various diseases. Its first line reads: "When an exorcist goes to the house of a patient." Structured in the typical "if-then" omen format, the omens in the series begin with *protases* ("if *x* happens") listing ominous things that might happen to the exorcist on the way to treat his patient and are followed by the *apodoses* ("then *y* will happen") give the corresponding prognoses for the recovery or death of the sick. This section is followed by others detailing medical symptoms and the prognosis for the course of the disease. Here the *protases* concern physical symptoms or the behavior of patients and a diagnosis of diseases and the offending gods or demons who caused them. The *apodoses* predict whether or not the patient will live or recover. Typically, the symptoms are organized by body part, going from head to toe. In other cases, they are arranged by the chronological order of the progress of the ailment.

Literary Texts. Literary texts also supply evidence about Mesopotamian medicine. In the Babylonian tale *The Poor Man of Nippur*, a destitute man seeking an audience with the mayor of his town poses as a physician. By saying that he is "a physician, a native of Isin," a city well known for its doctors, he infers that he is not just an ordinary doctor but one with special skills and knowledge. Isin was the cult center of Gula, the goddess of healing since earliest times. Her temple, the E-galmah, was renowned for its medical cures, and people traveled from all corners of Babylonia in search of treatment. Whether or not physicians were trained there is unknown, but being a "physician from Isin" was a distinct accomplishment. Gods could debilitate just as easily as they could cure. *The Poem of the Righteous Sufferer* tells the story of a thriving, successful man who has been brought to disgrace and ruin by the god Marduk. Sometimes referred to by scholars as the "Babylonian Job," the Sufferer has fallen into despair, lost his health, and suffered every possible malady. He expresses his discomfort by describing his ailments, going from head to toe, as in diagnostic omens:

> My eyes stare, they cannot see,
> My ears prick up, they cannot hear.
> Numbness has spread over my entire body,
> Paralysis has fallen upon my flesh.
> Stiffness has seized my arms,
> Debility has fallen upon my loins,
> My feet forgot how to move.
> (Foster)

Personal Correspondence. Letters include personal evidence about diseases and treatments. Letters from Old Babylonian Mari, from Middle Babylonian doctors, and from Late Assyrian court physicians have survived. The Assyrian kings, especially Esarhaddon (680–669 B.C.E.), tended to suffer from hypochondria, frequently requesting medical advice, not only about their own health but also about that of the entire royal family. In the following letter Esarhaddon's chief physician, Urad-Nanaya, offered advice on stopping nosebleeds:

> To the king, my lord. . . . Concerning the patient whose nose bleeds, [a high military official] told me that much blood flowed yesterday evening. They are handling those tampons ignorantly! They put them against the cartilage of the nose, pressing the cartilage, and that is why the blood keeps coming out. They should put them into the opening of the nostrils; it will cut off the breath but the blood will be held back. With the king's consent I will enter (the palace) tomorrow and give instructions. . . . (Parpola)

Sources:

Hector Avalos, *Illness and Health Care in the Ancient Near East: The Role of the Temple in Greece, Mesopotamia, and Israel* (Atlanta: Scholars Press, 1995).

R. D. Biggs, "Medicine, Surgery, and Public Health in Ancient Mesopotamia," in *Civilizations of the Ancient Near East,* 4 volumes, edited by Jack M. Sasson (New York: Scribners, 1995), III: 1911–1924.

Biggs, "Medizin," in *Reallexikon der Assyriologie und Vorderasiatischen Archäologie,* volume 7, edited by D. O. Edzard (Berlin & Leipzig: De Gruyter, 1987), pp. 623–629.

Jean-Marie Durand, "Maladies et Médicins," in *Archives épistolaires de Mari 1/1,* Archives Royales de Mari 26/1 (Paris: Editions recherche sur les civilisations, 1988).

Benjamin R. Foster, *Before the Muses: An Anthology of Akkadian Literature* (Bethesda, Md.: CDL Press, 1993).

Simo Parpola, ed., *Letters from Assyrian and Babylonian Scholars,* State Archives of Assyria, volume 10 (Helsinki: Helsinki University Press, 1993).

Erica Reiner, *Astral Magic in Babylonia,* Transactions of the American Philosophical Society, volume 85, part 4 (Philadelphia: American Philosophical Society, 1995).

E. K. Ritter, "Magical Expert (= āšipu) and Physician (= asû): Notes on Two Complementary Professions in Babylonian Medicine," in *Studies in Honor of Benno Landsberger on his Seventy-fifth Birthday, April 21, 1965,* edited by Hans Gustav Güterbock and Thorkild Jacobsen, Assyriological Studies, no. 16 (Chicago: University of Chicago Press, 1965), pp. 299–321.

Marten Stol, *Epilepsy in Babylonia,* Cuneiform Monographs, no. 2 (Groningen: Styx Publications, 1993).

SCHOLAR-SCRIBES OF THE FIRST MILLENNIUM B.C.E.

The Scribes of the Letters and Reports. It is hardly possible to overstate the importance of scholars to the kings of the late Assyrian Empire. Residing in cities all over the empire, Assyrian and Babylonian astral diviners in service to the Assyrian kings regularly watched the heavens, excerpted from the omen literature omens that they deemed appropriate to the observations, and sent this information back to the capital. Not only did their correspondence inform kings about what the scholars had observed and which omen from *Enuma Anu Enlil* and other omen sources could be derived from a particular celestial event, but the letters also advised rulers on propitious times for state activities and the precautions to be taken to avoid bad forecasts—thus influencing policy-making decisions. Their tablets reveal information about conditions within Assyria and Babylonia and diplomacy with bordering states. At the same time, the letters provide a window on the scholars' private lives and their relations with the Assyrian kings.

Master Scribes and Peripheral Scribes. The most influential scribes, called master (Akkadian: *ummanu*), lived in the capital. They were descended from scribal families who traced their lineage far back in time. They were constantly summoned to court to explain their interpretations of observed phenomena. Another group of scribes was deployed throughout Babylonia and Assyria. These scribes were farther away from the ear of the king, did not have as much influence, and were not held in as high esteem as the clique at court. Because they all owed their livelihood to the king and depended on his goodwill, they peppered their professional correspondence with flattery and expressions of loyalty and devotion. When there was disagreement among the scribes about interpretations of observations, the king was the first to know of it.

Late Babylonian Scribes. Many of the Late Babylonian scribes who worked in the astronomical archive in Babylon are known to modern scholars from their colophons, inscriptions at the end of scholarly texts that included the title of the text and the name of the scribe who copied it. Their names and names of their scribal families are preserved, but the exact location of what must have once been a vast astronomical center is still unknown. Almost all its texts were either directly sold to dealers by the local population or legally excavated but without proper records being made. Though these scribes regularly signed most other astronomical texts, only five diary authors are known. They were scholars, astronomers, and scribes, who kept the nightly watch and wrote their observations in astronomical diaries. A few might also have performed cultic duties, such as the recitation of incantations and the performance of rituals, and they likely worked on other kinds of astronomical texts and computed tables of mathematical astronomical calculations. More is known about the authors of these other advanced astronomical texts, because many of their tablets are inscribed with their names, titles, and patronymics. As well as being scholars, some of these scribes were lamentation singers and exorcists. Many were members of the scribal group called "Scribe of (the omen series) *Enuma Anu Enlil*." Possibly the scribes who prepared the diaries were also part of this group, but none described himself as such in the five colophons that have survived. The Late Babylonian scribes were still working at the Esangila Temple in Babylon into the early Common Era (C.E.), writing the latest known datable cuneiform text, an almanac for 75 C.E. Dating from possibly as late as the early third century C.E., a fragment of an incantation has also survived; it is written in Akkadian on one side, and on the other side is a transliteration in Greek, the common language of the day.

Anu-belshunu. One example of a scribe descended from a long line of scholars was Anu-belshunu, a prominent Hellenistic-period scribe who worked in the Anu temple in Uruk from at least 193 to 187 B.C.E. The son of another important scribe, Nidintu-Anu, Anu-belshunu and his father belonged to a family of scholars and scribes who traced their lineage back to Sin-leqe-unnini, the author of the unified version of the *Epic of Gilgamesh*, who lived in the Kassite period, during the latter half of the second millennium B.C.E. Anu-belshunu's son, Anu-ab-uter, held the prestigious title "scribe of *Enuma Anu Enlil*" and is well known from the colophons of astronomical texts, among them an impressive astral omen tablet inscribed with fanciful drawings of several constellations. Among the few surviving proto-horoscopes is one for a man named Anu-belshunu, born on the second day of the tenth month in the sixty-third year of the Seleucid Era (that is, 30 December 249 B.C.E.). Since his patronymic is not included in the proto-horoscope, no one can say with certainty that it was written for Anu-belshunu the scribe. If it is his proto-horoscope, as some scholars suggest, then Anu-belshunu would have been between fifty-five and sixty-one years of age when he worked on the astronomical texts on which his name appears as copyist.

Sources:
P.-A. Beaulieu and Francesca Rochberg, "The Horoscope of Anu-bēlšunu," *Journal of Cuneiform Studies*, 48 (1996): 89–94.

John Britton and C. B. F. Walker, "A 4th Century Babylonian Model for Venus: BM 33552," *Centaurus*, 34 (1991): 110–112.

M. J. Geller, "The Last Wedge," *Zeitschrift für Assyriologie und vorderasiatische Archäologie*, 87 (1997): 43–95.

Hermann Hunger, ed., *Astrological Reports to Assyrian Kings*, State Archives of Assyria, volume 8 (Helsinki: Helsinki University Press, 1992).

Otto Neugebauer, ed., *Astronomical Cuneiform Texts: Babylonian Ephemerides of the Seleucid Period for the Motion of the Sun, the Moon, and the Planets*, volume 1 (London: Published for the Institute of Advanced Studies, Princeton, N.J., by Lund Humphries, 1955).

Simo Parpola, ed., *Letters from Assyrian and Babylonian Scholars*, State Archives of Assyria, volume 10 (Helsinki: Helsinki University Press, 1993).

L. E. Pearce and L. T. Doty, "The Activities of Anu-belšunu, Seleucid Scribe," in *Assyriologica et Semitica. Festschrift für Joachim Oelsner anläßlich seines 65. Geburtstages am 18. Februar 1997*, edited by Joachim Marzahn and Hans Neumann, Alter Orient und Altes Testament, 252 (Münster: Ugarit, 2000), pp. 331–341.

Francesca Rochberg, *Babylonian Horoscopes* (Philadelphia: American Philosophical Society, 1998), pp. 79–81.

Rochberg, "Scribes and Scholars: The *tupšar Enūma Anu Enlil*," in *Assyriologica et Semitica. Festschrift für Joachim Oelsner anläßlich seines 65. Geburtstages am 18. Februar 1997*, edited by Joachim Marzahn and Hans Neumann, Alter Orient und Altes Testament, 252 (Münster: Ugarit, 2000), pp. 359–376.

Francesca Rochberg-Halton, Review of volume 1 (1988) of *Astronomical Diaries and Related Texts from Babylonia*, by Abraham Joseph Sachs and Hermann Hunger, *Orientalia*, 58 (1989): 551–555.

Abraham Joseph Sachs and Hermann Hunger, *Astronomical Diaries and Related Texts from Babylonia*, volume 1 (Vienna: Österreichischen Akademie der Wissenschaften, 1988).

Ivan Starr, ed., *Queries to the Sungod: Divination and Politics in Sargonid Assyria*, State Archives of Assyria, volume 4 (Helsinki: University of Helsinki Press, 1990).

TECHNOLOGY AND INVENTIONS

Accomplishments. The ancient Mesopotamians are credited with a host of original technological accomplishments. They built canal systems for irrigation and transportation, created the first man-made glass objects, and produced new wheeled war machines, movable siege towers, belfries with battering rams, and war chariots. They recorded the world's first recipes for perfume, beer, dyes, medicines, and bronze, and they invented a new cuisine.

Ziggurats. The Mesopotamian ziggurat stands out as a striking innovation in architectural design. Evolving from the early practice of building and rebuilding temples on earthen or brick platforms, the ziggurat resembled a multileveled, stepped pyramid. It was made of mud brick, clad in burnt brick set in bitumen mortar, and presumably topped with a temple or shrine. Ziggurats were a distinctive feature on the Mesopotamian skyline. The remains of more than thirty ziggurats have been found so far. Ur-Namma, king of Ur circa 2112 – circa 2095 B.C.E., was the builder of the first true ziggurats in southern Mesopotamia, and examples of his building projects can be found at Eridu, Nippur, and Uruk. His best-known ziggurat, and the best preserved today, is the one at Ur. Even though only two lower stages are partially preserved, images on reliefs and seals make it possible to reconstruct its original appearance. It was designed with a rectangular base and three stairways that converge midway up to become a single staircase leading to the top level, some fifty feet above the ground. A large ziggurat dedicated to the god Enlil was built during the fourteenth century B.C.E. at the fortified Kassite city of Dur-Kurigalzu (modern Aqar Quf), near Babylon. The remains of this ziggurat, now eroded to its core of mud brick and layers of reeds, lie within the remnants of a fortress once

Ziggurat at Ur (base 205 by 141¼ feet, height 54¾ feet), originally built by Ur-Namma (circa 2112 – circa 2095 B.C.E.) and substantially rebuilt by Nabopolassar (625–605 B.C.E.)

rich in Egyptian gold. In Babylon the ziggurat E-temenanki ("the foundation-platform of heaven and under-world") was built by Nebuchadnezzar II (604–562 B.C.E.) for the national god Marduk. It inspired Herodotus of Halicarnassus (fifth century B.C.E.) to write a glorious description of it in his *Histories,* and it may have served as the archetype for the Tower of Babel in the Hebrew Bible. It was laid out on the foundations of an Old Babylonian-period (circa 1894 – circa 1595 B.C.E.) ziggurat that had been successively rebuilt over the centuries. Nebuchadnezzar's ziggurat had seven stories that rose some three hundred feet to the top. The upper dwelling place of the god was said to have been clad with blue-glazed enameled bricks. According to Diodorus, a Roman historian of the late first century B.C.E., the ziggurat tower in Babylon was used for astronomical observation. This use is a distinct possibility, but there is no evidence to confirm it. Today only the foundations of the once-great tower survive. The largest ziggurat in Mesopotamia was the Anu ziggurat at Uruk, built during the Seleucid period (311–129 B.C.E.); only the remains of its sides, some one hundred meters in length, have survived.

The Amorite Wall. Incursions into Mesopotamia at the end of the third millennium B.C.E. by the Amorites (Akka-dian: *Amurru;* Sumerian: *Martu*), a Semitic-speaking peo-ple from the West, posed an imminent danger for the empire of the Third Dynasty of Ur. After rescuing his city from attack and causing the marauders to flee, Shu-Sin

(circa 2037 – circa 2029 B.C.E.) built an enormous defen-sive wall designed to fend off future infiltration. Called *Muriq-Tidnim,* "Keeping away the Tidnim" (one of the Amorite tribes), the Amorite wall was said to have been about 170 miles long. Although no remnant of the wall has been identified by archaeologists, it apparently stretched across both the Tigris and Euphrates Rivers at a point just north of the modern city of Baghdad. At the time of its construction, the wall was of such significance that its con-struction provided the names of Shu-Sin's fourth and fifth regnal years: "The year Shu-Sin the king of Ur built the Amurru wall, Muriq-Tidnim" and "The year after the year Shu-Sin the king of Ur built the Amurru wall, Muriq-Tidnim." For a brief period, even Shu-Sin's sixth regnal year was called "The year after the year after the year. . . ." In the end, this wall was a futile effort. Under Shu-Sin's son, Ibbi-Sin (circa 2028 – circa 2004 B.C.E.), the Ur III empire fell to the Amorites from the west, and Ur was sacked by the Elamites from the east.

Zimri-Lim's Icehouse. The palace of the Amorite king Zimri-Lim (circa 1776 – circa 1761 B.C.E.) at Mari on the middle Euphrates in Syria had nearly three hundred rooms at ground level and perhaps as many on the second floor. Many rooms were grouped around one of several large open courtyards. The palace included workshops, reception rooms, shrines, living quarters, storerooms, and kitchens. At Terqa, about seventy kilometers north of Mari, Zimri-Lim built an "icehouse" (Akkadian: *bit shuripim*) to store ice that was collected from the highlands during the winter. The ice was used to chill the royal family's wine, and it was presented at dinner to foreign diplomatic visitors and traveling merchants. A reference to the construction of the icehouse is found in Zimri-Lim's only surviving royal inscription. Two fragmentary letters from the governor of Terqa to Zimri-Lim mention the problem of preventing the ice from melting.

Synthetic Basalt. The southern alluvial plain of Mesopotamia lacks such basic raw materials as hardwoods, hard stone, and metal ores. By and large, such materials were obtained from the more-mountainous regions to the north and east through trade or plunder. However, a novel solution to the problem of obtaining hard stone was found at the site of Mashkan-shapir (modern Tell Abu Duwari), an early second millennium B.C.E. Old Babylonian city. All across the site, archaeologists recovered large rectangular slabs, whole and fragmentary, that appeared to be made of basalt, a dark-colored, fine-grained volcanic rock. Most of these stones were shaped for use as grinding stones, one of which was found with a handstone of the same material. A few pieces appeared to have been used for building construction. Chemical analysis revealed that the stones were not basalt, but rather must have been made from local alluvial silt that had been heated in a kiln to its melting point (about 1200°C) and then allowed to cool slowly. Such technology testifies to the abilities of the potters or metal workers of the day. Producing locally the stone needed for such everyday activities as grinding grain to make bread and beer must have been much more cost effective than having to import such stones, especially since grinding stones and handstones became worn with use and needed to be replaced periodically.

Water Clocks. The water clock (Akkadian: *dibdibbu*) is mentioned in both astronomical and mathematical texts. It was a container of water with a hole in the bottom. Time was measured by the amount of time it took the water to seep out of the opening. The original use of the water clock seems to have been marking off the three "watches" into which nighttime was divided. At sunset, the start of the first watch, water was poured into the water clock, and when the water clock was empty, the watch was over. Since the length of the night varies through the year, the water clock was filled with different quantities of water in each season. The earliest tables of quantities of water for the water clock date to the Old Babylonian period (circa 1894 – circa 1595 B.C.E.). They are based on an ideal year of 360 days, and the amount of water changed only four times a year. Later texts are less primitive. The astronomical compendium *MUL.APIN*, probably composed near the start of the first millennium B.C.E., changes water quantities at intervals of fifteen days, while a Late Babylonian tablet, dated about 500 B.C.E., specifies intervals of five days.

A Mobile Battering Ram. City walls were intended to provide protection from attackers. During the first millennium B.C.E., as it worked to implement the expansionist policies of the Neo-Assyrian kings, the Assyrian army developed methods to undermine the resistance of those

Drawing by Paul Emile Botta of stone palace-wall relief depicting the use of four-wheeled mobile battering rams during the siege of Pazashi; Palace of Sargon II (721–705 B.C.E.), Khorsabad (from Paul Emile Botta, *Monument de Ninive*, volume 1, 1849)

Artist's reconstruction of Sennacherib's aqueduct at Jerwan, 704–681 B.C.E. (from Thorkild Jacobsen
and Seton Lloyd, *Sennacherib's Aqueduct at Jerwan*, 1935)

seeking refuge within walled cities. These strategies included siege, storming the ramparts, breaching walls and gates, scaling walls, and tunneling under walls, as well as propaganda and psychological warfare. The palace reliefs of Ashurnasirpal II (883–859 B.C.E.) at Nimrud depict the use of a battering ram mounted on a mobile six-wheeled wooden frame covered by wicker shields. The machine appears to have been almost twenty feet long. Mounted at the front of the carriage was a round-domed, perhaps metal, turret, almost twenty feet tall, inside of which the battering beam was slung from a rope, like a pendulum. The head of the ram was shaped somewhat like that of an axe. It was apparently driven between the stones or bricks of the wall and then levered back and forth in an effort to dislodge them, ultimately bringing about the collapse of that portion of the wall. Additional protection for the ram operators was provided by archers perched within mobile fortified towers wheeled alongside the rams. Scenes of sieges in the palace reliefs of later Assyrian kings indicate that army engineers continued to develop the ram, experimenting with four- and six-wheeled versions and with a variety of different forms of armor.

Sennacherib's Aqueduct. When the Assyrian king Sennacherib (704–681 B.C.E.) moved his capital to Nineveh at the beginning of his reign, he restored the ancient city to magnificent splendor. At the same time, because the Tigris River was situated too low to be used for the large-scale irrigation his new city and parklands needed, he provided for the city's water supply with several ambitious building projects. In addition to an intricate system of canals to bring water from distant mountain streams to the city, he built an aqueduct of huge proportions. Bridging a valley, it was three hundred yards long and twenty-four yards wide. Standing on a layer of enormous rough boulders, it was built of some two million stone blocks, each weighing a quarter of a ton.

The Na-Gauge. The rise and fall of the level of the Euphrates River must have been observed since the earliest settlers made their home in Mesopotamia. Exactly when the height of the river began to be recorded can only be surmised. Certainly by the middle of the sixth century B.C.E., scribes were writing down changes of river levels in Babylon almost daily in astronomical diaries. Probably near the close of the fourth century B.C.E., the *na*-gauge was introduced as a means of accurately measuring the river level. From what little is known about the use of the *na*-gauge, it is assumed to have been something like a modern ruler. Measurement was taken relative to some benchmark, perhaps the top of a sluice gate in the Euphrates at Babylon, and read from top to bottom. There may have been more than one location at which *na* measures were taken. The two sluice gates mentioned in the astronomical diaries are possibilities. A high *na* value meant a low water level; a low *na* represented a high level; no *na* meant the water was ready to pour over the apertures of the sluice. Changes in river level were measured in units of fingers and cubits. During the Late Babylonian period, 1 cubit (approximately 50 centimeters or 20 inches) equaled 24 fingers. One *na*, which equaled four fingers or one-sixth of a cubit, is thought to have been the thickness of a layer of bricks, a standard measure. Recorded *na* values ran from 1 to 39.

Sources:

Stephanie Dalley, *Mari and Karana: Two Old Babylonian Cities* (London & New York: Longman, 1984).

Susan B. Downey, *Mesopotamian Religious Architecture: Alexander through the Parthians* (Princeton: Princeton University Press, 1988).

C. J. Gadd, "Babylonia *c.* 2120–1800 B.C.," in *The Cambridge Ancient History*, third edition, volume 1, part 2: *Early History of the Middle East*, edited by I. E. S. Edwards, Gadd, and N. G. L. Hammond (Cambridge & New York: Cambridge University Press, 1971), pp. 595–643.

Hermann Hunger and David Edwin Pingree, *MUL.APIN: An Astronomical Compendium in Cuneiform*, Archiv für Orientforschung, Beiheft 24 (Horn, Austria: Berger, 1989).

Abraham Joseph Sachs and Hermann Hunger, *Astronomical Diaries and Related Texts from Babylonia*, volume 1 (Vienna: Österreichischen Akademie der Wissenschaften, 1988).

E. C. Stone, D. H. Linsley, V. Pigott, G. Harbottle, and M. T. Ford, "From Shifting Silt to Solid Stone: The Manufacture of Synthetic Basalt in Ancient Mesopotamia," *Science*, 280 (26 June 1998): 2091–2093.

D. J. Wiseman, *Nebuchadrezzar and Babylon* (London: Published for the British Academy by Oxford University Press, 1985).

Yigael Yadin, *The Art of Warfare in Biblical Lands in the Light of Archaeological Study*, translated by M. Pearlman, 2 volumes (New York, Toronto & London: McGraw-Hill, 1963).

SIGNIFICANT PEOPLE

BULLUTSA-RABI

CIRCA SECOND HALF OF THE SECOND MILLENNIUM B.C.E.
EXORCIST-POET

Revered Author. Bullutsa-rabi was the author of a great hymn to Gula, the goddess of healing. The frame narrative of the poem, in which Bullutsa-rabi introduces Gula, is written in the third person, while Gula sings her own praise in the first person. In the third-person frame Bullutsa-rabi beseeched the goddess on his own behalf, and he even wrote his name in the last lines of the poem. The passage in which Gula enumerates her skills provides valuable information about how Mesopotamian physicians treated patients:

> I am the physician, I can save life,
> I carry every herb, I banish illness.
> I gird on the sack with life-giving incantations,
> I carry the texts which make (one) well.
> I give health to mankind.
> (My) clean dressing salves the wound,
> (My) soft bandage relieves the pain.
> At my examination, the moribund revives,
> At a word from me, the feeble one arises. (Foster)

Bullutsa-rabi's name appeared again, much later, among the authors listed in a catalogue of texts and authors found in the ruins of the library of the Assyrian king Ashurbanipal (668–627 B.C.E.) at Nineveh, destroyed by the Babylonians and Medes in 612 B.C.E.

Sources:
Benjamin R. Foster, *Before the Muses: An Anthology of Akkadian Literature*, 2 volumes (Bethesda, Md.: CDL Press, 1993), pp. 491–499.

W. G. Lambert, "The Gula Hymn of Bullutsa-rabi," *Orientalia*, new series 36 (1967): 105–132.

ESANGIL-KIN-APLI

CIRCA ELEVENTH CENTURY B.C.E.
ROYAL CHIEF SCHOLAR

Revered Scholar. Esangil-kin-apli was the chief scholar of Sumer and Akkad during the reign of the Babylonian king Adad-apla-iddina (circa 1068 – circa 1047 B.C.E.). Claiming descent from Asallulhi-mansum, a sage in the reign of Hammurabi (circa 1792 – circa 1750 B.C.E.), Esangil-kin-apli was not only an important citizen of Borsippa, holding many priestly titles, but was also the compiler of the medical omen series *SA.GIG*. More than a half millennium later, during the Seleucid period (311–129 B.C.E.), his name was included in the *List of Sages and Scholars*, a mark of his extraordinary status at a time when cuneiform texts circulated anonymously.

Source:
I. L. Finkel, "Adad-apla-iddina, Esagil-kin-apli, and the series SA.GIG," in *A Scientific Humanist: Studies in Memory of Abraham Sachs*, edited by Erle Leichty, Maria deJ. Ellis, and Pamela Gerardi, Occasional Publications of the Samuel Noah Kramer Fund, no. 9 (Philadelphia: University Museum, 1988), pp. 143–159.

KISIR-ASHUR

CIRCA SEVENTH CENTURY B.C.E.
EXORCIST

Tablet Collector. Kisir-Ashur, an exorcist of the temple of the god Ashur in the city of the same name, was a medical practitioner with his own personal library, found by archaeologists beneath the floors of his house. Many of these texts comprised incantations and prescriptions to counteract various sicknesses and evils. Also beneath the floors of several rooms were found apotropaic figurines of the sort used in conjunction with the rituals in the texts to ward off evil spirits. Of all the houses with private libraries in Ashur, Kisir-Ashur's had the largest collection of tablets and a rare writing board made of ivory.

Source:
Olof Pedersén, *Archives and Libraries in the Ancient Near East 1500–300 B.C.* (Bethesda, Md.: CDL Press, 1998).

NABU-ZUQUP-KENA

CIRCA LATE EIGHTH – EARLY SEVENTH CENTURY B.C.E.
SCRIBE AND ASTRONOMER-ASTROLOGER

Preserver of Ancient Texts. Nabu-zuqup-kena was an Assyrian scribe from Kalhu. In his time, all kinds of tablets, including those of the astronomical omen series *Enuma Anu Enlil*, were collected from all over Mesopotamia and brought to the various Assyrian capital cities to be copied for their libraries. Nabu-zuqup-kena was a copyist of Babylonian texts during the reigns of Sargon II (721–705 B.C.E.) and Sennacherib (704–681 B.C.E.).

Source:
A. Leo Oppenheim, "Divination and Celestial Observation in the Last Assyrian Empire," *Centaurus*, 14 (1969): 97–135.

URAD-NANAYA

CIRCA SEVENTH CENTURY B.C.E.
CHIEF ROYAL PHYSICIAN

A Favorite of the King. Urad-Nanaya was an exorcist who rose to the position of chief physician to the Assyrian king Esarhaddon (680–669 B.C.E.). Urad-Nanaya corresponded with the king regularly, and fourteen of his letters are preserved. He was especially favored because he was the son of one of the highest-ranking scholars at court, Adad-shuma-usur, personal exorcist and close confidant of Esarhaddon.

Source:
Simo Parpola, ed., *Letters from Assyrian and Babylonian Scholars*, State Archives of Assyria, volume 10 (Helsinki: Helsinki University Press, 1993).

DOCUMENTARY SOURCES

Astronomical Diaries (652–61 B.C.E.)—These predominantly observational astronomical texts were given the name *diaries* in modern times because they comprise day-by-day accounts of celestial, meteorological, and terrestrial phenomena. Their contents—including the economic and historical entries—can be dated to the exact day, making the diaries a rich source of all sorts of information. The long tradition of keeping these diaries is remarkable because they were composed not only when Mesopotamia was under the control of native dynasties but also later when the region was ruled by Achaemenid Persians, Hellenized Macedonians, and Parthians.

DUB.Ú.HI.A (circa 1000 B.C.E.)—This therapeutic medical tablet is filled with descriptions of symptoms listed by disease and matching prescriptive cures. Because this work includes detailed instructions for preparing and applying medications, this text was probably a valuable handbook for the professional healer.

Enuma Anu Enlil (circa 1000 B.C.E.)— This series of some seventy tablets is a collection of omens concerning the behavior of the moon, the sun, the planets, and stars, as well as weather conditions and earthquakes. This primary source of present-day information for astral omens was organized into a major series, which continued to be copied and augmented for many centuries.

Ephemerides (circa fourth century B.C.E.)—These theoretical astronomical texts of ephemerides (successive phenomena of the moon or planets) mark the beginnings of mathematical astronomy. The collection comprises some four hundred to five hundred tablets and fragments, some of which are procedure texts that give directions for computing the ephemerides.

Letters and Reports to Assyrian Kings (late eighth – seventh centuries B.C.E.)—The large number of surviving letters from Assyrian and Babylonian scholars to the later kings of Assyria underscores the important role of astrological experts in the Assyrian court. Because they were in charge of what had become the major branch of divination, these scholars wielded enormous influence on royal decision making. They observed and interpreted ominous celestial phenomena, then sent their astronomical observations, related predictions, and advice to the king, who relied heavily on their counsel in determining any course of action, personal or political. Because of the intimate nature of these texts, the letters and reports offer valuable insight into the personalities, foibles, and concerns of individual kings and scholars as well as the relations between them. The letters are also an important source of information about social, economic, and political conditions inside and outside of Assyria.

MUL.APIN (circa 1100 – circa 700 B.C.E.)—This three-tablet compendium of astronomical texts summarizes the sophisticated astronomical knowledge of its time, including intercalation schemes, catalogues of stars, and prediction schemes for risings and settings of planets.

SA.GIG (circa mid-eleventh century B.C.E.)—This series of forty diagnostic medical omen tablets provides diagnoses and prognoses for various diseases. It was known both by its Sumerian title, *SA.GIG*—"symptom(s)"—and its opening line, *Enuma ina bit mursi ashipu illaku* ("When the exorcist goes to the house of a patient"). Unlike therapeutic medical tablets—such as *DUB.Ú.HI.A*—*SA.GIG* does not include treatments for diseases. This series was compiled by Adad-apla-iddina's chief scholar, Esangil-kin-apli.

Venus Tablet of Ammi-saduqa (circa 1646 – circa 1626 B.C.E.)—The fifty-nine astrological omens of the so-called *Venus Tablet of Ammi-saduqa* were incorporated into *Enuma Anu Enlil* as Tablet 63. These omens deal with predicted outcomes based on pairs of last and first visibilities of Venus observed during the early years of the reign of Ammi-saduqa, a king of the First Dynasty of Babylon. This observational record has been studied carefully by modern historians interested in the chronology of the Old Babylonian period (circa 1894 – circa 1595 B.C.E.).

GLOSSARY

Abbuttu(m): (Akkadian) A characteristic hairstyle with a distinctive lock or curl worn by slaves.

Abzu: *See* **apsu.**

Adad: Akkadian (Sumerian: *Ishkur*) god embodying storms.

Agglutinative language: A language—such as **Sumerian** or **Hattic**—in which strings of monosyllabic prefixes and suffixes (affixes) are attached to simple fixed bases.

Ahura-Mazda: The sovereign deity in the Persian pantheon.

Akitu festival: Babylonian ceremonies celebrating the New Year, a sequence of rites held near the time of the Spring Equinox.

Akkadian: A term designating (1) the various East Semitic dialects of Assyria and Babylonia spoken during the third through first millennia B.C.E.; (2) the late third millennium B.C.E. political dynasty and its empire with its capital at Akkad (Agade); and (3) the style of the art of that empire.

Aleph-beth: The West Semitic writing system consisting of twenty-two consonantal signs.

Alluvium: The general name for all sediments, such as sand and clay, deposited in land environments by a stream.

Aluzinnu: (Akkadian; Sumerian loanword) A professional clown or buffoon.

Ama-ushumgal-ana: A local Sumerian god who came to be identified with the shepherd god **Dumuzi.**

Amorite: (Akkadian: *amurru;* Sumerian: *mar-du*) A term designating (1) the West Semitic–speaking nomadic inhabitants of Syria and their descendants; (2) their West Semitic dialects; and (3) the dynasties founded by them in Mesopotamia at the end of the third and beginning of the second millennium B.C.E.

An: *See* **Anu.**

Anu(m): The Akkadian (Sumerian: *An*) god of the heavens; his major cult center was at Uruk.

Anunnakku: A Sumerian term for the gods as a whole, later denoting the gods of the earth and underworld.

Anzud: (Sumerian; Akkadian: *Anzu*) The name of a divine lion-headed eagle, sometimes read as *Imdugud.*

Apkallu: (Akkadian; Sumerian loanword) In Babylonian tradition, the seven wise men or sages who lived before the Flood.

Apodosis: The main ("then") clause of an "if-then" conditional sentence (*see also* **protasis**); Mesopotamian omens were stated in the form of conditional sentences.

Apotropaic rites: Ritual attempts to ward off evil.

Apsu(m): (Akkadian; Sumerian: *abzu*) The freshwater ocean believed to lie below the earth.

Arabic: The West Semitic dialects spoken by the first millennium B.C.E. inhabitants of the Western and Arabian deserts.

Aramaic: The West Semitic dialects originally spoken by the late second and first millennium B.C.E. inhabitants of north Syria.

Arnu(m): Akkadian word for serious violations of the proper order created by the gods; sins.

A-sha: *See* **eqlu.**

Ashipu: An exorcist specializing in **apotropaic** ritual incantations.

Ashur: The Assyrian national god.

Asu(m): (Akkadian; Sumerian loanword) A "physician."

Augury: A method of soliciting omens by observing the flights of birds.

Awilu(m): Akkadian word for "man," especially a member of the highest, property-owning class in the Old Babylonian period (circa 1894 – circa 1595 B.C.E.).

Baetyl: A sacred upright stone.

Balag: Sumerian term for (1) a kind of song, perhaps a dirge; and (2) the stringed instrument played to accompany such a song.

Baru(m): An Akkadian word designating a diviner specializing in **extispicy, lecanomancy,** and **libanomancy.**

Ba'U: Sumerian goddess, the wife of **Ningirsu,** worshiped at Lagash during the third millennium B.C.E.

Bel: Akkadian word meaning "lord," also used as an epithet for the Babylonian god **Marduk.**

Belomancy: A method of soliciting omens by observing arrows shot into the air.

Belu(m): Akkadian word (Sumerian: *en*) meaning "lord," used to designate the head of the household.

Bulla (*plural:* **bullae**): Term used to denote (1) **prehistoric period** hollow spherical clay balls containing counting tokens; and (2) **Seleucid period** napkin-ring-like clay seals for rolled parchment and papyrus documents.

Celestial divination: Methods of foretelling the future based on observations of the positions and movements of the sun, moon, and planets among the stars.

Celestial equator: An imaginary circle representing the projection of the earth's equator onto the **celestial sphere.**

Celestial longitude: Angle measured eastward (right ascension) from the point where the **ecliptic** crosses the **celestial equator** (in Aries in the Hellenistic period; in Pisces in modern times) to the foot of a circle perpendicular to the ecliptic passing through the object.

Celestial sphere: An imaginary sphere with the earth located at its center and the stars located on its inner surface; there is no evidence that the ancient Mesopotamians envisioned such a construct.

Cledonomancy: A method of soliciting omens by analyzing chance responses or remarks overheard in a crowd.

Conjunction: The apparent closeness of two heavenly bodies at the same **celestial longitude.**

Corvée: Forced labor due the state or temple to ensure, for example, a speedy harvest or the maintenance of roads.

Cretula (*plural:* **cretulae**): Any small, solid, irregularly shaped lump of clay, often impressed with one or more seals, used to seal a knot on a string tied around a rolled papyrus or parchment document.

Cuneiform: The quintessential Mesopotamian writing system in which signs are formed from wedge-shaped impressions made on the surface of damp clay with a stylus that has a triangular or rectangular tip.

Damgar: *See* **tamkarrum.**

Damkina: Babylonian goddess, wife of **Ea** and mother of **Marduk.**

Dumuzi: Sumerian shepherd god, lover of **Inana.**

Ea: *See* **Enki.**

Eblaite: Local Semitic language recorded in cuneiform on clay tablets, dated circa 2300 – circa 2250 B.C.E., from Tell Mardikh (ancient Ebla) in western Syria.

Ecliptic: The great circle that is the apparent orbit of the sun among the stars.

Eduba: Sumerian name (literally "tablet house") for the Old Babylonian period (circa 1894 – circa 1595 B.C.E.) school for scribes.

E-gal: Sumerian word for temple (literally "great house").

Egitu: Akkadian word for "negligence" or "carelessness," especially toward a god.

Elamite: Language spoken in the region of Khuzestan in southwest Iran during the second and first millennia B.C.E. and the people who spoke it.

Emegir: The main literary dialect of Sumerian.

Emesal: A dialect of Sumerian apparently reserved for a special group of priests and for direct speech among women or goddesses in literary texts.

En: The head of a Sumerian temple, who is believed to have served the religious and political function of "priest-king" (*see also* **belu**).

Enki: Sumerian god (Akkadian: *Ea*) of the freshwater ocean beneath the earth (**Abzu**) and associated with wisdom and magic; his cult center was at Eridu.

Enlil: Supreme god of the Mesopotamian pantheon; god of the earth and air; his cult center was at Nippur.

Ennugi: Sumerian divine canal inspector of the great gods.

Ensi: Title of Sumerian city rulers during the third millennium B.C.E.

Entitlement monument: Inscribed and relief-carved stone stele or monument (so-called *kudurru*s) erected in temples to commemorate the permanent transfer of land to individuals.

Entu(m): Akkadian (Sumerian loanword) term for a high priestess.

Ephemerides: Tables of computed daily positions of the sun, moon, and planets.

Eponym system: Method used, especially by the Assyrians, for naming years after the holders of the annually appointed *limmu*-office.

Eqlu(m): Akkadian word (Sumerian: *a-sha*) for a field.

Equinox: The intersection of the **ecliptic** with the **celestial equator;** the sun crosses the *vernal equinox* about 21 March and the *autumnal equinox* about 21 September.

Ereshkigal: Sumerian goddess, queen of the Netherworld, and sister of **Inana.**

Ergative language: A language, such as Sumerian, in which the subjects of transitive and intransitive verbs bear distinctive case markers.

Erib-biti: Akkadian term, literally "one who enters the temple," designating a priest with access to restricted areas of a temple.

Erra: Akkadian warrior god whose chief weapon was famine and who became closely associated with **Nergal.**

Ershahunga: An **Emesal** lamentation prayer describing the worshiper's suffering and asking for divine relief.

Ershemma: A song in **Emesal** accompanied by a drum called a **shem** and including litanies and prayers to soothe the heart of a god.

Etemmu(m): Akkadian word for the spirit of the deceased that must be revered and propitiated with funerary offerings of food and drink lest it become restless and haunt the living.

Extispicy: The technique of predicting the future by examining the configuration of the entrails of sacrificial animals.

Faience: Glazed **frit.**

Frit: Partially fused quartz dust or sand that is modeled or molded to form beads, vessels, and figurines; *see also* **faience.**

Gagu(m): Akkadian (Sumerian loanword) term for a building or portion of a temple reserved for the **naditu-** priestesses.

Geshtinana: Sumerian goddess, sister of **Dumuzi.**

Grapheme: The basic unit of a written language, such as a letter in an alphabet, which represents a specific **phoneme.**

Hattic: An **agglutinative language** identified in the cuneiform tablets from Boghazköy (ancient Hattusa) in Anatolia.

Hemerology: A form of divination used to predict favorable days for acting on certain plans.

Hittite: An Indo-European language identified in the cuneiform tablets from Boghazköy (ancient Hattusa) in Anatolia.

Hurrian: A language, perhaps related to those of the modern Caucasus region, identifiable in **cuneiform** texts from north Syria and northern Mesopotamia during the third and second millennia B.C.E. (*See also* **Urartian.**)

Igigu: The ten great gods of the Old Babylonian pantheon; later all the gods of heaven collectively.

Ikkibu(m): The Akkadian (Sumerian loanword) term denoting a forbidden thing, place, or action; later broadened to include secular wrongs such as lying or stealing.

Ilku(m): In the Old Babylonian period the duty of a person holding land from a higher authority (such as the king) to work the land, and in later periods to deliver part of the harvest or some payment in silver.

Imdugud: *See* **Anzud.**

Inana: Literally "The Lady of Heaven," the supreme Sumerian goddess, the goddess of sexual love, who came to be associated with the Akkadian goddess **Ishtar.**

Intercalation: The periodic insertion of additional months into a **luni-solar calendar** to keep it synchronized with the seasons; initially performed on an ad hoc basis, the process was regularized during the Persian period.

Ishkur: *See* **Adad.**

Ishtar: Akkadian goddess of sexual love, warfare, and the planet Venus, identified with the Sumerian goddess **Inana.**

Ishum: Akkadian god whose name means "fire," a minor, generally benevolent deity who acted as a calming influence on the violent god **Erra.**

Kalu(m): Akkadian (Sumerian loanword) term for a lamentation-priest.

Karu(m): Akkadian term for a city's harbor, its harbor district, the city quarter occupied by traders, and a resident community of merchants.

Kiru(m): Akkadian (Sumerian: *kiri*) term for "garden" or "orchard."

Koine glossa: A simplified form of the Attic dialect of Greek; as the official dialect of the court of Macedon, *koine glossa* was the form of Greek spoken in Mesopotamia and throughout the Hellenistic world, following the conquests of Alexander III of Macedon in 331 B.C.E.

Kudurru: Akkadian word for "boundary"; the term is often applied to entitlement monuments.

Lama: *See* **lamassu.**

Lamashtu: (Akkadian) A female demon who preys on unborn and newborn babies; she is described and depicted as having a lion head, donkey teeth, naked breasts, a hairy body, and feet with bird talons. (*See also* **Pazuzu.**)

Lamassu: (Akkadian; Sumerian: *lama*) name for a protective spirit.

Language isolate: A language—such as Sumerian, **Elamite,** or **Hattic**—that has no close affinities to any other known language, living or dead.

Lecanomancy: A method of soliciting omens by observing the patterns formed by oil blobs dropped onto water.

Libanomancy: A method of soliciting omens by observing the behavior of smoke rising from burning incense.

Lilu: (Akkadian) Demonic spirits of young men who have died unmarried, especially dangerous to pregnant women and infants.

Limmu: *See* **eponym system.**

Linear zig-zag function: The method used in **System B** for calculating the mean value of a variable such as solar velocity, by reducing the variable to an arithmetic progression alternately increasing and decreasing by a constant amount in successive intervals of time between some fixed minimum and maximum values.

Lost-wax casting: A process for casting metal or glass objects; the artisan sculpts a wax model, which is then covered with clay and fired, causing the wax to melt out through channels pierced in the clay; molten metal (or glass) is then poured into the mold through these channels; when the medal or glass has cooled and solidified, the clay is broken away.

Lugal: Sumerian term for "king," literally "big man."

Luni-solar calendar: Calendar consisting of twelve lunar months of 29 or 30 days in length brought into synchrony with the seasons by the periodic addition of a thirteenth, or intercalary, month. (*See also* **intercalation.**)

Luwian: An Indo-European language related to **Hittite** spoken in Anatolia during the second and first millennia B.C.E., and recorded in cuneiform and in a native hieroglyphic system.

Mamitu: Akkadian word meaning an "oath" as sworn by the king and gods, and a "curse" for breaking such an oath.

Mar bane: Akkadian term designating a "free man," "citizen" of a city, or a member of the (land-owning) nobility during the seventh – fourth centuries B.C.E.

Mar shipri (*feminine:* **marat shipri):** Akkadian term that may be translated as "messenger," "envoy," "agent," "deputy," "ambassador," or "diplomat."

Marduk: Patron deity of the city of Babylon and chief deity in the Babylonian pantheon during the second and first millennia B.C.E.

Me: Sumerian term (pronounced "may") for divine powers and wisdom, the norms underlying all facets of human civilization.

Melammu: Akkadian term describing the awe-inspiring radiance, or superluminosity, inherent in things divine and royal.

Menology: A form of divination used to predict unfavorable days for acting on certain plans.

Meslamtaea: A Babylonian underworld deity, twin of Lugal-irra who was identified with **Nergal.**

Metonic cycle: Interval in which 235 lunar months equal 19 solar years, claimed to have been discovered by the Greek astronomer Meton about 432 B.C.E. (*See also* **period relations.**)

Mina: (Sumerian: *mana;* Akkadian: *manu*) A unit of weight (= 60 shekels) equivalent to approximately ½ kilogram or 1 pound.

Misharum (*or* **Mesharum):** Old Babylonian royal edict issued periodically to cancel debts.

Mother Hubur: *See* **Tiamat.**

Mushkenu(m): Akkadian term designating a commoner, poor person, or dependent.

Nabu: Babylonian scribe god and patron of writing, son of **Marduk.**

Naditu(m): (Akkadian) A cloistered holy woman.

Namburbu: (Akkadian; Sumerian loan word) A form of **apotropaic rite** to ward off a predicted evil event and transfer the evil to a disposable object.

Namma: Sumerian goddess, a deity of the subterranean waters, mother of **Enki.**

Nam-tag: Sumerian word for transgressions against the divine order.

Nanna: Sumerian moon god, also known as **Suena,** which was vocalized as **Sin** (pronounced "seen") in Akkadian; centers of his cult were at Ur during the third millennium B.C.E. and at Harran in Syria during the first millennium B.C.E.

Naru (*feminine:* **nartu):** Akkadian term (Sumerian loanword) for a "musician" or "singer" who performed in palace and temple accompanied by various musical instruments. (*See also* **zammeru.**)

Necromancy: The art of divining the future by communicating with the spirits of the dead.

Nergal: A Babylonian underworld deity who came to be equated with **Erra;** his cult center was at Kutha.

Ninazu: A Sumerian underworld deity, son of **Ereshkigal,** worshiped at Eshnunna.

Ningirsu: Patron god of Lagash who became assimilated with **Ninurta.**

Ninhursanga: Sumerian goddess also called **Ninmah,** mother of many gods and goddesses fathered by **Enki.**

Ninlil: Sumerian goddess, also known as **Sud,** wife of **Enlil.**

Ninmah: *See* **Ninhursanga.**

Ninni-ZA.ZA: A goddess worshiped in a temple dedicated to her at Mari during the third millennium B.C.E.

Nintu: A mother goddess and birth goddess, the "Lady of Births."

Ninurta: Sumerian warrior god, who became associated with **Ningirsu;** his cult center was at Nippur.

Nisaba: Sumerian goddess of the scribal arts; mother of **Sud.**

Obelisk: A tall four-sided stone pillar that tapers toward its pyramidal top.

Occultation: A celestial event in which the sun, the moon, or a planet passes directly in front of a star or planet.

Oneiromancy: The art of divining the future through the interpretation of dreams.

Opposition: The position of a planet when it rises in the east at sunset or sets in the west at sunrise.

Pabilsag: Sumerian deity whose associated constellation was later identified by the Greeks as Sagittarius.

Palaic: Indo-European language related to **Hittite** and **Luwian,** spoken in north central Anatolia and recorded in cuneiform at Boghazköy (ancient Hattusa).

Pashishu(m): Babylonian temple functionary who poured liquids during anointing ceremonies.

Patriarchy: Kinship structure in which the father is head of the family and descent as well as property ownership is traced from fathers through sons.

Patrilocal: A social system in which a woman who marries enters her husband's family and household.

Pazuzu: An Assyrian and Babylonian lion- or dog-headed demon capable of forcing **Lamashtu** back to the underworld.

Period relations: Mathematical relations stating that *s* intervals of one kind equal *t* intervals of another kind; for example, 235 lunar months equal 19 solar years (the so-called **Metonic cycle**).

Phoneme: In linguistics, the smallest distinguishable unit of speech such that a difference in sound makes a difference in meaning.

Physiognomic omens: Predictions derived from the appearance and behavior of individual people.

Piradazish: Old Persian term for a "fast courier."

Prehistoric period: The period before the invention of writing; in Mesopotamia the period prior to circa 3300 B.C.E.

Prognostic omens: Predictions about the courses and outcomes of diseases.

Prosopography: A means of studying the social history of a group of people having certain political or social characteristics in common through genealogy, onomastics, and demographics.

Protasis: The subordinate ("if") clause of an "if-then," or conditional sentence (*see also* **apodosis**); Mesopotamian omens were stated in the form of conditional sentences.

Proto-historic period: In Mesopotamia, the period during the earliest stages of development of the cuneiform writing system, circa 3300 – circa 2900 B.C.E.

Proto-horoscope: Late Babylonian cuneiform document that records the calculated positions of the planets at the moment of a person's birth but does not include predictions for the future.

Protome: Decoration shaped like the foreparts or upper parts of an animal, such as might be found in architectural decorations, on the arm or leg of a piece of furniture, or the base of a drinking **rhyton.**

Provenance (*also* provenience): In archaeology, the origin or derivation of an object; in art history, also the history of the ownership of the object.

Qingu: In the Babylonian creation epic *Enuma elish* the military leader of the demonic army of primeval goddess **Tiamat** in her war against **Marduk** and the younger gods.

Ramku(m): A Babylonian temple functionary concerned with ritual bathing.

Register: In art works, a distinct horizontal band within which a scene is depicted and separated from other scenes.

Repoussé: A technique in which a design is rendered in relief on a thin metal sheet by hammering from the underside.

Rhyton: A horn-shaped drinking vessel decorated with head and foreparts of an animal (*see* **protome**) and having a hole in the front for pouring.

Riemchen bricks: Small rectangular sun-dried or kiln-baked mud bricks of square cross-section mass produced in standardized molds, characteristic of Late Uruk period (circa 3300 – 2900 B.C.E.) architecture.

Saros cycle: A lunar eclipse cycle of 223 **synodic months,** approximately 18+ years, during which there is the possibility of 38 lunar eclipses with an average interval of 5+ months between eclipses.

Seah: (Akkadian: *sutu;* Sumerian: *ban*) A unit of capacity used to measure volumes of such commodities as barley and oil; equal to about 10 liters/quarts during the Old Babylonian period (circa 1900 – circa 1600) and about 6 liters/quarts during the Neo-Babylonian period (mid-first millennium B.C.E.).

Seleucid period: The historical period of ancient Mesopotamia during the reigns of the former Macedonian general Seleucus I and his successors, 312 B.C.E. – circa 129 B.C.E.

Sexagesimal system: A base 60 number system.

Shamash: Akkadian (Sumerian: Utu) sun god, god of justice; his two principal places of worship were at Sippar and Larsa.

Shangu(m): (Akkadian; Sumerian loanword) Chief temple administrator; priest.

Shara: The local warrior god of the Sumerian city of Umma.

Shaziga: (Sumerian; Akkadian: *nish libbi;* "sexual libido," literally "lifting the heart") Incantations to restore male potency.

Shem: A drum used to accompany an **ershemma.**

Sheqel: (Akkadian: *shiqlu*) A unit of weight equal to about 8 1/3 grams or 3/10 ounce.

Shuilla: (Sumerian; Akkadian: *nish qati;* "lifting the hand") A type of prayer consisting of praise for the deity, a list of complaints or pleas, and anticipatory thanks.

Sin: *See* **Nanna.**

Sipa: Sumerian word meaning "shepherd"; applied to the king's role as administrator of his people.

Solstice: Position of the sun on the **ecliptic** when it is furthest north (summer in the Northern Hemisphere) or furthest south (winter in the Northern Hemisphere).

Stationary points: The planets, when viewed from the earth, appear to speed up, slow down, and change direction of travel as a result of the differences between the earth's and the planets' velocities around the sun. The points in a planet's orbit where its apparent motion changes to retrograde motion and vice versa are termed its "first" and "second" stationary points, respectively.

Stele: An upright stone slab engraved with an inscription or design.

Step function: The method used in **System A** for calculating the mean value of a variable such as solar velocity, by reducing the variable to just two discontinuous values, one high, the other low, each held constant for two complementary periods or distances.

Sud: *See* **Ninlil.**

Suena: *See* **Nanna.**

Sumerian: (1) A **language isolate** spoken in southern Mesopotamia during the third millennium B.C.E., characterized as an **ergative language** and an **agglutinative language;** (2) the text written in that language from the third millennium B.C.E. through the first centuries C.E.; and (3) the people who spoke this language.

Synodic month: The period between two successive appearances of a phase of the moon, such as from one full moon to the next full moon.

System A: *See* **step function.**

System B: *See* **linear zig-zag function.**

Tamkarum: Akkadian (Sumerian: *damgar*) term for a "merchant" or "businessman."

Tammuz: The biblical name for **Dumuzi.**

Tell: (Arabic) A mound containing the remains of an ancient city, a composite of occupational and destruction levels and naturally deposited sediments.

Temenos: (Greek) A spacious sacred compound surrounding a temple, its altars, monuments, and gateways.

Teratological omens: Signs found in monstrous births of animals.

Terrestrial omens: Signs found in everyday occurrences.

Tiamat: Akkadian term for "sea" or "salt water"; personified as a primordial goddess in the Babylonian creation myth *Enuma elish.*

Tuppi maruti: (Akkadian, literally "tablet of sonship") A type of document from Nuzi recording the adoption of a man as a son and heir in exchange for his providing the adoptive parents with food, clothing, and other rations for the duration of their lives.

Udug: (Sumerian; Akkadian: *utukku*) A type of demon that could be either beneficial or malevolent.

Urartian: A language, perhaps related to those of the modern Caucasus region, identifiable in cuneiform texts from the vicinity of Lake Van in eastern Anatolia during the first millennium B.C.E. (*See also* **Hurrian.**)

Uttu: Sumerian spider-goddess associated with weaving.

Utu: *See* **Shamash.**

(W)ardu(m): Akkadian term for a "slave."

We: Sumerian minor god who is killed in the *Epic of Atra-hasis.*

Wilid bitim: (Akkadian, literally "house-born") Child born to chattel slaves.

Zababa: A local warrior god who later became associated with **Nergal;** his cult center was at Kish.

Zammeru: (Akkadian) An untrained singer or singer of popular songs. (*See also* **naru.**)

Ziggurat: (Akkadian: *ziqqurratu*) A monumental mudbrick stepped pyramid-like temple tower with steps leading to the top where rituals were performed.

GENERAL REFERENCES

GENERAL

Joan Aruz with Ronald Wallenfels, eds., *Art of the First Cities: The Third Millennium B.C. from the Mediterranean to the Indus* (New York: Metropolitan Museum of Art, 2003).

Piotr Bienkowski and Alan Millard, eds., *Dictionary of the Ancient Near East* (Philadelphia: University of Pennsylvania Press, 2000).

Jeremy Black and Anthony Green, *Gods, Demons and Symbols of Ancient Mesopotamia: An Illustrated Dictionary* (Austin: University of Texas Press, 1992).

Black, Graham Cunningham, Jarle Ebeling, Esther Flückiger-Hawker, Eleanor Robson, Jon Taylor, and Gábor Zólyomi, *The Electronic Text Corpus of Sumerian Literature*, The Oriental Institute, University of Oxford, 1998– <http://www-etcsl.orient.ox.ac.uk/>.

Stanley Mayer Burstein, *The Babylonaica of Berossus*, Sources and Monographs, Sources from the Ancient Near East, volume 1, fascicle 5 (Malibu, Cal.: Undena Publications, 1978).

The Cambridge Ancient History (London & New York: Cambridge University Press, 1970–)—includes volume 1, part 1, *Prolegomena and Prehistory*, third edition, edited by I. E. S. Edwards, C. J. Gadd, and N. G. L. Hammond (1970); volume 1, part 2, *Early History of the Middle East*, third edition, edited by Edwards, Gadd, and Hammond (1971); volume 2, part 1, *History of the Middle East and the Aegean Region, c. 1830–1380 B.C.*, third edition, edited by Edwards, Gadd, Hammond, and E. Sollberger (1973); volume 2, part 2, *History of the Middle East and the Aegean Region, c. 1380-1000 B.C.*, third edition, edited by Edwards, Hammond, and Sollberger (1975); volume 3, part 1, *The Prehistory of the Balkans; and The Middle East and the Aegean World, Tenth to Eighth centuries B.C.*, second edition, edited by John Boardman, Edwards, and Hammond (1982); volume 3, part 2, *The Assyrian and Babylonian Empires and Other States to the Near East, from the Eighth to the Sixth Centuries B.C.*, second edition, edited by Boardman, Edwards, Hammond, and Sollberger (1991).

Billie Jean Collins, ed., *A History of the Animal World in the Ancient Near East*, Handbuch der Orientalistik, volume 64 (Leiden: Brill, 2002).

Encyclopædia Britannica Online <http://www.search.eb.com>.

Benjamin R. Foster, *Before the Muses: An Anthology of Akkadian Literature*, 2 volumes (Bethesda, Md.: CDL Press, 1993).

H. Gasche, J. A. Armstrong, S. W. Cole, and V. G. Gurzadyan, *Dating the Fall of Babylon: A Reappraisal of Second-Millennium Chronology (A Joint Ghent-Chicago-Harvard Project)*, Mesopotamian History and Environment, Series II, Memoirs IV (Ghent: University of Ghent / Chicago: Oriental Institute of the University of Chicago, 1998).

William W. Hallo, *Origins: The Ancient Near Eastern Background of Some Modern Western Institutions*, Studies in the History and Culture of the Ancient Near East, volume 6 (Leiden: Brill, 1996).

Hallo and William Kelly Simpson, *The Ancient Near East: A History*, second edition (New York: Harcourt Brace Jovanovich, 1998).

Hallo, ed., and K. Lawson Younger Jr., associate ed., *The Context of Scripture* (Leiden & Boston: Brill, 2003)—volume 1, *Canonical Compositions from the Biblical World*; volume 2, *Monumental Inscriptions from the Biblical World*; and volume 3, *Archival Documents from the Biblical World*.

Herodotus, *The Histories*, translated by Aubrey de Sélincourt, revised, with an introduction and notes, by A. R. Burn (Harmondsworth, U.K.: Penguin, 1954).

Simon Hornblower and Anthony Spawforth, eds., *The Oxford Classical Dictionary*, third edition (Oxford: Oxford University Press, 1996).

Peter James, in collaboration with I. J. Thorpe, Nikos Kokkinos, Robert Morkot, and John Frankish, *Centuries of*

Darkness: A Challenge to the Conventional Chronology of Old World Archaeology (London: Cape, 1991).

Amélie Kuhrt, *The Ancient Near East, c. 3000–330 B.C.*, 2 volumes (London & New York: Routledge, 1995).

W. G. Lambert, *Babylonian Wisdom Literature* (Oxford: Clarendon Press, 1960).

Gwendolyn Leick, *Who's Who in the Ancient Near East* (London & New York: Routledge, 1999).

Eric M. Meyers, ed., *The Oxford Encyclopedia of Archaeology in the Near East*, 5 volumes (New York & Oxford: Oxford University Press, 1997).

Joan Oates, *Babylon* (London: Thames & Hudson, 1979).

A. Leo Oppenheim, *Ancient Mesopotamia: Portrait of a Dead Civilization*, revised edition, completed by Erica Reiner (Chicago: University of Chicago Press, 1977).

James Bennett Pritchard, ed., *Ancient Near East in Pictures Relating to the Old Testament*, second edition with supplement (Princeton: Princeton University Press, 1969).

Pritchard, ed., *Ancient Near Eastern Texts Relating to the Old Testament*, third edition with supplement (Princeton: Princeton University Press, 1969).

Michael Roaf, *Cultural Atlas of Mesopotamia and the Ancient Near East* (New York: Facts on File, 1966).

Martha T. Roth, *Law Collections from Mesopotamia and Asia Minor*, second edition, Society of Biblical Literature, Writings from the Ancient World Series, volume 6 (Atlanta: Scholars Press, 1995).

H. W. F. Saggs, *Babylonians*, Peoples of the Past, volume 1 (Norman: University of Oklahoma Press, 1995).

Jack M. Sasson, ed., *Civilizations of the Ancient Near East*, 4 volumes (New York: Scribners, 1995).

Ian Shaw, ed., *The Oxford History of Ancient Egypt* (Oxford: Oxford University Press, 2000).

Marc Van de Mieroop, *A History of the Ancient Near East ca. 3000–323 B.C.* (Malden, Mass.: Blackwell, 2004).

Ronald Wallenfels, ed., and Jack M. Sasson, consulting ed., *The Ancient Near East: An Encyclopedia for Students*, 4 volumes (New York, Detroit, San Francisco, London, Boston & Woodbridge, Conn.: Scribners, 2000).

GEOGRAPHY

Robert McCormick Adams, *Heartland of Cities: Surveys of Ancient Settlement and Land Use on the Central Flood-plain of the Euphrates* (Chicago: University of Chicago Press, 1981).

Pauline Albenda, *The Palace of Sargon of Assyria: Monumental Wall Reliefs at Dur-Sharrukin, from Original Drawings made at the Time of their Discovery in 1843–1844 by Botta and Flandin*, Synthèse, no. 22 (Paris: Éditions Recherche sur les Civilizations, 1986).

J. A. Brinkman, *Prelude to Empire: Babylonian Society and Politics, 747–626 B.C.*, Occasional Publications of the Babylonian Fund, 7 (Philadelphia: Babylonian Fund, University Museum, 1984).

Geoff Emberling and Norman Yoffee, "Thinking about Ethnicity in Mesopotamian Archaeology and History," in *Fluchtpunkt Uruk: Archäologische Einheit aus methodischer Vielfalt. Schriften für Hans Jörg Nissen*, edited by Hartmut Küne, Reinhard Bernbeck, and Karin Bartl, Internationale Archäologie Studia honoraria 6 (Rahden: Marie Leidorf, 1999), pp. 272–281.

Henri Frankfort, *The Art and Architecture of the Ancient Orient*, fifth edition, with supplementary notes and bibliography by Michael Roaf and Donald Matthews (New Haven: Yale University Press, 1996).

William W. Hallo, "The Road to Emar," *Journal of Cuneiform Studies*, 18 (1964): 57–87.

Alexander Heidel, *The Babylonian Genesis: The Story of Creation*, second edition (Chicago & London: University of Chicago Press, 1951).

Wayne Horowitz, *Mesopotamian Cosmic Geography*, Mesopotamian Civilizations, 8 (Winona Lake, Ind.: Eisenbrauns, 1998).

James Mellaart, *Earliest Civilizations in the Near East* (New York: McGraw-Hill, 1965).

A. R. Millard, "Cartography in the Ancient Near East," in *The History of Cartography*, volume 1: *Cartography in Prehistoric, Ancient and Medieval Europe and the Mediterranean*, edited by J. B. Harley and David Woodward (Chicago: University of Chicago Press, 1987), pp. 107–116.

Karen Rhea Nemet-Nejat, *Late Babylonian Field Plans in the British Museum*, Studia Pohl: Series Maior 11 (Rome: Biblical Institute Press, 1982).

Piotr Steinkeller, "New Light on the Hydrology and Topography of Southern Babylonia in the Third Millennium," *Zietschrift für Assyriologie und Archaeologie*, 91 (2001): 22–84.

Richard L. Zettler, *Nippur III: Kassite Buildings in Area WC-1*, Oriental Institute Publications, volume 111 (Chicago: Oriental Institute of the University of Chicago, 1993).

THE ARTS

Zainab Bahrani, *Women of Babylon: Gender and Representation in Mesopotamia* (London & New York: Routledge, 2001).

Dan Barag and Veronica Tatton-Brown, *Catalogue of Western Asiatic Glass in the British Museum* (London: Published for the Trustees of the British Museum, 1985).

Paul-Alain Beaulieu and Francesca Rochberg, "The Horoscope of Anu-bēlšunu," *Journal of Cuneiform Studies,* 48 (1996): 89–94.

John Boardman, *Persia and the West: An Archaeological Investigation of the Genesis of Achaemenid Art* (London: Thames & Hudson, 2000).

Luigi Cagni, *The Poem of Erra,* Sources and Monographs, Sources from the Ancient Near East, volume 1, fascicle 3 (Malibu, Cal.: Undena Publications, 1977).

Dominique Collon, *First Impressions: Cylinder Seals in the Ancient Near East* (London: British Museum, 1987).

John Curtis, ed., *Bronzeworking Centres of Western Asia, c. 1000–539 B.C.* (London & New York: Kegan Paul/ British Museum, 1988).

Stephanie Dalley, trans., *Myths from Mesopotamia: Creation, The Flood, Gilgamesh, and Others* (Oxford & New York: Oxford University Press, 1989).

O. M. Dalton, *The Treasure of the Oxus, with Other Examples of Early Oriental Metal-Work,* third edition (London: Trustees of the British Museum, 1964).

Susan B. Downey, *Mesopotamian Religious Architecture: Alexander through the Parthians* (Princeton: Princeton University Press, 1988).

Benjamin R. Foster, *Before the Muses: An Anthology of Akkadian Literature,* 2 volumes (Bethesda, Md.: CDL Press, 1993).

Henri Frankfort, *The Art and Architecture of the Ancient Orient,* fifth edition, with supplementary notes and bibliography by Michael Roaf and Donald Matthews (New Haven: Yale University Press, 1996).

Frankfort, *Cylinder Seals: A Documentary Essay on the Art and Religion of the Ancient Near East* (London: Macmillan, 1939).

Ian Freestone and David R. M. Gaimster, *Pottery in the Making: World Ceramic Traditions* (London: British Museum Press, 1997).

Andrew R. George, trans., *The Epic of Gilgamesh: The Babylonian Epic Poem and Other Texts in Akkadian and Sumerian* (London: Allen Lane, 1999).

McGuire Gibson and Robert D. Biggs, eds., *Seals and Sealing in the Ancient Near East,* Bibliotheca Mesopotamica 8 (Malibu, Cal.: Undena Publications, 1977).

William W. Hallo and J. J. A. van Dijk, *The Exaltation of Inanna,* Yale Near Eastern Researches, volume 3 (New Haven & London: Yale University Press, 1968).

Ernst Heinrich, *Die Paläste im alten Mesopotamien,* Deutsches Archäologisches Institut, Denkmäler antiker Architektur, 15 (Berlin: De Gruyter, 1982).

Heinrich, *Die Tempel und Heiligtümer im alten Mesopotamien,* Deutsches Archäologisches Institut, Denkmäler antiker Architektur, 14 (Berlin: De Gruyter, 1982).

Georgina Herrmann with Neville Parker, eds., *The Furniture of Western Asia Ancient and Traditional: Papers of the Conference held at the Institute of Archaeology, University College London June 28 to 30, 1993* (Mainz am Rhein: Philipp von Zabern, 1996).

W. G. Lambert, Alan R. Millard, and Miguel Civil, *Atra-Hasis: The Babylonian Story of the Flood, with the Sumerian Flood Story* (Winona Lake, Ind.: Eisenbrauns, 1999).

Gwendolyn Leick, *A Dictionary of Ancient Near Eastern Architecture* (London & New York: Routledge, 1988).

M. E. L. Mallowan, *The Nimrud Ivories* (London: British Museum Publications, 1978).

K. R. Maxwell-Hyslop, *Western Asiatic Jewellery, c. 3000– 612 B.C.* (London: Methuen, 1971).

P. R. S. Moorey, *Materials and Manufacture in Ancient Mesopotamia: The Evidence of Archaeology and Art: Metals and Metalwork, Glazed Materials and Glass,* British Archaeological Reports (Oxford: Oxford University Press, 1985).

Oscar White Muscarella, *Bronze and Iron: Ancient Near Eastern Artifacts in The Metropolitan Museum of Art* (New York: Metropolitan Museum of Art, 1988).

Jack Ogden, *Jewellery of the Ancient World* (London: Trefoil, 1982).

A. Leo Oppenheim and others, *Glass and Glassmaking in Ancient Mesopotamia: An Edition of the Cuneiform Texts Which Contain Instructions for Glassmakers, with a Catalogue of Surviving Objects* (Corning, N.Y.: Corning Museum of Glass, 1970).

Julian E. Reade, "Assyrian King-Lists, the Royal Tombs of Ur, and Indus Origins," *Journal of Near Eastern Studies,* 60 (2001): 1–29.

John Malcolm Russell, *Sennacherib's Palace without Rival at Nineveh* (Chicago: University of Chicago Press, 1991).

Edward W. Said, *Orientalism* (New York: Pantheon, 1978).

Ursula Seidl, *Die babylonischen Kudurru-Reliefs: Symbole mesopotamischer Gottheiten* (Freiburg: Freiburg University Press / Göttingen: Vandenhoeck & Ruprecht, 1989).

Jon Solomon, *The Ancient World in the Cinema,* revised and expanded edition (New Haven: Yale University Press, 2001).

Agnès Spycket, *La Statuaire du Proche-Orient ancien*, Handbuch der Orientalistik (Leiden: Brill, 1981).

Eva Strommenger, *5000 Years of the Art of Mesopotamia*, translated by Christina Haglund (New York: Abrams, 1964).

Jeffrey H. Tigay, *The Evolution of the Gilgamesh Epic* (Philadelphia: University of Pennsylvania Press, 1982).

E. Douglas Van Buren, *Symbols of the Gods in Mesopotamian Art* (Rome: Pontificum Institutum Biblicum, 1945).

John Van Seters, *In Search of History: Historiography in the Ancient World and the Origins of Biblical History* (New Haven: Yale University Press, 1987).

Ronald Wallenfels, *Uruk: Hellenistic Seal Impressions in the Yale Babylonian Collection I. Cuneiform Tablets*, Ausgrabungen in Uruk-Warka Endberichte 19 (Mainz am Rhein: Philipp von Zabern, 1994).

C. Leonard Woolley and others, *Ur Excavations*, 10 volumes, Publications of the Joint Expedition of the British Museum and the Museum of the University of Pennsylvania to Mesopotamia (London & Philadelphia: Published for the Trustees of the British Museum and the Museum of the University of Pennsylvania, 1927–1976).

Max Wykes-Joyce, *7000 Years of Pottery and Porcelain* (London: Owen, 1958).

Richard L. Zettler and Lee Horne, eds., *Treasures from the Royal Tombs of Ur* (Philadelphia: University of Pennsylvania, Museum of Archaeology and Anthropology, 1998).

COMMUNICATION, TRANSPORTATION, AND EXPLORATION

Julia Assante, "Sex, Magic and the Liminal Body in the Erotic Art and Texts of the Old Babylonian Period," in *Sex and Gender in the Ancient Near East. Proceedings of the 47th Rencontre Assyriologique International Helsinki, July 2–6, 2001*, part 1, edited by Simo Parpola and Robert M. Whiting (Helsinki: Neo-Assyrian Text Corpus Project, 2002), pp. 27–52.

Robert J. Braidwood, *Prehistoric Men*, eighth edition (Glenview, Ill.: Scott, Foresman, 1975).

Paul Collins, *The Uruk Phenomenon: The role of social ideology in the expansion of the Uruk culture during the fourth millennium BC*, BAR International Series 900 (Oxford: Archaeopress, 2000).

Dominique Collon, *First Impressions: Cylinder Seals in the Ancient Near East* (London: British Museum, 1987).

J. S. Cooper and W. Heimpel, "The Sumerian Sargon Legend," *Journal of the American Oriental Society*, 103 (1983): 67–82.

M. Dandamaev, ed., *Societies and Languages of the Ancient Near East: Studies in Honor of I. M. Diakonoff* (Warminster, U.K.: Aris & Phillips, 1982).

Peter T. Daniels and William Bright, eds., *The World's Writing Systems* (New York: Oxford University Press, 1996).

Israel Eph`al, *The Ancient Arabs: Nomads on the Borders of the Fertile Crescent 9th–5th Centuries B.C.* (Jerusalem: Magnes Press, Hebrew University / Leiden: Brill, 1982).

Irving L. Finkel and Julian E. Reade, "Assyrian Hieroglyphs," *Zeitschrift für Assyriologie und Archeologie*, 86 (1996): 244–268.

Douglas Frayne, "Šulgi, the Runner," *Journal of the American Oriental Society*, 103 (1983): 739–748.

Sally M. Freedman, *If a City is Set on a Height: The Akkadian Omen Series Šumma Alu ina Mēlê Šakin*, volume 1: Tablets 1–21, Occasional Publications of the Samuel Noah Kramer Fund, 17 (Philadelphia: University of Pennsylvania Museum, 1998).

Ignace J. Gelb, *Computer-Aided Analysis of Amorite*, Assyriological Studies 21 (Chicago & London: Oriental Institute, University of Chicago, 1980).

Gelb, "The Language of Ebla in the Light of the Sources from Ebla, Mari, and Babylonia," in *Ebla, 1975–1985: Dieci anni di studi linguistici e filologic. Atti del Convegno Internazionale (Napoli 9–11 ottobre 1985)*, edited by Luigi Cagni (Naples: University Oriental Institute, Department of Asian Studies, 1987), pp. 49–74.

M. J. Geller, "The Last Wedge," *Zeitschrift für Assyriologie und vorderasiatische Archäologie*, 87 (1997): 43–95.

David. F. Graf, "The Persian Royal Road System," in *Continuity and Change: Proceedings of the Last Achaemenid History Workshop April 6–8, 1990, Ann Arbor, Michigan*, edited by Heleen Sancisi-Weerdenburg, Amélie Kuhrt, and Margaret Cool Root, Achaemenid History, volume 8 (Leiden: Nederlands Instituut voor het Nabije Ooste, 1994), pp. 167–189.

Albert Kirk Grayson, *Assyrian and Babylonian Chronicles*, Texts from Cuneiform Sources, 5 (Locust Valley, N.Y.: J. J. Augustin, 1975).

William W. Hallo, "The Concept of Eras from Nabonassar to Seleucus," *Ancient Studies in Memory of Elias Bickerman*, special issue of *Journal of the Ancient Near East Society*, 16–17 (1984–1985): 143–151.

Hallo, "The Nabonassar Era and other Epochs in Mesopotamian Chronology and Chronography," in *A Scientific Humanist: Studies in Memory of Abraham Sachs*, edited by Erle Lichty, Maria deJ. Ellis, and Pamela Gerardi, Occasional Publications of the Samuel Noah

Kramer Fund, 9 (Philadelphia: University Museum, 1988), pp. 175–190.

Richard T. Hallock, *Persepolis Fortification Tablets*, Oriental Institute Publications, volume 92 (Chicago: University of Chicago Press, 1969).

John Huehnergard, *A Grammar of Akkadian*, third printing, corrected, Harvard Semitic Studies, no. 45 (Atlanta: Scholars Press, 2000).

Jacob Klein, "Šulgi and Išmedagan: Runners in the Service of the Gods (SRT 13)," *Beer-Sheva*, 2 (1985): 7*–38*.

C. C. Lamberg-Karlovsky, "The Archaeological Evidence for International Commerce: Public and/or Private Enterprise in Mesopotamia?" in *Privatization in the Ancient Near East and Classical World*, edited by Michael Hudson and Baruch A. Levine, Peabody Museum Bulletin, 5 (Cambridge, Mass.: Peabody Museum of Archaeology and Ethnology, Harvard University, 1996), pp. 73–97.

Mogens Trolle Larsen, *The Old Assyrian City-State and Its Colonies* (Copenhagen: Akademisk Forlag, 1976).

Samuel A. Meier, *The Messenger in the Ancient Semitic World*, Harvard Semitic Monographs, 45 (Atlanta: Scholars Press, 1988).

Cécile Michel, *Correspondance des marchands de Kanish au début du IIe millénaire avant J.-C.*, Littératures anciennes du Proche-Orient, 19 (Paris: Cerf, 2001).

Alan R. Millard, *The Eponyms of the Assyrian Empire 910–612 BC*, State Archives of Assyria Studies, 2 (Helsinki: Neo-Assyrian Text Corpus Project, 1994).

P. R. S. Moorey, *Ancient Mesopotamian Materials and Industries: The Archaeological Evidence* (Winona Lake, Ind.: Eisenbrauns, 1999).

Joseph Naveh, *Early History of the Alphabet: An Introduction to West Semitic Epigraphy and Palaeography* (Jerusalem: Magnes Press, Hebrew University / Leiden: Brill, 1982).

Hans J. Nissen, Peter Damerow, and Robert K. Englund, *Archaic Bookkeeping: Writing and Techniques of Economic Administration in the Ancient Near East*, translated by Paul Larsen (Chicago & London: University of Chicago Press, 1993).

Simo Parpola, Asko Parpola, and Robert H. Brunswig Jr., "The Meluhha Village: Evidence of Acculturation of Harappan Traders in Late Third Millennium Mesopotamia," *Journal of Economic and Social History of the Orient*, 20 (1977): 129–165.

Edith Porada, "The Cylinder Seals Found at Thebes in Boeotia," *Archiv für Orientforschung*, 28 (1981): 1–78.

Cemal Pulak, "The Cargo of the Uluburun Ship and Evidence for Trade with the Aegean and Beyond," in *Italy*

and *Cyprus in Antiquity: 1500–450 BC: Proceedings of an International Symposium held at the Italian Academy for Advanced Studies in America at Columbia University November 16–18, 2000*, edited by Larissa Bonfante and Vassos Karageorghis (Nicosia: Costakis and Leto Severis Foundation, 2001), pp. 13–60.

Michael Roaf and Annette Zgoll, "Assyrian Astroglyphs: Lord Aberdeen's Black Stone and the Prisms of Esarhaddon," *Zeitschrift für Assyriologie und Archeologie*, 91 (2001): 264–295.

Benjamin Sass, *The Genesis of the Alphabet and its Development in the Second Millennium B.C.*, Ägypten und Altes Testament, 13 (Wiesbaden: Otto Harrassowitz, 1988).

Denise Schmandt-Besserat, *Before Writing* (Austin: University of Texas Press, 1992)—volume 1, *From Counting to Cuneiform*; volume 2, *A Catalogue of Near Eastern Tokens*.

Marcel Sigrist and Peter Damerow, "Mesopotamian Year Names: Neo-Sumerian and Old Babylonian Date Formulae," *Cuneiform Digital Library Initiative*, University of California at Los Angeles and the Max Planck Institute for the History of Science <http://cdli.ucla.edu/>.

Rolf A. Stucky, *The Engraved Tridacna Shells*, Dédalo 19 (São Paulo: Museo de Arqueologia e Etnologia, Universidade de São Paulo, 1974).

Marie-Louise Thomsen, *The Sumerian Language: An Introduction to its History and Grammatical Structure*, third edition, Mesopotamia, volume 10 (Copenhagen: Akademisk Forlag, 2001).

Ronald Wallenfels, "Sealing Practices on Legal Documents from Hellenistic Uruk," in *Administrative Documents in the Aegean and their Near Eastern Counterparts. Proceedings of the International Colloquium, Naples, February 29–March 2, 1996*, edited by Massimo Perna (Turin: Paravia Scriptorium, 2000), pp. 333–348.

Irene J. Winter, "Phoenician and North Syrian Ivory Carving in Historical Context: Questions of Style and Distribution," *Iraq*, 38 (1976): 1–22.

Yigael Yadin, *The Art of Warfare in Biblical Lands in the Light of Archaeological Study*, 2 volumes, translated by M. Pearlman (New York, Toronto & London: McGraw-Hill, 1963).

SOCIAL CLASS AND THE ECONOMY

Kathleen Abrams, *Business and Politics under the Persian Empire: The Financial Dealings of Marduk-nasir-apli of the House of Egibi* (Bethesda, Md.: CDL Press, 2004).

Emin Bilgiç and Cahit Günbatti, *Ankaraner Kültepe-Texte III*, translated into German by Karl Hecker, Freiburger Altorientalische Studien Beihefte, volume 3 (Wiesbaden: Franz Steiner, 1995).

John A. Brinkman, Review of *Symbolae iuridicae Martino David dedicatae*, *Journal of Near Eastern Studies*, 32 (1973): 159–160.

Miguel Civil, *The Farmer's Instructions: A Sumerian Agricultural Manual*, Aula Orientalis-Supplementa 5 (Barcelona: Editorial Ausa, 1994).

M. I. Finley, *Ancient History: Evidence and Models* (London: Chatto & Windus, 1985).

Benjamin R. Foster, *From Distant Days: Myths, Tales, and Poetry of Ancient Mesopotamia* (Bethesda, Md.: CDL Press, 1995).

Ignace J. Gelb, Piotr Steinkeller, and Robert Whiting, *Earliest Land Tenure Systems in the Near East: The Ancient* kudurrus, Oriental Institute Publications, 104 (Chicago: Oriental Institute, 1981).

Andrew R. George, *The Babylonian Gilgamesh Epic: Introduction, Critical Editions, and Cuneiform Texts*, 2 volumes (Oxford: Oxford University Press, 2003).

McGuire Gibson and Robert D. Biggs, eds., *The Organization of Power: Aspects of Bureaucracy in the Ancient Near East* (Chicago: Oriental Institute, 1987).

Rivkah Harris, "The *nadītu*-woman," in *Studies Presented to A. Leo Oppenheim, June 7, 1964* (Chicago: Oriental Institute, 1964), pp. 106–135.

Harris, "The Organization and Administration of the Cloister in Ancient Babylonia," *Journal of the Economic and Social History of the Orient*, 6 (1963): 121–157.

Michael Hudson and Baruch Levine, eds., *Urbanization and Land Ownership in the Ancient Near East* (Cambridge, Mass.: Peabody Museum of Archaeology and Ethnology, 1999).

Leonard W. King, *Babylonian Boundary-Stones and Memorial Tablets in the British Museum* (London: Trustees of the British Museum, 1912).

Fritz R. Kraus, *Königliche Verfügungen in altbabylonischer Zeit*, Studia et Documenta ad iura orientis antiqui pertinentia, volume 11 (Leiden: 1984), pp. 168–183.

Hans Martin Kümmel, *Familie, Beruf und Amt im spätbabylonischen Uruk: prosopographische Untersuchungen zu Berufsgruppen des 6. Jahrhunderts v. Chr. in Uruk*, Abhandlungen der Deutschen Orient-Gesellschaft, 20 (Berlin: Mann, 1979).

Mario Liverani, "Half Nomads on the Middle Euphrates and the Concept of Dimorphic Society," *Altorientalische Forschungen*, 24 (1995): 44–48.

Alisdair Livingstone, *Court Poetry and Literary Miscellanea*, State Archives of Assyria, volume 3 (Helsinki: Helsinki University Press, 1989).

Kazuya Maekawa, "Female Weavers and their Children in Lagash: Pre-Sargonic and Ur III," *Acta Sumerologica*, 2 (1982): 81–125.

A. Leo Oppenheim, "The Seafaring Merchants of Ur," *Journal of the American Oriental Society*, 74 (1954): 6–17.

Susan Pollock, *Ancient Mesopotamia: The Eden that Never Was*, Case Studies in Early Societies (Cambridge: Cambridge University Press, 1999).

J. N. Postgate, *Early Mesopotamia: Society and Economy at the Dawn of History* (London & New York: Routledge, 1992).

Marvin A. Powell, "A Contribution to the History of Money in Mesopotamia Prior to the Invention of Coinage," in *Festschrift Lubor Matouš*, 2 volumes, edited by Bohuslav Hruška and G. Komoróczy, Assyriologia 5 (Budapest: Eötvös Loránd Tudományeggyetem, 1981), II: 211–243.

Powell, "Identification and Interpretation of Long Term Price Fluctuations in Babylonia: More on the History of Money in Mesopotamia," *Altorientalische Forschung*, 17 (1990): 95–118.

Powell, ed., *Labor in the Ancient Near East*, American Oriental Series, volume 68 (New Haven, Conn.: American Oriental Society, 1987).

Kathryn E. Slanski, *The Babylonian Entitlement* narûs (kudurrus): *A Study in Form and Function*, ASOR Books, volume 9 (Boston: American Schools of Oriental Research, 2003).

Alice Louise Slotsky, *The Bourse of Babylon: Market Quotations in the Astronomical Diaries of Babylonia* (Bethesda, Md.: CDL Press, 1997).

Piotr Steinkeller, *Sale Documents of the Ur III Period*, Freiburger Altorientalische Studien, volume 17 (Wiesbaden: Franz Steiner, 1989).

Elizabeth Stone, "The Social Role of the *nadītu*-woman in Old Babylonian Nippur," *Journal of the Economic and Social History of the Orient*, 25 (1982): 50–70.

Marc Van de Mieroop, *Crafts in the Early Isin Period: A Study of the Isin Craft Archive from the Reigns of Išbi-Erra and Šū-Illišu*, Orientalia Lovaniensia Analecta, 24 (Leuven: Departement Oriëntalistiek, 1987).

Van de Mieroop, "Gifts and Tithes to the Temples in Ur," in *DUMU-E₂-DUB-BA-A: Studies in Honor of Åke W. Sjöberg*, edited by Hermann Behrens, Darlene Loding, and Martha T. Roth, Occasional Publications of the Samuel Noah Kramer Fund, no. 11 (Philadelphia: Samuel Noah Kramer Fund, University Museum, 1989), pp. 397–401.

Van de Mieroop, *Society and Enterprise in Old Babylonian Ur* (Berlin: Dietrich Reimer, 1992).

Hermann L. J. Vanstiphout, "Disputations," in *The Context of Scripture*, volume 1: *Canonical Compositions from the Biblical World*, edited by William W. Hallo with K. Lawson Younger Jr. (New York & Leiden: Brill, 1996), pp. 575–578.

Raymond Westbrook, ed., *A History of Ancient Near Eastern Law*, 2 volumes, Handbuch der Orientalistik, volume 72 (Leiden: Brill, 2003).

POLITICS, LAW, AND THE MILITARY

Jean Bottéro, *Mesopotamia: Writing, Reasoning and the Gods*, translated by Zainab Bahrani and Marc Van de Mieroop (Chicago: University of Chicago Press, 1992).

Jerrold S. Cooper, *Reconstructing History from Ancient Inscriptions: The Lagash-Umma Border Conflict*, Sources from the Ancient Near East, volume 2, fascicle 1 (Malibu, Cal.: Undena Publications, 1983).

Muhammed A. Dandamaev, *Slavery in Babylonia: From Nabopolassar to Alexander the Great (626–331 B.C.)*, revised edition, translated by Victoria A. Powell, edited by Marvin A. Powell and David B. Weisberg (De Kalb: Northern Illinois University Press, 1984).

B. L. Eichler, "Literary Structure in the Laws of Eshnunna," in *Language, Literature, and History: Philological and Historical Studies Presented to Erica Reiner*, edited by Francesca Rochberg (New Haven: American Oriental Society, 1987), pp. 71–84.

J. J. Finkelstein, "Ammisaduqa's Edict and the Babylonian 'Law Codes,'" *Journal of Cuneiform Studies*, 15 (1961): 91–104.

Finkelstein, *The Ox that Gored*, Transactions of the American Philosophical Society, volume 71, part 2 (Philadelphia: American Philological Society, 1981).

Finkelstein, "Some New *Misharum* Materials and Its Implications," *Studies in Honor of Benno Landsberger on his Seventy-fifth Birthday, April 21, 1965*, edited by Hans Gustav Güterbock and Thorkild Jacobsen, Assyriological Studies, no. 16 (Chicago: University of Chicago Press, 1965), pp. 233–246.

Ilya Gershevitch, ed., *The Median and Achaemenian Periods*, volume 2 of *The Cambridge History of Iran* (Cambridge: Cambridge University Press, 1985).

McGuire Gibson and Robert D. Biggs, eds., *The Organization of Power: Aspects of Bureaucracy in the Ancient Near East* (Chicago: Oriental Institute, 1987).

Albert K. Grayson, *Assyrian Royal Inscriptions*, 2 volumes (Wiesbaden: Otto Harrassowitz, 1972, 1976).

Harry A. Hoffner Jr., *The Laws of the Hittites: A Critical Edition*, Documenta et Monumenta Orientis Antiqui, volume 23 (Leiden & New York: Brill, 1997).

Michael Hudson and Marc Van de Mieroop, eds., *Debt and Economic Renewal in the Ancient Near East* (Bethesda, Md.: CDL Press, 2002).

Bernard S. Jackson, "Principles and Cases: The Theft Laws of Hammurabi," *Irish Jurist*, 7 (1972): 161–170.

Thorkild Jacobsen, *Toward the Image of Tammuz and Other Essays on Mesopotamian History and Culture*, Harvard Semitic Series, volume 21 (Cambridge, Mass.: Harvard University Press, 1970).

Remko Jas, *Neo-Assyrian Judicial Procedures*, State Archives of Assyria Studies, volume 5 (Helsinki: Neo-Assyrian Text Corpus Project, 1996).

Mogens Trolle Larsen, *The Conquest of Assyria: Excavations in an Antique Land, 1840–1860* (London & New York: Routledge, 1996).

Brian Lewis, *The Sargon Legend: A Study of the Akkadian Text and the Tale of the Hero Who Was Exposed at Birth* (Cambridge, Mass.: American Schools of Oriental Research, 1980).

Mary A. Littauer and J. H. Crouwel, *Wheeled Vehicles and Ridden Animals in the Ancient Near East* (Leiden: Brill, 1979).

Mario Liverani, ed., *Akkad, the First World Empire: Structure, Ideology, Traditions* (Padua: Sargon, 1993).

William L. Moran, ed. and trans., *The Amarna Letters* (Baltimore: Johns Hopkins University Press, 1992).

Bustenay Oded, *Mass Deportations and Deportees in the Neo-Assyrian Empire* (Wiesbaden: Reichert, 1979).

A. T. Olmstead, *History of the Persian Empire* (Chicago: University of Chicago Press, 1948).

Samuel M. Paley, *King of the World: Ashur-nasir-pal II of Assyria 883–859 B.C.* (New York: Brooklyn Museum, 1976).

J. Nicholas Postgate, *The First Empires* (Oxford: Elsevier-Phaidon, 1977).

Martha T. Roth, *Law Collections from Mesopotamia and Asia Minor*, second edition, Society of Biblical Literature, Writings from the Ancient World Series, volume 6 (Atlanta: Scholars Press, 1995).

Roth, "Mesopotamian Legal Traditions and the Laws of Hammurabi," *Chicago Kent Law Review*, 13 (1995): 13–39.

Ronald H. Sack, *Images of Nebuchadnezzar: The Emergence of a Legend* (Selinsgrove, Pa.: Susquehanna University Press, 1992).

Claudio Saporetti, *The Middle Assyrian Laws* (Malibu, Cal.: Undena Publications, 1984).

Klaus R. Veenhof, ed., *Cuneiform Archives and Libraries. Papers read at the 30ᵉ Rencontre Assyriologique Internatio-*

nale. Leiden, 4–8 July 1983 (Istanbul, Turkey: Nederlands Historisch-Archaeologisch Instituut te Istanbul, 1986).

Raymond Westbrook, ed., *A History of Ancient Near Eastern Law,* 2 volumes, Handbuch der Orientalistik, volume 72 (Leiden: Brill, 2003).

D. J. Wiseman, *Nebuchadrezzar and Babylon* (Oxford & New York: Published for the British Academy by Oxford University Press, 1985).

LEISURE, RECREATION, AND DAILY LIFE

Robert McCormick Adams, *Heartland of Cities: Surveys of Ancient Settlement and Land Use on the Central Floodplain of the Euphrates* (Chicago: University of Chicago Press, 1981).

Paul-Alain Beaulieu, *The Reign of Nabonidus King of Babylon 556–539 B.C.,* Yale Near Eastern Researches, 10 (New Haven: Yale University Press, 1989).

Jean Bottéro, *The Oldest Cuisine in the World: Cooking in Mesopotamia,* translated by Teresa Lavender Fagan (Chicago & London: University of Chicago Press, 2004).

Bottéro, *Textes culinaire Mésopotamiens = Mesopotamian Culinary Texts,* Mesopotamian Civilizations, volume 6 (Winona Lake, Ind.: Eisenbrauns, 1995).

Miguel Civil, *The Farmer's Instructions: A Sumerian Agricultural Manual,* Aula Orientalis-Supplementa 5 (Barcelona: Editorial Ausa, 1994).

Mark E. Cohen, *The Cultic Calendars of the Ancient Near East* (Bethesda, Md.: CDL Press, 1993).

Dominique Collon, *Ancient Near Eastern Art* (London: British Museum Press for the Trustees of the British Museum, 1995).

Collon, "Banquets in the Art of the Ancient Near East," in *Banquets d'Orient,* Res Orientales, 4 (Bures-sur-Yvette, France: Groupe pour l'étude de las civilisation du Moyen-Orient / Louvain: Peeters, 1992), pp. 23–29.

Georges Contenau, *Everyday Life in Babylon and Assyria,* translated by K. R. and A. R. Maxwell-Hyslop (New York: St. Martin's Press, 1954).

Stephanie Dalley, "Nineveh, Babylon and the Hanging Gardens: Cuneiform and Classical Sources Reconciled," *Iraq,* 56 (1994): 45–58.

Wolfgang Decker, *Sports and Games of Ancient Egypt,* translated by Allen Guttmann (New Haven & London: Yale University Press, 1992).

Erich Ebeling, *Tod und Leben nach den Vorstellungen der Babylonier* (Berlin & Leipzig: De Gruyter, 1931).

Irving J. Finkel, *Ancient Board Games* (London: Welcome Rain, 1998).

Finkel, "The Hanging Gardens of Babylon," in *The Seven Wonders of the Ancient World,* edited by Peter A. Clayton and Martin Price (London & New York: Routledge, 1988), pp. 38–58.

William W. Hallo, "Games in the Biblical World," in *Avraham Malamat Volume,* edited by Shmuel Ahituv and Baruch A. Levine, Eretz-Israel Archaeological, Historical and Geographical Studies, 24 (Jerusalem: Israel Exploration Society, 1993), pp. 83–88.

Louis Francis Hartman and A. Leo Oppenheim, *On Beer and Brewing Techniques in Ancient Mesopotamia,* supplement to the *Journal of the American Oriental Society,* no. 10 (Baltimore: American Oriental Society, 1950).

Georgina Herrmann with Neville Parker, eds., *The Furniture of Western Asia Ancient and Traditional: Papers of the Conference held at the Institute of Archaeology, University College London June 28 to 30, 1993* (Mainz am Rhein: Philipp von Zabern, 1996).

Anne D. Kilmer, "Games and Toys in Ancient Mesopotamia," in *Actes du XIIe Congrès International des Sciences Prehistoriques et Protohistoriques,* 4 volumes, edited by Juraj Pavúk, Union Internationale des Sciences Prehistoriques et Protohistoriques (Bratislava: Institut Archéologique de l'Académie Slovaque des Sciences, 1993), I: 359–364.

Kilmer and others, "Musik," *Reallexicon der Assyriologie,* 8 (1995–1997): 463–469.

Samuel Noah Kramer, *The Sumerians: Their History, Culture and Character* (Chicago & London: University of Chicago Press, 1963).

Henri Limet, "The Cuisine of Ancient Sumer," *Biblical Archaeologist,* 50 (1987): 132–147.

Daniel David Luckenbill, *Ancient Records of Assyria and Babylonia,* 2 volumes (Chicago: University of Chicago Press, 1926, 1927).

K. R. Maxwell-Hyslop, *Western Asiatic Jewellery, c. 3000–612 B.C.* (London: Methuen, 1971).

Patrick E. McGovern and others, "A funerary feast fit for King Midas," *Nature,* 402 (December 1999): 863–864.

Lucio Milano, ed., *Drinking in Ancient Societies: History and Culture of Drinks in the Ancient Near East. Papers of a Symposium held in Rome, May 17–19, 1990,* History of the Ancient Near East Studies 6 (Padova: Sargon, 1994).

James D. Muhly, "Ancient Cartography," *Expedition,* 20, no. 2 (1978): 26–31.

Karen Rhea Nemet-Nejat, *Daily Life in Ancient Mesopotamia,* Daily Life through History (Westport, Conn.: Greenwood Press, 1998).

Simo Parpola and Robert M. Whiting, eds., *Sex and Gender in the Ancient Near East. Proceedings of the 47th Rencontre Assyriologique International Helsinki, July 2–6, 2001*, 2 volumes (Helsinki: Neo-Assyrian Text Corpus Project, 2002).

J. N. Postgate, *Early Mesopotamia: Society and Economy at the Dawn of History* (London & New York: Routledge, 1992).

Georges Roux, *Ancient Iraq* (London: Allen & Unwin, 1964).

John Malcolm Russell, *Sennacherib's Palace without Rival at Nineveh* (Chicago: University of Chicago Press, 1991).

Russell, *The Writing on the Wall: Studies in the Architectural Context of Late Assyrian Palace Inscriptions* (Winona Lake, Ind.: Eisenbrauns, 1999).

H. W. F. Saggs, *Civilization before Greece and Rome* (New Haven & London: Yale University Press, 1989).

Saggs, *The Greatness That Was Babylon: A Sketch of the Ancient Civilization of the Tigris-Euphrates Valley*, revised and updated edition (London: Sidgwick & Jackson, 1988).

Armas Salonen, *Die Fischerei im alten Mesopotamien* (Helsinki: Suomalainen Tiedeakademia, 1970).

Elizabeth C. Stone, *Nippur Neighborhood*, Studies in Ancient Oriental Civilization, no. 44 (Chicago: Oriental Institute of the University of Chicago, 1987).

Diane Wolkstein and Samuel Noah Kramer, *Inanna, Queen of Heaven and Earth: Her Stories and Hymns from Sumer* (New York: Harper & Row, 1983).

Richard L. Zettler and Lee Horne, eds., *Treasures from the Royal Tombs of Ur* (Philadelphia: University of Pennsylvania, Museum of Archaeology and Anthropology, 1998).

THE FAMILY AND SOCIAL TRENDS

Benjamin R. Foster, "The Birth Legend of King Sargon of Akkad," in *The Context of Scripture*, volume 1: *Canonical Compositions from the Biblical World*, edited by William W. Hallo with K. Lawson Younger Jr. (New York & Leiden: Brill, 1996), p. 461.

William W. Hallo and J. J. A. van Dijk, *The Exaltation of Inanna*, Yale Near Eastern Researches, volume 3 (New Haven: Yale University Press, 1968).

Maureen Gallery Kovacs, *The Epic of Gilgamesh* (Stanford: Stanford University Press, 1989).

Samuel Noah Kramer, *The Sumerians: Their History, Culture and Character* (Chicago & London: University of Chicago Press, 1963).

F. R. Kraus, "Von Altmesopotamischen Erbrecht," in *Essays on Oriental Laws of Succession*, Studia et Documenta, volume 9 (Leiden: Brill, 1969), pp. 1–57.

W. G. Lambert, "A Middle Assyrian Medical Text," *Iraq*, 31 (1969): 28–39.

Benno Landsberger, "Scribal Concepts of Education," in *City Invincible: A Symposium on Urbanization and Cultural Development in the Ancient Near East held at the Oriental Institute of the University of Chicago, December 4–7, 1958*, edited by Carl H. Kraeling and Robert McC. Adams (Chicago: University of Chicago Press, 1960), pp. 94–123.

Erle Leichty, "Feet of Clay," in *DUMU-E₂-DUB-BA-A*: *Studies in Honor of Åke W. Sjöberg*, edited by Hermann Behrens, Darlene Loding, and Martha T. Roth, Occasional Publications of the Samuel Noah Kramer Fund, no. 11 (Philadelphia: Samuel Noah Kramer Fund, University Museum, 1989), pp. 349–356.

Stephen J. Lieberman, ed., *Sumerological Studies in Honor of Thorkild Jacobsen on his Seventieth Birthday June 7, 1974*, Assyriological Studies, no. 20 (Chicago & London: University of Chicago Press, 1976).

R. McHale-Moore, "The Mystery of Enheduanna's Disk," *Journal of the Ancient Near Eastern Society*, 27 (2000): 69–74.

Karen Rhea Nemet-Nejat, *Cuneiform Mathematical Texts as a Reflection of Everyday Life in Mesopotamia*, American Oriental Series, volume 75 (New Haven: American Oriental Society, 1993).

Nemet-Nejat, *Daily Life in Ancient Mesopotamia*, Daily Life through History (Westport, Conn.: Greenwood Press, 1998).

Nemet-Nejat, "Women in Ancient Mesopotamia," in *Women's Roles in Ancient Civilizations: A Reference Guide*, edited by Bella Vivante (Westport, Conn.: Greenwood Press, 1999), pp. 85–114.

Hans J. Nissen, Peter Damerow, and Robert K. Englund, *Archaic Bookkeeping: Earliest Writing Techniques of Economic Administration in the Ancient Near East*, translated by Peter Larsen (Chicago & London: University of Chicago Press, 1992).

A. Leo Oppenheim, *The Interpretation of Dreams in the Ancient Near East* (Philadelphia: American Philosophical Society, 1956).

Simo Parpola and Robert M. Whiting, eds., *Sex and Gender in the Ancient Near East. Proceedings of the 47th Rencontre Assyriologique International Helsinki, July 2–6, 2001*, 2 volumes (Helsinki: Neo-Assyrian Text Corpus Project, 2002).

J. N. Postgate, *Early Mesopotamia: Society and Economy at the Dawn of History* (London & New York: Routledge, 1992).

Erica Reiner, *Your Thwarts in Pieces, Your Mooring Rope Cut: Poetry from Babylonia and Assyria* (Ann Arbor: Horace H. Rackham School of Graduate Studies, University of Michigan, 1985).

E. K. Ritter, "Magical Expert (= *āšipu*) and Physician (= *asû*): Notes on Two Complementary Professions in Babylonian Medicine," in *Studies in Honor of Benno Landsberger on his Seventy-fifth Birthday, April 21, 1965*, edited by Hans Gustav Güterbock and Thorkild Jacobsen, Assyriological Studies, no. 16 (Chicago: University of Chicago Press, 1965), pp. 299–321.

Martha T. Roth, *Babylonian Marriage Agreements 7th–3rd Centuries B.C.*, Alter Orient und Altes Testament, bd. 222 (Kevelaer: Butzon & Bercker / Neukirchen-Vluyn: Neukirchener, 1989).

Roth, "The Dowries of the Women of the Itti-Marduk-balāṭu Family," *Journal of the American Oriental Society*, 111 (1991): 19–37.

Georges Roux, *Ancient Iraq* (London: Allen & Unwin, 1964).

H. W. F. Saggs, *Civilization before Greece and Rome* (New Haven & London: Yale University Press, 1989).

Saggs, *Everyday Life in Babylonia & Assyria* (London: Batsford / New York: Putnam, 1965).

Wolfram von Soden, *The Ancient Orient: An introduction to the Study of the Ancient Near East*, translated by Donald G. Schley (Grand Rapids, Mich.: Eerdmans, 1994).

Niek Veldhuis, *A Cow of Sin*, Library of Oriental Texts, volume 2 (Groningen: Styx, 1991).

C. B. F. Walker, *Cuneiform* (London: Published for the Trustees of the British Museum by British Museum Publications, 1987).

RELIGION AND PHILOSOPHY

Bendt Alster, *The Instructions of Suruppak: A Sumerian Proverb Collection* (Copenhagen: Akademisk Forlag, 1974).

Alster, *Proverbs of Ancient Sumer: The World's Earliest Proverb Collections*, 2 volumes (Bethesda, Md.: CDL Press, 1997).

Alster, ed., *Death in Mesopotamia: Papers Read at the XXVIe Rencontre assyriologique internationale*, Mesopotamia, volume 8 (Copenhagen: Akademisk Forlag, 1980).

Robert D. Biggs, *ŠÀ.ZI.GA: Ancient Mesopotamian Potency Incantations*, Texts from Cuneiform Sources, volume 2 (New York: J. J. Augustin, 1970).

Jean Bottéro, *Mesopotamia: Writing, Reasoning and the Gods*, translated by Zainab Bahrani and Marc Van de Mieroop (Chicago: University of Chicago Press, 1992).

Bottéro, *Religion in Ancient Mesopotamia*, translated by Teresa Lavender Fagan (Chicago: University of Chicago Press, 2001).

Luigi Cagni, *The Poem of Erra*, Sources and Monographs, Sources from the Ancient Near East, volume 1, fascicle 3 (Malibu, Cal.: Undena Publications, 1977).

Miguel Civil, "Enlil and Ninlil: The Marriage of Sud," *Journal of the American Oriental Society*, 103 (1983): 43–66.

Mark E. Cohen, *The Canonical Lamentations of Ancient Mesopotamia*, 2 volumes (Bethesda, Md.: CDL Press, 1988).

Cohen, *The Cultic Calendars of the Ancient Near East* (Bethesda, Md.: CDL Press, 1993).

Jerrold S. Cooper, *The Curse of Agade* (Baltimore: Johns Hopkins University Press, 1983).

Benjamin R. Foster, *From Distant Days: Myths, Tales, and Poetry of Ancient Mesopotamia* (Bethesda, Md.: CDL Press, 1995).

Foster, ed. and trans., *The Epic of Gilgamesh* (New York: Norton, 2001).

Markham J. Geller, *Forerunners to Udug-hul: Sumerian Exorcistic Incantations* (Stuttgart: F. Steiner, 1985).

Andrew R. George, trans., *The Epic of Gilgamesh: The Babylonian Epic Poem and Other Texts in Akkadian and Sumerian* (London: Allen Lane, 1999).

Michael Haul, *Das Etana-Epos: Ein Mythos von der Himmelfahrt des Königs von Kiš*, Göttinger Arbeitshefte zur altorientalischen Literatur, 1 (Göttingen: Seminar für Keilschriftforschung, 2000).

Shlomo Izre'el, *Adapa and the South Wind: Language Has the Power of Life and Death*, Mesopotamian Civilizations, 10 (Winona Lake, Ind.: Eisenbrauns, 2001).

Thorkild Jacobsen, *The Harps that Once– : Sumerian Poetry in Translation* (New Haven: Yale University Press, 1987).

Jacobsen, *The Treasures of Darkness: A History of Mesopotamian Religion* (New Haven: Yale University Press, 1976).

Ulla Jeyes, *Old Babylonian Extispicy: Omen Texts in the British Museum* (Istanbul: Nederlands Historisch-Archaeologisch Instituut te Istanbul, 1989).

Jacob Klein, *Three Šulgi Hymns* (Ramat Gan, Israel: Bar Ilan University Press, 1981).

Ulla Koch-Westenholz, *Babylonian Liver Omens* (Copenhagen: Carsten Niebuhr Institute of Near Eastern Studies, University of Copenhagen, 2000).

Samuel Noah Kramer and John Maier, *Myths of Enki, The Crafty God* (New York & Oxford: Oxford University Press, 1989).

Jørgen Læssøe, *Studies on the Assyrian Ritual and Series "Bit Rimki"* (Copenhagen: Munksgaard, 1955).

W. G. Lambert, "Ancestors, Authors, and Canonicity," *Journal of Cuneiform Studies*, 11 (1957): 1–14.

Lambert, "A Catalogue of Texts and Authors," *Journal of Cuneiform Studies*, 16 (1962): 59–77.

Lambert, Alan R. Millard, and Miguel Civil, *Atra-hasīs: The Babylonian Story of the Flood, with the Sumerian Flood Story* (Winona Lake, Ind.: Eisenbrauns, 1999).

Erle V. Leichty, *The Omen Series Šumma Izbu*, Texts from Cuneiform Sources, volume 4 (New York: J. J. Augustin, 1970).

Guido Majno, *The Healing Hand: Man and Wound in the Ancient World* (Cambridge, Mass.: Harvard University Press, 1975).

A. Leo Oppenheim, *The Interpretation of Dreams in the Ancient Near East* (Philadelphia: American Philosophical Society, 1956).

Simo Parpola, *Assyrian Prophecies*, State Archives of Assyria, volume 9 (Helsinki: Helsinki University Press, 1997).

Parpola, ed., *Letters from Assyrian and Babylonian Scholars*, State Archives of Assyria, volume 10 (Helsinki: Helsinski University Press, 1993).

Olof Pedersén, *Archives and Libraries in the Ancient Near East, 1500–300 B.C.* (Bethesda, Md.: CDL Press, 1998).

Erica Reiner, *Astral Magic in Babylonia*, Transactions of the American Philosophical Society, volume 85, part 4 (Philadelphia: American Philosophical Society, 1995).

Reiner, *Šurpu: A Collection of Sumerian and Akkadian Incantations*, Archiv für Orientforschung, supplement 11 (Graz, 1958).

Reiner, *Your Thwarts in Pieces, Your Mooring Rope Cut: Poetry from Babylonia and Assyria* (Ann Arbor: Horace H. Rackham School of Graduate Studies, University of Michigan, 1985).

Brian B. Schmidt, *Israel's Beneficent Dead: Ancestor Cult and Necromancy in Ancient Israelite Religion and Tradition* (Winona Lake, Ind.: Eisenbrauns, 1996).

Yitzhak Sefati, *Love Songs in Sumerian Literature: Critical Edition of the Dumuzi-Inanna Songs* (Ramat Gan, Israel: Bar-Ilan University Press, 1998).

Ivan Starr, *The Rituals of the Diviner*, Bibliotheca Mesopotamica, volume 12 (Malibu, Cal.: Undena Publications, 1983).

Starr, ed., *Queries to the Sungod: Divination and Politics in Sargonid Assyria*, State Archives of Assyria, volume 4 (Helsinki: Helsinki University Press, 1990).

Karel van der Toorn, *Sin and Sanction in Israel and Mesopotamia: A Comparative Study* (Assen, Netherlands: Van Gorcun, 1985).

Moshe Weinfeld, *Deuteronomy 1–11: A New Translation with Introduction and Commentary*, The Anchor Bible, volume 5 (New York, London, Toronto, Sydney & Auckland: Doubleday, 1991).

Diane Wolkstein and Samuel Noah Kramer, *Inanna, Queen of Heaven and Earth: Her Stories and Hymns from Sumer* (New York: Harper & Row, 1983).

SCIENCE, TECHNOLOGY, AND HEALTH

Asger Aaboe, *Episodes From the Early History of Astronomy* (New York, Berlin & Heidelberg: Springer, 2001).

Aaboe, *Episodes From The Early History of Mathematics* (Washington, D.C.: Mathematical Association of America, 1964).

Hector Avalos, *Illness and Health Care in the Ancient Near East: The Role of the Temple in Greece, Mesopotamia, and Israel* (Atlanta: Scholars Press, 1995).

R. D. Biggs, "Medizin," in *Reallexikon der Assyriologie und Vorderasiatischen Archäologie*, volume 7, edited by D. O. Edzard (Berlin & Leipzig: De Gruyter, 1987), pp. 623–629.

John Britton and C. B. F. Walker, "Astronomy and Astrology in Mesopotamia," in *Astronomy Before the Telescope*, edited by Walker (London: Published for the Trustees of the British Museum by the British Museum Press, 1996), pp. 42–67.

Britton and Walker, "A 4th Century Babylonian Model for Venus: BM 33552," *Centaurus*, 34 (1991): 110–112.

Richard I. Caplice, *The Akkadian Namburbi Texts: An Introduction*, Sources from the Ancient Near East, volume 1, fascicle 1 (Malibu, Cal.: Undena Publications, 1974).

Stephanie Dalley, *Mari and Karana: Two Old Babylonian Cities* (London & New York: Longman, 1984).

Susan B. Downey, *Mesopotamian Religious Architecture: Alexander through the Parthians* (Princeton: Princeton University Press, 1988).

Robert Drews, *The End of the Bronze Age: Changes in Warfare and the Catastrophe ca. 1200 B.C.* (Princeton: Princeton University Press, 1993).

I. L. Finkel, "Adad-apla-iddina, Esagil-kīn-apli, and the series SA.GIG," in Erle Leichty, Maria deJ. Ellis, Pamela Gerardi, eds., *A Scientific Humanist: Studies in Memory of Abraham Sachs*, Occasional Publications of the Samuel Noah Kramer Fund, 9 (Philadelphia: University Museum, 1988), pp. 143–159.

M. J. Geller, "The Last Wedge," *Zeitschrift für Assyriologie und vorderasiatische Archäologie*, 87 (1997): 43–95.

Wayne Horowitz, *Mesopotamian Cosmic Geography*, Mesopotamian Civilizations, 8 (Winona Lake, Ind.: Eisenbrauns, 1998).

Jens Høyrup, "Babylonian Mathematics," in *Companion Encyclopedia of the History and Philosophy of the Mathematical Sciences*, 2 volumes, edited by I. Grattan-Guiness (London: Routledge, 1994), I: 21–29.

Høyrup, *Lengths, Widths, Surfaces: A Portrait of Old Babylonian Algebra and its Kin* (New York & Heidelberg: Springer, 2002).

Hermann Hunger, ed., *Astrological Reports to Assyrian Kings*, State Archives of Assyria, volume 8 (Helsinki: Helsinki University Press, 1992).

Hunger and David Edwin Pingree, *Astral Sciences in Mesopotamia* (Leiden & Boston: Brill, 1999).

Hunger and Pingree, MUL.APIN: *An Astronomical Compendium in Cuneiform*, Archiv für Orientforschung, Beiheft 24 (Horn, Austria: Berger, 1989).

Thorkild Jacobsen and Seton Lloyd, *Sennacherib's Aqueduct at Jerwan* (Chicago: University of Chicago Press, 1935).

Ulla Jeyes, "The Act of Extispicy in Ancient Mesopotamia: An Outline," *Assyriological Miscellanies*, 1 (1980): 13–32.

Ulla Koch-Westenholz, *Mesopotamian Astrology* (Copenhagen: Museum Tusculanum Press, 1995).

W. G. Lambert, "The Gula Hymn of Bullutsa-rabi," *Orientalia*, new series 36 (1967): 105–132.

Karen Rhea Nemet-Nejat, *Cuneiform Mathematical Texts as a Reflection of Everyday Life in Mesopotamia*, American Oriental Series, volume 75 (New Haven: American Oriental Society, 1993).

Otto Neugebauer, *The Exact Sciences in Antiquity*, second edition (Providence: Brown University Press, 1957).

Neugebauer, *A History of Ancient Mathematical Astronomy*, 3 volumes (Berlin & New York: Springer, 1975).

Neugebauer, ed., *Astronomical Cuneiform Texts: Babylonian Ephemerides of the Seleucid Period for the Motion of the Sun, the Moon, and the Planets*, 3 volumes (London: Published for the Institute of Advanced Studies, Princeton, N. J., by Lund Humphries, 1955).

Neugebauer and Abraham Joseph Sachs, eds., *Mathematical Cuneiform Texts*, American Oriental Series, volume 29 (New Haven: American Oriental Society / American Schools of Oriental Research, 1945).

A. Leo Oppenheim, "Divination and Celestial Observation in the Last Assyrian Empire," *Centaurus*, 14 (1969): 97–135.

Richard A. Parker and Waldo H. Dubberstein, *Babylonian Chronology: 626 B.C.–A.D. 75*, Brown University Studies, volume 19 (Providence: Brown University Press, 1956).

Simo Parpola, ed., *Letters from Assyrian and Babylonian Scholars*, State Archives of Assyria, volume 10 (Helsinki: Helsinki University Press, 1993).

Laurie E. Pearce, "Cuneiform Cryptography: Numerical Substitutions for Syllabic and Logographic Signs," dissertation, Yale University, 1982.

Pearce and L.T. Doty, "The Activities of Anu-belšunu, Seleucid Scribe," in *Assyriologica et Semitica. Festschrift für Joachim Oelsner anläßlich seines 65. Geburtstages am 18. Februar 1997*, edited by Joachim Marzahn and Hans Neumann, Alter Orient und Altes Testament 252 (Münster: Ugarit-Verlag, 2000), pp. 331–341.

Olof Pedersén, *Archives and Libraries in the Ancient Near East 1500–300 B.C.* (Bethesda, Md.: CDL Press, 1998).

Erica Reiner, *Astral Magic in Babylonia*, Transactions of the American Philosophical Society, volume 85, part 4 (Philadelphia: American Philosophical Society, 1995).

Reiner with David Edwin Pingree, *Enūma Anu Enlil. Tablet 63: The Venus Tablet of Ammisaduqa*, part 1 of *Babylonian Planetary Omens*, Bibliotheca Mesopotamica, volume 2, fascicle 1 (Malibu, Cal.: Undena Publications, 1975).

Reiner and Pingree, *Enūma Anu Enlil, Tablets 50–51*, part 2 of *Babylonian Planetary Omens*, Bibliotheca Mesopotamica, volume 2, fascicle 2 (Malibu, Cal.: Undena Publications, 1981).

Reiner and Pingree, *Babylonian Planetary Omens*, part 3, (Groningen: Styx Publications, 1998).

E. K. Ritter, "Magical Expert (= *āšipu*) and Physician (= *asû*): Notes on Two Complementary Professions in Babylonian Medicine," in *Studies in Honor of Benno Landsberger on his Seventy-fifth Birthday, April 21, 1965*, edited by Hans Gustav Güterbock and Thorkild Jacobsen, Assyriological Studies, no. 16 (Chicago: University of Chicago Press, 1965), pp. 299–321.

Eleanor Robson, *Mesopotamian Mathematics, 2100–1600 BC: Technical Constants in Bureaucracy and Education* (Oxford: Clarendon Press, 1999).

Francesca Rochberg, *Babylonian Horoscopes* (Philadelphia: American Philosophical Society, 1998).

Rochberg, "Scribes and Scholars: The *tupšar Enūma Anu Enlil*," in *Assyriologica et Semitica. Festschrift für Joachim*

Oelsner anläßlich seines 65. Geburtstages am 18. Februar 1997, edited by Joachim Marzahn and Hans Neumann, Alter Orient und Altes Testement 252 (Münster: Ugarit-Verlag, 2000), pp. 359–376.

Francesca Rochberg-Halton, *Aspects of Babylonian Celestial Divination: The Lunar Eclipse Tablets of Enuma Anu Enlil*, Archiv für Orientforschung, Beiheft 22 (Horn, Austria: Berger, 1988).

Rochberg-Halton, "Benefic and Malefic Planets in Babylonian Astrology," in Erle Leichty, Maria deJ. Ellis, Pamela Gerardi, eds., *A Scientific Humanist: Studies in Memory of Abraham Sachs*, Occasional Publications of the Samuel Noah Kramer Fund, 9 (Philadelphia: University Museum, 1988), pp. 323–328.

Rochberg-Halton, "Elements of the Babylonian Contribution to Hellenistic Astrology," *Journal of the American Oriental Society*, 108 (1988): 51–62.

Abraham Joseph Sachs and Hermann Hunger, *Astronomical Diaries and Related Texts from Babylonia*, volumes 1–3, 5 (Vienna: Österreichischen Akademie der Wissenschaften, 1988–2001).

W. H. van Soldt, *Solar Omens of Enuma Anu Enlil: Tablets 23 (24) – 29 (30)* (Istanbul: Nederlands Historisch-Archaeologisch Instituut te Istanbul, 1995).

Ivan Starr, *The Rituals of the Diviner*, Bibliotheca Mesopotamica, volume 12 (Malibu, Cal.: Undena Publications, 1983).

Starr, ed., *Queries to the Sungod: Divination and Politics in Sargonid Assyria*, State Archives of Assyria, volume 4 (Helsinki: University of Helsinki Press, 1990).

E. C. Stone, D. H. Linsley, V. Pigott, G. Harbottle, and M. T. Ford, "From Shifting Silt to Solid Stone: The Manufacture of Synthetic Basalt in Ancient Mesopotamia," *Science*, 280 (26 June 1998): 2091–2093.

Ronald Wallenfels, "30 Ajjaru 219 SE = 19 June 93 BCE," *Nouvelles Assyriologiques Brèves et Utilitaires* (1992): 37, no. 46.

Wallenfels, *Uruk: Hellenistic Seal Impressions in the Yale Babylonian Collection I. Cuneiform Tablets*, Ausgrabungen in Uruk-Warka Endberichte 19 (Mainz am Rhein: Philipp von Zabern, 1994).

D. J. Wiseman, *Nebuchadrezzar and Babylon* (Oxford & New York: Published for the British Academy by Oxford University Press, 1985).

Yigael Yadin, *The Art of Warfare in Biblical Lands in the Light of Archaeological Study*, 2 volumes, translated by M. Pearlman (New York, Toronto & London: McGraw-Hill, 1963).

CONTRIBUTORS

Paul Collins is Assistant Curator in the Department of Ancient Near Eastern Art at The Metropolitan Museum of Art, New York. He received his Ph.D. from the Institute of Archaeology, University College London, specializing in late fourth millennium B.C.E. Mesopotamia and the influence of ideology in the spread of culture. He has traveled widely in the Near East and has taught courses on the history and archaeology of the ancient Near East for the Universities of London and Oxford. He was part of the curatorial team for the landmark exhibition and catalogue *Art of the First Cities* at The Metropolitan Museum of Art in 2003. His publications include *The Uruk Phenomenon* (2000), contributions to *Atlas of World Art* (2004), and a forthcoming book about the collections of the Iraq Museum.

Karen Rhea Nemet-Nejat was the first woman to receive her Ph.D. degree in ancient Near Eastern Languages, History, and Cultures from Columbia University. Her thesis, *Late Babylonian Field Plans in The British Museum,* published in 1982, dealt with cartography and mathematics. Dr. Nemet-Nejat's interest in mathematics is evident in her many published articles and in *Cuneiform Mathematical Texts as a Reflection of Everyday Life in Mesopotamia* (1993). Her interests in other areas of ancient Near Eastern life are apparent in *Daily Life in Ancient Mesopotamia* (1998) and in articles on mirrors, women in the ancient Near East, and writing boards. She has held two fellowships at Yale University and has taught at Yale University and the University of Connecticut at Stamford. She is currently a research affiliate at Yale and is working on editions of cuneiform tablets from the reigns of the three minor Babylonian kings who ruled between Nebuchadrezzar II and Nabonidus.

Kathryn E. Slanski is a postdoctoral research fellow at Yale University, where she spends her time surrounded by cuneiform tablets in the Yale Babylonian Collection. Formerly an Assistant Professor at Tel Aviv University, she has led classes at Harvard, Tel Aviv, and Fairfield Universities, and she will begin teaching this year in the Directed Studies Program under the auspices of the Whitney Humanities Center at Yale. Her research seeks to integrate textual and visual evidence for the social and intellectual history of Mesopotamia, and she has written on ancient monuments, literary and religious traditions of the Hero, and representation of the gods. Dr. Slanski earned her Ph.D. in Near Eastern Studies at Harvard (1998), and has recently published her first book, *The Babylonian Entitlement narûs (kudurrus)* (2003).

Alice L. Slotsky is Visiting Assistant Professor of Assyriology in the Department of History of Mathematics at Brown University. She teaches the elements of the cuneiform writing system and all levels of the Akkadian language, and she specializes in Akkadian scientific texts. Dr. Slotsky is also a Research Affiliate in Assyriology in the Department of Near Eastern Languages and Civilizations at Yale University, from which she received her Ph.D. in Assyriology. Her fields of interest include Babylonian mathematics, astronomy, divination, and Late Babylonian commodity prices. She regularly lectures on and cooks from the Old Babylonian recipe tablets in the Yale Babylonian Collection. She is the author of *The Bourse of Babylon: Market Quotations in the Astronomical Diaries of Babylonia* (1997) and "The Uruk Solstice Scheme Revisited" (1993). Her current project is a collaborative study, with Ronald Wallenfels, of Late Babylonian tablets of prices in The British Museum.

Ira Spar is Professor of Ancient Studies at Ramapo College of New Jersey and Research Assyriologist in the Department of Ancient Near Eastern Art at The Metropolitan Museum of Art, New York. Dr. Spar received his doctorate in ancient history from the University of Minnesota and has specialized in the study of Neo-Babylonian commercial and legal texts.

He is editor and author of *Cuneiform Texts in The Metropolitan Museum of Art*, volumes 1–3.

Ronald Wallenfels is a former Associate Curator of Ancient Near Eastern Art at the Metropolitan Museum of Art, New York, and a retired New York City schoolteacher who is presently Adjunct Assistant Professor of Hebrew and Judaic Studies at New York University, where he teaches Akkadian. He earned his Ph.D. in Ancient Semitic Languages with a minor in art history and archaeology from Columbia University. Dr. Wallenfels specializes in the history and culture of the Neo- and Late Babylonian periods. In addition to many scholarly articles and book reviews, he is the author of *Uruk: Hellenistic Seal Impressions in the Yale Babylonian Collection I. Cuneiform Tablets* (1994) and *Seleucid Archival Texts in the Harvard Semitic Museum: Text Editions and Catalogue Raisonné of the Seal Impressions* (1998). He was the editor in chief of *The Ancient Near East: An Encyclopedia for Students* (2000) and, together with Joan Aruz, edited *The Art of the First Cities: The Third Millennium B.C. from the Mediterranean to the Indus* (2003).

INDEX OF PHOTOGRAPHS

INDEX

This index is sorted word by word. Page numbers in bold type indicate the primary article on a topic. Page numbers in italics indicate illustrations.

A

"A" Palace (Kish), 44, 162
Abortion, 280
Abu Temple (Eshnunna), *307*
Accounting, institutional, 158
Achaemenid period
    architecture, 47
    celestial omens, 341–342
    glass, 48
    images of kings, 53
    jewelry, 60–61, *61*
    metalwork, 71
    sculpture, 85
    seals and sealings, 89
Adad (deity), 58, *297*, 299, 348
    See also Ishkur (deity)
Adad-guppi, **262**
Adapa (mythical figure), 317, *318*
Admonitions, 288
Adoption, 169–170, 173, 273–274, 276–277, 279
Adultery, 277
Advice to a Prince, 156, 157, 174, 209
Agriculture, 21–22, 31, 146, **148–151,** *149, 150*
    See also Social class system and the economy
Akhenaten (king of Egypt), 104, 106
Akitu festival. *See* New Year's festival
Akkadian language, 112, 137, 272
Akkadian literature, 62, 64–65, 68
Akkadian period
    architecture, 45
    clothing, 233
    hairstyles, 256
    images of kings, *50,* 51
    images of the divine, *57,* 57–58, *304*
    kingship, 207
    metalwork, 68
    mythology, *312*
    sculpture, 79–80
    seals and sealings, 86–87, *87*
    transportation by land, 125
    transportation by water, 127
Aleph-beth, 113, 119, 133
Alewives, 281
Alexander, the Great (king of Macedon)
    and coins, 167
    and Greek alphabet/language, 114, 137
    kingship, 189
    and religion, 289
    warfare, 125–126, 222, 333

Alluvial plain, 146, 148
Almagest (Ptolemy), 332, 338
Almanacs, 334
Alphabet, Greek, 133, 137
Amenophis IV (king of Egypt), 104, 106
Ammi-saduqa (king of Babylon), 156, **178,** 330, 332
Amorite language, 113, 114
Amorite Wall, 353
Amorites, 160, 208, 298–299, 353
An (Sumerian deity), 298, 299, 308
    See also Anu (deity)
Anatolia
    banquets, 230, 231
    furniture, 250
    trade, 115–117, *118,* 165
Anatolian languages, 114
Ancestral sins, 302
Animal husbandry, *151,* **151–154,** *153*
    See also Social class system and the economy
Animal sacrifices. *See* Sacrifices, animal
Animals, for transportation, 125–126
Antiochus I (king of Seleucid Empire), 121
Anu (deity)
    in astronomy, 332
    and childbirth, 266
    in literature, 67, 174, 295
    in mythology, 317, 330
    numeral of, 299, 348
    syncretism, 299
    ziggurat, 353
    See also An (Sumerian deity)
Anu-ab-uter, 352
Anu-belshunu, 352
Anzu (deity), 57, 58, *94*
Anzud (Sumerian deity), 57, 58, *94*
Apkallu (sage), *56,* 58, *258,* 317, *318, 349*
Apodoses, 341, 350
Apotropaic figures and rituals, 257, *258,* 292, 340, 356–357
Appearance, physical, 32, *33*
Apprenticeship contracts, 155
Apsu, 23, 64, 246, 310
Aqueducts, 355, *355*
Arab family structure, 160
Arabic language, 113
Aramaean family structure, 160
Aramaic language, 112, 113, 133, 137
Aratta, Lord of, 99, 102, 117–118, 132, *135*
Archaic Ishtar Temple, Cult Room (Ashur), *320*

"Architect with Plan," 24, *27*
Architecture, 24, *27,* 42, **43–47,** *44, 46*
    See also Arts
Archives, 115, 265
    See also Libraries
Ardashir I (king of Persia), 190
Armenian clothing, *236*
Arrow in divination, 292, 339
Arts, **37–94**
    architecture, 42, **43–47,** *44, 46*
    Black Obelisk, 82, *82,* 83
    chronology, **38–40**
    documentary sources, **92–93**
    Flood stories, 63, 67, 91
    glass, faience, and glazed tiles, **47–50,** *48, 49*
    images of kings, 50, **50–53,** *51, 52*
    images of the divine, 42–43, **53–58,** *54, 55, 56, 57*
    influence of, 42, 43
    jewelry, 58, **60–61,** *61,* 70, 71
    literature, 41–42, **61–68,** *66,* 91, 92
    lost-wax casting, 68
    metalwork, **68–71,** *69, 70, 71*
    music and dance, 42, **71–72,** 91
    Nimrud ivories, 80, *81*
    overview, **41–43**
    painting, **72–74,** *73*
    pottery, *74,* **74–75**
    Royal Graves of Ur, 58, *59,* 60, 68, 72, 86, 90
    sculpture, 42, *59,* 60, *75–79,* **75–85,** *81–84,* 94
    seals and sealings, *57,* **85–89,** *86, 87, 88,* 92
    significant people, *91,* **91–92**
    wood carving, **90**
Ashur (Assyria)
    kingship, 209
    prices, 166–167
Ashur (Assyrian deity), *298,* 299, 356
Ashur (city)
    architecture, *46*
    deities, *298*
    tax exemptions, 174
    temples, *320*
    trade, 116–117, 165
Ashurbanipal (king of Assyria), **322**
    banquets, 231
    coronation prayer, 166–167
    furniture, 250, 252
    hunting, 259, *260*
    images of, 83–84, *260, 322*